11TH EDITION

The Dynamics of Mass Communication

Media in Transition

Joseph R. Dominick

University of Georgia, Athens (retired)

McGraw Hill

Connect
Learn
Succeed™

Published by McGraw-Hill, a business unit of The McGraw-Hill Companies, Inc., 1221 Avenue of the Americas, New York, NY 10020. Copyright © 2011, 2009, 2007, 2005, 2002, 1999 by The McGraw-Hill Companies, Inc. All rights reserved. No part of this publication may be reproduced or distributed in any form or by any means, or stored in a database or retrieval system, without the prior written consent of The McGraw-Hill Companies, Inc., including, but not limited to, any network or other electronic storage or transmission, or broadcast for distance learning. Some ancillaries, including electronic and print components, may not be available to customers outside the United States.

1 2 3 4 5 6 7 8 9 0 WCK/WCK 9 8 7 6 5 4 3 2 1 0

ISBN: 978-0-07-337888-6
MHID: 0-07-337888-7

Vice President, Editorial: *Michael Ryan*
Director of Development: *Rhona Robbin*
Sponsoring Editor: *Katie Stevens*
Development Editor: *Erika Lake*
Marketing Manager: *Leslie Oberhuber*
Media Project Manager: *Thomas Brierly*
Production Editor: *Anne Fuzellier*
Art Director: *Preston Thomas*
Art Manager: *Robin Mouat*
Design Manager: *Allister Fein*
Interior Designer: *Amanda Cavanaugh*
Photo Manager: *Brian J. Pecko*
Production Supervisor: *Louis Swaim*
Composition: *10/12 Palatino by Laserwords*
Printing: *45# New Era Matte Plus by World Color, Versailles*

Cover image: © *Mychal M. Richardson / Blend Images / Corbis*

Credits: The credits section for this book begins on page 473 and is considered an extension of the copyright page.

Library of Congress Cataloging-in-Publication Data

Dominick, Joseph R.
  Dynamics of mass communication : media in transition / Joseph Dominick. —11th ed.
      p. cm.
  Includes bibliographical references and index.
  ISBN-13: 978-0-07-337888-6 (alk. paper)
  ISBN-10: 0-07-337888-7 (alk. paper)
  1. Mass media. I. Title.
P90.D59 2010
302.23—dc22   2009048218

The Internet addresses listed in the text were accurate at the time of publication. The inclusion of a Web site does not indicate an endorsement by the authors or McGraw-Hill, and McGraw-Hill does not guarantee the accuracy of the information presented at these sites.

>> About the Author

Joseph R. Dominick received his undergraduate degree from University of Illinois and his Ph.D. from Michigan State University in 1970. He taught for four years at Queens College of the City University of New York before going to the College of Journalism and Mass Communication at the University of Georgia where, from 1980 to 1985, he served as head of the Radio-TV-Film Sequence. Dr. Dominick is the author of three books in addition to *The Dynamics of Mass Communication* and has published more than 40 articles in scholarly journals. From 1976 to 1980, Dr. Dominick served as editor of the *Journal of Broadcasting.* He has received research grants from the National Association of Broadcasters and from the American Broadcasting Company and has consulted for such organizations as the Robert Wood Johnson Foundation and the American Chemical Society. He served as interim department head from 2005 until his retirement in 2008.

>> Brief Contents

>> Contents

Chapter 9
Motion Pictures 200

Chapter 10
Broadcast Television 228

**> PART III   Specific Media
Professions   301**

Chapter 13

News Gathering and Reporting   302

Chapter 14
Public Relations   322

Chapter 15
Advertising   340

> PART IV   Regulation of the Mass Media   365

Chapter 16
Formal Controls: Laws, Rules, Regulations   366

>> Boxed Features

Media Talk

Need a good discussion starter? These boxes refer to Video clips at the Online Learning Center that introduce important issues in mass communication.

Media Tour

Go to the Online Learning Center to get a firsthand look at how various media operate and hear media professionals discuss significant concerns in their fields.

Social Issues

New Developments in mass communication raise new concerns. These boxes explore how the media operate in a social context.

Soundbyte

These boxes illustrate the unusual, the ironic, and the offbeat things that sometimes occur in the media world.

>> Preface

Those who have used the previous edition of *The Dynamics of Mass Communication* will notice that the 11th edition has a new subtitle: *Media in Transition.* This change seems highly appropriate given the singular transformations now engulfing the traditional media. Newspapers and magazines are struggling to stay alive; book publishers are digesting the implications of the e-book; the recording industry is scrambling for new business models; radio stations are coping with increased competition and searching for new revenue streams; TV networks are watching their audiences dwindle and wondering how to compensate for their loss of advertising dollars; and Hollywood is nervously watching as DVD sales slide and digital downloading threatens to do violence to the industry's bottom line.

Indeed, during mid-2009 there was a clever video circulating on the Internet called "The Year the Media Died," sung to the tune of "American Pie." Sample lyric:

> But the digital revolution fell like thunder
> With every newspaper that went under
> Bad news on the blogs
> The industry's gone to the dogs . . .
> Something touched me deep inside
> The year the media died.

Well, it may not be quite that bad and the situation may change when the economy recovers, but it's pretty obvious that five years from now the media landscape will be much different from today.

At the end of the decade, advertiser-supported media were hit with a double whammy. First, a deep recession dried up advertising dollars. Newspapers were the hardest hit since much of their revenue came from real estate and automotive ads, two of the areas most affected by the economic blues, but all the media suffered.

Second, a major change was taking place in advertising. For about 200 years, advertising and mass media went hand in hand. The media gathered an audience and the advertiser aimed messages at it. The process was inefficient since many in the audience were not prime prospects for what was being advertised, but marketers put up with the inefficiency since the media still offered the best way to get across a message. Then the Internet opened up new avenues, such as search engine advertising and social media marketing, which were much more efficient and focused. More advertising dollars left the traditional media and migrated to the Internet. Pretty soon, it was clear that there was no necessary hand-in-hand connection between advertising and the mass media. A new term emerged to describe this phenomenon: decoupling.

Media executives scrambled to offset their advertising revenue losses from traditional media by establishing a strong online presence, but they quickly relearned a basic lesson from Econ 101. Advertising supply on the Internet is virtually unlimited. During hard economic times, most companies cut their advertising budgets. What happens to price when supply is abundant and demand decreases? It declines. As one media executive put it, when it came to their online operations, media companies were trading analog dollars for digital dimes. The online revenue stream did not offset the losses from the decline of spending on traditional advertising.

Those media that do not depend on advertising have also been transformed by the digital revolution. The sound recording industry was forced to redefine itself because of digital downloads. The movie industry is currently coping with the same issue.

Even book publishing, the oldest mass media industry, which had managed to escape much of the impact of evolving technology, now finds itself dealing with the development of e-books and e-book readers, such as the Kindle. In short, the traditional way of doing business no longer works and all media are changing to cope with the new conditions. And that's a long explanation for the new three-word subtitle.

As you may have gathered by now, transition is a major theme of the 11th edition of *The Dynamics of Mass Communication: Media in Transition.*

In addition, since the last edition was published, social media—such as Twitter, MySpace, Facebook, YouTube, Flickr, and others—have become significant channels of communication. As of this writing, Facebook has more than 250 million members worldwide (that's more than the total population of Brazil), and YouTube contained more than 70 million videos with about 13 hours of content uploaded every minute.

Social media have become the first source of breaking news events. Much of the information about the postelection violence in Iran came from Twitter users and video posted on YouTube. Advertisers and public relations practitioners have embraced social media with gusto. It's rare these days to find an advertising or PR campaign that does not have a social media component.

The traditional media have also increased their use of social media. Among other examples, TV programs have Facebook pages; recording studios promote bands on their MySpace pages; magazines encourage readers to form their own communities; most newspapers allow readers to share pictures on the paper's Web site, and CNN reporters are frequent posters on Twitter. This increased use of social media is a second theme that runs through the new edition.

With the above as a general introduction, here's a more specific look at what's new in the 11th edition.

NEW TO THE 11TH EDITION

In addition to the new subtitle, there are several other changes. First, it's difficult for a textbook to provide up-to-the minute advice and information about careers, salaries, and upward mobility. Much of the career advice contained in the 10th edition no longer applies. Consequently, detailed information regarding the career outlook in the various media has been moved to the book's Web site, where it can be updated as conditions warrant.

Second, since everybody else in the world seems to be blogging, there is a blog that accompanies the book (http://dynamicsmasscomm.blogspot.com/) where you will find updates, class discussion starters, analysis, and wry asides. Finally, all tables now contain the latest information available.

Below are some of the changes that you will find in individual chapters.

- Part I: Chapter 1 now contains an extended discussion of the new media environment and how technology, economics, and social trends have contributed to the media's transition. There is also a new section on social media and their implications. Chapter 2 has an expanded discussion of functions of the new social media for the individual. Chapter 3 has been streamlined, and the development of social media is now included as the newest milestone.

- Part II: All of the chapters in Part II now include a new section called "Transition," which details how each medium is transforming itself to cope with changing economic, technological, and social conditions. All chapters also include a new section on social media. Chapter 4 has a discussion of the economic problems of newspapers, their search for a new business model, their transition to the Web, and an expanded discussion of the financial problems of papers. Chapter 6 discusses the challenges and potential of Amazon's new Kindle e-book reader. Chapter 8 includes a discussion of the RIAA's decision to stop suing file sharers and a description of new business models for the music industry. Chapter 10 incorporates a discussion of TV's transition to digital, while Chapter 11 has an expanded discussion of Web video.

- Part III: Chapter 13 features a new discussion on the problems of the traditional business model for news and a section on the "decoupling" of advertising from news. There is also an updated section on the differences and similarities of news media in light of their online efforts. Chapter 14 opens with an examination of the PR miscues of AIG. The chapter also contains an updated discussion of PR's use of social media and more details on the staffing of PR agencies. Chapter 15 also discusses the decoupling of advertising and media content. There is also an expanded treatment of the targeting of Internet ads.

- Part IV: Chapter 16 includes an updated status of legal issues mentioned throughout the chapter. Chapter 17 has a discussion of the ethical dimensions of the *Chicago Tribune*'s decision to hold back a story about the misdeeds of Illinois Governor Rod Blagojevich.

- Part V: Chapter 18 opens with an examination of differences in news coverage of President Obama's inauguration. The chapter also updates the media situation in Japan, Mexico, and China. Chapter 19 has a new section on video game violence and another on communication overload.

BOX SCORE

As in past editions, the boxed inserts in each chapter provide background material or extended coverage of topics mentioned in the text and raise issues for discussion and consideration. The 11th edition includes more than 90 new or revised boxes.

The boxes are grouped into several categories. The "Media Talk" boxes refer students to the Online Learning Center and introduce important issues in mass communication. Instructors can use these as discussion starters. The Media Tour boxes (also at the Online Learning Center) introduce video clips that look at how various media operate and feature media professionals discussing significant concerns in their fields.

The "Social Issues" boxes highlight matters of social concern that have generated some controversy. Some examples include a discussion of how journalists covered the financial crisis, an analysis of efforts to re-introduce the Fairness Doctrine, and whether we still need newsmagazines.

As the name suggests, "Ethical Issues" boxes raise questions about the proper way to act in difficult circumstances. For instance, what are the ethical problems raised by NBC's *To Catch a Predator* or by airbrushing photographs?

"Critical/Cultural Issues" boxes illustrate how this perspective can be used to further our understanding of mass communication. Examples include the influence of department stores on the development of radio and how the Food Network maintains traditional images of masculinity and femininity.

The "Media Probe" boxes take an in-depth look at subjects that have significance for the various media. Some examples include an examination of the role of Twitter in the postelection violence in Iran, the implications of the court decision concerning file sharing and the Pirate Bay Web site, and how the recession caused many newspapers to find themselves deeply in debt.

The "Decision Maker" boxes profile individuals who have made some of the important decisions that have had an impact on the development of the media. Examples include Ted Turner, Steven Spielberg, and Catherine Hughes.

And as before, the "Soundbytes" are brief boxes that highlight some of the strange, ironic, offbeat, and extraordinary developments that occur in the media, such as the MP3 player that includes a taser and a radio station that plays birdcalls.

CONTINUITY

The organization of the book has not changed since the 10th edition. Part I, "The Nature and History of Mass Communication," presents the intellectual context for the rest of the book. Chapter 1 compares and contrasts mass communication with other types of communication and notes that the distinctions are becoming fuzzier. Chapter 2 introduces two perspectives commonly used to understand and explore the operations of the media: functional analysis and the critical/cultural approach. Chapter 3 takes a macroanalytic approach and traces the general history of media from the invention of printing to the explosion of social media.

Part II, "Media," represents the core of the book. Chapters 4–12 examine each of the major media. The organization of each chapter follows a similar pattern. First, there is a brief history from the medium's beginnings to how it is transforming itself in the digital age. This is followed by sections that describe how the medium is becoming more mobile, how it has been affected by user-generated content, and how it is using social media. Next comes a discussion of the defining characteristics of each medium and a description of industry structure.

I have increased the emphasis on media economics. Since the major media in the United States exist to make a profit, it is valuable for students to appreciate where the money comes from, how it is spent, and why making a profit these days is harder than ever. This is even more important today as several media industries are struggling to survive as traditional revenue streams dry up and their online efforts cannot make up the shortfall.

Part III, "Specific Media Professions," examines three specific professions closely associated with the mass media: news reporting, public relations, and advertising. Similar to the approach in Part II, each chapter begins with a brief history, examines the structure of that particular profession, considers the changes brought about by the digital revolution, and discusses key issues in the field.

Part IV, "Regulation of the Mass Media," examines both the formal and informal controls that influence the media. These are complicated areas, and I have tried to make the information as user-friendly as possible.

The concluding Part V, "Impact, of the Media" continues to emphasize the social effects of the mass media. Chapter 18, "International and Comparative Media Systems," stresses the global influence of the mass media. Chapter 18, "The Social Effects of Mass Communication," looks at the impact media have on the individual as well as society.

Once again, I have tried to keep the writing style informal and accessible. Whenever possible I have chosen examples from popular culture that I hope all students are familiar with. Technical terms are boldfaced and defined in the glossary. The book also contains a number of charts, graphs, diagrams, and tables that I hope aid understanding.

SUPPORTING MATERIALS: COMPREHENSIVE

The Online Learning Center now houses the Media Talk video clips, Media Tours video clips, and all of the instructor resources (Instructor's Manual, Test Bank, and PowerPoint slides), and the traditional student quiz materials. The URL is **www. mhhe.com/dominick11e.**

ACKNOWLEDGMENTS

Thanks to all those instructors who used previous editions of *The Dynamics of Mass Communication* and were kind enough to suggest improvements. Several colleagues deserve special mention: Professors Noah Arcenaux and Paul Hillier provided boxed inserts; Professor Scott Shamp was kind enough to share his blog page; and Professor Michael Castengera's newsletter, "Message from Michael," was a valuable resource. In addition, thanks to researcher Meaghan Dominick for her efforts with the "Media Talk" boxes, and to Carole Dominick for helping with a number of tasks.

Once again I appreciate the sedulous efforts of all the reviewers who offered suggestions for the 11th edition:

Bridgette Colaco, Troy University

John Kerezy, Cuyahoga Community College

Robert M. Ogles, Purdue University

J. Mike Reed, Saddleback College

Roger A. Soenksen, James Madison University

And, as always, a big thanks to all the people at McGraw-Hill on publishing yet another edition: Editor-in-Chief Michael Ryan, Executive Editor Katie Stevens, Marketing Manager Leslie Oberhuber, Erika Lake for her comprehensive editorial development, Production Editor Anne Fuzellier, Media Project Manager Thomas Brierly, Photo Researcher Brian Pecko, Designer Allister Fein, Production Supervisor Louis Swaim, and Permissions Editor Karyn Morrison.

THE AUDIENCE

As most instructors will attest, the introductory course in mass communication attracts two types of students. One type is interested in following a professional career in some form of media (a career path made even more challenging by current market conditions). This student wants to know the nuts and bolts of the media—how they are organized, how they work, who does what, and what career possibilities are out there. The second type of student will probably never pursue a career in the media but will become a member of the audience and consume a great deal of media content. These students are more interested in analyzing and understanding how the media operate and what impact they have on society. To use an overworked expression, they want to become "media literate."

An original goal of the first edition of *Dynamics* was to present an up-to-date, detailed, and comprehensive look at contemporary media that would benefit aspiring media professionals and at the same time provide a useful foundation for those who will end up in other careers. A second goal was to help both students and faculty understand and appreciate the fast-changing world of mass communication a little better. As has been the case 10 times before, it is hoped that this new edition still fulfills both of those goals.

J. Dominick
Athens, Ga.

Your Guided Tour

CHAPTER 2

Perspectives on Mass Communication

This chapter will prepare you to:

- understand the differences between the functional approach and the critical/cultural approach to studying mass communication

- explain the value of each approach in the analysis of the mass communication process

- describe the functions mass media perform for society

- explain uses-and-gratifications analysis

- understand the concepts of meaning, hegemony, and ideology

People study mass communication for a variety of reasons. Scholars study it to better comprehend the process and to develop theories that explain and predict how the media operate. Critics study it to offer insights about its influence and to suggest improvements. Media consumers study it to become media literate, to be able to understand the elements involved in the mass communication process, and to analyze and critically evaluate information presented in the mass media. Those in the media industry study it in order to increase their operating efficiency and maximize their profits when they sell news and information products to the general public.

No matter what the reason for study, it is helpful to use a **paradigm** (a model or pattern used to analyze something) to guide the way we think about the mass communication process. A paradigm is useful for several reasons:

- It provides us with a consistent perspective from which to examine mass communication.
- It generates concepts that are helpful in understanding media behavior.
- It helps us identify what is or is not important in the process.

There are many paradigms that we could use to study mass communication. This chapter will introduce two that provide different ways of looking at media and society. The **functional approach** emphasizes the way that audiences use mass communication and the benefits people receive from media consumption. A second paradigm, which many have labeled the **critical/cultural approach**, examines the underlying power relationships in media exposure and stresses the many meanings and interpretations that audience members find in media content. (Chapter 19 introduces a third model, the empirical paradigm, an approach that has been commonly used to investigate the social effects of the mass media.)

A recent example highlights the difference between these two approaches. Released in 2008, *The Dark Knight*, the latest in the Batman series of movies, cost nearly $200 million to produce. The film was a huge commercial success, grossing more than $1 billion worldwide. In the movie, Batman, District Attorney Harvey Dent, and Lieutenant James Gordon battle a wave of chaos in Gotham City caused by a master criminal called the Joker. Batman eventually wins but is forced to question the morality of his methods.

A functional analysis would want to know several things. First, why did people choose to see the movie? Second, would people identify with Batman and, if so, why? Would viewers have a more positive view of violence after watching the film? Did younger viewers experience the film differently than older viewers?

A critical/cultural researcher would view the film as a text and deconstruct its various elements. For example, the only female character has little more than a minor role and is killed near the end of the film. A critical/cultural analysis might note that the film is another example of Hollywood encouraging a male-dominated society that marginalizes and de-powers women. Moreover, Batman is able to thwart the Joker by a hi-tech spy system that violates the privacy and civil rights of all Gotham City residents. From a critical/cultural perspective, the film appears to carry an ideological message that legitimizes authoritarian methods and encourages conservative political values.

All in all, this movie could serve as the springboard for many disparate avenues of inquiry. This chapter will look first at functional analysis and then examine the critical/cultural approach.

01

Chapter-Opening Previews

Chapter objectives and vignettes draw students in and help them concentrate on the important points of each chapter.

Media Tour Inside *Vibe*

You can access the Media World clips, with all new NBC videos, on the Online Learning Center home page. Go to www.mhhe.com/dominick11e, select Student Center and then Chapter 5. The first part provides a look at the magazine's operations, and the second part features the staff discussing a wide range of issues.

The original strategy was for *Vibe* to be another *Rolling Stone* but with different music. *Vibe*'s timing was good: Hip-hop, one of the primary music styles covered in the magazine, was just gaining popularity among both African American and white youths. As a result, the magazine was successful in attracting readers. Its circulation grew from about 100,000 in the early 1990s to 800,000 in 2002.

1. How does the business side of a magazine influence the editorial side?
2. What kind of companies might advertise in *Vibe*?
3. How do cultural trends play into the success of a magazine such as *Vibe*?
4. If you were the publisher of *Rolling Stone, Vibe*'s biggest competitor, how would you respond to *Vibe*'s success? How, if at all, would you change your magazine?
5. *Vibe* folded in 2009 but was resurrected under new ownership as a Web publication. Do you think the new online *Vibe* will succeed?

Media Tours

These boxes offer focus questions for viewing video tours of different media companies.

Media Talks

These margin notes offer focus questions for viewing NBC News videos related to chapter topics.

MEDIA TALK

TV Phenom *American Idol*

Clip 8: 6 minutes 25 seconds
You can watch Clip 8 *on the Online Learning Center home page,* www.mhhe.com/dominick11e. *Select* Student Center *and then* Chapter 8. This clip describes *American Idol*'s effect on the music industry. Note how this is another example of media symbiosis. Have you ever voted for someone on *American Idol*? Do you think that *American Idol* has hurt or helped the music industry? Have you ever bought or downloaded any of the songs by an *American Idol* contestant? When was the last time you went to the store and bought a CD? How do you get the music you want to listen to?

Ethical Issues · *Slumdog Millionaire:* Exploiting Poverty?

Slumdog Millionaire was the surprise film hit of 2008. Produced for a relatively cheap $15 million and without any major U.S. stars, it nearly missed getting to the big screen when its distributor wanted it to go directly to DVD. Fortunately for the movie, another distributor turned up and the rest of the story is well-known: *Slumdog* won the Oscar for Best Picture and is well on its way to grossing more than $200 million worldwide.

Not everything, however, was rosy. The film was not popular in India, and charges soon surfaced that *Slumdog* was exploiting poverty. The film is set in the slums of Mumbai and contains scenes of torture, misery, starving children, and other degradations. The cinematography, fast-paced editing, and music from M.I.A., however, make the scenes more surreal than real. The viewer is asked to dwell on scenes of filth and squalor but not quite accept them as authentic. It's set in the real world, but the story is a fairy tale.

Some critics have labeled the film an example of "poverty porn." These scenes of abject poverty, of course, make the audience feel much better about the hero's ultimate victory, but the film raises the issue of whether the moviemaker should take advantage of social deprivations in order to make a "feel good" movie that is ultimately aimed at a commercial market. When the film crew leaves, the poverty remains behind. The child stars in the film went back to the slums. If the film makes it big, as did *Slumdog,* does the filmmaker

have an ethical obligation to help those unfortunates who contributed to the film's success?

On the one hand, a person could argue that filmmakers aren't social workers and their prime mission is to create entertainment, not to cure the ills of the world. Moreover, shouldn't the responsibility for combating poverty rest on the government and not on film studios?

On the other hand, a commonly accepted ethical principle is that human beings should not be used as a means to an end (for more on ethics, see Chapter 17). The contributions of all to the success of a project should be acknowledged and fairly rewarded. Exploiting someone's weakness, powerlessness, or naïveté is a denial of that person's self-worth.

In the case of *Slumdog,* the filmmakers recognized some responsibility for those caught in the poverty shown in the film. They pledged about $1.5 million to a program designed to help the children caught in the Mumbai slums. They also promised to find better housing for the film's child stars and established an educational trust for them.

In a related development, a British TV production company was making plans to create a series called *Secret Slumdog Millionaire* in which rich persons would secretly go undercover in the slums of Mumbai, eventually reveal their identities, and give the poor large sums of money. Exploitation or not?

Ethical Issues

These boxes challenge students to think critically about ethical issues specific to mass communications industries.

Social Issues

New developments in mass communication raise new concerns. These boxes explore how the mass media operate in a social context.

Social Issues · Diversity in Television

Kweisi Mfume, president of the NAACP, speaking at his organization's national convention, criticized the four major TV networks for the lack of diversity in the new shows planned for the 1999–2000 season. He noted that none of the 26 series had a minority person in a leading or starring role. Mfume's criticism marked another chapter in the continuing controversy over the portrayals of minorities in prime time.

During the early years of TV, African American performers were difficult to find. And when they did appear, it was usually in a menial or subservient role. In 1965, however, a young Bill Cosby costarred with Robert Culp in *I Spy* and paved the way for more substantial roles for African American performers. By the 1970s several shows that featured black casts appeared in prime time—most were situation comedies, such as *The Jeffersons.* The number of African American performers increased slowly but steadily during the 1980s. For most of the 1990s, the proportion of black characters seen in prime-time TV was about the same as the percentage of African Americans in the general population. This increase, however, was due in part to the emergence of UPN and WB, two networks that targeted several of their series to African American viewers.

The apparent lack of diversity in the 1999–2000 season was especially troubling to Mfume. The NAACP noted that minorities were hard to find behind the camera as well. Of all the writers who worked on TV sitcoms and dramas, only 6 percent were black. FCC data show that minorities own about 2.8 percent of all broadcast stations.

Mfume threatened a boycott of the networks and their sponsors unless something was done. The networks responded by adding some minority characters to the casts of existing shows. CBS aired *City of Angels,* a drama set in an inner-city hospital, that featured a predominantly black cast and creative team. The networks also planned to increase minority hiring and to appoint executives in charge of their diversity efforts. These moves apparently satisfied Mfume, who called off plans for the boycott.

The 2000–2001 TV season did not spark similar protests. In addition to *City of Angels,* there were several new series with African Americans in major roles, such as *Boston Public.* The situation behind the camera and in minority ownership, however, was unchanged. Things improved a bit in the 2002 season when there were 43 series featuring multiethnic characters. Back in 1995, there were only 13 such shows on the air.

The diversity issues surfaced again in 2003, but this time the focus was on cable. Members of the Congressional Black Caucus sent a letter to the cable TV industry asking for more minority-themed programs and more minority-owned cable networks. It resurfaced when the NAACP noted that none of the situation comedies scheduled by the major networks for the 2006 season starred an African American actor or actress. A 2008 report compiled by the NAACP showed that the number of minority actors had actually decreased from 2006 to 2007.

Why should the networks present a diverse view of society? Many would argue that the networks have a social obligation to present an accurate view of society so that members of minority groups do not feel marginalized or disenfranchised from society. Others would suggest that TV should present role models for all groups. These high-minded reasons aside, it also makes economic sense for the networks to present a diverse menu of programs. The 2000 census showed that minorities constitute more than 35 percent of the U.S. population, and their buying power is increasing each year. Presenting shows that appeal to these groups is simply good business.

Further, some critics suggest that paying large amounts of attention to the way the broadcast networks portray minorities overlooks the gains minorities have made in cable. For instance, Black Entertainment Television draws a significant audience. Two Spanish-language networks, Galavision and Univision, are aimed at Hispanics.

Finally, consider the opinion of commentator Earl Ofari Hutchinson, who suggests that prime-time TV is not worth fighting for. He charges that the networks have oversaturated the airways with silly sitcoms and action shows designed to appeal to young, affluent whites. These types of programs, he argues, have no relevance for African Americans, who should focus their attention elsewhere. In a similar vein Cynthia Tucker, the African American former editor of the editorial page of the *Atlanta Journal-Constitution,* suggests that the NAACP is misplacing its efforts by concentrating on network TV programs. Instead, she argues, the organization should encourage young African Americans to stop watching TV. "Let prime-time TV keep its bland cast of characters," says Tucker. "There are plenty of good books in which black youngsters can find themselves reflected."[1]

---
[1]Quoted in Richard Breyer, "Color TV," *Word and I,* March 2000, 84.

Decision Makers

Profiles of people who have had a significant impact on contemporary mass media.

Decision Makers   Steven Spielberg

Steven Spielberg started making movies at age 12 using his father's 8mm camera. One of his earliest productions was a horror film starring his three younger sisters. He continued to make his own films during his college days, but he graduated with a degree in English because his grades were too low to get him into film school. One of Spielberg's independently made films

Steven Spielberg directing *Saving Private Ryan*.

caught the attention of an executive at Universal Pictures, who hired the young Spielberg to direct episodes of a TV series. The young director eventually wound up directing a made-for-TV movie, *Duel*, that won much critical acclaim.

On the basis of his success with *Duel*, Spielberg got approval to direct his first theatrical movie, *The Sugarland Express*. Although praised by critics, the movie did poorly at the box office. Nonetheless, the studio gave him a new assignment: directing the movie version of a best-selling novel about a huge shark. The movie, *Jaws*, released in 1975, marked a significant milestone in movie history. It was the first of

the big-budget summer action movies, a strategy that movie studios still follow (consider *Twister, Independence Day,* and *The Dark Knight*). *Jaws* was also the first of the movie blockbusters, raking in more than $250 million. Hollywood studios quickly adopted a "big budget equals big blockbuster" mentality.

Spielberg also hit upon a formula for making successful pictures that resonated with moviegoers: Take tried-and-true, classic adventure themes, and enhance them with cutting-edge special effects. The *Indiana Jones* trilogy, *Jurassic Park, E.T.,* and *Close Encounters of the Third Kind* are all examples of this formula. Spielberg also tackled more serious themes, as exemplified in *The Color Purple, Schindler's List, Amistad, Saving Private Ryan,* and *Munich*.

In a career that has spanned more than a quarter-century, Spielberg has won two Oscars and numerous other movie awards. Of the top 25 all-time movie hits, 4 were directed by Steven Spielberg.

Media Probes

Additional illustrations, examples, and background to chapter topics.

Media Probe   Radiohead: Groundbreaking or Gimmick?

Recording artists are well aware of the concept of **disintermediation** (a process that eliminates the distributor and delivers a product or service directly to the consumer). If a band could produce its own album and then promote and distribute it over the Internet, then there is little need for a record label. The band could simply sell direct to consumers and make a lot more money.

The British band Radiohead decided to take this route with the 2007 release of its album *In Rainbows*. The band had been under contract to recording company EMI but decided to try its hand at e-commerce after the contract expired. They announced that fans could download the whole album from Radiohead's Web site. And, in another novel twist, visitors to the site could pay whatever they wished, even nothing, for the album.

Pundits hailed the arrangement as groundbreaking and revolutionary, something that could shake the traditional recording industry to its core. Some even predicted that *In Rainbows* would mark the beginning of a trend that would put major record labels out of business.

It didn't quite work out that way. After 90 days, the band stopped the potentially free downloads and a message on

its Web site noted that the album would soon be available on a CD distributed by a major label and could be purchased through traditional outlets.

Why the change of tactics? Was offering the download a bad idea? We may never know for sure, but data gathered by an Internet audience rating service found that 60 percent of the people in the United States who downloaded the album paid nothing. Worldwide, the average price paid for a downloaded album was about $2.25. Although the official numbers were never released, sales of the CD at traditional stores and paid downloads from iTunes probably earned much more than the pay-what-you-will system.

Radiohead's tactics did not escape criticism. The voluntary payment plan was called a marketing gimmick, and fans were not pleased with the quality of the downloaded version. Many complained that they had to buy the higher-priced CD in order to fully appreciate the music.

The album, in all its forms, eventually sold more than 3 million copies, and the CD version opened at number one on all the major charts. Even so, the album was not the revolutionary force that many predicted.

Critical/Cultural Issues

These boxes illustrate the critical/cultural studies approach to mass communication in action.

Critical / Cultural Issues

The Meaning of Media

Cell phones, laptops, and PDAs belong to that broad class of devices known as *mobile information devices.* It's possible, however, that lumping these devices under one umbrella label may obscure differences in the way audience members perceive their functions. Communication scholars point out that communication technologies may be socially constructed in different ways by their users.

In an article in the June 2003 issue of *Critical Studies in Mass Communication,* Paul Leonardi argues that culture plays a major role in how media are perceived. Leonardi conducted focus groups (structured group interviews guided by a moderator) among Latinos living in the United States. He asked participants to discuss how cell phones, computers, and the Internet were perceived in Latino culture.

His results were somewhat surprising. Latino culture places a high value on consistent and close interpersonal contact, and the cell phone was seen as consistent with that value. Focus group participants revealed that the cell phone was an important tool for communication and was becoming a necessity for daily life. More than 90 percent of respondents had used a cell phone. Almost all of those who didn't currently own a cell phone planned to buy one within a year. Respondents recognized the utility of the cell phone in an emergency and the fact that cell phones represent an alternative way of reaching someone when the land lines are busy. Cell phones had become so ingrained in their daily lives that some participants mentioned that their children used cell phones to call them from another room in the house to ask what was being prepared for dinner. In short, the cell phone fit nicely with cultural values.

On the other hand, computers and the Internet were not such a good fit. Only 40 percent of the respondents had used a computer, and even fewer (27 percent) had ever used the Internet. Respondents appeared to think of computers and the Internet in the same way, treating them as similar.

They did not see the Internet as a communication medium. Instead, the Latinos in these focus groups perceived it as a tool with which to find information. The use of e-mail, chat rooms, and message boards as communication channels was seldom mentioned. Although computers were perceived as useful devices, they were also seen as inhibiting interpersonal communication among family members and friends. Surfing the Internet was perceived as a solitary activity that isolated people from each other. In short, respondents felt that computers and the Internet did not keep people connected. As a result, interpersonal values were jeopardized by these technologies.

Language also played a role in participants' preference for the cell phone over the computer. Spanish-language cell phones are readily available; Spanish-language computer platforms are harder to find. In addition, only a small portion of Internet content is in Spanish. This posed a cultural problem for Latinos. In order to access the Internet, it was necessary to forgo the use of one's native language.

Although many of the respondents said they planned to purchase a computer in the near future, their stated reasons for buying a computer had nothing to do with the computer's communication potential. Instead, the Latinos in Leonardi's study recognized that those who didn't have a computer would be in an inferior position to those in mainstream U.S. culture.

Leonardi's findings highlight that Latinos living in the United States do not view these information devices as homogeneous. Instead, they have distinct perceptions based on how cell phones, computers, and the Internet relate to their cultural values regarding communication. As Leonardi sums up: "[T]he communication goals of a particular group of users always play a crucial role in their uses and perceptions of technology. If we forget this, we may blindly adopt technologies because we believe they are a sign of progress without making sure they help us progress."

Full Range of Chapter Review Material

Clear, concise chapter summaries, key terms lists, and review questions provide students with essential study materials.

CAREER >> **Cable, Satellite, and Internet TV Industries**
OUTLOOK

The cable and satellite industry is smaller than the broadcast TV industry, employing about 90,000 people. The number working in Internet television is difficult to determine. The job prospects in this area, particularly Internet video, seem more positive than in the other media we have discussed. Specialized cable/satellite channels continue to premiere, and they will need people in production, sales, marketing, performance, and public relations. And, as the chapter indicates, Internet TV is a big growth area.

The career outlook in the various media industries changes quickly. For a more current description of conditions in the cable/satellite Internet business and a more detailed look at career options, please consult the book's Web site: www.mhhe.com/dominick11e.

MAIN POINTS

- Cable TV began in the 1950s as a way of bringing TV signals to places that could not otherwise receive them.
- Cable TV reached maturity by the turn of the century and was facing competition from DBS satellite systems.
- The Telecommunications Act of 1996 permitted cable and telephone companies to compete with one another.
- Internet TV developed in the late 1990s and became more popular with the growth of broadband.
- Cable and satellite systems are structured differently from those of conventional TV.

- Cable television is dominated by large multiple system operators. Two companies, DirecTV and the Dish Network, are the leading DBS providers.
- Internet video can be categorized by source (professional or amateur) and content (original or repurposed).
- User-generated video, such as those on YouTube, has become extremely popular.
- Internet video sites make money by charging a fee for their content or by selling advertising.
- Nielsen provides rating data for cable/satellite networks. Ratings for online video-sharing sites are provided by companies that measure Internet usage.

QUESTIONS FOR REVIEW

1. What are the defining features of cable/satellite TV? Of Internet TV?
2. Who are the major owners of cable and DBS systems?
3. How does cable/satellite programming compare to traditional broadcast network programming?

4. Trace the structure of a cable system from head end to home.
5. How can online video sites make money?

QUESTIONS FOR CRITICAL THINKING

1. How, if at all, will VOD change the cable TV industry?
2. Have you ever posted a video online? Why? Have you ever looked at online videos? Why?
3. Google paid $1.65 billion for YouTube. Do you think Google will get its money back?

4. Why do you think many presidential candidates opted to make their announcements using online video as opposed to a press conference?

KEY TERMS

multiple system operators (MSOs) (p. 261)
direct-broadcast satellites (DBS) (p. 261)
voice-over-Internet protocol (VOIP) (p. 261)

Internet TV (p. 262)
buffering (p. 262)
podcast (p. 262)
head end (p. 266)
distribution system (p. 266)
house drop (p. 266)

carriage fee (p. 268)
video-on-demand (VOD) (p. 268)
geosynchronous satellite (p. 269)
encrypted (p. 269)
microcasting (p. 274)

INTERNET RESOURCES

Online Learning Center

On the Online Learning Center home page, www.mhhe.com/dominick11e, select Student Center and then Chapter 11.

1. Use the Learning Objectives, Chapter Outline, and Main Points sections to review this chapter.
2. Test your knowledge of the chapter using the multiple choice and flashcard features of the site.
3. Expand your knowledge of concepts and topics discussed in the chapter with additional Questions for Critical Thinking and Internet Exercises.

Surfing the Internet

http://webcast.istreamplanet.com/lwc/whitechapel.asp
The Little White Wedding Chapel in Las Vegas has live and on-demand videos of its weddings.

www.blinkx.tv
Example of a video-sharing site that mixes professional and amateur content.

www.historychannel.com
Has more about history than it does about the cable network, but contains good examples of streaming video and interactivity.

www.multichannel.com
Multichannel News is the leading trade publication covering cable, satellite, and wireless companies.

www.ncta.com
Web site of the National Cable Television Association. Contains information about the latest issues facing the industry.

Springboards for Discussion and Research

Critical thinking questions based on the text and Internet resources engage students with issues affecting them as consumers and future professionals.

Online Learning Center: www.mhhe.com/dominick11e

This book-specific Web site features practice tests, learning objectives, chapter main points, key terms additional Questions for Critical Thinking, and an online glossary. For the instructor, the password-protected area of the Web site offers a teaching guide, detailed chapter summaries, and PowerPoint slides.

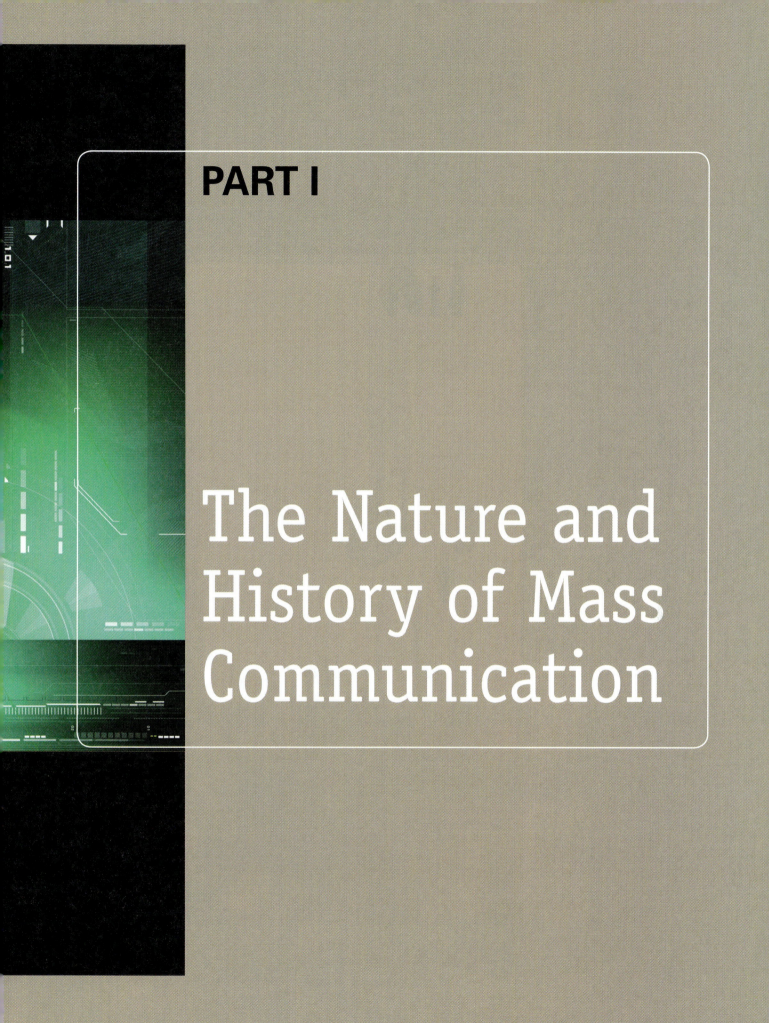

PART I

The Nature and History of Mass Communication

CHAPTER 1

Communication: Mass and Other Forms

This chapter will prepare you to:

- recognize the elements of the communication process

- understand the different types of communication settings

- identify the function of gatekeepers

- describe how the Internet has changed mass communication

- explain the various types of mass media convergence

- understand the technological, economic, and social forces that are transforming mass media

If these people unexpectedly show up on your doorstep, you may be the victim of a particularly dangerous Internet prank called SWATing.

New communication technologies bring great benefits to society, but they also bring new risks. Consider the following example:

Late one evening in California a husband, wife, and their two children were suddenly awakened by the roar of a helicopter and the wailing of police sirens. Thinking that perhaps a criminal was loose in the neighborhood, the husband grabbed a knife and went to the back porch to check on the backyard. Before he got very far he was blinded by the beams from several high-power flashlights. Angry shouts ordered him to drop to the ground. Suddenly he was surrounded by several SWAT team members who had their assault rifles pointed straight at him. The man was handcuffed and watched as the police stormed into his house.

Was the man a wanted criminal? No. Was there some terrible crime being committed in his house? No. Did the SWAT team make a mistake and arrive at the wrong address? No. The man and his family were the victims of a malicious Internet trick called SWATing. SWATing is a dangerous prank that exploits a weakness in the 911 emergency call service brought about by the development of telephone calls carried over the Internet using a process called VoIP, or Voice over Internet Protocol.

Before VoIP, calls from landline phones were registered to a fixed physical address. When a call came into a 911 call station, the address was displayed on a dispatcher's screen. A call made from a VoIP phone, however, is not routed from a fixed place but travels through Web servers located in a room that could be almost anywhere. VoIP providers have tried to solve this problem by attaching a customer's caller ID to a 911 call. Unfortunately, there are ways to "spoof" a caller ID so that it appears a call is originating from whatever number the caller wishes to display. This is apparently what happened to the California family. They were the victims of a SWATing call from a Washington teenager who picked their number at random and placed a 911 call that appeared to be coming from inside the California family's home. The teen pretended to be high on drugs and told the 911 dispatcher that he had just shot his sister and was about to murder someone else. Not surprisingly, the dispatcher sent the SWAT team to the address displayed on the caller ID. Luckily, no one was killed or injured. (Upgrading the entire 911 computer system would go a long way toward preventing these SWATing calls, but budgetary problems have so far prevented the improvement.)

Police eventually tracked down the Washington teenager and discovered that he had placed almost 200 bogus calls to 911 centers across the country. The teen pleaded guilty to five felony counts and was sentenced to three years in prison.

Communication between people is a fragile thing, particularly where technology is concerned. Even when there is no malicious intent, communication can go awry. The following examples may not be as disturbing as the SWATing case, but they are still illustrative.

- In Arizona an officer in a county sheriff's department pushed the wrong key while sending e-mail and sent a report on terrorist activity that was stamped "Do NOT release to the public or media" to all the media in the southern part of the state.

- A computer error at the company that published the alumni directory for the University of New Hampshire mistakenly listed 500 very much alive alumni as dead.

- A Georgia man received a letter from his bank informing him that he had overdrawn his account by $211 trillion.

- A technician at the Alaska Department of Revenue mistakenly erased a disc drive and deleted an account worth $38 billion.

- If you did a search on Google during the morning of January 31, 2009, all of your results might have displayed the warning "This site may be harmful to your computer." Somebody working for Google mistakenly added a "/" to a computer command that resulted in a warning message being displayed on everybody's search results.

- In Great Britain a taxi driver followed the directions given by his satellite navigation system and made a left turn into a river.

- An employee of the *Los Angeles Times* clicked on the wrong file and posted a story on the paper's Web site announcing that presidential nominee Barack Obama had chosen Hillary Clinton as his running mate.

- On December 31, 2008, thousands of owners of Microsoft's Zune digital music players discovered that their devices would no longer work because their software did not know how to handle a leap year.

- Thanks to a software glitch, 3,000 British citizens received a letter from their local elections office informing them that they were now officially residents of Guyana, South America.

- In 2008 Google's Web-trawling program found a six-year-old story in a newspaper's archive about United Airlines filing for bankruptcy and mistakenly placed it in Google News. An investment newsletter carried the story as current news and set off panic selling of United's stock. The stock lost 75 percent of its value before the error was corrected.

- In Canada a bank mistakenly sent hundreds of faxes containing confidential information about its customers to a junkyard operator in West Virginia.

Despite their apparent lack of similarity, these examples share certain elements common to human communication. They serve as a springboard for an examination of the differences between mass and other forms of communication. The mass media, however, are in transition, making these differences less clear. We will have more to say about this transition throughout the book, but in order to understand what is happening with mass communication we must first look at the basic process of human communication.

The Communication Process

Figure 1-1 depicts the communication process. We will refer to this figure as we examine the process more fully.

▲ Encoding: Transmitting the Message

To begin with, the **source** initiates the process by having a thought or an idea that he or she wishes to transmit to some other entity. Naturally, sources differ in their communication skills ("Garçon, I will have the Boeuf Haché Grillé au Charbon de Bois" versus "Gimmeaburger"). The source may or may not have knowledge about the receiver of the message. As I write these lines, I have only a general notion about the kinds of people who will read them, and I have no idea what you'll be doing while you're reading them (that's probably for the best). Sources can be single individuals, groups, or even organizations.

Encoding refers to the activities that a source goes through to translate thoughts and ideas into a form that may be perceived by the senses. When you have something to say, your brain and your tongue work together (usually) to form words and spoken sentences. When you write a letter, your brain and your fingers cooperate to produce patterns of ink or some other substance that can be seen on paper. Encoding in a communication setting can take place one or more times. In a face-to-face conversation, the speaker encodes thoughts into words. Over the telephone, this phase is repeated, but the phone subsequently encodes sound waves into electrical energy.

The **message** is the actual physical product that the source encodes. When you talk, your speech is the message. When you write a letter home, what you put on the paper is the message. When a television network presents *Lost* or *24*, the programs are the message.

FIGURE 1-1 Elements of the Communication Process

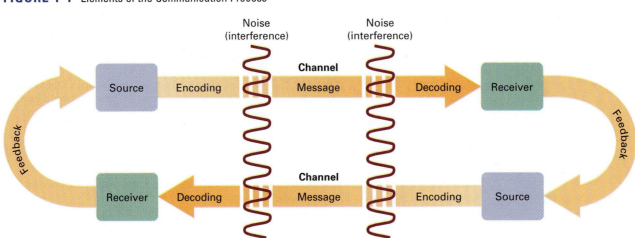

Human beings usually have a large number of messages at their disposal that they can choose to send, ranging from the simple but effective "No!" to something as complicated as Darwin's *On the Origin of Species.* Messages can be directed at one specific individual ("Dude!") or at millions (*People* magazine). Messages can be cheap to produce (the spoken word) or very expensive (this book). Some messages are more under the control of the receiver than others. For example, think about how hard or easy it is for you to break off communication (1) in a face-to-face conversation with another person, (2) during a telephone call, and (3) while watching a TV commercial.

Channels are the ways the message travels to the receiver. Sound waves carry spoken words; light waves carry visual messages. Air currents can serve as olfactory channels, carrying messages to our noses—messages that are subtle but nonetheless significant. What kind of message do you get from someone who reeks of Chanel No. 5? Of Brut? Of garlic? Touch is also a channel (such as braille). Some messages use more than one channel to travel to the receiver. For example, radio signals travel by electromagnetic radiation until they are transformed by receiving sets into sound waves that travel through the air to our ears.

▲ Decoding: Receiving the Message

The **decoding** process is the opposite of the encoding process. It consists of activities that translate or interpret physical messages into a form that has eventual meaning for a receiver. As you read these lines, you are decoding a message. If you are playing the radio while decoding these lines, you are decoding two messages simultaneously—one aural, one visual. Both humans and machines can be thought of as decoders. The radio is a decoder; so is a DVD playback unit; so is the telephone (one end encodes and the other end decodes); so is a film projector.

What we said earlier about encoding also applies to decoding: Some people are better at it than others. Many of you will not be able to decode "¿Dónde está el baño?"; others will. Some people are able to read 1,500 words a minute; others struggle along at 200.

The **receiver** is the target of the message—its ultimate goal. The receiver can be a single person, a group, an institution, or even a large, anonymous collection of people. The receivers of the message can be determined by the source, as in a telephone call, or they can self-select themselves into the audience, as with the audience for a TV show. It should also be clear that in some situations the source and receiver can be in each other's immediate presence, while in other situations they can be separated by both space and time.

▲ Feedback

Now let us examine the bottom half of Figure 1-1. This portion of the figure represents the potential for **feedback** to occur. Feedback refers to those responses of the receiver that shape and alter the subsequent messages of the source. Feedback represents a reversal of the flow of communication. The original source becomes the receiver; the original receiver becomes the new source. Feedback is useful to the source because it allows the source to

Carrie Underwood's "Before He Cheats" contains several examples of negative feedback.

answer the question "How am I doing?" Feedback is important to the receiver because it allows the receiver to attempt to change some element in the communication process. Communication scholars have traditionally identified two different kinds of feedback—positive and negative. In general terms, positive feedback from the receiver usually encourages the communication behavior in progress; negative feedback usually attempts to change the communication or even to terminate it.

Consider the following telephone call:

"Bambi?"

"Yes."

"This is Harold. I sit in front of you in econ class."

"Are you the one who keeps scratching your head with a pencil?"

"Gee, I never noticed it. I guess I do it unconsciously. Say, I was wondering if you would like to have coffee with me sometime after class."

"Are you kidding?"

Click.

This is *negative* feedback—the original receiver terminated the message. Here is another conversation:

"Bambi, this is Rod."

"Oh, hi, Rod. Has your leg healed up from the last game yet?"

"Yeah."

"How are your classes going?"

"I can't get econ."

"I'll be over in 20 minutes to give you some help. OK?"

"OK."

Click.

This is *positive* feedback—the original receiver encouraged the communication.

Feedback can be immediate or delayed. Immediate feedback occurs when the reactions of the receiver are directly perceived by the source. A speech maker who hears the audience boo and hiss while he or she is talking is getting immediate feedback. On the other hand, suppose you just listened to the latest CD by a popular group and decided it wasn't very good. To communicate that evaluation to the source, you would first have to identify the company that distributed the CD and find a mailing address, phone number, e-mail address, or Web site address. You would then have to send your feedback via the appropriate channel. If you got your message through to the company, it would still have to be passed on to the group, a process that might take several days or even longer.

▲ Noise

The final factor we will consider is **noise.** Communication scholars define *noise* as anything that interferes with the delivery of the message. A little noise might pass unnoticed, while too much noise might prevent the message from reaching its destination. There are at least three different types of noise: semantic, mechanical, and environmental.

Semantic noise occurs when different people have different meanings for different words and phrases or when the arrangement of words confuses the meaning. If you ask a New Yorker for a "soda" and expect to receive something that has ice cream in it, you'll be disappointed. The New Yorker will give you a bottle of what is called "pop" in the Midwest. An advertising copywriter penned the following slogan for a cough syrup company: "Try our cough syrup. You will never get any better." An article in a college newspaper included the following: "A panel of representatives from the sports world met to discuss performance-enhancing drug use at the Journalism School last night."

Noise can also be mechanical. This type of noise occurs when there is a problem with a machine that is being used to assist communication. A TV set with a pixillated picture, a pen running out of ink, and a static-filled radio are all examples of mechanical noise.

A third form of noise can be called environmental. This type refers to sources of noise that are external to the communication process but that nonetheless interfere with it. Some environmental noise might be out of the communicator's control—the noise at a restaurant, for example, where the communicator is trying to hold a conversation. Some environmental noise might be introduced by the source or the receiver; for example, you might try to talk to somebody who keeps drumming her or his fingers on the table.

As noise increases, message fidelity (how closely the message that is sent resembles the message that is received) goes down. Clearly, feedback is important in reducing the effects of noise. The greater the potential for immediate feedback—that is, the more interplay between source and receiver—the greater the chance that noise will be overcome.

Communication Settings

▲ Interpersonal Communication

Having considered the key elements in the communication process, we next examine three common communication settings, or situations, and explore how these elements vary from setting to setting. The first and perhaps the most common situation is **interpersonal communication,** in which one person (or group) is interacting with another person (or group) without the aid of a mechanical device. The source and receiver in this form of communication are within each other's physical presence. Talking to your roommate, participating in a class discussion, and conversing with your professor after class are all examples of interpersonal communication.

The source in this communication setting can be one or more individuals, as can the receiver. Encoding is usually a one-step process as the source transforms thoughts into speech and/or gestures. A variety of channels are available for use. The receiver can see, hear, and perhaps even smell and touch the source. Messages are relatively difficult for the receiver to terminate and are produced at little expense. In addition, interpersonal messages can be private ("Whassup?") or public (a proclamation that the end of the world is near from a person standing on a street corner). Messages can also be pinpointed to their specific targets. For example, you might ask the following of your English professor: "Excuse me, Dr. Iamb, but I was wondering if you had finished perusing my term paper?" The very same message directed at your roommate might be put another way: "Hey, Space Cadet! Aren't you done with my paper yet?" Decoding is also a one-step process performed by those receivers who can perceive the message. Feedback is immediate and makes use of visual and auditory channels. Noise can be either semantic or environmental. Interpersonal communication is far from simple, but it represents the least complicated setting.

▲ Machine-Assisted Interpersonal Communication

Machine-assisted interpersonal communication (or technology-assisted communication) combines characteristics of both the interpersonal and mass communication situations. The growth of the Internet and the World Wide Web has further blurred the boundaries

Microsoft's Bill Gates uses machine-assisted communication to get his point across at the annual meeting of the World Economic Forum. *(Raymond Reuter/Sygma)*

between these two types of communication. This section focuses on those situations that are closer to the interpersonal setting. The next section examines how the computer and the Internet have redefined many of the features of mass communication.

In the machine-assisted setting, one or more people are communicating by means of a mechanical device (or devices) with one or more receivers. One of the important characteristics of machine-assisted interpersonal communication is that it allows the source and receiver to be separated by both time and space. The machine can give a message permanence by storing it on paper, disk, or some other material. The machine can also extend the range of the message by amplifying it and/or transmitting it over large distances. The telephone, for example, allows two people to converse even though they are hundreds, even thousands, of miles apart. A letter can be reread several years after it was written and communicate anew.

The source in the machine-assisted setting can be a single person or a group of people who may know the receiver or not have firsthand knowledge of the receiver.

Encoding in this setting can be complicated or simple, but there must be at least two distinct stages. The first occurs when the source translates his or her thoughts into words or symbols. The second occurs when one or more machines encode the message for transmission or storage. When you speak on the telephone, for example, you choose and pronounce your words (stage 1), and a machine converts them into electrical impulses (stage 2).

Channels are more restricted in the machine-assisted setting. Whereas interpersonal communication can make use of several channels simultaneously, machine-assisted settings generally rely on only one or two. E-mail, for instance, relies on sight; a phone call uses electrical energy and sound waves.

Messages vary widely in machine-assisted communication. They can be tailor-made for the receiver (such as e-mail) or limited to a small number of predetermined messages that cannot be altered once they are encoded. Messages in this setting can be private or public and relatively cheap to produce.

Decoding can go through one or more stages, similar to the encoding process. Reading a letter requires only one stage, but reading e-mail requires two: one for the computer to decode electrical energy into patterns of light and dark, and another for your eyes to decode the written symbols.

The receiver in this setting can be a single person, a small group, or a large group. Receivers can be in sight of the source or out of view. They can be selected by the source (as with a phone call) or self-select themselves into the audience (as when taking a pamphlet from somebody on the street).

Feedback can be immediate or delayed. A band playing at a concert will hear the audience applaud following a song. A band that provides streaming audio of a new song on its Web site might have to wait for days to see if people liked it. In many situations feedback is limited to one channel, as in a phone conversation. In some situations feedback can be difficult if not impossible. If the automatic teller gives you a message that says, "Insufficient funds," you cannot tell it, "I just made a deposit this morning. Look it up."

Noise in the machine-assisted setting can be semantic and environmental as in interpersonal communication, but it can also be mechanical. Interference with the message might be due in part to difficulties with the machine involved.

In the future, machine-assisted communication will become more important. Mobile media, such as cell phones, personal digital assistants, and laptop computers, will become more and more popular and continue to expand the scope and impact of personal communication (see Chapter 3). The Internet may come to function more as an aid to interpersonal communication than as a mass medium (see Chapter 12). Finally, the differences between machine-assisted communication and mass communication will continue to blur. All of these trends will hasten the transition of traditional mass media into new forms of communication channels.

▲ Mass Communication

The third major communication setting is the one that we will be most interested in. The differences between machine-assisted interpersonal communication and mass communication are not that clear. Here is a traditional definition: **Mass communication** refers to the process by which a complex organization with the aid of one or more machines produces and transmits public messages that are directed at large, heterogeneous, and scattered audiences. There are, of course, situations that will fall into a gray area. How large does the audience have to be? How scattered? How heterogeneous? How complex must the organization be? For example, suppose a billboard is constructed on a busy street in a small town. Obviously, this would qualify as machine-assisted communication (a machine was used to print the billboard), but is this better defined as mass communication? An automatic letter-writing device can write thousands of similar letters. Is this mass communication? There are no correct answers to these questions. The dividing line between machine-assisted interpersonal communication and mass communication is not a distinct one.

The line is even less distinct when the Internet and the Web are considered. Take an e-mail message, for example. It can be addressed to one person, much like machine-assisted interpersonal communication, or it can go to thousands, a situation closer to mass communication. Or take the case of a chat room where one person might be communicating with dozens of others. If two people want more privacy, they can move to a "private" room, a situation that resembles machine-assisted interpersonal communication. On the other hand, feedback in the chat room is limited, a feature of mass communication. The usual clues from personal appearance, facial expressions, tone of voice, and gestures are not present.

Source   Until the advent of the Internet and the Web, the source in the traditional mass communication situation was typically a group of individuals who acted in predetermined roles in an organizational setting. In other words, mass communication was the end product of more than one person's efforts. For example, think about how a newspaper is put together. Reporters gather news; writers draft editorials; a cartoonist draws an editorial cartoon; the advertising department lays out ads; editors lay out all these elements on a sample page; technicians transfer this page to a master; other technicians print the final paper; the finished copies are given to the delivery staff; and, of course, behind all this is a publisher who has the money to pay for a building, presses, staff, trucks, paper, ink, and so on. This institutional nature of mass communication has several consequences that we will consider later in this book.

E-mail is fast and environmentally friendly; it uses no paper, and vehicles burn no gasoline delivering the message. It is no wonder, then, that American businesses send billions of e-mail messages every year.

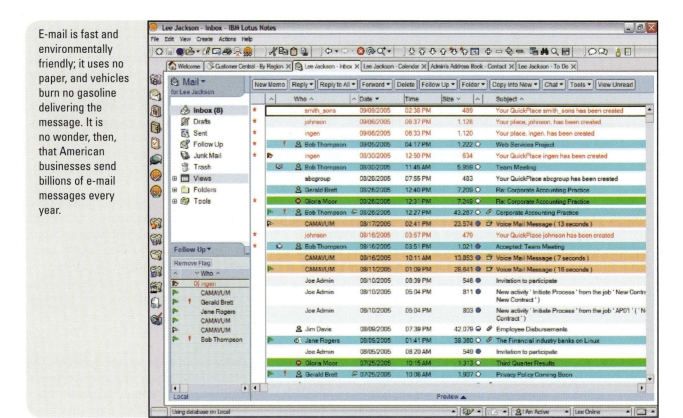

The advent of Internet-based mass communication changes this situation. Thanks to the World Wide Web, one person can become a mass communicator. The full implications of this change may take some time to become clear.

For both traditional and Internet-based mass communication, the source usually has little detailed information about its particular audience. The author of a blog has little detailed information about individuals who visit the site. Traditional mass media may have collective data, but these are typically expressed as gross audience characteristics. The newspaper editor, for example, may know that 40 percent of the readers are between 25 and 40 years old and that 30 percent earn between $20,000 and $50,000, but the editor has no idea about the individual tastes, preferences, quirks, or identities of these people. They are an anonymous group, known only by summary statistics.

Encoding/Sending   Encoding in mass communication is always a multistage process. Suppose a film producer has an idea. He or she explains it to a screenwriter. The writer goes off and produces a script. The script goes to a director, who translates it for the camera. Cinematographers capture the scenes on film. The raw film goes to an editor, who splices together the final version. The film is copied and sent to theaters, where a projector displays it on the screen, where the audience watches it. How many examples of encoding can you find in that oversimplified version of moviemaking?

Mass communication channels are characterized by the imposition of at least one, and usually more than one, machine in the process of sending the message. These machines translate the message from one channel to another. Television makes use of complicated devices that transform light energy into electrical energy and back again. Radio does the same with sound energy. Unlike interpersonal communication, in which many channels are available, mass communication is usually restricted to one or two.

Decoding/Receiving   Messages in mass communication are public. Anyone who can afford the cost of a newspaper or a CD player or a TV set can receive the message. Additionally, the same message is sent to all receivers. In a sense, mass communication is addressed "to whom it may concern." Of all the various settings, message termination is easiest in mass communication. The TV set goes dark at the flick of a switch; an automatic timer can turn off the radio; the newspaper is quickly put aside. There is little the source can do to prevent these sudden terminations other than bullying the audience ("Don't touch that dial!") or trying to stay interesting at all times ("We'll be back after these important messages").

Mass communication typically involves multiple decoding before the message is received. The CD player decodes patterns of light waves into sound waves for our hearing mechanism. The TV receiver decodes both sight and sound transmissions.

Receiver One of the prime distinguishing characteristics of mass communication is the audience. First, the mass communication audience is a large one, sometimes numbering in the millions of people. Second, the audience is also heterogeneous; that is, it is made up of dissimilar groups who may differ in age, intelligence, political beliefs, ethnic backgrounds, and so on. Even in situations where the mass communication audience is well defined, heterogeneity is still present. (For example, consider the publication *Turkey Grower's Monthly*. At first glance, the audience for this publication might appear to be rather homogeneous, but upon closer examination we might discover that members differ in intelligence, social class, income, age, political party, education, place of residence, and so on.) Third, the audience is spread out over a wide geographic area; source and receiver are not in each other's immediate physical presence. The large size of the audience and its geographic separation both contribute to a fourth distinguishing factor: The audience members are anonymous to one another. The person watching the *CBS Evening News* is unaware of the several million others in the audience. Lastly, in keeping with the idea of a public message, the audience in mass communication is self-defined. The receiver chooses which film to see, which paper to read, which Web site to visit, and which program to watch. If the receiver chooses not to attend to the message, the message is not received. Consequently, the various mass communication sources spend a great deal of time and effort to get your attention so that you will include yourself in the audience.

Feedback Feedback is another area where there are differences between interpersonal and mass communication. The message flow in mass communication is typically one-way, and feedback, in many instances, is more difficult than in the interpersonal setting. This situation, however, is rapidly changing because of the Internet. Newspapers often include e-mail addresses of reporters to encourage reader feedback. Producers of TV shows scan Web sites and blogs to glean the latest reaction to their episodes. People tweet (send Twitter messages) while they attend newsworthy events. Systematic, large-scale feedback conducted by media research companies, such as the Audit Bureau of Circulations for newspapers and MRI for magazines, tends to be more delayed, but there are exceptions. Nielsen Media Research, for example, provides overnight ratings for network TV shows.

Noise Finally, noise in the mass communication setting can be semantic, environmental, or mechanical. In fact, since there may be more than one machine involved in the process, mechanical noise can be compounded.

Table 1-1 summarizes some of the differences among the three communication settings that we have talked about.

Encoding at the movies. Director J.J. Abrams on the set of Star Trek. A motion picture goes through several stages of encoding before it gets to the audience: concept, story, script, filming, and editing.

TABLE 1-1

Differences in
Communication
Settings

Settings

Element	Interpersonal	Machine-Assisted Interpersonal	Mass
Source	Single person; has knowledge of receiver	Single person or group; has great deal of knowledge or no knowledge of receiver	Organizations or single person; has little knowledge of receivers
Encoding	Single stage	Single or multiple stage	Multiple stages
Message	Private or public; cheap; hard to terminate; altered to fit receivers	Private or public; low to moderate expense; relatively easy to terminate; can be altered to fit receivers in some situations	Public; can be expensive; easily terminated; same message sent to everybody
Channel	Potential for many; no machines interposed	Restricted to one or two; at least one machine interposed	Restricted to one or two; usually more than one machine interposed
Decoding	Single stage	Single or multiple stage	Multiple stages
Receiver	One or relatively small number; in physical presence of source; selected by source	One person or small or large group; within or outside physical presence of source; selected by source or self-defined	Large numbers; out of physical presence of source; self-selected
Feedback	Plentiful; immediate	Somewhat limited; immediate or delayed	Highly limited; usually delayed
Noise	Semantic; environmental	Semantic; environmental; mechanical	Semantic; environmental; mechanical

▲ Defining Mass Media

In the broadest sense of the word, a *medium* is the channel through which a message travels from the source to the receiver ("medium" is singular; "media" is plural). Thus in our discussion we have pointed to sound and light waves as media of communication. When we talk about mass communication, we also need channels to carry the message. **Mass media** are the channels used for mass communication. Our definition of a mass medium will include not only the mechanical devices that transmit and sometimes store the message (TV cameras, radio microphones, printing presses) but also the institutions that use these machines to transmit messages. When we talk about the mass media of television, radio, newspapers, magazines, sound recording, and film, we will be referring to the people, policies, organizations, and technologies that go into producing and distributing mass communication. A **media vehicle** is a single component of the mass media, such as a newspaper, radio station, TV network, or magazine.

In this book we will examine eight different mass media: radio, television, film, books, sound recordings, newspapers, magazines, and the Internet. Of course, these eight are not the only mass media that exist. Billboards, comic books, posters, direct mail, matchbooks, and buttons are some other kinds of mass media one could choose to examine. The eight types of media we have chosen, however, have the largest audiences, employ the most people, and have the greatest impact. They are also the ones with which most of us are most familiar.

Mass Media in Transition

It doesn't take a genius to see that the mass media five years from now will be significantly different than they were five years ago. A combination of technological, economic, and social factors has made some traditional business models obsolete, and several media are struggling to re-invent themselves for the digital era. Other media are dealing with a fundamental shift in the ways they reach their audiences.

The World Wide Web has changed the nature of mass communication: Get yourself a blog page like Professor Scott Shamp, Director of the New Media Institute at the University of Georgia, and you too could become a mass communicator.

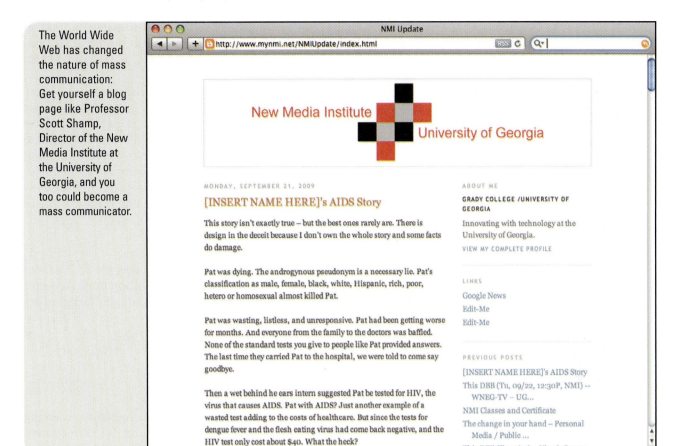

▲ Technology

On the technology level, the emergence of the Internet has created a new channel for mass communication. In the beginning, traditional media companies, such as newspapers and magazines, were unsure how to use this new medium and many posted content for free on their Web sites in an effort to promote the print editions. This ultimately siphoned off potential readers of the print edition, especially young readers, and circulation fell along with advertising revenues. Consequently, the traditional print media are looking for new ways to prosper in the digital age.

At the same time, the Internet opened the door for a host of new competitors for traditional media. Some Web sites simply replaced functions served by traditional media. Classified ads that might have gone to the newspaper went to Web sites such as Craigslist or autotrader.com. Online video sites, such as YouTube and hulu.com, cut into the audience and revenue of traditional TV networks and stations. Internet radio stations captured listeners at the office that previously had listened to broadcast stations. Other Web sites created new functions that captured audience attention and time. Instead of watching TV, many young people spent time on Facebook or MySpace or other social network sites. This increased competition forced the traditional media to reexamine their usual ways of doing business.

The primary reason behind this growth in competition is easy to see: The Internet brings down the cost of mass communication to a level at which almost anybody can afford it. A single individual can start a Web site for a relatively small sum (Facebook started in a Harvard dorm. Craigslist started as a hobby), and the Web site can reach a potential audience of millions. Furthermore, the low cost means that individual sites can be supported solely by those who create them, thus removing the profit consideration from the equation. It's probably fair to say that the vast majority of bloggers, for example, blog for reasons other than profit. To sum up, in the past, established media companies were shielded from new competition because the costs to enter the market were so high. That is no longer the case. A whole new type of mass communicator has emerged to compete with traditional media organizations, and the choices available for the audience have mushroomed.

Of course, not everybody who puts up a Web site is engaging in mass communication. If nobody or only a few people visit the site, no mass communication takes place. The fact that Uncle Harold publishes a blog does not mean that Uncle Harold is on the same level as the *New York Times* as a mass communicator. The *Times* has a lot more resources with which to draw a mass audience. But technically speaking, the same could be said about traditional media. If no one reads the *New York Times,* then no mass communication takes place. In short, although the potential to be a mass communicator exists for everybody—including Uncle Harold and the *New York Times*—actually becoming one is more difficult for Uncle Harold.

▲ Economics

This transition was further accelerated by the economic downturn during the last years of the decade. Advertising money dried up, and as noted above, competition from Web sites siphoned off the profits of traditional media. Organizations that expanded during an era of easy credit all of a sudden found themselves burdened by massive debt. Not surprisingly, cutbacks, layoffs, and severe cost-cutting followed. Several media organizations went bankrupt; others struggled to find new revenue streams; still others totally joined the digital era by ending their traditional forms and going online.

▲ Social Trends

Social change also hastened the transition. Consumers became accustomed to receiving their information and entertainment for free, and efforts to charge for Internet content met with resistance. Traditional passive media exposure was replaced by active participation in new social media such as Facebook, MySpace, and Twitter. The recording industry watched as person-to-person file sharing skyrocketed and sales of CDs plummeted. People began to spend their time creating media content (more than half of teens have created a social networking site; more than 100 million people have started blogs) and less time consuming media content.

The chapters in Parts II and III of this book will provide more details about how the various media are coping with this transitional era.

Characteristics of Media Organizations

Describing the characteristics of mass media organizations was a lot easier before the Internet came along. As mentioned above, thanks to the Internet, the distinction between machine-assisted interpersonal communication and mass communication has become fuzzy. When we try to identify the typical characteristics of mass communication organizations, the distinctions become fuzzier. Some Web sites engage in mass communication; some don't. The *New York Times* Web site gets more than 19 million unique visitors every month; we would expect the *Times'* Web site to possess the typical characteristics of a mass media organization (and it does). At the other end of the spectrum, the average blog has about 10–20 regular readers; most would agree that this is more like machine-assisted interpersonal communication. It is unlikely that these sites would share the same distinguishing features as www.nytimes.com. Nonetheless, at the risk of oversimplifying, and recognizing that some Web operations may represent exceptions, below are five features that have been traditionally used to define organizations that produce mass communication:

1. Mass communication is produced by complex and formal organizations.
2. Mass communication organizations have multiple gatekeepers.

3. Mass communication organizations need a great deal of money to operate.

4. Mass communication organizations exist to make a profit.

5. Mass communication organizations are highly competitive.

Let's examine each of these characteristics in turn and then examine how each has been transformed by the Internet and by the economic and social forces mentioned above.

▲ Formal Organizational Structure

Publishing a newspaper, making a movie, or operating a TV network requires control of money, management of personnel, coordination of activities, and application of authority. Accomplishing all of these tasks requires a well-defined organizational structure characterized by specialization, division of labor, and focused areas of responsibility. Consequently, traditional mass communication has been the product of a bureaucracy. As in most bureaucracies, decision making takes place at several levels of management, and channels of communication within the organization are formalized. Thus, many of the decisions about what gets included in a newspaper, TV program, or movie are made by groups. Further, decisions are made by several individuals in ascending levels of the bureaucracy, and communication follows predictable patterns within the organization.

The worsening economic climate of the last years of the decade has made many traditional media organizations less complex as entire departments were downsized or eliminated completely. Book publisher Random House axed two of its publishing groups. Time Inc. simplified its corporate structure and eliminated 600 jobs. Recording company EMI consolidated four divisions into one.

Turning now to the Web, a formal organizational structure is found with some Web operations but not with others. Web sites can be produced and maintained by a single individual or a small group, and decisions do not have to be filtered through a hierarchy. The Drudge Report, for instance, has only a handful of employees. Keep in mind, however, that many Web sites that attract a large audience have organizational structures that resemble those of a traditional mass media organization. To illustrate, Facebook has more than 700 employees, six main departments, and seven vice presidents. MySpace has 300 employees. YouTube has 13 separate departments.

▲ Gatekeepers

Another important factor that characterizes the traditional mass communication organization is the presence of multiple **gatekeepers.** A gatekeeper is any person (or group) who has control over what material eventually reaches the public. Some gatekeepers are more obvious than others, such as the editor at a newspaper, the news director at a TV station, or the acquisitions editor at a book publishing company. More complex organizations have more gatekeepers.

Once again, the dismal economic climate has had an impact on gatekeeping. When newspapers and magazines lay off employees, editors are likely to be included among those losing their jobs. When media companies consolidate and simplify their corporate structure, it usually means fewer gatekeepers.

Gatekeepers are far less numerous on the Web, but that doesn't mean they are nonexistent. Most newspapers, for example, have someone who scans comments posted on their Web sites and removes offensive or libelous posts. YouTube has several people who screen videos and

Getting past the gatekeepers in network television is difficult. ABC's hit series *Desperate Housewives* was first turned down by HBO, CBS, NBC, Fox, Showtime, and Lifetime.

remove the ones that are inappropriate or violations of copyright. Facebook removes illegal, offensive, and pornographic content as does MySpace. These sites exemplify a feature of gatekeeping that is unique to the Web—they rely on audience members to do the monitoring. Facebook and MySpace, for example, have links that allow members to report content that they find objectionable.

In general, however, gatekeeping is not a principal feature of many Internet sites, a situation that has both positive and negative consequences. On the one hand, individuals have the freedom to post whatever they want without too much fear of censorship. On the other hand, there is no guarantee that what is made available will be accurate or worthwhile. Rumors, conspiracy theories, vitriol, and truly tasteless content abound on the Internet. There are no editors to sort out the credible from the lies or to distinguish merit from the trash.

▲ Large Operating Expenses

Traditionally, it has taken a lot of money to get into the mass communication business and more money to keep going. In 2007, Rupert Murdoch's News Corporation bought Dow Jones & Company, publisher of the *Wall Street Journal*, for $5 billion and real estate mogul Sam Zell bought the Tribune Company, publisher of the *Chicago Tribune* and the *Los Angeles Times*, for more than $8 billion.

Once the organization is operating, expenses can also be sizable. A radio station in a medium-size market might spend around $1 million in operating expenses. A medium-market TV station probably spends $5–10 million annually.

As we have already noted, the Internet has reduced start-up and operating costs, but this does not mean that Web operations don't need cash in order to grow and prosper. Indeed, if an entrepreneur wants his or her Web site to reach a mass audience, somebody has to pay the bill. YouTube, for example, might not have gotten off the ground without an $11.5 million investment from a venture capital company. Facebook followed the same route, accepting about $40 million from two venture capital companies. Evan Williams, one of the founders of Twitter, raised $22 million from outside investors. (On the other hand, if your plans are less grandiose, Google gives members free blog space and Yahoo charges only $10 a month to host a Web site.)

Companies that have strong financial resources are the likeliest to survive high operating expenses and are more likely to survive in a down economy. In 2009, a number of global media giants dominated the field. Table 1-2 lists these "megamedia" companies; these names will turn up frequently in succeeding chapters.

▲ Competition for Profits

In the United States, mass communication organizations exist to make a profit. Although there are some exceptions (the Public Broadcasting Service, for example), most newspapers, magazines, record companies, film studios, book publishers, and TV and radio

TABLE 1-2	Company (home country)	2008 Revenue (in billion U.S. dollars)*
Global Media Giants	Time Warner (United States)	$46.9
	Walt Disney Co. (United States)	37.8
	Vivendi (France)	35.8
	Comcast (United States)	34.3
	News Corp. (United States)	32.9
	Sony** (Japan)	22.7
	Bertelsmann (Germany)	22.7

* To give some perspective to these data, General Motors' revenue for the same period was $149 billion; General Electric's was $182 billion.

** Includes only revenue from media divisions.

stations strive to produce a profit for their owners and shareholders. Broadcast stations are licensed to serve the public interest and newspapers assume a watchdog role for their readers, but if they do not make money, no matter how noble their goals, they go out of business (as was illustrated several times during the recession of the late 2000s.)

Profit ultimately comes from the consumer. When you download a song from iTunes or buy a movie ticket, part of the price includes the profit. Newspapers, radio, TV, and magazines make most of their profit by selling to advertisers the attention their audiences give them. The cost of advertising is then passed on to the consumer. The economics of mass communication is an important topic, and we will explore it throughout this book.

Since the audience is the source of profits, mass communication organizations compete with one another to attract an audience. This should come as no surprise to anyone who has ever watched television or passed a magazine stand. The major TV networks compete with one another for ratings, spending millions of dollars to promote their programs. Radio stations compete with other stations in their market. Record companies spend large sums promoting their recordings, hoping to outsell their competitors. Motion picture companies may gamble millions on films to compete successfully. As we have seen, the Internet has made competition even more severe.

As the first decade of the new millennium drew to a close, profits for media companies were especially hard to come by. The parent company of the *Chicago Tribune* filed for bankruptcy as did the *Minneapolis Star-Tribune*. Recording company EMI lost $221 million during the first part of 2008.

As for Web sites, many exist to make a profit. Perezhilton.com contains advertising and sales pitches for merchandise as does nytimes.com. Amazon.com makes its profit by selling hundreds of different products. Other Web sites do not share the profit motivation; some exist to serve the public (such as the .gov sites) or to gain attention and/or prestige for their owners (blogs). In this latter case, competition will not be much of a factor.

To sum up, the Internet is home to millions of Web sites. Many of them fit the definition of mass communication and exhibit all of the traditional characteristics of mass communication organizations (such as CNN.com, ESPN.com, nytimes.com). Other operations also engage in mass communication and exhibit some but not all of the five traditional features. (Thesmokinggun.com strives to make a profit. It attracts about 4 million unique views a month but has only a handful of employees and relatively small operating expense since it gets all its material from public records.) Other sites are better defined as machine-assisted interpersonal communication. Once again, the Internet has forced us to reexamine the way we traditionally think about mass communication and mass communicators.

The Internet: Mass and Interpersonal Channel?

As the Internet evolves, two distinct developments are becoming clear. The first suggests that the Web will become more important for interpersonal and social functions, as evidenced by the tremendous rise of social media. The operations that have been most successful on the Web most resemble interpersonal or machine-assisted communication. Blogs, e-mail, Skype, eBay, Facebook, Twitter, instant messages, MySpace, Wikipedia, and all of the Napster-like file-sharing programs are not so much examples of mass communication as they are of machine-assisted interpersonal communication, illustrating communication between single individuals (writing on someone's "wall" in Facebook) or among relatively small groups of people (such as occurs with Google Groups). In addition, virtually none of the successful operations mentioned above were started by a big media company (but big media companies bought in when these sites became successful).

Second, many experts have predicted that traditional mass media content (TV, movies, newspapers, magazines, sound recording, books, radio) will eventually be distributed mainly over the Internet, making the Net the single most important channel of mass communication. This trend is already taking shape with online newspapers and magazines; TV networks making their programs available on the Web (for example, hulu.com); movie studios making films available for download (for example, Netflix); downloadable books (for example, Amazon's Kindle e-book reader); and music (iTunes). There are dangers, however, associated with this development. If we become too dependent on the Internet, what happens if a natural disaster (such as a hurricane) or human-made calamity (such as a terrorist cyber attack) disables the system? In any event, the Internet is fostering both mass and machine-assisted communication at the same time.

Whatever its ultimate direction, the Internet has prompted mass communication scholars (and textbook writers) to rethink conventional definitions and categories of mass communication. It has also necessitated fresh models to describe the communication process, a topic that we will turn to next.

Models for Studying Mass Communication

The traditional model of mass communication was a "one-to-many" model. It suggested that information from the environment (both news and entertainment) is filtered through a mass media organization (newspaper, TV network, movie studio) where it is decoded, interpreted, selected, and finally encoded into a message that is reproduced many times over and distributed through the appropriate channel. For example, newspaper reporters cover events and encode stories that are evaluated by editors (gatekeepers) to see if they should make it into that day's edition of the paper.

Once through the gate, the paper is reproduced and physically distributed to readers. The readers, the receivers of the message, decode and interpret the message. Some audience behavior (buying a product, watching a TV show, subscribing to a magazine) is monitored by the media organization and is used as feedback to help shape future messages. Under the traditional model there is little direct interaction between sources and receivers.

Figure 1-2 is a rough attempt to represent Internet communication, a new arrangement that makes possible several different levels of communication: one source communicating with one receiver (e-mail), one source communicating with many receivers (CNN.com), a few sources communicating with a few receivers (chat rooms, blogs), and many sources communicating with many receivers (YouTube, eBay).

Note that in this simplified model, content is provided not only by organizations but also by individuals. In this circumstance there are no organizational gatekeepers. A single individual performs the decoding, interpreting, and encoding functions. Also note that Figure 1-2 is not a one-way model. Communication doesn't proceed from left to right but flows inward. The traditional mass communicator no longer necessarily initiates the process. Instead, it is possible for the receiver to choose the time and manner of the interaction. Suppose you want to find out what happened in a game involving your favorite baseball team that went into extra innings and finished late at night. With the traditional media you have to wait for a newspaper to be published or for your favorite TV station, cable network, or radio station to report the score. With the Internet you can visit a sports news Web site and find the information immediately. Furthermore, if you want to know more, you can visit your team's Web site for more details and check message boards for the reactions of others to the outcome. In short, the audience member has more control of the process.

Another area of contrast between the traditional and Internet models is that the messages that flow to each receiver are not identical. For example, you have many different choices about what you can use as your starting page when you access the Internet. In addition, it's possible to customize the information you receive. MSN.com, for example, offers many different configurations that allow you to choose specific sports scores, news headlines, stock market reports, weather forecasts, and entertainment news. Each receiver

FIGURE 1-2

Internet Mass
Communication Model

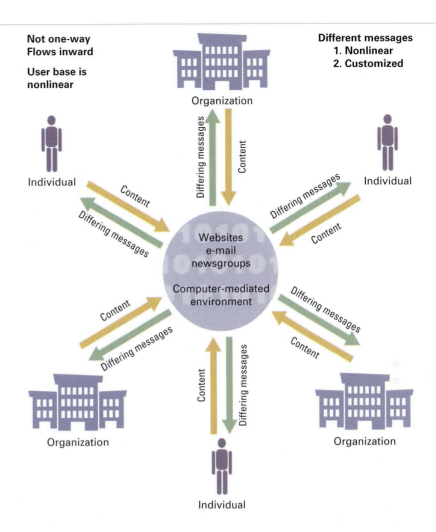

can customize the information that he or she receives. Some writers have characterized the traditional mass communication model as a "push" model (the sender pushes the information to the receiver), whereas the Internet model is a "pull" model (the receiver pulls only the information that he or she wants).

Finally, Figure 1-2 shows that both individuals and organizations are linked through a computer-mediated environment. This makes interaction and feedback much easier. The online magazine Slate.com, for example, has a site titled "The Fray," where readers can comment on stories in the magazine. This environment allows people and organizations to be linked in unprecedented ways, in totally new forms of interaction. The auction site eBay joins buyers and sellers all over the world. The newsgroup humanities.classics brings together people who were probably never aware of one another and lets them talk about Descartes and Wagner. The Internet links producers and customers and makes e-commerce possible (see Chapter 11). All in all, the new model, incomplete as it might be, suggests a new way of conceptualizing communication in the age of the Internet.

Transition: Emerging Media Trends

As media continue to evolve, several trends are already apparent: (1) audience segmentation, (2) convergence, (3) increased audience control, (4) multiple platforms, (5) user-generated content, (6) mobile media, and (7) social media. We will present a brief discussion of each term below, and subsequent chapters will point out additional examples.

▲ Audience Segmentation: The End of Mass Communication As We Know It?

Media audiences are becoming less "mass" and more selective. For example, in the 1930s nearly everybody tuned their radios to *Amos 'n' Andy*. Today the top-rated radio station in a major market is lucky if it captures 10 percent of the audience. In the 1950s *I Love Lucy* was a top-rated TV show with about 50 percent of viewers tuning in. In the 1980s *The Cosby Show* was number one with about a 33 percent share, and in 2009, top-rated *CSI* got about 12 percent.

About three out of every four adults read a newspaper in the 1960s; today that's down to about one out of two. *Reader's Digest* had a circulation of 18 million in 1976; today it's down to around 10 million.

All of these numbers illustrate the segmentation or fractionalization of the mass audience. What are some of the reasons for this change? First, for many in today's audience, time has become a scarce commodity, with much of it devoted to commuting, working, and child rearing. All of this means less available time for media, and when audience members do spend time with the media, they tend to look for content geared to their special interests.

Second, there are more media today to choose from: From just three TV networks in the 1950s to hundreds of cable and satellite channels, as well as DVDs, video games, and YouTube; from single-screen movie theaters to 18-screen multiplexes and movies on demand; and from a dozen or so local radio stations to hundreds of channels on satellite radio. Finally, advertisers have turned from mass to target marketing, paying a premium to reach those people most likely to buy their product or service. The ultimate consequence of all these factors is that the audience for any single media vehicle is reduced.

Does all this mean that *mass communication* is no longer a meaningful term? Should this book be titled *The Dynamics of Segmented Communication*? Well, not quite yet. First, the definition of *mass communication* given earlier still applies. Complex organizations still use machines to transmit public messages aimed at large, heterogeneous, and scattered audiences. Audiences are still large (President Barack Obama's inauguration drew a TV audience of about 40 million. The 2009 Super Bowl was viewed by 151 million total viewers, and even a flop TV show can reach a million households), scattered, and heterogeneous enough to justify using the term *mass communication*. Second, the channels of mass communication are unchanged, although there are more and more mass media using these channels: about 13,000 radio stations today compared with half that number a couple of decades ago, more than 3,000 new magazines in the past decade, hundreds of TV stations, and so on. The messages sent by these mass media through the channels of mass communication have become more specialized. Magazines, newspapers, radio, TV, and Web sites are aiming their content at more defined audience niches, in part to meet the demands of advertisers and in part because it's more cost-efficient. Consequently, it's harder for any one media vehicle to reach a large number of audience members. Nonetheless, the potential is still there for the right message in the right medium to transcend the limits of specialized content and to attract a mass audience in the broadest sense of the term.

▲ Convergence

The dictionary defines *convergence* as the process of coming together or uniting in a common interest or focus. Convergence is not a new idea (some past examples are sporks, clock radios, and brunch), but the word has enjoyed renewed popularity in recent years and has become the centerpiece in discussions about future trends in mass communication. It is a difficult term to discuss, however, because it has been used to refer to several different processes.

At one level it refers to **corporate convergence.** This trend started in the 1980s with synergy. Companies that were content providers, such as movie studios and record labels, acquired distribution channels such as cable TV. As digital technologies emerged, synergy turned into convergence, a vision of one company delivering every service imaginable.

The long tail theory was popularized by Chris Anderson of *Wired Magazine.* To understand its implications, take a look at the accompanying figure. Those readers who have taken an economics course will recognize it as a basic demand curve. Sales are measured on the vertical axis, and products on the horizontal. The part of the curve to the left of the dotted line represents products that are big sellers; the part of the curve to the right of the dotted line (the tail of the curve) represents all those products that sell only a little.

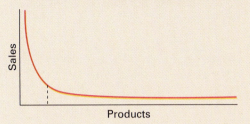

The Long Tail

Traditionally, media companies concentrated on the left part of the curve—the blockbuster movies, the platinum albums, the best-selling books. However, as Anderson points out, the new technologies, particularly the Internet, have made it easier for audience members to find niche products, items that a relatively small number of people demand.

For example, a traditional brick-and-mortar music store is limited by physical size and shelf space. Accordingly, it stocks only those CDs that are likely to sell in large numbers (the left part of the curve). CDs that only a few people want to buy aren't profitable; their shelf space is better occupied by more copies of a (potential) hit. With online merchants, however, physical space is not a problem. They can stock many thousands of titles (Amazon.com's virtual inventory consists of nearly 4 million books) and let customers browse their offerings online. If items are stored digitally, the cost of storing huge numbers is practically nothing. The iTunes inventory, for example, can theoretically run into the millions of songs, and there might be only a small demand for each of them. This means that the right side of the curve is theoretically infinite. Anderson suggests that merchants such as iTunes, Amazon.com, and Netflix can make just as much money (if not more) from sales on the right side of the curve as they can from the left. In short, rather than selling one song to a million people, iTunes can sell a million different songs to one person each.

Interestingly, this revenue distribution is already taking shape. Amazon.com has reported that less popular books already make up about 25 percent of its sales. Rhapsody, the online music company, makes 40 percent of its revenue from songs that wouldn't be stocked at Target or Wal-Mart.

The social and cultural implications of this trend are still unclear. On the one hand, there is more choice and more diversity available for audience members. Whereas the music-buying public was once restricted to what was on the shelves of the major retailers, now there is music to be downloaded to fit every conceivable taste and niche. When only three TV networks existed, entertainment had to be crafted to fit the lowest common denominator. As cable, satellite, and the Internet emerged as alternate channels of video, producers created programs that appealed to smaller groups, such as travel fans and devotees of courtroom drama. On the downside there may be the problem of having too much choice. How does a consumer decide which one of 100,000 movies to view? Will the browsing take more time than the actual viewing? There is also the problem of the loss of a common culture, something that everybody shares and can relate to and talk about. If everybody is wrapped up in his or her niche, there may be little left that draws us together.

(For more information on long tail theory, see Chris Anderson's book *The Long Tail: Why the Future of Business Is Selling Less of More.* As of 2007, its sales ranking on Amazon.com was 289 out of nearly 4 million books. That put it firmly in the left side of the curve.)

The early years of the new century saw several attempts at corporate convergence, but most were unsuccessful. For example, the merger between "old" media Time Warner and "new" media AOL didn't fulfill expectations. They finally split up in 2009. In France the convergence between "new" media company Vivendi and "old" media Universal Studios and Universal Music failed. In 2005 Viacom "de-converged," spinning off "old" media CBS, Infinity Radio, and a publishing house into a separate company while keeping "new" media MTV networks and a home video company.

Will corporate convergence reemerge when most Americans are connected to the Internet via broadband? Maybe, but for now the trend in corporate circles seems more toward divergence than convergence.

Another type of convergence is **operational convergence.** This occurs when owners of several media properties in one market combine their separate operations into a single effort. For example, in Florida, TV station WFLA, the *Tampa Tribune,* and TBO.com operate a converged news department. In Lawrence, Kansas, convergence occurred when the Lawrence *Journal-World* combined the news reporting functions of the paper, the paper's Web site, and its local cable news channel. All in all, an estimated 50 examples of this kind

Be forewarned. What follows may be somewhat discouraging to many who are planning a career in mass media. The declining fortunes of some traditional media are reflected in recent industry employment trends. The table below shows changes in the number of employees in selected media industries from the beginning of 2007 to the end of 2008. (All data come from the Bureau of Labor Statistics.)

Projections suggest that Internet companies will continue to hire new employees, perhaps not as many as in past years but their numbers are likely to increase. The PR industry is volatile but it also is expected to increase. The situation for newspapers and magazines will probably get worse. Of course, if the economy starts to rebound these numbers will obviously change, but for now the overall job outlook for the traditional media is pretty bleak.

Media	Employees 2007 (thousands)	Employees 2008 (thousands)	Percentage Change
Newspapers	352.9	311.2	−12%
Radio	109.8	102.1	−7%
Magazines	144.6	137.8	−5%
Broadcast TV	127.4	121.9	−4%
Cable TV	88.8	86.9	−2%
Ad agencies	182.3	181.8	(less than 1%)
Public relations	47.3	51.3	+8%
Internet companies	66.1	82.2	+22%

of convergence are currently under way. And if cross-media ownership rules are relaxed, this trend may accelerate.

The advantages of this type of convergence are obvious. It saves money because, rather than hiring a separate news staff for each medium, an operation can have the same reporters produce stories for the paper, Web site, and TV station. In addition, each medium can promote its partners. For instance, the TV newscast can encourage readers to visit the Web site or the print newspaper.

There are, of course, disadvantages as well. Reporters require additional training to master various media. This has generated some controversies among print reporters who are not eager to become "backpack journalists" (see Chapter 12) and carry around video cameras and audio recorders as part of their reporting tools. Further, many critics worry that converged operations mean fewer independent and diverse forms of journalism. Some conclude that, although operational convergence may be good for the media companies, it may not be good for consumers. In any case, the jury is still out on the merits of operational convergence.

Finally, what may be the most important type of convergence is **device convergence,** combining the functions of two or three devices into one mechanism. Apple's iPhone, for example, is a phone, an MP3 player, and a camera, and it can connect to the Internet. The latest model video game platforms can also play DVDs. Some cell phones incorporate navigation systems. Experts predict that eventually the home PC will converge with the TV set in one information appliance that will include e-mail, phone, Internet, DVD playback, and TV functions. Of course, the fact that the functions of more than one device can be combined doesn't mean that consumers will buy it. (There probably isn't much demand, for example, for a combination cell phone/electric razor.) In addition, there is always the danger that convergence will result in a piece of equipment that is too complex for consumers to operate.

Device convergence is manifesting itself in yet another way. All media seem to be converging on the Internet as a major channel of distribution. Newspapers and magazines have online editions. Music downloads are fast replacing CDs as the preferred delivery method. TV networks are making their episodes available for downloading as well as starting their own broadband channels. Movies and even books are also available in digital download forms.

▲ Increased Audience Control

Audience members are more in charge of what they want to see and/or hear and when they want to do it. Let's take television as an example. For many years viewers had to watch programs broadcast by local stations and the major networks according to the media's schedule. However, recent technological advances have given more power to the consumer. The VCR allowed time shifting, or recording a program to be viewed at a more convenient time. Remote controls made it easier for viewers to select what they wanted to watch. Cable and satellite channels offered hundreds of new viewing opportunities. Home video gave individuals the chance to make their own videos. In the past few years, digital video recorders (DVRs) such as TiVo have made time shifting easier and more efficient. Viewers can pause live TV, fast-forward through commercials, and store up to 80 hours of programming. Many cable companies now offer video on demand, enabling viewers to select content that they can watch at their convenience. In short, power has shifted from the source to the receiver.

The same trend is apparent in news. For many decades most Americans were dependent on the news provided by their local newspaper or TV network. Today audience members can choose from 24-hour cable news networks, Internet sites such as CNN.com that are devoted to news, and sites such as Google News that aggregate news from many different sources. If an audience member is not content with the traditional news outlets, she or he can read one of the hundreds of blogs that discuss news events.

Until recently, consumers were forced to buy recorded music packaged according to the wishes of industry executives. If an audience member wanted to buy just one or two songs by an artist, he or she was out of luck. The consumer had to buy an entire album. The success of Napster and other file-sharing programs clearly demonstrated that individuals were not satisfied with that arrangement. The music industry was slow to respond, but now consumers can download individual tracks from iTunes and other online sources.

Before the Internet, consumers with something to sell had to rely on the local newspaper's classified ad section. Now they can create their own ads on eBay or Craigslist. Similarly, employers once had to depend on the "Help Wanted" section of the paper. Now, however, they can scan the résumés of hundreds of potential employees on Monster.com.

Subsequent chapters will contain other examples of this trend, but by now the point is probably clear: The audience is gaining more control over the mass communication process. As one expert put it, mass communication has gone from a sit-down dinner with a fixed menu to a Vegas-style buffet.

▲ Multiple Platforms

"Everything. Everywhere": This has been the mantra at many media companies as they try to adapt to the changing world of media technology. The strategy is to make content available to consumers using a number of delivery methods to a number of receiving devices (or multiple platforms in the industry jargon).

Music videos may be the best illustration of this trend. For many years music video fans had to be content watching videos on MTV, VH1, Fuse, or one of the other cable/satellite networks. Then Web sites began streaming music videos. In 2008, Avril Lavigne's "Girlfriend" music video got more than 100 million views on YouTube. Recording companies realized that consumers were watching more videos on their computer screens than on their TV screens. Apple's video iPod and cell phones opened up

other possibilities. Today music videos still run on traditional TV screens, but the record labels have also struck deals with Apple and phone companies, such as Verizon, to take advantage of the new screens.

Television companies have also moved in this direction. NBC, for example, made entire episodes of *The Office* available for downloading on iTunes the day after their network broadcast. In addition, NBC partnered with Fox to start hulu .com, where visitors can watch hundreds of current and past TV series as well as dozens of shorter video clips. AT&T started a mobile TV service in 2008 that included live feeds from CNN, Comedy Central, and ESPN. In short, the networks are trying to make their content available on as many screens as possible.

Other media are also taking advantage of multiple platforms. Almost all major newspapers and magazines have Web sites for their digital versions that usually include video clips. The *Atlanta Journal-Constitution* and the *Seattle Post-Intelligencer*, like many other newspapers, deliver news to PDAs (such as a Blackberry) and to cell phones. Entertainment and news can be heard on a traditional radio set, a satellite receiver, or a computer and downloaded to an iPod.

We may not be quite there yet, but having everything available everywhere may not be that far in the future.

▲ User-Generated Content

User-generated content (UGC) or peer production has been the most celebrated trend over the past few years. The evidence is everywhere. Here are just a few examples: YouTube (acquired by Google for $1.65 billion in 2006), MySpace (acquired by News Corp for $580 million in 2005), Flickr (acquired by Yahoo! for about $30 million in 2005), and Wikipedia (not yet acquired), as well as 40 million bloggers.

This trend, so far at least, has shown no signs of slowing down. In California one TV station actually fired its news staff and now depends totally on items submitted by viewers. Even the Associated Press has an agreement with a Web site that lets "citizen journalists" contribute content. As this book went to press, there were about 80 of these "citizen" sites, ranging from Al Gore's Current.tv to Ourlittle.net, a site that lets residents in small towns post news about their neighborhoods.

Much of the popularity of UGC is due to user-friendly technology. Digital cameras have dropped in price, and video- and picture-sharing sites such as YouTube and Flickr have made it easy for audience members to upload their content. A person with just a minimum of technical skills can use a blogging program such as Movable Type or WordPress and be posting online in a matter of minutes. Creating content at Facebook or a MySpace page is ridiculously simple.

The move to UGC is one characteristic of what Web gurus call Web 2.0. What is Web 2.0? Here is the definition as provided (appropriately enough) by the user-generated Wikipedia: ". . . a phrase . . . that refers to a perceived or proposed second generation of web-based services such as social networking sites, wikis, [and] communication tools." In short, the new Web 2.0 encourages sharing and collaboration.

Whereas the old Web 1.0 was about companies, Web 2.0 is about communities. Whereas Web 1.0 was about pages, Web 2.0 is about people. Whereas Web 1.0 was about downloading, Web 2.0 is about uploading.

Of course, Web 2.0 and UCG might merely be a passing fad and might disappear as soon as the novelty wears off. Nonetheless, in subsequent chapters we will show how Web 2.0 and UGC are changing traditional media.

▲ Mobile Media

Much of modern mass communication involves people looking at screens. For the past couple of decades, the two main screens have been the TV screen and the computer screen. Now a parade of small screens has joined the lineup: the screen on a cell phone, personal digital assistant (PDA), iPod, or laptop computer. The emergence of the small screen has encouraged the emergence of the final trend: Mass media have become increasingly mobile.

The examples of this trend are everywhere. TV networks, magazines, and newspapers can send their content to phones, PDAs, and laptops. Many cell phones and PDAs can access the Internet. Laptops can connect to the Internet without wires. Consumers can subscribe to services that send TV shows to their cell phones. Newer models can double as MP3 players. In Japan individuals can download entire novels to their phones.

The movies have become mobile as well. A person can download a movie to a laptop computer or play one on a portable DVD unit. The new Sony portable Play Station can even show movies. Apple's iPod contains enough memory for thousands of songs and a screen that can display photographs and video. The iPod has spawned podcasting, which lets people take prerecorded audio programs with them. As suggested earlier, mobile media are another manifestation of the "anywhere" characteristic of multiple platforms.

The implications of this trend are of such great consequence that it is included in Chapter 3 as one of the significant milestones in the development of communication. In addition, the chapters in Part II of this book contain a section that details how each element of the mass media is becoming more mobile.

▲ Social Media

The last trend that is shaping the transition of the mass media goes by the name "social media." Although the label is simple, the concept is hard to define in a few words. At the risk of making things too simple, **social media** are online communications that use special techniques that involve participation, conversation, sharing, collaboration, and linkage.

Participation is the simplest technique that defines social media. It involves soliciting feedback from people about various issues or items. A news Web site that asks for opinions about a proposed new program and a Web operation such as Digg that lets people vote for their favorite online article or image are examples of participation.

Blogs and other Web sites that allow people to comment and to respond to one another are examples of the conversation function. Sharing is illustrated by YouTube, Flickr, and other sites where individuals can create and upload content for others to see. Wikis are social media that exemplify collaboration. The most elaborate social media involve linkage (more about linkage in Chapter 2). These are sites such as Facebook, MySpace, Google Groups, and Twitter where people can link up with friends (both close and distant) and form their own social networks and communities.

There is no doubt that social media have become popular. At the start of 2009, Facebook had more than 300 million users. If Facebook were a country, it would rank fourth in the world.

In addition to the Internet operations mentioned above, the Web sites of traditional media companies have incorporated the techniques of social media. On CBS.com, for example, there is a Social Viewing Room where you can watch your favorite program while interacting with other fans. About 75 percent of all newspapers allow readers to comment on stories, and about 60 percent allow readers to upload pictures and other content to their Web sites. The Web is filled with articles that explain how advertisers and public relations firms can use social media to promote their products and causes. (A Google search for "PR and social media" returned more than 21 million hits.)

Businesses are turning to social media to market their products. Home Depot, for example, sponsored a video contest that asked consumers to illustrate the home improvement project that they would like to undertake. The company created a Web site where people could view all the entries and discuss their projects on a home improvement bulletin board. Social media may also reshape politics. The 2008 presidential campaign of candidate Barack Obama relied extensively on social media. The future president created a Web site, my.barackobama.com, that encouraged people to post blogs and link with other supporters (more than 2 million did); he also accumulated nearly a million MySpace friends, placed videos on YouTube, and started his own photostream on Flickr. After his election, he continued to rely on social media with a new Web site, Change.gov, where people shared their opinions about important issues.

Social media have become influential in the mass communication process, and we will have more to say about them in subsequent chapters.

MAIN POINTS

- The elements in the communication process are a source, encoding process, message, channel, decoding process, receiver, feedback, and noise.

- The three types of noise are semantic, environmental, and mechanical.

- The three main settings for communication are interpersonal, machine-assisted interpersonal, and mass communication.

- Each element in the communication process may vary according to setting.

- *Mass communication* refers to the process by which a complex organization, with the aid of one or more machines, produces public messages that are aimed at large, heterogeneous, and scattered audiences.

- Traditionally, a mass communicator was identified by its formal organization, gatekeepers, expensive operating costs, profit motive, and competitiveness. The Internet has created exceptions to these characteristics.

- New models have been developed to illustrate Internet mass communication.

- Communication content has become more specialized in the past 40 years, but the channels of mass communication still have the potential to reach vast audiences.

- Seven trends that characterize modern mass communication are audience segmentation, convergence, user-generated content, increased audience control, multiple platform, more mobility, and social media.

QUESTIONS FOR REVIEW

1. What are the main elements in the communication process?

2. What are the three types of noise?

3. Compare and contrast interpersonal communication with machine-assisted interpersonal communication.

4. How has the Internet changed the characteristics of the sources of mass communication?

5. As far as the mass media are concerned, what is the difference between a fixed-menu dinner and a Vegas buffet?

QUESTIONS FOR CRITICAL THINKING

1. What's the most embarrassing communication breakdown that's happened to you? Analyze why it happened. Was it due to semantic noise? Environmental noise? Mechanical noise?

2. Keep a media diary for a day. Tabulate how much of your time is spent in interpersonal, machine-assisted interpersonal, or mass communication. What conclusions can you draw?

3. What are some of the shortcomings of the communication model in Figure 1-2? Are there some elements that are missing?

4. Find additional examples of the seven trends that characterize modern mass media? Are there some media that will be less affected by these trends? Do you think these trends are positive or negative developments?

KEY TERMS

source (p. 4)
encoding (p. 4)
message (p. 4)
channels (p. 5)
decoding (p. 5)
receiver (p. 5)
feedback (p. 5)

noise (p. 6)
interpersonal communication (p. 7)
machine-assisted interpersonal
  communication (p. 7)
mass communication (p. 9)
mass media (p. 12)
media vehicle (p. 12)

gatekeepers (p. 15)
corporate convergence (p. 20)
operational convergence (p. 21)
device convergence (p. 22)
social media (p. 25)

INTERNET RESOURCES

Online Learning Center

On the Online Learning Center home page, www.mhhe.com/dominick11e, *select* Student Center *and then* Chapter 1.

1. Use the Learning Objectives, Chapter Outline, and Main Points sections to review this chapter.

2. Test your knowledge of the chapter using the multiple choice and flashcard features of the site.

3. Expand your knowledge of concepts and topics discussed in the chapter with additional Questions for Critical Thinking and Internet Exercises.

Surfing the Internet

Listed here are sites that deal with interpersonal and mass communication.

www.aber.ac.uk/media/Documents/Short/trans.html
A thorough and lucid review and critique of the transmission model of communication. Contrast this model with the one in Figure 1-2.

www.mymissourian.com
As the site's slogan indicates ("Grassroots Journalism by Mid-Missourians"), a good example of user-generated content.

http://dcc.syr.edu
The latest research on and experiments about convergence, sponsored by the Convergence Center at Syracuse University.

http://social-networking-websites-review.toptenreviews.com
As the URL says, a site that reviews the top 10 social networking sites. Includes a side-by-side comparison and reader comments.

CHAPTER 2

Perspectives on Mass Communication

This chapter will prepare you to:

- understand the differences between the functional approach and the critical/cultural approach to studying mass communications

- explain the value of each approach in the analysis of the mass communication process

- describe the functions mass media perform for society

- explain uses-and-gratifications analysis

- recognize the dysfunctions of mass communication

- understand the concepts of *meaning, hegemony,* and *ideology*

The Dark Knight has been the subject of analyses by fans, critics, and mass media researchers.

People study mass communication for a variety of reasons. Scholars study it to better comprehend the process and to develop theories that explain and predict how the media operate. Critics study it to offer insights about its influence and to suggest improvements. Media consumers study it to become media literate, to be able to understand the elements involved in the mass communication process, and to analyze and critically evaluate information presented in the mass media. Those in the media industry study it in order to increase their operating efficiency and maximize their profits when they sell news and information products to the general public.

No matter what the reason for study, it is helpful to use a **paradigm** (a model or pattern used to analyze something) to guide the way we think about the mass communication process. A paradigm is useful for several reasons:

- It provides us with a consistent perspective from which to examine mass communication.
- It generates concepts that are helpful in understanding media behavior.
- It helps us identify what is or is not important in the process.

There are many paradigms that we could use to study mass communication. This chapter will introduce two that provide different ways of looking at media and society. The **functional approach** emphasizes the way that audiences use mass communication and the benefits people receive from media consumption. A second paradigm, which many have labeled the **critical/cultural approach,** examines the underlying power relationships in media exposure and stresses the many meanings and interpretations that audience members find in media content. (Chapter 19 introduces a third model, the empirical paradigm, an approach that has been commonly used to investigate the social effects of the mass media.)

A recent example highlights the difference between these two approaches. Released in 2008, *The Dark Knight,* the latest in the Batman series of movies, cost nearly $200 million to produce. The film was a huge commercial success, grossing more than $1 billion worldwide. In the movie, Batman, District Attorney Harvey Dent, and Lieutenant James Gordon battle a wave of chaos in Gotham City caused by a master criminal called the Joker. Batman eventually wins but is forced to question the morality of his methods.

A functional analysis would want to know several things. First, why did people choose to see the movie? Second, would people identify with Batman and, if so, why? Would viewers have a more positive view of violence after watching the film? Did younger viewers experience the film differently than older viewers?

A critical/cultural researcher would view the film as a text and deconstruct its various elements. For example, the only female character has little more than a minor role and is killed near the end of the film. A critical/cultural analysis might note that the film is another example of Hollywood encouraging a male-dominated society that marginalizes and de-powers women. Moreover, Batman is able to thwart the Joker by a hi-tech spy system that violates the privacy and civil rights of all Gotham City residents. From a critical/cultural perspective, the film appears to carry an ideological message that legitimizes authoritarian methods and encourages conservative political values.

All in all, this movie could serve as the springboard for many disparate avenues of inquiry. This chapter will look first at functional analysis and then examine the critical/cultural approach.

Functional Analysis

In its simplest form the functional approach holds that something is best understood by examining how it is used. In mass communication this means examining the use that audiences make of their interactions with the media.

By way of introduction, here are some actual responses given by college students to the question, Why do you use Facebook?

■   I use Facebook because it is a good way to keep in touch with people I otherwise wouldn't see. (It also lets me see how cute people are, if I was drunk when I met them.)
■   I use Facebook because I have no life and I'm compulsive about who my ex-boyfriends are conversing with.
■   I use Facebook because it gives me a way to put off studying.
■   I like to see the incriminating photos that people put up there.

Responses such as these, varied though they are, have led to several generalizations about the functions that media have for a society and for its individual members. This section will focus on cataloging and describing those functions.

▲   The Role of Mass Communication in Society

The mass media are a pervasive part of our lives. Just how pervasive might become clear if we charted the various functions the media perform for us. Before we do this, however, we need to realize that different media have different primary uses. Not many people, for example, listen to CDs to find out the latest news or read the newspaper while driving their cars. Moreover, different groups of people use the same mass media content for different reasons. History professors, for example, might read articles in scholarly journals in order to keep up with their profession. Others who pursue history as a hobby might read the same journals in order to relax and be diverted from their normal routine.

One more qualification needs to be mentioned before we begin examining the functions and uses of mass communication. It is possible to conduct this analysis on at least two levels. On the one hand, we could take the perspective of a sociologist and look through a wide-angle lens to consider the functions performed by the mass media for the entire society (this approach is sometimes called **macroanalysis**). This viewpoint focuses on the apparent intention of the mass communicator and emphasizes the manifest purpose inherent in the media content. On the other hand, we could look through a close-up lens at the individual receivers of the content, the audience, and ask them to report on how they use mass media (this approach is called **microanalysis**). Sometimes the end results of these two methods are similar in that the consumer uses the content in the way that the source intended. Sometimes they are not similar, and the consumer uses the media in a way not anticipated by the mass communicator—a phenomenon noted by both the functional and critical/cultural paradigms. Let's begin our analysis by using the wide-angle lens.

▲   Functions of Mass Communication for Society

For a society to exist, certain communication needs must be met. Primitive tribes had sentinels who scanned the environment and reported dangers. Councils of elders interpreted facts and made decisions. Tribal meetings were used to transmit these decisions to the rest of the group. Storytellers and jesters entertained the group. As society became larger and more complex, these jobs grew too big to be handled by single individuals. Throughout the following discussion we will examine the consequences of performing these communication functions by means of mass as opposed to interpersonal communication. Furthermore, there may be instances in which these consequences are undesirable from the point of view of the welfare of the society. These harmful or negative consequences are called **dysfunctions.** We will consider some of these as well. Lastly, these functions are not mutually exclusive; one example might illustrate several different categories.

This public-service campaign is an example of the warning function of the media.

Surveillance **Surveillance** refers to what we popularly call the news and information role of the media. The media have taken the place of sentinels and lookouts. The output of the thousands of media journalists in this country is impressive. The four major television networks provide about 600 hours of regularly scheduled news programs, and CNN, Fox, and MSNBC provide similar services. Web sites such as CNN.com update news continuously, and many big-city radio stations broadcast nothing but news. Newsmagazines reach nearly 5 million people, and approximately 1,500 daily newspapers and 7,000 weeklies also spread the news. The size of the news audience is equally impressive. On any given day about 60 million Americans are exposed to mass-communicated news.

The surveillance function can be divided further into two main types. Warning, or **beware surveillance,** occurs when the media inform us about threats from terrorism, hurricanes or volcanoes, depressed economic conditions, increasing inflation, or military attack. These warnings can be about immediate threats (a television station interrupts programming to broadcast a tornado warning), or they can be about long-term or chronic threats (a newspaper runs a series about air pollution or unemployment). There is, however, much information that is not particularly threatening to society that people might like to know about. **Instrumental surveillance** has to do with the transmission of information that is useful and helpful in everyday life. News about films playing at the local theaters, stock market prices, new products, fashion ideas, recipes, and teen fads are examples of instrumental surveillance.

Note also that not all examples of surveillance occur in what we traditionally label the news media. *People* magazine and *Reader's Digest* perform a surveillance function (most of it instrumental). In fact, the surveillance function can be found in content that is primarily meant to entertain. HBO's *Sex and the City* performed a surveillance function for fashions and designer footwear.

What are some of the consequences of relying on the mass media to perform this surveillance function? In the first place, news travels much faster, especially since the advent of the electronic media. It took months for the news of the end of the War of 1812 to travel across the Atlantic. In contrast, more than 90 percent of the U.S. population knew about the terrorist attacks of September 11, 2001, within 2 hours of the events. The initial air strikes in Operation Iraqi Freedom were reported on television minutes after they happened. Speed sometimes leads to problems, however; inaccuracies and distortions travel just as fast as truthful statements. During the 2008 presidential campaign MSNBC, the *New Republic,* and the *Los Angeles Times* reported that damaging leaks about the campaign of John McCain were coming from a McCain policy advisor named Martin Eisenstadt. Unfortunately, Martin Eisenstadt didn't exist; he was a fictional character created by a couple of filmmakers who created him in order to generate publicity for a planned TV show.

As many of you may already know, Twitter is a free social messaging service that allows people to communicate brief messages, called "tweets," in real time. Subscribers can read the tweets on their cell phones or Twitter Web site. Twitter has many interesting uses, but the one that is most relevant to this chapter is its role in breaking news events. In short, Twitter is taking over part of the surveillance process from traditional media.

When a U.S. Airways flight crash-landed in the middle of the Hudson River, many people first learned of the event from Twitter. Within minutes of the crash, there were hundreds of messages posted along with a picture of the crash sent by a person on a nearby ferry boat hurrying to rescue the passengers. The deadly attacks in Mumbai, India, were reported on Twitter before the traditional media got hold of the story. During the height of the crisis there were about 80 posts every 5 seconds from eyewitnesses and from others pleading for help. Much of the news about the postelection violence in Iran came from Twitter. For news junkies, Twitter has a site called Breaking News On, which, as the name suggests, is devoted only to breaking news.

Does this mean we no longer need journalists? Twitter opens up the journalistic process to anybody with a cell phone or computer and can replace traditional reporting. As we shall see in Chapter 13, this trend toward citizen journalism is reshaping the news business. Twitter allows almost instantaneous coverage of a news event and can get information out to the public before the traditional news media arrive on the scene.

Moreover, Twitter can be hyperlocal in focus. Friends can send news reports to friends. When a tornado warning was issued for portions of Colorado, one resident in Boulder heard about the warning not from the traditional media but from a tweet from a friend in California. During the California wildfires in 2008, Twitter users became neighborhood reporters, describing what specific houses had been saved and the addresses that were still threatened, information that traditional news organizations would have probably omitted.

Although Twitter has obvious strengths, we shouldn't be hasty in dismissing traditional journalism. When a news story breaks on Twitter, a torrent of unfiltered information comes at the user and it is difficult to keep up with the flow. There are no editors to make it manageable. In addition, tweets can be in error and quickly spread false information. Further, tweets of a breaking news story represent the fragmented views and comments of eyewitnesses who were fortunate enough (or unfortunate enough) to be at the scene of a breaking story. There are no journalists who could provide context and separate the meaningful from the trivial. And, of course, it's difficult to provide much thoughtful analysis in 140 characters.

Moreover, Twitter's popularity as a news source does not alter the point made in the text. We are still highly dependent on others for news. We still have to have a certain amount of trust in the media (or Twitterers) that do our surveillance. Credibility is still a chief concern. Just as with traditional media, we have to decide how much faith to invest in Twitter and behave accordingly.

The second consequence is a bit more subtle: Much of what we know about the world is machine-processed, hand-me-down information. News is prescreened for us by a complex arrangement of reporters and editors, and our conception of reality is based on this second-generation information, whose authenticity we do not usually question. For example, human beings have allegedly walked on the moon. Millions saw it—on TV. Not many saw it in person. Instead, we took the word of the TV networks that what we were seeing was fact, not fiction. However, some people feel that television staged the whole thing somewhere in Arizona as part of a massive, government-inspired publicity stunt. The same phenomenon occurred in 2004 with the rovers landing on Mars, as some people thought the pictures received from Mars were fakes. The point is this: In today's world, with its sophisticated system of mass communication, we are highly dependent on others for news. Consequently, we have to put a certain amount of trust in the media that do our surveillance. This trust, called **credibility,** is an important factor in determining which news medium people find the most believable. We will discuss the concept at length in Chapter 13.

The widespread use of the Internet to transmit news does not change this basic idea. The stories posted on CNN.com or other news-oriented Web sites have been screened by several reporters and editors. Other Web sites that deal with news, such as the Drudge Report or the many blogs that have recently appeared, may not have a layer of editors, a circumstance that may affect the sites' credibility. Information that is spread through e-mail and by lesser-known Web sites may be especially suspect. Whether the news is filtered or unfiltered, we still have to decide how much faith we invest in the media that provide it.

On the dysfunctional side, media surveillance can create unnecessary anxiety. In 2004 the media began reporting on an impending epidemic of bird flu that could kill anywhere from 5 million to 150 million people worldwide. As of early 2009, the epidemic had yet to materialize. (Of course, if an epidemic eventually occurs, this is a really bad example.)

Interpretation   Closely allied with the surveillance function is the interpretation function. The mass media do not supply just facts and data. They also provide information on the ultimate meaning and significance of events. One form of interpretation is so obvious that many people overlook it. Not everything that happens in the world on any given day can be included in the newspaper or in a TV or radio newscast. Media organizations select those events that are to be given time or space and decide how much prominence they are to be given. Stories that ultimately make it into the paper, on the newscast, or on a media organization's Web site have been judged by the various gatekeepers involved to be more important than those that did not make it.

Another example of this function can be found on the editorial pages of a newspaper. Interpretation, comment, and opinion are provided for the reader as an added perspective on the news stories carried on other pages. A newspaper might endorse one candidate for public office over another, thereby indicating that, at least in the paper's opinion, the available information indicates that this individual is more qualified than the other.

Interpretation is not confined to editorials. Articles that analyze the causes of an event or that discuss the implications of government policy are also examples of the interpretation function. Why is the price of gasoline going up? What impact will a prolonged dry spell have on food prices? When the president broadcasts a major political address, network correspondents usually appear afterward to tell us what the president "really said." After the 2008 presidential election, experts offered their opinions about the causes and consequences of the election of Barack Obama.

Interpretation can take various forms. Editorial cartoons, which originated in 1754, may be the most popular form. Other examples are less obvious but no less important. Critics are employed by the various media to rate motion pictures, plays, books, and records. Restaurants, cars, buildings, and even religious services are reviewed by some newspapers and magazines. One entire magazine, *Consumer Reports,* is devoted to analysis and evaluation of a wide range of general products. Political "spin doctors" try to frame the way media cover news events in a way that is positive for their clients. Many blogs interpret news events in line with their own political philosophy.

What are the consequences of the mass media's performing this function? First, the audience is exposed to a large number of points of view, probably far more than they could come in contact with through personal channels. Because of this, a person (with some effort) can evaluate all sides of an issue before arriving at an opinion. Additionally, the media make available to the individual a wide range of expertise that he or she might not have access to through interpersonal communication. Should we change the funding structure of Social Security? Thanks to the media, a person can read or hear the views of various economists, political scientists, politicians, and several hundred bloggers.

There are, however, certain dysfunctions that might occur. First, there is no guarantee that interpretations by experts are accurate and valid. In 2006, the media carried a report by the National Association of Realtors that analyzed sales trends and predicted that median new home prices would gain 1 percent in 2007. In reality, new home prices declined 2 percent. The same group predicted a 0.3 percent rise in sales in 2008. This prediction was even more off the mark as prices plummeted 9.5 percent. Second, there is the danger that an individual may, in the long run, come to rely too heavily on the views carried in the media and lose her or his critical ability. Accepting without question the views of the *New York Times* or Rush Limbaugh may be easier than forming individual opinions, but it might lead to the dysfunctional situation of audience passivity and of people allowing others to think for them.

Linkage   The mass media are able to join different elements of society that are not directly connected. For example, mass advertising attempts to link the needs of buyers with the products of sellers. Legislators in Washington may try to keep in touch with constituents' feelings by reading their hometown papers. Voters, in turn, learn about the doings of their elected officials through newspapers, television, radio, and Web sites. Telethons that raise money for the treatment of certain diseases are another example of this **linkage** function. The needs of those suffering from the disease are matched with the desires of others who wish to see the problem eliminated.

Another type of linkage occurs when geographically separated groups that share a common interest are joined by the media. Publicity about the sickness known as Gulf War syndrome linked those who claimed to be suffering from the disease, enabling them to form a coalition that eventually prompted government hearings on the issue.

The best examples of linkage, however, are on the Internet. The online auction site eBay lets a person who wants to sell a bronze cremation urn link up with potential buyers across the world. WebMD offers subscribers various "communities" where they can discuss their problems with others who have similar maladies. Craigslist.org lets users find jobs, roommates, dog walkers, and motorcycles for sale. Match.com boasts that it "gets singles connected to the millions of romantic possibilities out there, and often, to one very special someone." After a person finds that special someone, she or he can check out thenest.com, a blog where newlyweds share their experiences about the ups and downs of married life.

Facebook is another prime example of linkage. Facebook members can link up with friends, old and new, create interest groups, and share photos. The fastest-growing application of Facebook in 2009 was "Causes," which links people to causes and benefits. See the boxed insert "Accustomed to Your Face(book)."

Stephen Colbert offers his own, often offbeat, interpretations of current events.

A flash mob is a large group of people organized by social media that gathers quickly in a public place, performs an action for a short period of time, and then quickly disperses. Flash mobs are a rather bizarre illustration of the linkage function mentioned in the chapter. They have been around since the early part of the decade, but the growth of social media has made it much easier to get a mob together and to get larger numbers of people to join in.

In early 2009, thousands of people jammed Liverpool Street train station in London and danced for 15 minutes before dispersing. This particular flash mob was organized on Facebook. One person invited his friends, his friends invited their friends, and so on, and nearly 15,000 people showed up.

March 22, 2008, was billed as Worldwide Pillow Fight Day, and flash mobs were planned in 25 cities around the globe. At the appointed time, crowds showed up, had a pillow fight, then left. About 5,000 participated in the New York pillow fight.

Organizers of flash mobs say that they serve a positive function. They bring unexpected excitement to strangers, make people smile, and find new friends in the process. They do, however, have a dysfunctional side. A 2009 flash mob conducted a pillow fight in San Francisco's Justin Herman Plaza. As fate would have it, it started to rain during the pillow fight and all those feathers flying around turned into a white, feathery sludge that stuck to everything. City officials said it cost about $20,000 to clean up the mess. (I bet they weren't smiling.)

On the other hand, this linkage function may have harmful consequences. In 2009 it was estimated that there were more than 1,000 "hate" sites on the Internet. Terrorists can use these sites to spread hate propaganda and to recruit new members. Some Web sites provide password-protected online discussion groups in which veteran terrorists can persuade new members to join their cause.

Transmission of Values   The transmission of values is a subtle but nonetheless important function of the mass media. It has also been called the **socialization** function. *Socialization* refers to the ways an individual comes to adopt the behavior and values of a group. The mass media portray our society, and by watching, listening, and reading, we learn how people are supposed to act and what values are important. Consider the images of an important but familiar concept as portrayed in the media: motherhood. The next time you watch television or thumb through a magazine, pay close attention to the way mothers and children are presented. Mass media mommies are usually clean, pretty, cheerful, and affectionate. Ivory Snow laundry detergent typically adorns the packages of its products with a wholesome-looking mother and healthy child smiling out across grocery aisles.

Started in 1995 by Craig Newmark, craigslist.org gets about 3 billion page views per month.

There are no more-dramatic examples of the linkage and audience-building function than the social networking sites, such as MySpace and Facebook, that have recently become popular on the Web. Of the two, Facebook is probably better known to the readers of this book since it targets college students.

Facebook was started in 2004 by Mark Zuckerberg, then a sophomore at Harvard. It became instantly popular. In March 2005 the site had about 4 million unique visitors; by 2009 that number had zoomed to 300 million, and the number continues to grow.

The commercial potential of Facebook and MySpace has not been overlooked by the business community. The sites are gaining members while most traditional media are losing audience. They attract a young demographic that is particularly appealing to advertisers. It should come as no surprise, then, that MySpace was purchased by Rupert Murdoch's News Corp. for $580 million. (Facebook turned down an offer of $750 million, hoping for more.)

Facebookers don't seem to care too much about the business doings—they're too busy learning how to maneuver around the site. First, they have to learn a new vocabulary. As most of you already know, a "poke" is a way to get somebody's attention without actually sending a written message. The "pulse" is a list of what movies, books, and music are popular. "Tags" link photos to members' profiles. The "wall" is a place where friends post messages and have conversations. There are also rules of etiquette: Post a picture that actually looks like you; poke people before you ask them to be your boyfriend or girlfriend; and respond to messages in a timely manner.

Facebook obviously has many educational uses. Students studying *Beowulf* can chat about the deeper meanings of the text. Those who were absent from class can get notes and a general updating from classmates. News about what professor to avoid is quickly shared. The biggest use, however, is social. One survey found that 60 percent of students log on to chat, send messages to friends, and maybe even flirt with the cute guy or girl in their psych class.

There is, however, a dark side to all of this. Some students seemed to ignore the fact that the Internet is public. Anybody with an account can view your profile. Some underage students discovered this the hard way when they posted photos of themselves drinking alcohol and were disciplined by their universities. Others posted provocative photos of themselves and their class schedules, making it easy for potential stalkers to target them. Some colleges are examining ways to regulate speech on the site after discovering that some members were posting derogatory, demeaning, and inflammatory messages. Facebook recently tightened its security measures so that members have greater control over who sees what.

There's also the chance that what's on Facebook or MySpace now might have implications for the future. Employers have been known to check out the Facebook or MySpace profiles of job candidates to get clues to their personality and habits. Those students who contemplate a career in politics might find those racy party pictures they posted on Facebook coming back to haunt them.

Finally, Facebook is addictive. Members check into the site often and can easily spend large chunks of time on the site. It's easy to see how Facebook activity might wind up displacing studying or sleep. Too much linkage may be bad for you.

(Incidentally, the company was embarrassed back in the 1980s when one of their clean-cut, all-American types went on to star in X-rated films.) The Clairol company sponsored an ad campaign that featured the "Clairol Mother," an attractive and glamorous female who never let raising a child interfere with maintaining her hair. When they interact with their children, media mothers tend to be positive, warm, and caring.[1] Consider these media mommies drawn from TV: Marge Simpson, Nora Walker (*Brothers and Sisters*), Rochelle Rock (*Everybody Hates Chris*), and Lynette Scavo (*Desperate Housewives*). All are understanding, reasonable, friendly, and devoted to their children.

These examples show that the media portray motherhood and child rearing as activities that have a positive value for society. Individuals who are exposed to these portrayals are likely to grow up and accept this value. Thus, a social value is transmitted from one generation to another.

Mass Media and Socialization   Sometimes the media consciously try to instill values and behavior in the audience. Many newspapers report whether accident victims were wearing seat belts at the time of impact. In 1989, for instance, TV writers voluntarily agreed to portray alcohol usage more responsibly in their programs and to include references to designated drivers whenever possible. The next time you watch current TV shows, see if you can find anyone smoking a cigarette. The health concerns regarding smoking have prompted it to virtually disappear from prime-time TV.

---

[1]OK, Mrs. Costanza, George's mother on *Seinfeld,* might be an exception.

There are probably countless other examples of values and behavior that are, in part at least, socialized through the media. Let us examine some of the consequences of having the mass media serve as agents of socialization. At one level, value transmission via the mass media helps stabilize society. Common values and experiences are passed down to all members, thereby creating common bonds among them. On the other hand, values and cultural information are selected by large organizations that may encourage the status quo. For example, the "baby industry" in this country is a multimillion-dollar one. This industry advertises heavily in the media; it is not surprising, then, that motherhood is depicted in such an attractive light. To show mothers as harried, exhausted, overworked, and frazzled would not help maintain this profitable arrangement.

Mass media can also transmit values by enforcing social norms. In 2008 a video posted on YouTube showing the shoddy living conditions at a National Guard barracks was picked up by the media and became a national story. As a result of the publicity, the Defense Department appropriated nearly $250 million to fix the problem.

Not every attempt by the media to enforce social norms is successful. In an effort to combat binge drinking by college students, several campuses launched media campaigns designed to show that excessive alcohol consumption was not as widespread or normal as many students might think. The idea behind the campaign was to show college students that most of their peers drink only moderately or less, thus reducing pressure on them to drink to excess. A report released in 2003, however, found no drop in student binge drinking on university campuses that used a social norms media campaign in their prevention efforts.

TV and Socialization Of all the mass media, television probably has the greatest potential for socialization. By the time an individual is 18, he or she will have spent more time watching television than in any other single activity except sleep. A prime-time program that is popular with young people might draw an audience of 6 million 6- to 11-year-olds. Because of this wide exposure, several writers have warned of possible dysfunctions that might occur if television is the most important channel of socialization. For instance, since so many TV programs contain violence, it has been feared that young people who watch many such programs might be socialized into accepting violence as a legitimate method of problem solving. In one survey among grade schoolers, heavy TV viewers were more likely than light TV viewers to agree with this statement: "It's almost always all right to hit someone if you are mad at him or her." Another possibility is that the pervasiveness of television violence will encourage fearfulness about the "real world." One study, for example, found that children who were heavy TV viewers were more fearful of going out at night than were light TV viewers. We will discuss this topic at greater length in Chapter 19.

Finally, it has been argued that for many years the image of minority groups transmitted from one generation to the next by the mass media reflects the stereotypes held by those in power: white, Anglo-Saxon, Protestant males.

As a result, Native Americans and black Americans endured many years during which Native Americans were seen as savages who murdered civilized whites, and blacks were depicted in menial and subordinate roles. These stereotypes were slow to change, partly because it took a long time for members of these minority groups to influence the workings of large media organizations.

Entertainment   Another obvious media function is that of entertainment. Two of the media examined in this book, motion pictures and sound recordings, are devoted primarily to entertainment. Even though most of a newspaper focuses on the events of the day, comics, puzzles, horoscopes, games, advice, gossip, humor, and general entertainment features usually account for around 12 percent of the content. (If we considered sports news as entertainment, that would add another 14 percent to this figure.) Television is primarily devoted to entertainment, with about three-quarters of a typical broadcast day falling into this category. The entertainment content of radio varies widely according to station format. Some stations may program 100 percent news, while others may schedule almost none. In like manner some magazines may have little entertainment content (*Forbes*), while others are almost entirely devoted to it (*National Lampoon*). Even those magazines that are concerned primarily with news—*Time* and *Newsweek,* for example—usually mix some entertainment features with their usual reporting.

The scope of mass media entertainment is awesome. By 2009 approximately 53 million people in the United States had paid to see *The Dark Knight.* About 95 million people watched the 2009 Super Bowl. More than 11 million people bought copies of *Harry Potter and the Deathly Hallows.* Carrie Underwood's album *Some Hearts* sold 5 million copies. In a typical month about 3 million people read (or at least look at) *Playboy.*

The importance of the entertainment function of mass media has grown as Americans have accumulated more leisure time. The workweek has decreased from about 72 hours at the turn of the 20th century to the current 40 hours.

The emergence of mobile media (discussed in more detail in Chapter 3) has also amplified the entertainment function of the media. Specially equipped vehicles let children watch DVDs as they go on family trips. Travelers in airport terminals can play games on their cell phones or watch movies on their laptops or iPods while they wait. Commuters can play video games on handheld devices while they travel.

Troubadours, storytellers, court jesters, and magicians fulfilled the entertainment function in the centuries before the media. What are the consequences of having this task now taken over by mass communication? Clearly, the media can make entertainment available to a large number of people at relatively little cost. On the other hand, entertainment that is carried by the mass media must appeal to a mass audience. The ultimate result of this state of affairs is that media content is designed to appeal to the lowest common denominator of taste. More programs that resemble *Survivor* and *Jerry Springer* will find their way to TV than will opera performances. Newsstands are filled with more imitators of *Playboy* than imitators of *Saturday Review.* We are more apt to see sequels such as *Star Trek VIII, Wes Craven's New Nightmare,* and *Lethal Weapon VII* than we are to see *Much Ado About Nothing II* and *More King Lear.* Rock stations outnumber classical stations 20 to 1.

One other consequence of the widespread use of media for entertainment is that it is now quite easy to sit back and let others entertain you. Instead of playing baseball, people might simply watch it on TV. Instead of learning to play the guitar, an adolescent might decide to listen to a recording of someone else playing the guitar. Critics have charged that the mass media will turn Americans into a nation of watchers and listeners instead of doers.

▲ How People Use the Mass Media

It is probably clear by now that statements made about the functions of mass communication in society could be paralleled by statements about how the media function at the level of the individual. Consequently, we will now focus on how the individual uses

Violating a social norm: Deplorable conditions at Fort Bragg were revealed in a video on YouTube. Repairs began three days after the video was posted.

mass communication (in other words, we are moving from macro- to micro-analysis). At the individual level the functional approach is given the general name of the **uses-and-gratifications model.** In its simplest form the uses-and-gratifications model posits that audience members have certain needs or drives that are satisfied by using both nonmedia and media sources. This discussion will be concerned more with media-related sources of satisfaction. The actual needs satisfied by the media are called media gratifications. Our knowledge of these uses and gratifications typically comes from surveys that ask people questions about how they use the media (much like the questions at the beginning of this chapter). We can classify the various uses and gratifications into a six-category system: (1) cognition; (2) diversion; (3) social utility; (4) affiliation; (5) expression; and (6) withdrawal.

Cognition   Cognition is simply the act of coming to know something. When a person uses a mass medium to obtain information about something, he or she is using the medium in a cognitive way. Clearly, the individual's cognitive use of a medium is directly parallel to the surveillance function at the macroanalytical level. At the individual level researchers have noted that two different types of cognitive functions are performed. One has to do with using the media to keep up with current events, while the other has to do with using the media to learn about things in general or things that relate to a person's general curiosity.

Several surveys have found that many people give the following reasons for using the media:

- I want to keep up with what the government is doing.
- I want to understand what is going on in the world.
- I want to know what political leaders are doing.

These reasons constitute the current-events type of cognitive gratification. At the same time, many people also report the following reasons for using mass media:

- I want to learn how to do things I've never done before.
- I want to satisfy my curiosity.
- The media make me want to learn more about things.
- The media give me ideas.

These statements illustrate the second type of cognition—using the media to satisfy a desire for general knowledge.

Diversion   Another basic need of human beings is for diversion. Diversion can take many forms. Some of the forms identified by researchers are (1) stimulation, or seeking relief from boredom or the routine activities of everyday life, (2) relaxation, or escape from the pressures and problems of day-to-day existence, and (3) emotional release of pent-up emotions and energy. Let us look at each of these gratifications in more detail.

SOUNDBYTE

What . . . No Metallica?

Researchers who study the diversion function of the mass media focus on the process by which people seek rewarding media content. No less important is the opposite process: avoiding those forms of entertainment people cannot stand. For example, an Illinois high school teacher was looking for a way to cut down on the number of students who were kept after school as punishment. He started playing Frank Sinatra albums during detention. School behavior improved dramatically.

Stimulation   Seeking emotional or intellectual stimulation seems to be an inherent motivation in human beings. Psychologists have labeled these activities "ludic behaviors"—play, recreation, and other forms of activity that seem to be performed to maintain a minimum level of intellectual activity. Many people report that they watch, read, or listen simply to pass the time. The media have taken advantage of this need to avoid boredom in many creative ways. Airlines provide audio and video entertainment during long flights. Supermarkets have grocery carts with video screens that display the latest bargains. Restaurants and coffeehouses have computers on their tables to allow customers to surf before they sup. Special magazines are distributed only to doctors' waiting rooms. And advertisements can be found on walls and the backs of stall doors in restrooms.

Relaxation   Too much stimulation, however, is undesirable. Psychological experiments have indicated that human beings are negatively affected by sensory overload, in which too much information and stimulation are present in the environment. When faced with sensory overload, people tend to seek relief. The media are one source of this relief. Watching *American Idol* or reading *People* magazine represents a pleasant diversion from the frustrations and problems of everyday life. The choice of material used for relaxation might not always be apparent from surface content. Some people relax by reading articles about Civil War history; others read about astronomy or electronics. Still others might relax by listening to classical music. The content is not the defining factor, since virtually any media material might be used for relaxation by some audience members.

Emotional Release   The final manifestation of the diversion function is the most complex. On the one hand, the use of the media for emotional release is fairly obvious. For instance, the horror movie has had a long history of popularity in America. Starting with *Dracula* and *Frankenstein* and continuing through *The Creature from the Black Lagoon, Them,* and *The Thing* right up to *Nightmare on Elm Street, Friday the 13th, The Ring,* and *Scream,* people have sat in dark theaters and screamed their lungs out. Tearjerkers have also drawn crowds. *Broken Blossoms, Since You Went Away, The Best Years of Our Lives, Terms of Endearment, Dying Young, Titanic,* and *The Notebook* have prompted thousands, perhaps millions, to cry their eyes out.

On the other hand, emotional release can take more subtle forms. One of the big attractions of soap operas, for example, seems to be that many viewers are comforted by seeing that some people (even fictional people) have troubles greater than their own. Other individuals identify with media heroes and participate vicariously in their triumphs. Such a process evidently enables these people to vent some of the frustrations connected with their everyday lives.

Emotional release was probably one of the first functions to be attributed to media content. Aristotle, in his *Poetics,* talked about the phenomenon of **catharsis** (a release of pent-up emotion or energy) occurring as a function of viewing tragic plays. In fact, the catharsis theory has surfaced many times since then, usually in connection with the portrayals of TV violence. Chapter 19 contains a discussion of research that has dealt expressly with the catharsis notion.

Social Utility   Psychologists have also identified a set of social integrative needs, including our need to strengthen our ties with family, friends, and others in society. The media function that addresses this need is called **social utility,** and this usage can take several forms. Have you ever talked with a friend about a TV program? Have you ever discussed a current movie or the latest song you downloaded? If so, then you are using the media as

Media Probe · *American Idol* and Parasocial Relationships

Recall from the text that a parasocial relationship is one in which audience members treat a media character as though he or she is an actual friend. The one program that is the best example of how that concept can be utilized in a hit TV show is *American Idol*. How does the program promote parasocial interactions? Let's recount some of the ways.

First, parasocial relationships, as do real-life relationships, take time to develop. *Idol* recognizes this as each season lasts about five months. In addition, *Idol* is on twice a week, for at least 2 hours, giving viewers ample time to become familiar with the contestants and form relationships.

Second, just as people in real-life relationships are predictable, so are people on *Idol*. Take the judges, for example. Viewers can count on Simon Cowell to be brutally frank; Paula Abdul to be nice but unfocused, and Randy Jackson to fall somewhere in the middle.

Third, people in real-life are three-dimensional. On *Idol*, great care is taken to show the background of each finalist, their aspirations and dreams, their struggles with adversity, their families and friends, and their lives when they are not performing. The program fully fleshes out each contestant.

Fourth, real-life relationships are interactive. *Idol* achieves this quality by letting the audience vote for their favorites. This makes people choose a favorite contestant and root for him or her each week. Many people hope their favorites do a good job each week in the same way as for an actual friend.

Finally, all of us have friends and acquaintances who are unique, idiosyncratic, and maybe a little eccentric. *Idol* always seems to find one or two of these every season: Consider Sanjaya, William Hung, and Bikini Girl.

Granted, there are probably additional reasons why this show has been successful for nearly a decade, but parasocial interaction plays a big role.

conversational currency. The media provide a common ground for social conversations, and many people use things that they have read, seen, or heard as topics for discussion with others. There is a certain social usefulness in having a large repository of things to talk about so that, no matter where you are, you can strike up a conversation and be fairly sure that the person you are talking to is familiar with the subject. ("What did you think of the Super Bowl?" "How did you like *Star Trek?*")

Social utility is apparent in other instances as well. Going to the movies is probably the most common dating behavior among adolescents. The motion picture theater represents a place where it is socially acceptable to sit next to your date in a dark room without parental supervision. In fact, many times the actual film is of secondary importance; the social event of going out has the most appeal.

Other people report that they use the media, particularly television and radio, as a means to overcome loneliness. The TV set represents a voice in the house for people who might otherwise be alone. Radio keeps people company in their cars. In fact, some viewers might go so far as to develop feelings of kinship and friendship with media characters. This phenomenon is called a **parasocial relationship,** and there is some evidence that it actually occurs. For example, one study that examined parasocial relationships between the audience and TV newscasters found that more than half the people surveyed agreed with the statement "The newscasters are almost like friends you see every day."

Affiliation   This use is the individual counterpart to the linkage function mentioned earlier. Psychologists have recognized that one of the central needs of human beings is the need for affiliation. First described in the 1930s, the need for affiliation refers to a person's desire to feel a sense of belonging or involvement within a social group. The Internet is the primary medium that fulfills this function for many people. Facebook, MySpace, Twitter, LinkedIn, and Google Groups are the most obvious examples. Others include online gaming, instant messaging, dating and matchmaking Web sites, and text messaging. The need for affiliation is a powerful one as evidenced by the 300 million members on Facebook, the 110 million on MySpace, and the 35 million professionals on LinkedIn. How many Facebook friends do you have?

Expression   Self-expression refers to individuals' need to express their inner thoughts, feelings, and opinions. The first examples of the need for self-expression are the cave drawings done by early human beings. Since that time, the need for self-expression has been fulfilled primarily by creative and artistic activities such as music, painting, writing,

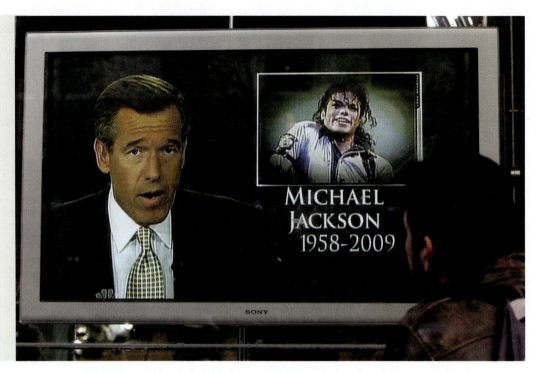

Many people turn to the media for breaking news events such as the death of Michael Jackson.

dance, and sculpture. The Internet has opened up new vistas for self-expression. Bloggers can express their opinions. Many sites let visitors comment on stories. Epinions.com is a site that is composed entirely of people's opinions. Budding musicians, actors, and filmmakers can post their efforts on YouTube or other photo- and video-sharing sites. MySpace and Facebook pages can be personalized to express a person's individuality. Several sites exist where budding digital artists can post their handiworks. The millions of blogs that have sprung up in the last few years suggest that expression is an important function for the individual.

Withdrawal   At times, people use the mass media to create a barrier between themselves and other people or activities. For example, the media help people avoid certain chores, as children are quick to learn. This hypothetical exchange might be familiar:

> "It's your turn to let the dog out."
> "I can't. I want to finish watching this program. You do it."

In this case attending to mass media content was defined as a socially appropriate behavior that should not be interrupted. In this manner other tasks might be put off or avoided entirely.

People also use the media to create a buffer zone between themselves and others. When you are riding a bus or sitting in a public place and do not want to be disturbed, you bury your head in a book, magazine, or newspaper. If you are on an airplane, you might pop in your iPod ear buds and tune everybody out. Television can perform this same function at home by isolating adults from children ("Don't disturb Daddy; he's watching the game") or children from adults ("Don't bother me now; go into the other room and watch *Sesame Street*").

Content and Context   In closing, we should emphasize that it is not only media content that determines audience usage but also the social context within which the media exposure

SOUNDBYTE

A Real Turnoff

The text mentions that the mass media can be used as a withdrawal mechanism that lets people isolate themselves from other people. But what if you're in a laundromat or a waiting room and there's a TV set blaring away? Suppose you want to withdraw from the mass media? One solution is TV-B-Gone, a device about the size of a package of gum that is really a universal remote control that turns off all TVs within a radius of 50 feet. Just don't use it at a sports bar.

occurs. For example, soap operas, situation comedies, and movie magazines all contain material that audiences can use for escape purposes. People going to a movie, however, might value the opportunity to socialize more than they value any aspect of the film itself. Here, the social context is the deciding factor.

It is also important to note that the functional approach makes several assumptions:

- Audiences take an active role in their interaction with various media. That is, the needs of each individual provide motivation that channels that individual's media use.

- The mass media compete with other sources of satisfaction. Relaxation, for example, can also be achieved by taking a nap or having a couple of drinks, and social utility needs can be satisfied by joining a club or playing touch football.

- The uses-and-gratifications approach assumes that people are aware of their own needs and are able to verbalize them. This approach relies heavily on surveys based on the actual responses of audience members. Thus, the research technique assumes that people's responses are valid indicators of their motives.

A great deal of additional research needs to be done in connection with the uses-and-gratifications approach. In particular, more work is needed in defining and categorizing media-related needs or drives and in relating those needs to media usage. Nonetheless, the current approach provides a valuable way to examine the complex interaction between the various media and their audiences.

Critical/Cultural Studies

The functional approach relies on empirical methods common to the social sciences. Researchers who use this approach ask people questions and tabulate the results or enumerate characteristics of media content. In contrast, critical/cultural researchers use a more qualitative and humanities-oriented approach. Although they use different methods, functional analysis and critical/cultural studies share some similarities. Both take a macroanalytic view of mass communication, both acknowledge that the media can be powerful forces in society, and both recognize that the media can operate in ways that can be dysfunctional. Unlike functional analysis, however, the critical/cultural approach examines such concepts as ideology, culture, politics, social structure, and hegemony as they relate to the role of media in society. Some background on this school of thought may be helpful.

▲ A Brief History

Most scholars suggest that the origins of the critical/cultural model can be traced to the Frankfurt School during the 1930s and 1940s. The Frankfurt School was a group of intellectuals committed to the analytical ideas of Karl Marx. (Keep in mind that we are discussing Marxism as a philosophical system and an analytical tool. Marxism as a political and economic system has fallen on hard times of late.) In simplified terms the core of this Marxist approach was that the best way to understand how a society worked was to examine who controlled the means of production that met the basic needs of the population for food and shelter. Marx noted that many Western countries had adopted a system of industrial capitalism in which mass production created wealth for the capitalists—the ones who owned the factories where the goods were produced. Mass production ensured that the basic needs of a society were met, but at a cost: tension between the haves (the wealthy) and the have-nots (the workers who labored in all those factories). In other words, the capitalist system exploited the working class and guaranteed their domination by the wealthy. Because capitalists were interested in creating more capital (or wealth), they had a vested interest in ensuring that the system stayed in place. Marx suggested that life would be better for all if some other, more equitable system of sharing wealth were in place.

The members of the Frankfurt School extended Marxist analysis into the cultural life of a society. They noted that, just as big firms controlled the production of economic goods, other big companies controlled the production of cultural goods. The radio industry, motion picture studios, newspaper and magazine publishers, and later the television business all adopted the capitalist model of production. According to the Frankfurt School, the culture industry exploited the masses just as capitalists did. They published and broadcast products based on standardized formulas that appealed to the mass audience and at the same time glorified and promoted the capitalist culture. For example, during the Depression of the 1930s, Hollywood did not make films that advocated a different economic or political system. Instead, the studios churned out glitzy musicals and comedies that portrayed common people who get a break and make it big despite bad economic times. The television sitcoms of the 1950s showed well-off families content with their lives in the suburbs: Ozzie and Harriet never agitated for a new economic system.

Much of the writing of members of the Frankfurt School was designed to show the exploitative character of mass culture and the way the culture industry helped destroy individuality by promoting the social dominance of large corporations. The object of the critical theory espoused by these writers was resistance to this mass culture and exploitation. The media were so powerful and pervasive, however, that critical resistance to these forces was nearly impossible. The media continued to reinforce the status quo.

The viewpoint of the Frankfurt School was criticized for being pessimistic and gloomy and for underestimating the power of the audience. Nonetheless, this perspective caused many to analyze the impact of the media industries on the political and economic life of society and to use interdisciplinary theories and methods in their investigations.

The next important stage in the development of the critical/cultural approach took place in Great Britain during the late 1950s and early 1960s. Scholars at the Centre for Contemporary Cultural Studies at Birmingham University noted that members of the British working class used the products of mass culture to define their own identities through the way they dressed, the music they listened to, the hairstyles they favored, and so forth. The audience did not seem to be manipulated by the media, as the Frankfurt School argued; instead, the relationship was more complicated. Audience members took the products of mass culture, redefined their meaning, and created new definitions of their self-image.

This emphasis on meaning was reinforced by studies of film and television. A theory developed by British film critics suggested that cinematic techniques (camera angle,

Moviegoers can find emotional release when they laugh and cry at movies such as *Marley and Me.*

During the Depression most Hollywood films refrained from making social or political statements about the hard times. Instead, films like *My Man Godfrey*, shown here, suggested that things were fine and that, with a little luck, everyone could afford the good life portrayed in the film.

editing, imagery) subtly but effectively impose on the audience the meanings preferred by the filmmaker.

This theory was later amended to acknowledge that, although films and TV shows could try to impose their preferred meanings on people, audience members were free to resist and come up with their own meanings. For example, although the dominant theme in a documentary about efforts to control pollution might be how hard industry is trying to control the problem, some in the audience might see the program as nothing more than an empty marketing gesture by big companies.

Important to the cultural studies group were the values that were represented in the content. Again drawing from Marx, the group noted that the values of the ruling class became the dominant values that were depicted in mass media and other cultural products. Marx analyzed dominant values in economic terms, but the cultural studies scholars extended the perspective to class, race, and, with the growth of feminist studies, gender. In Britain, and later in the United States, the dominant values that were represented were those of white, upper-class, Western males. The media worked to maintain those values by presenting versions of reality on TV and films that represented this situation as normal and natural, as the way things should be.

The audience, however, was not passive. The dominant values may have been encoded in complex and subtle ways (much critical/cultural research is aimed at describing and analyzing these subtle depictions), but viewers can supply their own meanings to the content (much critical/cultural research tries to catalogue how various audience members interpret content in different ways). One of the classic studies examined how the audience made sense of a British TV program, *Nationwide*. One group of viewers seemed to accept the dominant message of the program that British society was harmonious and egalitarian; another group "negotiated" their own, somewhat different interpretation; and a third group, young blacks who were not part of the mainstream, rejected it altogether.

The critical/cultural approach gained prominence in the United States during the 1970s and 1980s and was adopted by communication researchers and scholars engaged in feminist studies. Like Marxist analysis, feminist analysis saw inequalities in the way that wealth and power were distributed in society. Marx, however, argued that this inequality stemmed from industrial capitalism; feminist scholars suggested that it stemmed from male domination of women in society (sometimes referred to as *patriarchy*). Feminist critics examined how the media and other forms of culture contributed to the oppression of women. Advertising, for example, might suggest that the proper (or natural) place for a woman is in the home or that looking good is the preferred way for women to achieve success.

Not all critical/cultural scholars, however, emphasize power relationships. James Carey, for example, contended that researchers should study how communication creates, maintains, or modifies a culture. He argued that it is valuable to look upon communication as a ritual—how it draws people together and how it represents a sharing of beliefs. Someone interested in the ritual role of mass communication, for instance, might examine the cultural meanings of men gathering to watch *Monday Night Football* and how this rite illustrates the social bonds that help maintain society. Other critical/cultural scholars have examined how cultural myths are embodied in mass communication. A myth is an expressive story that celebrates a society's common themes, heroes, and origins. Studying the way popular media programs utilize the collective myths of a culture might help us understand their success. *Star Trek*, for example, has spawned a cult following, four TV series, and at least a half-dozen movie sequels. A mythic analysis of the TV show suggests that it draws upon a myth deeply rooted in American history—the myth of the frontier where a wagon train heads hopefully into uncharted and potentially dangerous territory in search of better horizons. Note that the *Star Trek* prologue describes space as "the final frontier," the *Enterprise* takes the place of the wagon train, Klingons take the place of hostile Indians, and Kirk becomes the wagon master while Spock serves as trusty sidekick.

As is probably obvious by now, the critical/cultural perspective is multidimensional and encompasses a wide variety of topics and analytic methods. It is difficult to summarize the important notions of such an eclectic approach, but the ones listed next have general relevance.

▲ Key Concepts

Like most other specialized ways of examining the audience, the critical/cultural approach has developed its own specialized vocabulary. We will examine some of the key terms.

Cultural studies, naturally enough, broaden the study of mass communication to encompass the notion of **culture.** Culture is a complex concept that refers to the common values, beliefs, social practices, rules, and assumptions that bind a group of people together. Hence, it is possible to identify a street culture or an Asian American culture or even a college student culture.

Culture is studied through the practices and texts of everyday life. A **text** is simply the object of analysis. Texts are broadly defined: They can be traditional media content such as TV programs, films, ads, and books, or they can be things that do not fit into the traditional category, such as shopping malls, T-shirts, dolls, video games, and beaches.

Texts have **meaning,** the interpretations that audience members take away with them from the text. In fact, texts have many meanings; they are **polysemic.** Different members of the audience will have different interpretations of the same text. Some may interpret it the way the source intended; others may provide their own unique meanings.

Ideology is contained in texts. Broadly, an ideology is a specific set of ideas or beliefs, particularly regarding social and political subjects. Mass communication messages and other objects of popular culture have ideology embedded in them. Sometimes the ideology is easy to see. Commercials, for example, illustrate the belief that consumption is good for you and for society. Other times the ideology is subtler and harder to detect.

Hegemony has to do with power relationships and dominance. In the United States, for example, those who own the channels of mass communication possess cultural hegemony over the rest of us. Groups with political and economic power extend their influence over those groups who are powerless or at the margins of society. Hegemony, however, is not based on force. It depends on the dominated group's accepting its position as natural and normal and believing that the status quo is in its best interest. Media rules, regulations, and portrayals all help the dominant class present the status quo as customary and desirable. Hegemony creates the positions of the superior and the inferior. This division is unstable and continuously being negotiated through interpretations of meaning.

A couple of examples will illustrate how these concepts are used in the critical/cultural approach. One critical/cultural study used the long-running TV show *60 Minutes* as its

PE Teachers in the Movies

Over the past 15 years many local school boards have cut physical education (PE) programs. In 2005 it was estimated that only about one in four students in the United States attended a daily physical education class. At the same time, teenage obesity has become a serious problem. In 2002 about 15 percent of children and teens were considered overweight, a 300 percent increase from 1980.

Is it possible that the deemphasis of PE programs could somehow be linked to the way that PE is portrayed in popular culture? A study in a 2003 issue of *Sports, Education and Society,* by Bryan McCullick, Don Belcher, Brent Hardin, and Marie Hardin, provided relevant information on this question by examining media portrayals of PE instructors.

The authors noted that popular culture can be meaningful in shaping how students and others view their relationship to education and educational programs. The article used a conceptual framework called *symbolic convergence theory,* which suggests that mass media provide stories with overarching themes that are shared by most members of a culture. These themes become part of the audience's notion of reality and can be more powerful than the "real thing." With this as a foundation, the researchers set out to find if there were common themes in the way PE instructors are depicted in the motion picture medium.

The authors identified 18 movies from 1990 to 2000 that portrayed physical education teachers. They included many that will probably be familiar to readers of this text: *Clueless, Mr. Holland's Opus, The Faculty, Scary Movie, Never Been Kissed,* and *Whatever It Takes.* The next step was to view the videotape of each movie and to identify common themes and representations.

Several themes emerged. First, PE teachers were seldom shown teaching. Instead, they were on the sidelines "cheering, chiding or deriding the students for lack of ability or machismo. The message is clear: teachers might be found in the classroom but not in the gymnasium."

Second, PE teachers were bullies. In several of the films, they enjoyed humiliating and verbally and physically embarrassing their students. In *Never Been Kissed* the main character becomes fatigued while running and drags herself to the teacher and asks for a drink of water. The teacher responds with "What do I look like, a waitress?" and threatens the student that if she doesn't finish running she will fail PE. In another movie the PE teacher repeatedly hits a male student with a baseball. Similar scenes occur throughout the film, and each time the teacher verbally abuses the student by calling him a girl.

Finally, there was a vast difference in how male and female PE teachers were depicted. Female teachers were portrayed as lesbians. In *Clueless* the main character describes her PE teacher as "in the grand tradition of PE teachers, same-sex oriented." In *Scary Movie* the teacher, Miss Mann, is a female with heavy facial hair and broad shoulders. On the other hand, male PE instructors were portrayed as sex-obsessed heterosexuals. In *Mr. Holland's Opus,* for example, the PE teacher continually talks to the main characters about sex.

The authors speculate about some of the possible consequences these stereotypes might have. The connection between physical education and sexuality might stop both males and females from entering the field because they might want to avoid what they might perceive as the negative connotations that go with the profession. Negative portrayals of PE might also reinforce an unfavorable image that school boards and school officials might have of the topic. As the authors put it: "If school administrators voted for the elimination of physical education after viewing . . . *Clueless, Sidekicks,* and *Never Been Kissed,* they could hardly be blamed."

The researchers acknowledge that their study provides no evidence of a causal link between their findings and the attitudes of audience members toward physical education. They argue, however, that their study provides students, educators, and administrators with information that might help them design strategies to combat these stereotypes and to help PE professionals develop more positive approaches for their chosen vocation.

text. The analysis found predictable themes and formulas in the program. One common type of *60 Minutes* segment can be interpreted as the classic American detective story. Somebody, maybe a business that is ripping off consumers, is committing a crime. The *60 Minutes* reporters have to hunt down clues and gather information. They may sneak in a hidden camera to catch the wrongdoers in the act. The reporters become the heroes; the businesspeople are the villains. The story is eventually resolved, and those who were committing the bad deeds are exposed or brought to justice.

This seems to be a meritorious service to the public. But upon closer inspection, this kind of *60 Minutes* story seems to be reinforcing the hegemony of the dominant class. Note that these stories go after companies or businesses that have violated some basic values of American capitalism: "Thou shalt not cheat the customer" and "thou shalt not promise more than thou canst deliver." The stories never question the basic ideology that capitalism is good for you. Instead, they imply that life would be fine if we could just expose all those companies that do not play by the rules of free enterprise and bring them back into the fold. Further, note how the program stands up for the "little person." The reporters are our friends and champions. Everything is fine with the system, and CBS can continue to make money selling ads in a top-rated program. It is easy for viewers to come away with an interpretation that simply reinforces the economic and social hegemony of the powerful.

A second example concerns arcade video games as a text. These games are typically played by a relatively powerless segment of society—younger teenagers. Nonetheless, these players can find a meaning in the games that lets them resist, for a rather short time, forms of social control, allowing them to form their own cultural identity. The arcade games, for instance, reverse the traditional relationship between machine and machine operator. In industry the two work together to produce some commodity; in the arcade the player plays against the machine. The idea is to consume, not to produce.

Playing arcade games is regarded by some with a certain amount of disapproval; some games are violent, and others have mature themes. There is also the view that game playing is a waste of time, and this disapproval on the part of *non*players probably plays a role in the games' attraction for those who *do* play. In addition, the joystick or steering wheel offers the player a direct means to control his or her environment, something that may not be possible in much of everyday life. These factors may account for the continuing popularity of this type of entertainment. Nonetheless, a closer look suggests that, although video games allow the player some freedom of cultural interpretation, the games still work to reinforce the dominant ideology—the social values contained in the games are the common ones in society. Thus, arcade players get a chance to blow away monsters, aliens, drug runners, thugs, and other assorted bad guys; there is no opportunity to show disfavor with the prevailing social norms. And, of course, many of those quarters from the arcade go back to the video game companies, which maintain their economic hegemony and make more games that teens can play to make them feel as though they are resisting the dominant ideology while they are actually supporting it.

This book presents a series of boxed inserts that illustrate the critical/cultural approach and demonstrate the range and diversity of critical/cultural topics. For example, see the boxed insert "PE Teachers in the Movies" in this chapter; in Chapter 5 you will find a critical/cultural analysis of teen magazine Web sites.

Some friction exists between those who choose the traditional effects or functional approaches and those who adopt the critical/cultural approach. This discord seems unnecessary since these various paradigms ask different questions about media and society and use different tools to look for answers. In addition, each approach can learn from the others. No technique is somehow better than the rest. All are useful in the quest to understand the complicated relationships between mass communication and its audience.

MAIN POINTS

- Functional analysis holds that something is best understood by examining how it is used.

- At the macro level of analysis, mass media perform five functions for society: surveillance, interpretation, linkage, transmission of values, and diversion. Dysfunctions are harmful or negative consequences of these functions.

- At the micro level of analysis, the functional approach is called *uses-and-gratifications analysis*.

- The media perform the following functions for the individual: cognition, diversion, social utility, and withdrawal.

- The critical/cultural approach has its roots in Marxist philosophy, which emphasized class differences as a cause of conflict in a society.

- The critical/cultural approach suggests that media content helps perpetuate a system that keeps the dominant class in power. It also notes that people can find different meanings in the same message.

- The key concepts in the critical approach are text, meaning, hegemony, and ideology.

- Although they are different approaches, both functional and critical/cultural studies can be valuable tools for the analysis of the mass communication process.

QUESTIONS FOR REVIEW

1. What is the difference between macroanalysis and microanalysis?

2. What is a dysfunction? What are some examples?

3. What is parasocial interaction? How does it work?

4. What is meant by the uses-and-gratifications approach? What are its assumptions?

5. What are the key terms in the critical/cultural approach?

QUESTIONS FOR CRITICAL THINKING

1. Compare and contrast the functional and the critical/cultural approaches. How does each view the audience? How does each view the media?

2. Compare your own reasons for using Facebook with those that appear at the beginning of the chapter. Are there any similarities?

3. Can you find any more current examples of status conferral? Linkage? Media dysfunctions?

4. As mentioned in the text, one of the assumptions of the uses-and-gratifications approach is that people can verbalize their needs. Suppose this assumption is false. Is the uses-and-gratifications approach still useful?

5. Review the boxed insert "PE Teachers in the Movies," an example of the critical/cultural approach. Are movie portrayals of teachers in general more positive than the portrayal of PE teachers? Why does Hollywood continue to perpetuate these stereotypes? Is it related to profits?

KEY TERMS

paradigm (p. 29)
functional approach (p. 29)
critical/cultural approach (p. 29)
macroanalysis (p. 30)
microanalysis (p. 30)
dysfunctions (p. 30)
surveillance (p. 31)
beware surveillance (p. 31)

instrumental surveillance (p. 31)
credibility (p. 32)
linkage (p. 34)
socialization (p. 35)
uses-and-gratifications model (p. 39)
catharsis (p. 40)
social utility (p. 40)
conversational currency (p. 41)

parasocial relationship (p. 41)
culture (p. 46)
text (p. 46)
meaning (p. 46)
polysemic (p. 46)
ideology (p. 46)
hegemony (p. 46)

INTERNET RESOURCES

Online Learning Center

On the Online Learning Center home page, www.mhhe.com/dominick11e, *select* Student Center *and then* Chapter 2.

1. Use the Learning Objectives, Chapter Outline, and Main Points sections to review this chapter.

2. Test your knowledge of the chapter using the multiple choice and flashcard features of the site.

3. Expand your knowledge of concepts and topics discussed in the chapter with additional Questions for Critical Thinking and Internet Exercises.

Surfing the Internet

The following are useful sites that are related to the material in this chapter. In addition, scan some of the newsgroups on the Net to see some of the special-interest topics that bring people together.

http://eserver.org
Page contains links to works using the critical/cultural approach in many disciplines.

www.aber.ac.uk/media/documents/short/usegrat.html
Site containing links to articles that discuss the uses-and-gratifications approach.

www.aejmc.net/ccs
Home of the Critical and Cultural Studies division of the Association for Education in Journalism and Mass Communication.

www.tandf.co.uk/journals/titles/07393180.asp
The Web site of one of the prominent journals that publishes critical/cultural research: *Critical Studies in Media Communication.*

CHAPTER 3

Historical and Cultural Context

This chapter will prepare you to:

- describe the major events and general trends in media history

- recognize the milestones in the development of human communication

- understand the role that these advances played in prompting significant changes in our culture and society

- learn that the emergence of new communications advances changes but does not make extinct those communications that came before

- understand that each advance in communication increases our power to convey and record information

This modern-day storyteller keeps alive the oral culture of our ancestors and introduces another generation to the art of verbal communications.

The historical and cultural contexts of media are important because history tends to be cyclical. This fact has been apparent for centuries. Many ancient civilizations relied on storytellers to hand down the history and culture of their society so that they might learn from the past. The same is true for modern society: Knowing what happened many years ago might help us understand what is going on now. For example, when radio first started in the 1910s and 1920s, its future was uncertain. Many thought radio would compete with the telephone and telegraph as a means of sending messages from point to point, while others saw radio's future in aviation, providing beacons for aircraft.

The first organization to recognize radio's importance was the military; the U.S. Navy led the way during World War I. After the war, as interest in the new medium increased, a totally new function emerged. Radio was used to broadcast information and entertainment to a mass audience. Many individuals and organizations scrambled to make use of this new means of communication: the telephone company, newspapers, businesses, and even universities. None had any clear idea how radio broadcasting would pay for itself. Eventually radio became a commercial medium, dominated by big business, that in less than 10 years reached an audience of 50 million. Radio changed America's news and entertainment habits and became a medium whose influence on popular culture is still being felt.

Compare radio's development with that of the Internet, which was started by the Department of Defense to improve military communication. When first developed, the Internet was envisioned as a means of point-to-point communication. It gained popularity through the efforts of scientists and amateur computer enthusiasts. When the World Wide Web and newsgroups offered a place where anyone could post messages and reach a large potential audience, businesses, educational organizations, government agencies, and individuals all scrambled to stake out a site. Everybody is currently trying to figure out how to make Web sites profitable. Will the Web eventually become primarily a commercial medium dominated by big business? (We're already seeing signs of this.) Will it change the way we get our news and entertainment? (Probably.) What sort of cultural impact will it have? (This may take a while to determine.) History may help us answer these questions.

You have probably heard the old joke about the guy who was annoyed because he couldn't see the forest because of all the trees, or couldn't see the blizzard because of all the snow, or couldn't see the city because of all the tall buildings (you probably get the idea by now). Well, sometimes it can be hard to see history because of all the names, places, dates, and events. Consequently, this chapter steps back and takes a broad view of media history, emphasizing major events and general trends.

Specifically, this chapter discusses seven milestones in the development of human communication: printing, telegraph and telephone, photography and motion pictures, radio and television, digital media, mobile media, and social media (see Figure 3-1). This overview of the historical and cultural context of mass communication will supplement and make more meaningful the specific histories of the various media presented in Parts II and III of this book.

FIGURE 3-1   Media Time Line

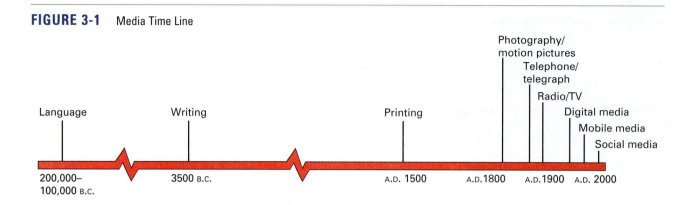

Before Mass Communication

Language developed about 200,000 years ago and led to the development of an oral culture—one that depended upon the spoken word. Such a culture is tremendously dependent on memory. The history and folklore of the culture was transmitted by individuals who memorized large amounts of information and recited it to those in the next generation who, in turn, passed it on to their offspring. Because there is a practical limit to what one person can remember, the growth of information and knowledge in an oral society was slow.

As humans developed further, it became harder to rely on oral communication to fulfill society's communication needs. The need to keep more detailed, permanent and accessible records spurred the next big development in communication—writing.

Writing probably developed in Sumeria (present-day Iraq) about 3500 B.C. A few hundred years later other systems of writing sprang up in Egypt and China. The emergence of the written word had many implications for early societies. It created a privileged class—those who could read and write—that had greater access to information, which led to greater access to power. Information was recorded on scrolls or eventually bound into books. Books and scrolls were stored in libraries, permanent repositories of knowledge that endured from one generation to the next. Writing helped establish empires by making it easier to keep records and to coordinate the movement of armies.

Books became more numerous during the Middle Ages. Most were hand-copied by scribes or monks working in monasteries. As trade and travel increased, the demand for information grew. Universities were founded in Paris around 1150 and in Oxford a few years later, making the demand for books even greater. There were not enough monks or scribes, however, to meet the demand, and books became expensive and even more of a medium of the elite.

This situation changed dramatically around 1450 with the invention of the printing press and movable type—the first of the communication milestones that we will examine.

Printing

The invention of printing is actually a story of many inventions. One of these was the development of paper by the Chinese. China was also responsible for the development of block printing—character outlines were carved out of a block of wood, and the raised parts were inked and pressed against a piece of paper. The oldest surviving block-printed book was published in 868. The Chinese also perfected a system of movable type, using first clay and later blocks of wood for individual characters. The Koreans were experimenting with movable metal type by the beginning of the 15th century.

The next major invention occurred in Germany, where Johann Gutenberg is generally credited with developing a printing press that used movable metal type. Gutenberg

Johann Gutenberg was a wine connoisseur as well as a metallurgist. His design for the printing press was borrowed from a similar device used in wine making.

published his famous Bible around 1453, and his new printing method quickly spread across Europe. Only 30 years after Gutenberg's Bible appeared, there were printing presses in more than 110 towns in western Europe alone. The total increase in the number of books available in Europe is impossible to calculate, but it is probably safe to say that by 1500 there were hundreds of times more books available than in 1450. As books proliferated, their cost went down. Although still expensive, books were no longer the exclusive possession of the very rich. The printed book could now be afforded by those who were simply relatively prosperous.

The consequences of the printing revolution are so far-reaching and extensive that it is impossible to discuss all of them. Most scholars seem to agree, however, on the most significant results.

▲ Effects of the Gutenberg Revolution

The printing press facilitated the development of vernacular (everyday) languages across the European continent. Most of the pre–printing press, hand-lettered books had been written in Latin—the language of the Catholic Church and of higher education. Reading these works therefore required the knowledge of a second language, which restricted potential readership to the educated elite. Many early printers, however, recognized that a broader market for their books would be available if they were published in French, German, or English. Many printers also felt closer ties to their home country than to the church, further encouraging the printing of books in native languages. This trend had other consequences. Bodies of information now became more accessible to more people, further encouraging the growth of literacy, and, in turn, prompting more books to be published. Finally, the use of the vernacular probably helped pave the way for the nationalism that swept Europe in succeeding centuries.

The printing press played a role in the religious upheaval that swept Europe in the 16th century. Before the press, those clerics who disagreed with the doctrines and policies of the church had limited channels for expression. Handwritten copies of their views were few, had limited circulation, and could easily be censored or confiscated by authorities. The situation was forever changed after Gutenberg. Theologian and religious reformer Martin Luther's writings were translated from Latin into the vernacular, printed as pamphlets, and distributed all over Europe. It has been estimated that it took only a month for his famous Ninety-five Theses (the ones he nailed to the church door in Wittenberg, Germany) to be diffused across Europe. One of his later pamphlets sold 4,000 copies in a month. Despite efforts by the church to confiscate and burn Luther's writings, the Reformation movement continued. In addition, the printing of the Bible in the vernacular meant that individuals now had direct access to the core of their religious belief system. The Bible could be read directly and interpreted individually; there was no need for clerical intervention. This increased access to information further weakened the power of the Catholic Church and helped the spread of Protestantism.

Moreover, the arrival of printing speeded up the publication of scientific research. Although it would still be considered agonizingly slow in the era of e-mail and the Internet, printing a book of scientific findings took far less time than it did when manuscripts were handwritten. Printing also ensured that identical texts would be read by scientists in different countries and helped them build on the work of others. Galileo and Newton made their contributions to science in the 17th century, after advances in 16th-century printing.

The printing press even helped exploration. The travels of the Vikings are little known, due in part to the fact that they explored during a time when it was difficult to record and publicize their exploits. Columbus visited America after printing developed, and his deeds were widely known in Europe a year after his return. Printed accounts of the discoveries of early explorers found a ready audience among those eager to find wealth and/or bring religion to the New World. Many early developers published glowing (and sometimes overly optimistic) accounts of life in the new lands, hoping to promote investments and help business. The journeys of the early voyagers were helped by printed books that contained navigational and geographic information about the Americas.

Further, the printing press had a profound effect on the growth of scholarship and knowledge. Whereas access to handwritten textbooks was difficult, university students now had printed texts. (Think how hard it would be to take this course if everybody in the class had to share just one textbook.) As the number of books increased, so did the number of students who studied at a university. Literacy increased further. Interest in the classical works of Greece and Rome was revived as they appeared in printed books that were read by many. Books based on the scholarship of other countries appeared. The advances in mathematics made by the Indians, Muslims, and Arabs were disseminated. Without the printing press the Renaissance of the 16th century might not have occurred.

Finally, the printing press led to the dissemination of what we would today call *news*. As will be discussed in Chapter 4, newspapers sprang up in Europe at the beginning of the 17th century. These early publications were primarily concerned with foreign news. It wasn't long, however, before these papers focused on domestic news as well. This development did not sit well with some monarchies, and government attempts to suppress or censor news content were not unusual. It took until the end of the 17th century to establish the notion of a press free of government control (more on this topic in Chapter 4). The early newspapers made government and political leaders more visible to the public and helped create a climate for political change in both Europe and America.

▲ Technology and Cultural Change

Before leaving this topic, we should note that it is easy to ascribe too much significance to the printing press, to assume that the printing press was the prime mover behind all the effects mentioned. Such a view is called **technological determinism**—the belief that technology drives historical change. A more moderate position suggests that technology functions with various social, economic, and cultural forces to help bring about change. Printing did not cause the Reformation, but it probably helped it occur. And vernacular languages were growing in importance before Gutenberg, but his invention certainly helped them along. In any case, the birth of printing marks the beginning of what we have defined as *mass communication,* and it is certainly a momentous event in Western history.

The next centuries brought further refinements to printing. A metal press was developed by the late 1790s; steam power to drive the press was added shortly thereafter. Advances in printing technology helped usher in the penny press, a truly mass newspaper (see Chapter 4). A better grade of paper made from wood pulp came into use in the 1880s, about the same time as the Linotype machine, a device that could compose and justify a whole line of metal type. Photoengraving brought better visuals to the paper in the 1890s, as did the development of halftone photography a few decades later. Hot-metal type gave way to photocomposition and offset printing in the 1970s and 1980s, and the computer ushered in an age of relatively cheap desktop printing a few years later. Printing has changed a great deal over the years, but its consequences are still very much with us.

The next two communication milestones occurred during what many have called the age of invention and discovery, the period roughly encompassing the 17th–19th centuries. The reasons behind the many achievements of this period are several. The great explorations of previous centuries had brought different cultures together, and scholars were able to share ideas and concepts. Further, there was a change in the way people generated knowledge itself. The traditional authority of the Catholic Church was eroding, and intellectuals looked less to faith and revelation as a source of knowledge and more toward reason and observation. Philosophers such as Bacon, Descartes, and Locke argued for systematic research based on what the senses could perceive. In addition, scientific societies in Italy, France, and Great Britain helped advance the frontiers of knowledge. And, as already mentioned, the printing press helped distribute news of current discoveries to all, prompting others to achieve new breakthroughs. Whatever the reasons, these three centuries saw such advances as Galileo's use of the telescope and notion of a heliocentric solar system, the theory of blood circulating through the body, Newton's theory of gravitation, the roots of modern chemistry, the utilization of electricity, and the discovery of microscopic bacteria. Inventions came along at a dizzying rate: the steam engine, the locomotive, the plow, the internal combustion engine, the automobile, the sewing machine, the dynamo, and a host of others. Not surprisingly, the field of communication also saw major developments, as the next two milestones demonstrate.

Conquering Space and Time: The Telegraph and Telephone

It is appropriate that we spend some time discussing the telegraph and telephone, two related technologies that presaged many of the features of today's media world. For instance, the telegraph harnessed electricity; it demonstrated the technology that would eventually be used in radio. It was also the first medium to use digital communication (dots and dashes). The telephone, with its interconnected network of wires and switchboards, introduced the same concept now at the core of the Internet: Everybody was linked to everybody else.

▲ Development of the Telegraph

It is difficult for people raised in an age of cell phones, cable TV, fax machines, e-mail, and the Internet to appreciate the tremendous excitement that greeted the development of the telegraph. Before the appearance of the telegraph in the early 19th century, messages could travel only as fast as the fastest form of transportation (with some minor exceptions). A messenger on horseback would clop along at around 15–20 miles per hour. A train carrying sacks of mail could travel about 30 miles per hour. The fastest form of message transportation was the carrier pigeon, which could cover more than 35 miles per hour. Then along came the telegraph, which sent messages traveling over wires at the almost unbelievable speed of 186,000 miles per second, the speed of light itself. No wonder that, when it first appeared, the telegraph was described as the great "annihilator of time and space." It was the first device that made possible instantaneous point-to-point communication at huge distances.

The technology necessary for the telegraph dates back to the discovery of electricity. Many early inventors realized that electricity could be used to send messages simply by varying the time the current was on and off. Experiments with early versions of the telegraph (*telegraph* comes from Greek words meaning "to write at a distance") were performed in the late 1700s. By the 1830s and 1840s, workable telegraph systems had been developed in England and the United States.

Samuel Morse was the principal force behind the creation of the telegraph in America. His device consisted of a sending key, a wire, and a receiver that made marks on a paper tape in concert with changes in the electrical current. Later versions did away with the paper tape and let the operator read messages by listening to the clicks made

After 155 years in the telegraph business, Western Union has pulled the plug. The yellow telegram with words typed on strips of paper no longer exists. In January 2006 the company discontinued its telegram service.

Western Union started sending telegrams back in 1851 when it was called the Mississippi Valley Printing Telegraph Company. It took the Western Union name after it acquired a number of competing telegraph services. For decades the telegram brought news, both good and bad, to millions of Americans. In 1929 alone, Western Union handled more than 200 million messages.

Advances in technology, however, ensured the telegram's demise. Faxes and cheaper long-distance telephone rates provided alternatives. The rise of e-mail, text messaging, and instant messages was the last straw.

Western Union, however, will still be around. The company has refocused its efforts into the financial area. Its formal name is now Western Union Financial Services, and it specializes in money transfers for businesses. Interestingly, the company chose to announce the end of its telegram service by posting a notice on its Internet site, taking advantage of the medium that helped make the telegram obsolete.

by the receiver. To simplify message transmission, Morse developed a code consisting of dots and dashes that is still in use today.

Morse demonstrated his device in the late 1830s and eventually received a grant from the government to continue his work. He constructed a line between Baltimore and Washington, D.C., and opened the nation's first telegraph service with the famous message "What hath God wrought?"

▲ The Cultural Impact of the Telegraph

Public reaction to the new machine was a combination of awe and amazement. The telegraph wires that swayed between poles were called *lightning lines.* The early telegraph offices set out chairs so that spectators could watch as messages came in from distant cities. Some people refused to believe that the new invention worked until they traveled to the source of the telegraphic message and verified it with the sender. Some were afraid that all that electricity flowing around above them posed a danger to their health, and they refused to walk under the wires.

Despite these fears the telegraph grew quickly, and lightning lines soon criss-crossed the nation. By 1850 almost every town on the expanding Western frontier could communicate with every other city. Maine could talk to Texas at the speed of light. By 1866 a cable had been laid on the floor of the Atlantic Ocean, linking Europe and America. Four years later, the overland wires and undersea cable carried more than 30 million telegraphic messages (telegrams).

The telegraph was changing communication at about the same time another invention was changing transportation—the railroad. Interestingly, the telegraph wires generally followed the railroad tracks, and stationmasters were often the first telegraphers. The telegraph made it possible to keep track of train locations and coordinate the complex job of shipping goods to various parts of the country—particularly to the West. The telegraph helped the train bring settlers to the frontier and played a role in the country's westward expansion.

The conduct of war was also changed by the telegraph. Troops could be mobilized quickly and moved, usually by railroad, in response to tactical and strategic developments. The significance of the telegraph for the military was demonstrated many times during the Civil War.

Morse's invention had an impact on commerce as well. It sped up communication between buyers and sellers, reported transactions, and organized deliveries. Instant communication brought about standard prices in the commodity markets. Before the telegraph the price of corn varied with local market conditions and might be several dollars cheaper in, say, Chicago than in St. Louis. After the telegraph connected all markets, local variations were evened out.

Further, as we will discuss in more detail in Chapter 4, the telegraph greatly enhanced newspapers' ability to transmit news. Information from distant places had previously taken weeks to reach the newspaper office. With the telegraph and Atlantic cable, even news from Europe could make the next day's edition. Newspaper publishers were quick to recognize the potential of this new device and used it heavily. Many incorporated the word "Telegraph" into their name. The telegraph also helped the formation of news agencies, or *wire services* as they were also called. The Associated Press made great use of the expanding telegraphic service to supply news to its customers. Finally, the telegraph changed the style of reporting. Because the early telegraph companies charged by the word, news stories became shorter. Rather than wordy, reflective, and interpretive reports, scoops, breaking news, and the bare facts began to characterize news reports.

▲ Government and Media

The telegraph also set the precedent for the relationship between the government and large media companies. In many other countries, since the telegraph was used to deliver messages, it seemed an extension of the post office, and the government agency that assumed responsibility for the postal service also administered the telegraph. However, this model was not followed in the United States. Although some in the government endorsed a federal takeover of the telegraph system, the prevailing sentiment was in favor of private, commercial development. By the end of the 19th century, telegraphic communication was dominated by one company, Western Union. As we will see in later chapters, other mass media—motion pictures, radio, television—were also developed as private rather than government enterprises and were dominated by one or a few large companies.

▲ A Change in Perspective

Another consequence of the telegraph was subtler and harder to describe. In some ways the telegraph changed the way people thought about their country and the world. By erasing the constraints of space, the telegraph had the potential to function as an instant linkage device (see Chapter 2) that tied people together. Morse wrote how the telegraph would make a neighborhood of the whole country. A Philadelphia newspaper, shortly after the successful demonstration of the device, wrote that the telegraph destroyed the notion of "elsewhere" and made everywhere "here." The paper declared that the telegraph would "make the whole land one being." An article in a magazine of the period was even more expansive: The telegraph "binds together by a vital cord all nations of the earth." It may not be too much of an overstatement to contend that the telegraph introduced the notion of a global village that was to be popularized a century later by Marshall McLuhan. It created a sense of unity among Americans and encouraged them to think in national and international terms.

Alexander Graham Bell demonstrates a version of his telephone for representatives of the business community. Bell and his colleagues eventually received 30 patents for telephone-related inventions.

The telegraph was joined by a companion invention, the telephone. Like the Morse invention the telephone conquered time and space and had the added advantage of requiring no special skills, such as Morse code, for its use. It transmitted the human voice from point to point. There was some confusion over the precise role the telephone would play in society, but the notion of linking phone users by wires and the development of the switchboard eventually made it possible to connect one place with many others. This arrangement helped the telephone become a fixture in businesses and homes across the nation. The telephone made private communication easier to

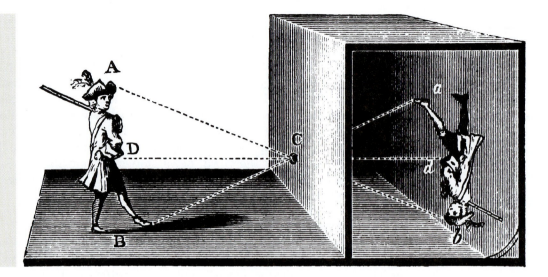

In the camera obscura a small opening containing a lens produces an inverted and reversed image of an object. Many artists used the camera obscura to help them draw precise images of people, landscapes, and buildings.

achieve. It was now possible for people to converse away from the watchful eyes of parents, bosses, and other authority figures. Finally, like the telegraph industry the telephone industry would be dominated by a large corporation, AT&T, which would eventually gain control of Western Union.

In sum, the telegraph and the telephone enabled people to communicate over vast distances in what we now call *real time* and had a far-reaching impact on the political, economic, and social development of the United States and the rest of the world. We will discuss this impact in detail throughout the book. In many ways it is still making itself felt today.

Capturing the Image: Photography and Motion Pictures

The telegraph and the telephone drew upon advances in the science of electricity. The next communication advance we will examine could not have occurred without advances in the field of chemistry.

▲ Early Technological Development

Two things are required to permanently store an image. First, there must be a way to focus the image on a surface. Second, the surface must be permanently altered as a result of exposure to the image. The first requirement was fulfilled in the 16th century with the creation of the camera obscura, a dark chamber with a pinhole in one wall. The light rays that entered the chamber through the small hole projected an image on the opposite wall. The second requirement took longer to achieve. In the 1830s two Frenchmen, Joseph Niepce and Louis Daguerre, experimented with various substances that changed upon exposure to light rays. Silver iodide provided the best results, and Daguerre sold this discovery to the French government. An English scientist, William Fox Talbot, working at about the same time as Daguerre, refined the process by capturing his images on paper in the form of negatives, permitting copies to be made. Other advances quickly followed, including the use of flexible celluloid film. George Eastman's company introduced the Kodak box camera in the 1890s with the slogan "You press a button. We do the rest." The Kodak was designed for the mass market. Amateur photographers simply loaded a roll of film in the camera, aimed the camera, pressed the button, and then sent the film off to Kodak to be developed and printed.

Mathew Brady's famous 1864 photo of a war-weary Abraham Lincoln. Part of this portrait was later used on the five-dollar bill.

There were several long-range consequences of these technological advances. Early photos (called *daguerreotypes*) required long exposure times, making them particularly suitable for portraits, for which the subject could remain still. These early portraits provided a way to preserve and humanize history. Our images of George Washington, for example, are from paintings that show him in an idealized manner, usually in noble poses making him appear distinguished and powerful. Our images of Abraham Lincoln, however, come from the many photographs that were taken of him during his term in office. The early photos, taken around 1860, showed him in flattering poses. The later photos, taken after years of war, showed a man grown visibly older, with lines creasing his forehead and tired eyes.

▲ Photorealism and Mathew Brady

The Civil War was the first American war to be photographed extensively. Before the camera the public's view of war was probably shaped mostly by paintings and etchings that showed magnificent cavalry charges and brave soldiers vanquishing the enemy, not the horror and carnage of actual combat. Mathew Brady persuaded the U.S. government to give him access to the battlefield. (Brady apparently thought the government would cover the costs of his venture, but his expectations were never met, and many of his photos were lost.) Because early photography was not able to capture action scenes, Brady was limited to photographing scenes of the aftermath of a battle. These images, however, were powerful enough. In 1862 Brady's colleagues photographed the battleground at Antietam just two days after the battle and before all the dead had been buried. The resulting photographs were the first to show the actual horrors of war. When the photos went on view in a New York gallery, they caused a sensation. The carnage of battle was revealed to all. As Oliver Wendell Holmes remarked, "Let him who wishes to know what war is like look at this series of illustrations." A hundred years later, other communication advances would bring scenes of horror from the Vietnam War directly into American living rooms.

Photography had an impact on art. Now that a means had been developed to preserve realistic images, artists were free to experiment and develop different ways of portraying the world. Again, although it is hard to say how much of a role photography played in influencing painting, the impressionist, postimpressionist, and cubist schools of painting came to prominence at about this same time. At the other end of the spectrum, photography itself became a fine art, as virtuosos such as Alfred Stieglitz, Margaret Bourke-White, and Edward Steichen created masterpieces of graphic reproduction.

▲ Photography's Influence on Mass Culture

One did not have to be an artist, however, to take pictures—everybody could and did. Advances in film and camera technology put cameras in the hands of the masses. Ordinary people took photos of significant people, objects, and events: marriages, new babies, new cars, pets, vacations, family reunions, proms, and so on. Photo albums quickly became a part of each family's library. Photography enabled each generation to make a permanent record of its personal history.

Advances in the printing process, such as halftone photography, also made it possible for photographs to be published in magazines and newspapers. By the beginning of the 20th century, dozens of illustrated dailies and weeklies were being published in the United States. This development created a new profession—**photojournalism**—and changed America's conception of news. Photojournalism reached new popularity in the

1920s when the pace of life quickened, and many innovations cropped up that promised to save time for the consumer—lunch counters for fast meals, express trains, washing machines, vacuum cleaners, and so forth. When it came to news reporting, the biggest time-saver was the photograph. Readers could look at photos much more quickly than they could read the long text of a story. As a consequence, printed columns decreased and space devoted to pictures increased, helping popularize the tabloids and picture magazines such as *Life* (see Chapter 5).

Photojournalism had subtler effects as well. First, it changed the definition of *news* itself. Increasingly, news became that which could be shown. Accidents, natural disasters, demonstrations, and riots were natural photo opportunities. This visual bias in news reporting remains a topic of concern even today. Second, as photo historian Vicki Goldberg put it, photography created "a communal reservoir of images." Certain historic events were fixed forever in the minds of the public by their photos: the fiery crash of the *Hindenburg*, the young girl screaming over the body of a dead student at Kent State, the smoking remains of the World Trade Center, the toppling of the statue of Saddam Hussein in Baghdad. All of these images have been etched permanently on the national consciousness.

Modern cell phone cameras have made photographers of everybody, and that, in turn, has raised privacy issues. Cell phones with cameras are banned in many locker rooms and health spas. Nearly every state has a law governing photographic voyeurism. Compounding the problem are the many Internet sites that showcase user-generated content, such as Flickr, Fotolog, and Phanfare. Unsuspecting people might be shocked to find that photos taken without their knowledge or permission all of a sudden show up on the Internet.

▲ Pictures in Motion

The technology behind photography led to the development of another way to capture an image. The goal behind this new milestone, however, was to capture an image in motion. Chapter 9 details the early history of the motion picture medium and traces how it evolved from a series of toys into a giant entertainment industry. It is significant that this new medium evolved while three significant trends were occurring in the United States. The first was industrialization. In the Industrial Revolution, which began in the early 19th century and continued into the 20th, production and manufacturing both increased significantly. Along with industrialization came the second trend, urbanization, as people moved into the cities to be near the plants and factories where they could find jobs. In the United States one-fourth of all Americans lived in an urban area by 1914. The third trend was immigration. About 25 million people immigrated to the United States between 1871 and 1914, and most of them wound up in cities where they went to work in manufacturing plants.

The culmination of these trends was the creation of a huge audience that was drawn to the new medium of motion pictures. The first movie houses sprang up in the cities. They were called *nickelodeons*, storefronts that had been turned into makeshift theaters, with uncomfortable benches or folding chairs for the audience, a tinkling piano, and poor ventilation. Nonetheless, nickelodeons were big hits among the newly arrived immigrants. By 1910 there were more than 10,000 of these nickelodeons around the country, and film exhibitors and filmmakers quickly recognized that there was a market for filmed entertainment. The motion picture business had started. Film eventually moved to plusher theaters and tried to appeal to the middle class, but it left its mark on the immigrant population. Many learned the customs and culture of their new country from nickelodeons.

▲ Motion Pictures and American Culture

The long-range impact of the motion picture lay mainly in the areas of entertainment and culture. As the demand grew for feature-length films, only very large companies were able to come up with the money needed to pay production costs. As will be noted in Chapter 9, these large companies came to dominate the production, distribution, and exhibition of movies. Today's film industry is controlled by global conglomerates that still follow many of the patterns established in the 1920s.

Edwin S. Porter's *The Great Train Robbery* was the first American film to tell a story. This classic Western was actually shot in New Jersey.

Movies forever altered America's leisure time. Vaudeville soon died out. Going to the movies became an important social activity for the young. Saturday afternoons that once were spent going to parks and friends' houses were now spent inside a darkened theater.

The movies became a major cultural institution. Photography and the mass-appeal newspaper had made it easier for people to recognize and follow the fortunes of their favorite celebrities, but motion pictures raised this process to a new level. Hollywood produced cultural icons, the movie stars. The popularity of motion pictures was based on their appeal to all social classes. Unlike serious drama, opera, and ballet, which appealed to the elite, movies attracted the masses. The movies helped bring about the notion of a popular culture, a phenomenon whose benefits and liabilities are still being debated.

In 1915 American poet Vachel Lindsay published *The Art of the Moving Picture,* which signaled the beginnings of a new popular art form. Lindsay's book was the first of many serious attempts to develop a theory of film. Although a popular entertainment form that blended business and art, film soon became a topic worth serious study, a trend still with us today as evidenced by the many universities that teach film as part of their curricula.

In the early 1930s the Payne Fund sponsored a series of studies on the possible harmful effects of attending motion pictures. This was the first of many studies that tried to establish just what impact film and, later, broadcasting have on society (see Chapter 19 for more details). The Payne Fund studies were significant because they marked the first time the public had decided that a medium, in this case motion pictures, had an effect on society and was deserving of serious examination.

Finally, although film played its most prominent role as a medium of entertainment, it is important to note that it had an influence on journalism as well. Started around 1910, newsreels appeared weekly or semiweekly and pictured the major events of the period. The big movie studios eventually controlled the production of newsreels. They standardized the content of the 10-minute reels so that audiences could expect to see something from Europe, some national news, some sports, a feature or two, and perhaps a human-interest story. The newsreels were discontinued in the 1950s and 1960s as pictorial journalism moved to television. These early news films, however, influenced many of the conventions and expectations of broadcast news reporting.

News and Entertainment at Home: Radio and Television Broadcasting

Radio, the first medium that brought live entertainment into the home, would not have been possible without advances in physics. The discovery of electromagnetic waves caught the attention of many scientists, who looked for ways to use this new discovery to send messages. Advances in wire telephony in the United States made it possible to send voice and music over the air and prompted AT&T to fund a massive research program in the area. Radio development, however, was stymied by patent problems. Had it not been for World War I, radio's development might have taken far longer. The war had a couple of major consequences for radio's development. The U.S. Navy solved the legal problem by asserting control over all patents that made possible major advances in technology.

Mathew Brady's decision to photograph dead soldiers on the Antietam battlefield started a controversy that persists even today: What is the proper way to cover the carnage caused by a war? Is it fitting to show dead American soldiers on the nightly newscast or in the newspaper? How about dead enemy soldiers or civilian casualties?

For many years the U.S. government forbade the photographing of dead U.S. soldiers for fear that it would demoralize the home front. Franklin Roosevelt reversed that policy during World War II when he felt that those at home had become too complacent and too removed from the realities of combat. Accordingly, in 1943 *Life* magazine published a photograph of the sand-covered bodies of three unidentifiable U.S. soldiers on an invasion beach in New Guinea. A short time later, John Huston's classic documentary film *The Battle of San Pietro* contained scenes of actual combat and resulting casualties. Decades later, during the Vietnam conflict, filmed scenes of wounded and dead GIs found their way onto the network news.

Operation Iraqi Freedom reopened the controversy. Since many reporters were embedded with combat troops, battlefield coverage was sometimes shown live or shortly after it occurred. For the most part the reporting on the part of the U.S. media was restrained. This led some observers to charge that the media were sanitizing the war and avoiding its harsh realities. On the other hand, when *USA Today* published a front-page photo of the bodies of two dead Iraqis, the paper received dozens of letters and more than a hundred phone calls criticizing the newspaper for its lack of judgment and accusing it of being antiwar.

Media professionals expressed different viewpoints concerning their responsibilities in time of war. Quoted in the *Washington Post,* ABC's Ted Koppel argued in favor of showing dead bodies: "One thing you cannot do is leave people with the impression that war is not a terrible thing." CNN's Walter Rodgers apparently felt the same way. During a live broadcast from outside Baghdad, Rogers showed the body of a dead Iraqi soldier next to a burned-out personnel carrier. Said Rodgers in a story in *Newsday,* "You ought to show even more than taste allows so no one has any illusions how terrible carnage and war are."

But does the audience really need to see grisly scenes to be reminded of the horrors of war? Doesn't everybody already know that war is horrible? Steve Capus, an NBC news producer, contended that a newscast should communicate the reality of war without wallowing in death or injury. News anchor Charles Gibson went further: "Any time you show dead bodies, it is simply disrespectful."

John Szarkowski, former director of photography at the Museum of Modern Art, offers another perspective. He argues that editors and reporters should not show every bloody scene they come across. After a while people become inured to the violence in the images, and each successive scene has less power than the one before it.

This issue is still with us today. For nearly two decades the Pentagon imposed a policy that forbade the taking of pictures of the caskets of returning war dead. This rule was relaxed in 2009 to allow photos and video footage as long as the families of the deceased agreed.

In sum, this debate will go on as long as reporters cover wars, and journalists will continue to struggle with their ethical obligations to their profession and to the audience.

Further, a large number of soldiers went into the Signal Corps, where they learned the fundamentals of the new medium. When they came back from the war, these men kept interest alive in radio, helping popularize many amateur radio clubs, and provided the basis for a ready-made audience for early broadcasting.

▲ Radio Broadcasting

The shift from using radio as a point-to-point communication device (like the telegraph) to using it as a point-to-many broadcasting medium caught many by surprise. Thanks to the popularity of early radio stations, broadcasting became a national craze, and by the early 1920s the stage was set for the emergence of another mass communication milestone. Radio was the first mass medium that brought sports, music, talk, and news into the living room.

In addition to World War I, other historical circumstances influenced radio's development. It is easy to overlook today, but when radio first started out, there was no system in place that permitted it to support itself. Many radio stations went on the air simply for the novelty of it, with little thought as to how to fund their operations. Significantly, modern radio emerged in the Roaring Twenties, when economic conditions were vigorous, consumer goods were easily available, stocks were soaring, and many people in the business world were accumulating fortunes. In the midst of this climate, it was easy for radio broadcasting to turn to commercials for its economic base. Accepting advertising brought quick profits and was in tune with the business-is-good philosophy of the times.

Business was so good, in fact, that the federal government generally kept out of it. Radio, however, needed government intervention. Overlapping signals from too many radio stations broadcasting on too few frequencies was a serious problem. In 1927 Congress created a Federal Radio Commission (FRC), whose main task was to regulate the technical side of the medium. Unlike the situation in some European countries, the FRC and its successor, the Federal Communications Commission, took a generally light-handed approach to regulation and favored the fortunes of commercial broadcasters.

It was also the era when newspaper chains and many other businesses were consolidating their operations. The development of radio networks fit nicely into this model, and it was not long before national programming was supplied by two, and later three, national radio networks. Further, tabloid newspapers were capturing readers, and Hollywood films were booming. These trends were to have an impact on the future of radio programming. In concert with its evolution as an advertising medium, radio moved toward mass-appeal programming that provided an audience of consumers for those who bought commercial time on the new medium.

Ironically, the Depression of the 1930s, which did some financial damage to radio, also helped its programming. Many performers from vaudeville, the recording industry, and the theater, rendered unemployed by the Depression, took their talents to radio, particularly network radio. As a result, the level of professionalism and the caliber of entertainment improved, and the networks solidified their grasp on the industry. By 1937 almost every powerful radio station in the country was a network affiliate. News broadcasting came of age about this same time, and radio soon became a more important source of news than the newspaper.

▲ The Cultural Impact of Radio

In terms of the long-term impact of this medium, several elements stand out. First, and most obviously, radio helped popularize different kinds of music. One of the early radio stations with a powerful signal was WSM in Nashville, which carried broadcasts of *The Grand Old Opry*, a program that introduced country music to many thousands. Broadcasts of black rhythm-and-blues music crossed the race barrier and gained listeners among whites. In more recent years radio helped popularize rock and roll, reggae, and rap.

Radio made its own contributions to the popular culture. Although early programs recycled many vaudeville acts, genres original to the medium soon developed. One of these was the soap opera, whose familiar formula later made the transition into television. In 1940 soaps accounted for more than 60 percent of all network daytime programming. Entertainment series aimed at children introduced youngsters to *Jack Armstrong—The All-American Boy* and *Captain Midnight*. The significance of these programs may be less in their style or content and more in the fact that they signaled the radio broadcasters' attitude that children were a viable market and that it was acceptable to send advertising their way. Situation comedies such as *Amos 'n' Andy* and action-adventure programs such as *Gangbusters* were other formats that persisted into television.

After a somewhat shaky start, radio news came of age in the 1930s and 1940s. Audiences tuned to the new medium for live coverage of the events leading up to World War II. Listeners could hear live the voices of world leaders, such as Adolf Hitler and British prime minister Neville Chamberlain. Commentators would then provide what in a more modern era would be called *instant analyses* of what was said. Radio personalized the news: Unlike newspapers, where a byline might be the only thing that identified a reporter, radio news had commentators and reporters with names, distinctive vocal styles, and personalities. A list of famous radio news personnel of the period includes H. V. Kaltenborn, Edward R. Murrow, and Lowell Thomas. These individuals became celebrities and introduced a new component into journalism—the reporter as star. This trend would also carry over into television as network anchors and reporters were able to command multimillion-dollar salaries, just like movie stars and sports heroes.

Finally, like the movies, radio changed the way Americans spent their free time. Radio was the prime source of entertainment and news. Families would faithfully gather around the radio set in the evenings to listen to the latest episodes of their favorite programs. By the 1940s household radio listening time averaged more than 4 hours per day, most of it in the early evening hours. A new phrase emerged to describe this period of peak listening activity. It was called *prime time,* another concept that passed over to TV.

▲ Television Broadcasting

Television, as will be discussed in Chapters 10 and 11, also had its beginnings in the 1920s and 1930s, and, as was the case with radio, a war interrupted its development. World War II halted the growth of TV as a mass medium. Early transmitting stations went off the air during the war, and TV receivers were no longer manufactured. The technology behind TV, however, received a substantial boost from the war effort, as new discoveries in the field of radar were translated into an improved TV broadcast system.

Also, like radio, television became popular during an age of relative prosperity. After a period of postwar retooling, American industry began churning out consumer goods. The self-denial of the war years gave way to a fulfillment of long-repressed desires, as Americans bought new cars, dishwashers, barbecue grills, and air conditioners. But the TV set was the most sought-after appliance. Television swept the country during the 1950s. It took the telephone about 80 years to reach 85 percent of the country's homes, and the automobile did it in 49 years. Television did it in 10. Approximately 10 million homes had TV in 1950; by 1959 that number had more than quadrupled. While new, labor-saving appliances increased leisure time, more often than not that leisure time was spent watching TV. Household furniture had to be rearranged to accommodate the TV set in the living room.

▲ The Cultural Impact of TV

Television grew up surrounded by other dramatic social trends and events. Americans were moving into the suburbs, and commuting thus became a ritual. Women were beginning to enter the workforce in greater numbers. The 1960s saw the emergence of the civil rights movement, the escalation of the war in Vietnam, and the growth of the counterculture. Television brought these happenings into the nation's living rooms.

Today, television is in 99 percent of all households, and the set is on about 8 hours every day. In an astoundingly short period, TV replaced radio as the country's most important entertainment and information medium and became a major cultural and social force. In fact, television probably has not been with us long enough for us to see all of its ultimate consequences. Some, however, are fairly obvious. Television has become a major consumer of time. Sleeping and working account for the most time in a person's day, but TV watching ranks third. Television also has transformed politics. Political conventions are staged for TV; candidates hire TV consultants; millions are spent on TV commercials; candidates debate on TV; and so on. TV has exerted a standardizing influence on society as well. Clothing, hairstyles, language, and attitudes seen on TV pervade the nation and, for that matter, the rest of the world. Further, television news became the most important and believable source of information. And, like the motion picture, television created a whole new slate of stars and celebrities. It has also been suggested that television has become an important source of socialization among children and that TV programs inspire antisocial and other undesirable behavior. (Chapter 19 reviews the evidence for these assertions.)

The cultural influence of television is sometimes subtle. Shows such as cable network TLC's *Trading Spaces* revived interest in home remodeling and interior design.

Although the telegraph was the first to be called the "great annihilator of time and space," television might be a better candidate for that title. Audiences have seen TV pictures live from Baghdad, Earth's orbit, the moon, and Mars (well, as live as they can be from a place so far away). In fact, today's TV viewer expects to see live reports of breaking stories, no matter where they are; no place seems far away anymore.

Photography was credited with creating a reservoir of communal experience. Television, however, has widened and deepened that reservoir. For example, televised images of President Kennedy's funeral, the *Apollo 11* moon landing, the *Challenger* explosion, and the planes striking the World Trade Center have all been indelibly impressed upon the national consciousness.

The Digital Revolution

In his book *Being Digital,* Nicholas Negroponte, director of MIT's Media Laboratory, summed up the digital revolution as the difference between atoms and bits. Traditionally, the mass media delivered information in the form of atoms: Books, newspapers, magazines, CDs, and DVDs are material products that have weight and size and are physically distributed. Negroponte maintains that this is rapidly changing: "The slow human handling of most information in the form of [recorded music], books, magazines, newspapers, and videocassettes is about to become the instantaneous transfer of electronic data that move at the speed of light." In short, atoms will give way to bits.

As an example, consider the difference between e-mail and traditional paper mail. In the traditional system a letter must be placed in an envelope with a postage stamp and given to the U.S. Postal Service, whose employees sort it, transport it, and deliver it a few days later to its recipient. E-mail needs no paper, no postage, and no delivery by postal carriers. It is a series of bits of information that travels electronically and is delivered in seconds rather than days. With e-mail the same message can be copied a thousand times and sent to a thousand different people much more quickly and cheaply than with paper mail.

At the risk of oversimplifying a rather complicated topic, we can describe **digital technology** as a system that encodes information—sound, text, data, graphics, video—into a series of on-and-off pulses that are usually denoted as zeros and ones. Once digitized, the information can be duplicated easily and transported at extremely low costs.

As will be discussed in Chapter 12, the computer was the first device to use the digital system to process information. The innovation quickly spread to other media. Digital technology makes possible the special effects now common in motion pictures and television,

All the communication milestones discussed in this chapter changed the way information was stored or transmitted. Starting with the printing press, they all expanded the scope of human communication by making it possible for people to share information with other people in other places or at other times. This achievement prompted a rather optimistic attitude toward the social benefits of the media. For example, the telegraph was viewed as a force for morality, understanding, and peace. Both radio and TV were touted as means of bringing education, high culture, and refinement to the masses. Cable TV was supposed to bring new forms of entertainment to minority groups and open the way for two-way TV that would aid the democratic process by making possible electronic polling. None of these things has yet come to pass. Nonetheless, the Internet, with its ability to connect everybody to everybody, is currently being touted as an information revolution that will affect society as deeply as the printing press. Whether this will happen is a matter of debate, but for now it might be useful to ask if new communication technologies automatically carry with them social benefits. Have they been liberating or constrictive?

A number of social critics have pointed out that new communication media expand the potential for freedom of expression and have greatly enlarged the scope of human culture. The cost of sending messages over long distances has dramatically decreased. Thanks to the telegraph, telephone, and Internet, people can do business, socialize, and argue with people all over the world. The new media have made information available to all. And, if information is power, the new media will empower more individuals. New means of communication make it easier for democracy to function. Film, radio, and TV have opened up new art forms and patterns of entertainment.

Others suggest a different interpretation. The new communication media have spurred the growth of large conglomerates whose main goal is profit, not cultural enrichment. Further, new communication media create an overload of information, some of it overpowering and pervasive, such as commercials, junk e-mail, and telemarketing. The information made available by the new technologies may be neither interesting nor useful nor profound, and it may interfere with people's attempts to identify the truly significant.

Moreover, although technological advances—such as the telegraph, telephone, and Internet—have expanded the scope of communication, is any of the communication worthwhile? Check out any chat room or Facebook page, and you will probably find that much of the communication consists of greetings, good-byes, flirting, and "how-are-you's." Newsgroups exchange recipes, talk about sports, review cigar brands, and discuss other information that most could live without. How much real dialogue actually occurs? Is it possible to have a meaningful conversation with people whom you can't see and who may not even be who they say they are? The new media have done little to promote political participation. Political apathy continues to increase. Most people would rather stay at home and watch TV than go to a political forum. Further, many critics would argue that the new media have provided little that is new and fresh in the arts and entertainment. Expanded TV channels have brought us more of the same.

In sum, advances in communication media have the potential for both positive and negative consequences.

as well as digital audio, digital video, digital photography, and digital equivalents of newspapers, magazines, and books.

The development of the Internet meant that computers could send digital information to all parts of the globe. All of a sudden, a new distribution medium was available that permanently changed the media environment. In short, digital technology and the Internet triggered a revolution in the way information is stored and transmitted. As a result, the traditional mass communication media found themselves in uncharted waters and had to figure out how to cope with this drastic development. Newspapers, for example, used to exist only on paper (atoms). Now they exist in both paper and digital form (bits). Big recording companies used to distribute music on tape or on disk (atoms). Napster and other music-sharing sites proved that individuals could download music files (bits) from other individuals on the Internet, totally bypassing the recording companies. The chapters in Parts II and III of this book discuss how the media are adapting to the digital age.

The digital revolution, of course, has had profound impact not only on the mass media but also on other institutions. It has, for example, transformed business. Even companies that deal in atoms rather than bits have found that they have to devise whole new marketing and distribution schemes to capitalize on the new digital age. It is not possible (yet) to have a tennis racket physically delivered over the Internet, but you can go online, search the various sporting goods sites for bargains, and order one that appeals to you. The Postal Service or a package delivery company, however, still has to deliver the racket

Almost everybody knows that Alexander Graham Bell was the inventor of the wired telephone, but not too many people know about Martin Cooper, the person generally given credit for inventing the cell phone. Cooper received a degree in electrical engineering, and after a stint in the Navy, he went to work for the Motorola Company in 1954. During his early years at Motorola, Cooper worked on developing portable communication devices. In 1967 he perfected a portable handheld police radio.

Motorola then gave Cooper the task of leading its research into cellular communication technology. At the time, Motorola was in a heated competition with rival Bell Labs to come up with a workable system. While the scientists at Bell worked to develop a bulky car phone, Cooper convinced Motorola to develop a personal phone, one small enough and light enough for people to carry around. After several years of experimentation, Motorola was ready to unveil its invention to the public. In April 1973, on his way to a press conference in New York City, Cooper decided to give the phone one last test. Standing outside a New York hotel, Cooper pulled out his prototype cell phone, which looked like a white brick with a number pad and an antenna. To the amazement of passersby, Cooper dialed a number and began talking out loud into his phone, thus making the first private personal cell phone call. Who was at the other end of Cooper's call? His rival at Bell Labs. Cooper can't remember his first words, but they were probably something like "Guess what? We did it." He does remember that there was a long period of embarrassed silence at the other end.

As of this writing, Cooper, now in his seventies, is still active in cellular technology. He is chairman of a company that is trying to improve wireless access to the Internet.

(atoms) to you. The importance of this new form of buying and selling has added a new noun, *e-commerce,* to our vocabulary.

Of course, for most people reading this book, the digital revolution is no longer a revolution—it's their life. Access to powerful information processing and storage tools is no longer earthshaking; it's taken for granted. Today's college students do most of their research online, store their music and photos digitally, communicate via text messages and Facebook, make their travel arrangements through the Web, and entertain themselves with video games, digital TV, streaming video, iPods, and DVDs.

The aftermath of this revolution, as has been mentioned previously, has been the empowerment of the individual audience member. Fledgling writers no longer need a publisher; they can create a blog, discussed in Chapter 12. New bands can bypass music companies and make their music available online. People with items to sell no longer have to pay a newspaper to run classified ads; they can find buyers for free on the Internet. Traditional news media no longer have monopolies over information. Many pictures of the 2009 U.S. Airways crash landing in the Hudson River and the postelection violence in Iran were taken by witnesses with digital cameras and shared over the Internet. All in all, the digital age has made technology accessible and cheap so that information may be obtained and shared.

The potential social and cultural implications of the digital age are considerable.

First, as mentioned in Chapter 1, digital technology has made it possible for everyone to be a mass communicator. This, in turn, is having a huge impact on how people are getting news, opinion, and entertainment. The trend toward user-generated content is one manifestation of this. In a typical month more than 30 million people visit YouTube to watch videos posted by other people—that's a bigger audience than most hit prime-time TV shows attract. And YouTube is not the only video-sharing site. At last count there were more than 60 similar Web sites. It would appear that we are all trying to entertain each other.

The number is hard to pin down, but there are probably more than 30 million blogs on the Internet. The Pew Internet and American Life Project estimated that a new blog is created every 6 seconds. Bloggers have become citizen journalists, reporting live from the scene of major news events such as the inauguration of President Barack Obama. They have also influenced debates on such topics as Social Security reform and party politics. Many blogs, such as Power Line and The Daily Kos, have become powerful editorial voices.

Second, consider what the digital age might mean for politics. A huge amount of political information—party platforms, candidates' positions, text of speeches—is available in digital form on the Web. A Pew Foundation survey found that the number of Americans

Critical / Cultural Issues

The Meaning of Media

Cell phones, laptops, and PDAs belong to that broad class of devices known as *mobile information devices.* It's possible, however, that lumping these devices under one umbrella label may obscure differences in the way audience members perceive their functions. Communication scholars point out that communication technologies may be socially constructed in different ways by their users.

In an article in the June 2003 issue of *Critical Studies in Mass Communication,* Paul Leonardi argues that culture plays a major role in how media are perceived. Leonardi conducted focus groups (structured group interviews guided by a moderator) among Latinos living in the United States. He asked participants to discuss how cell phones, computers, and the Internet were perceived in Latino culture.

His results were somewhat surprising. Latino culture places a high value on consistent and close interpersonal contact, and the cell phone was seen as consistent with that value. Focus group participants revealed that the cell phone was an important tool for communication and was becoming a necessity for daily life. More than 90 percent of respondents had used a cell phone. Almost all of those who didn't currently own a cell phone planned to buy one within a year. Respondents recognized the utility of the cell phone in an emergency and the fact that cell phones represent an alternative way of reaching someone when the land lines are busy. Cell phones had become so ingrained in their daily lives that some participants mentioned that their children used cell phones to call them from another room in the house to ask what was being prepared for dinner. In short, the cell phone fit nicely with cultural values.

On the other hand, computers and the Internet were not such a good fit. Only 40 percent of the respondents had used a computer, and even fewer (27 percent) had ever used the Internet. Respondents appeared to think of computers and the Internet in the same way, treating them as similar. They did not see the Internet as a communication medium. Instead, the Latinos in these focus groups perceived it as a tool with which to find information. The use of e-mail, chat rooms, and message boards as communication channels was seldom mentioned. Although computers were perceived as useful devices, they were also seen as inhibiting interpersonal communication among family members and friends. Surfing the Internet was perceived as a solitary activity that isolated people from each other. In short, respondents felt that computers and the Internet did not keep people connected. As a result, interpersonal values were jeopardized by these technologies.

Language also played a role in participants' preference for the cell phone over the computer. Spanish-language cell phones are readily available; Spanish-language computer platforms are harder to find. In addition, only a small portion of Internet content is in Spanish. This posed a cultural problem for Latinos. In order to access the Internet, it was necessary to forgo the use of one's native language.

Although many of the respondents said that they planned to purchase a computer in the near future, their stated reasons for buying a computer had nothing to do with the computer's communication potential. Instead, the Latinos in Leonardi's study recognized that those who didn't have a computer would be in an inferior position to those in mainstream U.S. culture.

Leonardi's findings highlight that Latinos living in the United States do not view these information devices as homogeneous. Instead, they have distinct perceptions based on how cell phones, computers, and the Internet relate to their cultural values regarding communication. As Leonardi sums up: "[T]he communication goals of a particular group of users always play a crucial role in their uses and perceptions of technology. If we forget this, we may blindly adopt technologies because we believe they are a sign of progress without making sure they help us progress."

who got campaign information online doubled from the 2000 to the 2004 elections. Ideally, this should result in a better-informed electorate. The confusion and bitterness surrounding the results of the 2000 presidential election in Florida prompted many to call for a system of online voting. Indeed, the Internet raises the possibility of true direct democracy. Our current representative democracy was conceived in part as a solution to the practical problem that all the people could not be physically present in one place to debate and vote. The Internet now makes it possible for computer owners to debate and cast a ballot at home. Do we still need representatives? Should we institute "digital democracy"?

The impact of the digital revolution on the economy cannot be overstated. In the United States around 90 million people buy something online every year. In 2008 it was estimated that e-commerce sales totaled $132 billion, up 88 percent from 2004. About $1 out of every $8 spent in the United States is spent online. Experts estimate that the Internet has created more than 6 million jobs.

Americans are already living in digital homes. They talk on digital telephones, play digital video games, watch digital TV, save programs on digital video recorders such as TiVo, rent DVDs, listen to digital music, take pictures with digital still and video cameras, and interconnect home computers via digital networks. The digital world touches everyone's life every day.

Finally, the arts have entered the digital age. There's a Digital Art Museum online that exhibits the work of leading artists. There are many other Web sites that feature digital artwork. Musicians, sculptors, and graphic artists have also embraced digital technology.

On the downside, now that the digital age has torn down the barriers to accessing and producing information, there is a whole lot of it. Enter "digital revolution" into a Google search, and you'll get about 15 million hits. The information is organized into not what you think is relevant but what the search engine thinks is relevant. Consequently, the results of the search seem chaotic, and you may have to scroll through several pages before you find something that is even remotely connected to what you are looking for. The digital revolution has resulted in an information glut. As scholar Neil Postman describes it in an article in the *Harvard International Journal of Press/Politics,* "Like the sorcerer's apprentice, we are awash in information without even a broom to help us get rid of it. Information comes indiscriminately, directed at no one in particular, in enormous volume, at high speeds, severed from import and meaning."

Finally, there is the problem known as the "digital divide." In the United States, although the gap shows signs of narrowing, families making more than $50,000 per year are more than twice as likely to have Internet access compared to those earning $30,000 or less. And whereas about 73 percent of the population of North America is connected to the Internet, in Africa it is about 6 percent. In the future those who have access to information will also have more access to power than those who do not. Will this digital divide translate into more serious social, economic, and political divisions?

Mobile Media

Sometimes it's hard to see a milestone when you're in the middle of it, but the signs are getting hard to miss. Walk around campus or on a busy main street, and see how many people are talking on cell phones. Check out any airport waiting lounge, and see how many people are laboring over laptop computers. What you see are indications that the next wave of communication technology is breaking over us.

The number of cell phone users in the United States topped 250 million in 2009. More than 60 million carry around laptops, and another 15 million use PDAs. All of these devices share common characteristics:

- They depend on wireless technology.
- They are portable, making it possible for people to access information from anywhere. The new portable media are the best illustration of one of the major themes of this book: increased media mobility.
- They are interconnected, making it possible for people to hook into the Internet or the worldwide phone network.
- They are blurring the distinction between mass and interpersonal communication.

Before the cell phone, two screens dominated American lives: the TV screen and the computer screen. Cell phones have become the third screen—a screen that has the potential to drastically transform traditional media and American culture. Let's first take a look at how mobile media are serving some of the traditional media functions discussed in Chapter 2.

We'll start with surveillance. Radio and TV stations have been providing traffic reports for decades, but now subscribers to a company called Traffic411 can hear the latest information tailor-made for their particular commute over their cell phone. Sports fans can receive scores, standings, and the latest news about games in progress over their phones if they subscribe to ESPN wireless. Several services offer the latest stock prices to their phone customers. Need to check ski conditions before heading out to the slopes? Motorola offers an Internet-ready cell phone that allows you to stay informed.

The newest generation of cell phones lets users take still pictures or video clips and post them on the Web in seconds. Imagine millions of Americans walking around with video-equipped cell phones. When breaking news occurs, people in the area can take video and still photos before the media even arrives on the scene. The most striking images of the 2004 Asian tsunami were taken by tourists, and many photos were placed directly on the Web. The news was transmitted without a traditional reporter or news organization. A cell phone video of Saddam Hussein's execution made its way onto the Web. In the future we will all be reporters.

Entertainment is firmly entrenched on the small screen. Almost all cell phones come with preloaded video games. New-generation phones are equipped with MP3 players so that subscribers can download and listen to music over their phones. Some companies are providing entertainment content specifically for the small screen. As part of the "Everything. Everywhere" trend discussed in Chapter 1, entertainment companies are supplying their content to mobile phones and laptops. Time Warner, for example, offers Mobile Access, a program that lets Time Warner Cable subscribers watch live TV on their phones. AT&T mobile subscribers can download segments of *Saturday Night Live.* Fox produced a spin-off program from its popular *24* expressly designed for cell phones. And there are several Web sites, including iTunes, where audience members can download full versions of movies to their iPods.

Turning now to linkage, it's obvious that being connected to millions of other people all over the world makes everyday life easier. What was once considered wasted time can now be used productively. Laptops enable people to read documents, send e-mail, prepare reports, and analyze data while waiting for a plane or even sitting on the plane itself. Businesspeople trapped in a traffic jam can make calls and stay in touch with the office through their cell phones and PDAs. A special use of the linkage function is achieving safety and security. A *Consumer Reports* survey found that security was the number-one reason people buy cell phones. Cell phone users can report accidents and other emergencies in seconds, no matter where they occur. More than 30 percent of all 911 calls come from a cell phone.

If you're late, you can call or send a text message alerting those at your destination. If you're lost, you can call for directions. If you're buying groceries for dinner, you can check to see if people want fish or chicken. There are many other examples, but the words of one 17-year-old pretty well sum it up: "With my cell phone I can order pizza from anywhere." This use vividly illustrates how wireless portable media are serving the linkage function of communication; thanks to the Internet and the cell phone network, everybody can be linked to everybody.

The new mobile media have already transformed American culture. Society has had to develop a new set of rules regarding cell phone etiquette. The LetsTalk.com Web site summarizes the most obvious ones: Turn off the phone in the movie theater, don't shout, pay attention when walking, and so on.

The cell phone is now the primary mode of socializing for teenagers. More than half of teens in the United States have their own phone.

The cell phone has taken on symbolic properties. Users customize their phone's appearance and ring tones to reflect their own individuality and/or status. Having the latest, thinnest model with all the bells and whistles has become "cool."

Family life has been forever altered because of cell phones. About 75 percent of all teenagers now have access to a cell phone, and more than 50 percent own one. The increasing number of teens with cell phones is due in part to parents who want their children to be prepared in the case of an emergency or who want to check up on them when they are out of the house. In a family in which parents are on the go because both hold jobs and children have to get to soccer or gymnastics or band practice, the cell phone provides a way for parents to monitor offspring by phone rather than in person. This new phenomenon is called **mobile parenting.**

Cell phones have even changed our culture's conception of time, a phenomenon called **time softening.** You've probably experienced this scenario several times. You're supposed to meet a friend at a restaurant at eight. A few minutes after eight, your friend calls you on your cell phone and says he's in his car only a couple of miles away and should be there in 10 minutes. If you're in contact, can you really be late?

Time softening also occurs when two people don't set a firm time for a meeting. Rather than saying, "I'll meet you at seven," PDA and cell phone users often say, "I'll call you when I'm leaving the office, and we'll set something up." The time-softening effect is an example of how wireless media, like traditional media, can have a socialization function. In this case they have changed the value that society has traditionally placed on punctuality.

Of course, like most revolutions mobile media have a downside. Most importantly. driving and talking on a cell phone don't mix. A study done at Harvard in 2002 suggested that cell phone use while driving might be linked to as many as 2,600 traffic deaths a year. Another study concluded that drivers on cell phones contribute to as many as 1.5 million accidents a year. It's no surprise, then, to find that as of 2008, legislatures in 35 states were considering laws to limit cell phone usage while driving.

The linkages provided by cell phones can be used for evil purposes. The attacks in Mumbai, India, were reportedly coordinated by individuals in Pakistan who guided the gunmen by cell phone and even in some cases decided the fate of hostages.

Camera-equipped cell phones have also raised privacy issues. Celebrities have to put up with star-obsessed fans (dubbed the "snaparazzi") taking their photos while they are eating, shopping, or walking down the street and posting them on the Web. In New York City several restaurants, clubs, and gyms frequented by celebrities have banned cell phones.

For every person who appreciates the convenience of a cell phone, there's another person who wishes that they would just shut up. Most professors are not amused by cell phones ringing during lectures. People eating at restaurants find their dining experience marred by people at other tables chatting loudly into their phones. Commuters relaxing or reading on trains and buses are disturbed by the loud conversations of cell phone users.

A conversation with someone who owns a PDA is always subject to frequent interruptions as e-mail appears. Some people have become fed up. "Cell phone rage" has been blamed for several altercations.

Finally, wireless mobile media can be expensive. The Motorola Z9 camera phone retails for $300. A new Blackberry PDA goes for around $400. If it turns out that only the rich can afford these devices, then the digital divide between rich and poor will only increase.

Social Media

We are in the midst of the last communication milestone that we will examine—social media. We discussed social media in general terms in Chapter 1. In this section we will trace their history and cultural impact.

The first tool for social media was the telephone. It connected friends and family and kept people in touch. When Bell Labs invented speed dialing, the telephone became an instrument of community building. The speed dial numbers programmed into a phone became a de facto community of people (and emergency services) that you felt were important to you. Speed dialing even introduced the notion of a preferred place within the community; if you were number one on a person's speed dial, you were probably number one in that person's life. (There is a classic Seinfeld episode about competing for the top spot on a person's speed dial.)

The birth of the Internet opened up new channels for social media. As we shall learn in Chapter 12, when the Internet first developed it was designed as a tool for the sharing of scientific data. Instead, scientists sent e-mails to their friends and colleagues. Linking several computers together made possible instant messaging, and in 1988 Internet Relay Chat allowed users to send real-time messages to others on the same channel.

The primary impetus behind the growth of social media was the development of the World Wide Web. The origins of social media on the Web can be found in the mid-1990s when personal Web pages became popular. A means of self-expression, these were pages where people could post photos, brief autobiographies, poems and essays, and links to other sites that they enjoyed. Visitors could sign a guest book, leave a brief message, and send e-mail to the site's owner, but personal pages did not lend themselves to building a social network.

The Web site that is generally acknowledged as the first social network site was SixDegrees.com. The site advertised itself as a tool to help people connect. It attracted

The Facebook Web site: "Giving people the power to share and make the world more open and connected." Facebook has more than 300 million active users.

a large audience but couldn't sustain itself and went under in 2000. Ryze.com debuted in 2001 as a site aimed at linking together business professionals and entrepreneurs but never achieved mass popularity. Friendster launched in 2002 and was originally designed to compete with online dating sites. The theory behind Friendster was that people would feel more comfortable dating friends of friends than they would strangers that they met online. It was immediately successful and soon had more than 3 million users. The quick growth led to technical problems, and its servers could not keep up with the demand. In addition, people began creating fake profiles and posting fake photographs. These problems led many to abandon the site.

Many social media sites launched in 2003. The most successful was MySpace, originally designed to appeal to those who had dropped Friendster. MySpace let users personalize their spaces and was a favorite of independent bands who used the service to promote their music. Teenage fans of these musical groups were then attracted to the site and encouraged their friends to join. By 2005 MySpace had millions of members and was purchased by the News Corporation for $580 million.

Facebook started in 2004 and was originally designed to serve only those at Harvard University. The service quickly expanded to other colleges (members had to have an .edu e-mail address to belong), and the service was seen as a private community. This did not last long as Facebook expanded to include high school students and corporate members and eventually was open to everybody. YouTube began operation in 2005, quickly became a popular site for user-generated content, and was acquired by Google for $1.65 billion. Twitter came on the scene a year later. The success of these sites is well-known, as evidenced by the hundreds of millions of people who visit them.

Social media are relatively new and their cultural impact is still evolving. Some preliminary observations, however, are possible. First, social media have changed the idea of community. In the past, people developed friendships based on local geography. Social media make possible virtual communities based on shared needs and interests rather than locale. Aspiring teen goths may identify more with the VampireFreaks.com community than with their high school friends. Global social neighborhoods are becoming just as familiar as the physical neighborhood we live in.

Second, social media are creating a surveillance culture. Digital cameras make everybody a reporter. Social media make it ridiculously easy to make what was once private information public and widely available. Events that might have gone unnoticed in the past are now easily made into causes célèbres. When Christian Bale launched into a rant against a crew member on a movie set, he probably never expected to see it on YouTube. When Miley Cyrus was photographed in a pose that was offensive to Asian people, it might have been quickly forgotten had it not been leaked to Internet sites where it was quickly shared. Facebook photos have come back to haunt many unsuspecting partygoers. It's possible that many activities that people think are private are actually being shared with thousands of people.

Next, social media have made history more permanent. Digital media are easily archived and easily accessible. Your tweets, blog entries, Facebook postings, and photos are all probably saved somewhere on some hard drive. Today's teenagers who apply for jobs in the next few years may find that much to their chagrin those embarrassing old party photos posted on MySpace have resurfaced. Candidates running for president in 2036 might have to explain why they made those controversial blog postings back in 2010.

Finally, it is usually a sign that some development has gained traction in society when it is adopted by commercial interests. Social media have become an indispensible marketing tool. It seems every product or service has some kind of social media tie-in. (In 2008 one Web site listed examples of more than 320 brands that were using social media. The number has undoubtedly grown since then.) Carnival Cruise Lines' Web site permits cruisers to form communities, share cruise photos, and give reviews and advice about cruises. Dunkin' Donuts has a Twitter account. (Sample tweet: @ ashkendo We call it "delicious" . . . full name, "Boston Kreme.") Southwest Airlines (and many

Lots of celebrities and politicians have joined social networks and created their own accounts. The problem for fans is that it's hard to tell who's for real.

Some celebrity accounts have been faked. Kanye West, Paris Hilton, and Lindsay Lohan have been victims of fake Twitter accounts. Politicians are not immune. Bogus accounts on Twitter were set up for George Bush, Dick Cheney, and the Dalai Lama.

Then there are the accounts that are managed by ghosts. When best-selling author John Grisham was being interviewed on the *Today* show, he was asked about his Facebook page. The question surprised Grisham because, as far as he knew, he didn't have a Facebook page. Turns out that Grisham was mistaken; he does have a Facebook page but he has nothing to do with it. In truth, his page was created by his publisher in an attempt to use social media to promote his books.

Grisham is not the only celebrity who has a Facebook or Twitter account that is actually managed by other people. In fact, it seems to be a status symbol to have somebody else handle your social media for you. Daytime TV stars Ellen DeGeneres and Kathie Lee Gifford have often given camera time to the people (usually interns) who handle their social media. Britney Spears recently advertised for a Harvard student who could manage her YouTube, Twitter, Facebook, and MySpace accounts. Said one of her assistants, "I think the majority of high profile celebrities aren't spending their time everyday updating their profile pages or responding to fans."

A lot of the fake celebrity accounts are simply ploys to get people to visit celebrity news sites. Many of the ghosted celebrity accounts are used for marketing and promotion. Sample tweet from *The Ellen DeGeneres Show:* "Don't forget to watch Better Off Ted tonight! They'll need the help; they're up against Idol."

There are some exceptions. Ashton Kutcher and Demi Moore tweet for themselves. Shaquille O'Neal tweets for himself and has more than 300,000 followers. Nonetheless, it appears that marketing is trying to take advantage of some of the popularity of social media.

other companies) has its own YouTube channel. Some experts suggest that commercialism might cause a backlash against social networks (see the boxed insert "Is That Really You?"). Keep an eye on social media over the next few years and see what other consequences might develop.

Concluding Observations: The Impact of New Media

In 1839 the director of the Paris Observatory, François Arago, was speaking to the French Parliament about a new technology that was then sweeping Europe: the daguerreotype, the ancestor of the modern photograph (see page 59). Many critics were hostile to the new technique because they feared it would have a harmful effect on French society by destroying the livelihood of thousands of French portrait painters and perhaps even put an end to the art of painting itself.

In defending the daguerreotype, Arago maintained that these fears were shortsighted. He voiced what we can call Arago's rule of technology: The greatest potential impact of a new invention is not how it changes or replaces old things but how it generates things that are entirely new. Arago's rule certainly held true for photography. It may have put a few portrait painters out of work, but more importantly, it led to the development of mechanically reproduced images, photojournalism, and the motion picture—developments that helped usher in the age of mass communication, something that the members of the 1839 French Parliament could not even have imagined.

One lesson we can learn from these milestones in the development of human communication is that, as Arago realized, it is impossible to predict the ultimate use of a new medium. When the telegraph was invented, many people thought it would have a profound effect on the world order. Since nations were linked by the telegraph and could send instant messages to one another, it was predicted that misunderstandings would cease, prejudices would vanish, and peace would reign. Things did not quite go in that direction. Alexander Graham Bell suggested that the telephone be used as a means of communication among the various rooms of a house or that phones be sold only in

Critical / Cultural Issues

Cell Phones, Religion, and Culture

Professor Heidi Campbell has studied the cultural implications of the widespread adoption of the cell phone.[1] She points out that the cell phone is more than a phone. It is a means of individual expression (personal ring tones, wallpaper, phone covers) as well as a tool for business, creating a social network of employees and clients. In fact, the cell phone has the potential for generating unexpected cultural impact.

The impact of the cell phone has spread to religion. Campbell argues that religious groups are using the cell phone to incorporate religious practices into society's new on-the-go lifestyle. For example, religious groups in many countries offer daily Bible text messages. Pope Benedict XVI sent out an inspirational text message to subscribers just a few days after his elevation. Catholics in the Philippines can receive the "Mobile Way of the Cross" and the "Mobile Rosary" on their cell phones. Muslims can buy a special phone that reminds them of prayer times and a digital compass that indicates the direction of Mecca. A British youth group uses cell phones to create a national prayer chain. All members receive a text message at specific times encouraging them to pray.

Of course, new technologies and religious culture do not always mesh smoothly. Muslims have criticized those who send text messages during Ramadan rather than making traditional personal visits. Hindus objected to an image of a Hindu god talking on a cell phone.

As Campbell points out, religious groups are receptive to those aspects of new technology that support their traditions but tend to resist those advances that cause friction with the traditional culture and beliefs. This process is a dynamic one, and often a new technology is shaped by a culture in order to fit in. Campbell presents a prime example of this process by analyzing the reactions of one ultra-orthodox religious group to the cell phone.

The average Israeli spends about 450 minutes per month talking on a cell phone, one of the highest rates in the world. Not all segments of Israeli society, however, have taken to the device. Ultra-orthodox Jews belong to a community that rejects modernity and its secular values. The cell phone is seen as a device that could be harmful to this community because it could easily deliver materialistic content to its users. At the same time, however, ultra-orthodox Jews note that the cell phone could possess certain benefits for the community.

What grew out of this tension is the "kosher phone," a specially designed handset that preserves the phone's calling function but disabled text messaging, Internet access, video, and voice mail applications. The kosher phone emerged after long negotiations between cell phone manufacturers and a council of rabbis. The council also drafted guidelines about how the technology would be used.

As Campbell concludes, if a technology with questionable features is deemed valuable to a community, a "culturing process" takes place. This culturing process may involve changes in both the culture of a community and the technology itself. In short, culture can influence both the form and function of any new technology.

[1]See Heidi Campbell, "Texting the Faith: Religious Users and Cell Phone Culture," in A. Kavoori and N. Arceneaux (eds.), *The Cell Phone Reader* (New York: Peter Lang, 2006).

---

pairs, linking just two specific points, such as a person's office and home. The phonograph was first used to record business dictation. When radio first started, most thought it would be used as a substitute for telegraph or telephone communication. All of these inventions became mass communication media that their creators never envisioned. We may be at the same point with the digital and wireless mobile milestones. We can see some of their possibilities, but their ultimate evolution is impossible for us to predict. Arago's rule may be validated all over again.

It appears that the emergence of a new communications technology changes *but does not make extinct* those advances that came before it. The telegraph and the telephone did not kill the printed word; nor did film, radio, TV, and the Internet. Television did not make radio extinct, but it did cause a major change in the way the medium was used. Likewise, the computer, the Internet, and mobile media will probably not cause any of the traditional media to evaporate, but they will probably change the way we use these "old" media.

Figure 3-1 (see page 52) is a time line that displays when each of the milestones occurred. A quick examination of the figure makes clear that the pace of communication innovations has accelerated. It took humans dozens of centuries to get from language to writing. The jump from writing to printing took about 5,000 years. The telegraph and telephone cropped up only 300 years later, followed quickly by photography and motion pictures. Radio was invented only a few years after that, as was TV. The computer followed on the heels of television. In fact, a person born in 1910 and who lived a hundred years (an accomplishment becoming increasingly more common) would have lived through several milestones: radio/TV, computers, mobile wireless media, and social media. Each advance in communication increases our power to convey and record information, and each has played a role in prompting significant changes in our culture and society. It is becoming difficult to digest fully the impact of one communication medium before another comes on the scene.

MAIN POINTS

- Printing made information available to a larger audience. It helped the development of vernacular languages, aided the Protestant Reformation, and contributed to the spread and accumulation of knowledge.

- The telegraph and telephone were the first media to use electricity to communicate. They marked the first time the message could be separated from the messenger. The telegraph helped the railroads move west and permitted the newspapers to publish more timely news. The telephone linked people together in the first instance of a communication network.

- Photography provided a way to preserve history, had an impact on art, and brought better visuals to newspapers and magazines. Motion pictures helped socialize a generation of immigrants and became an important part of American culture.

- Radio and TV broadcasting brought news and entertainment into the home, transformed leisure time, and pioneered a new, immediate kind of reporting. Television has an impact on free time, politics, socialization, culture, and many other areas as well.

- The digital revolution changed the way information was stored and transmitted and made e-commerce possible.

- Mobile media have changed American culture and taken over some of the functions of mass media.

- The next communication milestone is the expanding use of social media.

- In general, it is difficult to predict the ultimate shape of a new medium. New media change but do not replace older media. The pace of media inventions has accelerated in recent years.

QUESTIONS FOR REVIEW

1. Why was the telegraph labeled "the great annihilator of time and space"?

2. What exactly is the "communal reservoir of images" created by photojournalism? Can you think of other examples of images that are forever fixed by photographs?

3. What digits are used in digital technology? Why could the telegraph be considered the first digital device?

4. How have mobile media changed how we think about time?

QUESTIONS FOR CRITICAL THINKING

1. Suppose Henry David Thoreau (see page 55) were alive today. What do you think he would say about the Internet?

2. Many people would argue that, of all the communication media discussed in this chapter, television has had the greatest impact on society. Do you agree?

3. When the Internet was first developing, the term *information superhighway* appeared frequently in news stories about it. Now that the Internet has been around for a while, news stories rarely contain that term. Why is this so?

4. Do you own a cell phone? If so, how has it changed your life?

5. Consider the boxed insert "Cell Phones, Religion, and Culture." Can you think of other technological devices that have been subjected to a "culturing" process? How does the "kosher phone" relate to the concept of a community? Who should decide what features of a new technology are introduced to a particular culture?

KEY TERMS

technological determinism (p. 54)   digital technology (p. 65)   time softening (p. 71)
photojournalism (p. 59)   mobile parenting (p. 71)

INTERNET RESOURCES

Online Learning Center

On the Online Learning Center home page, www.mhhe.com/dominick11e, *select* Student Center *and then* Chapter 3.

1. Use the Learning Objectives, Chapter Outline, and Main Points sections to review this chapter.

2. Test your knowledge of the chapter using the multiple choice and flashcard features of the site.

3. Expand your knowledge of concepts and topics discussed in the chapter with additional Questions for Critical Thinking and Internet Exercises.

Surfing the Internet

Here are some sites that provide information on media history. Some of the sites mentioned in Chapters 4–11 are also of relevance here.

www.iath.virginia.edu/abell/homepage.html
Home page of Alexander Graham Bell. Reconstructs Bell's path to the invention of the telephone.

http://mediahistory.umn.edu
The best all-around site for media history. Contains an extensive time line, other links, book reviews, articles, archives, chat boards, and pages on the history of specific media.

www.archive.org
Home of the Wayback Machine. Surf the Web the way it used to be.

www.cln.org/themes/history_film.html
Provides links to many sites that contain information about film history.

www.gutenbergdigital.de
Gutenberg's Bible on the Web.

http://inventors.about.com/library/inventors/bltelegraph.htm
Page devoted to Samuel Morse and telegraphy. Contains diagrams of early telegraphs and relevant links.

PART II

Media

CHAPTER 4

Newspapers

This chapter will prepare you to:

- describe the challenges newspapers face in today's digital age

- recognize the conditions that had to exist before a mass press could come into existence

- understand the significance of the penny press

- explain the features that define both online and print versions of newspapers

- recognize the convergence of online and print newspapers

- understand the function of the Audit Bureau of Circulations (ABC)

- identify the various methods newspapers are using to stay in business

Scenes such as this are becoming all too common in the newspaper industry as many papers have cut employees or closed their print versions.

4

The state of the current newspaper industry may be best illustrated by what is happening with the American Society of Newspaper Editors (ASNE). Founded in 1922, the organization holds an annual convention that usually attracts hundreds of attendees. In 2009, for only the second time in its history, the ASNE canceled its convention because of the ongoing crisis in the newspaper industry. One of the items to be voted on at the convention was a proposal to drop the word "newspaper" from the organization's title.

The ASNE's problems mirror those of the entire newspaper industry. It seemed that every week during 2008–2009 brought more bad news: declining readership, declining advertising revenue, newspapers closing, layoffs, and bankruptcies. These problems weren't new; they've been around since the 1990s, but the economic downturn during the last part of the decade and the growing audience shift to the Internet as a news source changed things faster than anybody expected.

The state of the newspaper industry in 2010 resembles the state of the recording industry in 2000 when the business shifted from selling tangible items (CDs) to selling intangible items (digital downloads). The newspaper industry is now making the same transition. Its future may no longer lie with tangible items (papers) but with intangibles (Web sites). This chapter looks at the history, structure, economics, and future of the industry as it struggles to survive in the digital age.

A Brief History

▲ Journalism in Early America

Before we get to the details, it might be helpful to identify some general features of newspapers in early America:

- There were few papers.
- Printers and postmasters did most of the early publishing.
- News was not as timely as it is today.
- The idea of a free press was not endorsed by colonial governments.

In 1690 Boston printer Benjamin Harris published the first American newspaper, *Publick Occurrences both Foreign and Domestick*. One of the items in the paper alleged an affair between the king of France and his son's wife. This news story infuriated the Puritan officials of the colony, and they shut down the paper after one issue. The notion of a free press had yet to surface in America; most colonists believed that a paper had to have royal consent to be published.

Fourteen years later, John Campbell, the local Boston postmaster, put out the *Boston News Letter*. Published with royal permission, the paper was dull and lackluster, with many news stories simply reprinted from European papers. Campbell's paper had only about 300 subscribers and never made a profit.

A few years later, another Boston paper, the *New England Courant*, came on the scene. It was published by James Franklin, Ben's older brother, without government permission. Eventually, the elder Franklin's paper got him into trouble with the local authorities, and he was thrown into prison. Ben took over, and the paper prospered under his leadership. Ben eventually moved on to Philadelphia, where he started the *Pennsylvania Gazette,* which boasted such innovations as more legible type, headlines, and a cleaner layout.

Ben Franklin retired from a successful publishing career at the age of 42. During his career: he had started several papers, published one of America's first magazines, run the first editorial cartoon, proved that advertising copy could sell merchandise, and, perhaps most importantly, demonstrated that journalism could be an honorable profession.

▲ The Beginnings of Revolution

Newspapers grew in numbers during the Revolutionary War, and most were partisan, siding with the colonies or with the Crown. This period marked the beginnings of the **political press,** which openly supported a particular party, faction, or cause.

In 1776, when the Continental Congress adopted the Declaration of Independence, the text of the document was published in the *Pennsylvania Evening Post* on July 6. The next year the Continental Congress authorized Mary Katherine Goddard, publisher of the *Maryland Journal,* to print the first official copies of the Declaration with the names of the signers attached. Under Goddard's direction the *Journal* became one of the leading colonial papers during the war. Goddard was one of about 30 women who printed or published colonial newspapers.

Benjamin Franklin became the publisher of the *Pennsylvania Gazette* in 1729, when he was 24 years old. The paper became the most successful colonial newspaper, and Franklin the best-known colonial journalist and publisher.

Two early examples of the black press: *Freedom's Journal* was started in 1827 by John Russwurm, the first black person to graduate from a college in the United States, and by Samuel Cornish. Cornish later edited the *Colored American,* a paper that had subscribers from Maine to Michigan.

▲ The Political Press: 1790–1833

The politicization of newspapers did not end with America's victory in the Revolutionary War. Instead, partisan leanings of the press were transferred into another arena—the debate over the powers of the federal government.

At the vortex of this debate between Federalists and anti-Federalists was the Constitution of the United States. Although the original document made no mention of the right of a free press, the Bill of Rights did contain such a provision. The **First Amendment** held that "Congress shall make no law . . . abridging the freedom of speech, or of the press." Thus, the idea of a free press, which had emerged during the Revolutionary period, became part of the law of the new nation when Congress ratified this amendment in 1791.

Newspapers grew with the country in the first 20 years of the 19th century. The daily newspaper began in 1783 and developed slowly. By 1800, however, most large cities had at least one daily paper, and by 1820 there were 24 dailies, 66 semi- or triweeklies, and 422 weeklies. These newspapers were read primarily by the upper socioeconomic classes; early readers had to be literate and possess money to spend on subscriptions (about $10 per year or 6 cents per issue—a large sum when you consider that during those years 5 cents could buy a pint of whiskey). The content was typified by commercial and business news, political and congressional debates, speeches, acts of state legislatures, and official messages.

During this period several newspapers were formed in response to the needs and interests of minority groups. *Freedom's Journal,* the first of over 40 black newspapers published before 1860, was founded in the late 1820s by the Reverend Samuel Cornish and John Russwurm. Written and edited by blacks, the paper championed the cause of black people by dealing with the serious problems arising from slavery and by carrying news of foreign countries such as Haiti and Sierra Leone that appealed to its black audience.

At about the same time, in 1828, another minority group, the Cherokee Nation, published the *Cherokee Phoenix,* written in both Cherokee and English. When the Cherokees were evicted from their home in Georgia and forcibly resettled in Oklahoma, a new paper, the *Cherokee Advocate,* was started and continued to operate until 1906. The *Advocate* was revived in the 1970s and now publishes a monthly edition.

▲ Birth of the Mass Newspaper

Several conditions had to exist before a mass press could come into existence:

- A printing press had to be invented that would produce copies quickly and cheaply.
- Enough people had to know how to read to support such a press.
- A mass audience had to be present.

In 1830 the U.S. manufacturing firm R. Hoe and Company built a steam-powered press that could produce 4,000 copies per hour. This and subsequent steam-powered presses that were even faster made it possible to print an extremely cheap newspaper that everybody could afford.

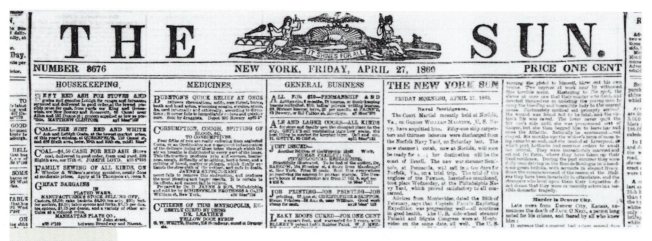

The second element that led to the growth of the mass newspaper was the increased level of literacy in the population. The first statewide public school system was established during the 1830s. The increased emphasis on education led to a concomitant growth of literacy as many people in the middle and lower socioeconomic groups acquired reading skills.

The final element was subtler and harder to explain. The mass press appeared during an era that historians call the age of Jacksonian democracy, an age in which ordinary people were first recognized as a political and economic force. Property requirements for voting had died out. Every state but one chose presidential electors by popular vote. In addition, this period was marked by the rise of an urban middle class. The trend toward democratization of business and politics fostered the creation of a mass audience responsive to a mass press.

▲ The Penny Press

Development of the Penny Press   Benjamin Day was only 22 years old when he launched the mass-appeal *New York Sun* in 1833. Day's idea was to sell his daily paper for a penny (a significant price reduction from the 6 cents a copy for other big-city dailies). Moreover, the *Sun* contained local news, particularly those items that featured sex, violence, and human-interest stories. Conspicuously absent were stodgy political debates. Day's gamble paid off as the *Sun* attracted readers, and the **penny press** was launched.

Others imitated the *Sun*'s success. The colorful James Gordon Bennett launched the *New York Herald* in 1835, which was an even more rapid success than the *Sun*. The *Herald* introduced a financial page, a sports page, and an aggressive editorial policy that emphasized reform.

Another important pioneer was Horace Greeley. His *New York Tribune* appeared in 1841 and soon ranked third behind the *Herald* and *Sun* in circulation. Greeley used his editorial pages for crusades and causes. He opposed capital punishment and gambling and favored trade unions and westward expansion.

Greeley also supported women's rights. In 1845 he hired Margaret Fuller as literary critic for the *Tribune*. In addition to providing commentary on the fine arts, Fuller wrote articles about the hard lot of prostitutes, women prisoners, and the insane. Greeley's decision to hire Fuller is typical of his publishing philosophy: Like Fuller he never talked down to the mass audience but rather attracted readers by appealing to their intellect more than to their emotions.

The last of the major newspapers of the penny-press era that we will consider began in 1851 and, at this writing, is still publishing. The *New York Times,* edited by Henry Raymond, promised to be less sensational than the *Sun* or the *Herald* and less impassioned than Greeley's *Tribune*. The paper soon established a reputation for objective and reasoned journalism.

All these publishers had one thing in common: As soon as their penny papers were successful, they doubled the price.

Significance of the Penny Press   At this point, we should consider the major changes in journalism that were prompted by the success of the mass press during the period from 1833 to 1860. We can identify several key changes:

- The basis of economic support for newspapers
- The pattern of newspaper distribution
- The definition of what constituted news
- The techniques of news collection

Prior to the penny press, most of a newspaper's economic support came from subscription revenue. The large circulation of the penny papers made advertisers realize that they could reach a large segment of potential buyers by purchasing space. Moreover, the readership of the popular papers cut across political party and social class lines, thereby assuring advertisers a broad-based audience. As a result, advertisers were greatly attracted to this new medium, and the mass newspapers relied significantly more on advertising revenues than did their predecessors.

Older papers were distributed primarily through the mail; the penny press, although relying somewhat on subscriptions, also made use of street sales. Vendors would buy a hundred copies for 67 cents and sell them for 1 cent each. Soon it became common to hear newsboys hawking papers on street corners in the larger cities. Since these papers had to compete with one another in the open marketplace of the street, editors went out of their way to find original and exclusive news that would give their paper an edge.

The penny press also redefined the concept of news, hiring people to go out and look for news. Reporters were assigned to special beats: police, financial, sports, and religion, to name a few. Foreign correspondents were also popular. And newspapers changed their emphasis from the affairs of the commercial elite to the social life of the rising middle classes.

This shift meant that news became more of a commodity, something that had value. And, like many commodities, fresh news was more valuable than stale news. Any scheme that would get the news into the paper faster was tried. Stories were sent by carrier pigeon, Pony Express, railroads, and steamships. The Mexican War of 1846 made rapid news transmission especially desirable, and many newspapers first used the telegraph to carry news about this conflict. All in all, the penny papers increased the importance of speed in news collection.

▲ Newspapers as Big Business

A new reporting technique emerged during the Civil War as telegraphic dispatches from the war zones were transformed into headlines. Because telegraph lines sometimes failed, the opening paragraphs of the story contained the most important facts. If the line failed during transmission of a story, at least the most important part would get through. Thus, the "inverted pyramid" style of reporting was developed.

After the war, from about 1870 to 1900, the total U.S. population doubled, and the urban population tripled. Newspapers grew even faster than the population; the number of dailies quadrupled, and circulation showed a fivefold increase. The thriving newspaper business also attracted several powerful and outspoken individuals who had a profound influence on American journalism. We will consider three: Pulitzer, Scripps, and Hearst.

Joseph Pulitzer came to the United States from Hungary and turned the *St. Louis Post-Dispatch* into a success. In 1883, he bought the *New York World*. In a little more than three years, Pulitzer increased the paper's circulation from 15,000 to 250,000.

What was Pulitzer's formula for success? Pulitzer stressed accuracy. He also introduced practices that appealed to advertisers: more advertising space and ads priced on the basis of circulation. Moreover, he aimed his paper at the large population of immigrants then living in New York by stressing simple writing and many illustrations. Pulitzer also reintroduced the sensationalized news format of the penny press, as the *World*'s pages carried

William Randolph Hearst, the successful publisher of the *San Francisco Examiner* and later the *New York Journal,* employed sensationalism (yellow journalism) to win the circulation wars of the late 1800s. He created a major publishing empire consisting of a chain of newspapers, a wire service, and four syndicates.

stories about crime, violence, and tragedy. Finally, Pulitzer endorsed the notion that a paper should promote the welfare of its readers, particularly the underprivileged.

Attempts to reach a working-class audience were not confined to the East. In the Midwest, E. W. Scripps started papers in Cleveland and Cincinnati, both growing industrial cities with large populations of factory workers. The Scripps papers featured concisely edited news, human-interest stories, editorial independence, and frequent crusades for the working class. Scripps pioneered the idea of a newspaper chain. By 1911 he owned 18 papers.

Perhaps the best-known of these three newspaper giants, thanks to the film *Citizen Kane,* is William Randolph Hearst. While Pulitzer was succeeding in New York and Scripps was acquiring papers in the Midwest, the 24-year-old Hearst was given control of the *San Francisco Examiner,* thanks to the generosity of his wealthy father. Hearst went after readers by appealing to their emotions. Fires, murders, and stories about love and hate were given splashy coverage. Hearst banked heavily on sensationalism to raise his readership level. His strategy worked: The *Examiner* shot to the number-one position.

▲ Yellow Journalism

Hearst, like Pulitzer before him, then invaded the big league—New York City. In 1895 he bought the *New York Journal.* Soon, Pulitzer and Hearst were engaged in a fierce circulation battle as each paper attempted to outsensationalize the other. As one press critic put it, the duel between these two spread "death, dishonor and disaster" all over page one. Sex, murder, self-promotion, and human-interest stories filled the two papers. This type of reporting became known as **yellow journalism,** and whatever its faults, it sold newspapers.

The battle between Pulitzer and Hearst reached its climax with the Spanish-American War in 1898. When the battleship *Maine* was blown up in Havana harbor, the *Journal* offered a $50,000 reward for the arrest of the guilty parties. Circulation promptly jumped over the 1 million mark. War was finally declared in April, and the *World* and the *Journal* pulled out all the stops. Hearst chartered a steamer and equipped it with printing presses. He also brought down his yacht and sailed with the U.S. fleet in the Battle of Santiago. The *Journal* put out 40 extras in a single day.

Although the period of yellow journalism was not the proudest moment in the history of the American newspaper, some positive features did emerge from it. First, it brought enthusiasm, energy, and verve to the practice of journalism, along with aggressive investigative reporting. Second, it brought wide exposure to prominent authors and led to some fine examples of contemporary writing. Stephen Crane, Frank Norris, Dorothy Dix, and Mark Twain all wrote for newspapers during this period (1880–1905). Further, yellow journalism helped popularize the use of layout and display devices—banner headlines, pictures, color printing—that would go on to characterize modern journalism.

▲ The Early 20th Century

From 1900 to 1920, consolidation characterized the newspaper business. Although circulation and profits went up, the number of daily newspapers decreased, and the number of cities with competing newspapers dropped by 60 percent. What happened?

First, the cost of new technology—Linotype machines, high-speed presses—proved too much for many marginal papers. Second, advertisers showed a preference for the paper with the largest circulation in the market. Smaller-circulation papers saw their revenues shrink to the point at which they could no longer compete. Third, consolidation had increased profits in the railroad, grocery, and hotel businesses, and newspaper publishers decided it could do the same for them. Consequently, newspaper chains—companies that owned several papers—grew quickly. By 1933 six chains—Hearst, Scripps-Howard, Patterson-McCormack, Block, Ridder, and Gannett—controlled 81 dailies with a combined circulation of more than 9 million, about one-fourth of all daily circulation.

Appearing with the consolidation trend and enjoying a short but lively reign was **jazz journalism.** At the end of World War I, the United States enjoyed a decade of prosperity known as the Roaring Twenties. The radio, Hollywood, the airplane, Prohibition, and Al Capone all captured national attention. The papers that best exemplify jazz journalism all sprang up in New York between 1919 and 1924. All were characterized by two features: (1) They were **tabloids,** printed on a page that was about one-half the size of a normal newspaper page; and (2) they were richly illustrated with photographs. The best example of this trend was the *New York Daily News.*

▲ The Impact of the Great Depression

The Depression had huge social and economic impact on newspapers and magazines. During the 1930s total daily newspaper circulation increased by about 2 million; the total population increased by 9 million. The total income of the newspaper industry, however, dropped about 20 percent in this decade. Marginally profitable papers were unable to stay in business, and approximately 66 dailies went under.

Although worsening economic conditions were one cause of the newspaper's decline, more important was the emergence of radio as a competitor for national advertising dollars. From 1935 to 1940, newspapers' share of national advertising revenues dropped from 45 to 39 percent, while radio's share jumped from 6 to more than 10 percent. By 1940, however, thanks to increased revenue from local advertisers, newspaper revenues had rebounded. Nevertheless, the economic picture was not rosy, and the number of daily papers declined to 1,744, an all-time low, in 1945.

▲ Postwar Newspapers

The postwar economy forced the newspaper industry to move even further in the direction of contraction and consolidation. Although newspaper circulation rose from approximately 48 million in 1945 to about 62 million in 1970, the number of dailies stayed about the same. There was actually a circulation loss in cities with populations of more than a million, and several big-city papers went out of business. Moreover, the number of cities with competing dailies dropped from 117 to 37 between 1945 and 1970. This meant that about 98 percent of American cities had no competing papers.

In 1945, 60 chains controlled about 42 percent of the total daily newspaper circulation. By 1970 approximately 157 chains accounted for 60 percent of total circulation. Why had the number of chains continued to grow? One factor was the sharp rise in costs of paper and labor. Newspapers were becoming more expensive to print. The large chains were in a position to share expenses and to use their presses and labor more efficiently. For instance, several papers could share the services of feature writers, columnists, photographers, and compositors, thus holding down costs.

The consolidation trend was present across media, as several media conglomerates controlled newspapers, magazines, and radio and TV stations. Black newspapers were also caught up in the trend toward concentration. In 1956 the *Chicago Defender* changed from a weekly to a daily, and its owner, John Sengstacke, started a group of nine black papers, including the Pittsburgh *Courier* and the Michigan *Chronicle.*

Another continuing trend was the competition among media for advertising dollars. The total amount of advertising revenue spent on all media nearly tripled between 1945 and 1970. Although the total spent on newspapers did not increase at quite this pace, the

When Lyndon Johnson signed the Civil Rights Act of 1964, he invited leaders of the civil rights movement to join him in the Oval Office. Only one woman was among the group that witnessed the historic moment—Ethel L. Payne, an African American journalist who had reported on civil rights issues for more than a decade.

Payne was the granddaughter of slaves. She originally wanted to become a lawyer but was denied admission to law school because of her race. In 1948 she went to Japan to work with African American troops who were stationed there. Two years later Payne showed excerpts from her personal journal about the problems of black soldiers to a reporter for the *Chicago Defender* who was visiting Japan. Her stories became a series in the newspaper and launched Payne on a journalism career.

Based in Chicago, Payne won awards for her coverage of problems in the African American community. She went to Washington in the mid-1950s to cover the beginnings of the civil rights movement. She wrote stories analyzing the historic *Brown* v. *Board of Education* Supreme Court decision. Payne made her presence felt at White House press conferences when she asked President Dwight Eisenhower pointed questions about the lack of progress on civil rights during his administration.

In 1956 Payne covered the arrest of Rosa Parks in Montgomery, Alabama, and the subsequent bus boycott. She reported the big stories of the civil rights movement, including the efforts to integrate the University of Alabama; the violence in Little Rock, Arkansas; the confrontation at Selma, Alabama; and the march on Washington in 1965. She was one of the first reporters to interview Dr. Martin Luther King Jr.

In 1966 she traveled to Vietnam to cover African American troops, who were involved in much of the fighting. She later accompanied Secretary of State Henry Kissinger on a six-nation tour of Africa. In 1978, at age 67, she ended her career with the *Chicago Defender* to write a syndicated column. Seven years later she became a leader in the effort to free South Africa leader Nelson Mandela.

Ethel Payne died in 1991. The *Washington Post* published a tribute to her on its editorial page. It praised her for being fair, straightforward, and independent, an assessment probably shared by her millions of readers.

---

amount spent on television increased by more than threefold. The rising TV industry cut significantly into the print media's national advertising revenue.

The biggest development of the 1980s was the birth of *USA Today* whose content was characterized by shorter stories, splashy graphics, and lots of charts and tables, innovations that were imitated by many local papers.

▲ Contemporary Newspapers: Struggling to Survive

The problems of the newspaper industry became apparent during the 1990s and intensified as the new decade progressed. Readership started a slow but steady decline; the Internet siphoned away advertising revenue, especially classified ad dollars, and young people in particular deserted the paper and went online for their news.

In addition, the industry was hurt by several bad management decisions. First, publishers did not know what to do with the Internet. Papers created online editions as an afterthought and used them primarily to steer readers to the print edition. From the beginning Web sites were seen as tangential to the paper's core business. Second, the online editions were free; readers paid nothing for the content. Predictably, some readers stopped subscribing to the print edition and circulation declined further. Moreover, the free content created an expectation that news online was free for the taking. Any future attempts to charge for this content would be met with resistance. Finally, the easy credit available during the midpart of the new decade prompted many papers to expand and to buy up existing properties. As a result, a number of newspaper companies were saddled with huge debts. (See the boxed insert on p. 101, "The Debt Trap.") During prosperous times this would have been a manageable situation, but the economic collapse during the last years of the decade cut into the bottom line and many papers could not meet their debt obligations.

All of this came together in 2008–2009 and resulted in a deluge of unfortunate developments. At the risk of spreading too much gloom and doom, here is just a partial sampling of the bad news:

- The Tribune Company, publisher of the *Chicago Tribune* and the *Los Angeles Times*, declared bankruptcy.
- The *Christian Science Monitor* stopped its daily print edition.

- Newspapers in Detroit and in several other cities cut home delivery to three times a week.
- The *Seattle Post-Intelligencer, Rocky Mountain Times,* and about 100 other daily and weekly papers shut down in 2008–2009.
- From 2007 to 2008, newspaper advertising revenue dropped an alarming 23 percent.
- In early 2009, the cost of a share of stock in the New York Times Company was under $5, less than the cost of a Sunday edition of the *Times.*

Now for the really bad news: Experts predict things will get worse. Nonetheless, newspapers were not ready to throw in the towel. There were a few bright spots. Newspapers still took in more than $38 billion in revenue, online readership was increasing, some small- and medium-market papers were still doing well, and the newspaper business was more willing than ever to consider new ways to increase revenue.

Newspapers in the Digital Age

▲ Transitions

Newspapers are experimenting with ways to stay afloat in the digital age. Their efforts are directed at two areas: cutting costs and increasing revenue. Cost-cutting efforts have ranged from the mild to the extreme. At one end of the spectrum, many newspapers are sharing content, something that would have been unheard of a decade ago. The *Washington Post,* for example, shares certain stories with the *Baltimore Sun.* Fierce competitors *Dallas Morning News* and *Fort Worth Star-Telegram* trade sports coverage. Content-sharing helps keep down the cost of news gathering. Numerous papers have cut costs by laying off employees or asking staff members to take unpaid furloughs.

Several big-city papers have stopped delivery to outlying areas, saving printing and delivery costs. Other papers have stopped home delivery on certain days of the week, suggesting that readers buy a newspaper at the newsstand or read the online edition to fill in the gaps. The most drastic cost-cutting step of all is dropping the print edition altogether and becoming an online-only publication. In Michigan, for example, the *Ann Arbor News* stopped its paper-and-ink operation and became AnnArbor.com, and as mentioned earlier, the century-old *Christian Science Monitor* dropped its daily print edition in 2009 and shifted to online.

At the same time, newspaper publishers are searching for new ways to make money. Some are exploring ways to charge readers a small sum for content, called a micropayment, which would imitate the business model pioneered by iTunes. Others are looking for ways to generate more income from advertising on cell phones and other mobile media. Finally, the industry is trying to figure out how to make more money from news aggregators, such as Google News, that use newspaper content to draw readers to their sites. We will examine the economics of the newspaper industry in more detail below.

Since it appears that the future of the newspaper business is closely tied to its online efforts, let's take a more detailed look at newspapers online.

▲ Online Newspapers

Online papers have certain advantages over traditional newspapers:

- Printed newspapers are limited by the **newshole,** the amount of news that can be printed in one edition. Online papers have no such limitations. The full text of lengthy speeches, transcripts of interviews, and extensive tables and graphs can be accommodated easily.
- Online papers can be updated continuously; there are no edition deadlines.
- Online papers are interactive. E-mail addresses, bulletin boards, and chat rooms allow readers to provide quick feedback to the paper. Many have searchable archives and links to other sites.

- Online papers can provide photos and video and audio clips to accompany news stories and advertisements. Some even offer social networking opportunities.
- Online papers can feature user-generated content.

In 1994 about 20 daily papers had Web sites. By 2009 it was rare for a paper not to have one.

During the early years of the Internet, online newspaper sites were slow to innovate. There was a fear that the Web site would steal readers from the print version. Thus, many of them simply took their print stories and placed them online, updating them only once a day. Some even withheld stories until they were published in the print edition. Newspapers, however, now realize that if they want to compete with other news sites such as CNN and CBS News, their Web sites have to do more.

A 2008 analysis of the top 100 newspaper sites revealed that newspapers were exploring new ways to connect with readers. All sites contained featured video and photos. Nearly all of the papers had blogs and provisions for readers to comment on blogs. User-generated photos were featured on 58 percent of the sites, but only 18 percent included user-generated videos. About 40 percent of the sites had podcasts. Social networking opportunities were relatively absent, appearing on only 10 percent of the sites.

▲ Mobile Media

Newspapers traditionally have been delivered to a place—a person's home or office. In the digital age newspapers are increasingly delivered to a person, thanks to the growing availability of wireless connections to the Internet and the increasing popularity of cell phones and laptops. About two of three Americans, for example, owns a cell phone (for more on wireless handheld media, see Chapter 3). These devices are becoming new delivery channels for newspapers. The *Wall Street Journal,* for example, offers a mobile edition to subscribers over their cell phones.

The number of people using mobile devices to access news on the Internet doubled from 2008 to 2009 to about 63 million per month. About 85 percent of iPhone users browse the mobile Web for news and information. The *New York Times* and big newspaper owner Gannett are both heavily into mobile news. The *Times* mobile news site was receiving more than 9 million page views a month in 2007. Gannett operates more than 100 mobile news sites and has more than 2 million subscribers.

The advertising potential of this channel is significant because ads delivered by cell phone reach already motivated consumers. Checking sports scores on your cell phone? While you're at it, click on a banner ad that sends you to a site where you can buy tickets for the next game. Further, young people are heavy users of cell phones, and these same young people are the ones most likely to abandon print newspapers. Mobile media offer publishers one way to reach this valuable audience. According to one research firm, the amount spent on mobile advertising will top $7 billion by 2013.

In sum, look for newspapers to be designed for multiple digital platforms, not just paper. As *New York Times* publisher Arthur Sulzberger Jr. put it, "Newspapers cannot be defined by the second word—paper. They've got to be defined by the first—news."

▲ User-Generated Content

Newspapers are joining the user-generated movement. The Tribune Company, a long-time member of the "old" media, recently hired a video-sharing company to manage user-generated videos on the company's 50 newspaper Web sites. The Gannett Company introduced a concept called "crowdsourcing" to bring readers into the news-gathering process. The publisher of the *Denver Post* has created YourHub.com, a series of local Web sites that feature user-generated content accessible from the newspaper's home page. Several papers have sponsored Saturday workshops for readers who want to know more about reporting. Even smaller papers, such as *Bluffton Today* in South Carolina, have started community blogs and sites where readers can post pictures.

Relying on citizen journalists, of course, carries some risk. The credibility and objectivity of the average citizen reporter may be suspect. It is difficult to know if citizen journalists are pursuing some personal agenda or how knowledgeable they are. The citizen who writes a story about a new school board policy might have children directly affected by the policy. The citizen journalist who calls *Pineapple Express* the best comedy film he ever saw may have seen only three comedy films in his life. There's no way of knowing.

▲ Social Media

As noted above, newspapers have made only limited excursions into the world of social media with only 10 percent of the Web sites of the top 100 papers using social networking tools. It is expected, however, that this percentage will grow as publishers become more familiar with the best ways to employ social media to build readership. One current use of social media is to provide Twitter headline feeds. To cite one example, the *New York Times*' main Twitter feed has more than a quarter-million followers. In Toronto, the *Globe and Mail* has created story-based communities. Using a live blogging/discussion tool, the Web site allows readers to interact during the coverage of breaking news and live events. Real-time comments and audio and video clips can then be incorporated into the final story. The Gannett Company has a different strategy. It bought Ripple6, the maker of social networking software, a move that will help Gannett improve its own social networking efforts.

Defining Features of Newspapers

The online and print editions of the newspaper share some defining features. First, the newspaper is made up of diverse content. Newspapers contain international, national, and local news. In addition, they feature editorials, letters to the editor, movie listings, horoscopes, comics, sports, film reviews, recipes, advice columns, classified ads, and a host of other material. Their range of content is extensive.

Second, newspapers are conveniently packaged. Both the print and online versions are organized according to content. There are sections devoted to general news, financial news, sports, and entertainment. In addition, each story contains a headline that makes it easy for readers to decide if they want to peruse the rest of the story.

Third, newspapers are local. Reporters cover meetings of the local school board, the city council, and the zoning commission. They cover the local police station and tell about the newest store openings in the local mall. Sports sections cover the hometown Little League and high school teams. Local people with merchandise to sell use the classified ads. Newspapers are the only medium with the resources to report all the neighborhood activities in a community.

Fourth, more than any other medium, the newspaper serves as a historical record. One writer described newspaper journalism as "the first draft of history." The typical paper contains a record of daily events, some profound, some not so profound, that influence our lives. If a person wants to get a sense of what life was like in the 1940s, for example, he or she can flip through some old issues of the paper and see what events were on people's minds, what movies they were seeing, and what products were being advertised.

Fifth, newspapers perform the watchdog role in our society. They monitor the workings of government and private industry for misdeeds and wrongdoings. They alert the public to possible threats and new trends.

Finally, newspapers are timely. News is not useful if it is stale. Recognizing this fact, the largest-circulation newspapers in the United States publish daily and online editions that can break news any time of the day. Getting the news out fast has always been one of the characteristics of the newspaper business.

Organization of the Newspaper Industry

This section will first examine the organization of the traditional ink-and-paper newspaper industry and then consider the online versions. The print newspapers that are published in this country are many and varied. They range from the *Wall Street Journal,* a nationally oriented financial daily, to the *Daily Journal of Commerce,* a small financial paper published in Portland, Oregon; from the *National Enquirer* to the *Daily Lobo,* the college newspaper of the University of New Mexico; from the million-plus-circulation *New York Times* to the 6,000-circulation Gallipolis *Daily Tribune* in Ohio. Obviously, there are many ways to categorize an industry as diverse as this one. For our purposes we will group papers by frequency of publication (dailies and weeklies), by market size (national, large, medium, small), and by their appeal to specialized groups. Table 4-1 shows the top 10 newspapers by circulation and the percentage change in circulation between 2007 and 2008.

TABLE 4-1

Top 10 Newspaper Circulation

Paper	2008 Circulation (millions)	2007 Circulation (millions)	Percent Change
USA Today	2.29	2.30	—
Wall Street Journal	2.01	2.08	−1.9
New York Times	1.00	1.13	−11
Los Angeles Times	0.74	0.84	−12
New York Post	0.63	0.67	−6
New York Daily News	0.63	0.68	−7
Washington Post	0.62	0.68	−9
Chicago Tribune	0.52	0.58	−10
Houston Chronicle	0.45	0.53	−15
Newsday	0.38	0.43	−12

Note: With few exceptions, newspaper circulation has seen a slow but steady decline.

▲ Print Dailies

To be considered a daily, a newspaper has to appear five times a week. In 2008 there were 1,422 dailies, down 4 percent from 2000 (see Figure 4-1) and about 6,500 weeklies. Whether a daily or a weekly, the chief concern of a newspaper is **circulation,** the number of copies delivered to subscribers, newsstands, and vending machines. Circulation figures reflect the crisis in the newspaper industry. Weekday morning circulation has decreased 5 percent since 2000, evening circulation has dropped 33 percent, and Sunday circulation is down 14 percent (see Figure 4-2). In addition, since the U.S. population has grown, the ratio of newspapers per household has dropped precipitously. In 1960, about 111 newspapers were sold per 100 households. In 2008, that number had declined to 40 newspapers sold per 100 households. The overall trend does not inspire optimism.

The circulation crunch, however, has not hit all papers with equal force. This becomes apparent when we divide daily newspapers into market groups.

National Newspapers   Only a few papers fall into this category. These are publications whose content is typically geared not for one particular region or city but for the entire country. These papers use satellites to transmit images and text to regional printing plants, where the papers are assembled and distributed. Gannett's *USA Today,* the *New York Times,* and the *Wall Street Journal* are the three national newspapers in the United States. Circulation for this group has not declined quite as much as in other segments.

FIGURE 4-1

Number of Daily Newspapers in the United States, 1950–2007

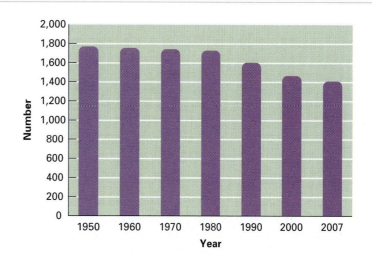

FIGURE 4-2

Daily Newspaper Circulation, 1980–2007

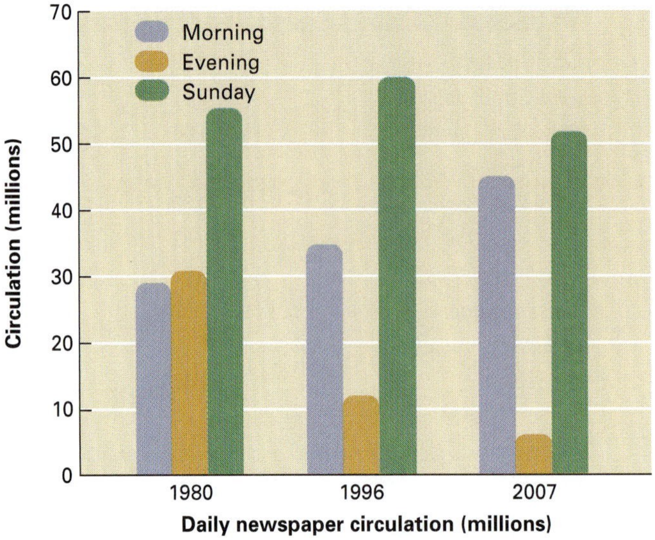

> **SOUNDBYTE**
>
> **Obits on the Web**
>
> The obituary section in the local newspaper can trace its roots back to at least the 19th century. The obits (as they are called in the trade) are one of the most-read parts of the paper, and most families make a practice of saving the published obituaries of loved ones as part of their family histories. It was only a matter of time before this section of the paper had its digital counterpart.
>
> Legacy.com is a Web site that offers "the next generation" of obituary. From its site: "Through this multimedia product families can share special stories and memories by adding extended text, video, audio, photos and music to their loved one's online obituary." Sounds a little like Facebook for the dearly departed . . . without the updates.

Large Metropolitan Dailies These are newspapers based in communities with a population of 500,000 or more. They are the group that is in the biggest trouble. Competition from the Internet for readers, a loss of advertising revenue to online sites, and the migration of young readers to the Web have all combined to hurt circulation and profits. In 2008, total circulation at the 10 largest metropolitan dailies dropped more than 6 percent. As we have already noted, several big-city papers have folded.

Medium-Sized Dailies Papers in this segment have circulations that range between 100,000 and 500,000, and their fortunes, particularly the papers at the top end of this range, are declining about as fast as their big-city counterparts. Circulation losses among this group averaged about 8 percent. There were, however, bright spots. Some medium-sized papers, particularly those in Florida and Arizona where the population is older, did not see such steep losses.

Small-Town Dailies Papers in this category generally have circulations under 100,000, and they are the ones that are doing the best job weathering the storm. Circulation losses in this group averaged about 2 percent. Some smaller papers even managed to gain circulation. The Madison, Wisconsin, *State Journal* increased circulation by more than 10 percent from 2007 to 2008. Why has the downturn been less severe in this group? They face less competition from other media outlets, their classified ad revenue is less likely to be hurt by sites such as Monster.com or Craigslist, and their emphasis on local news is more likely to keep readers.

▲ Print Weeklies

The number of weekly newspapers in the United States has remained fairly stable at about 6,500 over the past 10 years. The circulation of weeklies, however, increased from 29 million in 1970 to more than 45 million in 2008. Despite this increase in circulation, the rising costs of printing and distribution have made weekly publishers more cost-conscious.

Al Neuharth got into the newspaper business when he was 11 years old, delivering the *Minneapolis Tribune.* At 13 he had a part-time job in the composing room of a local weekly.

After serving in the military, he took a job as a reporter for a paper in South Dakota and later moved to the *Miami Herald.* Neuharth moved up rapidly through the ranks and eventually entered management. In 1960 he was appointed an assistant executive editor of the *Detroit Free Press.* His achievements there brought him to the attention of executives of the Gannett Company, who persuaded him to leave Detroit to manage two of Gannett's papers in New York. Neuharth's success there earned him a promotion to the position of chief of Gannett's operations in Florida. By 1970 Neuharth had become CEO of the company.

His emphasis was on the bottom line. During his tenure Gannett's annual revenue increased from $200 million to $3.1 billion. Neuharth continued the strategies of his predecessors by acquiring small- and medium-market dailies that enjoyed monopoly status in their markets and keeping costs down while raising ad rates. Stung by criticism that his papers emphasized profit at the expense of journalism, Neuharth strengthened the editorial operations of Gannett

Al Neuharth, the man responsible for making Gannett the nation's biggest newspaper company.

papers, and by 1980 many had won awards for excellence in reporting.

Neuharth's biggest gamble came in the early 1980s when he decided to use a network of communication satellites and regional printing plants to produce *USA Today,* a national general-interest newspaper. The new paper was greeted with derision by critics, who dismissed it as a "McPaper" that served up flavorless "fast-food" journalism. *USA Today* was an immediate hit with readers, however, and quickly garnered more than a million readers. Advertisers took a little longer to get on board, but the paper eventually turned a profit.

Now most experts agree that, after more than 25 years on the newsstands, *USA Today* has had a significant impact on the industry. Most newspapers have incorporated color, splashy page makeup, more charts and graphics, and shorter, more tightly written stories.

Neuharth retired in 1989 to become chair of the Freedom Foundation, an organization dedicated to furthering the cause of a free press in society. He also continues to write a syndicated newspaper column. The *Washington Journalism Review* named him the most influential person of the 1980s in print media.

▲ Maintaining Old and Attracting New Readers

No matter what their size and frequency of publication, all print newspapers face the task of maintaining their loyal readers while trying to attract new ones. This is proving to be a difficult job. In an attempt to attract younger readers, many papers are redesigning their print edition by adding more color, flashier graphics, shorter stories, and adding more "soft" news, such as fashion and entertainment articles. Many have changed their paper's layout so that it more resembles a Web page. These changes may cause a backlash among the most loyal newspaper readers—those between the ages of 45 and 62—who have become accustomed to the more traditional layout. In short, in their efforts to attract people who don't often read a newspaper, publishers may be driving away those who do.

Some big-city papers have adopted a different strategy to attract young readers. They are giving away free tabloids that present short news summaries but whose main emphasis is entertainment and lifestyle news. The *Chicago Tribune* distributes *RedEye* at mass transit stops and other places where young people may congregate. The *Washington Post* publishes a similar free tabloid called *Express.*

Are these efforts working? The results so far are not encouraging. Readership is still declining among the young people and also among older age groups.

▲ Special-Service and Minority Newspapers

Special-service newspapers are those aimed at several well-defined audience segments. There are, for example, many newspapers published specifically for the African American

The best-known member of the Spanish-language press is *El Diario*, published in New York City. The paper has a circulation of around 50,000.

community. The African American press in this country has a long history, dating back to 1827. Most early papers were started to oppose discrimination and to help gain equal rights and opportunities. The African American press reached its circulation peak in the 1960s when approximately 275 papers had a circulation of about 4 million. Since that time the African American press has seen a significant decline in both numbers of papers and circulation.

In 2009 approximately 190 African American papers, mostly weeklies, were publishing in 35 states and the District of Columbia. Papers such as the *Chicago Defender* and the *Philadelphia Tribune* are leading voices in their communities. Like their mainstream counterparts, African American papers are increasing their online presence.

Hispanics are the fastest-growing minority group in America, and the Spanish-language press has grown with them. According to the National Hispanic Media Directory, the number of daily Spanish-language newspapers grew from 14 in 1990 to more than 30 in 2008, while the number of weeklies increased from 152 to nearly 420. Some of the prominent Hispanic newspapers include *El Diario* in New York and *La Opinion* in Los Angeles. Like newspapers in general, the Hispanic press saw some circulation declines from 2006 to 2008 but not nearly as much as English-language papers.

There are many other ethnic newspaper publishers in the United States. Twelve cities have at least one Chinese-language newspaper, and eight cities have papers targeted to Polish Americans.

Another special type of newspaper is exemplified by the college press. Although numbers are hard to pin down, as of 2009 there were about 1,800 college papers published at four-year institutions, with a total circulation of more than 6 million. College newspapers are big business; consequently, more and more papers are hiring nonstudent professionals to manage their operations. Two of the largest college papers in terms of circulation are the University of Minnesota's *Minnesota Daily* and Michigan State University's *State News*, both with circulations of approximately 30,000. College newspapers get high readership scores. A 2005 survey found that 71 percent of college students read at least one issue of their college newspaper in the past week. The comparable number for the mainstream press was 41 percent. Even so, college papers are suffering from revenue losses. (See the boxed insert "College Newspapers Not Immune.")

▲ Organization of Online Newspapers

There are three main types of online newspaper Web sites: (1) news aggregators, (2) online Web sites associated with a local or national print newspaper, and (3) online-only sites.

News aggregators are sites that take information from many sources and meld it into a new presentation. Two of the best-known news aggregators are Yahoo!News and Google News. The sites typically carry headlines and maybe a lead sentence or two with a link that takes the reader back to the original source. They generally have no editorial staff that selects the stories, depending instead on a formula calculated by a computer program that scans a list of news Web sites.

The vast majority of online newspapers are affiliated with traditional print newspapers, either dailies or weeklies. Their structure varies, with some sites having a stand-alone organization with staffers who work only for the online site. Other sites combine the print and online operations so that one person may work for both. Most of these Web sites have a small number of employees, averaging about 5–10 people. The most popular newspaper Web sites are those that have a print counterpart. For example, the top five most visited newspaper Web sites in 2008 were nytimes.com (New York Times), washingtonpost.com (Washington Post), usatoday.com (USA Today), latimes.com (Los Angeles Times), and wallstreetjournal.com (Wall Street Journal Online).

Online-only sites have proliferated in the last couple of years. Many were started by journalists who were laid off from their print newspaper jobs. Others are the remnants of a print publication that went out of business, such as seattlepi.com, the online site of the defunct *Seattle Post-Intelligencer*. And to make it more complicated, some are run by newspapers that don't publish a print edition in the local market. Gatehouse Media, a newspaper company, started the Batavian in Batavia, New York, even though the local paper is published by another firm. Most online-only sites focus on local community news and events. Some examples are The Voice of San Diego, a nonprofit site staffed by 10 former journalists that gets about 60,000 unique visitors a month. The ChiTown Daily News has only four people on its staff and depends upon citizen journalists for its coverage of metro Chicago. So far, finding a profitable business model has been a challenge for most of these sites.

Newspaper Ownership

For many years the ownership story in the newspaper industry was big fish gobbling up smaller fish as large companies got bigger by acquiring smaller ones. The newspaper industry is still dominated by several large group owners, but the economic downturn has temporarily at least reversed the trend toward consolidation. The top five newspaper group owners are listed in Table 4-2. The biggest is the Gannett Company with 85 daily newspapers and a combined circulation of about 7 million.

TABLE 4-2

Biggest Newspaper
Groups, 2008,
by revenue

Name	Number of Papers Owned	Top Paper
Gannett Company	85	*USA Today*
Tribune Co.	10	*Chicago Tribune*
New York Times Co.	18	*New York Times*
McClatchy Co.	29	*Miami Herald*
Advance Publications	25	*Cleveland Plain Dealer*

The trend away from consolidation began in 2007 when the then second-largest newspaper chain, Knight Ridder, was purchased by the McClatchy Company, which in turn sold off a dozen of the papers to private owners. The Tribune Company was taken over by real estate tycoon Sam Zell in 2008 who then sold off one of the company's biggest papers, *Newsday,* to a cable TV company. The Dow Jones Company sold six papers to a small newspaper company in Alabama. As of mid-2009, many other papers were for sale, but there were few takers.

Why the reversal? Newspapers are no longer the profit centers they once were before the Internet. Their long-term prospects seem dim, and so far nobody has come up with a plan that would turn things around, a fact that scares away many buyers. Moreover, stock values have plummeted and shareholders have pressured management to sell papers that were losing money. In any event, for the short term at least, the trend is toward becoming smaller rather than getting bigger.

Producing the Print and Online Newspaper

▲ Departments and Staff

The departmental structure and staffing of a newspaper vary with its size. At the most general level, all papers are divided into three departments: (1) business, (2) production, and (3) news-editorial. The business department is in charge of selling advertising space in both the print and online editions and building the paper's circulation and Web site traffic. As the title implies, the production department handles the physical and electronic tasks necessary to get the news printed on paper and available on the Web site.

The most complex department is news-editorial. Note that these two functions—news and editorial—are kept separate in both the online and print versions. The editorial pages contain opinion, while the news pages contain objective reporting.

In the past, newspapers maintained separate departments for the print and online versions. At some papers the online staff was on a different floor or even in a different building. The current trend, especially among small papers, is toward merging the two. One recent survey noted that about 9 out of 10 small papers have newsrooms that combine the print and online operations. Bigger papers tend to be more likely to have a separate print and Web operation with about 6 out of 10 papers using a converged model.

There are several arrangements for a combined newsroom. One traditional arrangement is a newsroom directed by a managing editor who oversees and coordinates the day-to-day operations of the department. A city editor supervises local coverage, assigns reporters to beats (such as city hall, police, and health), and directs general-assignment reporters to handle a variety of stories. A wire editor edits international and national news from the Associated Press and other major news services. Most newspapers also have one or more people who are responsible for preparing the editorial pages.

A newer arrangement uses four defined roles: (1) a newsflow editor who manages the progress of a story through both the print and online version; (2) a storybuilder who combines print, audio, and video elements for a story; (3) a news resourcer who specializes in information, providing background, depth, and context to stories in both the print and online versions; and (4) "backpack" journalists (see Chapter 13) who conduct interviews, take photographs, and record audio and video footage for dissemination in print and online formats. Other staffing arrangements will probably emerge as the industry becomes more comfortable with the converged system.

▲ Prepublication Routine

Operational convergence is evident in the way the print and online editions are prepared. The traditional print newsroom had one deadline when all stories had to be ready. The modern converged newsroom is a 24/7 operation in which news on the paper's Web site is updated continuously.

There are two basic sources for news: local reporting and wire services. Early in the day the wire editor scans the outputs from the wire services and flags possible stories for the print and online editions. At the same time, the city editor is assigning reporters to various stories that will appear in print and online, and the managing editor is gauging the available space, the newshole, that can be devoted to news in that day's print edition. The greater the number of print ads, the greater the number of pages that can be printed, and the larger the newshole. The online edition, of course, has no such limitations.

Convergence is also showing up at the individual level. As the day progresses, reporters file stories for both the print and online editions. Many reporters also shoot and edit video for the Web site or record audio for a podcast. Since the Web version is continuously updated, some online stories may be rewritten several times. But this isn't all that is expected of the 21st-century newspaper reporter. She or he may be expected to write a blog, participate in chat rooms, and respond to reader e-mail. (These new duties have caused some problems; see the boxed insert "What's the Appropriate Job Description for a Converged Reporter?")

Editors for the print edition edit stories and design page makeup. Photos and graphics are added, and the finished pages are sent to a composing room. Eventually, the pages make their way to the press room, where they are printed and bundled together for delivery.

The above paragraph, of course, does not apply to the online version. Web editors post and update stories when needed. They also decide what photos and video and audio clips will accompany the day's stories. Many papers have instituted "early teams," an editor and one or more reporters, who start work around daybreak and work into the early afternoon reporting, writing, and posting stories exclusively for the Web site. About 8 out of 10 big newspapers have created early teams for their Web sites. The concept is less likely to be found in smaller papers, with only about 3 in 10 using early teams. When everything is in order, the story and related graphics are posted to the Web site. There is no need for a composing room, printing press, paper, or delivery truck.

The Economics of Newspaper Publishing

As mentioned earlier, the business model that has sustained the newspaper industry for the past few centuries is falling apart. Circulation is declining, but a far more serious problem is the decline in advertising revenue. In order to understand the situation, we need to take a close look at the economics of newspaper publishing. We'll start by examining revenues and expenses.

▲ Revenue

The traditional print newspaper has two sources of revenue: selling advertising space and circulation income—money from subscriptions and newsstand sales. Of these two sources, advertising is by far the most important, accounting for more than 80 percent of income.

There are four main types of advertising revenue:

- *Local retail:* advertising by local specialty stores, auto dealerships, grocery stores, and other local businesses
- *Classified:* employment ads, real estate ads, for-sale ads, and so forth, usually published in a special section of the paper
- *National:* ads bought by advertisers who need to reach a mass audience, such as ads for food, cell phones, and financial services
- *Prepaid inserts:* supplements put together usually by national chains such as Best Buy or Target that are inserted into the paper

Of these four types, classified and local retail are the most important. Historically, local retail has accounted for about 50 percent of all ad revenue and classified ads about 40 percent. Unfortunately for the newspaper industry, these two categories of advertising have been hit hard by increased competition and the economic downturn. Local retail advertising revenue dropped about 15 percent from 2006 to 2009. Much of this loss occurred because many local stores went out of business because they couldn't compete with companies such as Wal-Mart, an organization that does little newspaper advertising. Classified ad revenue fell a staggering 45 percent over the same period. Employment ads, real estate ads, and auto ads declined the most as competition from sites such as Monster.com and Craigslist and the bad economy ate into newspaper revenue. In other words, the industry's top two revenue streams have dropped by 60 percent over a three-year period. That spells trouble.

▲ Expenses

The costs of running a typical print newspaper can be viewed in several ways. One common method is to classify the costs by function:

- *News and editorial costs:* reporters and editors who cover and report the news
- *Printing costs:* such as newsprint (the paper), ink, and the cost of running the press
- *Mechanical costs:* composing and production expenses
- *Circulation and distributions costs:* gas, trucks, and delivery people
- *General administration costs:* clerical, secretarial, accounting, and so forth

These expenses are related to the circulation size of the paper. The more copies printed, the more the cost of ink, paper, delivery, and so on.

Newspapers have tried to cut these costs as much as possible by laying off people, shrinking the physical size of the paper, cutting delivery to outlying regions, and adopting more efficient production techniques. Costs, however, can be reduced only so far and long-term survival depends on increased revenue.

▲ Is Online the Answer?

About the only bright spot for newspapers in the last few years has been the increasing popularity of their Web sites. Overall, the newspaper industry averages 66 million unique visitors every month to its Web sites compared to about 51 million who get the print versions. The number of unique visitors to the top 10 newspaper Web sites increased by 16 percent from 2007 to 2008. Some individual papers showed even more impressive gains. The struggling *Chicago Tribune* had a 35 percent increase in unique visitors.

Will online papers save the newspaper industry? The jury is still out on that question, but the prospects don't look good. The big problem is that the increasing numbers of online readers are not translating into enough advertising dollars to stem the bleeding from the print version. Here's an example that might help explain the problem. Pretend that an employer is trying to find someone to fill a job opening. In the days before the Internet, the employer's choice would probably be limited to placing a classified "Help Wanted" ad in the local paper. In other words, the supply of advertising opportunities would be scarce. Now consider the current situation. The employer could advertise for a prospective employee on Craigslist, Monster.com, CareerBuilder.com, Yahoo!HotJobs, SimplyHired.com, and a few dozen other sites. In economic terms, the supply of online advertising opportunities is abundant. And what happens to the price when supply is abundant and demand stays about the same (or decreases as it has done the past few years)? You don't have to take Econ 101 to figure out that the price of online ads will go down. Additionally, advertisers know that people don't spend much time on newspaper Web sites. They spend more time looking through the print version. As a result, online ads generate much less revenue than print ads. For every dollar advertisers pay to reach a print newspaper reader, they pay about 5–10 cents to reach an online reader. This means that the print version still supplies most of the industry revenue. To illustrate, for a three-month period in 2007, the Tribune Company collected $66 million in online ad revenue; it collected about 10 times that amount from its print operation.

Newspapers are turning to automation to save money. These robot movers handle tons of paper.

To make the outlook even more pessimistic, online advertising may no longer be a growth area. For several years online advertising revenue was increasing at double-digit rates. From 2005 to 2006, the growth rate was 32 percent; from 2006 to 2007, about 18 percent. From 2007 to 2008, online revenue actually decreased by about 2 percent.

What about saving money by dropping the print version altogether and going online only? *The State of the News Media 2009,* a report by the Pew Project for Excellence in Journalism, noted that "Papers still make roughly 90% of their revenue from print and, although the numbers vary by paper, the cost of printing and delivering the printed newspaper averages 40% of costs. For now, it doesn't add up to sacrifice potentially 90% of revenues to save 40% of costs."

Given this depressing arithmetic, it is not surprising that newspapers are exploring other ways to generate income including charging for some content (a technique that has not been successful in the past) and striking advertising arrangements with Internet companies such as Yahoo!.

▲ Will Newspapers Survive?

The Pew Center's *State of the News Media Report* put it this way: "Newspapers are still far from dead, but the language of the obituary is creeping in."

Some newspapers will survive; some won't. Those that are in the best position are owned by big companies with other businesses whose profits can offset the newspaper losses. The Washington Post Company, for example, owns Kaplan Inc., a provider of educational and career services. In 2008, Kaplan was the Washington Post Company's fastest-growing division and its largest revenue producer. Those that are most at risk are those whose parent company took on large amounts of debt during the easy-credit years of the mid-decade. Towns with two newspapers will probably have a single survivor.

The traditional business model of newspapers is in trouble, and the industry is looking for different ways to structure the industry. There is no lack of suggestions.

One of the most interesting is the Low-Profit Limited Liability Company (L3C for short). An L3C is a business that strives to make a profit but is allowed to take investments from foundations and charities because the L3C is recognized as having a socially desirable benefit. The newspaper, say L3C supporters, performs in a way that benefits society: It promotes democracy by keeping its readers informed and encourages contributions to the marketplace of ideas. The big advantage of the L3C is that it opens up new investment potential. Big foundations, for example, are required to pay out at least 5 percent of their wealth every year into program-related investments. They can invest this money in for-profit organizations, such as an L3C, if they have a social benefit. The newspaper, of course, would still have to run a successful operation. The L3C structure has been approved in several states, but the Internal Revenue Service does not yet recognize newspapers as qualifying for that status.

Another alternative is to have newspapers adopt the model currently used by many universities: an endowed institution. Such an institution would not exist to make a profit but to serve society by promoting the general welfare. A huge advantage of this structure is that organizations that qualify are exempt from income tax and any donations made to the organization are tax deductible. Of course, the start-up costs for such an endeavor would be formidable. A newspaper might have to raise $1 billion or more just to cover the annual costs of publishing a paper. In addition, as an endowed institution the paper could no longer endorse political candidates.

A third alternative would keep newspapers as profit-making endeavors but would give them certain legal advantages. For example, the government could exempt newspapers from current antitrust laws, enabling a group of papers to negotiate among themselves to fix their prices. (Major League Baseball has gotten a similar break.) Or the government could do away with regulations that restrict papers from owning TV and radio stations in the same market or prevent two newspapers in the same market from merging.

Of course, there are compelling arguments against these arrangements. Why should a newspaper be given special privileges? All-news radio stations also promote social benefits. How about giving them special status as well? Further, do we really want to protect newspapers from the reality of the marketplace? The marketplace provides valuable feedback; it tells papers what is working and what isn't. Insulating papers from the marketplace makes it hard to tell if they are really serving their readers. Lastly, all of the above solutions assume that the newspaper is something worth keeping. A survey conducted by the Pew Center for Excellence in Journalism found that 42 percent would not miss their newspapers. If that's the case, it's going to be hard for any ownership model to succeed.

Maybe the most creative suggestion is for newspapers to declare themselves a religion and ordain reporters as priests. This would free newspapers from tax obligations and also qualify reporters for the priest-penitent privacy privilege. (It's probably unlikely that this will happen.)

The newspaper of the future will probably be a hybrid version that appears in print only a few days a week but with a Web site that is constantly updated. It's likely the online version will be delivered to a number of platforms including cell phones, iPods, and e-book readers such as Amazon's Kindle. Its main revenue source will be advertising, but it might also charge for specialized content. It will still employ journalists, but their daily routines will be unlike those in past decades. They will be audio reporters, photographers, video reporters, and bloggers.

All in all, it may be several years before new business models for the online print and newspaper industries are fully established. As the transition continues, look for more disruption and further challenges for this troubled industry.

Feedback for Newspapers

▲ The Audit Bureau of Circulations

The best-known feedback system for newspapers is that connected with the **Audit Bureau of Circulations (ABC).** During the early 1900s, with the growth of mass advertising, some publishers began inflating the number of readers in order to

TABLE 4-3	Year	All Daily Papers	Daily Circulation per 1,000 Adults
Daily and Weekly Newspaper Circulation	1960	58,882,000	475
	1970	62,108,000	428
Source: Compiled by author.	1980	62,201,840	360
	1990	62,327,962	329
	2000	55,772,847	287
	2008	50,700,000	225

attract more revenue from advertisers. In an effort to check this deceptive practice, advertisers and publishers joined to form the ABC in 1914. The organization's purpose was to establish ground rules for counting circulation, to make sure that the rules were enforced, and to provide verified reports of circulation data. The ABC audits about three-fourths of all print media in the United States and Canada—about 2,600 publications.

The ABC functions in the following manner: Publishers keep detailed records of circulation data. Twice a year, publishers file a circulation statement with the ABC, which the ABC in turn disseminates to its clients. Once a year, the ABC audits publications to verify that the figures that have been reported are accurate. An ABC representative visits the publication and is free to examine records and files.

Circulation scandals in 2004 prompted the ABC to reexamine its methods. The organization announced that more field auditors would be hired and the ABC staff would survey subscribers and newsstand operators to confirm that customers were actually paying for the copies that the newspaper reported as sold. The ABC also promised stiff punishment for any newspapers that deliberately faked their numbers. The ABC recently began to report both print and online readership for newspapers.

Those publishers who want more detailed feedback on their online audience size can subscribe to Nielsen/NetRatings (see Chapter 12). The company releases monthly reports on the number of unique visitors to various popular Web sites.

▲ Newspaper Audiences

As of 2009 approximately 51 million copies of morning and evening papers, either purchased at the newsstand or delivered to the doorstep, found their way into American homes every weekday. Daily newspaper circulation, in absolute terms, has decreased since 1990, as a glance at Table 4-3 shows. The population, however, has been increasing. To reflect this fact and to provide additional perspective, the final column of the table presents the ratio of daily circulation to the total adult population of the United States (expressed in thousands). As can be seen, daily newspaper circulation is not keeping pace with the overall growth of the population.

The percentage of adults reading one or more papers every day has declined from about 80 percent in the early 1960s to about 50 percent in 2008. The most pronounced decline has occurred in the 18–29 and 30–44 age groups and among those who have not attended college. The overall drop in daily circulation has been most noticeable in urban areas.

Why the overall decline? Some have attributed it to the increased mobility of Americans, the increase in single-person households, more expensive subscription and per-copy prices, a general decline in the literacy of young people, and competition from other media, especially the Internet.

Print newspapers are losing readers to online media. In 1995 about 4 percent of the U.S. population went online at least once a week to get their news. By 2008 the figure was almost 40 percent. A recent survey by the Pew Research Center found that one in seven Internet users have reduced the amount of time they spend with daily newspapers. The key demographic group that reads most of its news online is young adults—the same group that reads print papers the least. When people go online for news, however, they do not necessarily go to online newspapers. Many visit portals such as Excite or Yahoo!; some go to search engines such as Google; others check CNN.com or a TV network news Web site.

The Newspaper Industry

It's probably obvious by now that the traditional print newspaper is not a great place to look for a job. Since 2000, the total number of people employed in the news industry (newsroom employees, press operators, composers, delivery people, and so on) has declined by nearly 20 percent. The number of editorial employees (reporters, photographers, and editors) has decreased slightly more, and additional layoffs and paper closings are likely.

On the bright side, the online news area is one that will probably grow in the near future. Anybody who wants to become a reporter should make sure that his or her online skills are up-to-date and that he or she can report for a variety of platforms: audio, video, Web, and print.

The career outlook in the various media industries changes quickly. For a more current description of conditions in the newspaper industry and a more detailed look at career options, please consult the book's Web site: www.mhhe.com/dominick11e.

MAIN POINTS

- Newspapers in colonial America were published with permission of the local government. A free press did not appear until after the Revolution.

- The mass newspaper arrived in the 1830s with the publication of Benjamin Day's *New York Sun,* the first of the penny-press papers.

- The era of yellow journalism featured sensationalism, crusades, and human-interest reporting and introduced more attractive newspaper designs.

- Many newspapers were merged or folded during the early 1900s, as tabloid papers became popular. The trend toward consolidation would continue into the years following World War II.

- The newspaper industry is currently in a crisis as declining circulation and advertising revenue have made it difficult for many papers to stay in business.

- There are four types of daily papers: national newspapers, large metro dailies, midsize dailies, and small-town dailies. Other major types of papers are weeklies, special-service newspapers, and minority newspapers.

- All papers now have online versions.

- The trend toward consolidation in the newspaper industry has ended, and many newspapers are for sale.

- Newspapers are reexamining their business model and converging their print and online operations.

- Newspaper audiences are measured by the Audit Bureau of Circulations. Newspaper readership has declined for the past several decades, but online readership is growing.

QUESTIONS FOR REVIEW

1. Trace the changes in the definition of *news* from the 1600s to the 2000s.

2. What are the defining characteristics of newspapers?

3. What are some of the advantages the traditional ink-and-paper newspaper has over the online version?

What are some of the advantages the online version has over the print version?

4. Why are newspapers in trouble?

QUESTIONS FOR CRITICAL THINKING

1. Why don't young people read newspapers? What, if anything, could newspapers do to recapture this audience segment?

2. Should newspapers be allowed to own broadcast stations in their markets? Why or why not?

3. Will the online version eventually replace the print version of a newspaper? Why or why not?

4. What will the newspaper industry look like in 10 years?

5. Do we still need newspapers?

KEY TERMS

political press (p. 82)
First Amendment (p. 83)
penny press (p. 84)
yellow journalism (p. 86)

jazz journalism (p. 87)
tabloids (p. 87)
newshole (p. 89)
circulation (p. 93)

Audit Bureau of Circulations (ABC) (p. 102)

INTERNET RESOURCES

Online Learning Center

On the Online Learning Center home page, www.mhhe.com/dominick11e, *select* Student Center *and then* Chapter 4.

1. Use the Learning Objectives, Chapter Outline, and Main Points sections to review this chapter.

2. Test your knowledge of the chapter using the multiple choice and flashcard features of the site.

3. Expand your knowledge of concepts and topics discussed in the chapter with additional Questions for Critical Thinking and Internet Exercises.

Surfing the Internet

The following are examples of sites that deal with the newspaper industry. All listings were current as of late 2009.

http://graphicdesignr.net/papercuts/
This site keeps track of the layoffs and newspaper closings across the United States.

www.decaturdailydemocrat.com
A good example of a slick online paper published by a small-town daily.

www.naa.org
Site of the Newspaper Association of America, a major industry trade organization. Contains information on newspaper circulation, public policy, and diversity, as well as links to the organization's *presstime* magazine.

www.ojr.org
The *Online Journalism Review*, published by the Knight Digital Media Center, the best single source for the latest information on Internet journalism.

www.theonion.com
Looks like an authentic online paper but is actually satirical.

www.usatoday.com
Colorful site of the national daily *USA Today*. Note the emphasis on video, photos, and blogging.

CHAPTER 5

Magazines

This chapter will prepare you to:

- discuss the characteristics of magazines

- understand how the magazine industry is divided

- understand the function of Mediamark Research Inc. (MRI)

- appreciate the efforts of magazine publishers to incorporate the Internet into their business model

- understand the current financial difficulties of the magazine industry

- identify the five main magazine content categories

- describe the departments that produce magazines

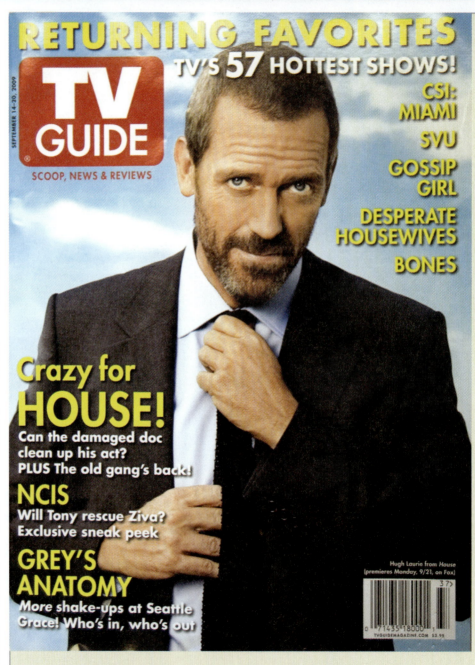

TV Guide tried to redefine itself from a channel-listing guide to a contemporary entertainment magazine. It even offered reviews of YouTube videos.

*T*V Guide debuted in 1953 and grew in popularity with the television medium. It soon became a familiar icon of American culture. By 1980, the magazine was selling nearly 20 million copies per week. In 1988, Rupert Murdoch's News Corporation bought the magazine for about $3 billion. After a series of deals and mergers over the next two decades, in early 2008 the TV Guide Company, consisting of the magazine, an interactive program guide, and several cable and online operations, wound up in the hands of Macrovision Solutions.

Of course, *TV Guide* was no longer the cultural or economic force that it was in past decades. The magazine was hurt by the proliferation of TV channels, which made its listings big and bulky. The on-screen guides used by cable companies were easier to use. The magazine lost readers to new publications that covered entertainment news. By 2008, its circulation had fallen to slightly more than 3 million and the magazine was losing about $20 million per year.

In late 2008, *TV Guide* was sold once again. The price: $1. No, that's not a typo. The whole magazine company was sold for one dollar, that's two dollars less than the cover price of a single copy. And that's not all. Macrovision agreed to loan the buyer $9.5 million at only 3 percent interest. In other words, Macrovision was paying somebody to take the magazine off its hands.

Are things that bad in the magazine business? Luckily no. No other magazines were sold for a buck. But as with the newspaper business discussed in Chapter 4, the Internet and the economic slowdown are having a dramatic effect on the traditional business model of the magazine industry. Although the print version seems secure for now, many publishers are betting that the future lies with more cost-effective online versions and with new distribution models that take advantage of the Internet and mobile media.

This chapter will explore the history, structure, economics, and organization of this industry as it progresses through a transitional period.

A Brief History

▲ The Colonial Period

In colonial times *magazine* meant "warehouse" or "depository," a place where various types of provisions were stored under one roof. The first magazines printed in America were patterned after this model; they were to be storehouses of varied literary materials gathered from books, pamphlets, and newspapers and bound together under one cover.

It was Ben Franklin who first announced plans to start a magazine in the colonies. Unfortunately for him, a competitor named Andrew Bradford got wind of his idea and beat Franklin to the punch. Bradford's *American Magazine* was published a few days before Franklin's *General Magazine* in 1741. The two publications carried political and economic articles aimed at an intelligent audience.

Both Franklin's and Bradford's magazines were ambitious ventures in that they were designed for readers in all 13 colonies and deliberately tried to influence public opinion; both quickly folded because of financial problems. The next significant attempt at magazine publishing occurred in Philadelphia when another Bradford (this one named William) started the *American Magazine and Monthly Chronicle* in 1757. This publication also contained the usual blend of political and economic articles mixed with a little humor; it was well edited and able to support itself for a year.

As America's political relations with England deteriorated, magazines, like newspapers, assumed a significant political role. Thomas Paine, who in his rousing pamphlet *Common Sense* argued for separation from England, became editor of the *Pennsylvania Magazine.* This publication strongly supported the Revolution and was a significant political force during the early days of the war. It became an early casualty of the conflict, however, and closed down in 1776.

All these early magazines were aimed at a specialized audience—one that was educated, literate, and primarily urban. Their overall impact was to encourage literary and artistic expression and to unify the colonies during America's struggle for independence from England.

▲ After the Revolution

Magazines popular during the late 18th and early 19th centuries contained a mix of political and topical articles directed primarily at an educated elite. The birth of the modern newsmagazine can be traced back to this period. *Niles Weekly Register,* which reported current events of the time, was read throughout the country.

Politics was also reflected in other magazines of the period. One of the most influential was the *Port Folio,* edited by the colorful nonconformist Joseph Dennie. Dennie's intended audience was a select one; he wished to reach "Men of Affluence, Men of Liberality, and Men of Letters." Although the major thrust of the paper was political, Dennie interspersed travelogues, theater reviews, satirical essays, and even jokes.

▲ The Penny-Press Era

While the penny press was opening up new markets for newspapers (see Chapter 4), magazine publishers were also expanding their appeal and coverage. The *Knickerbocker, Graham's Magazine,* and the *Saturday Evening Post,* all established between 1820 and 1840, were written not so much for the intelligentsia as for the generally literate middle classes. By 1842 *Graham's,* under the direction of Edgar Allan Poe, had a circulation of 40,000. The growing social and economic importance of women was illustrated by the birth of *Godey's Lady's Book* in 1830 and *Peterson's* in 1842. These two magazines offered articles on fashion, morals, diets, and health, and printed elaborate, hand-colored engravings in their pages. *Godey's,* under the editorship of Sara Hale, was a pioneer for women's rights and was the first magazine to campaign for wider recognition of women writers (see the boxed insert "Sara Josepha Buell Hale").

In 1850 *Harper's Monthly* was started as a magazine that would present material that had already appeared in other sources (rather like the *Reader's Digest,* except

Sara Josepha Buell Hale was responsible for having Thanksgiving declared an annual holiday and was the author of the popular nursery rhyme "Mary Had a Little Lamb." She was also one of the women who left a lasting impression on 19th-century American journalism.

Sara Josepha Buell married David Hale, a New Hampshire lawyer, who encouraged her to write articles and poems for local magazines. By the time she was 38, she had published 17 poems, many magazine articles, two short stories, a literary review, and a novel.

Her literary accomplishments brought her to the attention of Louis Godey, publisher of *Godey's Lady's Book,* who offered her the position of editor. She brought to the magazine an intimate editor-reader relationship that proved so popular that the magazine had a circulation of 150,000 by 1860, a remarkable figure for the time.

Sara Hale not only edited *Godey's Lady's Book* but also wrote about half of every issue. In addition, she found time to champion women's rights and was influential in persuading Matthew Vassar to start the college that still bears his name.

She spent 40 years editing the magazine and finally retired at age 89. Thanks to her efforts, *Godey's Lady's Book* is credited with being the best women's magazine of the period.

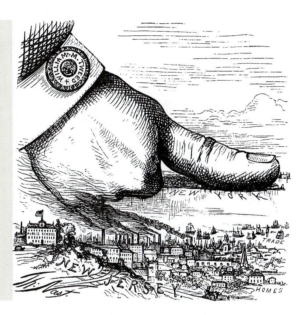

This political cartoon, titled "Under the Thumb," was created by Thomas Nast and appeared in *Harper's Weekly* during the summer of 1871.

that the articles were reprinted in full). *Harper's* also included elaborate woodcut illustrations along with its articles in double-sized issues. *Harper's Weekly* was instituted seven years later and was to become famous for its illustrations of the Civil War. In 1863 this magazine began publishing reproductions of Mathew Brady's war photographs.

The most famous example of the crusading approach of the penny press was the *Harper's Weekly* campaign against the corrupt political administration in New York in 1870. Under the control of William "Boss" Tweed, a group of unscrupulous politicians managed to bilk the city out of approximately $200 million. The editorial cartoons of Thomas Nast were credited with helping to bring down this ring.

▲ The Magazine Boom

In 1860 there were approximately 260 magazines published in the United States; by 1900 there were 1,800. Why the surge? The primary factors were more available money, better printing techniques that lowered prices, and especially the Postal Act of 1879, which gave magazines special mailing rates. It became possible to aim for a national market on a mass scale, and several magazines set out to do just that.

The most successful of the magazines seeking a mass market was *Ladies' Home Journal,* founded by Cyrus Curtis in 1881. The first issue, eight pages long, contained an illustrated short story, an article on growing flowers, fashion notes, child care advice, needlework hints, and recipes. Curtis was the first to recognize the potential for national advertising in the magazine industry.

The general crusading spirit of the press spilled over onto the pages of leading magazines of the late 1800s and early 1900s. Theodore Roosevelt dubbed the magazines that embraced this reform movement **muckrakers.** Corrupt practices in big business was the first issue to activate the muckrakers' zeal. *McClure's* ran an exposé of Standard Oil Company by Ida M. Tarbell. Although it carried the innocuous title "History of the Standard Oil Company," the article was filled with dynamite, for it revealed bribery, fraud, unfair business practices,

Time magazine celebrated its 75th birthday in 1998. Henry Luce, its creator, was only 24 years old when he published this first issue. (The person on the cover is Joseph Cannon, long-time Speaker of the House of Representatives.)

and violence. Shocking stories on political corruption in big cities and another series on crooked practices in the railroad industry followed Tarbell's initial effort. Other magazines joined in. *Cosmopolitan* published "The Treason of the Senate" in 1906 and followed up with attacks on the International Harvester Company. By 1912 the trend toward crusades and exposés had spent itself. Many of the problems uncovered by the muckrakers had been remedied. Most importantly, the public had grown tired of the crusades, and magazines had to search for other ways to attract readers.

▲ Between the Wars

Shifting economic conditions and changing lifestyles in the decades following World War I also influenced magazine development. Three distinct types evolved in the years between World War I and World War II: (1) the digest, (2) the newsmagazine, and (3) the pictorial magazine.

The finest example of the digest genre, *Reader's Digest,* appeared in 1922. Although this magazine reprinted articles that had appeared elsewhere, it first condensed and edited the material so that it could be read by people in a hurry.

The idea of a newsmagazine was not new—examples could be found in the 19th century. *Time,* however, borrowed little from its predecessors. From its beginning in 1923, *Time* based its format on an original concept: the distillation and compartmentalization of news under various departments. Other innovations included the use of the narrative

The beginning of life for *Life:* The magazine's first cover was shot by famous photographer Margaret Bourke-White.

style to report news stories; group journalism produced by the pooling of the efforts of reporters, writers, and editors into anonymous articles; the institution of a large research department; and a brash, punchy, jargonish writing style. The magazine grew slowly, but by 1930 it was turning a substantial profit. Two imitators, *Newsweek* and *U.S. News,* appeared in 1933.

In the mid-1930s two magazines, *Life* and *Look,* revived the tradition of the pictorial weekly originated by *Harper's* and *Leslie's. Life* was launched in 1936 and had almost a quarter-million subscribers before it even had a name. It featured public figures caught in unguarded moments, photo essays, occasional glamour shots, and articles on the arts. In this format *Life* would live for 36 years (it would reappear in the late 1970s in a totally different format). *Look* hit the newsstands in 1937, just a few months behind *Life.*

Hispanics are the largest minority group in the United States, numbering about 40 million. They are also becoming an economic force whose combined buying power will reach $1 trillion in 2010. Naturally, magazine publishers are taking notice of this market, but they are discovering that reaching Hispanic readers is a challenging task.

The number of Hispanic titles grew from 58 in 1996 to about 120 in 2008, but, given the size and growth rate of the Hispanic population, experts point out that the market is still underdeveloped. Similar to English-language publications, advertising revenue has also evaporated, and several magazines have folded, including *Shape en Espanol, Fuego,* and *Christina la Revista* (named after a Hispanic talk-show hostess).

Why haven't Hispanic magazines done better? First, the Hispanic community is made up of groups of smaller communities, such as Mexican, Cuban, Puerto Rican, and South American. It's difficult to find a magazine that will appeal to all groups.

Second, there is the language issue. There are many readers who speak only Spanish and prefer a Spanish-language magazine. Then there are those Hispanics who have lived in the United States for many years and have been educated in U.S. schools. They generally prefer to read in English. Finally, there are those who are bilingual, speaking Spanish at home but English everywhere else. They may prefer to read a magazine in either language. An advertiser who wants to reach a large segment of this market must spend money to construct and place English and Spanish versions of the ad. Many advertisers have decided to avoid this problem altogether and simply advertise on television. Figures from 2007 indicate that Hispanic magazines received only 2 percent of total Hispanic media spending while TV grabbed 64 percent.

Publishers, however, have not given up trying to attract this rapidly growing group of readers. *People en Espanol,* one of the leading Spanish-language publications, does continuous market research into readers' content preferences, demographics, and purchasing behavior. The magazine has also been helped by the growing number of Hispanic celebrities—Shakira, Eva Longoria, America Ferrera—who can be profiled. *Latina,* another successful title, sponsors tours and special events where copies of the magazine are given away.

Hispanic publishers are also paying more attention to magazine-related Web sites. *People en Espanol* embellishes its "100 Most Influential Hispanics" feature with additional content on its Web site. *Latina* recently set up its own social networking site.

Despite these innovations, advertisers are still unenthusiastic about devoting more ad dollars to magazines. Hispanic magazine publishers, just like any other publisher, must demonstrate to advertisers the value of reaching this target market before they can be successful.

Look lacked the current-affairs emphasis of its forerunner and concentrated more on personalities and features. Over the years it evolved into a family-oriented magazine. *Look* expired in 1972.

▲ The Postwar Period

Magazines of the postwar era reflected publishers' firm belief that the one way to become profitable was to specialize. Increased leisure time created a market for sports magazines such as *Field and Stream, Sports Afield, Golf Digest, Popular Boating,* and *Sports Illustrated.* Scientific advances also generated a resurgence of a popularized version of *Scientific American.*

The rapid expansion of urban communities and urban lifestyles gave rise to many specialized publications. Liberalized attitudes toward sex prompted such ventures as *Confidential* (1952) and the trendsetting *Playboy* (1953). During the 1960s the rebirth of an interest in urban culture encouraged the rise of "city" magazines, of which *New York* is probably the best example. For the black press the most significant development in the 1950s was the expansion of black magazines. John Johnson had started *Negro Digest* back in 1942 and used his profits to publish *Ebony,* whose format imitated that of *Life,* in 1945. In the early 1950s he added *Jet,* a weekly newsmagazine, and *Tan.* These were followed later by *Black World* and *Essence.*

▲ Contemporary Magazines

The last few years of the decade have brought difficult times to the magazine industry. The advertising revenue of consumer magazines dropped by about 14 percent from 2007 to 2009. Many print magazines folded—*House and Garden, Jane, PC Magazine, Domino, O at Home,* just to name a few—but most kept an online presence. Revenue projections for the next couple of years are not optimistic.

Teen Magazine Web Sites: What's the Message?

More and more teenage girls are going online, and among their top destinations are the Web sites of teen magazines. Much like their print counterparts, these Web sites contain articles on beauty, fashion, and relationships, but the Web sites offer additional features. They are interactive. Most have chat rooms, bulletin boards, and quizzes with instant feedback. In addition, they are private. Teenage girls looking for information about sexuality, for example, might feel more comfortable looking at this information online rather than reading it in a magazine. Finally, the information on the Internet can remain available indefinitely.

What are the messages that these Web sites are presenting to young women? Feminist theorists suggest that teen magazines may play an important part in teaching young girls about what it means to be feminine. They may emphasize the importance of physical appearance and stress that attracting men is the most important goal for teenage girls. Are teen Web sites doing the same?

This question was the focus of an article by Magdala Labre and Kim Walsh-Childers in the fall 2003 issue of *Mass Communication and Society*. The researchers analyzed the Web sites of *Cosmogirl, Teen People, Seventeen,* and *Teen* and identified the major themes present in the Web sites. One theme was that beauty was a requirement to be successful and to feel good about oneself. The researchers were quick to point out that the beauty presented in these Web sites was not natural beauty but beauty that had to be created. Young girls' body parts were portrayed as problem areas to be fixed. The underlying message seemed to be, "You are not OK as you are." As an illustration the authors pointed to a magazine Web site that offered help for eyebrows; another had an online poll that asked what girls hated most about their hair.

A second theme followed naturally from the first: Beauty is achieved through products. The Web sites offered a wide array of beauty products for those girls who were dissatisfied with the way they looked. Moreover, the sites portrayed the use of these products as the natural and accepted mode of behavior. The *Cosmogirl* site, for example, featured a survey that asked readers to name their favorite beauty products and to say why they love them. Another part of the site asked, "What's in your make-up bag?" The Web site seemed to assume that all its readers had favorite products and that owning a makeup bag was the norm.

A third theme, not unexpectedly, was that the Web sites could help teenage girls find the right products to make them beautiful. The sites took on the role of best friend or big sister, someone who knew about beauty problems and how to solve them. Some of the Web sites had experts, usually identified by just a first name, who offered tips on what to buy. The underlying lesson appeared to be that buying lots of cosmetics is the natural way for a young woman to become beautiful.

The authors conclude that the notion that beauty equals success sends the wrong message. Young women are being taught that they can gain power and happiness by purchasing the right brand of cosmetics, and not through personal achievements. The content of the Web sites also support one of the criticisms frequently voiced by feminist critics: These sites polarize gender roles by promoting the idea that women in society have roles restricted to making their bodies beautiful in order to attract male attention. Finally, the researchers point out that these sites capitalize on teenage girls' insecurities about their bodies to stimulate consumption. By defining beauty as physical perfection and urging the purchase of products to achieve that perfection, these sites (as well as their print counterparts) are creating unrealistic expectations in their young readers. Many young women may spend a good deal of time and money pursuing an ideal that can never be achieved.

Why were magazines struggling? First, they faced marketing problems. Supermarkets and big discount stores, such as Wal-Mart, were becoming more selective about the number of magazines they would display on their shelves. Sweepstakes competitions, such as the one sponsored by Publisher's Clearinghouse, have nearly disappeared because of legal problems, and the national do-not-call list has made it more difficult to recruit subscribers over the phone.

Second, cable TV and the Internet have encroached upon magazines' biggest selling point—attracting a specialized audience. Targeted cable channels, such as the Food Network and Oxygen, offer advertisers an alternative and sometimes more efficient way to reach their audiences. The Internet offers even more precise targeting. Doityourself. com., for example, is a natural place for Lowe's and Home Depot to advertise.

Publishers have been trying several strategies to improve their fortunes. They are strengthening their Web presence in an attempt to offset print advertising shortfalls. Other

Magazines are making use of social media. *Seventeen*'s Facebook page has more than 95,000 fans.

companies are branching out into ancillary activities, such as sponsoring conferences and trade shows. All are becoming more cost-conscious.

Finally, the weak economy meant that there were fewer advertising dollars to be had. The advertising categories that declined the most were those in the automotive, home furnishing, and financial sectors. Automobile ads, for example, dropped a disquieting 20 percent from 2007 to 2008.

There were some individual bright spots as some magazines bucked the trend. *Women's Health* increased its revenue by 60 percent. Parenting magazine *Cookie* and business publication *Fast Company* also scored impressive gains. New magazines continued to arrive on the scene. There were 191 start-ups in 2008, down 18 percent from 2007 but still an impressive number in a struggling economy.

The trend in magazine publishing for the last few decades has been to find a hot topic and quickly launch a magazine to take advantage of it. If the topic cools, then the magazines devoted to it are in trouble. For example, the booming real estate market during the middle of the decade prompted a host of home styling and decorating magazines. When the real estate market crashed, it took with it many of these publications (*Domino, Home, Country Home*, to name a few).

Finally, the magazine industry continues to be dominated by a few big companies that publish best-selling magazines. Table 5-2 contains a list of the leading companies as of 2008 (see page 124).

Magazines in the Digital Age

Magazines are still learning how best to use the Internet. In the early days of the Web, many magazines simply took articles from the print edition and posted them online. The main purpose of the online edition was to encourage people to subscribe to the print edition. Today, however, magazine Web sites have become more sophisticated and are treated as equal to their print counterparts. Many online magazines now have their own original content.

For readers a digital version of a magazine has obvious advantages. First, it may be available days before the print version arrives. Second, readers can easily e-mail articles to friends, order products advertised on the Web site, and search back issues. For the publisher the biggest advantage is cost. Producing and distributing an online edition is far cheaper than putting out a print edition.

Airbrushing is a general term that refers to touching up a photograph to remove imperfections or to enhance the image. Digital photography has made it extraordinarily easy to retouch photos. In fact, if you buy a digital camera and related software, it's likely that the software contains retouching tools that eliminate red-eye or make an image thinner or thicker.

An ethical issue arises when, without disclosing the alterations to the viewer, airbrushing is used to create images that are too ideal or too much of an improvement on reality. Magazines have been the source of several controversial examples. *GQ* admitted that a photo of Kate Winslet was airbrushed before appearing on its February 2003 cover. *Men's Fitness* thickened the biceps on a photo of tennis star Andy Roddick to promote a story about building stronger arms. *Glamour* was accused of slimming *Ugly Betty* star America Ferrera on its cover (the magazine denies any airbrushing was done). Perhaps the most famous example was *Redbook's* retouching of the cover photo of singer Faith Hill on its July 2007 cover. A Web site got hold of the original unretouched photo and ran it along with the airbrushed version. The differences were striking.

The ethical issue involved here is one of deception. Do readers have a right to know when photos have been digitally altered? The fashion magazine industry would argue that there's nothing wrong with airbrushing. After the Faith Hill controversy, a spokesperson for *Redbook* asserted that the retouching it did on her photo was "completely in line with industry standards." This admission suggests that deception is the industry standard and everybody does it. Of course, the fact that everybody does it does not make it right.

Another defense is that fashion photography should never be expected to tell the truth. Fashion is part fantasy and part art. Or as one fashion magazine executive put it, "They're not really photographs. They're images."

Others ask, What's the big deal? So cover girls (and guys) aren't as perfect as they are pictured. Where's the harm? Well, the harm may be to young girls' self-images. Several studies have found that women feel worse about their own body image after looking at fashion magazines. Further, these images might create unreal expectations. One survey found that almost half of third-grade girls wanted to be thinner, a wish brought on perhaps by hundreds of exposures to airbrushed models.

For its part, the American Society of Media Photographers makes its position clear. From its Code of Ethics: "Disclose any alteration and manipulation of content or meaning in editorial feature or illustrative photographs and require the publisher to disclose that distortion or any further alteration."

The home page of zinio.com, where you can subscribe to your favorite magazine in digital form.

▲ Transition

As of 2008, more than 6,000 consumer magazines had companion Web sites, up about 50 percent since 2004. The magazine industry is still trying to find the right balance between the online and the print version. As of 2009, it still appears that the print version is dominant. To illustrate, the Magazine Publishers Association publishes a comprehensive handbook for potential advertisers. Of the 70 or so pages in the handbook, only two pages were specifically devoted to magazine Web sites.

In 2007, the Web sites of *all* consumer magazines attracted about 68 million unique visitors per month. This may sound like a big number, but consider that just the top 10 newspaper sites attract the same number of unique visitors. Moreover, when compared to newspapers, magazine Web sites are less likely to have blogs, video, and reader comments—the popular interactive tools of Web 2.0.

The print version continues to bring in the bulk of the money. A 2007 survey found that the median digital share of revenue was 10 percent, about the same as the newspaper industry. In short, out of every 10 dollars a magazine takes in, 9 dollars come from the print version.

It appears that for the foreseeable future, despite the fact that many print magazines have gone out of business or gone Web-only, most magazine publishers think the print version will continue to be foremost in their operations. Time will tell if this philosophy changes.

▲ Replica Editions

The print version of many magazines is available digitally in replica form. A replica edition tries to duplicate the paper magazine reading experience as closely as possible. Unlike an online edition, where a reader can choose from a menu of stories and other features created expressly for the Web, a digital replica contains all the stories, graphics, fancy layouts, headlines, ads, and page numbers—and even those annoying little subscription cards—that the reader would find in the print edition. The replica version is displayed one page at a time, and the pages are side by side, just as in the print version.

Several companies offer electronic delivery of replica editions to subscribers. The biggest is Zinio Systems with about 750 titles available, including *Popular Science, TV Guide,* and *PC World.* Zinio's biggest competitor is Texterity, whose offerings include *Smart Money, Vibe,* and *Spin.*

▲ Mobile Magazines

Magazines, like newspapers, are making their publications available across a variety of mobile platforms. Consumers can now read magazines on their laptops and cell phones, as well as download video and audio podcasts. In the market for a car? *Car and Driver* publishes a version designed for cell phones that lets consumers check reviews, get the latest auto news, and even research prices, all while they are in the auto showroom. In 2007 publishing giant Hearst announced that *Seventeen* and *Cosmo Girl* were going mobile with sites where consumers could find fashion tips and dating advice and download ring tones. Zinio has an iPhone application that lets users examine about 20 magazines.

So far, the biggest use of these mobile publications is to promote the print edition of the magazine. Publishers know that most consumers will probably not read a whole issue on their cell phones. The mobile version gives them a chance to sample the content; if interested, they may subscribe to the print or digital edition.

Magazine publishers are also experimenting with making their content available on e-book readers such as Amazon's Kindle. In 2009 it was reported that big magazine publisher Hearst Corporation was working to develop a large-screen, wireless e-reader that would be tailored to magazines.

▲ User-Generated Content

Publishers are cautiously experimenting with user production of content. Part of their caution stems from their desire to maintain editorial control over the content on their Web site, and ensure that offensive or distasteful content does not appear. A second concern is the lack of a clear way to turn this content into a revenue generator. Nonetheless, some publishers have come up with ways to use reader-generated content to build their audience base and, if all goes according to plan, enhance their advertising revenue.

In the past few years some established magazines have given issues over to their readers. The June 2008 edition of *Budget Travel* consisted of articles submitted by readers. An issue of Time Inc.'s publication *This Old House* was retitled *Your Old House* and given over to user-generated content. Even the generally conservative *Business Week* let readers supply a good deal of an issue. None of these efforts rival *JPG,* a photography magazine that depends upon reader-generated content for every issue.

▲ Social Media

The magazine industry is exploring ways to use social media. Several magazine Web sites have incorporated Twitter, Facebook, and LinkedIn applications to help attract readers. With Twitter, for example, a magazine can set up an account for the publication itself along with accounts for various editors and writers. Many magazines, such as *Elle* and *Seventeen,* have their own Facebook pages. *Cooking Light* and *Prevention,* among others, have established reader communities. Expect to see more growth in this area as publishers discover the benefits of social networking.

Defining Features of Magazines

The first defining feature of magazines is that, of all the media discussed in this book, they attract the most specialized audiences. There are publications designed to reach specific demographic groups (*AARP Magazine, Maxim*), specific occupational groups (*Pointe*, the magazine for ballerinas, or *Builder*), specific interest groups (*Cigar Aficionado, American History*), specific political groups (*National Review, Mother Jones*), specific geographic groups (*Southern Living, Arizona Highways*), and a host of other very specific groups (*Latin CEO*).

The second defining feature is magazines' relationship with social, demographic, economic, and social trends. Of all the media, magazines are most in tune with such trends. As consumer and business needs change, some new magazines emerge, some old magazines cease publication, and others fine-tune their content. To illustrate, the Hispanic population in the United States rose more than 10 percent from 2000 to 2004, about four times the increase of the overall U.S. population. Magazine publishers were quick to offer publications aimed at this growing segment of U.S. society. *People en Espanol, Reader's Digest's Selecciones, Shape en Espanol,* and *Healthy Kids en Espanol* were just some of the titles launched in the past few years. To take another example, a poker craze swept the United States in 2004–2005. Magazine publishers were quick to respond with titles such as *All In* and *Bluff*. (Keep in mind that trendiness is a two-edge sword. Should the poker craze fade, so will the magazines.)

The third feature is that, as we have seen, magazines can *influence* social trends. Magazines helped fuel the American Revolution. The muckrakers at the turn of the 20th century prompted social reform. In the 1950s *Playboy* launched the sexual revolution in the United States. In the 1970s *Ms.* helped usher in the women's movement.

Will the digital magazine spell the end of the traditional print edition? As the preceding discussion suggests, probably not. Despite the advances in mobile technology, the print magazine is still the most convenient form to take with you. You can roll it up, or fold it, and it doesn't depend upon a wireless or a WiFi connection. Second, as noted in Chapter 1, audience segmentation is becoming more and more pronounced. Magazines were the first medium to adapt to this changing condition, and they remain well situated for the future.

This is not to say that there won't be changes. Magazines that aim for a large, undifferentiated audience, such as *TV Guide* and *Reader's Digest,* will have a harder time staying profitable. Some magazines will shift entirely to the Web. Finally, the magazine industry may find a totally different business model. One suggestion is the digital newsstand, sort of an iTunes for magazines, where readers can pick and choose the articles they want from one or more magazines and download them to their computers, phones, or PDAs. One thing is clear: The next few years will be challenging ones for magazine publishers.

A glance at any newsstand will illustrate that consumer magazines fall into major general-interest categories such as sports, health, computers, business, and women's interests.

Organization of the Magazine Industry

One of the problems in discussing the magazine industry is deciding what exactly is a magazine. The dictionary defines *magazine* as a "periodical publication, usually with a paper cover, containing miscellaneous articles and often with illustrations or photographs." This definition is broad enough to include *Reader's Digest,* with a circulation of more than 8 million; *Water Scooter,* a magazine for boating enthusiasts; *Sky,* given away to airline passengers by Delta Airlines; *Successful Farmer,* the magazine of farm management; *Go,* distributed to Goodyear tire dealers; *The Journal of Social Psychology;* and the *Bird Watcher's Digest.* There are around 19,000 magazines published in the United States. Both the number and the diversity of these publications are staggering. For example, *Burrelle's Media Directory,* a directory of advertising rates and other pertinent information about magazines, lists 116 automotive magazines, 68 horse-oriented publications, and 7 periodicals devoted to snowmobiling. There are more than 6,000 magazines sold regularly on newsstands, and the number of new consumer titles continues to rise. Obviously, classifying the magazine industry into coherent categories is a vexing problem. For our purposes we will employ two organizational schemes. The first classifies print and online magazines into six main content categories: (1) general consumer magazines, (2) business publications, (3) custom magazines, (4) literary reviews and academic journals, (5) newsletters, and (6) public relations magazines. The second scheme divides the magazine industry into the three traditional, functional components of manufacturing: production, distribution, and retailing.

▲ Content Categories

General Consumer Magazines A consumer magazine is one that can be acquired by anyone, through a subscription or a single-copy purchase or as a free copy. These magazines are generally shelved at the corner newsstand or local bookstore. (Other types of magazines are usually not available to the general public.) These publications are called *consumer magazines* because readers can buy the products and services that are advertised in their pages. One noticeable trend in the content of consumer magazines is, as mentioned, the movement away from broad, general-appeal to more specialized publications. Some of the better-known consumer magazines are *People, Time, Reader's Digest, TV Guide, Sports Illustrated,* and *Woman's Day* (see Table 5-1). Note that consumer magazines can

TABLE 5-1

Top 10 Consumer Magazines, 2008, by Circulation

Title	Circulation (millions)	Percent Change from 2007
AARP Magazine	24.1	−0.3
Reader's Digest	8.3	−14
Better Homes and Gardens	7.6	−0.3
National Geographic	5.0	0.2
Good Housekeeping	4.7	−0.2
Family Circle	3.9	−1.5
Woman's Day	3.9	−0.7
Ladies' Home Journal	3.8	−1.9
People	3.7	1.9
Time	3.3	−17

Note: With a few exceptions, magazine circulation has been declining.

exist in both print and online versions and that some magazines exist only online without a print counterpart. Salon.com, for example, covers politics and culture while Slate.com, owned by the Washington Post Company, usually focuses on current affairs. A more recent entry is The Daily Beast, published by former *Vanity Fair* editor Tina Brown.

Business Publications   Business magazines (also called *trade publications*) serve a particular business, industry, or profession. They are not sold on newsstands, and their readership is limited to those in the profession or business. The products advertised in these publications are generally those that would be purchased by business organizations or professionals rather than by the general public. *Business Publications Rates and Data* lists approximately 4,000 titles of business magazines. Most of these magazines are published by independent publishing companies that are not connected with the fields they serve. For example, McGraw-Hill and Penton are two private publishing companies that publish business magazines in a variety of areas. Other business publications are put out by professional organizations, which publish them as a service to their members. The degree of specialization of these magazines is seen in the medical field, which has approximately 375 publications serving various medical specializations. Some business publications are called *vertical* because they cover all aspects of one field. For example, *Pulp and Paper* reports on all segments of the paper mill industry. Other publications are called *horizontal* because they deal with a certain business function, no matter in what industry it exists. *Selling,* for example, would be targeted at salespeople in all industries. Leading business magazines include *Computerworld, Oil and Gas Journal,* and *Medical Economics.* Business publishers are also active in supplying databases and computer bulletin board systems to their clients. Like consumer magazines, business publications can exist in print and online.

Custom Magazines   Custom magazines are published by corporations that try to keep existing customers satisfied while attracting new clients. Some are distributed for free at various business locations; others can be purchased at newsstands. Lexus, for example, publishes a magazine that promotes its automobiles, while Hilton publishes *Grand Times,* enticing people to vacation at its resorts.

Custom magazines have been around for a while. Airlines have published them for decades, but in the last few years custom magazines have become more visible primarily because businesses have discovered that they are an effective marketing tool.

Custom magazines present at least two problems for the traditional magazine industry. First, they siphon off advertising dollars from more conventional magazines. If Lexus can target its potential customers with its magazine, it might reduce its advertising buys in *Time, Newsweek,* or other consumer publications. Second, a custom magazine editorial staff may have less independence than a traditional magazine. It would be highly unlikely that a story in Hilton's *Grand Times* would say something negative about the company. Be that as it may, custom magazines likely will be a more important factor in the years to come.

Literary Reviews and Academic Journals   Hundreds of literary reviews and academic journals, generally with circulations under 10,000, are published by nonprofit organizations and funded by universities, foundations, or professional organizations. They may publish four or fewer issues per year, and a large number do not accept advertising. These publications cover the entire range of literary and academic interests, and they include such journals as the *Kenyon Review, Theater Design and Technology, European Urology, Journalism and Mass Communication Quarterly, Poultry and Egg Marketing,* and the *Journal of Japanese Botany.* Some literary reviews and journals have online versions.

Newsletters   When some people hear the word *newsletter,* they think of a club, PTA, or church bulletin filled with helpful hints. Although these newsletters are important to their readers, we are talking about newsletters typically four to eight pages long and usually created by desktop publishing. They are sold by subscription, and in recent years they have become big business. In fact, there is even a *Newsletter on Newsletters,* published for those who edit newsletters. The coverage area of a newsletter may be broad or narrow. It might deal with one particular business or government agency, or it might report on a business function that crosses industry lines. The *Federal Budget Report,* for example, reports on just the president's budget and appropriations. On the other hand, the *Spear Report* covers financial developments that have an impact on many industries.

Newsletters are extremely specialized, with small circulations (typically under 10,000) but high subscription prices. Typical fees are about $200–300 a year, but fees of $600–800 are not unheard of, and some daily newsletters cost as much as $4,000 annually. Some influential newsletters are *Aerospace Daily & Defense Report, Oil Spill Intelligence Report,* and *Drug Enforcement Report.* Most newsletters are available online, and some can be delivered to PDAs and other mobile devices.

Public Relations Magazines   These are magazines published by a sponsoring company and intended specifically for one of its publics. An internal public relations (PR) magazine is aimed at employees, salespeople, and dealers. An external PR magazine is directed to stockholders, potential customers, and technical service providers.

These publications typically carry little advertising, apart from promotional items for the sponsoring organization. These publications also have their own professional organization, the International Association of Business Communicators. Most PR magazines exist only in print, but some have online counterparts.

▲ Functional Categories

A second useful way of structuring the print magazine industry is to divide it by function into the production, distribution, and retail segments.

Walk by the men's section of any newsstand in the United States, and you can see the influence that Felix Dennis has had on magazine publishing. You will see titles such as *Maxim, Stuff, FHM,* and *King* with scantily clad women on the covers and articles with titles such as "Get in Bed with Anna Kournikova," "The Girls of Reality TV," "The Ugliest Brawls in Sports History," and "The Best of E-Mail Pranks."

Before Felix Dennis, men's magazines in the United States were generally of two types: (1) general-interest magazines such as *Esquire* and *GQ,* and (2) magazines devoted to a single subject: cars, sports, health, nude women, and so on. The prevailing publishing wisdom was that men would not read a magazine that offered self-help advice. *Men's Health* redefined the category in 1986 when it offered service articles akin to those found in women's magazines, but it was Dennis who totally revamped the category by taking the "lad magazine" concept from Great Britain and introducing it in the United States.

At the risk of oversimplifying, the lad magazine's formula consists of sex, sports, beer, gadgets, clothes, and fitness. The unashamedly heterosexual *Maxim,* for example, seems based on the philosophy that the adult American male is simply an overgrown adolescent. A typical issue contains ample doses of sexy models, frat-boy humor, and "man-to-man" advice articles. Unlike *Esquire* and *GQ,* says Dennis, *Maxim* is for the man who likes sex better than he likes socks.

Dennis has been quoted as saying that his one talent is that he knows what people want minutes before they know it themselves, and his past history bears him out. Dennis got into the publishing business in the 1960s when he published an underground magazine in Great Britain. In the 1970s he published magazines based on current fads, such as kung-fu movies, and collectible items from films such as *Star Wars* and *E.T.* In 1985 he published *MacUser* just before Macintosh personal computers became popular. Dennis eventually sold the U.S. edition of the magazine for $25 million, which he used to finance the start of other computer magazines that proved successful, including *Computer Buyer* and *Computer Shopper.* By the mid-1990s Dennis was the fourth largest publisher in the United Kingdom.

In 1995 Dennis launched the British edition of *Maxim.* Once again, he was able to detect a popular trend. *Maxim* became profitable two years after its launch, about twice as fast as most successful magazines. Flushed with success, he launched *Maxim* in the U.S. market. The magazine quickly developed a readership. By 2002 its circulation hovered around the 2.5 million mark, making it the best-selling men's magazine. The magazine has also spun off a line of furniture and hair grooming products.

In the magazine business, however, nothing is certain, and the general decline in circulation has hit the men's category as well. By 2006 *Maxim's* circulation was down to about 2 million, and Dennis was considering selling the magazine.

If he sells, he will have plenty of other things to keep him busy. He publishes a political magazine and is a fan of high-end automobiles. He is also the author of a critically acclaimed book of poetry—not the sort of thing you'd expect from a publisher of a lad's magazine.

The Production Function   The production phase of the industry, which consists of approximately 2,000–3,000 publishers, encompasses all the elements necessary to put out a magazine—copy, artwork, photos, titles, layout, printing, and binding. A subsequent section will describe in more detail how a magazine is produced.

The Distribution Function   The distribution phase of the industry handles the job of getting the magazine to the reader. This is not a simple job. In fact, the circulation department at a large magazine may be the most complex in the whole company. As with newspapers, circulation of magazines means the total number of copies that are delivered through subscriptions or bought at the newsstand. There are two main types of circulation. In **paid circulation,** readers pay to receive the magazine, either through a subscription or at the newsstand. Paid circulation has two main advantages: (1) Periodicals that use paid circulation qualify for lower, second-class postal rates; and (2) paid circulation provides a revenue source to the publisher in addition to advertising. On the negative side, paid-circulation magazines must undertake expensive promotional campaigns to increase subscriptions or to sell single copies. Paid-circulation magazines have the added expense of collecting subscription payments and keeping records. Most consumer magazines use paid circulation.

The alternative to paid circulation is **controlled circulation.** Controlled-circulation magazines set specific qualifications for those who are to receive the magazine. Magazines that are provided to airline passengers or hotel/motel guests are examples. Controlled circulation has two main advantages: (1) Publications using it can reach all the personnel in a given field, and (2) these publications avoid the costs of promoting subscriptions.

The tremendous diversity of the magazine industry is illustrated by this magazine display in a bookstore. Magazine publishers compete vigorously for prime space (front row, eye level) in such a display.

On the negative side, controlled-circulation magazines gain no revenue from subscriptions and single-copy sales. Further, postage for these publications costs more. Controlled circulation has generally been used by business custom magazines and public relations magazines.

No matter what method is chosen, the circulation of a magazine is an important number. The larger the circulation, the more the magazine can charge for its advertising space.

For a paid-circulation magazine, distributing copies to subscribers is a relatively simple affair. The complicated (and expensive) part of this process is getting subscribers. There are no fewer than 14 methods used by magazines to build subscription lists. They include employing cash-field agencies, which have salespeople make house-to-house calls to sell subscriptions directly to consumers; employing direct-mail agencies; mounting direct-mail campaigns sponsored by the publisher; and, finally, using what are called *blow-in cards*, those annoying little cards that fall out of a magazine as soon as you open it.

Single-copy distribution to newsstands and other retailers is a multistep process. The publisher deals with only one party, the national distributor. The national distributor handles from a dozen to 50 or more titles. At least once every month, representatives of the magazine sit down with the national distributor and determine the number of magazines to be distributed for an upcoming issue. The national distributor then delivers the magazines to wholesalers who sell magazines and paperback books within specified areas. In any given month a wholesaler might receive 500–1,000 magazines to distribute to dealers.

The particulars of online magazine distribution, of course, are much different. Online magazines and newsletters can be distributed by e-mail or sent to cell phones, with "copies" going only to those who request them, or they can exist on a Web site, where they wait for readers. Whatever the arrangement, online magazines have no need for national distributors or wholesalers.

The late John Johnson was the founder and publisher of *Ebony* and *Jet* magazines.

The Retail Function   The retailer is the last segment of the industry. The best available figures indicate that there are approximately 140,000 retail outlets in the United States. Wal-Mart is the single biggest retailer, accounting for 20 percent of all magazines sales in 2008. Supermarkets accounted for about 40 percent. Supermarket sales have become so important that publishers pay the stores a premium of about $25 per checkout rack to have their titles prominently displayed. When a dealer receives a magazine, he or she agrees to keep the magazine on the display racks for a predetermined length of time (usually a week or a month). At the end of this period, unsold copies are returned to the wholesaler for credit.

Magazine Ownership

Recent mergers and acquisitions have resulted in a magazine industry dominated by large corporations. Many of the conglomerates (Time Warner, Hearst) have extensive holdings in other media. Table 5-2 contains a ranking of the top consumer magazine publishers by 2008 revenue and lists their well-known titles.

Rank	Company	Revenue (billions)	Top Magazines
1	Advance Publications	$3.6	*Parade, Vogue*
2	Time Warner	3.3	*People, Time*
3	Hearst Corp.	2.3	*Cosmopolitan, Good Housekeeping*
4	Meredith Corp.	.81	*Ladies' Home Journal, Better Homes and Gardens*
5	Reader's Digest Assn.	.76	*Reader's Digest*

Producing the Magazine

▲ Departments and Staff

The publisher is the chief executive officer at a magazine. He or she is responsible for budgeting, maintaining a healthy advertising position, keeping circulation high, and making sure the magazine moves in a consistent editorial direction. The publisher oversees four main departments:

1. *Circulation:* This department is responsible for keeping current readers satisfied and attracting new readers.
2. *Advertising and Sales:* As the name suggests, this department is responsible for selling space in the magazine to advertisers.
3. *Production:* This department oversees the actual printing and binding of the magazine.
4. *Editorial:* The head of this department supervises the editorial staff, plans topics for upcoming issues, and helps out with various public relations activities. The managing editor handles the day-to-day operation of the magazine, such as making sure articles are in on time, choosing artwork, and changing layouts.

Some magazines might have an additional department to handle their online operations, but declining revenues have compelled many publications to converge the online and print operations.

▲ The Production Process

Everything moves in cycles. Early magazine publishers were printers as well as writers, but during the 19th century the production function was divorced from the editorial function. Many magazines have now gone full circle: Computers enable writers and editors to set their words into type and make up pages, reuniting the production and editorial functions.

The first step in all print magazine production is preliminary planning and idea generation for upcoming issues. Once the overall ideas are set, the next step is to convert the ideas into concrete subjects for articles. At this point preliminary decisions concerning article length, photos, and accompanying artwork are made. Then the managing editor assigns certain articles to staff writers or freelancers.

The next step involves putting together a miniature **dummy,** a plan or blueprint of the pages for the upcoming issue that shows the contents in their proper order. This phase can now be done electronically, thanks to computer programs that allow editors to view 32 pages at a time.

At about this same time, schedules are drawn up to ensure that an article will get to the printer in time to be included in the forthcoming issue. A copy deadline is set—this is the day the writer must hand in the story to the editor. Time is set aside for editing, checking, and verifying all copy. A timetable is also set up for illustrations and artwork.

Articles are written and edited at the computer. Once they are in acceptable form, a computerized typesetter sets the copy in body and display-size type, and the articles are sent to the press or posted on the magazine's Web site.

The production process is different for the online version. One of the advantages of the Web version of a story is that it can contain more information than the print story. As a result, the transcript of lengthy interviews, background facts, and time lines may be incorporated into a Web story. Deadlines for weekly or monthly publications don't make sense for an online publication. Articles are frequently updated when new angles or new information appears. In addition to writers and editors, others also contribute to the process. A Web producer may incorporate audio and video into an online story. A graphics expert may look for the best screen layout for the story. Another editor may look for ways to include social media in the story. In short, publishing an online version requires additional skills and creates different challenges.

Economics

There are four basic sources of magazine revenue: (1) subscriptions, (2) single-copy sales, (3) advertising, and (4) ancillary services such as e-commerce, custom publishing, and database assistance. This section will concentrate on the first three of these.

The magazine industry was facing lean times as the decade came to an end. Advertising revenue dropped about 12 percent from 2007 to 2009. In addition, there were troubling signs on the horizon. Thanks to deeply discounted subscriptions, single-copy sales of magazines continued to fall, down about 11 percent from 2007 to 2008. Moreover, magazine circulation has declined about 3 percent from 2000. A glance at Table 5-1 shows that, of the top 10 consumer magazines, only 2 increased circulation from 2007 to 2008. Things were so bad that the publisher of the venerable *Reader's Digest* filed for bankruptcy in August 2009.

Another significant trend is the growing importance of advertising in the revenue mix. In 1995, advertising accounted for about 56 percent of all revenue with subscription income and newsstand sales making up the rest. In 2008, among the top consumer magazines, advertising accounted for about 75 percent. As is obvious, any slowdown in advertising, as happened in the latter part of the decade, will spell trouble for magazines. Magazines are increasingly turning to their online editions to help improve their bottom lines, but so far, as we have seen, the results have not been encouraging, with online revenue accounting for only about 10 percent of the typical magazine's income.

The relative importance of subscription impact, single-copy sales, and advertising varies tremendously from magazine to magazine. *Reader's Digest* gets almost all of its

TABLE 5-3

Breakdown of a
Consumer Magazine's
Dollar

Expense	Amount
Advertising expenses	$0.08
Circulation costs	0.31
Editorial costs	0.10
Manufacturing and distribution	0.40
Other costs	0.01
Administration	0.10

money from subscriptions and advertising. On the other hand, *Cosmopolitan* gets only a small proportion from subscriptions and relies mainly on advertising and newsstand sales. To gain some perspective on advertising, in 2008 it cost about $225,000 for a full page in *Ladies' Home Journal*. A full-page ad in *Forbes* cost about $100,000, but you could buy an ad on Forbes.com for about $200.

Yet another economic problem for the industry was a shift in the marketing environment. Big retailers such as Wal-Mart and supermarkets want to display only those titles that are best-sellers; cluttering up their shelves with unsold copies hurts their bottom line. As a result it was becoming more difficult for new magazines to find shelf space.

From the perspective of the consumer, it makes sense to subscribe to a magazine rather than to purchase it regularly at the newsstand. From 1996 to 2008, average annual subscription rates actually dropped from about $30 to $27. On the other hand, average cover prices during that same period shot up from $1.71 to about $4.50.

Where does the money go? The typical dollar breaks down approximately as shown in Table 5-3. Two items included in the manufacturing and distribution category of Table 5-3 have increased at the fastest rate: paper and postage.

Feedback for Magazines

The print magazine industry, like the newspaper industry, depends on the Audit Bureau of Circulations (ABC) for information about who is reading the publication. The ABC audits most consumer magazines and issues a "pink sheet"—so called because its report is printed on pink paper—every June and December. The ABC statement reports the magazine's average paid circulation and its **rate base.** The rate base is the number of buyers guaranteed by the magazine and is also the number that the magazine uses to compute its advertising rates. Other information in the report includes circulation for each issue in the past six months, state-by-state circulation data, and a report on five-year trends.

Another company, Business Publication Audit (BPA), specializes in business and trade magazines. It issues reports similar to those of the ABC, with additional information concerning the occupations of readers who receive controlled-circulation publications.

Although it is helpful to know the total circulation figure for a magazine, that number does not tell the whole story. Circulation measures the **primary audience,** those people who subscribe to the magazine or buy it at the newsstand. In addition, there is the **pass-along audience,** those people who pick up a copy at the doctor's office, at work, on the road, and the like. **Mediamark Research Inc. (MRI)** provides data on the total audience for magazines. This company selects a large sample of the magazine-reading public and conducts personal interviews with individuals to get an exposure score for each magazine. The reports issued by MRI are extremely detailed and encompass many volumes. They contain such specific information as the percentage of a particular magazine's readers who make more than $50,000 per year and detailed product use data, such as how many readers used a headache remedy in the past month. A small portion of an MRI report is reproduced in Figure 5-1.

BASE: FEMALE HOMEMAKERS	% TOTAL U.S. *000	% A *000	B % DOWN	C % ACROSS	D INDEX	A *000	B % DOWN	C % ACROSS	D INDEX	A *000	B DOWN	C ACROSS	D INDEX
			ALL			HEAVY & MEDIUM 3 OR MORE				LIGHT LESS THAN 3			
ALL FEMALE HOMEMAKERS	85323	6628	100.0	7.8	100	4397	100.0	5.2	100	2231	100.0	2.6	100
MONEY	2719	*310	4.7	11.4	147	*214	4.9	7.9	153	*95	4.3	3.5	134
MOTOR TREND	499	*18	.3	3.6	46	*2	-	.4	8	*16	.7	3.2	123
MUSCLE & FITNESS	1109	*99	1.5	8.9	115	*86	2.0	7.8	150	*13	.6	1.2	45
NATIONAL ENQUIRER	11898	1134	17.1	9.5	123	770	17.5	6.5	126	*364	16.3	3.1	117
NATIONAL GEOGRAPHIC	12588	692	10.4	5.5	71	*416	9.5	3.3	64	*276	12.4	2.2	84
NATIONAL GEOGRAPHIC TRAVELER	889	*19	.3	2.1	28	*7	.2	.8	15	*13	.6	1.5	56
NATIONAL LAMPOON	*313	*21	.3	-	-	*21	.5	-	-	-	-	-	-
NATURAL HISTORY	662	*76	1.1	11.5	148	*6	.1	.9	18	*70	3.1	10.6	404
NEWSWEEK	8286	637	9.6	7.7	99	*447	10.2	5.4	105	*190	8.5	2.3	88
NEW WOMAN	3214	*206	3.1	6.4	83	*129	2.9	4.0	78	*77	3.5	2.4	92
NEW YORK MAGAZINE	728	*117	1.8	16.1	207	*87	2.0	12.0	232	*30	1.3	4.1	158
NEW YORK TIMES (DAILY)	1355	*67	1.0	4.9	64	*31	.7	2.3	44	*36	1.6	2.7	102
NEW YORK TIMES MAGAZINE	2087	*159	2.4	7.6	98	*116	2.6	5.6	108		1.9	2.1	79
THE NEW YORKER	1189	*81	1.2	6.8	88	*51	1.2	4.3	83	*43	1.3	2.5	96
OMNI	975	*102	1.5	10.5	135	*47	1.1	4.8	94	*30	2.5	5.6	216
1,001 HOME IDEAS	3610	*315	4.8	8.7	112	*290	6.6	8.0	156	*55	1.1	.7	26
ORGANIC GARDENING	1904	*35	.5	1.8	24	*28	.6	1.5	29	*25	.3	.3	12
OUTDOOR LIFE	1864	*121	1.8	6.5	84	*107	2.4	5.7	111	*6 *15	.7	.8	31

Several companies including the ABC and Nielsen/NetRatings supply feedback about online readership. These reports usually tabulate the "unique visitors" to a Web site in some period of time, usually a month. The number of unique visitors to a magazine Web site may be much larger than its print circulation. *Sports Illustrated,* for example, has a print circulation of about 3 million; in contrast, si.com often receives more than 7 million visitors in a month. *Business Week* has a print circulation just under a million, but businessweek .com typically sees about 9 million visitors a month.

▲ Magazine Audiences

Although data on the audience of a particular magazine are readily available, information about the total audience for magazines is hard to come by, primarily because of the difficulty in defining what qualifies as a magazine. Nonetheless, some figures are available. In 2008, as reported to the ABC, total circulation of the top 589 magazines exceeded 368 million copies. Of these, about 11 percent were bought at the newsstand, while the remaining 89 percent were delivered as part of a subscription.

Almost everybody does some type of print or online magazine reading. In an average month, 85 percent of U.S. adults read at least one copy of a magazine. Most read more. One study reported that adults read or look through an average of 10 magazines per month. About 28 percent read a magazine on an average day, and the typical adult spends about 25 minutes daily reading magazines. As far as demographics are concerned, the typical magazine reader is more educated and usually more affluent than the nonreader. Magazine readers also tend to be joiners. One survey found them far more likely to belong to religious, scientific, and professional organizations than nonreaders.

You can access the Media World clips, with all new NBC videos, on the Online Learning Center home page. Go to www.mhhe.com/dominick11e, select Student Center and then Chapter 5. The first part provides a look at the magazine's operations, and the second part features the staff discussing a wide range of issues.

The original strategy was for *Vibe* to be another *Rolling Stone* but with different music. *Vibe*'s timing was good: Hip-hop, one of the primary music styles covered in the magazine, was just gaining popularity among both African American and white youths. As a result, the magazine was successful in attracting readers. Its circulation grew from about 100,000 in the early 1990s to 800,000 in 2002.

1. How does the business side of a magazine influence the editorial side?
2. What kind of companies might advertise in *Vibe*?
3. How do cultural trends play into the success of a magazine such as *Vibe*?
4. If you were the publisher of *Rolling Stone*, *Vibe*'s biggest competitor, how would you respond to *Vibe*'s success? How, if at all, would you change your magazine?
5. *Vibe* folded in 2009 but was resurrected under new ownership as a Web publication. Do you think the new online *Vibe* will succeed?

CAREER >> OUTLOOK

The Magazine Industry

At decade's end, the job outlook for the magazine industry is not optimistic. Layoffs and job cuts have hit magazines just as they have hit newspapers. Overall employment dropped 5 percent from 2007 to 2008. In one three-month period in 2008, the magazine industry lost 3,200 jobs. Online operations were not hit quite as hard, but job prospects were still dim. An economic recovery would improve the employment picture.

Those wishing to pursue careers in this area should develop strong writing and editing skills. Knowing how to prepare stories for the print and Web versions of a magazine is a big plus. Multimedia expertise is also an asset.

The career outlook in the various media industries changes quickly. For a more current description of conditions in the magazine industry and a more detailed look at career options, please consult the book's Web site: www.mhhe.com/dominick11e.

MAIN POINTS

- The first American magazines appeared during the middle of the 18th century and were aimed at an educated, urban, and literate audience.

- The audiences for magazines increased during the penny-press era as mass-appeal publications became prominent.

- Better printing techniques and a healthy economy helped launch a magazine boom during the latter part of the 19th century.

- The muckrakers were magazines that published exposés and encouraged reform.

- Magazines began to specialize their content following World War I. Newsmagazines, digests, and picture magazines became popular.

- The magazine industry is experiencing a difficult time due to declining advertising revenue.

- Magazines are specialized, current, influential, and convenient.

- The magazine industry is dominated by large publishing companies.

- The magazine industry can be divided into the production, distribution, and retail divisions.

- A typical magazine publishing company has several main departments, including circulation, advertising, production, and editorial.

- Magazines get revenues from subscriptions, single-copy sales, and print and online advertising.

- MRI is a company that measures magazine readership.

QUESTIONS FOR REVIEW

1. What are the four defining features of contemporary magazines? Should any other features be added to this list?

2. Why did the general-interest magazines *Look* and *Life* go out of business?

3. How is the magazine industry learning to coexist with the Internet?

4. What are the major departments at a magazine?

QUESTIONS FOR CRITICAL THINKING

1. Are there dangers in having large corporations dominate the magazine publishing industry?

2. *Playboy, Cosmopolitan,* and *Ms.*—three magazines that influenced social trends—all came on the scene before 1980. Are there any more current magazines that have been influential in shaping American culture and society? If not, why not?

3. Is it possible for a magazine to become too specialized? How big does a specialized audience have to be to support a print magazine? A Web-only magazine?

4. Muckraking by magazines never reappeared after its heyday in the early 20th century. Why not?

5. Read the boxed insert "Teen Magazine Web Sites: What's the Message?" (see page 114), and consider the following: Do these Web sites have a responsibility to present a more realistic and well-rounded view of young womanhood? How might the emphasis on beauty and beauty products affect young women who may not be able to afford the "right" cosmetics? Would the same messages be contained in Web sites for magazines targeted at adult women?

6. What's the future for print magazines?

KEY TERMS

muckrakers (p. 111)
paid circulation (p. 122)
controlled circulation (p. 122)
dummy (p. 124)
rate base (p. 126)
primary audience (p. 126)
pass-along audience (p. 126)
Mediamark Research Inc. (MRI) (p. 126)

INTERNET RESOURCES

Online Learning Center

On the Online Learning Center home page, www.mhhe.com/dominick11e, *select* Student Center *and then* Chapter 5.

1. Use the Learning Objectives, Chapter Outline, and Main Points sections to review this chapter.

2. Test your knowledge of the chapter using the multiple choice and flashcard features of the site.

3. Expand your knowledge of concepts and topics discussed in the chapter with additional Questions for Critical Thinking and Internet Exercises.

Surfing the Internet

The following are examples of sites of or related to magazines. All sites were current as of late 2009.

http://money.cnn.com
A cooperative venture between CNN and *Money* magazine, both owned by Time Warner. Note the interactive tool you can use to look up a stock price.

www.people.com
Makes extensive use of photos and video. Also available on iPhone and Blackberry.

www.magazine.org
The site of the major trade association of the industry, the Magazine Publishers of America. Contains statistics, FAQs, press releases, and research reports.

www.zinio.com
Provides digital delivery of magazines. Download the software and a sample issue to see for yourself how this process works.

www.magazinedeathpool.com
Gloomy blog that chronicles magazines that didn't survive the economic crunch.

CHAPTER 6

Books

This chapter will prepare you to:

- understand that books are the oldest form of mass communication

- recognize the factors that led to the commercialization of book publishing

- explain how the digital revolution may change the underlying structure of the book industry

- identify the main parts of the book industry

- understand how the economic recession is affecting the book industry

30 Rock star Tina Fey had never written book, but that didn't stop a publishing company from paying her $5 million to write her first one.

The book publishing industry is facing difficult financial times. Sales are flat, and many big companies are laying off employees. So why did Little, Brown and Company pay Tina Fey about $5 million to write her first book?

Most people reading this book are already familiar with Ms. Fey, the Emmy-winning star of NBC's *30 Rock* and spot-on impersonator of vice presidential candidate Sarah Palin. She has written TV and movie scripts, but never a book. Industry insiders estimate that her first attempt will have to sell about a million copies, a huge number for what promises to be a book of humorous essays, to make a profit for the company.

Little, Brown and Company's deal is characteristic of today's book publishing industry. Increasingly, publishers are placing big bets on one or two books that are likely to be huge blockbusters rather than investing in several smaller projects.

In many ways, today's publishing industry resembles the movie industry. They both try to hit home runs rather than singles, and they both like properties that resemble other big successes. If a movie about a comic book hero is successful (*Ironman*), then a movie about another hero (*Wolverine*) should also be a good bet. Likewise, if a book about a lovable dog is a best-seller (*Marley & Me*), then a book about a lovable cat should also do well (*Dewey*). If Stephen Colbert's *I Am America (And So Can You)* can sell a million copies (and he's only on a cable channel), then why not a book of humor by Tina Fey?

Of course these big bets can easily fail. In 2006 Henry Holt & Company spent nearly $1 million for *The Interpretation of Murder*, which was rumored to be the next *Da Vinci Code*. The book sold fewer than 30,000 copies in the United States.

Nevertheless, despite hard economic times, the book industry will keep trying to find the next superseller and will keep shelling out the big bucks for projects that look a lot like other proven or potential winners. In that connection, it should come as no surprise that in late 2008 publisher HarperCollins paid comedian Sarah Silverman about $2.5 million for her first book—a collection of humorous essays, just like Tina Fey's book.

Many early medieval manuscripts, such as this hymn book, were "illuminated" with colorful drawings and graphics.

A Brief History

Early books were inscribed by hand and lavishly decorated; many were valued as works of art. Until approximately the 12th century, most books in Europe were produced by monks in monasteries. As noted in Chapter 3, all this changed with the invention of movable type that worked with a printing press.

The invention of movable metal type suitable for printing is generally credited to Johann Gutenberg. Trained as a metalworker, Gutenberg developed a way to cast metal type and to encase it in a wooden mold that could then be attached to a printing press. In about 1455 Gutenberg printed his first book—the Bible. First put on sale at the Great Frankfurt Fair, the book cost the equivalent of three years of wages for the typical laborer of that time.

Gutenberg's innovations spread quickly throughout Europe. The Protestant Reformation and the writings of Martin Luther spurred the printing of religious books. Printed books appeared in England in 1476. Although book publishing was not considered a socially important force, Henry VIII recognized its potential as a political force and required all printers to obtain government approval before setting up shop.

▲ Colonial America

By the early 17th century, book publishers had followed the early immigrants to North America. In 1640 the Puritans in Cambridge, Massachusetts, printed the *Bay Psalm Book*. About 90,000 other titles were to follow it as book publishing took hold in the American colonies. Early publishers functioned as printers and sometimes as authors. One of the early printer-publishers who went on to fame was Benjamin Franklin. His *Poor Richard's Almanack* sold about 10,000 copies a year. Most book content was religious, such as that in *The Practice of Piety* and *Day of Doom.* Sentimental novels, many of them imported from England, also sold well. As the Revolutionary War approached, many book printers turned out political pamphlets. Thomas Paine's *Common Sense* sold 100,000 copies in just 10 weeks.

▲ The Penny-Press Era

The change in printing technology and the growth of literacy mentioned in Chapter 4 also helped the book publishing industry. Many of the publishing companies still active today can trace their roots to the early 1800s. Many publishers specialized in professional and educational books, while others addressed their efforts to the general public. Book prices declined and authors such as James Fenimore Cooper and Henry Wadsworth Longfellow became popular, as did the works of English authors. Public education and the penny newspaper created a demand for reading materials. The number of public libraries tripled between 1825 and 1850. Book reading became a symbol of education and knowledge.

The novels of Charles Dickens and Walter Scott were best-sellers during this period, as were books by Herman Melville and Henry David Thoreau. Specialized books also appeared. In the late 1840s textbooks were profitable, as were reference, medical, and engineering books. The most significant book of the period, however, was probably Harriet Beecher Stowe's *Uncle Tom's Cabin,* published in 1852. It sold 300,000 copies in its first year and was credited with converting many readers to an antislavery position.

▲ The Paperback Boom

During the Civil War soldiers turned to reading to fill the idle time between campaigns. This created a demand for cheap reading materials, and before long a series of paperbacks priced at 10 cents apiece flooded the market. These "dime novels" included the popular Frank Merriwell and Horatio Alger stories. By 1880 about one-third of all books published in the country were paperbacks, and 15 firms were selling the softbound volumes at prices ranging from 5 cents to 15 cents. Many of the best-selling paperbacks were pirated editions of best-sellers in England and other European countries. By the late 1880s this problem was so bad that a new copyright law was adopted. The effect of this new law, combined with years of cutthroat competition and price cutting, spelled the end of this era of paperback popularity.

▲ The Early 20th Century

The period from 1900 to 1945 saw the commercialization of publishing. Prior to this time, many publishing companies had been family-owned and specialized in publishing one particular kind of book. Publishers had been a close-knit group, and their dealings with one another resembled what might take place in a genteel private club. However, several events altered this situation. First, a new breed of literary agents, concerned with negotiating the best bottom line for their authors, entered the scene. Forced to pay top dollar for the rights to books, the publishing business became more businesslike. Second, many publishing houses expanded into the mass market, publishing popular works of fiction. To compete in the mass marketplace, these publishing houses introduced modern promotion and distribution techniques to the book industry. Third, a depression in the 1890s and a subsequent sluggish economy meant that the book industry was forced to depend more on banks for finance capital. The banks, of course, insisted that the book companies be run with the utmost efficiency, with an eye toward increasing profits. By World War II all these factors combined to make the book industry more commercially oriented.

The content of popular books was highly variable during this period. Outdoor adventures written by such authors as Jack London and Zane Grey were popular at the turn of the century. During the Roaring Twenties light fiction such as *The Sheik* and P. G. Wodehouse's Jeeves stories were best-sellers. Detective fiction by Erle Stanley Gardner (Perry Mason was his hero) and Ellery Queen sold well during the Depression. In 1936 two books broke the 2-million mark in sales: Dale Carnegie's *How to Win Friends and Influence People* and Margaret Mitchell's *Gone with the Wind.*

▲ Postwar Books: Paperbacks and Consolidation

Margaret Mitchell's *Gone with the Wind* was turned down by 25 publishers before Macmillan published it.

Shortly after the end of World War II, new paperbacks published by Bantam, Pocket Books, and New American Library appeared. These books were popular because of their 25-cent price and because new channels of distribution were used to market them. Wire racks filled with paperbacks appeared in train stations, newsstands, drugstores, and tobacco shops. A whole new audience was thus exposed to paperbacks. In 1950 the "quality" paperback appeared. These were serious nonfiction or literary classics that found their prime markets in education.

Moreover, expanded leisure time and more disposable income made book reading a popular means of recreation. In short, the book publishing business looked like a good investment for the future. Consequently, large corporations began acquiring book companies. Between 1958 and 1970, there were 307 mergers or acquisitions of publishing companies. These mergers brought new financial and management resources to the book industry, which helped it stay profitable during the 1970s.

The cutbacks at newspapers have caused collateral damage to the book industry. As a cost-saving measure, many papers have downsized or completely eliminated the book review section. The *Chicago Tribune,* for example, shrank its book section and moved it from its high-circulation Sunday edition to low-circulation Saturday. The *Los Angeles Times* dropped its stand-alone book section, and the *Atlanta Journal-Constitution* eliminated the position of book review editor.

Part of the reason for the disappearance is money. Economic times are tough, and book publishers have cut back on print advertising in favor of point-of-purchase displays. Consequently, book review sections don't bring in much revenue and are the first to be chopped when things get tough.

What are the consequences of this trend? For one, it might ultimately hurt the newspaper even more in the future. Book readers are also newspaper readers. Encouraging reading, especially book reading, encourages reading the newspaper as well. The trend also signals that newspapers see their societal function differently. Newspapers initially carried book review sections not because they were profitable but as a public service to their readers. The book section was a contribution to the country's ongoing intellectual and cultural conversation.

There are some observers who suggest that the loss of newspaper book reviewers is not something to bemoan. In recent years, many blogs devoted to book reviewing have emerged (such as curledup.com). The authors of these blogs argue that reviewing has become less elitist and more democratic. Motivated readers can seek out dozens of different opinions rather than relying on the viewpoints of a privileged few. (Note that this is another example of how the interpretation function is shifting from the traditional media to the Internet.)

Can bloggers do the job as well as traditional reviewers? It's difficult to tell. Bloggers need no special training or education to write a review. You can have more confidence that a review in a newspaper was written by somebody who has some experience and expertise in the area. Book sections also tried to present a wide range of reviews, including books from all genres, from well-known and not-so-well-known authors and from major and not-so-major publishers. Bloggers may not display that same range.

The disappearance of the book review section is especially hard on authors. In the past, getting a book reviewed by a prestigious newspaper usually meant increased sales, visibility, and prestige. Getting reviewed by a blogger in Boise does not have the same cachet.

The content of popular books during this period was varied. The first big paperback best-seller following World War II was Dr. Benjamin Spock's *Baby and Child Care.* Other notable paperbacks followed. Mickey Spillane's Mike Hammer was a hard-boiled private eye who appeared in six novels during the 1950s that sold 17 million copies. *Peyton Place,* a novel famous for its racy (for the time) parts, sold 10 million in paperback. All in all, from 1946 to 1970, paperback sales were dominated by light fiction and an occasional how-to book.

▲ The Contemporary Book Industry

The wave of consolidation that began in the 1970s continued into the new century. Bertelsmann acquired Random House, and HarperCollins bought Morrow. Consequently, as of 2009, book publishing was dominated by a few big companies.

The 1990s and early 2000s ushered in major changes in the way books are marketed. Amazon.com was the first major company to offer books for sale online direct to consumers, with no trip to the bookstore necessary. Barnesandnoble.com and bordersstores.com provide similar services. In 2006 online sellers sold more than $2 billion worth of books.

The contemporary book industry has also seen a jump in the number of outlets where books are sold. In addition to chain and independent bookstores, consumers can buy books at mass marketers, such as Wal-Mart, and at grocery stores, hardware stores, cheese shops, and office supply stores. Walk into any Starbucks and you're likely to find books for sale.

Along with other mass media, book publishing suffered from the economic downturn near the end of the decade. After a respectable 3 percent increase in revenue from 2006 to 2007, book industry income declined by about 3 percent from 2007 to 2008, and for the near future the outlook wasn't optimistic. Bookstores were also having problems making a profit.

As is discussed more below, book publishers were exploring new ways of getting books to the reader, including digital books that were downloaded to e-book readers and placing a selection of audio books on iTunes for downloading. Publishers also experimented with putting portions of a book on the Web, where it could be downloaded for free in the hopes that the sample would prompt people to buy the whole book.

The content of contemporary books is remarkably varied. At decade's end, fiction books by established writers James Patterson, Stephen King, and John Grisham were on the best-seller lists along with newcomer Stephenie Meyer (the Twilight series featuring vampires). In nonfiction, the 2008 presidential election created a host of politically oriented best-sellers. President Barack Obama authored two of the top 20 best-selling books of 2008. Conservative talk-show hosts Glenn Beck and Bill O'Reilly along with columnist Thomas Friedman also had top-selling books. Diet and self-help books, such as *A New Earth,* continue to be popular. All in all, the varied content of the book industry reflects the specialized tastes of today's reading public.

Books in the Digital Age

▲ Transition

Books are the last stronghold of the analog age. Although the digital age has transformed newspapers and magazines, it has yet to significantly change the book publishing industry. Digital technology, however, has made some changes in the way books are produced: Authors submit text in digital form, editors prepare digital text for publication, and publishers set type from digital text. But most readers still purchase a tangible object, ink on paper bound between covers. There are indications, however, that books may be about to enter a transitional period.

▲ The E-Book

There have been attempts to introduce digital books, called **e-books,** for almost a decade. The early e-book readers were expensive and difficult to use, and they had poor image quality. On top of that, there weren't enough titles in electronic form to spur consumers into trying the new technology.

The situation changed dramatically when Sony introduced its e-book reader in 2006. Using a new technology called e-ink, the Sony reader could hold more than 100 average-sized books. Readers could increase the type size for easier viewing and bookmark individual pages. Sony also created an online store where readers could purchase digital books for about 20 percent less than print versions. Books were first downloaded to a person's computer and then side-loaded to the e-reader. By 2009, Sony had sold about 400,000 e-readers, not a huge amount but enough for the industry to take notice.

In 2007 online retailer Amazon entered the e-book arena with its Kindle. About the same size as a Sony e-book reader, the Kindle can hold about 200 books and boasts wireless connectivity that enables a book to be downloaded directly to the reader, usually in less than a minute. Readers can also subscribe to newspapers and magazines that arrive over a wireless connection. On top of that, Kindle owners can search within individual books, compile digital clippings, and make marginal notes. If your eyes are tired, a text-to-speech feature lets Kindle read the book out loud. Amazon, of course, has access to a large number of books and about 245,000 are available in digital form. As of 2009, best-sellers were priced at $9.99. Sony responded to the Kindle by making a deal with Google that gives Sony e-book owners free access to more than 500,000 books in the public domain.

E-books make possible things that print books can't match. An e-book, for example, can be continually updated. There's no need to buy a new edition if all the changes can be downloaded to the reader. Think of the advantage this would be for professional and reference books, not to mention college texts. Fiction authors might even make alternate endings available or further develop minor storylines.

A company called E ink has developed a process that might improve the quality of the e-book experience. A big problem with e-book readers is the quality of the display. Consumers complain that it is not bright enough, lacks contrast, and is hard to read in bright light. E ink's new technology consists of millions of tiny microcapsules, each about the diameter of a human hair, that contain positively charged white particles and negatively charged black particles suspended in a clear fluid. The capsules are overlaid on a thin film of plastic circuitry. In response to a negative electric field, the white particles zoom to the top of the capsule where they are visible to the reader. Reversing the process sends the black particles to the top, which makes the surface appear dark.

Electronic ink can be printed on any surface, including cloth and paper. It is a high-contrast medium, just like regular ink and paper; is legible in both bright and low light; and uses little power. It has applications not only for e-books but also for other areas. One of the company's first products was a large indoor sign that could be programmed by pagers controlled through the Internet. The potential for electronic ink is huge. E ink's Web site reads, "Electronic ink will lead to a new generation of 'expressive surfaces'—intelligent displays that are built right into everyday products. In the future, clothing, buildings, household objects, and information appliances all will have the ability to communicate." What would Gutenberg think?

E-books have their disadvantages. E-book readers are expensive. Color images are lacking, charts and graphs are difficult to read, and battery life could always be improved. Big, lavishly illustrated "coffee table" books don't translate well to digital form, and it's tough to lend an e-book to a friend. Finally, if you happen to drop a book, nothing much happens to it; if you drop an e-book reader, you might be out a couple hundred dollars.

E-books have yet to make a big financial impact. They account for not quite 1 percent of all book industry revenue, but that is expected to grow in the next few years. In any case, it looks as though the digital revolution is slowly making its way into book publishing.

▲ Printing on Demand

Another possibility thanks to digitalization is **printing on demand.** This publishing method is a little less radical than that of the e-book. In this approach traditional publishers are still part of the mix, but books are printed and distributed differently.

Here's how it works: Publishers create a huge database of books in digital form. A customer goes to a bookstore, browses through a catalogue, and selects a book. A machine in the bookstore then downloads the book and prints it while the customer waits.

The implications of printing on demand are impressive. Traditional book publishers look for books that will sell enough copies (usually a large number) to make a profit. They then print thousands of books, ship them to bookstores, and hope that most of them are not returned as unsold copies. With printing on demand, however, publishers do not have to guess how many books they should print. They simply print one whenever somebody orders it. This eliminates all the production and shipping costs and guarantees that no books will be returned unsold. Eliminating these costs and the guesswork involved in forecasting demand means that publishers can make money on a book that sells only a few hundred copies. This might open up the way for a multitude of special-interest books that would be too expensive to publish with the traditional method.

Printing on demand has yet to make its way into the local bookstore. It was estimated that, as of 2008, printing on demand accounted for about 1 percent of total book sales. Nonetheless, the technique has gained ground. Much printing on demand takes place between printers and publishers of scientific and medical books. In difficult economic times many aspiring authors are turning to printing on demand to give their books visibility and perhaps lead to a contract with a major publisher.

No one is suggesting that the e-book and printing on demand will ever totally replace the traditional ink-and-paper book. People will still be drawn to the feel and texture of books and the unique experience of reading paper pages bound between covers. Even so, the digital age has already opened up a number of possibilities for the book industry, and even more will become apparent as technology continues to evolve.

Would-be novelists in Japan have found a new channel for their works—the cell phone. Some of these mobile novels, as they are called, are written at a computer keyboard and posted on a Web site for downloading to a cell phone. Many are pecked out (usually by using the thumbs) on a cell phone keypad.

Using a new art form calls for new conventions. The mobile novels have lots of dialogue and short paragraphs, making them easier to read on the cell phone screen. Big empty spaces between sentences suggest that the characters are lost in thought. The stories are typically about love, friendships, and other problems of young life. Teenage girls tend to be the biggest readers.

A couple of these cell phone novels have been turned into paper-and-ink books and have topped the Japanese best-seller lists. The biggest success, called *Love Sky,* has sold more than a million copies and is being made into a movie.

How many people are writing cell phone books? The Web site where these works are stored, Magic Island, contained more than a million novels as of early 2009.

▲ Mobile Books

The e-book is just as portable as the paper-and-ink version. Digital books can be downloaded to a dedicated book reader, such as Sony's e-book reader or Amazon's Kindle, or to other handheld devices, including cell phones. The Kindle has a feature that synchs it to an iPhone so that readers can start reading on the Kindle and continue reading on their iPhones. Amazon also announced plans to make their books available for Blackberrys and other brands of phones. Readers in Japan have been able to download full-length novels to their cell phones for several years (see the boxed insert "Thumbing Your Way Through a Novel").

▲ User-Generated Content

There have been a few beginning steps in the area of user-generated content as publishers begin to explore its potential and pitfalls. The British division of Penguin Books announced the creation of a wiki-novel, *A Million Penguins,* in 2007. Visitors wound up creating about 400 pages in the first month, but what they produced might charitably be described as disorganized. Random House is planning a user-generated book focusing on business uses of the Internet. Harlequin, the publisher of romance books, launched a Web site where readers could provide their own answers to evocative questions such as "What is love?" The best answers will be published in an e-book.

▲ Social Media

The book publishing industry is experimenting with social media in a variety of ways. In the marketing area, several publishers have utilized social media to promote their books. Many books have their own Facebook pages. Authors are also using social media. Patricia Cornwell's Web site has message boards and a feature that lets her readers submit questions and then vote on the ones that the author will respond to. A British author, R. N. Morris, made one of his crime novels available on Twitter—in 140-character chunks.

Social networking sites for people who write and read books have also sprung up. Shelfari.com, for example, describes itself as ". . . a gathering place for authors, aspiring authors, publishers, and readers, [that] has many tools and features to help these groups connect with each other in a fun and engaging way." Library Thing and GoodReads are similar sites. HarperCollins recently started Authonomy, a Web site where aspiring authors could submit manuscripts and ideas and have them critiqued by other members of the community.

Defining Features of Books

Books are the least "mass" of the mass media. It took about 40 years to sell 20 million copies of *Gone with the Wind,* but more than 50 million people watched the movie version in a single evening when it came to television. Even a flop TV show might have a million people in its audience, whereas a popular hardcover book might make the best-seller list with 125,000 copies sold. Even a mass-market paperback might sell only about 5 million copies.

Books, however, can have a cultural impact that far outweighs their modest audience size. *Uncle Tom's Cabin* is credited with helping to change a nation's attitude toward slavery. Dr. Spock and his *Baby and Child Care* altered the way parents brought up their children and became the target of critics who blamed him and his methods for the social unrest of the 1960s. Rachel Carson's *Silent Spring* changed the nation's attitudes toward the environment.

Finally, books are the oldest and most enduring of the mass media. Gutenberg printed his first book in the 15th century. Public libraries have been around for hundreds of years. Many individuals have extensive collections of books in their own home libraries. People throw away newspapers and magazines shortly after reading them, but most save their books.

Organization of the Book Industry

The book publishing industry can be divided into three segments: publishers, distributors, and retailers.

▲ Publishers

The publishing segment consists of the 3,000 or so establishments that transform manuscripts submitted by authors into books that are sought by readers. Every year these companies publish 100,000 to 150,000 new titles. Book publishing is a highly segmented industry. Publishers have developed a classification system for the industry based upon the market that is served. The following are the 10 major divisions suggested by the Association of American Publishers:

Amazon's Kindle can wirelessly download a novel in less than a minute.

1. *Trade books:* Titles aimed at the general consumer and sold primarily through bookstores. They can be hardbound or softbound and include works for juveniles and adults. Trade books include hardcover fiction, nonfiction, biographies, cookbooks, and art books.

2. *Religious books:* Includes Bibles, hymnals, prayer books, theology, and other literature of a devotional nature.

3. *Professional books:* Titles aimed at doctors, lawyers, scientists, accountants, business managers, architects, engineers, and all others who need a personal reference library in their work.

TABLE 6-1

Sales by Publishing
Industry Division, 2008

Division	Percentage of Sales
Trade	33
Elhi	24
Higher education	16
Professional	14
Book club/mail order	2
Mass-market paperback	5
E-books	1
Audio books	1
All other	4

4. *Book club and mail order:* These may at first sound more like part of a distribution channel than a division of the publishing segment, but some book clubs publish their own books, and almost all prepare special editions for their members. Mail-order publications consist of books created for the general public and marketed by direct mail. These are different from book clubs because the books are marketed by the publisher, and customers do not incur any membership obligations in an organization.

5. *Mass-market paperbacks:* Softbound volumes on all subjects that achieve their major sales in places other than bookstores. Typically, these are the books sold from racks in supermarkets, newsstands, drugstores, airports, chain stores, and so on.

6. *Elementary and secondary textbooks:* Hard- and softcover books, workbooks, manuals, and other printed materials, all intended for use in the classroom. Logically enough, schools are the primary market for these publishers. (This division is also referred to as *elhi* publishers—from *el*ementary and *hi*gh school.)

7. *Higher education:* Texts and workbooks for the college market.

8. *Audiobooks:* Books released on disc that consist of a person reading the text of a book.

9. *E-books:* As mentioned above, those digital versions available for downloading to computers or special readers.

10. *Other:* These include university presses, reference books, and standardized tests.

Table 6-1 shows the relative importance of each of these segments to the industry. As can be seen, trade, professional, and textbook publishing are the major divisions, accounting for 87 percent of sales.

▲ Distributors

The Internet has drastically changed the book distribution system. There are now three main channels by which books get to consumers. In the traditional method the publisher usually ships copies of the book to a wholesaler or distributor who, in turn, sends the books to a retail outlet where consumers can buy them. Online booksellers such as Amazon.com use a different approach. The consumer orders a book from the Web site, and the book is shipped from the seller's warehouse directly to the consumer, bypassing the distributor and retail outlet. E-books, of course, go directly from publisher to consumer, bypassing everything in between. Figure 6-1 illustrates these distribution arrangements.

▲ Retailers

There are around 10,000 bookstores in the United States plus the big online booksellers. As of 2008, Amazon.com was the biggest bookseller in the United States and the rest of the world. The Barnes and Noble chain was in second place followed by Borders/Waldenbooks.

FIGURE 6-1

Channels of Book
Distribution

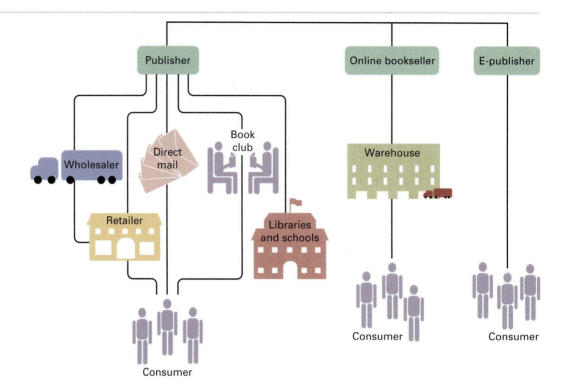

In 2008, these three big chains accounted for about $12 billion in revenue (this figure includes magazine sales, stationery, coffee, and so on). Other retail channels include college bookstores and direct-to-consumer sellers such as book clubs. The economic downturn in 2008–2009 has cut into bookstore profits, and Borders/Waldenbooks was in financial trouble in 2009.

Ownership in the Book Industry

The book industry is dominated by large conglomerates with interests in other media. The top five companies as of 2008 were the following:

1. *Pearson Publishing:* A global media company that is the world's largest educational publisher, with imprints such as Scott, Foresman and Prentice-Hall. It also owns the Penguin Group of consumer publishing firms (Penguin, Dutton, and Viking) as well as the *Financial Times* business newspaper.

2. *Random House:* Part of the Bertelsmann media empire, which includes interests in 600 companies in 63 countries and is engaged in books, magazines, TV, and radio.

3. *HarperCollins:* Rupert Murdoch's worldwide communications company, which owns HarperCollins as well as 20th Century Fox, the Fox TV network, and various newspapers and magazines.

4. *Simon & Schuster:* Part of the CBS Corporation, a conglomerate that has TV networks, radio stations and a radio network, and cable networks.

5. *Hachette Book Group:* Formed in 2006, when a French company, Hachette Livre, acquired Time Warner Books. The book group includes Little, Brown and Company, Grand Central Books, and Hachette Audio.

Producing the Book

▲ Departments and Staff

There are four major departments in a typical publishing company: (1) editorial, (2) production, (3) marketing, and (4) general administration or business.

The editorial department is in charge of dealing with authors; it is responsible for selecting manuscripts and preparing them for publication. Some editors specialize in procuring new manuscripts, and some read manuscripts, write reports on them, and recommend acceptance, revision, or rejection. Other editors work with accepted manuscripts, checking grammar, language, accuracy, and so on.

As its name suggests, the production department oversees the physical design of the book. This department is responsible for type style, composition, paper, printing, and binding.

The marketing department supervises sales, promotions, and publicity. The actual type of marketing depends on the book and its intended audience. Publishers of elhi textbooks sell mainly to school systems. Mass-market paperbacks are sold to retailers who, in turn, sell them to the public. Advertising in trade magazines, television interviews, and reviews in respected publications are common marketing tools.

The business manager at a publishing company is responsible for several functions. One of the most important is accounting. Further, this department prepares budgets and makes long-range financial forecasts. Other responsibilities include dealing with internal personnel policies and supervising the general day-to-day operational needs of the company.

▲ The Publication Process

Editors get their books in three ways: (1) through submissions by agents, (2) as unsolicited books sent in by authors, and (3) as book ideas generated by the editor. Most trade manuscripts are submitted through literary agents. Agents are known quantities and will not generally submit manuscripts that they know are unacceptable to the editor. Unsolicited manuscripts are given an unflattering name in the business: "slush." As they come in, these manuscripts are put in the slush pile and eventually read, if the author is lucky, by an editorial assistant. Most of the time they are rejected with a form letter, but every once in a while an author gets through. For instance, E. D. Baker's *The Frog Princess* has sold well and has been translated into several languages. Editors also generate ideas for books. If an editor has a good idea for a book, he or she will generally talk to one or more agents who will suggest likely candidates for the assignment. This is another good reason writers should have

Jeff Bezos was always tinkering with things. When he was three, he took apart his bed. Eleven years later, he tried to make a hovercraft out of a vacuum cleaner. Sixteen years after that, he tinkered with the way books were sold and totally revolutionized the business by starting Amazon.com.

After growing up in Houston and Miami, Bezos enrolled at Princeton, where he studied computer science and engineering. After a couple of jobs in the financial marketplace, he wound up at a Wall Street investment company. One day in 1993, while doing financial research, he came across a startling statistic: The Internet was growing at a rate of 2,300 percent a year. Bezos recognized the tremendous selling potential of the Net and decided to launch an online business. He reasoned that things that are big mail-order sellers should also do well online. Accordingly, he made a list of the top 20 mail-order products and determined that books would be the best item to sell. A virtual bookstore would have the space to list all the millions of books in print; no brick-and-mortar store could do that. Further, book wholesalers had already produced CD-ROMs that listed all available titles. Bezos recognized that the existing book databases could easily be put online.

Bezos's family and friends invested $300,000 in his idea, and Bezos moved to Seattle, the home of many Net-savvy programmers who would be needed to get the business online. Seattle was also the home of one of the biggest book wholesalers in the country.

Working out of his garage, Bezos created a Web site that he tested among his friends. It seemed to work well, and Bezos decided to open the site to everybody. But what to call it? He originally wanted to call it Cadabra.com, as in "abracadabra," the magic incantation. When he tried this name out on his lawyer, however, the lawyer thought Bezos said "Cadaver.com" and wanted to know why he would name his site after a dead body. Bezos went back to the drawing board and eventually settled on Amazon.com, after one of the world's longest and most powerful rivers.

The rest, as they say, is Internet history. The company grew quickly. In 1996 Amazon.com had 300 employees. In 2008 it had about 17,000. From a few thousand customers in its first year, it now has more than 20 million in about 150 countries. Sales in 2008 exceeded $19 billion. Its brand name is more recognizable than Burger King or Barbie. Amazon.com has also branched out from books and now sells CDs, toys, electronics, and gifts from its Web site. Amazon.com is now the biggest bookseller in the world.

Bezos is trying to shake things up again by offering the Kindle e-book reader. For now, the Kindle can only be used to buy e-books, but it could evolve to offer other services, such as ordering other merchandise from the Amazon.com site or a new platform for video games. In any case, Amazon.com has reached iconic status as a marketing channel.

agents. In any case, the author typically submits a proposal consisting of a cover letter, a brief description of the planned book, a list of reasons it should be published, an analysis of the potential market, an outline or a table of contents, and perhaps one or two sample chapters. The proposal usually goes to an acquisitions editor and is evaluated. If the publishing decision is favorable, a contract is signed, and the author begins work in earnest.

Editorial work starts as soon as the author submits chapters to the publisher. Editors look at the overall thrust of the book to make sure it makes sense and achieves its original intent. Moreover, the mechanics of the book are checked to make sure that the general level of writing is acceptable, that all footnotes are in order, that all necessary permissions to reproduce material from other sources have been obtained, and that all artwork is present. Eventually, both author and editors will produce a manuscript that is mutually satisfactory.

While all this editing is going on, other decisions are being made about scheduling, designing the interior look of the book, and designing the cover. When everything is in order, the book is printed, bound, and sent to the warehouse to await distribution, or it is distributed online.

The Economics of Book Publishing

The economic recession at the end of the decade caused financial problems for the book industry. Revenue dropped about 3 percent from 2007 to 2008 (see Figure 6-2). Additional declines were forecast for 2009. Audiobooks showed a sharp fall-off as did books in the adult hardcover category.

FIGURE 6-2

Book Publishing
Revenue, 1983–2008

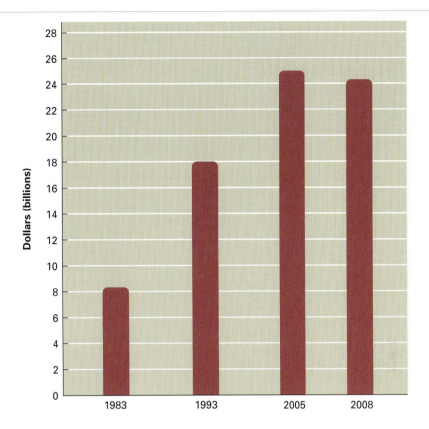

All publishers instituted cost-cutting measures, and staff cuts were common. Publishing companies eliminated 1,200 jobs in 2008. One major publisher even stopped acquiring new manuscripts.

At the consumer level it is obvious that books have become more expensive. In 2007, a hardcover copy of *Harry Potter and the Deathly Hallows* had a list price of $35, while best-selling paperbacks went for $9.99. The high prices have prompted many consumers to buy from discount sellers and the used-book market.

A publisher has two main sources of income: (1) the money that comes from book sales and (2) money from **subsidiary rights** (sales to book clubs, foreign rights, paperback rights, and reprint permissions). Of these two the income from book sales is more important. It should be noted, however, that the publisher does not get all the money from the sale of a book. The list price is discounted for wholesalers and booksellers. These discounts might amount to 40 percent for many books.

The costs a publisher incurs are many. First, there is the cost of manufacturing the book: printing, typesetting, and paying royalties to the author. These costs are variable and are tied to the number of books printed. For example, paper costs would be more substantial on a book with a press run of 20,000 than on one with a run of 2,000. There are also operating expenses, including editorial, production, marketing, and general administration expenses. Table 6-2 shows a hypothetical operating statement for an adult trade hardcover book published by a typical publishing company. The book has a list price of $20 (all numbers are rounded for convenience), and 10,000 copies were printed. After a year, 2,000 copies were unsold and were returned to the publisher for a credit. This means that 8,000 copies were sold. Allowing a 40 percent discount from the list price leaves the publisher with revenues of about $12 per book. Multiplying 8,000 by $12 gives us the gross sales amount: $96,000. From this are subtracted the costs of returns and allowances, leaving a balance of $77,000 in net sales

Critical / Cultural Issues

Labor Versus Management in Journalism Textbooks

As mentioned in Chapter 2, the critical/cultural approach examines texts, broadly defined. In a paper presented at the 2000 convention of the Association for Education in Journalism and Mass Communication, Dr. Jon Bekken took a more literal approach and examined textbooks—in this case, journalism textbooks—to discover if these texts were instilling a professional ideology in their readers.

Bekken notes that studies of the coverage of business conflicts have generally found that the media cover these disputes from a perspective that does not favor labor or labor unions. For example, labor reporting focuses on the inconvenience strikes cause for consumers rather than on the issues that lead to a strike. Wages rather than health and safety are portrayed as the central concern of labor. In addition, there is a trend toward ignoring labor news altogether. Fewer than a dozen newspapers employ even one full-time labor reporter.

Bekken wondered if these attitudes might have been fostered during a reporter's academic training. He was specifically interested in the way organized labor was portrayed in 29 media writing and reporting textbooks. After performing a critical/cultural analysis, he concluded that the texts marginalized labor, making it seem unimportant. For instance, he noted that some textbooks have exercises that ask students to write articles about layoffs or hiring freezes based on press releases or notes from interviews with corporate or government officials. The subtle lesson conveyed in these exercises is that the important perspectives do not include those of labor. Other texts simply make little or no mention of labor or labor unions despite the fact that many newspaper workers belong to the International Typographical Union, and several newspapers have been plagued by labor-management troubles.

Most texts generally gloss over labor problems in the newspaper industry itself. Health risks such as carpal tunnel syndrome, poor working conditions, and inadequate pay are seldom mentioned. The idea that joining a union might help address some of these issues is not discussed.

Bekken chronicles other examples of how labor is almost trivialized. One textbook devotes as many words to covering labor as it does to covering weddings. Another urges reporters to avoid an antibusiness attitude in their stories and to rely on corporate officials, financial analysts, and government regulators as sources for business news. When textbooks do discuss how to cover labor, their emphasis is on covering strikes, violence connected with strikes, or unfair labor practices.

What are some of the results of the way these texts depict labor? As Bekken says,

> Students carry blind spots towards labor inculcated in their academic training into newsrooms across the country. Editors and publishers have slashed the number of labor reporters. . . . Reporters and editors typically do not look to the labor movement for news—rather they wait for strikes, or include labor in discussions of special interest groups said to dominate the political system.

Bekken ends his analysis by noting that in recent decades textbook authors have tried to remove sexist language and pay more attention to cultural sensitivity. Moreover, newer editions of reporting texts have been expanded to cover topics such as religious news and consumer news. Nonetheless, he points out, most journalism textbooks do not do a good job covering that large number of Americans who labor for a living. The fact that many of the students who read these books go on to ignore labor in their own reporting ought not surprise us.

revenue. Manufacturing costs and author royalties amounted to $45,400. This sum is subtracted from the net sales to find the gross margin on sales (the amount that net sales exceeded the cost of sales)—in this case, $31,600. Table 6-2 also assumes that the publisher sold some subsidiary rights (to a book club or a paperback publisher) and received $6,900 in return. So far, the total income from the book is $38,500 ($31,600 + $6,900). Subtracting the total operating expense of $34,600 from $38,500 yields a net income of $3,900.

These figures, of course, would vary for other publishers and for other segments of the book industry. Profit margins typically varied from 2 to 20 percent during the period between 1999 and 2006. Advances and acquisition rights are two of the big expenses in publishing. For example, Random House paid Charles Frazier, author of the best-seller *Cold Mountain,* an $8 million advance for his second novel, *Thirteen Moons,* and, of course, $5 million for Tina Fey's yet untitled effort.

TABLE 6-2

Profit-Loss Statement
of Trade Hardcover
with $20 List Price

Press run	10,000 copies		
Returned	2,000 copies		
Gross sales	8,000 copies	@ $12 per	$96,000
Returns and allowances			(19,000)
Net sales			77,000
Cost of sales			
Manufacturing			27,700
Royalties			17,700
Total cost of sales			45,400
Operating expenses			
Editorial			4,500
Production			1,600
Marketing and fulfillment			18,500
Administration			10,000
Total operating expenses			34,600
Margin of net sales over cost of sales			31,600
Other income			6,900
Net income			3,900

Feedback in Book Publishing

The most important form of audience feedback in the book industry is the best-seller lists compiled by newspapers such as the *New York Times* and *USA Today* and the trade publication *Publisher's Weekly*. These organizations use slightly different methods to tabulate a rank ordering of the best-selling books, but all involve collecting data from a sample of the various channels of book distribution—chain bookstores, independent bookstores, newsstands, and price clubs—and then assigning various weights to the numbers to come up with the rankings. Making the best-seller list is important since many bookstores automatically order large numbers of all books that make the list. Consequently, appearing on the list can mean added sales for a book.

In addition to best-seller lists, the industry uses Nielsen BookScan, a service that measures actual sales data from about 6,500 major retailers across the United States, including big chains and independent stores. In a typical week the service tabulates sales figures on more than 300,000 different titles. Companies that subscribe to BookScan can access sales data broken down by region, subject, and format.

Champion boxer, cook, and author George Foreman signs books on a book tour.

▲ Audiences

According to a 2008 survey by the National Endowment for the Arts, about 119 million Americans reported reading at least one book in the past year. In 2002, the comparable number was about 116 million. The increase, however, did not keep pace with the increase in the adult population for those years. In percentage terms, about 54 percent of Americans read books in 2008, down from 57 percent in 2002.

Literary reading—defined as reading novels, short stories, plays, and poems—jumped about 4 percent

Comedy Central's Stephen Colbert introduced the word *truthiness* to the American people during one of his reports. As defined by the *Urban Dictionary*, *truthiness* means the quality of stating concepts that one wishes or believes to be true rather than the facts. Odd as it may seem, truthiness was at the core of one of the most publicized controversies in the book publishing industry in 2006.

At issue was James Frey's *A Million Little Pieces*, a powerful memoir about the author's struggles with addiction, the law, and himself, concluding with his eventual rehabilitation. The book was published in 2003 and became a huge best-seller when Oprah Winfrey chose it as one of her book club selections. Shortly thereafter, thesmokinggun.com reported that it was unable to find any record of Frey's alleged run-ins with the law and subsequent prison time. Faced with these discrepancies, Frey admitted that parts of his memoir were, in fact, based on fiction. For example, Frey wrote that he spent three months in jail; the actual police records showed that he spent only a few hours in custody. He also admitted that he lied when he wrote about running over a police officer and undergoing a root canal without Novocain, nor could he produce any records that supported his claims of struggles in rehab.

The reaction to these revelations ran the gamut from condemnation to support. Oprah Winfrey initially supported Frey, claiming that, even with the fabrications, the "underlying message" of the book was still valid. Other literary types sounded a similar theme. They argued that a memoir was based not on what actually happened but on how the author remembered what had happened. It was the "essential message," or the "essence of the experience," or "the larger truth," or the "inner core of the story" that counted, not factual matters.

Readers, however, thought otherwise. Many said they felt betrayed. Even Oprah changed her stance, removed the book from her reading list, and berated the author for his transgressions during an episode of her program. Two

readers even filed a lawsuit against the publisher for breach of contract and deceptive advertising for calling the book a work of nonfiction.

What are the ethical implications of this situation? Does the author of a personal memoir have an ethical obligation to his or her readers to inform them that what they are reading might contain some exaggerations or embellishments or even outright fiction? What about the publisher? Should it publish a disclaimer about the accuracy of a memoir? Is it under any ethical obligation to check on the veracity of the information it publishes? (Interestingly, courts have held that publishers are not legally bound to check facts, but what is their ethical obligation to their readers and to other memoirists who actually write the truth and whose reputation may be sullied by those who don't?)

In the aftermath of the scandal, several things occurred. Some publishers conceded that they will be looking more closely at some of the more extreme claims made by authors who submit memoirs. James Frey was dropped by his publisher and his contract for additional books was canceled. Plans for a movie based on the book (Brad Pitt and Jennifer Aniston bought the film rights) were put on hold. Despite all of these developments, "truthiness" can still be profitable. Frey's royalties for *A Million Little Pieces* amounted to more than $4 million.

It appears, however, that the lessons of the James Frey saga were not taken to heart. Truthiness, unfortunately, is still around. In 2008, it was revealed that *Love and Consequences,* published by Penguin, was a fake. The book purported to be about a racially mixed woman, raised in poverty by an African American mother, who sold drugs for a tough Los Angeles street gang in order to survive. In truth, the author was a middle-class white woman who went to private school and admitted making up the whole story.

The publisher recalled all the books and canceled a proposed book tour. It is not known if the author got to keep any advance money.

---

from 2002. Interestingly, the survey found that the biggest increase in literary reading was among 18- to 24-year-olds, reversing an earlier trend. In addition, the survey found that about 15 percent read some form of literature online.

The Book Publishing Industry

Book publishing is a relatively small industry. There are only about 70,000–75,000 jobs in the entire business. Like the other print media, the book industry has been hard hit by the economic downturn. Consequently, the career outlook, at least for now, is depressing. On the bright side, despite all the pundits who keep saying that reading is a lost art, the recent readership figures released by the National Endowment for the Arts show that book reading is still holding its own. If the economy bounces back, then career prospects should improve.

The career outlook in the various media industries changes quickly. For a more current description of conditions in the book publishing industry and a more detailed look at career options, please consult the book's Web site: www.mhhe.com/dominick11e.

MAIN POINTS

- The book is the oldest form of mass communication. Early books were printed by hand until the invention of movable type and the printing press.

- In early America publishers were also printers. Books became more popular during the 17th and 18th centuries.

- From 1900 to 1945, the book publishing industry became more commercialized. Continuing consolidation has resulted in a modern book industry that is dominated by a few large companies.

- The digital revolution has yet to have a drastic effect on the book industry. E-books and printing on demand have yet to become important parts of the industry. Despite the slow progress of digital content, there are signs that it is moving forward.

- The book industry consists of publishers, distributors, and retailers. The emergence of online booksellers has changed the way books are sold and distributed.

- The book publishing industry is trying to cope with unfavorable economic conditions.

QUESTIONS FOR REVIEW

1. How has the content of popular books changed from the 17th to the 21st century?

2. What are the defining features of books?

3. What are the main revenue sources for book publishers?

4. What is the difference between a trade book and a mass-market paperback?

QUESTIONS FOR CRITICAL THINKING

1. What would you prefer—a traditional ink-and-paper book (such as this one) or an e-book? Why?

2. Book sales have not increased in the last couple of years. What might be some of the reasons? What impact, if any, do you think the Internet has had on book reading?

3. What advantages and disadvantages are connected with a book industry dominated by a few big firms?

4. Read the boxed insert "Labor versus Management in Journalism Textbooks," on page 144, and then consider the following. To what extent—and why—does it matter whether such texts avoid discussing labor problems in the media industry or carry a promanagement bias? If you are taking a course in writing/reporting, look at the text you are using. Does it marginalize or trivialize labor? What can students do to raise awareness of these issues in class?

KEY TERMS

e-book (p. 135)   printing on demand (p. 136)   subsidiary rights (p. 143)

INTERNET RESOURCES

Online Learning Center

On the Online Learning Center home page, www.mhhe.com/dominick11e, *select* Student Center *and then* Chapter 6.

1. Use the Learning Objectives, Chapter Outline, and Main Points sections to review this chapter.

2. Test your knowledge of the chapter using the multiple choice and flashcard features of the site.

3. Expand your knowledge of concepts and topics discussed in the chapter with additional Questions for Critical Thinking and Internet Exercises.

Surfing the Internet

Remember, Web sites change all the time; some move, some evaporate, and some transform.

www.bookweb.org
The home page of the American Booksellers Association, the trade group representing independent bookstores. Contains the current best-sellers list.

www.bookwire.com
Takes a look inside the book business. Includes news, features, and links to other related sites.

www.bisg.org
The home page of the Book Industry Study Group. Provides research information about the industry.

www.arts.gov/research/readingontherise
A link to the National Endowment for the Arts survey of literary reading in America.

www.publishersweekly.com
The online version of *Publisher's Weekly,* the leading trade magazine. Includes job listings.

CHAPTER 7

Radio

This chapter will prepare you to:

- explain how radio broadcasting developed in the 1920s

- recognize how television affected radio

- discuss the defining features of radio

- understand that radio gets programming from local stations, networks, and syndication companies

- explain how the digital age is affecting radio

- appreciate the potential of HD radio

- understand how the Internet has affected the radio industry

Radio towers such as this carry the programs of terrestrial radio stations. This one also carries microwave relay dishes.

It used to be a lot easier to talk about radio. There was only one kind—the analog kind that was transmitted over the airwaves by stations on the ground. In the mid-1990s, a new kind appeared: digital radio stations on the Internet. This meant that a person talking about radio had to distinguish between over-the-air radio and online radio. Then in 2001, a satellite was launched that delivered high-quality digital radio to compatible radio receivers. A person now had to distinguish among earth-bound, over-the-air radio (labeled terrestrial radio), digital online radio, and digital satellite radio. Then, to make things even more difficult, terrestrial stations started broadcasting high-quality digital radio (labeled HD radio). Now a person had to distinguish among terrestrial analog radio, terrestrial HD radio, satellite radio, and online radio. If that wasn't complicated enough, terrestrial stations started digital broadcasting on the Internet. Now a person had to distinguish among terrestrial analog radio, digital terrestrial HD radio, terrestrial radio stations online, satellite radio, and stations that were only on the Internet with no terrestrial counterpart (labeled online-only stations).

Two things should be apparent from the above paragraph. One, a chapter that talks about radio has to be careful to distinguish exactly what kind of radio it's talking about, and two, radio has definitely moved into the digital age. In fact, radio is doing a good job making the transition to the digital age—but we're getting ahead of ourselves. Let's gain some perspective by first taking a look at the development of radio—we'll start with the terrestrial analog kind.

A Brief History

In 1887 Heinrich Hertz, a German physicist, successfully sent and detected radio waves. Guglielmo Marconi used Hertz's efforts to build a wireless communication device that could send Morse code—dots and dashes—from a transmitter to a receiver. Marconi started a wireless telegraphy company that would play an important part in early radio's development.

Reginald Fessenden and Lee De Forest provided the breakthroughs that would make broadcasting—as opposed to sending dots and dashes—possible. Fessenden, with the help of General Electric (GE), built a high-speed, continuous-wave generator that could broadcast the human voice and music. De Forest invented the vacuum tube, originally called the *audion*, which made it much easier to receive radio signals.

The development of early radio was hampered by legal battles over patent rights to various inventions. When World War I broke out, the U.S. Navy assumed responsibility for all relevant patents, and radio made great technical strides during the war.

▲ The Birth of Commercial Radio

Big Business   After the war corporate America recognized the potential of radio. A new company, the Radio Corporation of America (RCA), was formed and acquired the assets of the U.S. division of the Marconi Company. Stock in RCA was held by some of the biggest companies of the period: AT&T, GE, and Westinghouse. Note that these companies thought RCA would be in the wireless telegraphy business. Despite the efforts of Fessenden and De Forest, it was hard to envision that broadcasting news and entertainment to the general public could make money.

Some individuals, however, were more prescient. David Sarnoff, an employee of the Marconi Company who later became head of RCA, suggested that one day this new invention would become a "radio music box." Sarnoff himself would be one of the central figures in the development of this new medium.

A Mass Audience   Frank Conrad, an engineer for Westinghouse in Pittsburgh, tinkered with radio as a hobby. He built a radio transmitter in his garage and started broadcasting recorded music, reporting sports scores, and showcasing the musical abilities of his sons. In a short time he had attracted an enthusiastic audience of radio fans. A local department store started selling radio sets so that more people could hear Conrad's programs. Westinghouse built a station so that Conrad's signal would be heard by more people. Westinghouse also built the radio sets and received "free" advertising because of its connection with the station. The station, KDKA, signed on in 1920 and is still on the air, making it the country's oldest station.

KDKA was a success. In response, RCA, GE, and AT&T, along with many other companies and organizations, started radio stations. Radio listening became a national craze. By discovering that an audience existed for broadcast programs intended for the general public, radio found the role it would play for the foreseeable future.

A young boy listens to an early radio set.

Better Receivers   Early radio receivers were not user-friendly. They were powered by an assortment of large, bulky, and sometimes leaky batteries. Tuning required patience, a steady hand, and a knowledge of electronics.

Critical / Cultural Issues

Department Stores and the Early Days of Radio

Contributed by Noah Arceneaux, Assistant Professor of Media Studies, San Diego State University. In 1922, the year of the famed "broadcasting boom," a few dozen department stores built their own radio stations. These stations were not as numerous as those operated by newspapers or universities, though they warrant a close examination. Radio, as a new technology, could have developed in a number of ways, though department stores promoted the idea that it should be used to deliver non-offensive entertainment, mixed with advertisements. The success of their stations helped to pave the way for the advertising-supported, commercial system of broadcasting that would eventually dominate the American radio industry.

The fact that department stores were early adopters of radio is not surprising given their prior uses of electrical lighting, elevators, and telephones. Many individuals in the late 19th century, for example, first encountered these technologies inside the stores. These retailers also had a history of developing new forms of promotion, such as full-page, illustrated newspaper advertisements. Stores also organized elaborate promotional events, fashion shows, musical concerts, and parades to impress their customers. When Horne's department store in Pittsburgh promoted Frank Conrad's experimental broadcasts in an advertisement, it was not trying to inspire a national phenomenon. It was simply doing what department stores had done all along.

For their radio programming, stores favored opera, classical, and conservatory music. In an attempt to support the least offensive kinds of content, they avoided radical political views as well as jazz, which was considered vulgar by some elite members of society at the time. Their radio advertisements were not overt, though whenever the announcer identified the station, he would always mention the name of the store (and sometimes the address). In order to maximize the publicity value, the stores presented lectures based on specific types of merchandise, such as shoes or women's clothing. It was hoped that a listener would associate the store with this particular item, an association that might result in a sale.

The balance between commercial advertisements and editorial content is a delicate issue for all forms of media, though many store stations were praised for the high quality of their programming. Most listeners did not object to the indirect advertising, and some of the stations, such as WOR in Newark and WIP in Philadelphia, established national reputations. In the second half of the 1920s, resistance to advertising decreased, and more stations adopted this practice. The number of store stations decreased at this time, as retailers discovered that it was easier to buy airtime on other stations than to establish their own.

Department stores also made a deliberate effort to bring women into the radio audience. The majority of listeners in the early 1920s were male, many of whom had built their own receivers from spare parts. The stores, which catered to female shoppers, sold attractively designed, factory-built receivers intended for the living room. In the midmorning hours, when presumably all the men were at work, the store stations aired cooking, sewing, or fashion programs to entertain housewives. The hosts of these programs were women, while announcers for other kinds of shows were almost exclusively men.

This brief history illustrates a critical/cultural approach to media in that it does not take a dominant system—in this case, commercial broadcasting—to be natural or logical. The goal rather is to explain how this particular system came to be and how it was promoted by specific institutions, such as department stores. The groups that supported the commercial system of broadcasting did not simply impose their vision on a passive public. Listeners enjoyed the programming from the first commercial stations and accepted the indirect approach to advertising. The success of these stations, including the ones from department stores, encouraged other broadcasters to mix advertisements with content. In this regard the commercialization of American radio broadcasting should be understood as a hegemonic process in which coercion mingled with consent.

The ways in which women were incorporated into the radio audience also illustrate a critical/cultural perspective. It may seem a positive development that the early radio industry sought to appeal to women, though we must consider the narrow range of identities offered to women. They could cook, mend clothing, and otherwise look beautiful for their husbands. Similarly, when women presented lectures on the radio, the topics had to be suitably "feminine." This restrictive vision on what it meant to be a woman reveals the patriarchal view that was dominant in the 1920s, a view that is still evident in many contemporary radio and television programs.

(*Note:* Adapted from "Department Stores and the Origins of American Broadcasting, 1910–1931," Ph.D. dissertation, University of Georgia, 2007.)

By 1926, however, set manufacturers had improved their product. New radios ran on household current, could be tuned with just two knobs, had better antennas, and looked like a fashionable piece of furniture. Between 1925 and 1930, 17 million radio sets were sold, and radio was becoming truly a mass medium.

▲ The Commercialization of Radio

One of the curious things about early radio broadcasting was that very little of it was done by broadcasters. The early stations were owned by a polyglot of organizations. WLS in Chicago was owned by Sears, Roebuck (*World's Largest Store*); WGN by the *Chicago Tribune* (*World's Greatest Newspaper*); WSM in Nashville by the National Life and Accident Insurance Company (*We Shield Millions*); and WHB in Kansas City by the Sweeney Automotive and Electrical School.

Early broadcasting was not expensive, and radio station owners figured they got their money's worth through the exposure they received through the station. Before long, however, operating expenses began to pile up, and stations searched for a way to have their stations turn a profit.

Nobody knew quite how to do it. Some felt listeners should send in voluntary contributions; others wanted a tax on radio tubes. It was the phone company that finally came up with a workable plan. AT&T began selling time on WEAF, their flagship station in New York, to anybody who wanted to broadcast a message. The most logical customers for this new service were companies that had things to sell. Thus, in 1922 the Queensboro Realty Company paid $300 for five radio talks that extolled the benefits of living in the country, preferably on a lot bought from Queensboro Realty. Other companies quickly recognized the advertising potential of this new medium and bought time on WEAF and other stations. The problem of financing radio broadcasting was solved—broadcasting would be supported by advertising.

Networks   Linking radio stations into a **network** made good economic sense. Rather than having each individual station pay the costs of producing its own program, it was much cheaper for all stations to share the cost of a single program and broadcast the same show on all stations. Moreover, a linked network of stations gave advertisers the ability to reach a larger audience in a wider geographic area.

The first network was the National Broadcasting Company (NBC), a subsidiary of RCA, set up in 1926. NBC actually started two networks. One consisted of stations originally owned by RCA, and another was made up of stations acquired from AT&T when the phone company decided to get out of the broadcasting business. NBC got a competitor when the Columbia Broadcasting System (CBS) went on the air the next year. William S. Paley, whose career with CBS would last into the 1980s, headed the new network.

Radio receivers in the 1930s no longer required a knowledge of electronics to operate. A family could simply sit back and listen.

The two networks grew quickly. By 1937 NBC had 111 affiliated stations, while CBS had 105. Advertisers were spending more than $27 million annually on network radio. It was obvious that the network-affiliate arrangement would persist for some time to come.

Revenues from advertising permitted the networks to hire big-name entertainers. Jack Benny, Ed Wynn, and George Burns and Gracie Allen were all well-known vaudeville entertainers who successfully made the transition to radio. The most successful program, however, was *Amos 'n' Andy*, a comedy starring Charles Correll and Freeman Gosden, two white comedians working in blackface. Although considered racist today, it was a top-rated show during the late 1920s and early 1930s, and listening to it became a national habit.

"This . . . is London." Edward R. Murrow's famous opening was familiar to millions of Americans who listened to his reports from the British capital during World War II. Murrow went on to a distinguished career in TV journalism.

Government Regulation The early success of radio broadcasting had unanticipated consequences. As more and more stations went on the air during the 1920s, interference became a tremendous problem, and the government lacked the authority to do anything about it.

Congress finally acted to resolve this situation by passing the **Radio Act of 1927.** This act set up the Federal Radio Commission (FRC), a regulatory body that would issue licenses and try to clean up the chaos that existed. The commission defined the AM broadcast band, standardized channel designations, abolished portable stations, and moved to minimize interference. By 1929 the situation had improved, and the new radio medium was prevented from suffocating in its own growth.

Thus, by the end of the 1920s, the framework for modern radio broadcasting was in place. It would be a commercially supported mass medium dominated by networks and regulated by an agency of the federal government.

▲ The Depression Years and World War II

By most standards radio was not hit as hard by the Depression as were other industries. In fact, the amount of money spent on radio advertising tripled from 1930 to 1935. Profits may not have been as high as they would have been in better economic times, but the radio industry was able to weather the Depression with relatively little hardship.

The FCC The most significant legal development for radio during the Depression years was the formation of the **Federal Communications Commission (FCC).** President Roosevelt wanted to create a government agency that would consolidate the regulatory functions of the communications industry. In response to the president's demands, Congress passed the **Communications Act of 1934,** which consolidated responsibilities for broadcast and wire regulation under a new seven-member FCC. The expanded commission had increased responsibilities, but the fundamental philosophy underlying the original Radio Act of 1927 remained unchanged.

The Birth of FM In the mid-1930s Edwin Howard Armstrong, a noted inventor, demonstrated frequency-modulated radio, or FM, to his friend David Sarnoff, head of RCA. At the time, Sarnoff was more interested in promoting the development of television and, despite the technical advantages of FM, was not interested in backing Armstrong's creation. Armstrong tried to develop FM on his own. He set up his own transmitter for demonstrations and by 1940 had sold the rights to manufacture FM receiving sets to several companies. Sarnoff then offered Armstrong $1 million for a license to his invention, but Armstrong, probably still angry over Sarnoff's earlier rejection, refused. FM's further development was interrupted by the start of World War II.

Radio Programs Depression-era programs reflected a need for diversion and escape. Action-adventure series, such as *The Lone Ranger*, were popular, as were daytime soap operas. Network radio news grew during the 1930s, and live coverage of special events, such as the abdication speech of Edward VIII of England, drew huge numbers of listeners. Broadcasts from Europe on the eve of World War II kept many listeners glued to their radio sets for the latest bulletins. During the war Edward R. Murrow gained fame through his reports from war-torn London.

World War II   Radio did well during the war. The number of dollars spent on radio ads nearly doubled from 1940 to 1945. Helped by a newsprint shortage and an excess-profits tax that encouraged companies to advertise, radio broadcasting outpaced the newspapers as a national advertising vehicle in 1943.

The shape of modern broadcasting would be significantly altered by a court ruling that came in the middle of the war. In 1943 the Supreme Court ruled that NBC must divest itself of one of its two networks. NBC chose to sell the weaker network to Edward Noble, who had made his fortune selling Life Savers candy. Noble renamed his network the American Broadcasting Company (ABC), and by the end of the war, ABC had 195 affiliates and was a full-fledged competitor for the older networks.

▲ Innovation and Change: 1945–1954

The nine-year period following World War II was marked by great changes in both the radio and recording industries, changes that ultimately drove them closer together. The development of television delayed the growth of FM radio, altered the nature of network radio, and forced the radio industry to rely on records as the most important part of a new programming strategy.

The Growth of FM   Despite the fact that FM sounded better than AM, was static free, and could reproduce a wider range of sound frequencies, AM broadcasting had started first, and FM struggled to catch up. FM had the misfortune of beginning its development at the same time as TV. In addition, because of technical considerations, both FM radio and TV are suited for about the same place in the electromagnetic spectrum, and in 1945 the FCC decided to give the rapidly expanding TV service the space formerly occupied by FM. The commission moved FM "upstairs" to the 88- to 108-MHz band (where it is today), thus rendering obsolete about half a million FM radios.

The Emergence of Television   Of course, the biggest change in radio's fortunes came about because of the emergence of television. (Chapter 10 has more to say about the development of TV.) By 1948 it was apparent that TV would take over the mass entertainment function served by network radio. The emergence of TV meant changes in the content, economics, and functions of radio. Although many individuals believe that television cut into the revenues of the radio industry, no such thing happened. In fact, radio revenues rose steadily from 1948 to 1952 and, after a brief drop from 1953 to 1956, continued to rise. The part of the industry upon which TV did have a drastic effect was network radio. The percentage of local stations with network affiliations dropped from 97 percent in 1947 to only 50 percent by 1955. Network revenue dropped by 60 percent in approximately the same period. Faced with this loss, stations relied more heavily on revenue from ads for local businesses. In short, they redistributed the makeup of their revenue dollar. As TV became the new mass medium, local stations cut back on their budgets; relied more heavily on music, talk, and news; and began searching for a formula that would allow them to coexist with television.

Specialized Formats   By 1956 it was obvious that the radio networks would no longer be the potent programming source they had been in the past. In that year radio networks were carrying only about 35 hours of sponsored evening programs each week. Finally, by 1960 all the once-popular evening programs and daytime serials had come to an end. Radio network service was limited primarily to news and short features, usually amounting to no more than 2 or 3 hours of time a day.

Local stations soon adapted to this change. Now that they no longer were tied to the networks for the bulk of their programming, they were free to develop their own personalities. Most did so by adopting a specialized format, a sound that had distinctive appeal to a certain segment of the audience. The most successful experiment occurred in the Midwest, where a station began monitoring the sales of records and sheet music and playing those tunes that were selling the most. Hence, the Top 40 format was born.

In the 1950s the DJ became an important figure in radio programming. In fact, many became stars in their own right. DJs sent out glossy pictures of themselves to their fans; they appeared at supermarket openings and record hops; they were the emcees at personal appearances by rock-and-roll groups. As the DJs became more influential, they also began to program their own shows. They picked the records that they would play during their shifts.

Record promoters also recognized the tremendous importance of airplay in the marketing of a hit. The more a record was played on the radio, the more copies it sold. Naturally, record promoters and DJs began to develop close ties. In the beginning the relationship was innocent enough. Promoters would make sure that DJs got the latest releases their companies were offering, and they also put in a good word or two about their companies' products. Competition grew intense, however, and by 1959 about 250 new records were being released every week. Some unscrupulous promoters resorted to more than words to advance their records. At first, they would send DJs an elaborate Christmas gift. If that did not work, some even "hired" the DJ as "creative consultant" and paid him or her a fee every month. Others would cut the DJ in on the action and offer to pay a penny to the DJ for every record sold in the market. Eventually, most promoters stopped these charades and simply passed the DJ an envelope filled with cash in return for airplay of their company's songs. In 1958 and 1959, record distributors reportedly spent over a quarter-million dollars in the larger markets on payola.

The news of this illicit business practice did nothing to help the image of rock and roll or of broadcasting. Section 508 was added to the 1934 Communications Act to stop this practice, but it was not altogether successful. New payola scandals broke out in the industry in the early 1970s. At least one record company was accused of offering drugs to station personnel in return for increased airplay, and some concert promoters were accused of offering monetary bribes. Payola resurfaced in 2000 when 80 program directors at Spanish-language stations were investigated for allegedly taking bribes from Fonovisa Records.

The most recent twist in the payola saga involves independent promoters who charge music labels a fee to promote their records and pay money to radio stations for access to their programmers and playlists. The money involved can be substantial. In large markets the promoters might funnel as much as $300,000 to the stations. Record labels consider this just another promotional cost in getting their songs on radio. This arrangement is perfectly legal since no covert money flows directly from the labels to the stations. Despite its legitimacy the practice has drawn criticism from several sources. *Rolling Stone* labeled it "legal payola," and congressional leaders found the practice troubling. In response Clear Channel and other radio group owners announced in 2003 that they were cutting their ties with independent promoters. But in 2005 Sony BMG was involved in yet another payola scandal.

Most recently, the nation's four largest radio companies agreed to a $10 million deal in payments and other considerations in order to settle a year-long FCC investigation into claims that stations owned by the companies accepted cash and other gifts from music companies in return for playing their releases. Part of the money in the 2007 agreement would go to a fund to be used in training stations to avoid payola.

Only time will tell if this latest development will stop the practice. Payola seems to be one problem that will not disappear.

Featuring a bright, continuous, and upbeat sound, the format was ruled by the **clock hour,** which specified every element of programming. The success of the Top 40 sound encouraged radio stations to experiment with other specialized formats. By 1964 at least a dozen different formats, ranging from country to rock to classical, had sprung up.

▲ Growth and Stabilization: 1955–1990

The number of radio stations continued to grow during these years, from 3,343 in 1955 to more than 7,000 in 1970. More and more stations adopted the Top 40 format, and it very quickly became the format of choice among young listeners—who, as it happened, had a good deal of money to spend on the records they heard played by their favorite disc jockey, or DJ. Since at this time the DJ had control of what songs were played on the air, he or she became the focus of promotional efforts by record companies to gain airplay for their new songs. All too soon this arrangement led to the growth of **payola** (see the boxed insert "Payola").

The most significant development in radio during the 1970s and 1980s was the emergence of FM. By the early 1960s AM stations were becoming harder to obtain; it was easier to get an FM license. The FCC passed the **nonduplication rule,** which prevented an AM-FM combination from duplicating its AM content on its FM station for more than 50 percent of the time. Faced with this ruling, FM stations developed their own kind of sound (many went to a rock format) that capitalized on FM's better technical

FIGURE 7-1

Division of AM and FM
Audiences

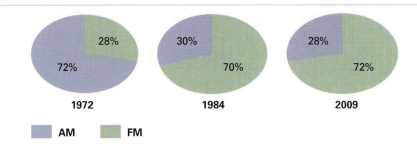

qualities. As a result the number of FM stations tripled between 1960 and 1970, and profits began to increase. By 1990 FM accounted for about 70 percent of listening time. Many AM stations switched to a news/talk format in order to stop the audience erosion (see Figure 7-1).

A noncommercial radio network, **National Public Radio (NPR),** went on the air in the early 1970s with an 80-station network. Over the next few years its number of affiliates doubled, and by 1980 it was reaching a cumulative audience of more than 5 million people per week. Its most successful programs were its daily news programs *Morning Edition* and *All Things Considered.*

▲ Contemporary Radio

The pivotal event for radio in the 1990s was the passage of the **Telecommunications Act of 1996.** The act was concerned primarily with encouraging competition in the new communication technologies, but the radio industry, through skillful lobbying, was able to include itself in the bill. Only a few sentences in the final version of the act concern radio, but those few sentences had an impact out of proportion to their length. A key provision completely erased the cap on the number of stations a company could own and increased to eight the number of stations a company could own in a single market.

The new law caused an avalanche of buying and selling of radio properties, and some stations were sold several times in a single year. In a typical year before the act, about $2 billion was spent on radio acquisitions and mergers. In 1996 the number hit $14.4 billion. That figure was eclipsed the next year when $15.3 billion was spent. New radio giants sprang up almost overnight. The radio industry became even more consolidated as a few large group owners dominated the industry.

On the programming front, talk became the hottest format on AM radio, thanks to the success of such performers as Rush Limbaugh, Dr. Laura Schlessinger, Tom Joyner, and Sean Hannity. The trend toward format specialization continued on FM as stations recognized that attracting as little as 2–3 percent of the audience was enough to keep them profitable.

The first decade of the new century saw several important developments. Two satellite radio companies, XM and Sirius, began operation, transmitting digital signals to subscribers and offering dozens of talk and commercial-free music channels. The two companies struggled financially and finally merged in 2008.

The recession at the end of the decade slowed the trend toward consolidation in the radio industry. Clear Channel, owner of more than 1,200 radio stations, was acquired by a group of private investors in 2008 and sold off more than 400 of its stations. Other radio station groups were also up for sale, but the bad economy scuttled potential deals. The radio industry also saw its advertising revenue decrease.

The radio industry introduced HD radio, a high-quality digital signal, but the innovation was slow to catch on. Even though more than 1,700 stations were broadcasting HD by 2010, HD radio set sales were minuscule and many consumers were unaware that HD radio even existed.

Thousands of Internet-only radio stations were in operation, and many terrestrial broadcasters expanded their offerings on the Web. The economic future of online radio is closely tied to the amount of copyright fees that stations must pay to play music. Recent legislation called for rates to be negotiated by Web stations, and by 2009 some stations had worked out arrangements with copyright organizations.

Radio stations—satellite, terrestrial, and online—faced increasing competition from iPods, iPhones, and other devices that let people listen to their favorite music on MP3 players rather than on the radio. Other listeners turned to podcasts for information and entertainment. The increased competition is one of the factors that has caused the average amount of time a person spends listening to radio to decrease steadily since 1994.

Despite these difficulties, the radio industry is still a significant advertising medium. More than 230 million Americans listen to terrestrial and satellite radio every day, and many more tune in online. Radio gives advertisers a chance to reach potential customers in their cars and at work. Radio stations are learning how best to use the Web to increase their audiences and their income. In short, radio, in some form, will be around for many more years.

Radio in the Digital Age

▲ Transition

Terrestrial radio stations were slow to enter the digital age, but there are now signs that they are catching up. Early radio station Web sites simply streamed the audio from the station's analog broadcast and posted their playlists and maybe the bios of the DJs. All in all, they were seen as adjuncts to the over-the-air service.

The increased competition from online radio and declining ad revenues prompted terrestrial radio stations to come up with new Web strategies. The result was that traditional radio moved online in a big way.

▲ Terrestrial Stations on the Web

CBS Radio, owner of about 150 terrestrial stations, acquired Web broadcaster Last FM, where listeners can create and share their own playlists with others. CBS then made a deal with AOL Music that put CBS in charge of AOL's Internet radio service. A visitor to the AOL music site can select from about 150 CBS stations or from the 200 or so channels offered by AOL. CBS Radio also made a similar arrangement with Yahoo!'s Music Launchcast Radio, making CBS, one of the first terrestrial broadcasters, a major player online.

Clear Channel Radio took a more local approach and expanded the online versions of eight of its large-market stations as well as adding erockster, a site where listeners can listen to a nationwide service, tune in to one of Clear Channel's local stations, or listen to music-on-demand. Citadel Broadcasting launched Right Now Radio in 2006, a site that has links to the streaming audio of about 180 Citadel stations and interviews with music industry performers. Other group owners also expanded their online operations.

These moves are evidently paying off. At the start of 2008, traffic at terrestrial radio stations' Web sites had increased by about 20 percent from the previous year. Meanwhile, unique visitors to Internet-only stations decreased by about 10 percent. As more and more advertising dollars move online, it is likely that terrestrial radio broadcasters will devote even more energy and money to their online versions.

Radio talk show host Sean Hannity. His syndicated program reaches about 12 million people.

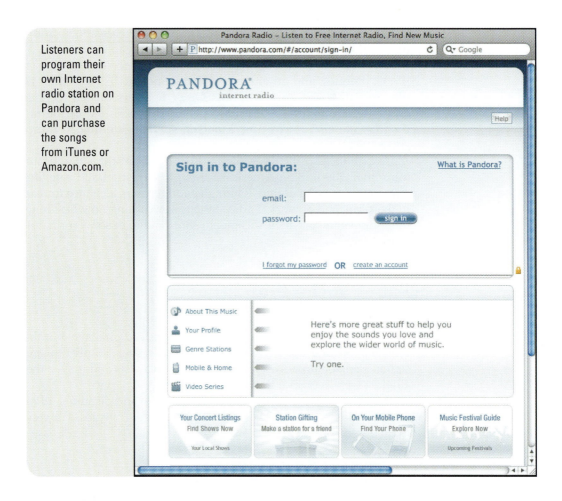

Listeners can program their own Internet radio station on Pandora and can purchase the songs from iTunes or Amazon.com.

▲ Internet Radio

There are thousands of **Internet-only radio stations** (or, as they are called in the business, pure-play Internet stations) on the Web. Some are one-person operations run out of a bedroom or garage, such as Blablaradionet. Many offer formats that would never be heard on traditional radio. One Internet station, for example, plays only accordion music; another broadcasts air traffic control transmissions. Others, like Pandora or slacker.com, are music services where users create their radio stations by generating playlists based on their favorite artists or songs. Slacker has about 2 million songs in its database. Other popular online radio sites are Live 365 and Radio Tower.

The biggest problem facing online radio is a financial one. Web stations must pay royalty fees to music performers, songwriters, composers, and record labels. (Terrestrial radio does not pay fees to performers or labels. The recording companies, however, were lobbying to change this situation. See below.) In 2007, the Copyright Royalty Board significantly increased the rates paid by Internet stations. For 2008, for example, Internet stations were scheduled to pay $0.0011 cent per song per listener. This may not sound like much, but the numbers quickly add up. One calculation found that AOL Music would wind up paying more than $1 million a month under the new arrangement. Smaller Web stations would be hard-pressed to stay in business. In 2008 Congress gave Internet stations additional time to negotiate rates with the Recording Industry Association of America, the group representing performers.

The situation is complicated because some Internet-only radio services would prefer to pay a flat percentage of their revenues, while others that have additional revenue streams prefer a per song/per listener system. Most Web radio services owned by terrestrial stations have negotiated their own per song arrangements. In July 2009, an agreement was reached that called for large commercial Webcasters to pay a reduced fee per song/per listener while smaller Web stations would pay a fee based on a percentage of their revenues or a percentage of their expenses.

▲ HD Radio

HD radio is a digital service that greatly improves the signal qualities of terrestrial radio stations. With HD radio an FM station sounds as good as a CD, while AM stations sound as good as current FM stations and are static free. Moreover, digital signals can be compressed so that a single station can broadcast several programs at once. For example, a station might play Top 40 music on its main analog and digital signal while broadcasting jazz or classical on its digital-only subchannels.

Consumers have to buy a special receiving set to receive the HD signals. Sets used to cost several hundred dollars, but many are now available for $80. Some automakers offer HD radio as an option in their new models. Many new HD radio receivers have an option called tagging that lets listeners press a button to tag a song that they heard on the radio. The tagged song is stored in an iPod that is cradled in the HD receiver. The next time the consumer synchs his or her iPod, he or she is given the option to purchase the song.

HD radio is still struggling in the marketplace. About a million HD sets were sold in 2008, but that's only about 1 percent of all radio sets that were sold. One of the problems is that HD radio hasn't broken any new ground. It simply offers more of the same with better sound quality.

▲ Satellite Radio

Sirius XM is the name of the new satellite company formed by the merger of Sirius and XM satellite radio services in 2008. About 18 million people subscribe to the new combined service. For about $13 a month, subscribers can listen to more than 70 music channels along with more than 30 talk channels. Listeners can also tune in over the Internet.

Commuters are the primary market for satellite radio. Sirius XM has introduced local traffic and weather channels in major cities that broadcast continuous updates. The company has also expanded beyond the automobile by offering portable receivers that can be used in the home.

Financial difficulties continue to plague satellite radio. Both XM and Sirius spent hundreds of millions of dollars attracting talent such as Howard Stern and Oprah Winfrey to their service as well as spending large sums for the rights to professional sports games. As a result, Sirius XM was struggling to reach profitability. The company was also hurt by the downturn in new car sales. Much of the company's growth was due to factory-installed satellite radio as an option for new car buyers.

▲ Mobile Radio

As noted below, mobility and portability have always been part of the defining features of traditional radio. Now both satellite and Internet radio are becoming more mobile. Sirius XM markets car and in-home receivers.

Radio is also showing up on cell phones. Since there are about 2 billion cell phone users worldwide, radio broadcasters are seriously looking at ways to reach this audience. Motorola, for instance, offers iRadio, a service that lets subscribers listen to a preselected lineup of stations on their cell phones. In 2006 Clear Channel revealed plans to stream radio content to AT&T subscribers, and Infinity Radio announced a similar plan in cooperation with Nokia. There is also an iPhone application for mobile radio. Market research indicates that about 50 percent of people would like to have radio on their cell phones.

▲ User-Generated Content

The most obvious example of user-generated content is podcasting—recording an audio program and making it available for downloading from a Web site. Many traditional radio broadcasters, such as NPR and the BBC, produce hundreds of podcasts per year, but audience members can also get into the act. Podcast. net lists thousands of available programs ranging from personal rants to teen fashions. A public radio station in Chicago, called Vocalo, depends on user-generated content for almost all of its programming.

▲ Social Media

Radio stations, both terrestrial and online, have embraced social media. DJs at stations in large and small markets have started Facebook and MySpace pages along with Twitter accounts. DJ blogs with listener comments are standard on radio station Web sites. Entercom Communications started video channels on the Web sites of 70 of its stations where viewers can comment and contribute content. Clear Channel launched social network sites for a dozen of its music stations. The sites resemble mini MySpace pages but are geared for the local market served by the station. Users can create a profile, upload photos, and add friends.

Online radio service Pandora has a feature that allows listeners to keep track of their friends and exchange messages. Live 365 offers message boards and chat rooms and has a Twitter account. Last FM has similar features. In sum, social media are a significant part of the strategy used by radio stations to attract and keep an audience.

> **SOUNDBYTE**
>
> **Radio for the Birds**
>
> When a new British digital radio station first went on the air, it broadcast a looped, 20-minute recording of birdcalls so that engineers could correctly adjust the signal. The birdcalls were supposed to be temporary and were scheduled to be replaced by the station's permanent format. The station was totally surprised when a half-million listeners tuned in to hear the calls of pigeons, swallows, robins, and blackbirds. The format was so successful that the station renamed itself Birdsong Radio.

Defining Features of Radio

Radio is portable. Some radio sets, like the Walkman, are small and personal. Others, like the boom box, are big and public. No matter their size, radio sets are easily transported and go everywhere—the beach, sporting events, jogging trails, the workplace. Car radios provide news and entertainment to commuters on their way to and from work. In fact, it is hard to find a place where radio cannot go.

Radio is supplemental. Most radio listening occurs while we are doing something else—driving, working, studying, falling asleep, waking up, cleaning, and so on. Radio rarely is the prime focus of our attention; it provides an audio background for our activities.

Radio is universal. Virtually every household has at least one working radio. In fact, the average house has about six. Almost every car is equipped with a radio. In an average day about 70 percent of Americans listen to radio.

Radio is selective. Much like the magazine industry (see Chapter 5), the radio industry has become a niche medium. Radio stations choose formats that attract a small, narrowly defined audience that is attractive to advertisers. As mentioned earlier, if a radio broadcaster can find a formula that attracts just 2–3 percent of the audience, odds are that the station will turn a profit.

Organization of the Terrestrial Radio Industry

There are more than a half-billion working radio sets in the United States. That works out to about two radios per person. There are about 13,970 radio stations in operation. Thanks in part to an FCC philosophy that encouraged competition, the number of stations increased 100 percent from 1970 to 2008. To understand how this rapidly growing business is organized, we will examine it from several perspectives: programming, technology, and format.

▲ Local Stations, Nets, and Syndicators

Local radio stations operate in cities, towns, and villages across the country. Big cities have many stations. New York City has about 90; Los Angeles, about 60. Smaller towns may have only one or two. Whitefish, Montana, for example (population 4,000), has four stations. Programming for these stations is provided by networks (nets), program syndication companies, and locally produced music and talk. Technically, the distinction between a net and a syndication service is that all stations on a network carry the net program at the same time, while syndicated programming is carried at different times by the stations. In practice, however, much syndicated radio programming is satellite-delivered and carried simultaneously, and many network affiliates record net programming and broadcast it later. To make things even more complicated, the traditional networks also offer syndicated programs. Consequently, the distinction between the two services may no longer be meaningful.

Some of the most popular syndicators and networks are the Premiere Networks, operated by Clear Channel, which carries, among others, Glenn Beck and Bob Costas; Dial Global Networks, home of the American Comedy Network, Clark Howard, and Ed Schultz; and the Westwood One Networks, home of Charles Osgood and Dennis Miller. The syndicated shows of Rush Limbaugh, Sean Hannity, and Tom Joyner continue to be popular. Many radio stations also subscribe to syndicated shows in specialized areas. The Motor Racing Network, for example, supplies coverage of major NASCAR races to more than 700 stations.

▲ AM and FM Stations

Broadcast radio stations are either AM or FM. **AM** stands for *amplitude modulation*, and **FM** stands for *frequency modulation*. As we saw earlier in the chapter, since about 1975 the fortunes of FM radio have been increasing while those of AM stations are on the decline. In 2009, almost three-quarters of listenership went to the FM stations. Keep in mind, however, that some AM stations, particularly those in large markets, are doing quite well. In 2009, AMs were the top-rated stations in Boston (WBZ), St. Louis (KMOX), and Cincinnati (WLW).

All physical factors being equal, radio signals sent by AM travel farther, especially at night, than signals sent by FM. The AM dial on a typical radio set illustrates

The WYNK humvee on a remote in Baton Rouge, Louisiana. Remotes are an important part of promotion for a local radio station.

FIGURE 7-2 Simplified Diagram of the Electromagnetic Spectrum

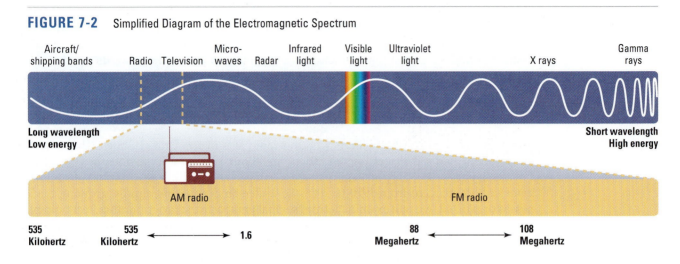

the precise frequencies in the electromagnetic spectrum where the AM station operates. AM stations are further classified by channels. There are three possible channels: clear, regional, and local. A clear channel is one with a single dominant station that is designed to provide service over a wide area. Typically, these dominant stations have a strong signal because they broadcast with 50,000 watts of power. For example, the 720 spot on the AM dial is a clear channel with WGN, Chicago, the dominant station, operating at 50,000 watts. The 770 position is also a clear channel with WABC, New York, dominant. A regional channel is one shared by many stations that serve fairly large areas. A local channel is designed to be shared by a large number of stations that broadcast only to their local communities.

FM signals do not travel as far as AM, but FM has the advantage of being able to produce better sound qualities than AM. FM radio is also less likely to be affected by outside interference such as thunderstorms. Similar to AM, FM stations are organized in classes. Class C FM stations are the most powerful, operating at 100,000 watts. Class B and Class A stations are less powerful. A glance at the FM radio dial reveals that FM stations operate in a different part of the electromagnetic spectrum than does AM. Figure 7-2 is a simplified diagram of the spectrum showing where AM, FM, and television signals are located.

Much of a radio station's operation is automated. A computer sequences when songs play, when commercials run, and when the DJ talks. Modern radio broadcasting equipment has become so compact that a radio station could easily fit inside the average dorm room (except for the antenna tower).

When radio stations broadcast a digital signal, the old analog transmission is replaced by a series of 0s and 1s that represent various sound frequencies. The digital receiver translates these numbers back into sound waves. Obviously, the analog AM and FM distinctions do not apply to digital radio.

▲ **Station Formats**

Perhaps the most meaningful way we can organize radio stations is according to their **format,** a type of consistent programming designed to appeal to a certain segment of the audience. A format gives a station a distinctive personality and attracts a certain kind of audience that advertisers find desirable. In fact, the development of radio after 1960 is marked by the fine-tuning of existing formats and the creation of new ones that appeal to people in distinct demographic and lifestyle categories. Most modern stations can offer an amazingly precise description of the kind of listener they want their format to attract. An adult contemporary station, for example, might set its sights on men and women, ages 25–45, with college educations, making more than $80,000 a year, who read

Rolling Stone, drive either a BMW or a Volvo, and go to the mall at least twice a week. In our discussion we will cover three basic categories of radio formats: music, ethnic, and news/talk.

The Music Format

The music format is the largest category and includes many subdivisions and variations. In 2009 the two most listened-to formats were adult contemporary (AC) with about 14 percent of the audience and contemporary hit radio (CHR) with about 11 percent. The main appeal of the AC format is to 25- to 49-year-old females. AC stations play the "hits of the '80s, '90s, and today" with a blend of about 80 percent oldies and 20 percent current tunes. Coldplay, The Fray, and Nickelback are artists who are likely to be heard on AC stations.

CHR (also called Top 40) features a small playlist of hits in a fast rotation. The format does best with the 16–24 age group. Artists whose songs were frequently played on CHR stations in 2009 included Gwen Stefani, Beyoncé, and Britney Spears.

Other top formats are urban and country. The urban format showcases a large number of African American artists and plays rap, hip-hop, and dance music. The format is aimed at city dwellers but has attracted listeners in rural areas as well. As of 2009, some prominent urban artists were Ne-Yo, Kanye West, and Jay-Z.

Country stations, as the name suggests, play hit country-and-western singles and employ DJs who are down-home, friendly, and knowledgeable about country music. The country format has two main divisions: (1) traditional country stations that play mainstream classic, twangy country music and (2) contemporary country stations that play more current artists who might use synthesizers and other modern sounds. A country station's audience still mainly comprises adults ages 35–55.

Black and Ethnic Formats

These formats aim for special audiences that are defined primarily by race and nationality. There are about 175 stations that program for the black audience, and about 260 stations that serve the Hispanic audience. Many of the black and Hispanic stations feature urban contemporary music and run news, features, and special programs of interest to their audiences. In addition, about 60 stations have formats aimed at other ethnic groups: Polish, German, Italian, French, Irish, and Greek.

Format Homogenization

Radio stations sound pretty much alike no matter where you are. Almost all the major music formats are represented in the large and medium markets, and it seems that every market has its morning "zoo crew"; an AC station that specializes in "the classic hits" of the 1980s, 1990s, and today; a modern rock station that calls itself "Power" or "Z" or "Q" something or other; an easy-listening station with a "warm" format that dedicates love songs at night; and maybe even an AM station that specializes in "golden oldies." Even the DJs sound pretty much the same.

Hits by artists such as Jay-Z are a mainstay on the playlists of urban contemporary stations.

There are several reasons for this trend toward homogenization. The most important is the increasing consolidation in the industry. Big radio companies own stations in all the big markets. What works in one market is likely to work in another. In addition, it is cheaper to program the same music from market to market. Finally, radio has become so competitive that programming decisions are based on the recommendations of program consultants and on surveys and focus groups. Since the same records are generally tested in all markets and usually score high, the recommendations about what to play are the same from market to market. Not surprisingly, many stations prefer to adopt a "safe" format, one that has worked in other markets, rather than risking a sizable amount of money on a new and untested format.

News/Talk Format   This format is becoming more and more popular on the AM band and accounts for 17 percent of all radio listening time. Some stations emphasize the news part of the news/talk format. National, regional, and local news reports are broadcast periodically throughout the day. Sports, traffic, weather, editorials, public affairs programs, and an occasional feature round out the programming day. News stations appeal primarily to a male audience in the 25- to 54-year-old age category.

The talk format attracts listeners in about the same age group. Common types of programs that appear on stations using the talk format are call-in shows, usually hosted by an opinionated and maybe even abrasive host; interview shows; advice shows; and roundtable discussions. News, weather, traffic reports, and other feature material are blended in with these programs. Unlike the music formats, which do not demand their listeners' close attention, the talk format requires that its audience concentrate on the program in order to follow what is being said.

▲ Noncommercial Radio

Many of the early radio stations that went on the air during the 1920s were founded by educational institutions. As the commercial broadcasting system became firmly established, many educational stations were bought by commercial broadcasters, and

Ira Glass is producer and host of NPR's *This American Life.*

the fortunes of noncommercial radio dwindled. In 1945, with the coming of FM broadcasting, the FCC set aside several frequencies for educational broadcasting. This action sparked a rebirth of interest in this kind of broadcasting, so that by 2009 there were about 2,400 noncommercial radio stations on the air.

Most noncommercial radio stations are owned by educational institutions or private foundations. Noncommercial radio gets its support from the institutions that own the stations. Ultimately, much of this support comes from tax revenue since taxes support most public educational institutions. Other sources of support are endowments (gifts), grants from foundations or the federal government, and listener donations.

Noncommercial stations are served by National Public Radio (NPR). Founded in 1970, NPR provides program services to about 850 affiliates around the country. Member stations pay a fee based on audience reach and annual budget and receive in return about 50 hours of programming per week. Many of these shows are produced at NPR headquarters; others are produced at NPR stations and distributed by NPR. Probably the best-known NPR programs are *All Things Considered* and *Morning Edition.* About 33 million people listen to NPR every week.

The public radio stations that help support NPR receive financial support from the Corporation for Public Broadcasting (CPB), a private, nonprofit organization funded by Congress. Member stations receive money from the CPB, and those that decide to affiliate with NPR pay some of this money to the network as a fee. NPR also receives grants directly from the CPB. Congress, however, has threatened to cut the CPB's budget, which, in turn, would lead to less money for stations and for NPR. Consequently, many public radio stations have resorted to underwriting, a practice in which the station accepts money from a person or an organization in return for an acknowledgment on the air. In some cases these acknowledgments sound suspiciously like commercials. In contrast, NPR for the most part has resisted the pressure to air these minicommercials. In 1995, however, NPR relented a bit and allowed underwriters to broadcast brief slogans. NPR's financial fortunes were helped in 2003 when Joan Kroc, widow of McDonald's founder Ray Kroc, donated $200 million to the network.

Unlike commercial radio networks, NPR has found a way to generate significant revenue from the digital revolution: The network is one of the biggest podcasters in the world. Apple's iTunes lists more than 50 NPR shows in its menu, with more than 300 titles available to download. NPR sells sponsorship of these podcasts to advertisers who wish to reach the network's relatively affluent listeners. Podcasts sponsored by the auto maker Acura, for example, have been downloaded more than 25 million times. The success of NPR's podcasts has caused some controversy, however. Local NPR affiliates worry that people will download the podcasts and not listen to the local station, thus hurting the local station's chances to raise money during on-air fund drives.

The other noncommercial radio network, Public Radio International (PRI), was formerly known as American Public Radio. The Minneapolis organization is a network that acquires and distributes programming from station-based, independent and international producers. Unlike NPR, PRI does not produce any of its programming, but it does finance program production at member stations. A noncommercial station can be an affiliate of both NPR and PRI.

Organization of Online Radio

Unlike terrestrial broadcasting, online radio is streamed directly to a computer. After a brief lag time, the signal starts to play. Anybody who has access to content and the appropriate hardware and software can start an Internet radio station. This fact makes it difficult to construct a comprehensive organizational arrangement. Nevertheless, there are three major types of stations:

1. *Online stations that are affiliated with a terrestrial station.* Many of these simply simulcast what is currently playing on the terrestrial station; others may simulcast part of the time and depart from the terrestrial station's format part of the time.

2. *Choice-based stations,* such as Pandora and Last FM, that let listeners choose their favorite artists and types of music in order to create their own playlists. In effect, listeners program their own unique radio station.

3. *Format-specific Internet-only stations.* These are stations that play narrowly focused genres of music, such as dr-love.com, specializing in rap and rhythm and blues; Radio Free Kansas, specializing in progressive rock; and CityBeat Radio, specializing in trance and electro. There are hundreds of these stations on the Internet; some are one-person operations; others are part of larger organizations.

Most online stations depend upon advertising for support. Others may run ads but also ask for listener contributions. To get some idea about the diversity of radio stations on the Internet, visit www.radiotower.com for a list of more than 5,000 stations.

Ownership in the Radio Industry

As mentioned earlier, the 1996 Telecommunications Act drastically changed the landscape of the radio industry by producing a wave of consolidation that left the industry controlled by a few big media companies. Clear Channel, for example, managed to acquire more than 1,200 radio stations. As of 2009, the trend toward consolidation in terrestrial radio had stopped, at least for the moment, as Clear Channel sold hundreds of its radio stations after being bought by a group of independent investors. Nonetheless, the radio industry was still dominated by big companies. In addition to Clear Channel, other big owners were Cumulus (more than 300 stations) and Citadel (more than 200 stations).

The trend for satellite radio was in the other direction as Sirius and XM merged into a single company. The merger was not an easy one, requiring two years to gain approval by the Federal Communications Commission and the Justice Department.

SOUNDBYTE

13,000 Radio Stations in the Palm of Your Hand

The Aluratek Company has introduced a thumb drive, called Jukebox, which allows users to listen to 13,000 Internet radio stations. Jukebox stores station information and listening software in its memory. All a user has to do is plug the device into a USB port and start listening. There's even a search function that allows a person to search by format and location. So, if you're in the mood for some Scandinavian rap, Jukebox will find you a station.

Producing Radio Programs

▲ Departments and Staff

The departmental structure of a terrestrial radio station varies according to its size. Obviously, a small station with five or six employees has a departmental setup different from that of a large station with a hundred-person staff.

The two top management positions are the general manager and the program director. The manager has the responsibility for planning and carrying out station policy, maintaining contact with the community, and monitoring program content, audience ratings, and sales information. The program director is responsible for the station's sound. He or she supervises the music or other program material that the station broadcasts and also hires and fires announcers and DJs. Other staff members take responsibility for maintaining the online operation.

The sales department consists of the sales manager and the station's sales force. The news department is responsible for compiling the station's local newscasts and rewriting the wire service reports of national and regional news. The engineering department, under the supervision of the chief engineer, is staffed with technicians responsible for keeping the station on the air and maintaining the equipment.

▲ Putting Together a Program

This section will concentrate on how traditional radio programs are produced for the music, talk, and news formats.

Music Format   When the staff of a local station puts together their program, the first step is generally to lay out a **format wheel** (also called a *format clock*), a pie chart of an hour divided into segments representing different program elements. Figure 7-3 is a simplified version of a wheel for a contemporary rock station. (Note that Figure 7-3 is a visual aid, not something you would find at a radio station. All of the sequencing and scheduling represented in Figure 7-3 is handled by computers.)

Note that the music is structured to flow from one segment to another. Album cuts and hits from the past are spread around the wheel. Additional wheels would be constructed for the various parts of the broadcast day (that is, one wheel for morning

FIGURE 7-3

Format Wheel for a
Contemporary Rock
Station

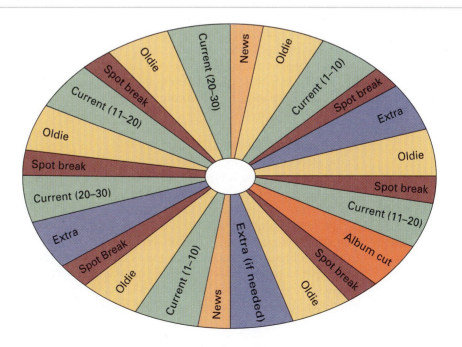

drive time, another for 10 A.M.–4 P.M., another for evening drive time, and another for 7 P.M.–midnight).

Talk Format   Most of the content of the talk format is produced by the local station. As is the case with the music format, the makeup of the audience is taken into account. During drive time, talk segments should be relatively short and liberally interspersed with news, weather, and traffic reports. The audience for the 10 A.M.–4 P.M. segment tends to be primarily female, and therefore, topics for discussion reflect the interests of that group. The early-evening audience is generally younger and contains more males.

Producing a talk show requires more equipment than does producing a simple DJ program. Speaker telephones and extra telephone lines are needed, as is a delay system. This device gives the talk-show moderator a 7- to 30-second delay period during which he or she can censor what is said by the caller. Another important part of the talk show is the telephone screener. The screener ranks the waiting calls by importance, letting the most interesting callers go first, and filters out crank calls or calls from regulars who contact the station too frequently.

All-News Format   The all-news station also works with a programming wheel, similar to that of the music format. Instead of music, however, the news wheel shows the spacing between headlines, weather, news, sports, business reports, and commercials. It also illustrates the **cycle,** the amount of time that elapses before the program order is repeated.

The all-news format is the most difficult to produce. A large staff, consisting of anchorpersons, a managing editor, local reporters, editors, rewrite people, a traffic reporter, and stringers (freelance reporters who are paid per story), is needed. The list of necessary equipment and facilities is also long: radio wire services, sports wire, weather wire, mobile units, police- and fire-frequency scanners, short-wave receivers, and perhaps even a helicopter.

The Economics of Radio

Radio was affected by the economic recession at the end of the decade. Total revenue in 2008 was $19.5 billion, down about 9 percent from 2007. Further, radio's share of the total amount spent on advertising in the United States also declined during that same period. In short, money that used to be spent on radio ads is now being spent in other media.

On the bright side, terrestrial radio still reaches about 235 million people a week and its drive-time audience is growing, thanks to longer commuting times. Another 13.5 million per week listen online. Radio also attracts targeted audiences, something that appeals to advertisers. Music programming is cheap since much of it comes free courtesy of the recording companies. (The recording industry is trying to change this. See the boxed insert "Should Radio Pay More?")

▲ Sources of Revenue

Radio stations earn their money by selling advertising time. The amount that a radio station charges for time is included in its rate card. A typical radio commercial costs several hundred dollars in large cities. The same commercial in a small town might cost only a few dollars.

The radio industry has four sources of income from the sale of commercial time. The first comes from the sale of spots on network programs to national advertisers trying to reach a broad market. The second is the sale of time on local stations to advertisers who wish to reach a specific region (such as the Northeast) or a specific type of market (such as rural areas). This is called *national spot advertising.* The third source is advertising purchased by local establishments that want their commercials to be heard only in the

For about the last 80 years terrestrial radio stations have paid royalties to songwriters, publishers, and composers, but they have never paid royalties to performers or record labels. In 1995 the U.S. Copyright Office authorized a recording industry organization called SoundExchange to collect and distribute performance royalties for artists and labels when their recordings are played on satellite radio, the Internet, and cable and satellite television. Terrestrial radio was exempt from this ruling.

The rationale behind this arrangement is that radio stations are giving performers and labels free advertising and promotion by playing their songs. When listeners buy songs after hearing them on the radio, part of the purchase price goes to the performer and label. The radio industry argument is this: The more radio exposure, the more sales and the more money earned by the artist and label. We're already helping the artists and labels make money, so why should we pay more?

This deal worked fine as long as both the radio and recording industry were making money, but times are different now, especially for the record companies who have seen their revenues drop because of file sharing and a shift away from profitable CDs to less-profitable single-track downloads.

The recording industry argues that radio air play is not that important anymore when it comes to promoting sales. There are plenty of places where consumers can hear music—Internet stations, satellite radio, Facebook pages, and so on. Radio is no longer the only engine for driving sales, so the exemption for terrestrial radio no longer makes sense.

Terrestrial broadcasters respond that if they have to start paying more fees to play music, many stations will no longer be able to make a profit and will shut down or shift to formats that don't require payments. Some in the broadcasting industry also point out that there are still quite a few rich recording artists who have done quite well without being paid performance royalties.

The recording industry took its case to Congress in 2007 as bills to end terrestrial radio's exemption from paying performance royalties were introduced in both the House and Senate. The recording industry has tried this tactic in previous years but has not been successful. The broadcasting industry has a strong lobby and is likely to vigorously oppose this proposed legislation. In any case, the next few years will be pivotal.

immediate community. The fourth is off-air income, mainly derived from revenue generated by advertising on the station's Web site and merchandising. In 2008, each of these sources represented the following amounts of each dollar of radio revenue:

- Local: 70 cents
- National spot: 15 cents
- Off-air: 9 cents
- Network: 6 cents

The numbers indicate that the overwhelming amount of revenue in radio came from local commercials. It is interesting to note, however, that only the off-air category showed an increase from 2007 to 2008.

▲ General Expenses

Expenses in radio are divided into five areas: (1) technical, (2) programming, (3) sales, (4) general administration, and (5) news. Technical expenses include the payroll for the engineering staff and the cost of maintaining and replacing equipment. Program costs cover salaries paid to talent, outlays for tapes and CDs, and music fees paid to the music licensing organizations. Sales costs are made up of the salaries of the sales staff and all the other expenses that go with selling. General administrative expenses include the salaries of all management, secretarial, and clerical personnel; the depreciation of physical facilities; the cost of office supplies; and any interest that is due on loans to the station. News expenses consist of the costs involved in covering local and national stories.

As of 2008, general administration expenses ranked first, accounting for about 40 percent of all expenses. Programming came next, making up about 20 percent of the expense dollar, followed closely by costs associated with sales. News and technical expenses taken together accounted for about 15 percent.

Radio and the Local Community

The philosophy that guided the development of radio in the United States was based on localism. Radio stations were licensed to serve the public interest of those who could hear their signals. Stations were expected to be integral parts of their local communities and responsive to the needs of local residents. The Federal Radio Commission set aside a number of AM channels that were dedicated to lower-power stations serving a particular town. Over the years other regulations were enacted that favored localism. To encourage the development of roots in the community, owners were required to hold on to stations for three years before they could be sold. Stations had to survey their listeners and ascertain the needs of their community, and then provide programs to address those needs. Caps were placed on the number of stations one company could own to discourage large corporations from becoming out-of-town station owners with little or no ties to the community. In an effort to ensure access for many voices, there were further caps on the number of stations that could be owned in one market.

As pointed out by Charles Fairchild in his article "Deterritorializing Radio: Deregulation and the Continued Triumph of the Corporatist Perspective in the USA," which appeared in a 1999 issue of *Media, Culture and Society,* this localist philosophy is not much with us today. His analysis of changes in the radio industry in recent decades is a good example of a critical/cultural investigation that focuses on ideology and power relationships in society.

In essence, Fairchild argues that recent changes have removed the connection between a radio station and its local community. He suggests that there are two dominant ideologies in force that compete as definitions of the *public interest.* One, the statist position, conceives of government as the protector of the public interest and an agency that ensures that the broadest number of people benefit from the medium. The other, the corporatist view, holds that the

market is the best determiner of the public interest. The most economically successful service is that which succeeds best in the marketplace. In other words, the public interest is what interests the public.

Fairchild notes that the corporatist view has been the dominant model in recent radio operations. Due in part to an active industry lobby and the economic power wielded by large communications corporations, recent changes have almost erased the notion of local service. Following are just a few of those changes: The three-year ownership rule has been dropped; the requirements for ascertaining the needs of the community have been minimized; and perhaps most importantly, the cap on the total number of stations that can be owned has been removed, and the limit on the number of stations that can be owned in a market has been raised to eight.

What are the effects of this change in ideology? The radio industry has become consolidated, with big corporations controlling hundreds of stations. Locally owned stations that had deep roots in the community have been gobbled up by big companies whose headquarters are in some faraway city and whose main interest is the bottom line. Consequently, local programming has been reduced in favor of standardized entertainment and news fed from some central location nowhere near the local community. Programming decisions are left to consultants and syndicators who have no local ties whatsoever. Hence, as Fairchild suggests, radio has become "deterritorialized," detached from a community connection.

Fairchild concludes that the corporatist ideology has triumphed: "local radio stations are the objects of unaccountable control from outside local communities and neither the government nor the public have any levers of power with which they can influence broadcasters to provide access to those voices which cannot gain any serious measure of volume elsewhere."

Feedback for Radio

▲ Meters and Diaries

For the last several decades **Arbitron** has provided measurement of the radio audience. Arbitron surveyed approximately 280 radio markets and reported its results to stations, networks, syndication companies, and advertisers.

Individuals who were chosen at random from telephone listings were mailed pocket-sized diaries and asked to record their in-home and out-of-home listening (see Figure 7-4). Arbitron mailed out 3,000 to 4,000 diaries in a given market, and despite several reminders, usually less than 40 percent of the diaries were returned in usable form. The returned diaries underwent about three to four weeks of analysis before the data were sent to stations and other customers.

Arbitron changed its method in 2007 by introducing the **portable people meter (PPM).** The new device is similar to that used to compile television ratings (see Chapter 10). The PPM is clipped to an individual's clothes while that person goes about his or her daily

FIGURE 7-4

Sample Arbitron Radio Diary

Source: Arbitron Ratings: Your Radio Ratings Diary. Copyright © Arbitron Ratings Company. Reprinted by permission.

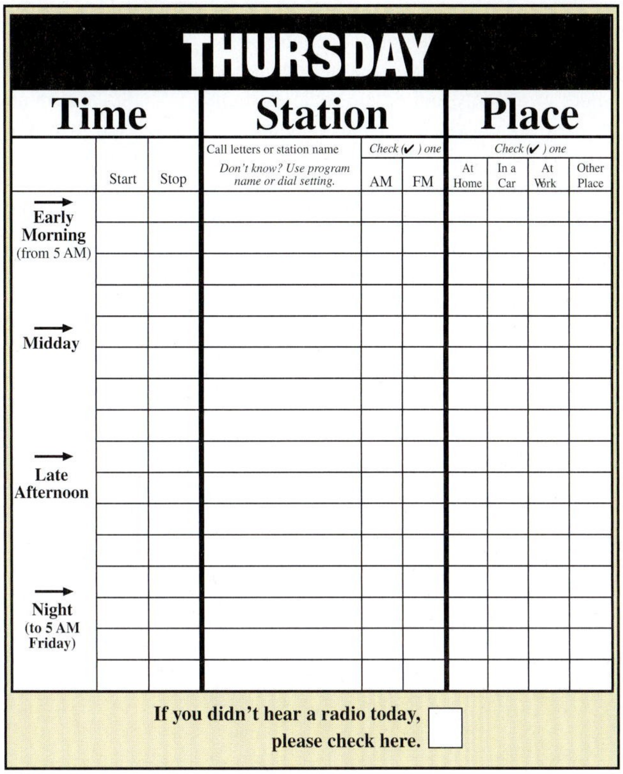

THURSDAY

Time			Station			Place			
	Start	Stop	Call letters or station name *Don't know? Use program name or dial setting.*	Check (✔) one: AM	FM	Check (✔) one: At Home	In a Car	At Work	Other Place
Early Morning (from 5 AM)									
Midday									
Late Afternoon									
Night (to 5 AM Friday)									

If you didn't hear a radio today, please check here. ☐

routine. Participating radio stations encode an inaudible unique signal as part of their broadcasts. The PPM "hears" the signal and records the station and the time spent listening. At the end of the day, a person slides the PPM into a docking device and the data are transmitted to a central computer where they are analyzed. Such a device requires far less effort than filling out a diary. Arbitron plans to have PPMs in all of the top 50 markets by the end of 2010. Smaller markets will still be measured by the paper diary.

When the first PPM ratings reports appeared in late 2007 and early 2008, they contained some surprises for radio broadcasters. Compared to the old diary method, the PPMs indicated that more total people were listening to radio but were spending less time with individual stations. Morning drive time did not draw as big an audience as previously thought, but more people were listening on weekends. Moreover, some stations saw their ratings plummet while others improved. In New York, for example, the number-one station as determined by the diary method dropped to 12th place after the PPMs were introduced, and the number-16 station jumped to number 8.

Many radio stations claimed that Arbitron's PPM sample underrepresented key demographic and ethnic groups. Under pressure from local broadcasters, attorneys general in New Jersey and New York sued Arbitron to prevent it from making its data commercially available. (See the boxed insert "PPM Unfair to Minority Radio Stations?") Amid continuing dissatisfaction with the PPM from stations, the A. C. Nielsen Company announced in late 2008 that, after a 46-year absence, it was reentering the radio ratings business to compete with Arbitron. Nielsen plans to use the diary method.

▲ Ratings and Shares

Measurements of radio and television audiences gathered by the diary or PPM method are usually expressed in terms of two related concepts: (1) ratings and (2) share of the audience. A **rating** is simply the ratio of listeners of a particular station to all people in the market. Suppose that in a market with 100,000 people, 20,000 listen to radio station

Technological innovations are often greeted with controversy. The PPM was no exception. When it was first introduced in major markets, owners of minority and ethnic radio stations noticed that it was their station's ratings that declined the most from the old diary method. In New York, for example, two stations were tied for second place using the diaries: One was a Spanish-language station and the other was a rhythm and blues station. After the PPM, the Spanish-language station dropped to 11th and the other station fell all the way to 17th. Declines such as these can cost stations significant amounts in advertising revenue and might even drive some stations out of business.

The ratings drops in New York and other markets prompted owners of ethnic stations to question the methods used by Arbitron in drawing its sample. For instance, owners of Hispanic stations questioned Arbitron's method of including only homes with traditional telephone lines, suggesting that many minority homes that have only cell phones are left out of the sample. They also questioned if the PPM sample was large enough to accurately reflect the listening behavior of all Hispanics. It was also noted that the PPM method used in some markets, such as New York, had not been accredited

by the Media Ratings Council, an industry organization that validates audience measurement.

Several minority radio broadcasters formed the PPM Coalition in order to petition the Federal Communications Commission to investigate Arbitron's methods. In addition, the minority broadcasters brought pressure in the political arena as well. Then–presidential nominee Barack Obama wrote a letter to Arbitron asking the company to postpone using the PPM until it was endorsed by the Media Ratings Council. In New York and New Jersey, the attorneys general filed suit against Arbitron to stop the commercial use of the devices.

Eventually, Arbitron worked out an agreement with both states. The company agreed to pay $100,000 to a project to support minority radio and agreed to modify its methods in order to include more minorities in its sample. It also will fund an ad campaign to promote minority radio and study ways to avoid bias against minorities when using the PPM methods. Minority broadcasters called Arbitron's decision a good first step but continued to press for additional changes in the company's procedures. This is a controversy that will probably persist for some time.

KYYY from 9:00 A.M. to 9:15 A.M. The rating of KYYY would be 20,000/100,000, or 20 percent. A **share of the audience** is the ratio of listeners of a particular station to the total number of radio listeners in the market. For example, again suppose that 20,000 people are listening to KYYY from 9:00 A.M. to 9:15 A.M. and that in the total market 80,000 people are listening to the radio during the same period. KYYY's share of the audience would be 20,000/80,000, or 25 percent. Shares of the audience divide the listening audience among all stations in the market. When they are summed, shares should total 100 percent. Ratings are important to stations because they are used to establish the rates stations will charge advertisers.

▲ Radio Audiences

There are almost twice as many radio sets in this country as there are people. As of January 2009, there were more than 575 million radio receivers scattered around the United States, with car radios accounting for about one-third of this number. On a typical day at least three-fourths of all adults will listen to radio, and the average person will listen, or at least have the radio on, for about 3 hours. Most people listen to radio in the early morning when they are getting ready for and driving to work and in the late afternoon when they are driving home. These two "day parts," consisting roughly from 6 A.M. to 10 A.M. and 4 P.M. to 7 P.M., are called *drive time*.

The precise audience makeup for a given station depends on that station's format. Top 40 stations draw an audience composed primarily of 12- to 24-year-olds, with females outnumbering males by about three to two. Modern rock attracts 18- to 34-year-olds, in about equal proportions of men and women. Jazz, classical, alt-country, and all-news formats generally attract an older crowd, with most of their audience coming from the 45-and-over age group. Country music stations seem to have an across-the-board appeal to those over 25. As a person gets older, he or she tends to evolve out of the audience for one format and move on to another.

CAREER >> OUTLOOK

The Radio Industry

The poor economy at decade's end has made the career outlook in radio somewhat pessimistic. The total number of employees in the traditional radio industry dropped by about 12 percent from 2000 to 2009. Much of this drop was caused by consolidation, the decline of radio news, and voice tracking. The outlook for radio news jobs and DJs is not bright. Careers in the sales department have somewhat better prospects. Online radio also seems to be a growth area, albeit a modest one.

The career outlook in the various media industries changes quickly. For a more current description of conditions in the radio industry and a more detailed look at career options, please consult the book's Web site: www.mhhe.com/dominick11e.

MAIN POINTS

- Radio started out as point-to-point communication, much like the telephone and telegraph. The notion of broadcasting did not come about until the 1920s.

- The decade of the 1920s was an important one in radio. Big business took control of the industry, receivers improved, commercials were started, networks were formed, and the FRC was set up to regulate radio.

- The coming of TV forced local stations to adopt formats, such as Top 40 or country.

- FM became the dominant form of radio in the 1970s and 1980s. Sparked by a loosening of ownership rules, a wave of consolidation took place in the industry during the 1990s.

- Radio is moving slowly into the digital age. Satellite radio and Internet radio are two digital services that will compete with traditional radio. Radio stations are introducing HD radio.

- Radio programming is provided by local stations, networks, and syndication companies.

- Stations have refined their formats to reach an identifiable audience segment.

- Most radio revenue comes from local advertising. Big companies now dominate large-market radio.

- Radio advertising revenue has recently declined.

- National Public Radio is the best-known public broadcaster.

- Radio audiences are measured by Arbitron using a diary method or the new personal people meter. The demographic characteristics of the radio listener vary greatly by station format.

QUESTIONS FOR REVIEW

1. What were the key developments during the 1920s that helped shape modern radio?

2. What impact did the Telecommunications Act of 1996 have on the radio industry?

3. What are the defining features of radio?

4. What is the function of a format wheel?

5. How is radio listening measured?

6. How do Internet stations differ from terrestrial stations?

QUESTIONS FOR CRITICAL THINKING

1. What might have happened if radio had developed during the 1930s—the Depression years—instead of the Roaring Twenties?

2. What formats might radio stations have developed if rock and roll had not come along?

3. The radio industry is highly concentrated. Consolidation may have helped radio's bottom line, but is the listener better served? Why or why not?

4. Listen to the radio stations in your market. Are there audience segments in the market that are not being served?

5. Read the boxed insert "Radio and the Local Community" on page 170, and consider the following: What effect might the Internet have on the amount of local news, information, and other services in a given community? Will the Internet allow access to "those voices which cannot gain any serious measure of volume elsewhere"? Who owns the radio stations in your hometown? How do the locally owned stations compare with those that are corporate owned?

KEY TERMS

network (p. 152)
Radio Act of 1927 (p. 153)
Federal Communications Commission (FCC) (p. 153)
Communications Act of 1934 (p. 153)
clock hour (p. 155)
payola (p. 155)
nonduplication rule (p. 155)

National Public Radio (NPR) (p. 156)
Telecommunications Act of 1996 (p. 156)
Internet-only radio station (p. 158)
AM (p. 161)
FM (p. 161)
format (p. 162)
voice tracking (p. 164)

format wheel (p. 167)
cycle (p. 168)
Arbitron (p. 170)
PPM (p. 170)
rating (p. 171)
share of the audience (p. 172)

INTERNET RESOURCES

Online Learning Center

On the Online Learning Center home page, www.mhhe.com/dominick11e, *select* Student Center *and then* Chapter 7.

1. Use the Learning Objectives, Chapter Outline, and Main Points sections to review this chapter.

2. Test your knowledge of the chapter using the multiple choice and flashcard features of the site.

3. Expand your knowledge of concepts and topics discussed in the chapter with additional Questions for Critical Thinking and Internet Exercises.

Surfing the Internet

Web sites devoted to radio are about as changeable as the medium itself. With luck these will still be functioning.

www.otr.com
A site devoted to radio's Golden Age. Listen to clips from kids' after-school serials, radio dramas, and classic comedy shows.

http://pandora.com
Program your own radio station.

www.entercom.com
Entercom Communications Corporation home page. Click on "radio stations" to locate all of Entercom's holdings.

www.kisw.com
KISW-FM, a Seattle rock station. Includes streaming media, links to video, and stuff you can buy.

www.npr.org
The home of National Public Radio. Note the links to podcasts.

www.rab.com
Home page of the Radio Advertising Bureau. Filled with useful statistics and facts about radio.

CHAPTER 8

Sound Recording

This chapter will prepare you to:

- understand the development of the recording process

- explain the impact of the Depression and World War II on the industry

- recognize the significance of the CD

- discuss the impact of file sharing

- explain how the digital age is affecting the recording industry

- describe the departments that make up the recording industry

- understand the current economic problems of the industry

Fans of Marié Digby have tuned in to her YouTube Channel more than 4 million times.

Singer-guitarist Marié Digby has been called an Internet phenomenon: a virtual unknown who used the Internet to make it big. Her songs have been viewed millions of times on YouTube. Her success, along with that of other Internet rags-to-riches stories such as Esmee Denters and Sandi Thom, has been cited as evidence that aspiring stars no longer need the help of the recording industry to become successful; they can simply use the Internet in general and YouTube in particular to build an audience.

In the case of Ms. Digby, however, the story is a bit more complicated. Her success on the Internet was orchestrated by Hollywood Records, part of the huge Walt Disney Company.

Before she became a YouTube phenomenon, Marié Digby was singing at nightclubs around the Los Angeles area where she caught the notice of an agent who eventually linked her with the Hollywood label. The recording company and Ms. Digby produced a debut album of original songs. They also decided upon a marketing and promotion plan: They would make Marié Digby an Internet sensation.

Following the record company's advice, Ms. Digby posted videos on YouTube of her singing cover versions of hits by Maroon 5, Nelly Furtado, and others. The recording company knew that people who were searching for the songs by other artists would stumble on the songs by Ms. Digby and listen to hers as well. The strategy worked, and before long her songs were getting thousands of views. Her version of Rihanna's "Umbrella" peaked at number 10 on the charts.

Ms. Digby's rising popularity also caught the attention of mainstream media. She was interviewed by a Los Angeles radio station where the DJ claimed that the station discovered her on YouTube. She appeared on Carson Daly's late-night TV show where the host claimed that she was discovered through the Internet. Well, those statements might have been true, but Ms. Digby's appearances on both shows were arranged by Hollywood Records' promotion department. On Ms. Digby's MySpace page, where visitors could hear her music, the box marked "Type of Label" was filled in with "None." (After a reporter questioned the entry, it was changed to "Major" and finally to "Hollywood Records.")

By 2009, Ms. Digby's career was well on its way to success. Her YouTube channel has been viewed more than 4 million times; one of her songs was featured on MTV's *The Hills*. A new album was scheduled to be released in late 2009. The Internet surely played a role in her success and maybe some singers can become stars based only on YouTube videos, but in Ms. Digby's case, it helped to have a big record label operating behind the scenes.

This episode also illustrates that traditional recording companies understand the promotional power of the new social media such as MySpace and YouTube, and will try their best to capitalize on it. The next "Internet star" might be the creation of a recording label's promotions unit.

Of all the media discussed in this book, the recording industry was the first to be drastically affected by the shift from tangible atoms (such as CDs) to intangible bits of information (such as MP3 files). The recording industry was blindsided by the digital revolution and is now trying to cope with an innovation that has transformed its distribution system, its economic base, and its traditional business model. This chapter will examine the history, structure, organization, and economics of this rapidly changing industry.

A Brief History

▲ Early Technologies

Thomas Edison recited "Mary Had a Little Lamb" into a primitive recording machine consisting of a tinfoil-wrapped cylinder, needle, microphone, and crank. It is interesting to speculate what might have happened if Edison had sung the nursery rhyme rather than recited it. Perhaps innovators would have been more aware of the music potential of this new medium, and the history of the recording industry might have been different. As it was, Edison and others thought his **phonograph,** the name he gave his 1877 invention, might best be suited to recording the spoken word. He eventually tried to sell it to the business community as an aid to dictation. At the time, the idea of using the phonograph to bring musical entertainment into the home was too wild to imagine.

Edison's phonograph faced new competition when Chichester Bell and Charles Tainter patented a device called the **graphophone,** in which Edison's foil was replaced by a wax cylinder. In 1887 more competition emerged when Emile Berliner patented a system that used a disk instead of a cylinder. He called his new invention a **gramophone.**

By 1890 three machines that recorded and played back sound were on the market. At about this time big business entered the picture as Jesse Lippincott, who had made a fortune in the glass tumbler business, purchased the business rights to both the phonograph and the graphophone, thus ending a bitter patent fight between the respective inventors. Lippincott had dreams of controlling the office-dictating market, but stenographers rebelled against the new device, and the talking-machine business fell upon hard times. Strangely enough, relief appeared quickly and financial solvency returned, a nickel at a time, thanks to a new idea: using the phonograph to record music instead of the spoken voice.

One of Lippincott's local managers hit upon the idea of putting coin-operated phonographs in the many penny arcades and amusement centers that were springing up all over America. For a nickel you could listen through a pair of stethoscope-like earphones to a cylinder whose 2-minute musical recording had a technical quality that could only be described as awful. Still, these **nickelodeons** were immensely popular, and the demand for "entertainment" cylinders grew. Companies quickly scrambled for a share in the new recording production business.

▲ Rivalry and Growth

The two decades spanning the turn of the 20th century were a time of intense business rivalry in the recording industry. While the two major companies, the Columbia Phonograph Company and Edison's North American Phonograph Company, fought one another, Berliner's United States Gramophone Company perfected the process of recording on flat disks. Ultimately, Columbia recognized the superiority of the disk and attempted to break into the market by selling the zonophone, its own version of the disk player. As for Berliner, along with machinist Eldridge Johnson, he formed the Victor

The phonograph is just one of Thomas Edison's inventions. His 1877 model was hand-cranked, and the sound waves were preserved as scratches in tinfoil.

Talking Machine Company, which had as its trademark a picture of a dog peering into the bell of a gramophone and the slogan "His Master's Voice." Thanks to aggressive marketing, this new company was highly successful and in 1906 introduced the Victrola, the first disk player designed to look like a piece of furniture. By 1912 the supremacy of the disk over the cylinder had been established.

The 100th anniversary of phonograph recording on a flat disk was 1988. This technology was created by Emile Berliner, an immigrant from Germany, who worked as a stock clerk in a clothing store while investigating the intriguing new world of sound amplification and recording. Berliner quickly noted that the cylinders used by Edison had too many disadvantages to be practical. He perfected a way to encode sound on a flat disk that could be easily duplicated by using a master mold, much like pressing waffles in a waffle iron.

His invention was slow to catch on in the United States because of competition from Edison, but it was a success in Europe. Eventually, Berliner introduced to the American market the phonautograph, which he renamed the gramophone. This eventually replaced the cylinder.

In one area Berliner clearly saw the future. He predicted that prominent singers and performers would collect royalties from the sale of his disks. He was wrong on another count, however. He thought that musicians and artists who were unable to appear at a concert would simply send a record to be played on stage instead.

Berliner also developed the prototype of the modern microphone, and both his inventions—the disk and the microphone—came together when electronic recording was perfected during the 1920s. Even the modern CD owes him a debt. Like his original invention the CD stores information in a spiral on a flat, rotating surface.

On the eve of World War I, record players were commonplace throughout America. A dance craze in 1913 sent profits soaring, a trend that was to continue throughout the war. In 1914, 27 million records were manufactured; 107 million were produced in 1919 following the end of the war. The record industry had entered a boom period.

The boom continued when the years after World War I ushered in the Jazz Age, a period named after the spirited, popular music of the Roaring Twenties. **Jazz,** which emerged from the roots of the black experience in America, was spontaneous, individualistic, and sensual. Because of its disdain for convention, jazz was widely denounced as degenerate during its early years (about 30 years later, another spontaneous and sensual musical innovation, rock and roll, would also be denounced).

The good times, however, did not last. In the beginning no one in the record industry regarded radio as a serious threat. Record company executives were sure that the static-filled, raucous noise emanating from radios would never compete with the quality of their recordings. They were wrong.

▲ The Impact of Radio on the Recording Industry

Radio gained popularity in the 1920s, and the recording industry felt the effects. By the end of 1924, the combined sales of players and records had dropped 50 percent from those of the previous year. In the midst of this economic downturn, the recording companies quietly introduced electronic recording, using technology borrowed from their bitter rival, radio. The sound quality of records improved tremendously. But despite this improvement, radio continued to be thought of as the medium for "live" music, and records were dismissed as the medium of "canned" music.

In 1926 the record industry began to market radio-phonograph combinations, an obvious testament to the belief that the two media would coexist. This attitude was also prevalent at the corporate level. In 1927 rumors were flying that the Victor Company would soon merge with the Radio Corporation of America (RCA). Frightened by this prospect, Columbia, Victor's biggest rival, tried to get a head start by merging with the new (and financially troubled) radio network United Independent Broadcasters. All too soon, however, the record company became disillusioned and dissolved the deal. The much-discussed RCA and Victor merger came about in 1929, with the new company dominated by the radio operation.

▲ The Depression Years

The Great Depression of the 1930s dealt a severe economic blow to sound recording. Thomas Edison's record manufacturing company went out of business in 1930. Record sales dropped from $46 million in 1930 to $5.5 million in 1933, and several smaller labels folded. The entire industry was reeling.

During the 1940s the local record shop was the place to hang out with friends and listen to the latest releases.

In the midst of all this gloom, the recording industry was saved once again by the nickel. Coin-operated record players, called *jukeboxes* (the origin of this term is obscure), began appearing in the thousands of bars and cocktail lounges that sprang up after the repeal of Prohibition in 1933. These jukeboxes were immensely popular and quickly spread to diners, drugstores, and restaurants. Starting in 1934, total record sales began to inch upward; by 1939 sales had increased by more than 500 percent.

▲ World War II and After

The record industry did not do well during the war. First, the U.S. government declared shellac—a key ingredient of disks—vital to the national defense, and supplies available for making records dropped drastically. Second, the American Federation of Musicians, fearful of losing jobs because of canned music, went on strike. The strike lasted from 1942 to 1944, and as a result, record sales increased slowly during the war years. However, it was also during the war that Capitol Records embarked on a novel approach to record promotion. The company mailed free records to radio stations, hoping for airplay. This action marked formal recognition of a new industry attitude: Radio could help sell records. This new philosophy would revolutionize the recording industry.

In 1948 Columbia introduced the 33⅓-rpm long-playing record (LP). The new disks could play for 25 minutes a side and were virtually unbreakable. Rather than adopt the Columbia system, RCA Victor introduced its own innovation, the 45-rpm extended-play record. The next few years were described as the "battle of the speeds," as the record-buying public was confronted by a choice among 33⅓, 45, and 78 records. From 1947 to 1949, record sales dropped 25 percent as people waited to see which speed would win. In 1950 RCA conceded and began issuing 33⅓ records. Columbia won only a partial victory, however. The 45 would become the preferred disk for single pop recordings, and the 33⅓ would dominate album

Elvis Aaron Presley sold more than 250 million records, starred in 33 movies, and forever changed American popular music.

sales. The 78 became obsolete. There were also changes in record players. High-fidelity sets came on the market in 1954, followed four years later by stereophonic record players. Record sales more than doubled during this period.

The mushrooming popularity of television during the 1950s had an impact on both radio and the recording industry. Television took away the big national stars from radio and forced local stations to experiment with new formats in an attempt to keep their audiences. One of the most popular radio formats that emerged was Top 40, a sound that relied on a set playlist based on record sales. The emergence of rock and roll helped the new Top 40 format become popular with a young audience. As we saw in Chapter 7, this young audience had a good deal of money to spend on the records they heard played by their favorite DJs.

▲ The Coming of Rock and Roll

Rock had its roots in black rhythm and blues, commercial white popular music, country and western, and jazz. In July 1955, Bill Haley and the Comets moved into the number-one spot on the charts with "Rock Around the Clock." Less than a year later, another performer who would enjoy a far more substantial career came on the scene. "Heartbreak Hotel," recorded by a then relatively unknown Elvis Presley, would stay at the number-one position for seven straight weeks. It was with Elvis that rock and roll first blossomed. Combining a country-and-western style with the beat and energy of black rhythm-and-blues music, Elvis's records sold millions. He appeared on Ed Sullivan's network TV show (from the waist up—Sullivan thought Elvis's pelvic gyrations too suggestive). Through Elvis rock and roll gained wide recognition, if not respectability.

Presley's success inspired other performers from the country-and-western tradition. Jerry Lee Lewis combined Mississippi boogie-woogie with country music to produce a unique and driving style. His "Whole Lotta Shakin' Going On" sold 6 million copies from 1957 to 1958.

Several rock pioneers came from traditional black rhythm-and-blues music. Perhaps the most exciting (certainly the most energetic) was Richard Penniman, or, as he called himself, Little Richard. Except for a period of three months, Little Richard had a record in the Top 100 at all times from 1956 to 1957 (best known are "Long Tall Sally" and "Tutti Frutti"). About the same time, on the South Side of Chicago, Chuck Berry was singing blues in small nightclubs. Discovered by the owner of a Chicago-based record company, Berry was the first artist who paid more than passing attention to the lyrics of rock and roll. His style would later influence many musical groups, including the Beatles.

▲ The Commercialization of Rock

By 1959, through a combination of bizarre events, all the pioneers of rock had disappeared. Elvis had enlisted in the Army. Jerry Lee Lewis had married a 13-year-old girl said to be his cousin and dropped from sight. Little Richard was in the seminary. And Chuck Berry was incarcerated in federal prison. Thus, the way was open for a whole new crop of stars. Economics dictated what this new crop would look and sound like.

Record companies recognized that huge amounts of money could be made from the rock-and-roll phenomenon if it was promoted correctly. Unfortunately, rock and roll had an image problem. In 1959 the record industry was shaken by the payola scandals (see Chapter 7) that, arriving on top of years of bad publicity and criticism of rock and roll as responsible for most of society's ills, threatened rock's profitability. Since rock and roll had too much moneymaking potential to be abandoned, the record companies decided to clean up rock's image.

As the 1960s opened, the new look in rock was characterized by middle-class, white, clean-cut, wholesome performers. Rock stars were young men and women you would not hesitate to bring home and introduce to your parents. On the male side Ricky Nelson, Bobby Vee, Bobby Vinton, Fabian, Paul Anka, Frankie Avalon, and the Four Seasons were popular. There were fewer examples on the female side. Those who had hits included Annette Funicello, Connie Francis, Brenda Lee, and Lesley Gore. All fit the new image of rock and roll. Consequently, the early 1960s saw few musical innovations. In 1963, however, the music changed again.

▲ The British Invasion

Their name was inspired by Buddy Holly and the Crickets, but instead of choosing the entomologically correct "Beetles," the group decided to spell their name "Beatles" (which incorporated the word *beat*). In early 1964 they took the United States by storm. Musically, the Beatles were everything that American rock and roll was not. They were innovative, especially in vocal harmony, and introduced the harmonica as a rock instrument. Ultimately, they would change the shape of the music business and American popular culture. The Beatles had seven number-one records in 1964; they held down the top position for 20 of the 52 weeks that year.

Berry Gordy began as an assembly-line worker in Detroit but ended up as the head of one of the largest black-owned businesses in America. Along the way he introduced black performers to a wider audience and permanently shaped the evolution of American popular music.

In 1957 Gordy wrote a hit song for R&B artist Jackie Wilson. While Gordy and Wilson were in the studio working on other projects, a group called the Matadors auditioned for Wilson. Although Wilson was unimpressed with their songs, Gordy noticed the potential of their lead singer, a young man named Smokey Robinson.

Over the next few years, Gordy continued to write and produce songs for a number of black artists. Unsatisfied with the way his songs were handled by the major record labels, Gordy decided to start his own. He took an $800 loan from his family and in 1959 opened what would later become Motown Records. The company released its first single in 1959 and had its first number-one hit two years later with the Marvelettes' "Please Mr. Postman."

Motown star Diana Ross and Berry Gordy Jr.

In its early years Motown appealed primarily to black audiences, but Gordy's strategy was to appeal to both whites and blacks. Motown's advertising slogan was "The Sound of Young America." During the mid-1960s Gordy's company pioneered the Motown sound, which revolutionized the music industry. Artists such as Stevie Wonder, Marvin Gaye, Smokey Robinson, and Diana Ross and the Supremes became popular with both black and white record buyers. A few years later Gordy introduced the Jackson Five, featuring a young Michael Jackson as lead singer.

In 1988 Berry Gordy was inducted into the Rock and Roll Hall of Fame along with the Supremes, Bob Dylan, and the Beatles. That same year, Gordy sold Motown Records to MCA for more than $60 million. He continued, however, to head Motown's record publishing division and its film and television sections. The sound Gordy created will continue to influence the musical tastes of future generations.

Their success paved the way for a veritable British invasion. Most British rock at this time resembled American rock: cheery, commercial, and white. Not surprisingly, some of the first groups that followed the Beatles represented this school (Herman's Hermits, Freddie and the Dreamers, the Dave Clark Five, and Peter and Gordon, to name a few). There was another style of British rock, however, far less cheery, as represented by the Rolling Stones and the Animals. This style was blues-based, rough-hewn, slightly aggressive, and certainly not bouncy and carefree.

American artists were not silent during this influx of British talent. Folk music, as performed by Bob Dylan and Joan Baez, was also popular. It was only a matter of time before folk merged with rock to produce folk rock. Soul music, as recorded on the Motown label, also made its mark during the 1960s.

The Beatles have more gold albums—47—than any other group in the history of sound recording. The Beatles were on top of the charts again in 2009 thanks to the release of the video game *The Beatles: Rock Band*.

▲ Transitions

The late 1960s was a time of cultural transition. Freedom, experimentation, and innovation were encouraged in almost all walks of life, and popular music was no exception. Sparked by the release of the Beatles' *Sgt. Pepper* album, a

The 1960s was a decade of change in American music. Compare early-1960s recording star Annette Funicello (shown in her Mouseketeer costume) with late-1960s star Janis Joplin.

fractionalization of rock began to take place. Several trends of this period are notable. In 1968 Blood, Sweat and Tears successfully blended jazz, rock, and at times even classical music. The Band introduced country rock. The Who recorded a rock opera, *Tommy*. In the midst of all this experimentation, commercial formula music was also healthy. The Monkees, a group put together by ads in the newspaper, sold millions of records. Bubblegum rockers the Archies kept "Sugar, Sugar" at the top of the charts for a month in 1969 (it replaced a song by the Rolling Stones, "Honky Tonk Woman").

Toward the end of the 1960s and the beginning of the 1970s, rock music became part of the counterculture; in many instances it went out of its way to break with the establishment. Musically, many of the songs of this era were characterized by the **heavy metal** sound; amplifiers and electronic equipment began to dominate the stage. The artists also broke sharply with tradition. The pioneers in this style of rock were all vaguely threatening, a trifle unsavory, and definitely not the type you would bring home to the folks.

▲ Industry Trends: 1970s–1990s

The recording industry enjoyed a boom period during the mid-1970s, resulting in large measure from the popularity of disco. A downturn during the early 1980s reversed itself during the second half of that decade thanks to Michael Jackson's *Thriller* album and a few popular movie soundtracks. The 1990s saw the CD replace tape as the preferred playback medium. Record companies were happy about this since the profit margins on CDs were greater than for tape. As a result recording industry revenues showed some fluctuation but generally increased during the 1990s.

▲ The Contemporary Sound Recording Industry

The biggest development in the past decade has been the emergence of portable MP3 players, such as Apple's iPod, and their impact on the industry. By the start of 2009, more than 6 billion songs had been downloaded from Apple's iTunes Web site. This single fact has put the industry on notice that its old business model is outdated. Consumers no longer want to pay $16–17 for a CD with only a couple of songs on it that they like; they would rather purchase songs individually by downloading them to their computers and MP3 players.

One of the strangest trends in the evolution of popular rock-and-roll music has been a small but persistent genre of records that can only be classified under the somewhat macabre title of "morbid rock." Although its roots probably go back further, it became especially notable in the 1960s. Among the first songs to become a hit was "Teen Angel," the tale of an unfortunate couple whose car stalled on the railroad tracks. Although the young man of the song is smart enough to run like crazy, the young woman goes back to the car to retrieve her sweetheart's high school ring. The train arrives at the same time. End of romance.

Another early example was J. Frank Wilson's "Last Kiss," a tragic tale of a guy and girl out on a date who plow into a disabled car. He survives. She doesn't. End of romance. "Tell Laura I Love Her" told the teary story of a young man who needs money to continue his romance with his girlfriend and so resorts to stock car racing to provide extra income. He totals his car and himself. End of romance. "Patches" concerned the romance between a young woman from the wrong side of the tracks and a middle-class young man. Despondent, the young woman drowns herself in the river. At the end of the song, the young man is contemplating the same thing. Even wholesome Pat Boone got into the act with "Moody River," a song that also told the story of two people who throw themselves into the river and drown.

The trend was less noticeable in the early 1970s, but a song titled "Billy, Don't Be a Hero" enjoyed wide popularity. This song was about a boy who goes off to war, against the wishes of his girlfriend, and gets killed. End of romance. (For those who are true fans of this genre, Rhino Records has collected 10 teen tragedy songs ranging from "Last Kiss" to the little-known but nonetheless moving "The Homecoming Queen's Got a Gun." Incidentally, the back cover of the LP doubles as a tissue dispenser.)

The trend hasn't resurfaced since 1999 when Pearl Jam's remake of "Last Kiss" went to number two on the charts. Perhaps it's . . . dead.

Thus, there was a slow but steady decline in the number of CDs purchased from 2005 to 2009. Meanwhile, digital downloads have increased significantly. In sum, the industry is moving away from selling shiny discs (atoms) to consumers and embracing the notion that its future is selling music online (bits).

Despite best-selling albums by performers such as Taylor Swift, recording industry revenues are still being hurt by illegal downloading.

The downturn in sales has meant problems at the retail level. Tower Records and Musicland both filed for bankruptcy in the mid-2000s. At the same time, competition was increasing in the digital download market. In addition to iTunes, Wal-Mart, MTV, Yahoo!, Virgin, and Amazon all started music downloading services.

The industry continues to fight against illegal file sharing, but it is difficult to tell if their efforts are paying off. Lawsuits effectively put the original Napster out of business, and subsequent legal efforts against successors such as Grokster were also successful. The industry also started suing individuals who had illegally downloaded large numbers of songs and were sharing them online. Many people paid cash settlements to the recording companies to settle the lawsuits.

In late 2008, the Recording Industry Association of America (RIAA) announced a change in strategy and declared that it would no longer pursue legal action against those allegedly sharing music illegally on the Internet. Instead, the RIAA plans to work with Internet Service Providers, (ISPs) to curb the practice. The RIAA's new tactic is to inform ISPs when one of their customers may be illegally sharing music online. The ISP will either forward this information to the customer or send the customer a request to stop the practice. If the customer continues to share music files, the ISP may eventually cut off the customer's Internet access. (Of course, there is nothing to stop the customer from signing up with another ISP and once again begin file sharing.)

As the recording industry continues to search for a solution to illegal file sharing that would also help its bottom line, one idea keeps popping up: a surcharge, maybe around $5, on a consumer's monthly Internet bill that would cover the cost of pirated music.

There are several variations to this plan. In one version, the surcharge would allow consumers to download all the music they wanted from the recording companies' catalogues. The charge would be mandatory; everybody would pay a little extra whether they downloaded music or not. The money would be collected by an industry organization and doled out to labels and artists by some predetermined formula. The model for this would be the radio industry, where stations pay a compulsory license fee to the industry in return for the right to play music. The Internet Service Provider (ISP) would assume the role of the radio station and collect and pay the fee. ISPs might be persuaded to go along with the plan because they are afraid that they could be sued by the recording industry and eventually be held liable for copyright infringements on their networks.

The plan is strongly opposed by consumer groups. Why should someone who doesn't download music have to pay a surcharge? That seems to violate the basic principle of fairness. In response, the recording industry notes that Americans pay for public broadcasting whether they watch it or not. And what about all those cable channels that people never watch? Consumers still pay for them on their monthly bill. But what about people who legally download music from places such as iTunes? Do they pay twice? Would this system put iTunes out of business?

Another potential problem is that a music surcharge would create guaranteed income for the record labels. This might remove any incentive for innovation or to spend money on the development of new artists. Why take risks when the reward is guaranteed?

And if ISPs collect a surcharge for the music industry, shouldn't they also collect a fee for the movie industry to cover the cost of pirated movies? Or how about another fee tacked on to ISP bills to compensate for illegally shared computer software?

Despite all the problems, the recording industry is still willing to put its support behind this idea. This shows how far the industry will go to shore up its faltering business model.

Why did the RIAA change its tune, so to speak? For one thing, the mass lawsuits against alleged illegal file sharing brought a lot of bad publicity to the recording industry. In addition, although suing file sharers brought some additional revenue to the industry, it did little to halt the practice. One study found that file-sharing volume increased 19 percent from 2006 to 2007. Time will tell if the new RIAA strategy has any impact.

On the business side, record labels explored new ways to make revenue, including selling snippets of music to be used as cell phone ringtones, licensing songs to video games, such as Guitar Hero, and striking new deals with performers that give the record companies a percentage of the performer's concert and merchandise proceeds.

Efforts on the promotion front centered on using the Internet, particularly the social media sites, to promote and sell music, as noted in the chapter opener. Facebook, MySpace, YouTube, and music blogs have all become important in the marketing of music.

Moreover, the industry remained highly concentrated. Sony bought out its partner Bertelsmann in 2008 to form Sony Music, one of four big companies that account for more than 85 percent of industry revenue.

The growing concentration of the recording industry had an effect on what music people heard. The quest for a better bottom line puts the emphasis on turning out releases that sell big numbers. The music that racks up big sales tends to be predictable and formulaic rather than new and original. Indeed, many observers have blamed the drop in music sales not so much on illegal downloading as on the lack of any new and compelling musical styles.

Sound Recording in the Digital Age

▲ Transition

As we have seen, throughout most of its history, sound recording used the analog technique. Sound waves were first etched into grooves of a vinyl disk or into rearranged particles on a magnetic tape. In both cases the recording industry manufactured and distributed the products (disks or tapes) that consumers purchased. The digital technique

Recording industry profits slipped steadily from 2000 to 2003. Most experts concede that part of this decrease (some would say most of it) was due to downloading free music. With only a few exceptions, almost everybody in the recording industry considers downloading songs from file-sharing sites such as Pirate Bay and eDonkey to be stealing (or "pirating" as the industry calls it). On the other hand, with few exceptions, people who download music feel quite the opposite.

In that connection, I often asked my students the following question: Would you go to a store and walk out with a CD without paying for it? Aside from a couple of sarcastic replies, almost all students answered in the negative and conceded that taking a CD without paying for it is stealing. I next asked them this: Would you download music from the Internet and share it online without paying for it? Almost everybody answered this in the positive. I then asked them what the difference is between the two situations. Their answers reveal a lot of the complexities involved in developing an ethical stance about file-sharing programs.

Their rationales for their behavior generally fall into these broad categories:

- It's okay to download and share music because the record companies have been overcharging us for CDs and have been exploiting performers for years (just listen to Courtney Love), and the companies deserve it. File sharing is a righteous protest, just another way to "stick it to the Man," a philosophy that was popular during the 1960s.

- It's okay to download and share music because on the Internet all information should be free.

- It's okay to download and share music because I only download stuff that I wouldn't buy anyway, so I'm not really hurting anybody.

Let's look in turn at each of these arguments from an ethical point of view.

Taken to its logical extreme, the first argument suggests that it's okay to steal from any individual company that you think charges too much for its goods or services or somehow mistreats its workers. Would you steal a Buick because you think GM has been pricing its cars too high? Even assuming the premise about exploiting performers is correct (and it should be noted that many of these "exploited" performers have a rather impressive lifestyle), is it okay to steal from companies whose conduct you disapprove of? Suppose some clothing company pays its workers in Thailand only a couple of dollars an hour. Should you steal its goods? Would that make it become less exploitive? This sounds like endorsing the policy that two wrongs actually do make a right. One well-known ethical principle is Kant's Categorical Imperative (see Chapter 17), which states that you should act in the same way that you want others to act toward you. If you ran a business, would you want people who decide they disapprove of your business to steal from you?

The argument that "information should be free" is a common one. At its core is the belief in some sort of entitlement to information, that somehow the existence of the Internet means we have a right to share freely the works of others. In the first place, information doesn't simply appear; somebody has to create it. It would seem more reasonable to argue that the individual who created the information (music, movies, or video) should be the one to decide if it's free. If members of a musical group think that free exposure on the Internet will help them charge more for their concert appearances, they should be able to post their music on file-sharing systems. (Many groups have done this.) On the other hand, if a group decides that it wants people to pay to hear its music, it should have that right. This is the notion behind the legal doctrine of intellectual property. Take an example: Suppose you create a clever new video game and share the software with some friends. Suppose further that Microsoft hears about it and offers you a large sum of money to market the game. In the meantime, however, suppose one of your friends, a strong believer in the idea that information should be free, posts your game on the Web, and it becomes so popular that Microsoft decides the market is already saturated and withdraws the offer. Shouldn't you have the right to decide what to do with your creation?

The argument about downloading only stuff that otherwise wouldn't be bought raises an interesting question. In the first place, if you share files, other people who might have otherwise bought the record might download it and not buy it. This would seem to hurt those who created the music. Second, your decision not to buy might have been influenced by the presence of the music for free on the Internet. Who's to say that you might have a different attitude toward the music if it weren't freely available on the Net? Maybe you would buy it after all.

Putting aside the various legal arguments about downloading, it would appear that all the common arguments justifying downloads from file-sharing systems don't stand up to an ethical analysis. Indeed, now that legal downloading services are available as an alternative, the common rationalizations seem even weaker. Nonetheless, many students appear to be unfazed and continue to download. They apparently don't believe it's stealing.

Why the ethical disconnect between walking out of a store without paying for a CD and downloading a CD without paying? Part of the explanation is the gap between action and consequence. Taking a CD from a store has an immediate and clear effect: The retailer loses the money that he or she paid for the CD. There is a visible victim. Downloading music from the amorphous and impersonal Web separates the act from its harmful consequence. There is no apparent victim. The record companies and the artists who are harmed by downloading are removed and abstract. Would downloading be as popular if the downloader had a clear idea about how his or her act directly affected the artist?

changed that by encoding music as pure information, a string of binary numbers, from which music could be recovered. As a result consumers no longer needed to buy the product from the record companies. All they needed were the numbers and their hard drives or blank CDs. This development would not have been a problem for the industry as long as there was no efficient way of getting those numbers to the consumer. The development of the personal computer and the Internet, however, made it easy for consumers to download digital information to their home computers and other portable devices.

As we have already seen, the recording industry was thrust into the digital age before it was fully prepared for the consequences. At first, music executives dismissed downloading from the Internet as something only a few geeks would be interested in. Then came Napster, Kazaa, and their progeny, and the business was forever changed. Never had so much music been available to so many for free. All of a sudden, as recording industry expert John Kennedy put it, the recording industry had to figure out a way to make music easier to buy than to steal. Now, with iPod and iTunes and similar devices and services, it appears as if the industry may have found a way to survive the digital revolution.

▲ The Rise of the iPod

More than 170 million iPods had been sold by the beginning of 2009, and more than 6 billion songs have been downloaded from iTunes. In addition to introducing a new business model, the iPod brought about other changes. First, it created a new cottage industry. More than 200 accessories can be purchased for the iPod, including nylon carrying cases, external speakers, a remote control, and a mechanical iDog musical companion that moves to the beat of the music. Many new cars carry an "aux" outlet that lets drivers plug their iPods into the car's sound system. Then, of course, there are podcasts, prerecorded programs that people download to their devices. Podcasts didn't exist before the iPod became popular. Second, the iPod gave birth to a whole new radio format. Drawing upon the fact that iPod owners store a wide range of music on their devices, many FM stations switched to a format called "Jack FM" or "Dave FM" that resembled an iPod set to random shuffle, capitalizing on the unpredictability of what would be played next.

In 2007, Apple announced the iPhone, a device that, among other things, blended the iPod with a cell phone. It was an instant success and by the end of 2009, Apple had sold about 20 million of the devices. The iPhone permitted consumers to download music directly from the iTunes store to their iPhones, a feature that further helped spark digital music sales.

▲ The Decline of the CD

The digital revolution has caused a seismic shift in the way consumers buy and store music. Throughout much of recent history, the recording industry sold collections of songs, called *albums,* in a variety of formats: vinyl records, tape cassettes, and plastic CDs. Typically, consumers found that there were only two or three songs per album that they actually liked, but they were still forced to buy the whole collection. The digital revolution put more power in the hands of consumers, who could now buy and download only those songs that they liked. Needless to say, consumers began abandoning the album format.

Sales of CD albums have been slowly declining since 2000. They dropped 19 percent from 2007 to 2008. Meanwhile, the number of digital downloads increased an impressive 45 percent in that same period. It doesn't take a genius to see that the old way of selling music is on the way out. Unfortunately for record companies, the increased revenue from downloading of individual tracks is not enough to make up for the losses from the decrease in CD album sales.

Recording artists are well aware of the concept of **disintermediation** (a process that eliminates the distributor and delivers a product or service directly to the consumer). If a band could produce its own album and then promote and distribute it over the Internet, then there is little need for a record label. The band could simply sell direct to consumers and make a lot more money.

The British band Radiohead decided to take this route with the 2007 release of its album *In Rainbows*. The band had been under contract to recording company EMI but decided to try its hand at e-commerce after the contract expired. They announced that fans could download the whole album from Radiohead's Web site. And, in another novel twist, visitors to the site could pay whatever they wished, even nothing, for the album.

Pundits hailed the arrangement as groundbreaking and revolutionary, something that could shake the traditional recording industry to its core. Some even predicted that *In Rainbows* would mark the beginning of a trend that would put major record labels out of business.

It didn't quite work out that way. After 90 days, the band stopped the potentially free downloads and a message on its Web site noted that the album would soon be available on a CD distributed by a major label and could be purchased through traditional outlets.

Why the change of tactics? Was offering the download a bad idea? We may never know for sure, but data gathered by an Internet audience rating service found that 60 percent of the people in the United States who downloaded the album paid nothing. Worldwide, the average price paid for a downloaded album was about $2.25. Although the official numbers were never released, sales of the CD at traditional stores and paid downloads from iTunes probably earned much more than the pay-what-you-will system.

Radiohead's tactics did not escape criticism. The voluntary payment plan was called a marketing gimmick, and fans were not pleased with the quality of the downloaded version. Many complained that they had to buy the higher-priced CD in order to fully appreciate the music.

The album, in all its forms, eventually sold more than 3 million copies, and the CD version opened at number one on all the major charts. Even so, the album was not the revolutionary force that many predicted.

▲ New Products

The recording industry has developed a symbiotic relationship with the cell phone industry. People like to personalize their ringtones, and the recording companies are eager to help them. Individuals can download snippets of songs from several places on the Web to their cell phones, where they play every time a call comes in. Some of these short segments of music can cost about $2.50 (pretty expensive when you consider that a person can download a whole song from iTunes for 99 cents). In 2008 ringtone sales exceeded $510 million, but it appears that sales are leveling off.

▲ Mobile Music

The Sony Walkman was the first device that enabled consumers to take their recorded music with them. The iPod, iPhone, and related devices, such as the Nokia XpressMusic Phone and the Samsung i450, continue this tradition. Mobile music can be accessed in two ways. Consumers can purchase tunes from an online source and download the song to their computer and then sideload the song to a digital player. The second method is direct downloading to specially equipped mobile phones, called smartphones, such as the iPhone or Google's Android. The iPhone dominates this market, accounting for more than 80 percent of downloads.

An application called Shazam makes it easy for smartphone owners to acquire music by allowing them to identify and purchase songs using their mobile phones. Shazam uses music recognition technology and, after "hearing" a short segment of a song, displays the name of the song, the artist, and links that let the owner buy and download the track. By mid-2009 Shazam had about 100 million requests to identify songs.

▲ User-Generated Content

There are two types of user-generated content that are relevant to the music industry. The first involves artists and record labels that make their content available for others to incorporate into their homemade productions. Universal Music Group and Warner Music Group have agreements with YouTube to let users include their music in user-created videos that are then posted on the site. Some performers, including Nine Inch Nails, have posted raw recording tracks online and allow fans to remix them.

The second type of content includes all of the user-generated music videos posted on YouTube and other video-sharing Web sites. It's difficult to tell how much of this content exists, but a search of YouTube using the terms "new bands 2008" returned about 200,000 hits.

▲ Social Media

As noted in the chapter opener, both recording companies and individual artists realize that social media are becoming more important. Fledgling artists produce their own videos (or, as in the case of Marié Digby, get a little help from a record company) for sites such as MySpace and YouTube in the hope of generating buzz and attracting the attention of a big record label. In fact, when MySpace first started, one of its big draws was the fact that many new bands posted samples of their music on their MySpace pages. People could visit the site, hear new acts, and share their favorites with their friends. Since then the site has become an important place for both new and established acts. MySpace Music has a comprehensive list of music according to genre. As of 2009, the "rock" category had nearly 2 million listings. Many artists also make use of the social networking possibilities on Facebook. The site hosts dozens of music forums where members can discuss artists and trade favorites.

Defining Features of Sound Recording

Sound recording is a cultural force. Its products help characterize social groups and define movements and trends in American society. Recorded music has been at the center of a great deal of cultural and social controversy. Sound recording helped usher in the Jazz Age during the Roaring Twenties. This new style of music was condemned as corrupting the nation's morals. The same criticisms were heard during the 1950s when rock-and-roll music became the rallying point for a new youth culture. During the 1960s recorded music joined the counterculture, and big record companies (benefiting from the status quo) earned huge profits from selling albums that challenged the status quo. In the 1990s rap music recordings introduced the hip-hop culture to the rest of America. All in all, the sound recording industry has played a major role in shaping modern culture.

Sound recording is also an international enterprise, with recording artists selling their music worldwide. For instance, Ricky Martin's eponymous album sold 14 million copies worldwide and 7 million in the United States. Celine Dion's greatest-hits album sold 5 million in the United States and 9 million internationally. Recording artists also tour all around the globe.

The recording business is a unique blend of business and talent. Recording companies are continually searching for new artists and new sounds that will succeed in the marketplace. The singers and musicians may be the stars, but the recording companies are the star makers. Most hit recordings owe much of their success to the marketing and promotion efforts of their record labels.

> ## SOUNDBYTE
>
> **Why Would You Ever Get out of Bed?**
>
> The Leggett & Platt Company now offers the Starry Night Sleep Technology Bed for media fans of all ages. The bed has a built-in 5.1 channel sound system with 8-inch subwoofers, 2,500 watts of power, an HDTV projector in the headboard, an iPod docking station, wireless Internet connection, and a hard disk that holds 1.5 terabytes of information. That's enough space for around 2,000 hours of video or for about 400,000 of your favorite songs. The price: depending on how many extras you want, between $20,000 and $50,000 (and that doesn't include pillows).

Organization of the Recording Industry

The recording industry consists of the various creative talent and business enterprises that originate, produce, and distribute records to consumers. Rock music accounts for more than 45 percent of the total sales of the recording industry; rhythm and blues and hip-hop account for another 24 percent; country, about 20 percent; Latin about

Country group Sugarland's first album sold more than a million copies.

8 percent; and jazz, classical, and gospel make up the rest. Although this chapter concentrates on rock, remember that the other music styles are also part of the industry. For our purposes we will divide the business into four major segments: (1) talent, (2) production, (3) distribution, and (4) retail.

▲ Talent

The talent segment of the industry consists of all the singers, musicians, songwriters, arrangers, and lyricists who hope to make money by recording and selling their songs. The phrase "hope to make money" is important because far more performers are laboring in virtual obscurity in and around Detroit, Seattle, Nashville, New York, and Los Angeles than are cashing royalty checks from their recordings. Exactly how many people are "out there" hoping to make it big is impossible to pinpoint.

Performers start out as a beginning act. The initial motivation may be simply personal pleasure. Many begin performing during high school. For example, Bob Dylan (then known as Bob Zimmerman) started out with a high school band in Hibbing, Minnesota.

In years past the next step for the novice musician or musical group was to form a traveling act that played anywhere and everywhere to gain experience, a little money, and recognition. Weezer, for example, kicked around southern California for several years, playing in places with names such as Club Dump and Bob's Frolic Room before finding commercial success. Although some bands and artists still go this route, many others, such as Marié Digby, turn to the Internet and post videos on YouTube, Facebook, or MySpace. If the act is good (and lucky), it may be noticed by a talent scout or producer from a major recording label (the record companies keep an eye on the Web and regularly check out anybody who has created an Internet "buzz"). If things go well, the act is signed to a recording contract.

▲ Production

The recording company brings the act to a recording studio, where a large number of songs are recorded. Audio engineers and elaborate sound-mixing facilities are used to get exactly the right sound. Eventually, a single or an album is put together. The company also supplies publicity, advertising, merchandising, and packaging expertise. Promotion—which in the recording industry consists primarily of getting the record played on influential radio stations and prominently displayed on iTunes and social media sites, and getting the music video on YouTube and other video outlets—is also the responsibility of the company. There are dozens of record companies, but a handful dominate the business: Warner, Sony, Universal, and EMI.

▲ Distribution

There are six main outlets for music distribution: (1) direct retail, (2) rack jobbers, (3) one-stops, (4) direct consumer sales, (5) online sales, and (6) direct download (see Figure 8-1). Of these six outlets, mass marketers and rack jobbers are most important, accounting for more than 60 percent of all sales.

FIGURE 8-1

Music Distribution
Channels

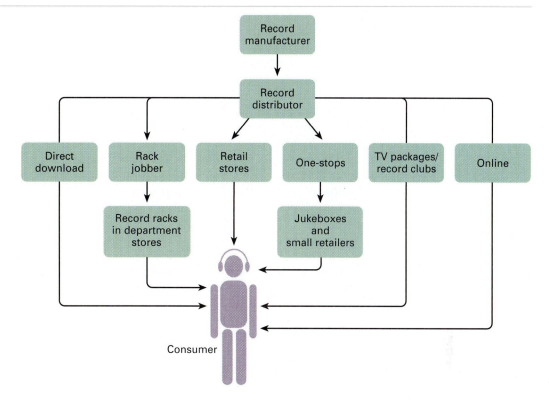

Direct retail refers to stores that specialize in the sale of CDs, and related products. Many retail stores are chain operations with several outlets in different parts of the country.

Rack jobbers service the CD racks in variety or large department stores. Wal-Mart has, for example, its CD shelves serviced by rack jobbers. The rack jobber chooses the records that are sold in these locations, thus relieving store management of the task of keeping up with the latest Eminem CD and such other tasks as reordering titles and returning unused merchandise.

One-stops purchase records from record companies and resell them to retail stores. For example, a small, independently owned retail store might not qualify for credit from the record companies and so might purchase its records from a one-stop.

TV packagers and record clubs sell directly to the consumer. You have probably seen TV ads for collections of music (*The Best of Heavy Metal, Connie Francis's Greatest Hits, Zamfir and the Pan Flute*). Record clubs have become less important in recent years.

Online distribution is direct: The consumer deals directly with an online retailer, such as Amazon.com, and the product is delivered to his or her door.

The mechanics of digital downloading are also relatively simple: A consumer visits one of the many sites that offer downloads for sale, such as iTunes, MSN Music, or Wal-Mart, and selects a single track or album that he or she wishes to download. Most sites now offer a single download for less than a dollar, although this price will probably go up. For example, iTunes raised the price for many of its popular downloads to $1.29 in 2009. The price to download an album varies depending on how many songs are available to download.

▲ Retail

The times are not good for traditional record stores. Competition from online music sites and mass-market stores such as Wal-Mart has made it difficult for many retailers to survive. Wherehouse Music filed for bankruptcy in 2003 followed by Tower Records in 2004. Big retailer HMV closed dozens of stores. Transworld Entertainment (TWE), which operates nearly a thousand FYE, Coconuts, and Strawberries stores, has seen its revenue plummet. And Tower eventually folded in 2006, as did Musicland.

While the importance of the traditional record stores declined, the importance of mass marketers such as Target and Wal-Mart increased. In 1992, according to the Recording Association of America, 25 percent of all CDs and tapes were purchased at mass merchandise stores. In 2008 that figure rose to 40 percent. Over that same period the percentage sold in traditional record retail stores dropped from 53 to less than 10 percent. iTunes is the biggest record retailer, accounting for nearly 25 percent of the market. Wal-Mart is in second place.

Retailers are aware that if online downloading becomes the preferred way of delivering music to consumers, there will be little need for brick-and-mortar retail stores. Some retailers now stock DVDs, video games, magazines, and electronic equipment as well as gift cards that let people download from iTunes and other sources. In some retail outfits music accounts for less than half of all sales. Moreover, some electronics retailers, including Best Buy, have gotten into the music-downloading business.

Ownership in the Recording Industry

The recording industry is one of the most concentrated of all media industries. As shown in Table 8-1, big companies dominate the business, accounting for more than 85 percent of the market. The four companies that dominate the industry are (1) Universal Music Group, owned by the French conglomerate Vivendi; (2) Sony, a large Japanese conglomerate; (3) EMI, owned by a British private investment group; and (4) Warner Music, formerly part of the Time Warner empire but now owned by a private investment group.

Producing Records

There are seven departments within a typical recording company:

1. *Artists and Repertoire (A&R):* This department serves as the talent scout for the industry. A&R personnel monitor influential Internet music Web sites and keep an eye on local markets to see who's hot. Once in a while, they might also venture out on the road to check out acts (called *garage bands* in the trade) in the hopes of finding the next superstar.

2. *Sales and Distribution:* As the name suggests, this department sells the company's products and then makes sure the CDs get to the stores and digital tracks get to downloading sites where consumers can buy them.

3. *Advertising and Merchandising:* This division is responsible for planning media ad campaigns and point-of-purchase displays in sales outlets. The efforts of this department are coordinated with those of the promotion department.

TABLE 8-1

Top Four Recording Companies, 2009

Company	Major Labels	Top Stars
Universal Music Group	Geffen, Island Def Jam, Motown	Kanye West, Fall Out Boy, Gwen Stefani
Warner Music	Atlantic, Warner Bros., Maverick	James Blunt, Rob Thomas, Madonna
Sony	Arista, Epic, Jive	Beyoncé, Britney Spears, Jessica Simpson
EMI	Virgin, Capitol, Blue Note	ColdPlay, Keith Urban, Katy Perry

4. *Promotion:* This department helps market and promote the company's artists. Although getting a song played on an influential radio station is still an important part of the promotion process, other strategies are effective as well. A song played during a hit TV show (such as the Fray's "How to Save a Life" on *Grey's Anatomy*) can significantly boost sales. Having a presence on social media is also a necessity.

5. *Business:* This department includes lawyers, accountants, market researchers, financial analysts, and secretarial and clerical staffers. It functions in the recording industry the same as in any other business or industry.

6. *Publicity:* This department attempts to get press coverage for new performers and new releases and also has the job of getting new acts and albums reviewed by influential publications such as *Rolling Stone* and *Billboard* and by influential bloggers.

7. *Artist Development:* The duties of this department include coordinating tour dates, making sure the act has a well-produced concert show, and arranging for TV appearances.

▲ Making a Recording

For a performer or a group to win a recording contract, they first must convince someone in a record company that they have a sound that will sell. Some artists produce a **demo,** a disc that provides a sample of their sound. Others post videos on the Internet and hope that they catch on. Still others bombard the A&R department with e-mails and MP3 attachments or links to music Web sites. These initial efforts don't have to be professional grade, but they do have to highlight the strengths of the performer or group.

If things work out, the performer or group is signed to a contract to produce an album or perhaps just one or two tracks. At that point the act moves into a recording studio to make a master recording.

Resembling something you might see at NASA's mission control center, with banks of modern equipment, blinking lights, and digital readouts, the modern recording studio does multitrack recording. Professional studios have machines capable of recording up to 48 different tracks. This means that different instruments and vocals can be recorded on different sections of a disc. Thus, a piano might be recorded on one track, drums on another, bass on another, lead vocals on another, background vocals on yet another, and so on. So that one track does not leak onto another, the studio is set up with careful placement of microphones and wooden baffles—soundproof barriers that keep the sound of one instrument from spilling over into the mikes recording the other instruments. Once the session starts, the producer makes most of the creative decisions. The producer decides when the performers take a break, when the tune has to be played over because of a bad note, when the music should be played back so the group can hear itself and perhaps make changes in the arrangement, and so on.

The advent of multiple-track recording has revamped the music-making process. Currently, it is not even necessary for band members to record together. The instrumentalists can come in one at a time and "lay down" their tracks, the lead singer or singers can add the vocals later, and everything can be put together at the mixing console.

A sophisticated mixing board such as this one handles as many as 48 separate sound tracks that contain recordings of instruments and vocals. Note the computer monitors. Computer programs remember previous mixing setups, making the process faster and easier.

After the recording session the next step is the mix down, the technically exacting job of mixing down the multiple tracks onto a two-track stereo master. In the mix down each track is equalized; echo, overdubbing, or other special effects are added; and certain passages are scheduled for rerecording. If an album is being produced, each track has to be precisely placed on the stereo spectrum. A track can be placed in the left or right speaker or in the center, where it is heard equally in both speakers. Mixing a 16- or 24-track tape down to 2 tracks can take several days. The job has been made somewhat easier in recent years thanks to computerized mixing boards. After the mix is completed, the master is stored on a disc for possible manufacturing and distribution. At the same time, the promotion department is given a preview of the new release, and the advertising and publicity departments begin their efforts.

The Economics of Sound Recording

We will approach the topic of economics at two levels. First, we will examine the economic structure of the industry as a whole. Next, we will investigate the financial ups and downs of a typical musical group trying to make it in the recording business.

▲ Economic Trends

As can be seen from Figure 8-2, the economic outlook for the recording industry is not encouraging. After peaking in 2000, revenues have steadily declined. From 2000 to 2008, revenues fell by nearly 40 percent. (Industry experts are quick to point out that 2000 was the year that Napster and other file-sharing services became popular.)

Digital downloading is the only bright spot in this gloomy picture. According to Nielsen SoundScan (see below), there were more than 1 billion digital tracks sold in 2008 and another 66 million digital albums, both up significantly from 2007. In the meantime, sales of CDs continued to fall, dropping 19 percent from 2007. As is the case with other media, the increased revenue from digital sales does not totally offset the loss from the decline of CD sales since the record labels make more from a CD sale (see Table 8-2).

▲ New Business Models

Faced with declining revenues, the recording industry is exploring other ways to make money. One new arrangement is called a 360 deal, in which a company agrees to make a large cash payment to a performer and in return gets a percentage of all revenue generated

FIGURE 8-2

Recording Industry
Revenues, 1980–2008

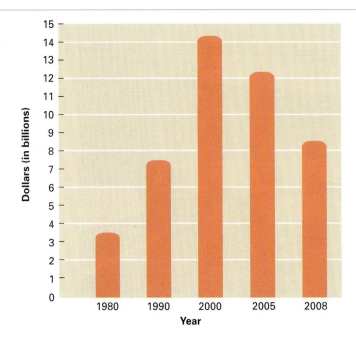

TABLE 8-2

Where the Money
Goes

Source: Compiled by
author from industry
trade publications.

Destination	Typical CD ($16 price)	Destination	Downloaded Track (99 cents price)
Record label overhead and profit	$7.04	Record label	$0.50
Retailer overhead and profit	4.64	Service provider	0.14
Artist royalty	1.60	Artist royalty	0.11
Distributor/Manufacturer	1.76	Distributor	0.09
Publisher	0.80	Publisher	0.08
Miscellaneous	0.15	Miscellaneous	0.07

by the performer, including income from record sales, touring, merchandise, endorsement deals, and any other activity that takes in money. The theory behind this contract is that although consumers are unwilling to pay for CDs, they will buy concert tickets, T-shirts, signature clothing, and other items. For example, Madonna signed a 360 deal with concert promoter Live Nation for a reported $120 million.

The industry has also capitalized on the success of video games such as Guitar Hero, Rock Band, and related games. Record labels license their songs to the games in return for a fee. These games have also given some performers new life. Aerosmith reportedly made more money from Guitar Hero: Aerosmith than from any of their albums. Vivendi, the conglomerate that includes Universal Music, showed its confidence in the future earning potential of these games by acquiring Activision, the company that makes Guitar Hero.

▲ Rock Performers: The Bottom Line

Most of the people who read this book will not go on to be rock stars. Nonetheless, examining the financial arrangements that surround the production of popular music is useful for all readers as it can tell a lot about the economics of the business.

There are many stories about the fantastic sums of money earned by pop music stars. Some stars do make a lot of money. (R.E.M.'s most recent contract with Time Warner was for $80 million.) Others, however, are not quite so lucky. A new artist or group will receive a royalty rate of about 9–12 percent of the suggested retail price of a CD. A more established act might negotiate a rate that is a little higher, maybe 15 percent. Really successful performers might get 20 percent or more. Royalty rates on downloads run to about 11 percent. For simplicity, let us say a hypothetical group of four performers is getting a 15 percent royalty rate on CDs and digital album sales and 11 percent on single-track downloads. They also get a $1-million advance from their record company (totally unrealistic for a new group, but this is a best-case scenario). They spend half of the advance to record the album, leaving $500,000. They have to pay $100,000 to their manager and $25,000 to their business manager and their lawyer. After $170,000 in taxes, the group has $180,000 to split four ways, or $45,000 a person. And the group has to live on that for a year before the album gets released.

Again, let us take the best-case scenario and say the CD sells 500,000 copies, the digital album is downloaded 200,000 times, and there are a million downloads of single tracks from the album. The group would get about $1 million from sales of the CD, $300,000 from the digital album downloads, and $100,000 from single-track downloads. The band also goes on tour. The record company kicks in $200,000 to cover expenses, recoupable from royalties. A lot of tours lose money, but we'll be optimistic and say this tour makes $100,000 in profit. Total income for the group equals $1.5 million. Sounds good so far.

There are, however, expenses involved. The $1-million advance is recoupable by the record label. The label spends about $300,000 promoting the band; costs are charged against royalties. The record company spends $100,000 making a music video. A typical contract would charge half of that to the band. What's left after about a year of work and all this accounting? No more than $150,000, divided four ways, or $37,500 apiece—before taxes. Not exactly the kind of riches the band was probably dreaming about.

There's no question that iTunes has become a huge success. It's the biggest record retailer and has sold more than 6 billion songs. With facts like those, one would think that recording artists would be eager to get their songs on iTunes. Most are, but a growing number are shunning iTunes because they feel that releasing single tracks for downloading cuts into their more profitable album sales. Performers also dislike the iTunes policy of not allowing album-only downloads; with few exceptions, iTunes requires that tracks be available separately.

In 2008, two established performers, Kid Rock and AC/DC, insisted that their albums only be sold whole and did not allow their music on iTunes. Shunning iTunes did not seem to matter for Kid Rock. His album was the third best-selling album of 2008, at 1.7 million units. AC/DC released its album through Wal-Mart and sold 1.6 million copies. Clearly, not everybody needs iTunes.

But for many artists, making tracks available on iTunes is a huge advantage. The best-selling album in 2008 belonged to Lil Wayne and sold 2.7 million copies. Single tracks from the album were available on iTunes and were downloaded millions of times. The best-selling digital downloaded single in 2008 belonged to Leona Lewis with 3.3 million downloads. These downloads didn't seem to hurt as her album sold 1.2 million units. Counting 10 single-track sales as the equivalent of one album sale (a common industry metric), brings Lewis's total to about 1.5 million, without taking into account the sales of any other single track from the album. That puts her sales pretty close to those of Kid Rock and AC/DC.

What can we conclude from all of this? Does selling single tracks on iTunes cannibalize album sales? It appears that the answer is a less-than-satisfying "it depends." Established acts, such as Kid Rock, that have a fan base will probably be fine because loyal fans will purchase the music no matter how it is made available. On the other hand, a new act might not be so lucky.

The new pricing structure adopted by iTunes in 2009 means that many artists will get more income from digital singles and may persuade some to make their songs available to the service. But there will probably still be some who prefer the old-fashioned way of making consumers buy the entire album.

Of course, the band might make a little money from TV appearances, overseas sales, and merchandising. Most artists, however, do not see much money until they have had a couple of back-to-back hits. And even such luck is no guarantee of riches. The group TLC, for example, declared bankruptcy after selling $175 million in CDs.

The truth is that relatively few acts are able to command large sums of money. The riches in the music industry are disproportionately divided, with a small number of artists at the top making most of the money. According to the RIAA, of the 27,000 or so new recordings released every year, only 10 percent are profitable.

Feedback for Sound Recording

▲ *Billboard* Charts

Every week disk jockeys, program directors, and record company executives scan the *Billboard* charts, the most important channel of feedback in the sound recording industry (see Figure 8-3).

How is the *Billboard* chart put together? In general, the *Billboard* charts are based on two components: (1) exposure and (2) sales. To measure sales, *Billboard* relies on Nielsen SoundScan, a data-reporting system that keeps track of sales and digital downloads in the United States and Canada. Sales data are collected weekly from about 14,000 retail stores, mass merchandisers, and online outlets.

To measure exposure, *Billboard* uses data from Nielsen Broadcast Data Systems (NBDS). This organization monitors airplay on more than 1,600 radio stations in the United States, Canada, and Puerto Rico that play a variety of formats. NBDS reports that it detects more than 100 million songs every year. For some of its charts—the Hot 100, for example—*Billboard* combines the two measures and winds up with a single index number for each song and rank-orders it accordingly.

Note that another mass medium, radio, plays an important part in the feedback mechanism for sound recording. Radio stations with a music format rely on the *Billboard* charts to determine what songs they should play. Thus, sound recording also functions as a feedback mechanism for radio.

FIGURE 8-3   Excerpt from a *Billboard* Chart

▲ Sound Recording Audiences

Information regarding the audience for sound recording (records and CDs) is somewhat difficult to uncover, partially because the recording industry is supported by audience purchases and not by advertising. This means that recording companies concentrate on compiling overall sales figures and that detailed demographic information about the audience is typically not sought after. True, some record companies have sponsored market research to find out more about their audiences, but the results of these studies are usually not made available to the general public. It has been estimated that more than 90 percent of all households in the country have some means of playing a CD or a downloaded music track.

In general, those people who have a sound system have paid about $500–800 for their equipment. They listen to discs and downloads about an hour a day.

Record buying is related to age. Older consumers are accounting for more record purchases. In 2006, people over 30 accounted for about 55 percent of the total dollar value spent on prerecorded music, a 25 percent increase from 1988. At the same time, consumer spending by those ages 19 and under declined from 32 percent to 21 percent. The percent of the dollar values of all purchases is currently split about evenly between males and females.

The Recording Industry

These are difficult times for the recording industry, and the outlook for the near future at least is not good. All of the major recording labels have cut jobs and downsized some departments. Employment chances might be better with companies that offer digital music downloads, such as Apple and Amazon, or with companies that sponsor tours and concerts.

The career outlook in the various media industries changes quickly. For a more current description of conditions in the recording industry and a more detailed look at career options, please consult the book's Web site: www.mhhe.com/dominick11e.

MAIN POINTS

- Thomas Edison pioneered the development of the phonograph, which was first used as a device to record voice. Emile Berliner perfected the modern technique of recording music in a spiral pattern on a disk. By the end of World War I, record players were found in most American homes.

- The coming of radio and the Depression hurt the development of the recording industry, but the business was able to survive because of the popularity of jukeboxes.

- After World War II the industry grew quickly because of the development of magnetic tape recording and the LP record and, most of all, because radio stations began to play recorded music as part of their formats.

- Rock-and-roll music helped spur record sales and made young people an important part of the market for recorded music.

- File-sharing software and legal digital downloading may transform the basic way the music industry conducts business.

- There are four segments in the recording industry: talent, production, distribution, and retail.

- Four big companies dominate the record business.

- *Billboard* magazine's charts are the most important form of audience feedback for the industry.

- After several years of growth, the recording industry's revenue has declined, due in part to file sharing on the Internet.

QUESTIONS FOR REVIEW

1. Trace the various media that have been used to record sound, from Edison's time to the present.

2. How do legal downloading sites such as iTunes work? Why are they examples of disintermediation?

3. Trace the distribution arrangement in the sound recording business. How many of the distribution channels have you personally used?

4. If the chance of financial success is so small, why do so many people still try to make it in the recording industry?

QUESTIONS FOR CRITICAL THINKING

1. Why did it take the recording industry so long to figure out that radio airplay helped record sales? Will the same be true with file sharing?

2. What are the implications of large corporate ownership in the record business? Are big companies less likely to promote new acts and risky musical styles?

3. What are the ethical implications of downloading and sharing music from file-sharing services? If you have

ever downloaded music, did you feel guilty doing it? Why or why not?

4. What will be the future of the retail record store in the digital era? If you can download music directly to your computer, why go to a store? Do people go to record stores for purposes other than simply buying an album?

KEY TERMS

phonograph (p. 178)
graphophone (p. 178)
gramophone (p. 178)
nickelodeons (p. 178)

jazz (p. 179)
heavy metal (p. 183)
disintermediation (p. 188)
rack jobbers (p. 191)

one-stops (p. 191)
demo (p. 193)
Billboard (p. 196)

INTERNET RESOURCES

Online Learning Center

On the Online Learning Center home page, www.mhhe.com/dominick11e, *select* Student Center *and then* Chapter 8.

1. Use the Learning Objectives, Chapter Outline, and Main Points sections to review this chapter.

2. Test your knowledge of the chapter using the multiple choice and flashcard features of the site.

3. Expand your knowledge of concepts and topics discussed in the chapter with additional Questions for Critical Thinking and Internet Exercises.

Surfing the Internet

Web sites for the recording industry are just as evanescent as the industry itself. The following were current as this book went to press.

www.billboard.com
Billboard magazine's online version. Contains the latest news about the industry plus recent charts.

www.sonymusic.com
Home page of Sony Music. Lists all top artists and has links to the company's various labels.

www.apple.com/itunes
You probably already know about this one.

www.recording-history.org
A comprehensive look at the evolution of recording technology.

www.riaa.org
Site of the Recording Industry Association of America. Contains industry data, the latest news, and legal information.

CHAPTER 9

Motion Pictures

This chapter will prepare you to:

- explain how the motion picture industry developed

- describe how the studios dominated the industry

- discuss how television affected the film industry and its audience

- understand the implications that digital moviemaking holds for the industry

- explain how the digital age is affecting film

- describe the components of the movie industry and how a motion picture is produced

During tough economic times, Americans tend to go to movies to escape. Movies such as *Paul Blart, Mall Cop* helped Hollywood earn record revenues in 2008.

As far as the movie industry is concerned, history might not be repeating itself but it's coming fairly close. As we shall see below, when the Depression hit in the 1930s, movies generally weathered the crisis better than other mass media. Starting in 1933, when the Depression was at its deepest, film revenue increased every year but one up to the start of World War II in 1941. One of the explanations for this surprising trend was that Americans went to the movies to escape from the bleak realities of life during the Depression. A look at some of the movies popular in the 1930s seems to support this reasoning. Big, lavish musicals, such as the films of Busby Berkeley, were big hits as were broad comedies, many directed by Frank Capra, and escapist action-adventure films such as *The Prisoner of Zenda, Tarzan,* and *King Kong.*

As of this writing, the economic difficulties at the end of the 2000s were not nearly as severe as those 70 years earlier but once again Hollywood is doing quite well during an economic downturn. Even as times were getting tight, domestic box office revenue rose to $9.8 billion from 2007 to 2008, an all-time high. Then, in the first half of 2009, revenue really took off. Ticket sales jumped about 18 percent, and attendance climbed by about the same number. It seemed that Americans were once again forgetting their troubles by going to the movies. And once again, they were enjoying escapist fare. Musicals such as *Mamma Mia, Step Up,* and *Hannah Montana* were box office successes. Comedies were big (*Paul Blart, Mall Cop; Marley and Me*) along with the rags-to-riches *Slumdog Millionaire.* Action-adventure heroes such as Batman, Ironman, and Indiana Jones drew big crowds.

This is not to say that Hollywood wasn't touched by the economic downturn. Many studios cut staff, reined in budgets, and instituted other cost-cutting measures. The digital revolution was also causing concern as sales of DVDs began to fall and digital downloading of movies increased. By the time you read this, the situation might have changed, but for now, the movie industry has done the best job dealing with hard financial times.

This chapter will examine the history, structure, and economics of the movie business as Hollywood prepares for a challenging future.

A Brief History

Motion pictures and television are possible because of two quirks of the human perceptual system: the phi phenomenon and persistence of vision. The **phi phenomenon** refers to what happens when we see one light source go out while another one close to the original is illuminated. To our eyes it looks like the light moves from one place to another. In **persistence of vision,** our eyes continue to see an image for a split second after the image has disappeared from view. In the early 19th century, a host of toys that depended on this principle were created in Europe. Bearing fanciful names (the Thaumatrope, the Praxinoscope), these devices made a series of hand-drawn pictures appear to move.

▲ Early American Cinema

The Edison Lab   Before long, some key inventors realized that a series of still photographs on celluloid film could be used with these devices instead of hand drawings. In 1878 a colorful Englishman (later turned American), Edward Muybridge, attempted to settle a $25,000 bet over whether the four feet of a galloping horse ever simultaneously left the ground. He arranged a series of 24 cameras alongside a racetrack to photograph a running horse. Rapidly viewing the series of pictures produced an effect much like that of a motion picture. Muybridge's technique not only settled the bet (the feet did leave the ground simultaneously in certain instances) but also demonstrated, in a backward way, the idea behind motion picture photography. Instead of 24 cameras taking one picture each, what was needed was one camera that would take 24 pictures in rapid order. It was Thomas Edison and his assistant, William Dickson, who finally developed what might have been the first practical motion picture camera and viewing device. Using flexible film, Dickson solved the vexing problem of how to move the film rapidly through the camera by perforating its edge with tiny holes and pulling it along by means of sprockets. In 1889 Dickson perfected a machine called the **Kinetoscope** and even starred in a brief film demonstrating how it worked.

These early efforts in the Edison lab were not directed at projecting movies to large crowds. Edison thought the device could make money by showing brief films to one person at a time for a penny a look. He built a special studio to produce films for this new invention, and by 1894 Kinetoscope parlors were springing up in major cities. However, the long-range commercial potential of this invention was lost on Edison. He reasoned

An early version of the Praxinoscope. Later models would be able to project a moving image onto a large screen for many people to view at once.

D. W. Griffith's *Birth of a Nation* was made to commemorate the 50th anniversary of the end of the Civil War. The film was based on a novel titled *The Clansman.* In 1906 a stage play based on the novel had caused disturbances in Philadelphia when it opened, but Griffith chose to go ahead with his plans to turn the work into a movie.

The story paints the prewar South as a happy and idyllic place whose serenity is disrupted by the war. At the war's conclusion, Southern whites are shown being victimized by renegade African Americans, northern carpetbaggers, and corrupt politicians. In response, whites form the Ku Klux Klan, which exacts vengeance on black people and restores the prewar utopia.

The NAACP objected to the film when it opened on the West Coast. About 40,000 African Americans demonstrated in California. In response the San Francisco city censor (several big cities had film censorship boards in this era) ordered a couple of the film's more controversial scenes cut out. A delegation called on the mayor of New York City to stop the premiere but was rebuffed. When the movie opened in Boston, several brawls broke out outside the theater. Unrest was averted in Chicago when the mayor agreed to seat a black man on the city's film censorship board. Griffith, for his part, never understood the feelings of black people toward the film. He responded to these actions by issuing a pamphlet about free speech.

Birth of a Nation is rarely screened today. Modern audiences find the racial depictions unacceptable. The film is remembered not so much for its content as for its technical achievements and because it served notice that motion pictures could exert a political and social force.

that the real money would be made by selling his peep-show machine. If a large number of people were shown the film at the same time, fewer machines would be needed, so he was not interested in adapting the machine for larger audiences.

Developments in Europe proved Edison wrong as inventors there devised large-screen projection devices. Faced with competition, Edison perfected a projector called the *Vitascope* and unveiled it in New York City in 1896.

Early movies were simple snippets of action—acrobats tumbling, horses running, jugglers juggling, and so on. Eventually, the novelty wore off, and films became less of an attraction.

The Nickelodeons   Public interest was soon rekindled when early filmmakers discovered that movies could be used to tell a story. In France, Alice Guy Blache produced *The Cabbage Fairy,* a 1-minute film about a fairy who produces children in a cabbage patch, and exhibited it at the Paris International Exhibition in 1886. Blache went on to found her own studio in America. Better known is the work of a fellow French filmmaker and magician, Georges Méliès. In 1902 Méliès produced a science fiction film that was the great-great-grandfather of *Star Wars* and *Star Trek;* it was called *A Trip to the Moon.* Méliès, however, did not fully explore the storytelling freedom afforded by film. His films were basically extravagant stage plays photographed by a stationary camera. It was an American, Edwin S. Porter, who in his *Great Train Robbery* first discovered the artistic potential of editing and camera placement. This and other new narrative films were extraordinarily popular with audiences and proved to be financially successful. Almost overnight, 50- to 90-seat theaters, called *nickelettes* or *nickelodeons* because of the 5-cent admission price, sprang up in converted stores throughout the nation.

Nickelodeons depended on audience turnover for their profits. Keeping the audience returning required that films be changed often—sometimes daily—to attract repeat customers. This policy created a tremendous demand for motion pictures, and new production companies were quickly formed. (In these early days films were regarded as just another mass-produced product; hence, early film studios were called *film factories.*) New York and New Jersey served as the bases for these early film companies.

Adolph Zukor and D. W. Griffith   Adolph Zukor decided to copy European filmmakers who were making longer, more expensive films aimed at a middle-class audience. He acquired the four-reel French film *Queen Elizabeth,* starring Sarah Bernhardt, the most famous actress of the period, and distributed it in the United States at the then-exorbitant price of a dollar a ticket. His experiment was successful, proving that American audiences would pay more and sit still for longer films. Nevertheless, *Queen Elizabeth* remained essentially the filming of a stage play.

It was an American, D. W. Griffith, who eventually took full advantage of the film medium and established film as its own art form. Although controversial and racist in its depictions (see the boxed insert "Birth of a Controversy"), his brilliant Civil War drama, *Birth of a Nation,* was released in 1915 and became the most expensive American film produced to that date ($110,000). The 3-hour movie, which was shot without a script, introduced history as a film topic. Griffith went on to top *Nation*'s figures with an even bigger epic, *Intolerance,* a piece comprising four scenarios dealing with life's injustices. The movie was completed in 1916 at a cost of about $2 million (the same film made in the 2000s would easily cost $90–110 million).

In response to the controversy generated by *Birth of a Nation,* two African American brothers, George and Noble Johnson, made films that presented a more realistic and accurate view of African Americans. The first of these, *The Realization of a Negro's Ambition,* demonstrated that there was an African American audience that would support films that spoke to their community. The Johnsons' company, Lincoln Motion Pictures, stayed in operation until the early 1920s, when a lack of capital and an inability to secure bookings at white theaters forced it out of business.

Birth of the MPPC Events in moviemaking during the decade of 1908–1918 had far-reaching effects on the future shape of the film industry. As the basic economic structure of the film industry developed, the center of filmmaking moved to the West Coast, and independent film producers, having survived attempts by the major studios to stamp them out, became an important force in the industry. The tremendous demand for new pictures brought enormous competition into the field. Small film companies cut corners by using bootlegged equipment (for which they paid no royalty fees) and started making films. Competition quickly reached the cutthroat level; lawsuits were filed with alarming frequency. In an effort to bring order to the business (and to cut down on legal expenses), the leading manufacturers of films and film equipment banded together, pooled their patents, and formed the **Motion Picture Patents Company (MPPC)** to restrict moviemaking to the nine companies that made up the MPPC. Film exhibitors were brought into line by a $2-per-week tax, which entitled the theaters to use projection equipment patented by the MPPC. Failure to pay this tax meant that the theater owners would no longer be supplied with MPPC-approved films. Eventually, to accommodate the growing industry, a new role, that of film distributor, was created. The film distributor served the function of a wholesaler, acquiring films from the manufacturers and renting them to exhibitors. This three-level structure—production, distribution, and exhibition—is still with us today. The MPPC was quick to take control of film distribution as well.

Instead of squelching competition, the MPPC actually fueled it. Annoyed by the repressive regulations, independent producers began offering films to exhibitors at cheaper rates than MPPC members. Full-length feature films, several reels in length, were imported from Europe. In response the MPPC declared war. "Outlaw" studios were raided and equipment smashed. In an effort to escape the harassment of the MPPC, independent producers fled New York and New Jersey. They were looking for a location with good weather, interesting geography, low business costs, and proximity to a national border so that the independents could avoid the MPPC's subpoenas. Florida proved to be too humid; Cuba was too inconvenient; Texas was too flat. Finally, they found the perfect environment—a rather sleepy suburb of Los Angeles called Hollywood. By 1913 this new home had so encouraged independent filmmaking that the MPPC could no longer contain its growth. And so, by 1917, for all practical purposes, the patents organization had lost its power.

The Star System The aura of glamour surrounding Hollywood and its stars might not have emerged if the MPPC had not been so stubborn. Whereas the patents company refused to publicize its performers, the independents quickly recognized that fan interest in film actors and actresses could be used to draw crowds away from the movies offered by the MPPC. Carl Laemmle, an independent producer, shrewdly publicized one of his actresses with a poetic name—Florence Lawrence—until she became what we might call the first movie star. As Florence's fame grew, her pictures brought in more money, spurring other independents to create their own stars to keep pace. The two artists who best exemplified the growth of the star system were Mary Pickford and Charlie Chaplin. In 1913 Chaplin was working in movies for $150 a week, a good salary in those days. Just four years later he was paid a million dollars for making eight pictures. Mary Pickford, nicknamed "America's Sweetheart," was paid $1,000 per week in 1913. By 1918 she was making $15,000–20,000 per week in addition to earning a cut of up to 50 percent of her films' profits.

In 1919 the star system reached its natural conclusion. Both Chaplin and Pickford joined with other actors and filmmakers to start their own production company—United Artists. The employees now owned the shop.

The star system had other, subtler effects. Once stars became popular, the public demanded to see them in longer movies. However, feature-length films that ran 1–2 hours were more expensive to make. Further, audiences could not be expected to sit for several hours on the wooden benches found in many of the nickelodeons. A need had been created for large, comfortable theaters that could accommodate thousands of patrons and, at the same time, justify higher admission costs. In 1914 the Strand opened in New York. With seats for more than 3,000 people, it occupied a whole city block and had space for an entire symphony orchestra. On the West Coast, Sid Grauman opened his Egyptian Theater (across from the Chinese Theater) in 1922 at a cost of almost a million dollars. His ushers were dressed in Cleopatra costumes. Clearly, the nickel was no longer the symbol of the movies.

Consolidation and Growth The increased cost of filmmaking made it imperative for producers to make sure that a company's movies were booked into enough big, new theaters to turn a profit. Under this economic pressure the film industry moved in the direction of consolidation. Adolph Zukor, whose company would ultimately become Paramount Pictures, combined the production and distribution functions into one corporate structure.

Charlie Chaplin, one of the first movie superstars created by the Hollywood star system, delighted film audiences throughout the world. This scene is from one of his earlier works, a 1916 short called *One A.M.*

Paramount and its chief rival, Fox, began building their own theaters, and Marcus Loew, owner of a large chain of theaters, purchased his own studio (later to become MGM). Studio owners could exert control over independent exhibitors through another policy known as **block booking.** To receive two or three topflight films from a studio, the theater owner had to agree to show five or six other films of lower quality. Although this policy was not very advantageous to exhibitors, it assured the production companies of steady revenue for their films.

All this was taking place as World War I devastated Europe. When the war ended in 1918, the American film industry was the dominant film force in the world, accounting for upwards of 80 percent of the worldwide market. By the beginning of the 1920s, the major production companies were comfortable and prosperous and enjoyed as firm a lock on the film business as had the old MPPC, which they had replaced only a few years earlier.

▲ The Roaring Twenties

The prosperity boom that followed the war exploded in Hollywood with more force than in other business sectors. Profits were up, and extravagance was the watchword as film-makers endorsed the principle that the only way to make money was to spend money. Between 1914 and 1924, the cost of a feature film increased 1,500 percent. Salaries, sets, costumes, props, and rights to best-sellers all contributed to the mushrooming costs. Even the lawyer for United Artists was paid $100,000 a year. By 1927 the average film cost about $200,000, and many films easily topped that. *Ben Hur* (1925) was made for a reported $6 million.

Huge salaries created a boomtown atmosphere in Hollywood, and many people—some still quite young—were unprepared to deal with the temptations that came with sudden wealth. Before long, newspapers were reporting stories about orgiastic parties, prostitution, studio call girls, bootleg whiskey, and drugs. Hollywood was dubbed "Sin City." In 1922, within a few short months, comedian Fatty Arbuckle was involved in a rape case, two female stars were implicated in the murder of a prominent director, and popular actor Wallace Reid died while trying to kick his drug addiction. Public reaction to these revelations was predictable: indignation and outrage. By the end of the year, politicians in 36 states had introduced bills to set up censorship boards for films. The motion picture companies hired a well-respected former postmaster general, Will Hays, to head a new self-regulatory body for the industry. Called the Motion Picture Producers and Distributors Association, this organization was successful in heading off government control, and the basic standards it laid down would be in force for almost four decades.

Al Jolson in *The Jazz Singer.* This film convinced the industry that audiences wanted to see "talkies," or films with sound, thus ushering in a new era in Hollywood.

▲ The Coming of Sound: The Late 1920s

Since optical recording of sound on film had been feasible since 1918, why did Hollywood wait until the late 1920s to introduce sound films? Money.

Business was good during the 1920s, and the major studios did not want to get into costly experimentation with new techniques. Warner Brothers, however, was not as financially sound as the other studios. Since Warner did not own movie theaters in the big cities and could not exhibit all its pictures in the most lucrative markets, the company was willing to try anything to get its films into theaters. In 1927 Warner released *The Jazz Singer,* in which Al Jolson not only sang but spoke from the screen. Within two years the silent film, for all practical purposes, was dead.

The novelty of sound gave a boost to the film industry, despite the devastating economic effects of the Depression. In 1929 average weekly movie attendance was 80 million; by 1930 it had reached 90 million—a fact that led many to regard filmmaking as a Depression-proof industry. They were quickly proved wrong as attendance dropped in 1931 and again in 1932. The industry generated several innovations to attract audiences. *Becky Sharp* was filmed in the new Technicolor process in 1935. Theaters also began the practice of showing double features, two feature films on the same bill. Animated cartoons began to draw sizable audiences. All this new activity called for Hollywood to produce even more films—almost 400 per year during the 1930s—to meet the demands of the market. This high production volume was a boon to major studios since they could churn out larger numbers of films more economically. Moreover, the tremendous amount of money needed to convert to sound and the poor financial conditions created by the Depression forced many small companies out of business, leaving eight major studios with a lock on the industry.

▲ The Studio Years: 1930–1950

The 20 years from 1930 to 1950 were the studio years, with MGM, 20th Century Fox, RKO, Warner Brothers, Paramount, Universal, Columbia, and United Artists dominating the industry. These studios created hundreds of acres of back-lot movie sets, constructed elaborate soundstages, and built up showy stables of creative talent, carefully groomed for stardom. Audiences adored and emulated their favorite screen idols, who were presented as larger-than-life gods and goddesses inhabiting a glamorous fantasyland.

Individual studios left their imprint on the films of the period as each studio's products took on a distinct personality. For example, during this period Warner Brothers became best known for its gangster films, 20th Century Fox for its historical and adventure films, and MGM for its lavish, star-studded musicals.

Orson Welles in a scene from the 1941 film *Citizen Kane.* Welles was 25 when he directed, produced, and starred in this film, considered by many critics the best American movie ever made.

The most significant period for motion picture achievement were the years from 1939 to 1941. *Gone with the Wind,* which showcased the new Technicolor film process, was released in 1939. In that same year two other soon-to-become-classics, *The Wizard of Oz* and *Stagecoach* (starring John Wayne in his first major role), were released. Just two years later, Orson Welles directed and starred in *Citizen Kane,* which some critics consider the best American film ever made.

The financial backing and diverse holdings of the studio system helped the film industry survive the Depression. Attendance and profits began climbing in 1934 and held steady throughout World War II. During the 1940s going to a movie was just as much a part of American life as watching television is today. In fact, the all-time peak for film-going was 1946, when average weekly attendance reached over 90 million. By 1948, however, all this was to change.

Back in 1938, the Justice Department had filed suit against Paramount and the other major film companies, charging that the industry's vertical control of production, distribution, and exhibition constituted restraint of trade and monopolistic practices. The case had been set aside during the war, but by 1948 the courts had ordered the major studios to get rid of at least one of their holdings in these three areas. Most chose to divest themselves of their theater chains. The court also eliminated the block booking system and thus deprived the studios of guaranteed exhibition for all their films. As a result the studios had to cut back on film production and reduce costs.

▲ The Reaction of the Film Industry to TV

When television began building a sizable audience during the late 1940s, it cut into the motion picture industry's profits. The first reaction of the film industry was to fight back. Studios stubbornly refused to advertise their films on TV, and they would not release old films for showing on the newer medium. Many studios wrote clauses into the contracts of their major stars forbidding them to appear on TV. None of their efforts had an appreciable effect on television's growing popularity; more and more Americans bought TV sets, while film attendance slipped.

One of the problems with 3-D movies was the uncomfortable plastic glasses that audience members had to wear to appreciate the three-dimensional effects. New production techniques spurred a comeback for 3-D movies in the 2000s.

Hollywood looked for ways to recapture some of its audience from TV. By the early 1950s the film industry thought it had found the answer—technical wizardry. The first technical gimmick was 3-D (three-dimensional film). The audience wore special polarized glasses to perceive the effect and were treated to the illusion of spears, trains, arrows, knives, birds, and even Jane Russell jumping out at them from the film screen. Unfortunately, the glasses gave some people headaches, the equipment was too expensive for most theater owners to install, and audiences quickly became bored with the novelty. It was soon apparent that 3-D was not the answer. The second technical gimmick concerned screen size. Cinerama, which involved the use of three projectors and curved screens, surrounded the audience with film. Less expensive techniques that enlarged screen size, such as Cinemascope, Panavision, and Vistavision, were ultimately adopted by the industry but did little to stem Hollywood's loss of money.

The attitude of the movie companies toward TV during those early years was a clear example of shortsightedness. What the film companies failed to see was that they could have played a dominant role in TV's evolution. Because the major networks were not eager to supply early TV shows, film companies would have been logical sources for programming. Somewhat belatedly, Hollywood recognized that it was in its best interest to cooperate with television. In the late 1950s the studios began to release their pre-1948 films to TV and to supply programs to the networks. In 1960 post-1948 theatrical films were made available to the smaller TV screens.

By the 1950s, when it became clear that TV would be a formidable competitor, the film industry cast about for new ways to draw audiences back to the theaters. It tried big-budget, spectacle movies, such as *Cleopatra*, as well as films that addressed more adult subjects, such as adultery and homosexuality, that could not be shown on TV.

▲ Realignments: The Film Industry from 1960 to 1990

The 1960s were marked by the waning power of the major studios and by a closer affiliation with their old competitor, television. The continued rise of the independent producer led to a concomitant loss of power by the studios. As major production houses cut back operations, they released many actors, writers, and directors who, naturally enough, formed small, independent production companies. Using the big studios for financing and distribution, these independents and the artists they employed frequently took small salaries in exchange for a percentage of a film's profits. By the mid-1960s roughly 80 percent of all American films were independent productions.

The poor economic climate brought about other changes. Large studios, faced with ever-worsening financial conditions, were absorbed by larger conglomerates. In the early 1970s both the MGM and 20th Century Fox studios were sold to make room for real estate developers.

The late 1960s also saw a change in the regulatory climate that surrounded films. The Supreme Court issued several decisions that loosened controls on content, and filmmakers were quick to take advantage of their new freedom. In 1968 the Motion Picture Association of America (MPAA) liberalized its attitudes toward self-regulation. Whereas the old production code attempted to regulate content, the new system attempted to regulate audiences by instituting a G-PG-R-X labeling system.

The relationship between film and television became even closer in the 1960s, as movies made expressly for TV appeared in the middle of the decade. In 1974 about 180 of these TV movies were shown on network television. In that same year the major film companies distributed only 109 films to theaters.

Film history from 1970 to 1990 was marked by several trends: Revenue went up, as did the budgets of many feature films, and several motion pictures racked up astonishing

During the 1950s Hollywood introduced 3-D movies in an attempt to lure viewers away from their TV sets and back into theaters. Each major studio released a few films in the 3-D format, and although some were successful, including the horror classics *House of Wax* and *Creature from the Black Lagoon,* the format was quickly abandoned, primarily because it gave many audience members a headache.

The early 3-D films were produced using the anaglyphic method. Two versions of the same scene were superimposed on the same frame of film. One version was red and the other blue. The audience wore special glasses with a red filter for one eye and a blue filter for the other. Because of these filters, a separate image entered each eye and the brain did the rest, creating a 3-D effect. The problems with this method were that it interferes with the natural colors of a scene and if the projectors in the theater were out of synch the image would become fuzzy and jittery, causing a lot of eyestrain among viewers.

The newer method of 3-D uses polarized light and two synchronized digital movie projectors. One projector shows images intended for the right eye, the other for the left. A polarized filter is placed over one projector that filters out light waves moving in an up-down direction but lets through those moving in a left-right direction. The other projector has a filter that does the opposite. The audience wears glasses that also contain filters so that the left eye sees only the light from the left projector and the right eye sees light only from the right projector. The result is two separate images that your brain turns into a 3-D image. The images are sharp and clear with no scratches or jittery images.

Hollywood is seriously exploring this new technique. Several 3-D pictures opened in theaters in 2009 including *Monsters vs. Aliens,* concert films featuring Hannah Montana and the Jonas Brothers, and the horror film *My Bloody Valentine.* The biggest test of 3-D's appeal may come at the end of 2009 when director James Cameron (*Titanic*) is scheduled to release his big-budget 3-D *Avatar.* In addition, studios are planning to issue 3-D versions of some of their successful 2-D films, such as *Titanic* and *Toy Story.*

If the new 3-D method is a success, those strange-looking glasses with the polarized lenses may become the next hot fashion accessory.

gross receipts. Foremost among the trends was a reversal of the slump in box office receipts that began in 1946 and finally bottomed out in 1971. With the exception of temporary declines in 1973 and 1976, the general trend has been upward. In 1977 the total box office gross came to about $2.4 billion; by 1981 it had risen to nearly $3 billion, although some of this increase could be attributed to inflation.

With more cash flowing into the box office, more money became available for the budgets of feature films. In fact, films of the late 1970s and early 1980s were reminiscent of the extravaganzas of the 1920s. Perhaps the most interesting film phenomenon of the era was the rise of the blockbuster. From 1900 to 1970 only two films (*The Sound of Music* and *Gone with the Wind*) managed to surpass $50 million in film rentals; between 1970 and 1980, 17 films exceeded this mark (see Table 9-1).

On another front, in 1985 the MPAA instituted a new rating category—PG-13. This category was designed for those films for which parental guidance for children under 13 was recommended. Yet another new category, NC-17, replaced the X rating in 1990.

TABLE 9-1

All-Time Box Office Leaders, 2008

The figures are based on film rentals, that is, the money received by film distributors from motion picture theaters. This figure is not the same as box office receipts, nor does it include DVD or videocassette rentals and sales. The table includes only data from the United States and Canada.

Rank	Title	Year	Rental Income (millions)
1	*Titanic*	1997	$601
2	*The Dark Knight*	2008	533
3	*Star Wars*	1977	461
4	*Shrek 2*	2004	441
5	*E.T.*	1982	435
6	*Star Wars—Phantom Menace*	1999	432
7	*Pirates of the Caribbean—Dead Man's Chest*	2006	423
8	*Spider-Man*	2002	404
9	*Star Wars—Revenge of the Sith*	2005	380
10	*Lord of the Rings—Return of the King*	2003	377

▲ Contemporary Trends

The motion picture industry continues to be concerned about piracy and illegal file sharing. Movie executives saw what the original Napster did to the music industry and do not want their industry to share the same fate. The problem is even more pressing now that file-sharing programs such as BitTorrent speed up the process so that even large movie files can be downloaded in a relatively short time. A visit to the MPAA Web site reveals that much of it is devoted to stopping piracy.

DVD sales still make up most of the income for the film industry, but revenues declined for the first time ever from 2006 to 2007 and continued to decline again in 2008, a trend that has many in the industry worried that the market has become saturated. Rather than buying or renting a DVD, many consumers were turning to digital downloads or video-on-demand. In a related matter, the format battle over the industry standard for high-definition DVDs was resolved in favor of Sony's Blu-ray disc. Sales of Blu-ray DVD players were still sluggish.

On the financial front, more studios were limiting their risks by striking co-financing deals and spreading the cost of making and distributing a film among several companies. (To get an idea of how this works, next time you go to a movie, count the number of company logos that appear before the film starts.) Co-financing reduces a company's possible loss but also limits its profits.

As mentioned earlier, film industry revenues continued to rise in the last half of the decade, reaching an all-time high in 2008 with indications that 2009 might be even better. Much of this increase has come from higher ticket costs as the number of tickets sold has remained constant or slightly declined. Hollywood, however, was not immune to the economic slowdown at the end of the decade. Studios trimmed costs and cut the number of films scheduled for release.

The motion picture industry remains dominated by six big companies: Sony/MGM, NBC Universal, Disney, Fox, Warner Brothers, and Paramount. These firms finance, produce, and distribute motion pictures and typically control about 80 percent of the market.

Modern film content is highly varied. The top two films of 2008 were based on action-adventure comic book heroes (*The Dark Knight* and *Ironman*). Four of the top 10 were animated features geared for children (including *Wall-E* and *Kung Fu Panda*), and one was about vampires (*Twilight*).

Motion Pictures in the Digital Age

▲ Transition

Most films are still produced the analog way by capturing images on film. Nonetheless, the digital revolution is affecting the production, distribution, and exhibition of motion pictures.

▲ Making Digital Movies

Digital moviemaking is already a reality. In fact, anybody who shoots video with a digital camera and edits on a computer is making a digital movie. Many big-budget Hollywood movies, such as *Get Smart* and *Jumper,* were shot with digital cameras. Animated films, such as *Bolt,* were created entirely by digital effects. A new technology, called motion capture, makes it possible to record the movement of human actors in order to animate digital human characters. Films such as *Beowulf* and *The Curious Case of Benjamin Button* relied heavily on this technology.

▲ Digital Distribution to Theaters

The current system of distributing films hasn't changed much in the last 90 years. Hundreds of copies of a celluloid film are printed, checked for quality, put into big metal cans, and shipped to theaters across the country. Each of these copies can cost more than $2,000.

Digital distribution is much cheaper. Movies can be copied to a hard drive and shipped to theaters or transmitted electronically by satellite, optical fiber, or the Internet. Experts calculate that digital distribution might save the industry as much as $1 billion annually. Moreover, digital distribution eliminates the scratches, dust, and "gate jitter" that often occur with traditional film.

▲ Digital Distribution to the Home

Buying or renting a DVD from Blockbuster or Netflix is one form of digital distribution, but the method that has attracted the most recent attention is digital downloading. Apple TV, for example, lets consumers download a movie to their computer and wirelessly sends the film to a TV set. Blockbuster offers a service that enables consumers to rent or buy a movie that is then downloaded to a computer. Thanks to a process called buffering, viewers can start watching the beginning of a movie while the rest of it continues to download. In addition, both Blockbuster and Netflix offer real-time streaming movies over the Internet that can be played on big-screen TV sets. Consumers have to purchase a special player (Blockbuster's is called a Mediapoint Player; those using Netflix have several options, including a Roku media player or even an Xbox 360 game console) and need a high-speed Internet connection. Note that this is another example of the transition from atoms (tangible DVDs) to bits (intangible digital bits of information).

▲ Digital Projection

Once the digital movie is sent to the theater, it has to be shown on a special digital projector. The industry has been slow to change to digital because of cost—about $100,000 per screen. For a 16-screen megaplex theater, that's a lot of money. Theater

Many movies, such as *The Curious Case of Benjamin Button,* depend heavily on digital special effects.

owners argued that film distributors should pay part of the cost; film distributors were reluctant to chip in, citing increased costs during the transition period when they would have to supply both analog and digital versions of movies. In late 2008, however, theater owners and five major studios worked out a deal in which the studios would help defray the cost of the changeover. Given the poor economic climate, however, it may take a while for the transition to occur. Currently, only about 5,000 out of 40,000 movie screens in the United States and Canada are equipped with digital projection equipment.

Digital projection may also revive an old movie idea—three-dimensional (3-D) films (see the boxed insert "What's Old Is New"). Studio executives think that 3-D movies on the big screen will boost ticket sales by drawing audiences away from their living rooms and back into theaters, a development that would also help theater owners since it would mean more people at the concession stand. As of mid-2009, only 1,200 screens were capable of 3-D projection.

▲ Mobile Movies

Movies are probably the least portable of all media. They were designed to be seen in a large hall on a large screen. Nonetheless, the digital age has opened new possibilities. Portable DVD players that weigh less than 2 pounds and are not much bigger than this book are becoming popular. Many SUVs and vans have video screens installed so that passengers in the back can watch DVDs during a trip. And, as we have already mentioned, there are many services that give subscribers the ability to download movies onto their laptops.

Mobile movies keep getting smaller—in screen size, that is. Owners of an iPhone, iPod Video or iPod Touch, and other devices can download and view movies on a 3.5-inch screen. Sprint offers a pay-per-view service that streams full-length movies to consumers' cell phones for about $4–5 each. There are even services that offer porn films delivered to a cell phone.

▲ User-Generated Content

Given the nature of film production, user-generated content is not yet a significant factor in the movie industry. Nonetheless, there are some examples. During the production of the cult classic *Snakes on a Plane*, New Line Cinema reshot some scenes incorporating suggestions from fans across the Internet. In early 2009, an independent film, *Perkins 14*, premiered at a national horror film festival. The film was created on Massify, an online collaboration site for filmmakers, and users were involved in making all decisions, from scripting to postproduction. *Faintheart* was a similar project that relied on MySpace members to choose a director and music and to develop some storylines. Independent filmmakers hope the Internet will help movie fans reconnect with moviemakers.

▲ Social Media

The movie industry was one of the first to appreciate the marketing power of social media. Back in 1999, the makers of *The Blair Witch Project* used the Internet to promote their movie using viral marketing techniques. Information about the movie spread quickly through chat rooms and bulletin boards. The movie *Cloverfield* used many of the same techniques in 2008 when the movie promoters created a series of fake Web sites that were used to spread rumors about the film. Fan communities quickly sprang up and debated theories about the film's plot. During the period right before the movie's release, *Cloverfield* was one of the most "blogged" words on the Internet.

There are numerous other examples. Leonardo DiCaprio posted a trailer for one of his new movies on his MySpace page. It got so many views, it broke the page's visit counter. Michael Moore posted videos on YouTube to promote his documentary *Sicko*. Marvel Entertainment routinely places trailers for its upcoming films on MySpace and Facebook.

Trailers are those snippets of scenes from an upcoming movie that are shown before the main feature. Trailers date back to 1913 and have always been a key part in the marketing of a soon-to-be-released film. In years past, the only place you could see a trailer was at a local movie theater or maybe on a cable network. Now the Internet has provided a potent new channel for movie promotion.

Trailers are routinely placed on MySpace, YouTube, Facebook, Yahoo!, iTunes, and a film's Web site. The trailer for the vampire hit *Twilight* got 55 million views online. Movie studios also like the fact that on the Internet they can show "red band" trailers, the ones that contain content a bit too edgy for the theater venue.

The growing importance of the Internet does not mean that film studios are overlooking the traditional in-theater trailer. In fact, trailers are more important than ever. Short "teaser trailers" are released to movie theaters about six months before a film is due to be released. The main trailer is ready to hit theaters three months later. Studios try to aim their trailers at the film's target audience. Thus, a raunchy comedy usually contains a trailer for another raunchy comedy.

The Motion Picture Association of America's guidelines suggest that trailers should run no longer that 2½ minutes. Theaters usually run about four to six trailers before the feature and limit the total time allotted to trailers to about 10–11 minutes.

There's even an awards show: The Golden Trailer Awards. In 2008, the best trailer of the year was the one for *The Dark Knight*.

The trailer for *The Incredible Hulk* was viewed 14 million times online, and the film made more than $135 million at the box office. Social media have given filmmakers new channels to promote their projects directly to the audience.

Defining Features of Motion Pictures

The most noticeable characteristic of motion pictures is their potential cost. Many big-budget Hollywood movies have production expenses that routinely top the $100-million mark. Tack on another $20 million or so for marketing and distribution, and you're talking real money. No other media product—book, magazine, TV series, CD—costs as much as motion pictures. (Of course, filmmakers sometimes put together films for much less and sometimes make big money—*Paranormal Activity,* for example—but these tend to be rare events.)

Partly because commercial moviemaking is so expensive, the industry has become dominated by big conglomerates. As noted earlier, six major companies now control most of the market. These companies have the financial resources to risk $100 million or so on a few dozen films each year in hopes of finding a blockbuster. Making motion pictures tends to be only one of many media interests in which these conglomerates are involved. Some have holdings in TV and the Internet; others own publishing companies and recording companies.

Film has a strong aesthetic dimension. Of all the media discussed in this book, film is the one most often discussed as an art form. My university library lists 110 entries under the heading "motion picture aesthetics." This characteristic introduces a tension in the field because most big-studio films are produced to make a profit rather than to showcase their artistic merit. Many independent filmmakers, however, make films not because of the bottom line but because they find their efforts artistically satisfying. Although this chapter discusses primarily mainstream Hollywood moviemaking, keep in mind that thousands of freelance filmmakers work outside the established corporate structure and produce films of varying length on a myriad of topics.

Going to the movies continues to be a social experience. It is the only medium that facilitates audiences gathering in large groups to be exposed to the same message. And, of course, moviegoing is still a popular dating activity. In fact, the social dimension of moviegoing might be the most important one.

Steven Spielberg directing *Saving Private Ryan.*

Steven Spielberg started making movies at age 12 using his father's 8mm camera. One of his earliest productions was a horror film starring his three younger sisters. He continued to make his own films during his college days, but he graduated with a degree in English because his grades were too low to get him into film school. One of Spielberg's independently made films caught the attention of an executive at Universal Pictures, who hired the young Spielberg to direct episodes of a TV series. The young director eventually wound up directing a made-for-TV movie, *Duel,* that won much critical acclaim.

On the basis of his success with *Duel,* Spielberg got approval to direct his first theatrical movie, *The Sugarland Express.* Although praised by critics, the movie did poorly at the box office. Nonetheless, the studio gave him a new assignment: directing the movie version of a best-selling novel about a huge shark. The movie, *Jaws,* released in 1975, marked a significant milestone in movie history. It was the first of the big-budget summer action movies, a strategy that movie studios still follow (consider *Twister, Independence Day,* and *The Dark Knight). Jaws* was also the first of the movie blockbusters, raking in more than $250 million. Hollywood studios quickly adopted a "big budget equals big blockbuster" mentality.

Spielberg also hit upon a formula for making successful pictures that resonated with moviegoers: Take tried-and-true, classic adventure themes, and enhance them with cutting-edge special effects. The *Indiana Jones* trilogy, *Jurassic Park, E.T.,* and *Close Encounters of the Third Kind* are all examples of this formula. Spielberg also tackled more serious themes, as exemplified in *The Color Purple, Schindler's List, Amistad, Saving Private Ryan,* and *Munich.*

In a career that has spanned more than a quarter-century, Spielberg has won two Oscars and numerous other movie awards. Of the top 25 all-time movie hits, 4 were directed by Steven Spielberg.

Organization of the Film Industry

Although film is an art form, the film industry is in business to make a profit. If an occasional moneymaking film also turns out to have artistic merit, so much the better, but the artistic merit is usually a by-product rather than the main focus. Our analysis of the film industry divides its structure into three areas: (1) production, (2) distribution, and (3) exhibition.

▲ Production

Films are produced by a variety of organizations and individuals. For many years the major studios controlled virtually all production, but independent producers have recently become prevalent. The major studios now finance and distribute many films made by independent companies.

Film studios differ in their arrangements, but a typical setup involves four main departments: (1) film production, (2) distribution, (3) TV production, and (4) administration. The film production department handles all those elements that actually go into the making of a film, including story development, casting, art, makeup, and sets. The distribution department handles sales and contracts for domestic and worldwide duplication and delivery of films to theaters and to home video. As its name suggests, the TV division develops and produces movies and series for first-run and syndicated television. Sales, financial deals, and legal arrangements are the provinces of the administration department.

▲ Distribution

The distribution arm of the industry is responsible for supplying prints of films to the thousands of theaters located across the United States and around the globe. In recent years distribution companies have also supplied films to TV networks and to makers of DVDs. Distribution companies maintain close contact with theater owners all over the world and also provide a transportation and delivery system that ensures that a film will arrive at a theater before its scheduled play date. In addition to booking the film at local movie houses, the distribution company is responsible for making the multiple prints of a film that are necessary when the film goes into general release. They also take care of advertising and promotion for the film. Most of the distribution of motion pictures is handled by the large studios, which are firmly entrenched in both the production and distribution aspects of the business.

The nature of film distribution ensures that the large companies will control a large portion of the business. First, it is too expensive for an independent producer or a small distribution company to contact theaters and theater chains spread all over the globe. The big studios already have this communication network set up and can afford to maintain it. Second, the large studios can offer theater owners a steady stream of films that consistently feature big-name stars. A small company could not withstand that competition for long.

Distribution companies also serve as a source of financing for independent producers. These companies lend money to a film's producer to cover all or most of the estimated cost of a film. In this way the major studios acquire an interest in films that they did not directly produce. This arrangement will be discussed further in the section on film economics.

▲ Exhibition

In 2009 there were about 40,000 movie screens in the United States, an all-time high. Multiplex theaters, featuring 12 or 18 screens clustered around a central concession stand, are still the rule. Most new theaters seat 200–400 patrons. The massive movie palaces of the 1920s and 1930s have not reemerged, but there are noticeable changes inside the motion picture theater as exhibitors go after a slightly older demographic. Soundproofing to prevent spill from adjoining theaters is now common, and concession stands are putting real butter on popcorn, with a few even offering mineral water, cappuccino, and valet parking (see the boxed insert "Deluxe Theaters").

Ownership in the Film Industry

Big conglomerates, many of them mentioned in earlier chapters, dominate the film industry. As of 2009 the top six were as follows:

1. *The Walt Disney Company:* Headquartered in California, Disney has two movie enterprises: Touchstone, for mature-audience films, and Buena Vista, for general films. Disney has holdings in television, cable, and publishing in addition to its interests in theme parks, hotels, music, real estate, golf courses, and cruise ships. Disney also makes money licensing Disney characters for use by other companies.

2. *Time Warner:* Warner Brothers is the motion picture arm of this huge conglomerate, which has interests in the Internet, magazine publishing, recorded music, motion picture theaters, and cable TV, among other media.

The trend in movie exhibition is big 18- and 24-screen multiplexes. Increased competition and declining profits forced some movie theaters to close during 2006 and 2007.

3. *Paramount (Viacom):* In addition to owning and making motion pictures, Viacom owns cable TV networks, motion picture theaters, and music publishing companies.
4. *Sony/MGM:* In 2004 Sony added MGM to its list of properties that include movie theaters, TV production facilities, consumer electronics, and video games.
5. *NBC Universal:* NBC acquired Universal from Vivendi, a French company, in 2003. GE, the parent of NBC, now has interests in cable and broadcast TV, a motion picture studio, and a recording company.
6. *News Corporation:* Rupert Murdoch's Australian-based company owns 20th Century Fox. The company is also involved in satellite broadcasting and publishing and owns a TV network and a cable news channel.

Producing Motion Pictures

▲ Preproduction

How does a film get to be a film? The three distinct phases in moviemaking are (1) preproduction, (2) production, and (3) postproduction.

All films begin with an idea. The idea can be sketchy, such as a two-paragraph outline of the plot, or detailed, such as a novel or a Broadway play.

The next step of the preproduction process is writing the screenplay. In general, the route to a finished motion picture script consists of several steps:

■ *Step 1: treatment.* This is a narrative statement of the plot and descriptions of the main characters and locations; it might even contain sample dialogue.

■ *Step 2: first-draft script.* This version contains all the dialogue and camera setups and a description of action sequences.

■ *Step 3: revised script.* This incorporates changes suggested by the producer, director, actors, and others.

■ *Step 4: script polish.* This process involves adding or subtracting scenes, revising dialogue, and making other minor changes.

While all this is going on, the producer tries to find actors (in the film industry, people who act in films are described by the generic term "talent," whether they have any or not)

The budget for *Quantum of Solace*, the 22nd in the series of James Bond films, was more than $200 million.

who will appear in the film. The contracts and deals that are worked out vary from astronomical to modest. One common arrangement is for the actor to receive a flat fee. These fees have been rising in the past few years and are one of the reasons films cost so much to produce. For example, Jim Carrey gets around $20 million per picture, and Nicole Kidman receives about $15 million. At the other end of the scale, the Screen Actors Guild has a contract that spells out the minimum salary that must be paid to talent in minor roles and walk-on parts.

Meanwhile, the producer is also trying to secure financial backing for the picture. We will say more about the monetary arrangements in film in the section on economics. For now, it is important to remember that the financial arrangements have to be worked out early in the preproduction process.

At the same time, the producer is busy lining up skilled personnel to work behind the camera. Of these people the film's director is central. When all the elements have been put together, the director will determine what scenes get photographed from what angle and how they will be assembled in the final product. Working closely with the director are the cinematographer (the person responsible for the lighting and filming of the scenes) and the film editor (the person who will cut the film and assemble the scenes in the proper order). A movie crew contains dozens of other skilled people: set designers, makeup specialists, electricians, audio engineers, crane operators, painters, plumbers, carpenters, property masters, set dressers, caterers, first-aid people, and many others.

Shortly after the director has been signed for the project, he or she and the producer scout possible locations for shooting the film. Some sequences may be shot in the sound studio, but others may need the authenticity that only location shooting can provide. As soon as the locations have been chosen, the producer makes the necessary arrangements to secure these sites for filming. Sometimes this entails renting the studios of a major motion picture production company or obtaining permits to shoot in city streets or other locales. The producer must also draw up plans to make sure that the filming equipment, talent, and technical crew are all at the same place at the same time.

▲ Production

Once all these items have been attended to, the film moves into the actual production phase. Cast and crew assemble at the chosen location, and each scene is shot and reshot until the director is satisfied. The actors and crew then move to another location, and the process starts all over again. Overriding the entire production is the knowledge that all this is costing a great deal of money. Shooting even a moderate-budget film can cost $400,000–500,000 *per day*. Therefore, the director tries to plan everything so that each dollar is used efficiently.

The average shooting schedule for the typical film is about 70 days. Each day's shooting (and some days can be 16 hours long) results in an average of fewer than 2 minutes of usable film.

▲ Postproduction

The postproduction phase begins after the filming has been completed. A film editor, working with the director, decides where close-ups should be placed, what angles scenes should be shown from, and how long each scene should last. The elaborate special effects that some films require are also added during postproduction. Once the scenes have been edited into an acceptable form, postproduction sound can be added. This might include narration, music, sound effects, and original dialogue that, for one reason or another, has to be redone. (About 10–15 percent of outside dialogue has to be rerecorded because of interfering noises.) Finally, the edited film, complete with final sound track and special effects, is sent to the laboratory where a release print of the film is made.

The Economics of Motion Pictures

There are several revenue streams for the motion picture industry: (1) money taken in at the U.S. box office, (2) revenue from the international box office, (3) sales and rentals of DVDs and tapes, and (4) miscellaneous video sources such as pay-per-view and video-on-demand.

As far as the U.S. box office is concerned, film revenue set a record in 2008 at $9.8 billion. The international box office was also at a record high. On a less optimistic note, movie attendance actually declined slightly from 2007 to 2008. Also troubling to the industry is the fact that revenue from DVD sales and rentals dropped for the first time from 2006 to 2008, from $24 billion to about $22.5 billion. (Note that DVD income far exceeds box office revenue.) Movie executives were hoping that the emergence of the Blu-ray high-definition DVD would help sales, but so far that has not materialized.

Here's a rough approximation of how much money movie studios make on the following:

Transaction	Studio Revenue
DVD rental at video store (@ $5.00)	$2.25
Movie box office admission (@ $7.00)	$3.50
DVD sale (@ $19.98)	$14.00

Not surprisingly, Hollywood is concerned about the recent lack of growth in DVD sales.

In short, Hollywood is not yet in need of a bailout, but its future fortunes remain hard to predict. Many studios have cut back on the number of films they are releasing and are no longer giving movie stars the generous paydays of years past.

Movies are an expensive medium. In 2007 the cost of producing and marketing the typical film was nearly $106 million, up about 30 percent from 2002. And some films cost much more. *Superman Returns* and *Spiderman 3* both topped the $250-million mark. If you've been to the movies lately, you're also aware that movies are getting expensive for consumers. The average ticket price in 2009 was $7.20, and in many cities a ticket to an evening performance costs more than $10. Add in another $5 for a medium popcorn (about 90 percent of that is profit for the movie theater) and $4 for a soft drink, and a night at the movies can be an expensive proposition—but still less expensive than attending a professional sporting event or going to a theme park.

▲ Financing a Film

Where do producers get the enormous sums of money necessary to make a film? Let us take a look at some common financing methods. If a producer has a good track record and a film looks promising, the distributor might lend the producer the entire amount needed to make the film. In return the distributor gains distribution rights to the film. Moreover, if the distributor also has studio facilities, the producer might agree to rent those facilities from the distributor.

A second method is to arrange for a **pickup.** Under this arrangement a distributor agrees to "pick up" the cost of a finished picture at a later date for a set price. Although this agreement does a producer little immediate good, he or she can take the pickup to a bank to help secure a loan for the cost of the film.

A third method is a **limited partnership,** an arrangement whereby the film is financed through outside investors. Each limited partner puts up a set amount, and his or her personal liability is limited by the amount invested; that is, a partner cannot lose any more money than he or she put up even if the film goes over budget.

A fourth method is a **joint venture.** Under this setup several companies involved in film production and distribution pool their resources and agree to finance and distribute one or more films. Given the increasing cost of motion pictures, this arrangement is becoming more common as several companies share the risk and potential rewards of a movie. *Ironman,* for example, was financed by a joint venture between Paramount and Marvel Entertainment.

The producer and distributor also agree on how to divide the distributor's gross receipts from the film (the money the distributor gets from the theater owners, TV networks, pay-TV operations, and DVD revenues). Since the distributor takes the greatest risk in the venture, the distributor is the first to be paid from the receipts of the film. Distribution companies charge a distribution fee for their efforts. In addition, there are distribution expenses (cost of making multiple prints of the film, advertising, necessary taxes, insurance). Lastly, the actual production cost of the film must be repaid. If the distributor or a bank lent the producer $50 million to make the film, that loan has to be paid off (plus interest). Because of all these expenses, it is estimated that a film must earn two and one-half to three times its production cost before it starts to show a profit for the producers. Hollywood accounting tends to be complicated, however, and sometimes it is hard to determine when a film is profitable.

▲ Dealing with the Exhibitor

The distributor is also involved in other financial dealings, specifically with the exhibitors. An exhibition license sets the terms under which the showing of the film will occur. The license specifies the run of the film (the number of weeks the theater must agree to play the picture), holdover rights, the date the picture will be available for showing, and the clearance (the amount of time that must elapse before the film can be shown at a competing theater).

The license also contains the financial terms for the film's showing. There are several common arrangements. The simplest involves a specified percentage split of the money taken in at the box office. The exhibitor agrees to split the money with the distributor according to an agreed-upon formula—perhaps 50/50 the first week, 60/40 the second, 70/30 the third, and so on—with the exhibitor keeping more money the longer the run of the film. Another alternative is the **sliding scale.** Under this setup, as the box office revenue increases, so does the amount of money the exhibitor must pay the distributor. For example, if a week's revenue was more than $30,000, the exhibitor would pay the distributor 60 percent; if the revenue was between $25,000 and $29,999, the distributor would receive 50 percent; and so on. Another common approach is the 90/10 deal. Under this method the movie theater owner first deducts the house allowance (called the *nut*) from the box office take. The house allowance includes all the operating expenses of the theater

Back in the 1930s the Catholic Church formed the Legion of Decency, whose members were urged to boycott films that the Church found objectionable. The Legion was a powerful force for several decades but eventually lost power by the 1970s. (See Chapter 17 for more information on the Legion of Decency.) Since that time the Catholic Church has generally been careful about condemning specific films.

In 2006, however, the Church chose to speak out against the film version of the blockbuster novel, *The Da Vinci Code*. A church official said the film contained "slander, offenses, and errors" and that Christians should reject lies and "gratuitous defamation" aimed at their religion. The official noted that if a film about the Holocaust or the Qur'an had been released that contained equally egregious errors, there would have been a worldwide uprising. Religious groups called for a boycott of the film.

In light of the controversy, Ron Howard, the film's director, was asked to put a disclaimer at the beginning of the film stating that the story was fiction. He refused but stated that film was not theology and was not meant to offend.

The controversy surrounding *The Da Vinci Code* was another example of what Christians in general and Catholics in particular suggest is Hollywood's recent propensity to denigrate faith and religion. Consider such films as *Dogma, The Last Temptation of Christ, The Omen,* and the recent *Elizabeth: The Golden Years*. All contained a definite anti-Catholic perspective.

The issue was raised again in 2009 with the impending release of *Angels and Demons,* the "prequel" to *The Da Vinci Code*. Once again, the Vatican spoke out against the film. The film's producers were banned from entering the Holy See or any church in Rome, a move that forced them to construct expensive sound stages to stand in for famous churches.

Church authorities exercised caution, however, about a boycott, fearing that the publicity would simply prompt more people to see the film. *The Da Vinci Code* was apparently not hurt by the calls for a boycott. Despite lukewarm critical reviews, the film wound up with worldwide gross revenue topping $750 million.

(heating, cooling, water, lights, salaries, maintenance, and so on), plus a sum that is pure profit for the theater (this sum is called *air*). From the revenues (if any) that remain, the distributor gets 90 percent and the house 10 percent.

As suggested earlier, concession stand sales are a significant source of income for movie theater owners. If the average moviegoer spends $20 on popcorn, candy, soft drinks, nachos, and other munchies, and a billion or so tickets are sold every year, that works out to about $20 billion in annual revenue.

Movie theaters now have an additional revenue stream from on-screen advertising. Theaters love this since the cost involved in this process is minimal. In order to clear time to show in-theater commercials, however, the exhibitor often cuts back on the time devoted to showing movie previews, a move that doesn't sit well with the studios.

▲ Promoting a Film

A well-known film executive once said that a film is like a parachute: If it doesn't open, you're dead. The first week that a film is in release is crucial; in fact, since most films open on a weekend, the first three days are even more crucial. Films that open badly seldom do well.

Consequently, a good deal of promotion, marketing, and advertising is targeted to getting people into theaters for that opening weekend. The most common strategy is to launch a media blitz that touts the film weeks before it opens. These campaigns are not inexpensive. For instance, Warner Brothers reportedly spent nearly $100 million promoting *The Dark Knight*.

Feedback for Motion Pictures

▲ Box Office

Feedback in the movie industry revolves around the weekly box office figures compiled and reported in various trade publications including **Variety.** Each week *Variety* reports the top-grossing films in the American and foreign markets. An example of this listing is reproduced in Figure 9-1.

FIGURE 9-1   *Variety* Box Office Revenue Chart

TITLE (DISTRIBUTOR/PARTNER)	Reported Box Office 9/4-9/7 (weekend)	Percent Change in Box Office*	Number of Theaters This Week	Number of Theaters Last Week	Weeks Avg $ Per Theater	No. of Weeks in Release	Domestic Box Office Cumulative	Foreign Box Office Cumulative	Worldwide Box Office Cumulative
The Final Destination (WB)	$15,295,069	-44%	3121	3121	$4901	2	$50,435,066	$32,500,000	$82,935,066
Inglourious Basterds (Weinstein)	14,950,489	-23%	3358	3165	4452	3	95,146,096	83,985,645	179,131,741
All About Steve (20th)	14,058,106	—	2251	—	6245	1	14,058,106	—	14,058,106
Gamer (Lionsgate)	11,203,761	—	2502	—	4478	1	11,203,761	—	11,203,761
District 9 (Sony)	9,114,591	-11%	3139	3180	2904	4	103,388,712	24,777,311	128,166,023
Julie and Julia (Sony)	7,077,574	+1%	2528	2503	2800	5	80,717,968	1,175,818	81,893,786
Halloween II (Weinstein)	6,872,800	-58%	3088	3025	2226	2	26,928,692	—	26,928,692
G.I. Joe: The Rise of Cobra (Par)	6,705,288	-13%	2846	3467	2356	5	141,021,754	139,750,923	280,772,677
Extract (Miramax)	5,513,634	—	1611	—	3422	1	5,513,634	—	5,513,634
The Time Traveler's Wife (WB)	5,465,925	-15%	2803	2961	1950	4	55,809,927	7,000,000	62,809,927
Shorts (WB)	3,845,717	-15%	2631	3105	1462	3	18,272,777	2,500,000	20,772,777
G-Force (Disney)	2,842,407	+1%	1477	1926	1924	7	115,469,113	76,996,000	192,465,113
Harry Potter and the Half-Blood Prince (WB)	2,502,248	+1%	1091	1508	2294	8	297,614,366	619,600,000	916,500,000
500 Days of Summer (Fox Searchlight)	2,381,148	+19%	935	909	2547	8	28,449,326	2,523,667	30,972,993
Taking Woodstock (Focus)	1,916,451	-45%	1395	1393	1374	2	6,442,111	181,460	6,623,571

To compile these data, *Variety,* in cooperation with Nielsen Entertainment Data Incorporated, collects box office results from 50,000 movie screens in 14 countries, including the United States, Canada, Mexico, and several countries in South America, Europe, and Asia. Most of the column headings in *Variety*'s chart are self-explanatory. Each film's title is listed, followed by the distributor. The remaining columns show box office revenue, number of screens showing the picture, average revenue per screen, and domestic and foreign revenue estimates. Note that this chart reports only a film's gross earnings; it does not show how much profit, if any, a film has made.

The economic feedback contained in *Variety* is extremely important in the movie industry. One or two blockbuster films can improve the financial position of an entire company. In addition, a film successful at the box office is apt to inspire one or more sequels and several imitators.

▲ Market Research

Audience research has become more influential in the movie business because of the tremendous cost of motion pictures. At most studios the first step is concept testing to find promising plotlines. The next step is an analysis of the script. If the script seems promising, the studio will go ahead and film it and make a rough cut. The rough cut is then used by movie researchers in a series of test screenings. In addition, **focus group** sessions are held. A focus group is a small sample (usually about 10–15 people) of the target audience that is asked detailed questions about what the viewers liked and did not like. With this information the studio can add or drop a scene, modify the ending, change the musical score, or make other alterations. Once these changes are completed, the movie is released for a sneak preview. Audience members fill out preview cards that summarize their reactions to a film, its characters, and its stars. It is possible for the director to make

FIGURE 9-2

Average Weekly Film Attendance in the United States

Source: Motion Picture Association of America. Used by permission

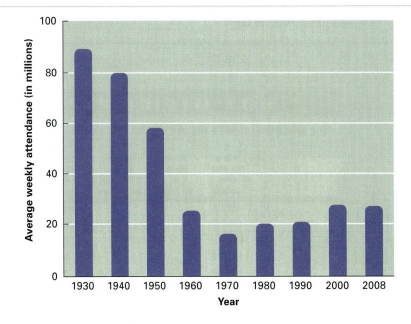

limited changes in the film in response to this feedback, but it is usually too late to make wholesale changes.

▲ Motion Picture Audiences

Average weekly attendance had been slowly rising from 1980 to 2002, but admissions fell slightly from 2006 to 2008. As shown in Figure 9-2, attendance is nowhere near the levels of the 1930s and 1940s when film was in its heyday.

The movie audience tends to be young. About 60 percent of filmgoers are under 40. Frequent moviegoers (those who see at least 12 films a year) account for about three-quarters of all film admissions. They tend to be young, single (going to movies continues to be a popular dating activity), from middle-class families, and from urban areas. The average person in the United States attends about five films a year.

The audience for movies is largest in July and August and smallest in May. The worst two weeks of the year for moviegoing are the first two weeks in December, when attendance drops 30–50 percent.

Movies at Home

Home video has become Hollywood's biggest revenue source. In 2008 combined income from the sales and rentals of DVDs topped the $22-billion mark, more than double the amount taken in at the box office. DVD revenue, however, has recently declined, suggesting to many in the industry that the DVD market has matured and that there is little room left for growth. Hollywood is hoping that new high-definition DVD players and discs will reinvigorate the DVD market. These DVDs, however, have been slow to catch on because of high prices for high-definition playback units and discs.

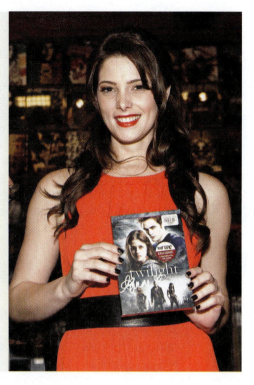

DVDs have reshaped the home video industry. Vampire fans bought 3 million copies of *Twilight* the first day of its release.

The home video market, like the theatrical market, is driven by big hits. Movies that were popular on the big screen are almost invariably popular on the home screen. *Kung Fu Panda,* for example, sold 8 million DVDs. At the other end of the spectrum, some films that are box office bombs do significantly better in the home market. *Office Space* took in only $10 million at the box office but more than $45 million from DVD sales and rentals.

Moreover, the DVD is shrinking the amount of time between the release of a movie in theaters and its appearance on disc. Historically, there was a six-month gap between theatrical release and entry into the home video market. That interval has shrunk to just three months and even less in some instances, thanks to better duplication and distribution facilities that make DVDs easier to manufacture and deliver to retail shelves. In addition, more films are opening on larger numbers of screens, saturating the market much more quickly than before. The shorter interval helps movie studios take advantage of the movie advertising campaigns that are still fresh in consumers' minds.

Pay-per-view (PPV) television provides another revenue stream for movie companies. More than 30 million homes are equipped with PPV, and the number is growing steadily. In addition, the number of channels available on cable and satellite systems is increasing, and many of these new channels are devoted to PPV. Finally, Hollywood gets income from licensing its movies to premium cable channels, such as HBO and Showtime, in addition to receiving money from selling the rights to movies to traditional over-the-air broadcasters. Given these numerous video aftermarkets, it is no surprise that TV generates more revenue for the movie industry than does the box office. Chapter 10 contains more information on home video.

The Film Industry

Job prospects in the film industry are highly volatile, but most college students who are interested in a career in film are not discouraged by the difficulty involved in becoming successful. Film students tend to be dedicated and passionate about their interest in film and will try to succeed no matter what the employment forecast.

Taking college courses in film is great preparation for a career since it provides students an opportunity to become familiar with the hardware and software used in the industry. In addition, purchasing a good digital camera, investing in professional editing software, and making a couple of films on your own can build a good foundation for later efforts.

The career outlook in the various media industries changes quickly. For a more current description of conditions in the film industry and a more detailed look at career options, please consult the book's Web site: www.mhhe.com/dominick11e.

MAIN POINTS

- The motion picture developed in the late 19th century. After being a main attraction in nickelodeons, films moved into bigger theaters, and movie stars quickly became the most important part of the new industry. Sound came to the movies in the mid-1920s.

- Big movie studios dominated the industry until the late 1940s, when a court decision weakened their power. Television captured much of the film audience in the 1950s. By the end of the 1960s, however, Hollywood had adapted to television and was an active producer of TV shows. A major trend in modern movies is the rise of big-budget movies.

- The transition to digital moviemaking may transform the film industry.

- The movie industry consists of production, distribution, and exhibition facets. Large conglomerates control the business. Producing a motion picture starts from a concept, proceeds to the production stage, and ends with the postproduction stage.

- Movie revenues have shown small but steady growth over the past 10 years. DVD sales and rentals and foreign box office receipts are important sources of movie income.

- Movie audiences are getting older, but a significant part of the audience is still the 30-and-under age group.

QUESTIONS FOR REVIEW

1. What are the defining features of motion pictures?
2. What caused the rise and fall of the Motion Picture Patents Company?
3. How did the film industry react to TV?
4. What are the three main segments of the motion picture industry?
5. What are the various ways films are financed?

QUESTIONS FOR CRITICAL THINKING

1. Suppose the movie industry had never moved to Hollywood, staying instead on the East Coast. How might films be different?
2. What are the potential advantages and disadvantages of big corporations controlling motion picture production?
3. Do filmmakers have an obligation to be socially responsible for what they present on the screen? Why or why not?
4. Will any of the antipiracy tactics adopted by the film industry be effective in stopping the illegal copying and distribution of films? Why or why not?
5. Someone once said that Hollywood producers don't make films; they make deals. Comment on the validity of this statement and its implications.

KEY TERMS

phi phenomenon (p. 202)
persistence of vision (p. 202)
Kinetoscope (p. 202)
Motion Picture Patents Company
   (MPPC) (p. 204)

block booking (p. 206)
pickup (p. 220)
limited partnership (p. 220)
joint venture (p. 220)
sliding scale (p. 221)

Variety (p. 222)
focus group (p. 223)
pay-per-view (PPV) (p. 225)

INTERNET RESOURCES

Online Learning Center

On the Online Learning Center home page, www.mhhe.com/dominick11e, *select* Student Center *and then* Chapter 9.

1. Use the Learning Objectives, Chapter Outline, and Main Points sections to review this chapter.
2. Test your knowledge of the chapter using the multiple choice and flashcard features of the site.
3. Expand your knowledge of concepts and topics discussed in the chapter with additional Questions for Critical Thinking and Internet Exercises.

Surfing the Internet

These represent a variety of movie theme sites.

www.imdb.com
The Internet Movie Database. Contains everything you ever wanted to know about movies. Has information about stars, cast, plot, and box office performance for just about every movie.

www.mpaa.org
The official Web site of the Motion Picture Association of America. Contains industry statistics and the latest news releases. Has an extensive section that deals with copyright issues.

www.mrcranky.com
An offbeat review page featuring a reviewer who has high standards and a caustic style. Mr. Cranky rates movies by assigning a number of bombs. For example,

four bombs means "As good as a poke in the eye with a sharp stick."

www.variety.com
The Web site of the trade paper that is the bible of the entertainment industry. Includes the latest industry news, global box office charts, film reviews, and profiles of production companies.

www.videobusiness.com
Find out the latest trends in home video, satellites, and video-on-demand. Access is free, but you have to register.

www.Warnerbros.com
The Warner Brothers Web site. Check out new releases, view movie trailers, and see which Warner products are available on DVD.

CHAPTER 10

Broadcast Television

This chapter will prepare you to:

- trace the development of television

- describe the evolution of the networks

- explain the impact of the Telecommunications Act of 1996

- detail the implications of the digital age for broadcast television

- explain how television ratings are formulated

- describe the departments of the television industry and how programs are produced

NBC's scheduling of Jay Leno's talk show in prime time illustrated the changing world of network TV programming.

I n late December 2008, the NBC television network announced a move that signaled a fundamental change in the broadcast television industry: NBC was giving late-night talk show host Jay Leno a prime-time program that would air five nights a week at 10 P.M. Running a show five days a week (called "stripping" in the business) is common during the day but unprecedented in prime time.

Why did NBC make such a radical move, and what does it tell us about the changing world of broadcast TV? NBC's decision was primarily a cost-cutting move. The network was mired in last place in the ratings and hadn't had a big hit in the 10 P.M. time slot since *ER* back in 1994. Since producing hour-long scripted shows can cost $3 million or more an episode, scheduling a scripted series at 10 P.M. would cost around $15 million a week. In contrast, an hour of Leno's talk show would run about $2 million a week. Over the course of a year, NBC would save tens of millions of dollars.

Several weeks into the 2009–2010 season it appeared that NBC's strategy was paying off. Leno's program ranked third in its time slot, but its ratings were high enough to ensure a modest profit for NBC. (Local NBC affiliates, however, weren't happy. They claimed Leno's show was a weak lead-in to their late evening local newscasts.)

NBC's move also illustrated some of the realities of today's broadcast TV business. Shrinking advertising revenues and declining network viewership are changing the traditional network–local station relationship and threatening the basic business model that has fueled broadcast television since the 1940s. For decades, the networks dominated prime-time and daytime TV programming. During their heyday, they programmed 3½ hours nightly in prime time and were responsible for such mega-hits as *Gunsmoke, Seinfeld, MASH,* and *Friends.* Advertisers were lining up to buy network ads. At any given minute in prime time, more than 90 percent of the audience was watching a network program. Today, the four major networks are lucky if they get 40 percent. Further, the networks program only 3 hours on a weeknight (Fox programs only 2 hours) and the next mega-hit has yet to emerge. With NBC's announcement, the opportunities for scripted drama and comedy shows decreased even more. To make matters worse, advertising revenue was drying up.

Times are also changing for local stations. A network affiliation contract used to be a huge plus for a local station. It gave them commercial time to sell adjacent to high-rated network shows and also compensated them for giving up their time for network programs. Network affiliation is still important, but current network shows no longer have the same high ratings as previously and local stations may have to pay the network for programs. At least one network was discussing dropping the local affiliates all together and becoming a cable-only network.

Clearly, broadcast TV is in a time of transition.

This chapter will examine broadcast TV, and the next chapter will look at other forms of television: cable, satellite, and Internet. (This is not a totally neat division because broadcast stations are also carried via cable and satellite, and stations and networks both have a Web presence.) Although the distinction between traditional broadcast TV and the newer forms doesn't concern most people, there are some areas where the distribution channel does make a difference. In addition to variations in programming strategies, broadcast TV is regulated differently from the other forms of TV while cable, satellite, and Internet TV have different revenue sources than broadcast TV. Most importantly, broadcast, cable, satellite, and Internet TV are all coping differently with the digital revolution.

A Brief History

The two men who developed television in the United States could not have been more different. At the age of 16, Philo Farnsworth diagrammed his idea for a television system on the chalkboard in front of his somewhat amazed high school teacher. Farnsworth, an individualistic and lone-wolf inventor, worked at developing his new device, which he called an *image dissector,* and eventually patented it in 1930. In contrast, Vladimir Zworykin was an organization man, working first for Westinghouse and then for RCA. By 1928 he had perfected a primitive camera tube, the iconoscope.

Picture quality of the early television systems was poor, but technical developments during the 1930s improved performance. RCA, with Zworykin's help and with a patent arrangement that permitted it to use Farnsworth's invention, set out to develop TV's commercial potential. NBC, owned by RCA, gave the first public demonstration of broadcast commercial television at the 1939 World's Fair.[1]

The initial public response to TV was lukewarm. Sets were expensive, and there were not many programs for people to watch. Even early TV actors were somewhat skeptical about the future of the new medium. They had to wear green makeup to look normal for the TV camera and swallow salt tablets because the intense heat of the lights necessary for TV made them perspire constantly.

World War II interrupted TV's development. When peace returned in 1945, new technology that had been perfected during the war greatly improved both TV reception and working conditions for the performers. New TV cameras required much less light. TV screens were bigger. There were more programs available, and stations were being linked into networks. All the signs pointed to big things for TV. In 1945 there were only eight TV stations and 8,000 homes with TV in the entire United States. Ten years later, there were nearly a hundred stations, and 35 million households (about 67 percent of the country) had TV.

TV's rapid success caught the industry and the Federal Communications Commission (FCC) off guard. Unless technical standards were worked out, the TV spectrum was in danger of becoming overcrowded and riddled with interference, just as had happened with radio 30 years earlier. To guard against this possibility, the FCC imposed a freeze on all new applications for TV stations. The freeze, which went into effect in 1948, would last for 4 years while the FCC gathered information from engineers and technical experts. When the freeze was lifted in 1952, the FCC had established that 12 VHF and 70 UHF channels (see page 242) were to be devoted to TV. In addition, the commission drew up a list that allocated television channels to the various communities in the United States and specified other rules to minimize interference. Also, thanks largely to the efforts of Frieda Hennock, the first woman to serve on the commission, TV channels were set aside for educational use.

▲ The 1950s: Television Takes Off

Networks, Tape, UHF, and Color   The early television industry was modeled after radio. Local stations served their communities and, in turn, might be affiliated with networks. There were four TV networks during this period: CBS, NBC, ABC, and DuMont, a smaller network that went out of business in 1956. Also much like early radio networks, TV networks quickly became the primary programming sources for their affiliates. NBC and CBS were usually the most popular networks, with ABC trailing behind. Most early network programs were game shows, sports events, and interviews, with a few comedies and dramas interspersed throughout the schedule.

In the early days of TV, most network prime-time programs were produced by advertising agencies that retained control over their content. The agencies also decided on the length and placement of the commercials. After the 1959 scandal that followed the discovery that some quiz shows had been "fixed," the networks reasserted their control

---

[1]In fairness to Farnsworth, the inventor demonstrated his system in 1934 using what today would be called a *closed-circuit telecast.*

Mr. Television, Milton Berle, dressed in one of the costumes that were his trademark on *Texaco Star Theater.*

over programming. Most programs were produced by independent production companies, with much of the financing provided by the networks, an arrangement that would be in place for the next several decades.

Most programs were broadcast live from New York or were filmed in California. Live programs, of course, could not be repeated and often had to be performed again for the West Coast. In 1956 the Ampex Corporation developed videotape, a cheap and efficient way of storing TV programs. By the beginning of the 1960s, most of TV's live programming had switched to tape.

After the FCC-imposed freeze ended, TV stations and TV sets multiplied rapidly. The new UHF channels, however, did not do so well. Few sets equipped with UHF receivers were made during the 1950s. The UHF stations had smaller coverage areas than the VHF stations, and most advertising dollars went to VHF stations. As a result, UHF TV, much like FM radio, started off at a disadvantage.

Color television was introduced during the 1950s. Led by NBC (RCA, the parent company, was manufacturing color TV sets), the networks were broadcasting 2–3 hours of color programming per day by 1960.

The Golden Age of Television   Many broadcast historians refer to the 1950s as the golden age of TV. Many shows that aired during the decade became extremely popular. *Toast of the Town*, hosted by Ed Sullivan, is still regarded as the exemplar of the variety series. *Texaco Star Theater*, starring ex-vaudevillian Milton Berle, prompted many people to buy TV sets just to see what wacky stunts Berle would pull off on his next program.

Live prestige dramas were also run in prime time. Programs such as *Studio One* featured plays by Rod Serling, Gore Vidal, and Reginald Rose. Broadway stars such as Rex

The Beverly Hillbillies was the most popular of the "bucolic" situation comedies. It was the number-one show during the 1961–1962 TV season and spent 9 years on the air.

Harrison and Tallulah Bankhead performed in live TV drama. The growing popularity of videotape, however, put an end to these live productions.

By the end of the 1950s, a new genre, the adult Western, in which character and motivation overshadowed gunfights, dominated TV. By 1959, there were 26 Westerns in prime time, including *Gunsmoke*, *The Life and Legend of Wyatt Earp*, and *Wagon Train*.

▲ Coming of Age: Television in the 1960s

By the early 1960s TV had lost its novelty and become just another part of everyday life. The number of TV stations continued to increase, and by the close of the decade, more than 95 percent of all American households owned at least one TV.

Television journalism came of age during the 1960s. NBC and CBS expanded their nightly newscasts from 15 to 30 minutes in 1963, and ABC followed suit shortly thereafter. In November of that year, TV journalism earned praise for its professionalism during its coverage of the assassination and funeral of President John F. Kennedy. The networks also covered the civil rights movement and the growing social unrest across the country. Perhaps the most exciting moment for television news came in 1969 with its live coverage of Neil Armstrong's historic walk on the moon.

Noncommercial broadcasting also evolved during the 1960s. About 69 educational stations were broadcasting by 1965. A report issued by the Carnegie Commission proposed that Congress establish a Corporation for Public Broadcasting. The commission's recommendations were incorporated into the **Public Broadcasting Act of 1967,** which set up the Public Broadcasting Service.

Another segment of the video industry was also experiencing growth during this time period—cable television. We will discuss the history of cable TV in the next chapter.

Television programs popular in the early 1960s included a number of rural comedies, such as *The Beverly Hillbillies* and *Green Acres.* After the Kennedy assassination, however, fantasy and escapist programs dominated prime time. In 1964, for example, some of the shows that premiered included *Bewitched* (about a friendly witch), *My Favorite Martian* (about a friendly Martian), and *My Mother the Car* (self-explanatory).

▲ The 1970s: Growing Public Concern

As the 1970s began, public concern over the impact of television programming was growing. A panel of scientists set up by the Surgeon General's office to investigate the impact of exposure to TV violence suggested that TV violence was related in a modest way to aggressive behavior in some young children. We'll explore this topic further in Chapter 19.

The early 1970s were also characterized by the growth of citizen group involvement in FCC decisions. Groups such as Action for Children's Television and the Office of Communication of the United Church of Christ and coalitions of minority groups became influential in shaping broadcasting policy.

The three networks continued to dominate the industry during the early-to-mid-1970s, but by the end of the decade, they were beginning to feel the competition from the growing cable industry. Friction between the traditional over-the-air broadcasters and the cable companies continues today.

The biggest trend in television programming during the early 1970s was the growth of law-and-order programs, such as *The FBI, Charlie's Angels,* and *Mannix.* By the middle of the decade, these shows were replaced by a number of adult situation comedies, shows

Live TV coverage of the first man landing on the moon in 1969 reached hundreds of millions of viewers.

that dealt with more mature themes. *All in the Family, M*A*S*H,* and *Sanford and Son* typified this trend. By the end of the decade, prime-time soap operas such as *Dallas* and *Dynasty* topped the ratings.

▲ The 1980s and 1990s: Increased Competition

The biggest trends in the TV industry in the 1980s and 1990s were the continuing erosion of the three big networks' audiences and the increased competition from new networks and cable channels. In the early 1970s the three networks routinely pulled down about 90 percent of the prime-time audience. By the late 1990s their share had dropped to less than 60 percent. In addition, a fourth network, the Fox Broadcasting Company, owned by Rupert Murdoch's News Corporation, started broadcasting in 1987. In the early 1990s two other networks started up: the United Paramount Network (UPN) and the Warner Broadcasting Network (the WB). Both began with limited schedules but had plans to expand their offerings. (In 2006, the WB and UPN would merge to form a single network, CW.)

In 1995 the world of network broadcasting was shaken by two megadeals. First, the Walt Disney Company acquired CapCities/ABC for $19 billion. Then, with the ink barely dry on that deal, Westinghouse disclosed that it was buying CBS for $5.4 billion and eventually changed its name to CBS Corporation.

▲ Cable's Continued Growth

Cable reached more than 68 percent of the population by 2000. As cable systems increased their capacity, new cable programming services rushed to fill the new channels. By 2000 there were six national pay-per-view services; six premium services, including HBO and Showtime; and more than 75 cable networks, including the Sci Fi Channel, Animal Planet, and the Outdoor Channel. Many cable systems were providing more than 100 channels of television to their subscribers. Some new cable networks were having trouble because there was no room left on local systems to carry them. The growing popularity of cable channels further eroded the audiences of the traditional TV networks.

Advertising revenue also grew, topping the $11-billion mark in 1999. By the turn of the century, it was obvious that the cable industry was a full-fledged competitor of traditional broadcasting.

Decision Makers Ted Turner

R. E. "Ted" Turner inherited his family's outdoor advertising company in 1963, when he was 24. The Atlanta-based business was in poor economic shape, but the young Turner managed to turn it around. Six years later, Turner learned that a financially troubled UHF television station was for sale. Disregarding the fact that the station's signal was so weak that he could not pick it up on his own TV set, Turner bought the station, renamed it WTCG, and began to advertise it on his unused billboards around Atlanta. With a skillful programming mix of TV reruns and old movies, the station eventually became one of the few UHF stations in the country at the time to turn a profit. Turner, however, was not content with merely turning the station around. He had much bigger plans for it.

One day in 1976, at a meeting of the station's managers, Turner placed a beat-up model of the RCA Satcom I satellite on the table and proclaimed that WTCG would soon be competing with CBS, NBC, and ABC. Turner had decided that he would use the new communication satellites to beam WTCG to cable systems all over the country, making it a national network. Not surprisingly, his managers were incredulous. Almost everybody dismissed Turner's idea as totally impractical.

There were many reasons to think this bold move would not work. First, cable TV had not yet caught on; it was available in only 16 percent of the country, mostly in rural areas. Second, cable systems relied on terrestrial microwave signals; not many were equipped to receive satellite feeds. Third, the FCC had a rule against leapfrogging that prohibited cable systems from importing signals from distant cities unless they also took the signals of stations closer to their market. Additionally, FCC regulations permitted cable systems to use only expensive 10-meter satellite dishes, which most systems could not afford. Undaunted, Turner pitched his idea to big cable operators. They were not impressed.

As fate would have it, however, two weeks later, the FCC dropped its leapfrogging rules and permitted stations to use smaller and cheaper satellite dishes. All of a sudden, Turner's idea did not seem so far-fetched. In December, Turner renamed his station WTBS and started distributing it by satellite, thus creating the first superstation.

WTBS caught on slowly. When it first went on the satellite, the station was received by a grand total of four cable systems. Turner helped its fortunes by purchasing the Atlanta Braves baseball team and making their games available on WTBS. The new superstation continued to grow in popularity, eventually reaching 74 million homes. The success of WTBS inspired the creation of other cable networks and totally changed the cable TV industry. Turner proved that people would subscribe to cable not just to get good reception but also to get programming.

Turner had other ideas. He had encouraged cable systems to carry WTBS by promising them that he would also provide them with additional cable networks. In 1980 he launched the first of those networks—CNN. Cable operators were lukewarm toward the new project. Most refused to provide money to cover start-up costs. Turner invested $21 million in the new venture, which was immediately derided by competitors for its bargain-basement approach to news. Critics labeled CNN the Chicken Noodle Network.

CNN started off losing money, but Turner kept the network alive with the profits from WTBS. Finally, CNN went into the black in 1985. Six years later, during the Gulf War, CNN scooped the other networks by having reporters on the scene in Baghdad when the war broke out. CNN's success spawned several 24-hour news service competitors, including MSNBC and Fox News Channel.

Several other Turner decisions have also paid off. In 1986 he paid more than a billion dollars for the MGM/United Artists film library. Turner used the films to help launch two other cable networks—Turner Network Television and Turner Classic Movies. Turner also bought the Hanna-Barbera animation studio and started the Cartoon Network.

However, some of Turner's ventures did not work out so well. After Time Warner merged with AOL, Turner became a vice chair of the new company. The merger was a disappointment, and AOL Time Warner's stock suffered a huge drop in value. Turner lost millions as a result. In 2003 he resigned his position with the company.

Turner also has an interest in philanthropy. His United Nations Foundation grants money to organizations that are interested in population control and the environment. His Turner Foundation concentrates on improving life in the United States. The decline in AOL Time Warner's stock, unfortunately, has meant a cutback in funding for both organizations.

Turner has made some good decisions and some that have not been successful. Regardless, his decisions have had an enormous impact on television and have been key contributors to the design of the modern TV industry landscape.

▲ New Technologies

A development that had a significant impact on both traditional TV and the cable industry was the spectacular growth of videocassette recorders (VCRs). Fewer than 5 percent of households had VCRs in 1982. By 2000 that figure was 90 percent. In fact, the VCR was adopted faster than any other appliance except television. The effects of the VCR were many.

First, the renting of movies on cassettes became a multibillion-dollar business, with motion picture studios depending on cassettes for a large part of their revenue.

Second, the VCR encouraged **time shifting,** playing back programs at times other than when they aired. Although this increased total audience by allowing people who might not otherwise have viewed a program to do so, it caused some new problems for advertisers since viewers fast-forwarded through commercials.

Finally, the proliferation of the handheld remote-control device has also caused problems for advertisers and programmers. Remote units have encouraged the tendency toward *grazing,* rapidly scanning all the channels during a commercial or dull spot in a program in search of greener pastures.

After a slow start, direct broadcast by satellite (DBS) got a big boost in 1994 when two companies, DirecTV and United States Satellite Broadcasting (USSB), offered subscribers about 150 channels of programming beamed directly to their homes via a small (18-inch diameter) receiver.

On the legal side the biggest development was the Telecommunications Act of 1996 (discussed in Chapter 17), which introduced program ratings and the V-chip while encouraging competition between cable and phone companies and easing ownership restrictions on TV stations.

Contemporary Broadcast Television

As mentioned at the beginning of the chapter, broadcast television is in a state of change. Network and local station audiences continue to shrink, and advertising dollars are finding their way to the Web. The big-four networks—ABC, CBS, NBC, and Fox—have made programming available on the Internet. NBC Universal and Fox launched hulu.com where viewers could watch clips and full-length programs (more on Hulu in Chapter 11). ABC.com offers streaming versions of its hit programs a few hours after they are broadcast. Viewers can watch episodes of CBS shows on its Web site and on TV.com.

Digital Video Recorders (DVRs) such as Tivo have changed the way Americans watch TV. The DVR makes it easy for viewers to record programs and watch them at more convenient times and to fast-forward through commercials, a development that advertisers find troubling. About 30 percent of U.S. households were equipped with DVRs in 2009, and that number is expected to climb in the future.

Also on the technology front, the DVD player has replaced the VCR as the preferred playback medium for home video. As of 2009, nine out of ten households were equipped with a DVD player. And those DVD players are increasingly connected to big-screen TV sets capable of receiving **high-definition television (HDTV),** an innovation that offers far better picture and sound quality than ordinary standard-definition TV. About 35 percent of households had HDTV in 2009, but that number is expected to quickly increase as prices for HD sets continue to fall.

Network audience erosion continued as viewers migrated to cable channels, the Web, and video games. The four major networks' share of the TV viewing audience in 2008 was down to less than 40 percent. Network advertising revenue dropped 3.5 percent from 2007 to 2008 and was basically flat from 2008 to 2009. As revenue dropped, costs increased, resulting in significant profit declines. Local stations' ratings also dropped as did ad revenue.

The drop in ad revenue and the bad economic climate prompted the networks to cut costs. ABC cut its workforce by about 175 and NBC laid off 750. The networks also cut back on program development and looked for ways to trim the production costs of their series. In that connection, all the networks were relying more on lower-cost reality series, such as *American Idol, The Biggest Loser,* and *Dancing with the Stars,* and less on scripted programs. In 2008–2009, the four major networks scheduled nearly 20 hours of nonscripted programs per week.

On a more positive note, even though their audiences are declining, broadcast networks and local stations are still the best means for advertisers to reach a large audience in a hurry. Some hit TV shows, such as *American Idol,* can reach more than 30 million viewers. In addition, online ad revenue has been increasing.

If Hollywood is taking an interest in developing 3-D movies (as noted in Chapter 9), can television be far behind? Not surprisingly, the TV industry is exploring 3-D movies for the smaller screen.

There have already been some experiments. NBC broadcast an episode of the series *Chuck* in 3-D, and a commercial during the 2009 Super Bowl for the 3-D movie *Monsters vs. Aliens* also appeared in 3-D. Thanks to a deal with Sobe Life Water, viewers who wanted to watch the 3-D effect could pick up glasses at participating grocery stores. The National Football League and the National Basketball Association have broadcast games in 3-D to movie theaters.

More and more TV set makers are producing sets capable of displaying 3-D pictures. At a recent consumer electronics show, Panasonic demonstrated a 103-inch, plasma screen 3-D TV that showed high-definition 3-D scenes from the animated movie *Bolt*. Blu-ray players are also capable of producing 3-D images. A 3-D version of *Journey to the Center of the Earth* was released on Blu-ray discs in 2008.

In addition, engineers are fervently working to develop a system where the viewer doesn't have to wear special glasses to get the 3-D effect. The Phillips Company has demonstrated a prototype of an autostereoscopic display that provides nine slightly different views of an image and combines them into a single 3-D screen image, no glasses needed.

Will 3-D TV be the next big craze, or will it simply be a gimmick that is quickly forgotten? Set manufacturers and TV networks hope it will catch on. Set makers need something to spur sales, and the TV networks need something to draw people back to their programs.

Television in the Digital Age

▲ Transition

Broadcast television is now fully digital. As of June 19, 2009, all television stations were broadcasting **digital television (DTV)**. DTV offers many advantages over analog TV. Digital pictures are clearer and sound quality is better. DTV makes possible high-definition television, plus the DTV picture has an aspect ratio more like that of a motion picture screen. Finally, since digital signals can be compressed and take up less space in the electromagnetic spectrum, broadcasters can subdivide the digital channel and offer several different programs in the same space. For example, a station might broadcast a network program on its main channel, a local newscast on a digital subchannel, and weather on another subchannel.

▲ Broadcasters and the Web

Broadcast networks are putting more effort into making their Web sites attractive to visitors. In addition to full episodes of ABC programs, ABC.com runs promotional videos and presents additional background material, such as a time line for *Lost* and games and quizzes based on its popular programs. CBS.com offers an HDTV player, full episodes of CBS programs, previews, and special features, such as how to build the perfect sandwich to accompany your favorite CBS show. Although these efforts increase the viewership of network programs, they may hurt a network affiliate. A local affiliate understands that if people watch net programs on hulu.com or a net Web site, they probably won't be tuning in to a local station.

Speaking of local stations, they were slow to realize the importance of a Web presence. Many stations simply used their Web sites to promote the on-air operation. As a result, local-market newspaper Web sites generated significantly more revenue than TV station sites. In response, local stations have improved their Web sites, adding breaking news stories, more video clips, and social media. Rather than an adjunct to the broadcast station, the Web sites have become stand-alone sites with content and features not available on the over-the-air operation. Forecasts for 2009 predicted that local TV station Web sites would generate $1.3 billion in revenue in 2009, a 26 percent jump over 2008.

▲ Broadcasters and Broadband

A high-speed broadband connection, such as with a cable modem or DSL, makes it possible for networks and local stations to create their own specialized shows that are distributed only through the Web site. Disney-ABC, for example, operates ESPN 360, an online sports channel available to certain Internet Service Providers that streams live

Jericho was a TV series about survivors in a small Kansas town following a nuclear war. It premiered on the CBS network during the 2006–2007 season and, like many new programs, was canceled at season's end. The show, however, had developed a number of passionate fans, and many had started Web sites dedicated to the program.

When *Jericho* was canceled, the fans were angry and started their own campaign, fueled by blogs and fan Web sites, to bring the show back. Drawing upon a scene in the last episode of the season, when one of the characters says "Nuts," repeating the response made famous by General Anthony McAuliffe when he was asked to surrender during

the Battle of the Bulge, fans started sending pounds and pounds of nuts to CBS network headquarters. After receiving more than 20 tons of nuts (that's about 8 million individual peanuts), CBS relented and renewed the program for the 2007–2008 season.

Unfortunately for *Jericho* fans, the ratings continued to fall and CBS canceled the show a second time. As is probably obvious by now, *Jericho* fans don't give up easily. Fan Web sites are trying to drum up support for a *Jericho* full-length movie and a comic book.

(By the way, CBS donated all those nuts to charitable organizations.)

coverage of sporting events. CBS.com has *Heckle U,* a Web series about a slacker who excels at heckling during basketball games. NBC.com features *Nowhere Man,* a Web series companion to the network's *Heroes.*

Broadband series, however, have yet to generate a profit for broadcasters, and the networks do not invest a lot of money in their development. Nonetheless, they do represent a place where the networks (and maybe a few local stations) can experiment with new programming forms and new creative personnel without risking a lot of money. Occasionally a Web series makes it to broadcast TV. *Quarterlife,* for example, started out as a Web series and was picked up by NBC in 2008. The show was canceled after one episode. In the 2009 season, ABC premiered *In the Motherhood,* a series that started on MSN.com.

▲ Mobile TV

There are two kinds of mobile TV. One type consists of video clips, TV shows, and movies that a person downloads from iTunes and other sources. The second type consists of live broadcasts directly to a cell phone or other mobile device. Live broadcasting to mobile devices is the method that is generating the most excitement, and it will be the focus of this section.

Mobile phone users can receive live TV in one of two ways. They can pay a monthly subscription fee and get a lineup of preselected channels from their cell phone provider, or they can receive free broadcasts that are supported by advertising. MobiTV, for example, is available to Sprint and AT&T subscribers for about $10–15 a month and carries programming from NBC, CBS, ESPN, Fox, and many other channels. As of 2008, MobiTV had about 4 million subscribers. News, weather, and live sports broadcasts are among MobiTV's most popular programs. A company called MediaFlo, a subsidiary of Qualcomm Communications, offers a similar service. Subscription services were hurt by the recession at the end of the decade as consumers cut back on spending.

In early 2009, TV stations in 22 cities across the United States announced that they had joined a network that will provide a free television service designed to be received by cell phones and other mobile devices using a technology called Mobile Pedestrian Handheld (MPH). Washington, D.C., was the first city to premiere the MPH service that offered live broadcasts, complete with commercials, from the local NBC, CBS, and Fox stations. The biggest problem with the MPH system is getting phones that can receive the signals into the hands of consumers, since the big cellular companies already sell phones that work with the rival MobiTV and MediaFlo subscription systems. Nonetheless, the Open Mobile Video Coalition, the group that is backing the free mobile service, is confident that they can work out an arrangement.

▲ User-Generated Content

Broadcasters were the first to realize the potential of user-generated content. *America's Funniest Home Videos* premiered in 1989 and, as of this writing, is still on the air. The growth of video on the Internet, however, has opened up new possibilities for the industry, and broadcasters are experimenting with other ways to capitalize on the do-it-yourself video boom. (A lot of broadcast content is used by amateurs to make "mash-ups," whereby video from several sources is edited together to make a new video.) The biggest problem facing broadcasters (as well as cablecasters) with regard to user-generated content is how to relate to video-sharing giant YouTube. All are trying different strategies. CBS has a deal with YouTube to post news, entertainment, and sports videos on the site. On the other hand, Viacom, owner of several cable channels, sued YouTube for $1 billion and removed more than 100,000 clips from the site, claiming copyright violations. Disney, parent of ABC, has also voiced concern about illegal uploading of its content on YouTube. On the other other hand, News Corp., parent of Fox, and NBC Universal have started their own video-sharing site, hulu.com, with content from most of their hit programs. Although the future is always murky, most professionally produced content may wind up on Web sites owned by the copyright holders while the amateur stuff stays with YouTube.

▲ Social Media

When Dr. Lawrence Kuttner unexpectedly committed suicide, mourners could go to his Facebook page and read glowing tributes to Dr. Kuttner from his coworkers and post their own messages about the deceased. Interestingly enough, Dr. Kuttner wasn't a real person and neither were his coworkers. Kuttner was a character on the hit Fox TV series *House,* and his Facebook page was the creation of Fox's promotion department.

Fox's effort is just one example of how the broadcast TV industry has embraced the new social media. Visitors to NBC's *30 Rock* Web site can play interactive games, post questions for the stars to answer, and join the *30 Rock* community. The producers of ABC's *Lost* would occasionally drop hints about the show's future storylines on the program's Web site that would cause intense analysis and speculation by fans on the show's message boards. The title character of NBC's *Chuck* had a MySpace page and used Twitter to communicate with fans of the show. Dunder Mifflin, the fictional paper company of *The Office,* has its own Web site where fans can apply for a position at one of the company's make-believe branches.

Are social media effective marketing tools for the networks? In a week's time the *Office* Web site got about 8 million page views, and the fictional Dunder Mifflin site had more than 40,000 unique visitors.

Local TV stations were slow to adopt social media, but that situation is changing. About two dozen TV stations owned by Hearst-Argyle have a feature on their Web site that lets visitors engage in discussions and share their videos and photos. Many stations offer blogs and message boards. Some local-station TV reporters have started Twitter accounts. In short, look for local TV to capitalize on social media even more in the next few years.

Defining Features of Broadcast Television

Like radio, TV is a universal medium. About 99 percent of the homes in the United States have at least one working TV set. In fact, most homes have more than one. Although not quite as portable as radios, miniature TV sets make it possible to take TV anywhere.

Television has become the dominant medium for news and entertainment for Americans. Surveys have consistently revealed that most people choose television as their main source of news. In addition, in the average American household, the TV set is on for about 8 hours every day. Prime-time television series may draw an audience of 20 million households. In short, TV has become an important part of our society.

Further, TV, especially network television, is an expensive business. It costs the production company more than $3 million to produce one episode of a typical one-hour scripted prime-time series. Most series produce about 20–22 original episodes a year. A little math reveals that the total cost for one season of one prime-time hour for one network is about $60 million. Some more math discloses that the total tab for prime-time programming for the four major networks is more than $2 billion. Added to that is the cost of daytime programs and newscasts. TV advertising is also costly, averaging more than $200,000 for a 30-second spot in network prime time.

Finally, over the past several decades, the broadcast television industry has watched its audience fragment. Back in 1970, the major networks' share of the audience was about 90 percent. Today, the increase in cable networks, DVD usage, video games, and home video has cut that share in half.

Organization of the Broadcast Television Industry

The **commercial television** system consists of all those local stations whose income is derived from selling time on their facilities to advertisers. **Noncommercial television** consists of those stations whose income is derived from sources other than the sale of advertising time.

A local TV station is licensed by the FCC to provide TV service to a particular community. In the industry these communities are customarily referred to as *markets*. There are 210 markets in the United States, ranging from the number-one market, New York City, with about 7.4 million homes, to number 210, Glendive, Montana, with about 4,000 homes. Some of these local TV stations enter into contractual agreements with TV networks. As of 2009, six commercial networks in the United States supplied programs to local stations: the American Broadcasting Company (ABC), the Columbia Broadcasting System (CBS), the National Broadcasting Company (NBC), the Fox Broadcasting Company (FBC), the CW, and My Network TV. The Public Broadcasting Service (PBS) serves as a network for noncommercial stations. A local station that signs a contract with one of the networks is an affiliate. ABC, CBS, and NBC have about 200 affiliates scattered across the country; Fox has slightly fewer; and the CW and My Network TV have still fewer. Local stations that do not have network affiliation are independents.

Much like the film industry, the TV industry is divided into three segments: (1) production, (2) distribution, and (3) exhibition. The production element is responsible for providing the programming that is ultimately viewed by the TV audience. The distribution function is handled by the TV networks and cable and syndication companies. The exhibition of television programs—the element in the system that most people are most familiar with—is the responsibility of local TV stations.

▲ Production

Pretend for a moment that you are the manager of a local TV station in your hometown. Your station must provide 24 hours of programming every day, or approximately 8,800 hours of programming each year. Where does one get all this programming? There are three basic sources: (1) local production, (2) syndicated programming, and (3) for some stations, network programs.

Local production consists of those programs that are produced in the local station's own studio or on location with the use of the station's equipment. The most common local productions are the station's daily newscasts, typically broadcast at noon, in the early evening, and in the late evening. These newscasts attract large audiences, which in turn attract advertisers. As a result the local news accounts for a major proportion of the ad revenue that is generated by a local station. Not surprisingly, local stations devote a major share of their production budgets to their news shows. Other locally produced programming might consist of local sporting events, early-morning interview programs, and public affairs discussion shows. It would be difficult, however, for a local station to fill its entire schedule with locally produced programming. As a result most stations turn to programming produced by other sources.

If the station is affiliated with a network (and most stations are), much of its programming problem is solved. Networks typically supply about 65–70 percent of the programming carried by their affiliates. Many of the programs supplied by the networks are produced by the networks themselves. News, sports, early-morning talk

A local TV news program. News is the most common form of production at a local station and also produces the most revenue.

shows, and an increasing number of prime-time dramas and sitcoms are network productions. Independent production companies or the TV divisions of major motion picture studios supply other programs. Table 10-1 lists some programs and their production companies.

Many independent production companies sell their shows to syndication firms. For instance, King World Productions handles *Wheel of Fortune, Jeopardy, The Oprah Winfrey Show,* and *Inside Edition.* Programs that have already played on the networks (called *off-net series*) are also distributed by syndication companies. These programs usually air during the late afternoon or early evening, not in prime time. In addition, packages of movies, made up from some of the 30,000 films that have been released for TV, can be leased from syndication companies.

▲ Distribution

The three main elements in the distribution segment of television are the broadcast networks, cable and satellite networks, and syndication companies. The network distributes programs to its affiliates by transmitting them via satellite. The station then transmits them to its viewers as they are received, or it records them and airs them at a later time. The affiliation contract between a local station and the network is a complicated document that specifies the terms by which the station agrees to carry the network's programs.

TABLE 10-1	**Production Company**	**Programs**
Examples of Production Companies and Their Programs for the 2008–2009 Season	Networks	
	ABC	*20/20, Grey's Anatomy*
	CBS	*60 Minutes, 48 Hours Mystery*
	NBC	*The Office*
	Fox	*Cops*
	Independents	
	Mark Burnett Prods.	*Survivor, Celebrity Apprentice*
	Endemol	*Deal or No Deal, Extreme Makeover, Home Edition*
	TV Divisions of Film Companies	
	Warner Bros.	*Two and a Half Men, Chuck*
	20th Century Fox	*My Name Is Earl, 24*

For many years, the networks compensated the stations for turning over their airtime so that the networks could air network commercials, but that model is now changing. As network revenue declined and the networks found that they could effectively distribute their programs via the Web, the networks asked for "reverse compensation," charging the local stations a fee to carry net programs. As of 2009, Fox, the CW, and NBC have adopted this system and it's likely the other networks will follow suit. This is not a positive development for local stations since it increases their costs when many are struggling to stay profitable.

Syndication companies provide another kind of program distribution. These organizations lease taped or filmed programs to local television stations in each local market. Sometimes, as mentioned, the syndication company also produces the program, but more often it distributes programs produced by other firms. Local stations that purchase a syndicated program receive exclusive rights to show that program in their market (a situation complicated by cable TV systems that bring in distant stations). Usually, a station buys a package of programs—perhaps as many as 120 episodes or more—and the contract specifies how many times each program can be repeated.

Syndication companies try to sell their shows in as many TV markets as possible. The greater the coverage of the show, the more appealing it is to national advertisers. Top-rated syndicated shows, such as *Wheel of Fortune* and *Jeopardy,* are seen in nearly all TV markets.

Syndication functions as an important aftermarket for prime-time TV shows. In fact, some prime-time series are produced at a deficit, sometimes $200,000 or more for each one-hour episode. Production companies gamble that they can make back this money in the syndication market. It is a risk, but if a show hits it big in syndication, it might earn half a billion dollars or more. To be attractive in the syndication market, however, a prime-time show must have enough back episodes stockpiled so that stations can run episodes for a long time without showing repeats. Since 100 seems to be the magic number, series usually have a big party to commemorate the production of their hundredth episode. Since only 22 or 24 new shows are produced each season, it is obvious that those series that last four or five years are the best bets for syndication success.

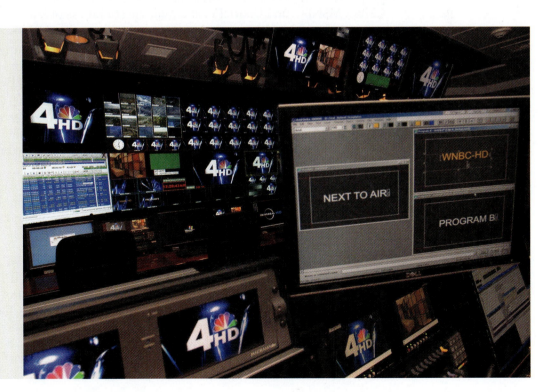

Inside a TV control room: The director scans the bank of monitors before deciding what to put on the air.

▲ Exhibition

In June 2009 all U.S. broadcast stations switched from analog to digital transmission. Before the transition, analog stations were divided into two types: **VHF** stations, broadcasting on channels 2–13, and **UHF** stations, broadcasting on channels 14–69. The digital transition, however, has scrambled things a bit because all of the existing VHF and UHF stations were assigned new digital channel numbers, and some old VHF stations got UHF channels and vice versa. Luckily, the new digital arrangement includes a feature that changes the new digital channel back into the old channel number that everybody is used to. So viewers in Madison, Wisconsin, used to watching analog Channel 3, the CBS affiliate, still see their station identified as Channel 3 even though the new digital channel is actually Channel 50.

As suggested earlier, another important difference among stations concerns their affiliation with national networks. As of 2009, more than 90 percent of all commercial stations were affiliated with CBS, NBC, ABC, or Fox. Of the remaining 10 percent, many are affiliates of the CW or My Network TV.

Those stations not affiliated with networks are called **independents.** For many years independents were hampered because most were UHF stations and had less coverage area than VHFs. The emergence of cable, however, gave UHF independents more of a competitive advantage, since unlike the situation with over-the-air signals, with cable both UHF and VHF stations have the same audience reach. Recently, most independent stations signed on with either the CW or My Network TV. "Pure" independents are now hard to find.

Ownership in the Television Industry

As of 2009, all the major networks were under the control of large conglomerates:

- NBC Universal is owned by General Electric. In addition to its holdings in non-media areas, such as aerospace, aircraft engines, consumer products, and financial properties, GE has interests in TV stations; cable/satellite networks, including CNBC, MSNBC, and Court TV; and a movie studio. As of late 2009, there were reports that cable giant Comcast was interested in acquiring NBC.

- ABC is owned by the Walt Disney Company, which also owns theme parks, a cruise line, retail stores, and media holdings that include magazines, film production companies, radio networks, record companies, cable networks, and TV stations.

- Fox is controlled by Rupert Murdoch's News Corporation, which owns a major film and TV production company, more than 20 TV stations, cable networks, satellite networks, a record company, newspapers, magazines, and a book publishing company.

- CBS is part of CBS Corporation, a company that was spun off from media conglomerate Viacom in 2005. In addition to the network, the CBS Corporation includes the CBS-owned TV and radio stations, a TV production company, and book publisher Simon & Schuster.

The two newest networks, the CW and My Network TV, are also part of large organizations. The CW is a joint venture between the CBS Corporation and media giant Time Warner. My Network TV is owned by the News Corporation, parent of Fox.

At the station level the Telecommunications Act of 1996 (see Chapter 17) allowed a person or organization to own an unlimited number of TV stations as long as the combined reach of the stations did not exceed 35 percent of the U.S. population (later amended to 39 percent). By the end of 2008, big groups controlled most of the TV stations in the top 100 markets. Table 10-2 lists the top five group owners.

TABLE 10-2

Top Five Owners of TV
Stations, 2009

Group	Percentage of U.S. Households Reached (as calculated by the FCC)
CBS Corp.	35.5
Ion Media Networks (Paxson)	32.4
Fox TV Stations	31.2
NBC Universal	30.3
Tribune	27.5

Producing Television Programs

▲ Departments and Staff

There are many different staffing arrangements in television stations. Some big-city stations employ 300–400 people and may be divided into a dozen different departments. Small-town stations may have 20–30 employees and only a few departments.

In one common arrangement, a station manager is ultimately responsible for all station activities. The rest of the station is organized into five departments:

1. *Sales:* Is responsible for selling time to local and national advertisers, scheduling ads, and billing clients.
2. *Engineering:* Maintains technical equipment.
3. *Production/Programming:* Puts together locally produced programming; also acquires programming from outside sources and is responsible for scheduling.
4. *News:* Is in charge of producing the station's regularly scheduled news programs.
5. *Administration:* Consists of clerical, accounting, and personnel segments that help in the day-to-day running of the station.

At the network level the divisions are somewhat more complicated. Although the major networks differ in their setups, all seem to have departments that perform the following functions:

1. *Sales:* Handles the sale of network commercials and works with advertising agencies.
2. *Entertainment:* Works with producers to develop new programs for the network.
3. *Owned and operated stations:* Administers those stations owned by the networks.
4. *Affiliate relations:* Supervises all contracts with stations affiliated with the network (and generally tries to keep the affiliates happy).
5. *News:* Is responsible for all network news and public affairs programs.
6. *Sports:* Is responsible for all sports programming.
7. *Standards:* Checks all network programs to make sure they do not violate the law or the network's own guidelines for appropriate content.
8. *Operations:* Handles the technical aspects of actually sending programs to affiliates.

▲ Getting TV Programs on the Air

At the local level the biggest effort at a TV station goes into the newscast. Almost every station has a studio that contains a set for one or two anchorpeople, a weather forecaster, and a sportscaster. The station's news director assigns stories to reporters and camera crews, who travel to the scene of a story and videotape a report. Back at the station, the newscast producer and news director are planning what stories to air and allotting time to each. In the meantime the camera crews and reporters return; the reporters write copy and editors prepare videotape segments. When the final script is finished (this may be only a few minutes before airtime), it is given to a director, who is responsible for pulling everything together and putting the newscast on the air.

Ethical Issues   *American Idol* and Responsibility

Fox's *American Idol* has been a huge hit. In its eighth season in 2009, the show regularly tops the Nielsen ratings. Fans are familiar with the show's format. Four judges (a new judge was added for 2009) critique amateurs who think they can sing. The opening weeks feature auditions where the judges roundly disparage several performers who obviously have an overrated opinion of their talent.

During 2006 one of the performers who didn't make it was Paula Goodspeed. Her performance of "Proud Mary" was soundly criticized by judges Paula Abdul and Randy Jackson. Judge Simon Cowell went further, noting that Paula was singing with braces on her teeth and wondered aloud how she could sing with "that much metal" in her mouth. Cowell was chastised by many fans for being too harsh.

In late 2008, Ms. Goodspeed committed suicide by over-dosing on drugs in front of Paula Abdul's house. Speculation immediately arose over the role her *Idol* experience played in her suicide. Did her rejection start her on the road to suicide?

The program was criticized for using the early rounds as a showcase for frivolous performers who were merely looking for attention and for generating entertainment value from putting down people in front of a national audience. From an ethical standpoint, the key question involved responsibility. As in medicine, the first rule of a show that thrusts amateurs,

even willing amateurs, into the national spotlight should be "Do no harm." Did the show have an obligation to make sure that all who appeared on the show were not psychologically harmed by the experience?

In Ms. Goodspeed's case, her problems began long before her *Idol* appearance. She was apparently obsessed with Paula Abdul and had been stalking her for perhaps as long as six years, and she had a history of other psychiatric problems. Did the insensitive comments during her audition send her over the edge? She seemed to react rationally to her rejection. Comments on her MySpace page indicated that she knew she wasn't emotionally ready to try out in a national competition.

Does *American Idol* have an obligation to research the mental history of all its contestants? Such a task would seem unreasonable. Even trained psychologists have trouble identifying someone who might be suicidal. Contestants are required to sign a release form that allows the show to release private information about them that may expose them to embarrassment or ridicule. The release seems fair warning to contestants that their experience might not be pleasant.

In any event, for the 2008 season, the early audition rounds that featured the somewhat bizarre performers were shortened and Simon's comments seemed a bit softer.

In addition to the news, the local station might produce one or two interview programs. Some stations also produce a "magazine" program consisting of segments videotaped on location and later edited into final form. Aside from these kinds of shows, most local stations do little other production.

Because they are responsible for filling the hours when the biggest audience is watching (called *prime time,* 8–11 P.M., Eastern Standard Time), the networks must pay special attention to cultivating new shows. For the moment we will concentrate on how a prime-time series is produced.

Everything starts with an idea. Network executives receive hundreds of ideas every year; some come from independent producers, some from TV departments of motion picture companies, some from network employees, and a good many from amateurs hoping for a break. From this mass of ideas, the networks select perhaps 50–75, usually submitted by established producers or companies, for further attention. After examining plot outlines and background sketches of the leading characters for these 50–75 potential series, the networks trim the list once again. For those ideas that survive, the networks request a sample script and a list of possible stories that could be turned into scripts. If the idea still looks promising, the network and producer enter into a contract for a **pilot,** the first episode of a series. In a typical year perhaps 25 pilots are ordered by each network. If the pilot show gains a respectable audience, the network may order five or six episodes produced and may place the program on its fall schedule. From the hundreds of ideas that are sent to the network, only a few ever make it to prime time.

The process does not stop with the fall season. If a program does well in the ratings, the network will order enough episodes for the rest of the season. If the show does not do well, it will be canceled and replaced with another show. Meanwhile, network executives are sifting through the hundreds of program ideas for the next season, and the cycle begins once again.

The Economics of Broadcast Television

The television industry has been profitable since 1950, and its total income has increased every year since 1971. In 2008, according to the Television Bureau of Advertising, television advertising revenue amounted to about $46 billion. The changing structure of the television industry, however, has had a significant economic impact on both local stations and the networks. We will explore more about this after we look at the traditional sources of television advertising revenue.

▲ Commercial Time

Where did the $46 billion in revenue come from? It came from the sale of commercial time by networks, local stations, and cable systems to advertisers. A station, network, or cable system makes available a specified number of minutes per hour that will be offered for sale to advertisers. There are three different types of advertisers who buy time on TV: (1) national advertisers, (2) national spot advertisers, and (3) local advertisers.

National advertisers are those that sell general-consumption items: soda pop, automobiles, deodorant, hair spray, and so on. These advertisers try to reach the biggest possible audience for their messages and usually purchase commercial time on broadcast network programs or cable networks.

In contrast, other advertisers have products that are used mainly in one region or locale. For example, a manufacturer of snowmobiles would gain little by having his or her ad seen in Miami or New Orleans. Likewise, a manufacturer of farm equipment would probably not find many customers in New York City. These companies turn to national spot buying. The snowmobile manufacturer would buy spots in several northern markets, such as Minneapolis, Minnesota; Fargo, North Dakota; and Butte, Montana. The farm equipment company would place ads in primarily rural markets.

Finally, many local businesses buy advertising time from TV stations. They purchase time on one or more TV stations located in a single market. Network spots (national advertising) account for 36 percent of the total amount of advertising dollars, and the remainder is divided about equally between national spot and local advertising.

Revenues depend upon the amount of money a station charges for its commercial time. The larger the audience, the more money a station can charge. The prices for 30- and 60-second commercials are listed on the station's rate card. The cost of an ad will vary tremendously from station to station. A 30-second ad might cost only $100–200 in a small market, but the same ad would cost thousands in a major market. The same general pricing principles apply at the network level. Shows with high ratings have higher advertising charges than shows with low ratings. For example, in 2008, the average network 30-second spot in prime time cost about $200,000. On top-rated shows, spots were going for about $300,000; on lower-rated shows, the cost was about $100,000. To gain some perspective on how expensive it can get, consider that for the 2008 Super Bowl, a 30-second spot was going for about $3 million.

Some television shows are finding novel ways to generate income. Product

A 30-second spot on *Grey's Anatomy* during the 2008–2009 season cost about $250,000.

Kweisi Mfume, president of the NAACP, speaking at his organization's national convention, criticized the four major TV networks for the lack of diversity in the new shows planned for the 1999–2000 season. He noted that none of the 26 series had a minority person in a leading or starring role. Mfume's criticism marked another chapter in the continuing controversy over the portrayals of minorities in prime time.

During the early years of TV, African American performers were difficult to find. And when they did appear, it was usually in a menial or subservient role. In 1965, however, a young Bill Cosby costarred with Robert Culp in *I Spy* and paved the way for more substantial roles for African American performers. By the 1970s several shows that featured black casts appeared in prime time—most were situation comedies, such as *The Jeffersons*. The number of African American performers increased slowly but steadily during the 1980s. For most of the 1990s, the proportion of black characters seen in prime-time TV was about the same as the percentage of African Americans in the general population. This increase, however, was due in part to the emergence of UPN and WB, two networks that targeted several of their series to African American viewers.

The apparent lack of diversity in the 1999–2000 season was especially troubling to Mfume. The NAACP noted that minorities were hard to find behind the camera as well. Of all the writers who worked on TV sitcoms and dramas, only 6 percent were black. FCC data show that minorities own about 2.8 percent of all broadcast stations.

Mfume threatened a boycott of the networks and their sponsors unless something was done. The networks responded by adding some minority characters to the casts of existing shows. CBS aired *City of Angels,* a drama set in an inner-city hospital, that featured a predominantly black cast and creative team. The networks also planned to increase minority hiring and to appoint executives in charge of their diversity efforts. These moves apparently satisfied Mfume, who called off plans for the boycott.

The 2000–2001 TV season did not spark similar protests. In addition to *City of Angels,* there were several new series with African Americans in major roles, such as *Boston Public*. The situation behind the camera and in minority ownership, however, was unchanged. Things improved a bit in the 2002 season when there were 43 series featuring multiethnic characters. Back in 1995, there were only 13 such shows on the air.

The diversity issues surfaced again in 2003, but this time the focus was on cable. Members of the Congressional Black Caucus sent a letter to the cable TV industry asking for more minority-themed programs and more minority-owned cable networks. It resurfaced when the NAACP noted that none of the situation comedies scheduled by the major networks for the 2006 season starred an African American actor or actress. A 2008 report compiled by the NAACP showed that the number of minority actors had actually decreased from 2006 to 2007.

Why should the networks present a diverse view of society? Many would argue that the networks have a social obligation to present an accurate view of society so that members of minority groups do not feel marginalized or disenfranchised from society. Others would suggest that TV should present role models for all groups. These high-minded reasons aside, it also makes economic sense for the networks to present a diverse menu of programs. The 2000 census showed that minorities constitute more than 35 percent of the U.S. population, and their buying power is increasing each year. Presenting shows that appeal to these groups is simply good business.

Further, some critics suggest that paying large amounts of attention to the way the broadcast networks portray minorities overlooks the gains minorities have made in cable. For instance, Black Entertainment Television draws a significant audience. Two Spanish-language networks, Galavision and Univision, are aimed at Hispanics.

Finally, consider the opinion of commentator Earl Ofari Hutchinson, who suggests that prime-time TV is not worth fighting for. He charges that the networks have oversaturated the airways with silly sitcoms and action shows designed to appeal to young, affluent whites. These types of programs, he argues, have no relevance for African Americans, who should focus their attention elsewhere. In a similar vein Cynthia Tucker, the African American former editor of the editorial page of the *Atlanta Journal-Constitution,* suggests that the NAACP is misplacing its efforts by concentrating on network TV programs. Instead, she argues, the organization should encourage young African Americans to stop watching TV. "Let prime-time TV keep its bland cast of characters," says Tucker. "There are plenty of good books in which black youngsters can find themselves reflected."[1]

---

[1]Quoted in Richard Breyer, "Color TV," *Word and I,* March 2000, 84.

placement in TV shows, for example, has become a big business with companies sometimes paying millions of dollars to get their product prominently displayed. In the first three months of 2008, there were more than 100,000 instances of product placement on prime-time TV. NBC's *The Biggest Loser* led the way with nearly 4,000 instances, followed by *American Idol*.

▲ Where Did the Money Go?

At the network level, one of the biggest expenses is programming. For example, a typical half-hour sitcom costs about $1.5 million. Hit shows cost much more. An hour-long show might have a price tag approaching $3 million. Quiz and reality shows are much cheaper to produce, and it's not a surprise to find that networks are relying on them more and more.

At the local level, the costs are broken down differently, but the heavy cost of programming is evident there as well. Programming costs account for about 35–40 percent of the local station expense dollar, followed by administrative costs and expenses for news.

Public Broadcasting

▲ A Brief History

Public broadcasting in the United States has been in existence for more than 40 years. Over that time its achievements have been considerable, but its evolution has been hampered by political infighting, a lack of a clear purpose, and, most of all, insufficient funding.

Until 1967 noncommercial TV was known as educational television. In 1967, following the recommendations of the Carnegie Commission, Congress passed the Public Broadcasting Act, which authorized money for the construction of new facilities and established the Corporation for Public Broadcasting (CPB) to oversee noncommercial TV and distribute funds for programs. The government also created the Public Broadcasting Service (PBS), whose duties resemble those of commercial networks. Although this arrangement seemed to work well at first, internal disputes soon surfaced concerning which of these two organizations had final control over programming.

In addition, several cable channels began to offer programs that competed for public TV's audience. Many experts felt that much of the traditional programming on public TV would eventually move to cable or to videocassette. On top of this came further reductions in federal funds for public broadcasting.

Then things started to change. Somewhat surprisingly, cable turned out to be more of a friend than a foe to public TV. Since two-thirds of all public stations are in the UHF band, carriage by local cable systems increased their coverage area and helped public TV double its audience from 1980 to 1984. Public TV wound up as the primary cultural channel in the nation, with 90 million viewers every week.

In the mid-1980s, however, the Reagan administration cut funds for public broadcasting and proposed to freeze future funding at current levels. Congress restored some of the cuts, but in 1987 the system was struggling to get along on about the same amount of money it had in 1982. PBS funding became a major political issue again in the early 1990s. Faced with this financial uncertainty, public TV looked to other sources for funding: corporate underwriting, auctions, viewer donations, and sales of program guides.

Public television's problems continued into the new century. PBS's average prime-time ratings are down 37 percent over the past 10 years. (PBS has about the same level of viewing as the Cartoon Network cable channel.) To make matters worse, PBS's loyal audience is getting older (the average viewer is in his or her mid-50s), and younger viewers are not flocking to public TV. Any attempt to attract younger viewers risks alienating public TV's core audience of mature Americans.

Money is still a problem as well. Public stations have moved to digital transmission, a conversion that cost millions. Dwindling revenues have meant layoffs at local stations and at the network level. Congressional funding continues to be tight. The 2008 budget for the Corporation for Public Broadcasting totaled $410 million. That is about what ESPN collects every two months in subscriber fees. In short, public TV faces significant challenges if it is to remain a viable alternative for television viewers.

▲ Programming and Financing

In 1990 PBS presented an 11-hour documentary titled *The Civil War*, which became the highest-rated program in the history of PBS. Although it might be a bit of an exaggeration, much of the history of PBS programming can be described as a civil war between the local public stations and the centralized PBS organization. Each side has scored significant

The debate about PBS has been going on since the growth of cable television in the 1980s and 1990s. Many of the new channels featured content that was previously the province of PBS. The History Channel, the Discovery Channel, Animal Planet, Nickelodeon, the Hallmark Channel, and others fragmented the audience for PBS programs. PBS ratings have been declining (along with the ratings of many other networks) for the past decade. From 2000 to 2009, PBS's ratings have dropped 37 percent.

What should be the role of PBS in a 500-channel television universe? A mission statement adopted by PBS stations in 2004 says in part that "public television is more essential than ever in the cluttered media landscape." It goes on to point out that in an age of conglomerate media ownership, PBS stations may be the only locally owned stations in the community and are better suited to responding to local needs. The document goes on to state:

> Public television . . . strives for impact and measures its success by the extent of its ability to educate and inform, to enlighten and entertain. In short, public television strives to:

- ■ Challenge the American mind.
- ■ Inspire the American spirit.
- ■ Preserve the American memory.
- ■ Enhance the American dialogue.
- ■ Promote global understanding.

Those are lofty goals. Does the programming on PBS stations fulfill them? Critics suggest that PBS programs have grown musty with age. *Nova, Masterpiece,* and *NewsHour* have all been on the air for 30 to 40 years. The American version of *Antiques Roadshow* has been around for more than a decade. (The U.S. program was based on a British series that premiered in 1979.) Typical prime-time programming includes reruns of old British sitcoms such as *Keeping Up Appearances* and *Are You Being Served?* Critics also suggest looking at the schedule of the local PBS affiliate. How much local programming is aired during the typical week?

The programmers at PBS, however, face a dilemma. If their shows venture too far away from mainstream, such as programs that examine gay and lesbian lifestyles or global warming, PBS is criticized as being too liberal. If their shows stick with the familiar, they are branded as obsolete or redundant with those of the commercial networks.

A second issue concerns the drift of public television toward its commercial counterparts. That 2004 mission statement proclaims the goal of commercial television is to attract as many viewers as possible and expose them to advertising but suggests that PBS is different. In the past decade, however, PBS has opened up its programs to an expanded program of underwriting, whereby a sponsor donates money to a station or PBS in return for a 30-second message at the beginning of the program. Many of these messages look exactly like ads playing on commercial TV. In addition, underwriters would rather reach a large audience than a small one. This means that public TV, if it wants to continue to attract underwriting revenue, will try to air programs that attract a large audience, much like commercial TV.

The transition to digital will make the questions about the role of PBS even more complicated. Does PBS really need a Facebook fan page or a YouTube channel? Check out the PBS Twitter feed. Does it fulfill the goals of the mission statement? This is a debate not likely to end soon.

victories in this fray over the years, but most recently, the tide has turned in favor of the centralized authority. Let us quickly review how the system used to work and how it has changed.

Prior to 1990 PBS used a mechanism called the Station Program Cooperative (SPC) to determine which programs were carried by its member stations. The SPC system represented a decentralized decision-making process. Member stations were given a ballot that contained the descriptions of possible programs, and they voted for those they wished to broadcast. After several rounds the initial list was pared down and stations voted again, but this time each station had to promise that it would help pay for the programs it voted for.

This system encouraged the broadcast of programs that already had some funding or series that could be acquired cheaply. Innovative or daring series that were expensive and had no prior funding commitments were seldom produced. The system also leaned heavily on a few big public TV stations that did the bulk of the production work. Finally, PBS had no cohesive national scheduling system.

In 1990, faced with declining funds and viewers, PBS suspended the SPC and moved toward more centralized programming. An executive vice president for national programming was appointed with the power to develop and schedule new programs. By any measure the first PBS season under the new centralized system was a success, exemplified by the fact that the *Civil War* series was watched by millions.

Educational programs, such as *Nova*, make up a significant part of the PBS schedule.

Successive seasons, however, were not as successful. For the entire decade of the 1990s, despite being one of the most established TV networks, PBS got an average prime-time rating of 2.0 (of all the TV homes in America, about 2 percent watched PBS in prime time). PBS's average rating dropped even further during the new decade. In addition, PBS occasionally lands in political hot water. In the late 1990s, Congress grilled PBS executives when it was learned that PBS stations, which are supposed to be politically neutral, were providing Democratic and Republican groups with their donor lists. Political parties could then use these lists to solicit donations. In 2005 a congressional subcommittee chastised PBS for producing a children's program in which a cartoon rabbit visited real-life children whose parents were lesbians.

PBS programs have earned numerous awards and substantial praise from critics. *Sesame Street* revolutionized children's TV by presenting educational content in an entertaining format. *Nova* and *Cosmos* introduced millions to the wonders of science. However, PBS programs have also come in for their share of criticism. Many critics have charged that PBS displays a liberal bias, and they have complained about the size of the salaries PBS pays to some of its performers.

Like commercial stations, public TV stations receive licenses from the FCC. As of 2009, there were 356 PBS stations operated by 168 licensees. About half of these licensees are community organizations, another one-third are colleges and universities, about 12 percent are state-operated networks, and the remainder belong to local educational or municipal authorities.

In 2009, more than a third of the homes in America watched public TV at least once a week. Viewing times, however, are far lower than those for commercial TV. Average household daily viewing time for public TV is about 25 minutes, compared with more than 4 hours for commercial TV.

Unlike commercial TV, public television is funded by a number of sources. About one-third of the support for public television comes from federal, state, and local governments; about one-fourth comes from member contributions; another 15 percent comes from corporations; and the rest comes from foundation grants, auctions, and other miscellaneous sources.

Public broadcasting is inching slowly into the digital age. Previews of upcoming programs are streamed from the PBS site, which also contains blogs and message boards. PBS also makes portions of its popular *NewsHour* available on iTunes, and the network is considering a video-on-demand service. One of the problems that PBS will have to solve is that much of its programming is long-form, an hour in length, a format that doesn't easily download to laptops and cell phones.

Home Video

The home video industry came into existence because of the tremendous growth of VCR sales. By 2005 about 92 percent of homes in the United States were equipped with the device. Recently, the VCR was replaced by DVD (digital videodisc) players. DVD offers

Personal video recorders, such as TiVo, will change the future of TV viewing.

better pictures and sound than videotape; can contain additional video material, such as outtakes and interviews with a director; and can feature multiple-language soundtracks. DVD sales have skyrocketed; it is estimated that there are now more than 85 million in U.S. homes.

DVD players are used to play back prerecorded discs that can be purchased or rented from video stores such as Blockbuster. There are more than 40,000 prerecorded titles on the market, and many more are introduced each month.

A new entry in the home video market is the **digital video recorder (DVR),** such as TiVo, which allows viewers to record television programs on a hard drive. Sales of DVRs were slow in the early years of the new century but picked up in recent years.

Like most other businesses, home video can be divided into three segments: production, distribution, and retail. The production side of the industry consists of those companies that produce prerecorded discs. Since much of the home video market consists of movies, many of the large motion picture studios also dominate the DVD business.

These companies sell to distributors, who form the bridge between production and retail. Currently, some 90 distributors in the United States handle DVDs. Major companies include Disney, Fox, Columbia, and Paramount. Moreover, the DVD distribution business now resembles record distribution as a new breed of rack jobber is making it easy for many retail and department stores to get into the video-renting business.

The DVD has opened up a new aftermarket for television. Boxed sets of an entire season of such contemporary series as *Sex in the City, The Simpsons,* and *24* have generated increased revenue for production companies. Moreover, classic TV series also do well. *I Love Lucy—The First Year* and *The Dick Van Dyke Show—Season One* were best sellers. Even shows that didn't do all that well when they first aired, such as *Sports Night* and *The Family Guy,* have found new life on DVDs.

Sales and rentals are big business. Consumers spent about $22.5 billion on DVDs in 2008. Retailers are concerned about the competition posed by video-on-demand and the growing number of premium movies available through direct-broadcast satellites.

Feedback for Broadcast Television

▲ Measuring TV Viewing

Let us examine how the ratings for both network programs and local stations are determined.

Network Ratings   Nielsen Media Research, serving the United States and Canada, provides the networks with audience data through its Nielsen Television Index (NTI). To compile these ratings, Nielsen uses a device called a *People Meter,* introduced in the late 1980s. The People Meter consists of an apparatus about the size of a clock radio that sits on top of a TV set and a handheld device that resembles a TV remote-control unit. Demographic data are gathered from each household member, and then each is assigned a number. While watching TV, each family member is supposed to periodically punch in his or her number on the handheld device to indicate viewing. People Meters can be used to tabulate all viewing—network, syndicated shows, and cable—and can even tabulate DVD or DVR playbacks. There are more than 12,000 households in the Nielsen People Meter sample (the sample size will increase to 37,000 by 2011), and usable data are obtained from more than 90 percent of the meters. The sample is replaced every two years. The People Meter service is not cheap. Networks pay millions of dollars annually for the service.

Nielsen is also testing other systems. The **Portable People Meter (PPM)** is a device about the size of a pager that detects inaudible signals that are encoded into radio and television programs. It requires little effort on the part of the respondent (a person simply clips the PPM to an article of clothing), and there are no buttons to push. The PPM can measure viewing or listening both in and out of the home. Preliminary tests of the device are being carried out in several U.S. cities.

Local-Market TV Ratings   Nielsen surveys more than 200 markets in the United States at least four times a year, using a combination of diary and electronic meter techniques. A computer selects phone numbers at random from all telephone directories in the area. The households selected into the sample are asked to keep a diary record of their television viewing.

Households that agree to participate receive one diary for every working TV in the household. The diary provides a space for entering the viewing of the head of the household as well as that of other family members or visitors. Participants are asked to record their viewing every quarter-hour. In addition, the respondents are asked to record the sex and age of all those who are watching. At the back of the diary are questions concerning how big the family is, where the household is located, and whether the family subscribes to cable. Diaries are kept for seven days and then returned to the ratings company. Nielsen reports that it is able to use approximately 40–50 percent of all the diaries it sends out.

Nielsen uses two kinds of electronic devices to measure local TV viewing. Set meters record any time a sample household TV is turned on and what channel is being viewed. The meters also record DVR usage. Meter data are supplemented by information from diaries.

In the 50 largest markets, Nielsen has introduced the Local People Meter, the same device used with its national sample, but in the local-market situation the sample is drawn only from the local viewing area.

Nielsen's long-term plans call for the phasing out of paper diaries. The company will use Local People Meters in the top 25 markets while the remaining markets will use electronic meters or Internet diaries. Nielsen's ultimate goal is to measure media usage on all media platforms: MP3 players, cell phones, and Internet video.

In addition to measuring the audience for TV programs, Nielsen now reports viewership of commercial minutes that interrupt the programs. Starting in 2007, Nielsen calculated the **C3 rating,** defined as the rating of the average commercial minute including live viewing and DVR playback within three days. Note that this is an average rating for commercial minutes; it is not a rating for each commercial in the program. Advertisers now buy time based on these C3 numbers.

Finally, Nielsen's monopoly on TV ratings may end. In mid-2009, the Arbitron company announced plans to use its Portable People Meter, currently used to measure radio listening, to also measure TV viewing. In addition, NBC, CBS, and several other media companies formed the Coalition for Innovative Audience Measurement in 2009 in an attempt to find the most effective way to measure traditional TV viewing and online and mobile phone viewing.

▲ Ratings Reporting

Television viewing data are reported essentially the same way as for radio. The following formula is used to calculate the **rating** for a TV program in a local market:

$$\text{Rating} = \frac{\text{Number of households watching a program}}{\text{Number of TV HH}}$$

where "TV HH" equals the number of households in a given market equipped with television.

Similarly, the **share of the audience** is found by using the following formula:

$$\text{Share of audience} = \frac{\text{Number of households watching a program}}{\text{Number of HUT}}$$

where "HUT" equals the number of households using (watching) television at a particular time.

Four times every year (February, May, July, and November), Nielsen conducts a "sweep" period during which every local television market in the entire country is measured. Local stations rely on these ratings to set their advertising rates. As Nielsen moves away from diaries to local-market People Meters, demographic audience data will be available year-round, thus making the traditional sweep periods less meaningful.

Determining the Accuracy of Ratings   Because the numbers in the rating books are the basis for spending vast amounts of money, it is important that they be as accurate and reliable as possible. During the early 1960s, in the wake of quiz show and payola scandals, Congress took a close look at the broadcasting industry. In response to one congressional committee's criticism of audience measurement techniques, advertising and broadcasting leaders founded the Electronic Media Ratings Council, subsequently renamed the Media Ratings Council (MRC). The task of the MRC is threefold: It monitors, audits, and accredits broadcast measurement services. The council monitors performance of ratings companies by making sure that reported results meet the minimum standards of performance set by the MRC. Audits are performed on a continuing basis. If the ratings company passes the audit, it is accredited and is allowed to display the MRC's seal of approval on its ratings reports.

Despite the MRC's work, broadcast ratings are still subject to widespread criticism. One common complaint, voiced by many who evidently do not understand the statistical theory that underlies sampling, is directed at Nielsen's national survey. How can a sample of only 12,000 homes, these critics ask, accurately reflect the viewing of more than 100 million television households? In actuality, this sample size will generate tolerably accurate results within a specified margin of error. Other criticisms, however, deserve closer attention.

First, it is possible that the type of person who agrees to participate may have viewing habits different from those of the viewer who declines to participate. Second, in

Critical / Cultural Issues

The Bachelor

One of the interesting things about the critical/cultural approach is the range of items that can serve as texts for analysis. From popular mail-order catalogues to mass-marketed toys, critical/cultural scholars have mined all sources for insights on our society. Popular TV shows have also come under scrutiny. For example, a doctoral dissertation by Dr. Amanda Hall about ABC's *The Bachelor* illustrates how audiences use this program to construct meaning.

Hall looked at both the program and its audience. She performed a textual analysis of the program. She interviewed viewers about their impressions of the program and what it meant to them, and she observed groups of viewers as they watched the programs.

What did she discover about the program? She argued that *The Bachelor* is a modern fairy tale. The man is Prince Charming. The competition itself, with the lavish trimmings and carefree lifestyle, is the Big Ball. All of the women are vying to be Cinderella. Moreover, like many fairy tales, there is an element of melodrama (a melodrama has a simplified plot, stereotypical characters, exaggerated emotion, and a happy ending) in *The Bachelor*.

The audience apparently recognized and embraced both the fairy tale and melodramatic dimensions of the program. Hall's research revealed that viewers vicariously helped Prince Charming by participating in discussions with other viewers about whom the bachelor should choose.

She also found evidence of patriarchy in the program. The man was active and dominant and had a voice. The women were passive and subservient and were given a voice only when they were talking about the bachelor and their chances to be the chosen one. Further, the whole program was told from the masculine point of view. The

words of the bachelor gave direction and a story line to the program.

The patriarchy was evident on other levels as well. The bachelor was controlled and rational. The women were portrayed as emotional and frequently teary. The competition among them became fierce and resulted in catfights and "bitchy" behavior. As Hall concluded, the program "sends a strong patriarchal message about heterosexual relationships—a woman's place is to serve in a subordinate (and emotional) position to her husband."

Finally, the theme of domestication was vividly present. The ideal wife, the choice of Prince Charming, had to be a mate and potential mother who knew how to behave. Women who did not fit this characterization were often removed early in the competition. Women who understood this requirement and acted accordingly generally lasted longer.

Young women who viewed *The Bachelor* used the program as an aid in understanding themselves and their own relationships. Messages from the program serve to illustrate socially prescribed expectations of gender roles. Viewers enjoyed the show even while recognizing the patriarchal elements. Indeed, many seemed to reject the dominant theme of the program and instead chose to focus on ways that they could reject the patriarchal interpretations and substitute more liberating ones of their own.

In sum, Hall's research underscored a key point in the critical/cultural approach. As she concluded, "A central argument for this study is that text and audience are both powerful—one does not overpower the other. As such, it is necessary to study both in order to effectively engage with issues of consumption and representation."

the case of the Nielsen reports (based on about 55 percent of the diaries sent out), it is possible that "returners" behave differently from "nonreturners." Third, people who know that their viewing is being measured may change their behavior. Fourth, ratings companies admit that they have a problem measuring the viewing of certain groups. For example, minorities—particularly blacks and Hispanics—may be underrepresented in the ratings companies' samples. Finally, the stations that are being measured can distort the measurement process by engaging in contests and special promotions or by running unusual or sensational programs in an attempt to "hype" the ratings. The distinction between hype and legitimate programming, however, is somewhat fuzzy. Clearly, the ratings are not perfect. Nonetheless, despite all their flaws, they present useful information at an affordable price to advertisers and to the television industry. As long as the United States has a commercial broadcasting system, some form of the ratings will be around.

▲ Television Audiences

The TV set has become firmly entrenched in the life of Americans. As of 2009, some 99 percent of all homes in the country had at least one working television set. About 75 percent had more than one.

You can access the Media World clips, with all new NBC videos, on the Online Learning Center home page. Go to www .mhhe.com/dominick11e, select Student Center and then Chapter 10.

CBS Affiliate 35WSEE-TV provides programming to Erie, Pennsylvania. The Erie market ranks 143rd out of 210 markets with about 158,000 television households. As such, it is probably typical of a smaller-market TV station. The first part of the video introduces you to key members of the station staff.

The next segment raises some issues for you to consider:

1. Most of the discussion focuses on the news operation. Why? How important is news to a local station?

2. What challenges do these professionals face in practicing quality journalism?

3. How is technology affecting the station? Could the lack of a "human element" hurt or help newscasting? What are the arguments on each side?

4. Would stations in bigger markets face the same issues?

5. Go to www.wsee.tv and see what the station looks like today.

The set in the average household is on for about 8 hours a day, with each individual watching an average of more than 3 hours daily. The TV audience changes throughout the day, steadily growing from 7 A.M. until it reaches a peak from 8 to 11 P.M., Eastern Standard Time. After 11 P.M., the audience drops off dramatically. Figure 10-1 details this pattern of audience viewing.

Not surprisingly, the television audience is largest during the winter months and smallest during July and August, when people spend more time outdoors. The composition of the television audience changes during the day. Preschool and female viewers tend to predominate during the daytime hours from Monday to Friday. On Saturday mornings most of the audience is under 13. Prime time is dominated by those in the 18- to 49-year-old age group.

Various demographic factors, such as age, sex, social class, and education, affect viewership. For example, teenagers watch the least. People in low-income homes generally watch more television than their middle-income counterparts. People with more education tend to watch less, and women watch more often than men.

FIGURE 10-1

Household Viewing of Television at Various Times of the Day

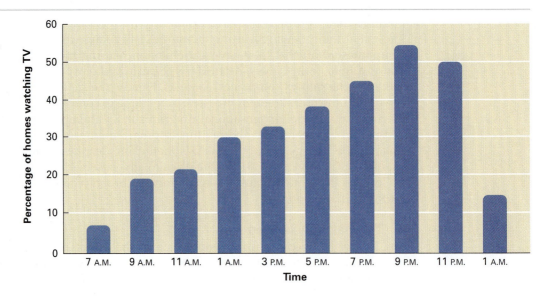

The Broadcast Television Industry

Like most of the media industries at the end of the 2000s, career prospects in the broadcast media were not bright. There were about 120,000 people employed in the industry in 2008, down from about 129,000 in 2005. Further declines are expected. Job opportunities seem to be a bit better at the local level than at the networks. Those interested in production jobs should consider looking at companies that specialize in nonscripted reality programs.

The career outlook in the various media industries changes quickly. For a more current description of conditions in the broadcast television industry and a more detailed look at career options, please consult the book's Web site: www.mhhe.com/dominick11e.

MAIN POINTS

- Electronic television developed during the 1930s. After World War II it quickly grew in popularity and replaced radio as the main information and entertainment medium.

- Three networks—NBC, CBS, and ABC—dominated early TV. Live drama, variety, and quiz and game shows were popular during the 1950s.

- Television matured in the 1960s, and its content became more professional. The public television network began in 1967. Cable TV grew slowly during this decade.

- The 1970s saw TV programs criticized for excessive violence.

- In the 1980s and 1990s, the three traditional TV networks lost viewers to cable and to VCRs. The Fox network became a major competitor.

- The Telecommunications Act of 1996 had a significant impact on TV station ownership and also introduced program content ratings. Rules for the eventual conversion to digital TV were announced in 1997.

- Changing from analog to digital signals will mean better pictures and sound. Consumers have to buy a new TV set or a converter to receive the new signals. TV stations may use the digital signal to broadcast high-definition television or lower-definition programs among which viewers may choose.

- TV is universal, dominant, and expensive. Its audience is currently fragmenting into smaller segments.

- The broadcast TV industry consists of program suppliers, distributors, and local stations.

- Big conglomerates own the major TV networks, and large group owners control most of the stations in large markets.

- Public broadcasting relies less on tax revenues and more on private sources of funding.

- The Nielsen Company compiles both network and local-station television ratings.

QUESTIONS FOR REVIEW

1. What are the defining features of the TV medium?
2. What are some of the advantages of being an affiliate of a major TV network?
3. Who owns the TV networks?
4. Trace the evolution of U.S. noncommercial TV programming.
5. How has the DVR affected TV viewing?

QUESTIONS FOR CRITICAL THINKING

1. What should be the goal of public television? Should the government support public broadcasting?
2. Large companies control the broadcast television industry. What are some of the good points and bad points of large corporate ownership?
3. The major broadcast networks have been losing viewers for the past two decades or so. Will they still be around 10–15 years from now? Why or why not?
4. In addition to the Nielsen People Meter, what are some ways that television viewing can be measured?
5. Review the boxed insert *"The Bachelor,"* on page 253. Next, consider the following. *The Bachelor* has a female counterpart in *The Bachelorette.* Ratings for *The Bachelorette* have not been as good. Can you think of any reasons why? Are there other reality programs that utilize a fairy tale theme?

KEY TERMS

Public Broadcasting Act of 1967 (p. 232)   noncommercial television (p. 239)   Portable People Meter (PPM) (p. 251)
time shifting (p. 235)   VHF (p. 242)   C3 ratings (p. 251)
high-definition television (HDTV)   UHF (p. 242)   rating (p. 252)
   (p. 235)   independents (p. 242)   share of the audience (p. 252)
digital television (DTV) (p. 236)   pilot (p. 244)
commercial television (p. 239)   digital video recorder (DVR) (p. 250)

INTERNET RESOURCES

Online Learning Center

At the Online Learning Center home page, www.mhhe.com/dominick11e, *select* Student Center *and then* Chapter 10.

1. Use the Learning Objectives, Chapter Outline, and
   Main Points sections to review this chapter.

2. Test your knowledge of the chapter using the multiple
   choice and flashcard features of the site.

3. Expand your knowledge of concepts and topics
   discussed in the chapter with additional Questions
   for Critical Thinking and Internet Exercises.

Surfing the Internet

www.abc.com
Watch hit ABC shows in full screen and high resolution—
along with a few commercials.

www.museum.tv
Home page of the Museum of Broadcast Communication.
Site contains clips from old TV programs.

www.nbcnewyork.com
The Web site of the local NBC affiliate in New York City.
Note the large number of choices for the user, ranging from
news headlines to traffic information.

www.turnoffyourtv.com
If you do not like TV, this is the site for you. Includes a
page that suggests things to do instead of watching TV.

www.nielsenmedia.com
Information about Nielsen Media Research, the firm
that rates TV programs. Check out the Inside Ratings
link for a basic description of how the TV audience is
measured.

CHAPTER 11

Cable, Satellite, and Internet Television

This chapter will prepare you to:

- trace the development of cable, satellite, and Internet television

- describe the implications of the digital age for these media

- understand the structure, content, and finances of cable, satellite, and Internet TV

- appreciate the potential of Internet TV

- explain the audience measurement techniques used for these media

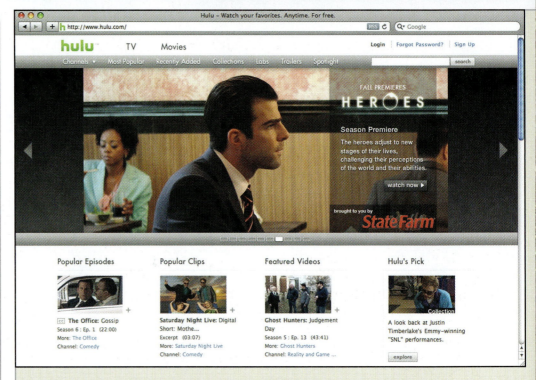

Watch full-length movies and network TV shows on hulu.com. *Time* named the site the fourth-best invention of 2008. (The retail DNA test kit was number one.)

Let's call this a tale of two sites. Internet giant Google acquired YouTube in 2006 in a deal that was worth about $1.65 billion. YouTube is by far the biggest source of Internet video. In March 2009, YouTube accounted for 5.5 billion (that's *billion* with a *b*) video streams—and that was just for one month. Thirteen hours of content *per minute* is uploaded to the site each day. Despite this huge popularity, YouTube has yet to make any money for Google. In fact, analysts suggest that the site probably loses at least $200 million each year.

Hulu.com, a joint venture between NBC Universal and the News Corporation, owner of Fox, went public in March 2008. ABC joined in 2009. (The name "hulu" has no meaning in English, but there is a Mandarin word "hu-lu" that literally means "gourd." Hulu's founders say they chose this word because in ancient times gourds were hollowed out and used as containers for precious items.) In one year, Hulu became the number-two online video site on the Web, accounting for about 350 million streamed videos in March 2009, still far behind YouTube's total but an impressive achievement in just a year. Even more impressive, analysts project that Hulu will probably turn a profit in 2010, a small one but a profit nonetheless.

How come the site running a distant second can make money while the clear leader keeps burning through millions? Hulu can "monetize" nearly all of its content since it carries programs and clips that appeal to advertisers. YouTube can monetize only a small fraction of its videos, usually only the content that is professionally produced. The millions of user-generated videos on YouTube have no attraction for advertisers, who are afraid an ad for their product might be paired with a video of some teenager in his underwear playing air guitar, or worse. YouTube realized its dilemma and in 2009 created a new area on its site devoted to long-form professional content.

What lessons can we learn from this tale? First, huge popularity on the Web does not necessarily translate into profits. Second, to make money from Web video a site needs a viable business model, such as Hulu's. The third lesson is more subtle, as explained below.

The ultimate winner in the Hulu vs. YouTube competition may take years to emerge. But one thing is clear: For every winner there is usually a loser, and in this case there may be more than one. The tremendous success of Hulu and YouTube demonstrated that people were willing to go directly to the Web to watch programs instead of viewing them on the local broadcast TV station, or on satellite or cable. If the Internet becomes the preferred vehicle for watching TV, who needs broadcast TV, cable, or a satellite system? Needless to say, broadcasters, cablecasters, and satellitecasters are looking very carefully at the long-term implications of Internet video.

The last chapter examined traditional broadcast TV. This chapter will examine the history, economics, structure, and potential of the newer forms of television—cable, satellite, Internet—as they face the challenges posed by the digital age. We'll start with a look at how they came to be.

A Brief History

Cable TV began modestly in the 1950s as a device used to bring conventional television signals to areas that could not otherwise receive them. As cable grew, some systems imported signals from distant stations into markets that were already served by one or two local stations. The local stations, as you might imagine, were not pleased, since their audiences were being siphoned off by the imported signals. This situation caused some political maneuverings as stations affected by cable appealed to the FCC and to Congress for help. The FCC vacillated over the question of cable regulation before issuing, in 1965, a set of rules that retarded the growth of cable in large markets. In 1972 the FCC enacted a new set of less restrictive rules for cable. By 1980, in a move toward deregulation, the FCC had dropped virtually all rules governing cable.

This deregulation move helped systems grow as cable companies scrambled to acquire exclusive franchises in communities across the nation (see Figure 11-1). Some companies made extravagant promises to win these contracts: a hundred or more channels, local-access channels, community channels, shopping and banking at home, two-way services—and all at bargain prices. After the smoke cleared, the industry recognized the economic reality dictating that its performance would fall short of promises.

While all this was going on, the United States and the Soviet Union were competing in the "space race" that culminated with the lunar landing in 1969. One of the by-products of the space race was the development of rockets that could launch communication satellites into Earth orbit. The first satellite TV transmission occurred in 1962 using *Telstar I* (this satellite has the distinction of being the only satellite commemorated by a rock song). In the early 1970s more communication satellites circled the Earth.

Satellite TV transmission came of age in 1976 when a little-known pay-TV cable service, HBO, used a satellite to transmit the "Thrilla in Manilla" heavyweight championship fight between Muhammad Ali and Joe Frazier to cable systems across the United States. That

FIGURE 11-1

Growth Within the U.S. Cable TV Industry

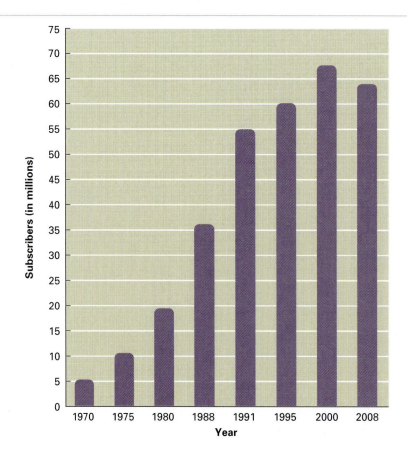

same year, media entrepreneur Ted Turner started transmitting "superstation" WTBS to cable systems. Other satellite-distributed channels quickly followed, and cable subscribers could now receive a host of new programming, including CNN, MTV, and ESPN. This gave people in urban and suburban areas a compelling new reason to subscribe to cable, and the industry grew quickly during the 1970s and 1980s. For example, the percentage of homes with cable increased from about 14 percent in 1975 to more than 50 percent in 1987. By the end of the 1980s, the cable industry was dominated by large **MSOs (multiple system operators)** such as TCI. Locally owned cable systems were quickly disappearing.

As of 1991, 7,500 cable systems served about 55 million households. Keep in mind that this growth occurred despite the fact that cable companies generally avoided expensive urban installations. The growth rate slowed somewhat during the mid-1990s, but by 2007 about 66 million households subscribed to cable.

Cable also scored several programming coups. ESPN signed a contract with the National Football League to carry prime-time pro football games. CNN's coverage of the Gulf War, the O. J. Simpson trial, and 9/11 attacks demonstrated that it could be a formidable competitor to network news. Big-ticket network series bypassed the traditional syndication route and premiered first on cable.

Cable got a competitor in the mid-1990s thanks to the development of high-powered **direct-broadcast satellites (DBS)** that could send a signal directly to a small home satellite dish, bypassing the cable system altogether. Two companies, Echo Star (Dish Network) and DirecTV, eventually dominated the industry. The number of households subscribing to satellite companies increased from about 2 million in 1995 to more than 30 million in 2008.

On the economic side, cable advertising revenues exceeded $2 billion in 1990 and rose to about $27 billion by 2008. Although still small in comparison with the ad revenues generated by traditional television, the 2008 figure represents an increase of almost 42 percent over that of 2004.

The most significant developments in the cable industry in the past three decades have been legal ones. In 1984 Congress deregulated the rates cable systems could charge consumers. Eight years later, in response to subscriber complaints, Congress reregulated the industry by passing the Cable Television Consumer Protection and Competition Act, which caused about a 17 percent reduction in rates and mandated that broadcasters choose between *must carry* (the local cable system had to carry the station's signal) and *retransmission consent* (the local station had the right to negotiate compensation for carriage of its signal). Most broadcasters opted for consent and were compensated with promotional time on the system or were granted space for their own existing or planned cable networks. But this situation changed in the mid-2000s when broadcasters, facing declining ad revenues and looking for new sources of revenue, began demanding payment from cable companies in order to carry their programs. Satellite systems and phone companies that offer video already pay a fee to the broadcasters. It is likely that cable will eventually follow suit, a move that would mean increased monthly bills for subscribers.

The next major piece of legislation was the Telecommunications Act of 1996 (discussed in more detail in Chapter 16). The new law gave telephone companies the right to enter the cable business and gave cable companies the right to provide telephone services. In addition, both telephone and cable companies could own competing systems in the same community. Finally, the act allowed most cable companies to once again set their own rates. Significant competition between phone companies and cable companies did not materialize for several years, but by the middle of the decade, the situation was changing. Thanks to a new technology, **voice-over-Internet protocol (VOIP),** cable companies were able to offer an alternative to the traditional phone lines. For their part the telephone companies are moving into the television business. Verizon offers TV programming over its fiber optic system (FiOS). As of mid-2009, FiOS subscribers could receive 348 digital channels, including 100 in high-definition, along with high-speed Internet access.

For many of you reading this, Judy McGrath would seem to have the ultimate dream job: She is the president of the MTV Networks Music Group and is responsible for MTV, MTV2, VH1, CMT, and all of the company's digital media services. Under her direction MTV has grown from a small niche cable network to an international brand that symbolizes a unique attitude and lifestyle.

Always a music fan, McGrath first tried to get a job writing for *Rolling Stone.* When her efforts proved unsuccessful, she turned to writing advertising copy and then went to work for *Mademoiselle* and *Glamour.* In 1981 she heard about a new cable channel launched by Warner Entertainment that would be devoted to rock music. Despite the fact that she could not even get the channel on her home TV, McGrath joined the newly created MTV as a copywriter and on-air promotion person. (She was one of the ones responsible for using all the space film footage to promote the channel.) To the surprise of many people, MTV was successful in attracting 16- to 24-year-olds, an audience coveted by advertisers. MTV became part of the huge Viacom conglomerate, and McGrath quickly moved up the ranks to creative director, executive vice president, and eventually chair and chief

executive at MTV Networks. Under her direction MTV expanded all over the world.

When the music video novelty began to wear off in the mid-1980s and ratings started to sag, McGrath introduced programs that became popular culture icons: *Beavis and Butt-Head, The Real World, The MTV Music Awards, MTV Unplugged*, and *Total Request Live.* She also introduced political coverage to MTV and was instrumental in the development of the 1992 *Choose or Lose* get-out-the-vote campaign. More recently, McGrath has led MTV into other media: movies, books, and the Internet.

What does she see in MTV's future? Since a high proportion of MTV viewers are also Web surfers and spend a good deal of time on MTV.com, look for more integration of the music on MTV and MTV2 with the Web site. MTV.com will be used to highlight some of the artists or genres featured on the cable channels. In addition, plans are under way for more international expansion, particularly in Asia. Finally, it is likely McGrath will continue to provide special programming that deals with important social issues, such as the 17 hours the channel devoted to hate crimes. And, of course, there will always be music videos.

Cable was experiencing problems resulting from its own growth. There were more cable networks around than available space on local systems. In addition, like the broadcast networks, cable TV was becoming a victim of audience fragmentation.

Despite these difficulties, the long-range outlook seems positive. Cable continues to draw viewers away from the broadcast TV networks. In addition, thanks to their existing coaxial cable and fiber optic cables, cable companies can offer subscribers high-speed Internet connections.

The late 1990s saw the development of a different way to distribute TV signals: **Internet TV** or Webcasting. The key to this process was an innovation called *streaming*, in which a computer stores video signals—a process known as **buffering**—and plays them back while at the same time storing new, incoming signals. In short, the head end of the video is playing while the tail is being extended.

Video on the Web grew slowly, primarily because most people had slow, dial-up connections, and it took a long time to play even a short clip. But the increasing popularity of high-speed broadband connections and the ease with which video could be uploaded on the Web helped fuel an explosion of user-generated content. By mid-decade, sites such as YouTube and Blinkx, where audience members upload and share their videos, became the hip places to visit. Experts predict that by 2010 more than half of the video content on the Web will be user-generated. The broadcast networks and cable companies started their own broadband channels, as did many private companies and individual entrepreneurs.

The huge success of Apple's iPod sparked another channel for Web video—the **podcast.** A podcast is a media program that is downloaded from a Web site and played back at an individual's convenience over a computer or an MP3 player such as an iPod. By 2009 thousands of video podcasts were available on the Internet.

The phone companies were also moving with more enthusiasm into the video business. AT&T, for example, offers U-Verse TV, a new Internet-based system that provides 200 channels of video and music.

Critical / Cultural Issues

Who's That in the Kitchen?

Cooking has often been associated with "women's work." There are signs, however, that the roles of men and women in the domestic arena, particularly in the kitchen, are shifting. One of the factors influencing this transition may be television. In an article published in the March 2009 issue of *Critical Studies in Media Communication,* Rebecca Swenson takes a close look at how one cable channel, the Food Network, might be contributing to a change in the ideologies associated with men, women, food, and cooking.

Ms. Swenson notes that the way cooking tasks are divided within the home and portrayed on television is important because our ideas of "who does what" often reflect deeply held beliefs about significant social categories such as "man" and "woman." If men are doing more in the kitchen, our cultural notions about what is traditionally women's work might also be changing. Is the Food Network reflecting any change in long-established male and female roles in the kitchen?

In order to answer this question, the researcher examined Food Network series during 2006 and 2008, focusing on themes, narratives, and social cues contained in the programs. Her results indicate that the programs are structured to show that men can cook and still retain their masculinity. Ms. Swenson identified several ways in which male cooks are portrayed differently than female cooks that help to maintain a more masculine image.

In the first place, men were more likely to be portrayed as professional cooks who prepare complicated dishes and educate their audiences about food-related topics, whereas women are portrayed as approachable, domestic cooks who prepare food for friends and family members. Male hosts often made references to their formal training or business experiences; female hosts, although equal in expertise and experience, rarely made such statements. Male cooks usually appeared wearing the traditional chef's white jacket. Female cooks were often casually dressed and wearing an apron. Other male hosts preserved their masculinity by appearing as more than cooks. Alton Brown, for example, takes on the roles of historian, food scientist, and anthropologist during his program.

Second, when males cook on the Food Network, it is generally for leisurely entertainment. When males enter the kitchen, it's usually for some special event, such as Sunday dinner, holiday entertaining, or for some kind of festive occasion. For example, on *Guy's Big Bite,* the host usually is cooking food for his "posse" in preparation for some upcoming party. In contrast, female cooks are typically shown preparing weekday family meals.

A third theme was to portray cooking as a journey. Although both male and female hosts went on the road during this type of program, female hosts were more likely to act as practical, budget-conscious trip advisors (such as Rachel Ray's *$40 a Day)* while male hosts were searching for "real" American food to satisfy their manly appetites. In short, males were more like adventurers; females more like thrifty homemakers.

A final theme portrayed cooking as a competitive contest. In programs such as *Iron Chef America* and *ThrowDown with Bobby Flay,* male chefs are no longer cooks: They take on the traditional male role of athlete as they compete against others and against the clock. Portraying cooking as an activity that depends on speed, cunning, power, and stamina runs counter to the traditional feminine model, whereby cooking is nurturing, democratic, and family centered. Ms. Swenson does acknowledge, however, that both male and female contestants compete in these programs, a fact that suggests a more nongendered division of labor.

In sum, as the author concludes: "The Food Network does construct food preparation as gendered work, and cooking is negotiated in ways that protect traditional understandings of masculinity and femininity. . . . To protect the concept of masculinity, men enter the kitchen as scientists, chefs, athletes and entertainers."

Cable, Satellite, and Internet TV in the Digital Age

▲ Transition

All three of these delivery systems are firmly established in the digital age. Cable and satellite systems now use digital techniques to distribute their programming. Internet TV has always been digital.

For cable and satellite systems, digital signals make possible video-on-demand, interactive program guides, high-definition TV, and digital video recorders (DVRs). Digital signals create sharper and crisper video and can be compressed, increasing the number of channels that can be transmitted over a single system.

In addition to television programs, cable systems use digital technology to provide telephone service to their customers as well as Internet access. Telephone companies

Talk about striking it rich. In the digital age one good idea can be worth money—an awful lot of money.

Chad Hurley was raised in Birdsboro, Pennsylvania. He attended Indiana University of Pennsylvania where he first majored in computer science and later switched to graphic design. After graduating in 1999, he took a job with a new company based in California called PayPal. Steve Chen was born in Taiwan but moved to the United States when he was 15. He majored in computer science at the University of Illinois—Urbana-Champaign. He too wound up working at PayPal in the late 1990s. Jawed Karim also attended the University of Illinois but dropped out to move to Silicon Valley where he too took a job at PayPal.

At a dinner party one night in 2004, the three were talking about how easy it was to share photographs on the Internet but how hard it was to share video clips. They decided to work on that problem and started meeting at Karim's apartment and in Hurley's garage. Karim was impressed by a site called HotorNot.com that let users post pictures of potential dates and rate them on a 1–10 scale. This site was unique because up to this point only the people who owned the site could post content whereas with HotorNot anybody could post photos for everybody else to see.

The three young men managed to cobble together a simple routine that allowed users to post their own videos in any format and play them back using any Web browser. In addition, they built in a search function and allowed people to rate and tag other people's videos. They also incorporated a feature that let people insert a video directly into a Web page. They came up with a name for the site—YouTube—and a slogan—"Broadcast Yourself."

As is sometimes the case with breakthrough technologies, the creators had no idea about the ultimate use of their invention. They thought that people would use it to illustrate items for sale on eBay or to show travel videos. What happened next was totally unexpected: The audience took over the site. They posted karaoke sessions, snowboarding wipeouts, amateur stand-up comedy routines, stupid pet tricks, and introspective soliloquies. Some posted news footage, such as the aftermath of Hurricane Katrina and rocket attacks in Afghanistan. Others lifted clips from *The Daily Show* and the Cartoon Network and posted them (raising an issue with copyright holders that would become a continuing problem for YouTube). A couple of clips—one featuring Diet Coke and Mentos and another a skit from *Saturday Night Live*—were viewed by millions. Many used YouTube to post videos on their MySpace pages. Less than a year after it was launched, YouTube became a media phenomenon. It now airs more than 100 million videos, and about 70,000 are added every day.

YouTube was lucky to capitalize on two developments that fed on each other. The first was the revolution in digital video made possible by cheap cameras and simple editing software. The second was the rise of the Internet as an interactive social network where users generated and shared information. It was not coincidental that YouTube grew at the same time as Wikipedia, Facebook, MySpace, Flickr, and other, similar sites.

What about the three guys who made YouTube happen? They're a lot richer now. In 2006 Google bought YouTube for $1.65 billion.

---

are doing the same. This makes it possible for telephone and cable companies to offer a "bundle" of services—Internet, TV, phone—for a lower price. Satellite systems have trouble matching this feature.

▲ Mobile Media

As noted in the previous chapter, broadcast TV has moved into the mobile TV market, and cable/satellite networks have done the same. MobiTV sends ESPN, Fox News, C-SPAN, and other networks to subscribers' cell phones. The cable companies, however, have a problem with mobile media because the big wireless networks that are used to send video to phones are controlled by the phone companies, such as AT&T and Sprint. In that connection, Comcast, Time Warner, and Google are partners in a project to build the nation's fastest wireless network. Cox Communications is taking another course, based on short-range WiFi technology that would allow users to access video within an area served by Cox Cable.

▲ User-Generated Content

Like the broadcast industry, networks carried by cable and satellite are increasingly turning to user-generated video. CNN has a feature called I-Report that lets individuals send video to the news channel, where it might make it on the air. The cell phone video recorded by a student while the Virginia Tech shootings were in progress was played on CNN dozens of times. MSNBC features FirstPerson, where users can submit news video. ESPN has something similar called Sports Center Home Video.

The biggest place, of course, to find user-generated video is the Internet. Thanks to the success of YouTube (see the boxed insert "The Guys Behind YouTube"), user-generated content has exploded on the Web. There were at least 150 video-sharing sites on the Web in mid-2009. YouTube, the most popular with more than 80 million videos, streams about 125 petabytes of data per month (a petabyte is a "1" followed by 15 zeros). YouTube also has what media gurus call "stickiness," the amount of time a person spends visiting a site. Visitors to the video-sharing site spend an average of nearly 15 minutes per session. Most sites are lucky if their stickiness number gets above 5 minutes.

YouTube has become so popular that it is used by politicians, advertisers, recording hopefuls (remember Marié Digby from Chapter 8), aspiring actresses (lonelygirl15), comedians, and others hoping for their 15 minutes of fame. MySpace, the social networking site, contains a tutorial on how users can post a YouTube video into their profile. Many apparently do, as a significant number of visitors to YouTube are MySpace subscribers embedding video on their MySpace site.

▲ Social Media

Cable/satellite network Web sites, like their broadcast counterparts, are making extensive use of social media. One of the most popular sites, Comedy Central, features blogs and interactive games. The Web site of the Travel Channel includes a travel community link where visitors can share their top restaurant picks and favorite destinations. Sports fans can join ESPN's SportsNation to discuss questions such as what pro team did best in the draft or what baseball team is likely to win the pennant.

CNN is heavily involved with Twitter. In 2009, the cable network joined a competition with celebrity Ashton Kutcher to see who could be the first to amass 1 million followers (Kutcher won but it was close). TNT relied heavily on Facebook and Twitter to promote their coverage of the 2009 NBA playoffs. Dish Network and DirecTV have teams that monitor their Twitter accounts.

Defining Features of Cable, Satellite, and Internet TV

Obviously, a person needs at least one extra piece of equipment in order to receive video from these sources. Cable subscribers rent set-top boxes or use cable "smart cards" to receive their programs. Satellite viewers need a receiver and a satellite dish. Internet TV viewers have to have a computer and a modem.

A second obvious feature is that the consumer has to pay extra to receive these services. Unlike broadcast TV, where a rabbit-ears antenna connected to the set is enough to bring in their programs, cable and satellite subscribers must pay a monthly fee to receive their programs. On the Internet, viewers can watch some programs for free but must pay to receive others (such as the $1.99 on iTunes). All, however, have to pay extra for Internet access.

A third feature is that these services carry many channels that appeal to niche or highly differentiated audiences. Unlike broadcasters, who still try to aggregate the biggest possible general audience, cable/satellite systems carry such specialized channels as the History Channel, the Weather Channel, and the Documentary Channel. And even the niche audiences are being divided up. There are two cable networks devoted to health programming, for example, and five devoted to home and lifestyle topics.

Organization of the Cable and Satellite Industries

We'll first focus on the organization of the cable and satellite industries and then take a look at Internet television.

FIGURE 11-2

Diagram of the Transmission of HBO Programming from Studios, via Satellite, to the Pay Subscriber's Television Set.

At the head end the signal is assigned to a cable TV channel before being sent on its way to the subscriber's home.

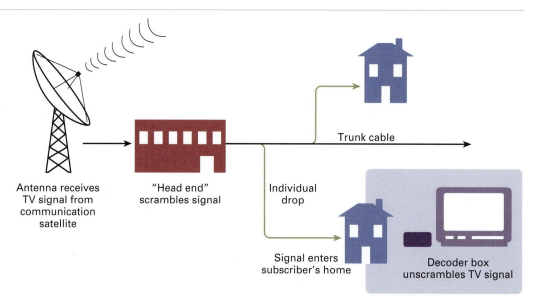

Antenna receives TV signal from communication satellite

"Head end" scrambles signal

Trunk cable

Individual drop

Signal enters subscriber's home

Decoder box unscrambles TV signal

▲ Structure: Cable TV

Cable systems are structured differently than those of conventional TV. There are three main components in a cable system: (1) the head end, (2) the distribution system, and (3) the house drop (see Figure 11-2).

The **head end** consists of the antenna and related equipment that receive signals from distant TV stations or other programming services and process these signals so that they may be sent to subscribers' homes. Some cable systems also originate their own programming, ranging from local newscasts to weather dials, and their studios may also be located at the head end.

The **distribution system** consists of the actual cables that deliver the signals to subscribers. The cables can be buried or hung on telephone poles. In most systems the main cable (called the *trunk*) has several feeder cables, which travel down side streets or to other outlying areas. Finally, special amplifiers installed along the distribution system boost the strength of the signal as it comes from the head end.

The **house drop** is that section of the cable that connects the feeder cable to the subscriber's TV set. Drops can be one-way (the signal travels in only one direction—from the head end to the house) or two-way (the signal can also be sent back to the head end by the subscriber). Fiber optic cables make it possible to carry 500 or more channels.

▲ Programming and Financing: Cable TV

We will examine these topics from two perspectives: (1) that of a local cable system operator and (2) that of a national cable network.

Local Operators   There are six basic sources of programming for a local system:

1. *Local origination:* This programming might include local news, high school football, and discussions. A local government channel may carry city council meetings or zoning board hearings. Some systems have set aside public access channels for anyone to use for a modest fee.

2. *Local broadcast television stations:* Some cable systems carry signals from nearby cities in addition to local channels.

3. *Superstations:* These are local stations whose signals are carried by many systems nationwide. Major superstations include WGN, Chicago; KTLA, Los Angeles; and WPIX and WWOR, New York. The original superstation, WTBS, Atlanta, changed its status in 1998 to that of a cable network.

4. *Special cable networks:* These are services distributed by satellite to cable systems. Most of these networks are advertiser supported. Examples include MTV, the Weather Channel, USA Network, Black Entertainment Television, and the noncommercial C-SPAN (which covers Congress).

5. *Pay services:* These are commercial-free channels that typically provide theatrical movies and original programming. HBO, Showtime, the Movie Channel, and Cinemax are examples.

6. *Pay-per-view:* These are channels set aside for the showing of recently released theatrical films and special sports and entertainment events. Subscribers receive the programs for a specified price. Movies, for example, might cost $4.95; special events, such as Wrestlemania, might run $20–30.

A local cable system has two basic sources of income: (1) subscription fees from consumers and (2) local advertising. Most systems charge a fee for local stations, superstations, and special cable networks. In addition, consumers might pay an additional fee to receive one or more pay channels. Cable is a capital-intensive industry: It takes a lot of money to start a system. The operating costs of a typical system are more reasonable. A good part of the basic cable monthly subscription fee goes to cover construction and maintenance costs.

Cable systems must also pay for their programming. In the case of pay services, the consumer fee is split between the cable system and the cable network. There has been a recent shift in the composition of cable system revenue. Pay-cable and pay-per-view receipts now account for more than half of cable operators' income. Local advertising on cable represents another source of income for operators. This sum is growing, but it still represents less than 20 percent of total income for local systems. In addition, cable systems that carry home shopping networks generally receive a percentage of the sales revenue generated in their market. Figure 11-3 illustrates the growth in cable TV revenue.

FIGURE 11-3

Cable Industry
Revenue, 1996–2008
(millions of dollars)

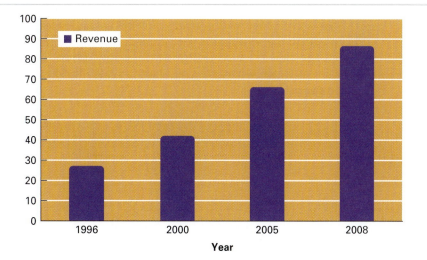

Speaker of the House Nancy Pelosi appears on C-SPAN. Special-interest channels such as C-SPAN have fragmented the cable TV audience.

National Operators   At the national level cable networks draw upon three major sources for their programming: (1) original production, (2) movies, and (3) syndicated programs. The all-news channel CNN relies upon original production for virtually all its content. Most of ESPN's programming is also original, as is C-SPAN's. Movies make up most of the content on HBO and Showtime. Superstations program a mix of all three sources, while channels such as USA Network and Lifetime depend heavily on syndicated programs.

There are three main revenue sources for national cable services: (1) advertising, (2) carriage fees, and (3) subscription fees. Pay-TV channels such as Showtime and HBO make their money from subscription fees paid by consumers. Some cable networks, such as MTV and ESPN, charge local operators a **carriage fee.** As of 2005, for example, ESPN charged $2.90 per subscriber, Fox Sports about $1.68, and CNN about 47 cents. Cable companies pass these charges along to their customers. Some channels, such as C-SPAN, support themselves entirely from this money. Other networks sell advertising in addition to the carriage fee, and still others support themselves almost entirely through ads. As mentioned earlier, advertising revenues for cable are growing, but cable still accounts for only a small percentage of the total TV ad dollars. Table 11-1 lists the top cable channels.

▲ Pay-per-View (PPV)

PPV makes most of its money from sporting events (mainly high-profile boxing matches), movies, concerts, and adult content. Subscribers pay fees ranging from $5 to $50 to see these events. After racking up impressive revenue figures during the late 1990s, PPV has fallen on difficult times. Increasing competition from video-on-demand and digital cable channels has forced many cable system operators to reexamine the long-range future of this service. Still, the potential for big money exists. The Oscar de la Hoya–Floyd Mayweather boxing match brought in $134 million and was the biggest moneymaker in PPV history.

▲ Video-on-Demand (VOD)

Cable and satellite operators are hoping that **video-on-demand (VOD)** will provide a big boost to their bottom lines. VOD works like this: A cable or satellite company stores movies or TV shows on a huge server. A searchable index contains a list of everything that is available. A subscriber scans the list and selects the program that he or she wants to watch; the selection is sent immediately to the person's TV set. A special set-top box lets the viewer pause, fast-forward, or rewind. In short, you get to watch whatever you want to watch whenever you want to watch it. Most cable/satellite services offer a per-program fee.

TABLE 11-1

Top Cable Services, 2008

Network	Number of Subscriber Households (in millions)
Discovery	98.0
TNT	98.0
ESPN	97.8
CNN	97.5
USA	97.5

A subscriber to the basic cable package offered by Comcast can receive about 100 channels (it varies by location). Of course, not everybody watches all 100 channels. Some are popular, such as the four broadcast networks and ESPN, TNT, and CNN. Others don't attract much of an audience. The Golf Channel, Retro TV, and the Real Estate Channel, for example, would seem to attract a loyal but small following. But if you want to receive ESPN and your other favorites, you have to pay for the channels that you don't watch as well. Does this model sound familiar? Does it remind you of the recording industry's traditional approach whereby a consumer had to buy an entire album just to get the one or two songs that were personal favorites?

What if some adventurous entrepreneur came up with a plan to let consumers pay for only those channels that they wanted to see and not bother with the ones that the consumer would never watch? This "a la carte" approach would require special deals with the content providers and might depend on the Internet for distribution. It would be a challenge, but not an insurmountable one.

An initiative by the Federal Communications Commission to investigate the a la carte option got nowhere, and cable companies have so far resisted any attempt to make them change their pricing structure. Does this sound a little bit like the situation in the recording industry? The Internet totally upset the traditional way of doing business for the recording industry. Will it do the same for cable and satellite?

VOD has been around for a number of years but was slow to catch on because of a lack of content and a complicated user interface. Its fortunes have improved a bit recently as cable/satellite companies have simplified the ordering process and added more movies and TV shows to VOD libraries. Movies are still popular, but TV show episodes are the fastest-growing genre. Analysts predict VOD could bring in more than $2 billion in 2010.

In the past few years, however, VOD has been less of a priority for cable and satellite companies as they turn their attention to the Web. VOD does not create the same kind of "buzz" as a popular video on YouTube. Further, cable and satellite services are facing competition from other companies. Apple sells TV shows and other content on its iTunes Web site. Hulu.com offers hundreds of TV episodes for free.

▲ Structure: Satellite TV

A satellite system consists of five elements (see Figure 11-4):

1. Content providers, such as ESPN, Nickelodeon, or local broadcast stations, who send their signals to
2. A broadcast center, which takes the programming and transmits it to
3. Geosynchronous communication satellites (a **geosynchronous satellite** is one whose orbit keeps it over the same spot on Earth), which receive the programs from the broadcast center and send them back down to
4. A small satellite receiving dish, which picks up the signal and transmits it to
5. A satellite receiver, which transforms the signal so that it can be viewed on a conventional TV set.

Satellite signals are compressed in order to allow a greater number of channels to be transmitted to and from an orbiting satellite. To prevent people from receiving the signals without a subscription, the signals are **encrypted** (scrambled so that only those with a proper decoder can view them). The satellite receiver decrypts the signals and distributes them to one or more TV sets.

▲ Programming and Financing: Satellite TV

The same programming carried by the major cable companies is also distributed by satellite, including local broadcast stations; superstations; nonbroadcast networks such as MTV, USA, and CNN; pay services such as HBO; and pay-per-view. Unlike cable, satellite networks are national in focus; there is no local origination of programs.

FIGURE 11-4

Diagram of a Satellite Broadcasting System

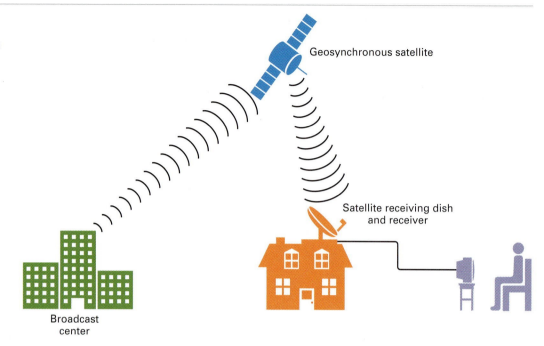

Geosynchronous satellite

Satellite receiving dish and receiver

Broadcast center

Similar to cable, the biggest source of revenue for satellite companies is the monthly subscription fees paid by their customers. In addition, DirecTV and Dish charge extra for DVRs, HDTV, and additional receivers. Unlike cable, local advertising is not a significant revenue stream.

Also similar to cable, satellite providers' biggest expenses are related to hardware. It costs a lot of money to launch, maintain, and eventually replace a communication satellite. Installing, servicing, and replacing dishes and receivers constitute another significant expense. DirecTV and Dish also pay content producers for the right to carry their programs.

As mentioned above, DirecTV and the Dish Network are having trouble competing against the cable industry's ability to bundle voice, video, and high-speed Internet access. In response, the satellite providers have explored alliances with phone companies.

▲ Ownership of Cable and Satellite TV

The ownership trend in cable, as in other media, has been toward consolidation. Comcast acquired the assets of AT&T Broadband in 2002 to become the nation's largest cable provider. Comcast and number-two Time Warner serve more than half of all cable customers. The five largest cable companies are listed in Table 11-2.

There are two major companies that dominate the U.S. satellite TV market: DirecTV and Dish Network. DirecTV, with about 18 million subscribers, is controlled by Rupert Murdoch's News Corporation. The Dish Network is owned by EchoStar and has about 14 million customers.

TABLE 11-2

Five Largest Cable System Operators, 2008

Company	Number of Subscribers (in millions)
Comcast	24.2
Time Warner	13.1
Cox Communications	5.3
Charter Communications	5.0
Cablevision Systems	3.1

Internet Video

Compared to starting a cable or satellite TV channel, starting an Internet TV channel is relatively easy. No expensive studios and pricey equipment are needed. All it takes is a camera, a computer, some software, and a Web site, and you're in business. It's no wonder that this is a hot area.

Further, the explosion of video on the Internet in recent years is another indication that the convergence between television set and computer is well on its way. Of course, an explosion is a difficult thing to analyze. Internet video is still expanding, and its final configuration is up in the air. This section will try to make some sense out of this rapidly changing area by examining its structure and finances.

▲ Structure: Sources and Content

One way to analyze Web video is to classify it first by source—professional or amateur, or as they say in the business, "pro or Joe" (as in the average Joe)—and then by its content—original or repurposed. Let's first look at professionally produced content.

Professionally Produced Content   This has been a huge growth area. Today it's unusual to find a major company or organization that does not have video available on its Web site. Professional video sources include the following:

- Media companies such as the broadcast and cable/satellite networks, newspaper and magazine publishers, and movie studios
- Corporations that produce video for their company Web sites or for internal communication and training
- Marketing and advertising companies
- Product manufacturers
- Service organizations, such as the USO and Rotary International
- Government agencies, such as Social Security and the Food and Drug Administration

These organizations typically have their own in-house production facilities or hire an outside production company to put together their video.

Professional content can be repurposed or original. Current or past television programs available at network Web sites or at video sites such as Hulu and Joost are examples of repurposed content. These programs reach (or reached) the majority of their viewers through traditional television, and the Internet provides a supplemental channel that attracts additional viewers. An episode of ABC's *Grey's Anatomy*, for example, draws about 12 million viewers when it is broadcast over-the-air and close to another million online. Parts or all of these programs may be available on video-sharing Web sites where their presence can cause copyright issues.

There are abundant examples of professionally produced original online series. Here are just a few. Sony's Crackle.com has a slate of several original series produced for the Web site. *Rockville, CA,* a Web series with a music theme, is available at TV.com and other sites. More than a dozen original series are available at Vimby.com

Advertisers and marketers are another source of professionally produced original video. Ford, along with many other companies, has a YouTube channel, where you can follow the company's latest efforts at achieving fuel economy. Coca Cola includes several short video features on its Web site as does Wrigley's Gum. French Maid TV offers "how to" instructions on various topics (geared to the needs of marketers) that feature a trio of French maids (who else?).

The candidates in the 2008 presidential campaign made heavy use of Internet video. Hillary Clinton announced her candidacy with a video posted on her Web site. Eventual winner Barack Obama's site included BarackTV, complete with clips of speeches and campaign rallies. After the election, video of President Obama's weekly address was regularly posted on the White House's official Web site.

A recent *Wall Street Journal* article profiled a family in Kentucky who are part of a major threat to the cable and satellite TV industries. No, they weren't plotting some foul play. The family simply canceled their cable subscription and started to watch their favorite programs online for free. Numbers are hard to come by, but experts suggest that the family is just one of about a million who have "cut the cord," so to speak. It's quite possible that the weak economy will make this number grow even more.

Naturally, cable and satellite operators are worried. They get about half their revenue from subscribers' monthly fees. The content providers are also worried since they get a fee per subscriber from the cable and satellite services, but they can make up for some of their losses by selling advertising in the online versions. Broadcast networks aren't worried. Their programming is free to begin with, and online viewing gives them an additional place to run commercials. For a cable or satellite service, however, there's no way to make up for losing a subscriber.

It appears, however, that the cable/satellite industry has a plan. The industry is pushing a subscriber-only approach to online video. Under the plan, Web sites that offer video would get access to cable/satellite programs but visitors would have to prove that they subscribe to a cable or satellite service in order to view the programs. For example, if a person wanted to watch TNT's *The Closer* on hulu.com, the person would have to confirm that he or she subscribes to Comcast or some other cable or satellite service before the program would play. The system might rely on account numbers, passwords, registration, or some other security check. If you're not a subscriber, too bad.

Such a scheme has great appeal for cable/satellite companies. They would no longer give away their content for free—a mistake made by the newspaper industry that many think led to its current crisis. Will consumers go for it or will it simply make them mad and encourage piracy? That's an open question, but one thing is clear: If this system goes into effect, consumers will quickly learn the difference between free broadcast TV and TV you have to pay for.

The White House is not the only branch of government producing original Web content. In mid-2009, Patty Duke was starring in an original video on the Web site of the Social Security Administration urging people to apply for benefits online. The U.S. Census Bureau and the National Oceanic and Atmospheric Administration have started YouTube channels.

Videos on YouTube have been viewed nearly 2 billion times. It has been estimated that the total amount of time people have spent watching YouTube since it first started is more than 9,000 years.

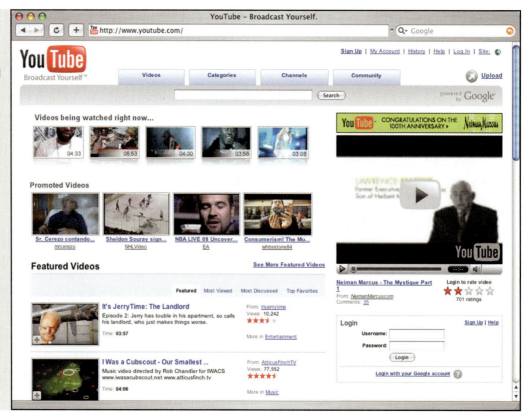

You can get Internet access on your desktop PC, your laptop, your netbook, your cell phone, your Nintendo DSi, and even in the backseat of some New York taxicabs. How come you can't get it on your big-screen TV?

Some have tried. Apple TV and Akimbo's video player let viewers download content form the Web and play it back on a TV set, but both offered limited content. Sony manufactures an add-on for its Bravia series HDTV sets that provides access to a restricted number of Web sites. Nintendo's Wii game system can display some Web content, but image quality is poor and not all video formats are supported. Note that all of these systems require a person to hook up another device to his or her TV set. Internet company Yahoo! is trying a different tactic. In 2009 it demonstrated an Internet-enabled TV that used what the industry calls widgets, small programs that allow access to some Internet content such as news, weather, and sports.

What is lacking is a TV set with built-in Internet access that allows the consumer to surf the whole Web, not just a walled-off garden of preselected content. Everyone knows that such a device is inevitable, but so far not much progress has been made. Why the slow pace? Several reasons.

First, TV set manufacturers think that consumers don't want such a device. They point to a 2006 survey that found that 80 percent of U.S. households were not interested in a device that would display the Internet over their TV screens. But that was 2006, before YouTube and Hulu got to be so popular and thousands of movies and TV shows became available for viewing.

A second reason is cost. Set manufacturers are already looking at reduced profits. Adding Internet access would probably bump up the cost of a TV by at least $100–150. Increasing the price of a product in the midst of an economic slowdown doesn't make sense.

Third, there are technical problems. Slow Internet connections can be a problem. Plus, the Internet occasionally crashes, and while most people don't get too excited when that happens on their personal computers, what if the Internet went out in the middle of a blockbuster movie? Or during the Super Bowl?

Finally, some content providers are afraid that giving consumers unfettered access to the Internet and its available video options might lead them to give up their cable or satellite service since they could watch all their favorites online. Since cable and satellite systems charge for their content, this development would immediately hurt their bottom lines.

The issue here is the old chicken-and-egg dilemma. Consumers say they don't want an Internet-enabled TV set because they haven't seen one in action. But consumers can't see one in action because set manufacturers are unwilling to manufacture them because consumers say they don't want them. Eventually, however, someone will figure out a way around this dilemma, and the Internet-connected set will become a common item on TV showroom floors.

Amateur-Produced Content   Some amateur-produced content is repurposed, such as posting a homemade wedding or birthday party video on YouTube, but most "Joe-produced" content is original. One study indicated that about half of all online videos are amateur productions. The subject matter of these amateur clips is so diverse that it defies categorization. A quick scan of some of the more popular video-sharing sites reveals clips that range from serious to funny, from mundane to bizarre, and from intriguing to absolutely boring. In addition, they are almost always short clips, seldom more than 5 minutes long—"bite size entertainment," as suggested by a recent issue of *Wired*.

Homemade video, of course, is the ultimate example of user-generated content, and it has spawned a whole new Web industry—video sharing. Why is video sharing so popular? Three possible reasons: (1) We are inherently nosey and want to find out what's happening in other people's lives, (2) we have lots of free time, and (3) we all want our 15 minutes of fame.

YouTube, of course, is the best example of what can be done with user-generated content, but it has numerous competitors. Revver, for example, promises to share advertising revenue with its contributors. Google Video requires a verification process to make sure user-generated videos meet its legal and technical requirements. MySpace makes it easy to add a video to a person's profile. Jumpcut offers extensive video editing tools; Vimeo lets subscribers upload 250 megabytes of video every week. No matter how many video-sharing sites appear, there always seem to be videos to fill them up. No wonder *Time* magazine named the user-generating audience its 2006 Person of the Year. Not everybody, however, wants to post his or her videos along with everybody else's on these sites; some prefer a more limited approach. Porsche encourages its customers to post their homemade videos to its Porsche.magnify site. Even the New York Hamster House, a haven for homeless hamsters in New York City, has user-generated videos on its Web site.

Internet video can also be used for microcasting.

▲ Microcasting

When the Brookwood High School Marching Bronco Band of Snellville, Georgia, spent a few days at band camp in South Carolina, parents back in Georgia could check up on their progress thanks to a Web cam that sent video of their practices over the Internet. People who board their dogs at Camp BowWow can see how their pooches are doing via Web cam. As its name suggests, HighSchoolPlaybook.com aggregates amateur videos of high school sports. Relatives can't get to the wedding? Vowcast offers a live Webcast. Relatives can't get to the funeral? Around 60 funeral parlors offer live (?) Webcasts.

The word *broadcasting*, as first used with early radio and then TV, meant sending a message to a large, heterogeneous group of people. When format radio and cable TV networks came into being, the word *narrowcasting* was coined for targeting your message to appeal to a small, well-defined subsegment of the total audience. Top 40 radio stations, for example, narrowcast to 12- to 22-year-olds; ESPN, primarily to male sports fans; and C-SPAN, to aficionados of politics. Video sent over the Internet takes this process one step further by making possible **microcasting,** sending a message to a small group of interested people. This is another example of the "few-to-few" model of communication mentioned in Chapter 1.

Internet video is in the peculiar position of moving in two directions at once. At one end of the spectrum, it is becoming more like a traditional mass media channel as people turn to it to watch TV shows and Hollywood movies. But the Internet is moving in the other direction as well. The most successful applications on the Web are examples of improved forms of machine-assisted interpersonal communication: e-mail, social media such as Facebook and Twitter, instant messaging, peer-to-peer file sharing. Interestingly, these applications were created by end-users and not by big mass media companies. Microcasting is yet another example of this trend.

Before long, Internet-capable cell phones will be equipped with video cameras. When that happens, the possibilities for Web microcasts will become endless. Dad could microcast Scott's and Buffy's soccer games or band recitals to the grandparents in another state.

Fergerson Funeral Home microcasts funerals on the Web.

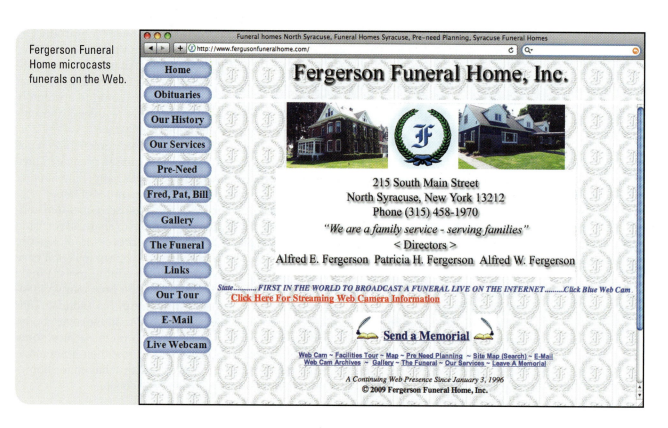

High schools could microcast the prom to interested parents. How about video of the local Little League games? Microcasting, of course, will raise all sorts of questions about privacy that will have to be resolved in the near future.

Feedback for Cable, Satellite, and Internet TV

Networks distributed by cable and satellite are measured by Nielsen Media Research. The techniques are the same as reported for broadcast TV in Chapter 10. A national sample using People Meters provides viewing data that are reported in terms of ratings and shares. Ratings for cable/satellite-distributed networks tend to be smaller than for broadcast networks. Nielsen also publishes a *Cable Network Audiences Composition Report* that provides more detailed information about audience demographics.

Gathering feedback on Internet video is a new and difficult area. The Nielsen company reports video viewing using its VideoCensus service, which combines panel data with usage data. Clients tag each of their videos with a sort of electronic watermark that allows Nielsen to track viewings. A second firm, comScore, tracks video viewing using a sample of about 2 million people worldwide who agree to install tracking software on their computers. The numbers from the two services sometimes differ widely.

▲ Audience

About 85 percent of American households get their television from either a cable or a satellite provider. Those who subscribe tend to be younger, have more children, and be more affluent than those who are not subscribers. Cable/satellite networks are more specialized than over-the-air networks, and their demographic makeup varies according to their target market. ESPN, for example, attracts a male audience; Oxygen, a female one. Nickelodeon aims for youngsters while CNN and MSNBC try for a more mature audience.

Some preliminary data about the audience for online video are available from Nielsen and comScore. About 150 million Americans watch online video. Men are more likely than women to be viewers, and men tend to watch short, amateur-produced videos while women watch more full, professionally produced episodes. Young people are more likely to watch than older people, with 18- to 24-year-olds watching the most. The two most preferred places to watch Web video are YouTube and the networks' Web sites. Although the time spent with online video is increasing, about 70 percent of all television viewing time is spent in front of a traditional TV set. Finally, the average time spent watching online video is about 10–20 minutes a day. (Compare this figure to the 4-hours-a-day average time spent watching conventional TV.)

Cable, Satellite, and Internet TV Industries

The cable and satellite industry is smaller than the broadcast TV industry, employing about 90,000 people. The number working in Internet television is difficult to determine. The job prospects in this area, particularly Internet video, seem more positive than in the other media we have discussed. Specialized cable/satellite channels continue to premiere, and they will need people in production, sales, marketing, performance, and public relations. And, as the chapter indicates, Internet TV is a big growth area.

The career outlook in the various media industries changes quickly. For a more current description of conditions in the cable/satellite Internet business and a more detailed look at career options, please consult the book's Web site: www.mhhe.com/dominick11e.

MAIN POINTS

- Cable TV began in the 1950s as a way of bringing TV signals to places that could not otherwise receive them.

- Cable TV reached maturity by the turn of the century and was facing competition from DBS satellite systems.

- The Telecommunications Act of 1996 permitted cable and telephone companies to compete with one another.

- Internet TV developed in the late 1990s and became more popular with the growth of broadband.

- Cable and satellite systems are structured differently from those of conventional TV.

- Cable television is dominated by large multiple system operators. Two companies, DirecTV and the Dish Network, are the leading DBS providers.

- Internet video can be categorized by source (professional or amateur) and content (original or repurposed).

- User-generated video, such as those on YouTube, has become extremely popular.

- Internet video sites make money by charging a fee for their content or by selling advertising.

- Nielsen provides rating data for cable/satellite networks. Ratings for online video-sharing sites are provided by companies that measure Internet usage.

QUESTIONS FOR REVIEW

1. What are the defining features of cable/satellite TV? Of Internet TV?

2. Who are the major owners of cable and DBS systems?

3. How does cable/satellite programming compare to traditional broadcast network programming?

4. Trace the structure of a cable system from head end to home.

5. How can online video sites make money?

QUESTIONS FOR CRITICAL THINKING

1. How, if at all, will VOD change the cable TV industry?

2. Have you ever posted a video online? Why? Have you ever looked at online videos? Why?

3. Google paid $1.65 billion for YouTube. Do you think Google will get its money back?

4. Why do you think many presidential candidates opted to make their announcements using online video as opposed to a press conference?

KEY TERMS

multiple system operators
  (MSOs) (p. 261)
direct-broadcast satellites
  (DBS) (p. 261)
voice-over-Internet protocol
  (VOIP) (p. 261)

Internet TV (p. 262)
buffering (p. 262)
podcast (p. 262)
head end (p. 266)
distribution system (p. 266)
house drop (p. 266)

carriage fee (p. 268)
video-on-demand (VOD) (p. 268)
geosynchronous satellite (p. 269)
encrypted (p. 269)
microcasting (p. 274)

INTERNET RESOURCES

Online Learning Center

On the Online Learning Center home page, www.mhhe.com/dominick11e, *select* Student Center *and then* Chapter 11.

1. Use the Learning Objectives, Chapter Outline, and Main Points sections to review this chapter.

2. Test your knowledge of the chapter using the multiple choice and flashcard features of the site.

3. Expand your knowledge of concepts and topics discussed in the chapter with additional Questions for Critical Thinking and Internet Exercises.

Surfing the Internet

http://wedcast.istreamplanet.com/lwc/whitechapel.asp
The Little White Wedding Chapel in Las Vegas has live and on-demand videos of its weddings.

www.blinkx.tv
Example of a video-sharing site that mixes professional and amateur content.

www.historychannel.com
Has more about history than it does about the cable network, but contains good examples of streaming video and interactivity.

www.multichannel.com
Multichannel News is the leading trade publication covering cable, satellite, and wireless companies.

www.ncta.com
Web site of the National Cable Television Association. Contains information about the latest issues facing the industry.

CHAPTER 12

The Internet and the World Wide Web

This chapter will prepare you to:

- describe how computers were invented

- explain how the Internet and the World Wide Web were developed

- understand the advantages of broadband Internet access

- realize the potential impact of Web 2.0

- recognize the economic impact of the Internet

- discuss the social concerns raised by the Internet

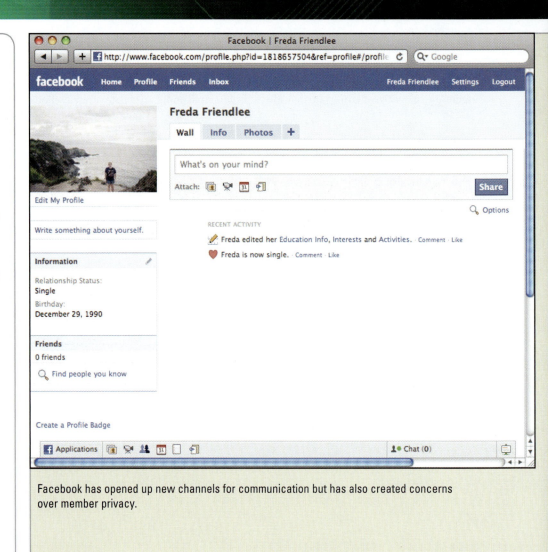

Facebook has opened up new channels for communication but has also created concerns over member privacy.

In late 2007, a young woman with a Facebook account was surprised when a friend who lived several states away congratulated her on her purchase of a new dress. Another woman was shocked to discover that her friends saw information about her video rentals at Blockbuster.

These were just two of the many consumers who were part of a Facebook advertising program called Beacon. The program sent data from external Web sites to Facebook, where the information could be shared with friends. There were 44 Web sites that initially signed on to the Beacon project including Blockbuster, Overstock.com, and Fandango. So anytime that a person bought a movie ticket through Fandango, the purchase would appear on the person's Facebook News Feed section.

The program used an opt-out arrangement, whereby default members were part of the program unless they requested to be left out. Opting out of the program was difficult and required a Facebook member to make four clicks before he or she could be totally removed from Beacon.

The program ran into immediate controversy. Members claimed it was an invasion of privacy and that the process of opting out was poorly explained and too complicated. One Web site organized a group to complain about the program; within a short time, the group had 70,000 members.

Opposition grew quickly and within a month's time Facebook CEO Mark Zuckerberg apologized for the program and announced that Beacon would become an opt-in program. Beacon's problems, however, did not go away. In 2008, Beacon participant Blockbuster became the target of a class-action lawsuit that charged the video company with violating a federal privacy law by being part of Beacon.

What can we learn about the Internet from this ill-fated venture? First, extremely popular Web sites such as Facebook are still trying to translate their popularity into profits. Facebook hoped to increase advertising income by offering marketers the kind of ads they most desire: ads targeted to people already interested in a product. If a woman bought an outfit from Overstock.com, Clarks might want to sell her some shoes to go with it.

Second, consumers are now a powerful force. The Internet and social networking sites such as Facebook make it easier for consumer groups to link together and make their complaints heard. Dell, Motrin, and other companies have found this out the hard way. Advertising expert Bob Garfield summed it up this way: "The herd will be heard."

Finally, Facebook and other sites illustrate how easily someone's privacy can be threatened by modern Internet technology. A person may never know what information a Web site may collect and with whom it is shared. Sites such as Facebook are all about sharing information, but users should make sure that they are the ones in charge of how that information is shared.

This chapter will examine the history, structure, economics, and social implications of this evolving medium.

A Brief History of the Computer

The earliest versions of the computer were basically adding machines designed to take the drudgery out of repetitive arithmetical calculations. In the 17th century, French mathematician and philosopher Blaise Pascal (a modern computer language was named for him) created the *arithmétique,* a machine the size of a shoebox filled with interconnected 10-toothed wheels that could add numbers up to one million. A few decades later, the German mathematician Gottfried Wilhelm von Leibniz explored the subject of binary arithmetic, a system with just two possible values, 0 and 1. The binary system is the one used by modern computers.

During the 19th century, English inventor Charles Babbage, working with Augusta Ada Byron, the daughter of Lord Byron, the English poet, worked out plans for an "analytical engine," a steam-powered device about the size of a football field, that would quickly perform complicated mathematical operations. The existing technology, however, was not sufficient to build this machine, and after 19 years of trying, Babbage and Byron gave up.

In America, Herman Hollerith developed a tabulating machine to help process data collected in the census of 1880. His machine used punched cards and electrical circuits to do calculations, and it worked so well that businesses all over the country clamored for it, prompting him to start his own company, International Business Machines (IBM).

In 1940 a Harvard University mathematician, Howard Aiken, made the next major breakthrough when he created a digital computer—one that worked with binary numbers, 0 and 1, or in Aiken's case, switch closed or switch open. Aiken's computer, the Mark I, was 50 feet long and 8 feet tall and had 750,000 parts. When it was running, it sounded like thousands of knitting needles clicking together. A few years later, researchers at the University of Pennsylvania constructed the first all-electronic computer, ENIAC. Although ENIAC was much faster than any previous mechanical computer, its size was a drawback—it stood two stories tall, weighed 30 tons, and used about 18,000 vacuum tubes.

SOUNDBYTE

Spam

Ever wonder why there is so much spam on the Internet? Because the more spam that is sent, the more likely the spammer will get a response. One study in 2008 found that spammers get only one response for every 12.5 million spam messages. In order to get 100 responses, a spammer would need to send more than a billion spam e-mails.

ENIAC, completed in the late 1940s, was the world's first general-purpose, digital, all-electronic computer. The device took up most of the space in a good-sized room. ENIAC is a far cry from today's laptop computers.

Most people think the Internet has an unlimited amount of space. That may be true on a theoretical level, but on a practical level we are running out of room. YouTube, high-definition TV over the Web, "cloud" computing (whereby individuals store information on a data center, such as Google, rather than their own computers), online gaming, and video conferencing are all huge users of network space.

The numbers are so large that they are difficult to comprehend. To start with, Internet traffic is measured in exabytes. An exabyte is a quintillion bytes (or a million trillion bytes or 1,000,000,000,000,000,000 bytes). Or, to put it another way, an exabyte is 50,000 times larger than the digitized version of the Library of Congress. In 2008, Internet traffic amounted to about 75 exabytes.

Let's say that Netflix converted its DVD-by-mail operation to high-definition TV downloads (the company is studying this option). Netflix ships about 1.8 million DVDs every day. If they converted to high-definition video downloads, it would amount to about 6 exabytes, or about 8 percent of the entire Internet in 2008. What would happen if all the video on YouTube was converted to high-def? That would mean about another 15–20 exabytes per year (more as the number of videos on YouTube keeps growing). In sum, just converting Netflix and YouTube to high-definition video would increase Internet traffic by about one-third. Add in the increase in traffic that would result if Hulu, TV.com, and the other video-sharing sites, as well as the social media sites, introduced high-def, and it's plain to see that the total traffic would spike. And this example just includes converting to high-definition video; it doesn't include the normal growth of the Internet as more people around the world gain access. Some estimate that by 2015, Internet traffic may reach more than one zettabyte (that's 1,000 exabytes).

The trouble is that the network may not be able to handle all that traffic. As a result, computer users may face "brownouts" when their machines access Web pages at a much slower pace, or they may encounter instances where their computers simply go offline for several minutes. Internet service companies are working hard to increase capacity, but for every increase that comes along there is some new application that uses more and more bandwidth.

The invention of the transistor in the 1950s led to new electronic computers that were smaller, cheaper, and easier to maintain. Integrated circuits made it possible for many transistors to be embedded in a tiny silicon chip, which paved the way for the microprocessor. These advances opened up new markets for computer manufacturers. In the late 1970s, personal computers (PCs), using packaged software, appeared in stores. Designed for home use, these computers were used primarily for word processing, financial management, and game playing.

A few years later, developments in hardware and software expanded the communication function of the computer. The **modem,** from *mod*ulate and *dem*odulate, enabled PCs to converse with one another and with larger computers located in other places over telephone lines. New communications software facilitated the development of local area networks (LANs), which linked several computers into a network. As miniaturization continued, laptop computers and wireless modems became more common.

The next major development in the continuing evolution of the computer will be a move from the office to the living room. Most families keep their computer in an office or den where they use it to read the latest news, check e-mail, manage their money, and do word processing. Computer companies, however, are creating new machines that will make the computer the centerpiece for home entertainment. These new entertainment PCs will allow consumers to record and play back TV shows, look at digital photos, play CDs and DVDs, and participate in online video games all on a large digital display that can double as a TV set. The initial price tag for this new generation of computers will be steep, but experts predict that sales will grow over time.

Laptop computers have become more popular, smaller, and more portable. By decade's end, annual sales of laptops exceeded 30 million. In 2008, Toshiba introduced a laptop that weighed only 2.4 pounds. Netbooks, small laptop computers designed just for Internet access and basic functions, appeared in 2009 and cost only around $250 to $400.

The explosion in computer communication continues today. Every day, billions of pieces of electronic mail (e-mail) are carried over the Internet. Every night millions of individuals log on to social networking sites, check bulletin boards, shop, read the news, share video, and download music.

The Internet

The Internet is a network of computer networks. Think of it as a system that combines computers from all over the world into one big computer that you can operate from your own PC. Some computers are run by government agencies (like the National Aeronautics and Space Administration), some by universities, some by libraries, some by school systems, some by businesses, and so on. The connections among these networks can be ordinary phone lines, microwaves, fiber optic cables, or wires built specially for this purpose. A related example might be the phone system. When you call somebody in Cleveland, the call is routed through several different phone networks in different parts of the country. You really do not care what route it takes or what companies handle it as long as your call gets there. So, too, with the Internet. When you search for information, send e-mail, or chat online, several different networks may handle your messages. Just as there is no one phone company, there is also no one Internet company.

The Internet's seemingly chaotic structure arose from its somewhat fractured history. A little background will help to clarify.

▲ From ARPANET to Internet

Back in the early 1970s, when the Cold War was still raging, the U.S. Department of Defense was concerned about the vulnerability of its computer network to nuclear attack. The Pentagon did not want to lose all its computing and communication ability to one well-placed atomic bomb. Consequently, defense computer experts decentralized the whole system by creating an interconnected web of computer networks. The net was designed so that every computer could talk to every other computer. Information was bundled in a packet, called an Internet Protocol packet, which contained the destination address of the target computer. The computers themselves then figured out how to send the packet. Thus, if one portion of the network happened to be disabled, the rest of the network could still function normally. The system that the Pentagon eventually developed was called ARPANET.

At about the same time, companies developed software that enabled computers to be linked to local area networks (LANs) that also contained the Internet Protocol programs. Not surprisingly, many of these LANs were also connected to ARPANET, causing the network to grow even more.

The users of this early network were primarily scientists and computer experts, and most observers thought that it would continue to be of interest only to high-tech types. (The network was once uncharitably labeled a "Disneyland for geeks.") In the late 1980s, however, the National Science Foundation, whose own network was already connected to ARPANET, created supercomputing centers at U.S. universities. Since they were so expensive, only five could be built. This meant that they had to be shared and interconnected. The ARPANET seemed like the obvious choice for interconnection, but there were too many problems involved. Instead, the National Science Foundation built its own system using the Internet Protocol and hooked together chains of regional networks that were eventually linked to a supercomputer. Thus, the Internet, or Net, was born.

Now that students, scientists, government workers, and others had access to supercomputers, the amount of information at their disposal increased tremendously. The Internet also served as a communications link that enabled scientists from all over the country to share data. Doctors, lawyers, journalists, authors, and business owners recognized the potential of the Net, and traffic increased.

The Internet was still used by only a small fraction of computer owners. Three developments, however, contributed to a meteoric rise in the Internet's popularity.

The first was the development of the World Wide Web (WWW, or Web) in 1990. Engineers working at a physics laboratory in Switzerland created an interconnected set of computers on the Net that all used the same communications program. This program took advantage of **hypertext,** a navigational tool that linked one electronic document, either text or graphics, with another, thus creating a virtual web of pages. The Web started off as an electronic information resource for scientists but was quickly discovered and utilized by the entire Internet community. Any organization or individual could create a page on the Web as long as the person or organization used the communication rules developed in Switzerland. It was not long before conventional media companies, businesses, organizations, and individuals got involved with the Web. By 1998 it was estimated that there were more than a million Web sites in operation.

The second development made it easier for consumers to find what they were looking for on the Web. This happened in 1993 with the creation of user-friendly navigation tools that helped further spur the growth of the Web. The first of these **browsers,** called Mosaic, was able to retrieve data, determine what they were, and configure the data for display. Mosaic created a graphical display for users that simplified navigating the Internet. In 1994 one of the developers of Mosaic formed a commercial company that was eventually named Netscape. Software giant Microsoft introduced its own browser, Internet Explorer, a few years later.

The third development was the **search engine,** a utility that scans the Internet for terms selected by the user and displays the results according to some predetermined criterion, such as relevance. Some well-known search engines are Google and Yahoo!. These advances helped users make sense of the Internet and turned it into a useful information tool.

The mid-2000s saw the development of easy-to-use software programs that made it simple to upload content to the Internet. This encouraged the growth of blogs (see below), social networking sites, and video-sharing sites, all of which combined to make the Internet more popular than ever.

The first decade of the new century saw the Internet continue to grow at a fast pace. More Americans were accessing the Internet using high-speed broadband connections, and WiFi hot spots made the Net more mobile. As of 2009, about 70 percent of U.S. adults were Internet users. The average American was online more than 27 hours in a month and viewed more than 1,600 Web pages.

Web 2.0 became a common term as the Web became more interactive, with users uploading and sharing information. Video-sharing sites and social networking sites were the two hottest properties at decade's end. Big companies have acquired several popular Web destinations. MySpace was acquired by the News Corporation in 2005, and Google bought YouTube a year later. Obviously, the Internet has grown into a powerful mass communication medium.

Structure and Features of the Internet

As mentioned earlier, the Internet is a global network of computer networks. In more technical terms, this means that a group of two or more networks is electronically connected and able to communicate with one another. Together, they act as a single network. For this to work, however, the computers have to speak a common language. The common language, called a **protocol** by computer programmers, that was developed for the Internet is called the Transmission Control Protocol/Internet Protocol (TCP/IP). It is actually a set of protocols that govern how data travel from one machine to another over networks. IP is sort of like the address on an envelope. It tells a computer where to send a particular message. TCP breaks up the information into packets that can be transmitted efficiently and then reassembles them at their destination.

Individuals gain access to the Internet through an Internet service provider (ISP), a company that connects a subscriber to the Net and usually charges a fee (many companies, including some local phone and cable companies, function as ISPs). As of 2009, the biggest ISPs were AT&T and Comcast with about 15 million subscribers each.

Once connected to the Internet, an individual can make use of a variety of tools for information, entertainment, and communication. Three of the more popular applications are (1) e-mail, (2) newsgroups, and (3) the World Wide Web.

▲ E-Mail

Millions of people are connected to the Internet, and you can send mail to one of them or to many of them. **E-mail** works on the client/server arrangement. To send and read e-mail, users (clients) must access another computer (the server), where their mailbox resides. E-mail messages are not limited to text. Attachments, such as graphics or spread-sheets, can also be sent.

E-mail is usually fast, cheap, and reliable. It is the most widely used Internet resource. In 2008, more than 50 trillion e-mail messages moved through the Net.

E-mail is helpful, but it also has some drawbacks. First, it is not as formal as a printed letter, so there may be some tasks for which it is inappropriate (like telling someone he or she has been fired). Second, e-mail is not as private as a letter in an envelope. Your message may travel through several computers where others might have access to it. At some companies employee e-mail might also be available to management. Third, e-mail comes with the ever-present nuisance called **spam.** Spam, the cyber equivalent of junk mail, includes unsolicited messages touting low mortgage rates, porno sites, and miracle cures; clogs up people's mailboxes; and takes time to delete. Spam is on the increase; the Internet carries more spam messages than legitimate e-mail. If that were not bad enough, about one in every 200 spam messages contains a virus. Fourth, there is the problem of information overload. In many businesses, memos that used to go to a small group of people now get sent to everybody, and every decision—no matter how small—gets circulated via e-mail. As a result, the average worker at a Fortune 500 company sends and receives nearly 200 messages every day, taking up a big chunk of the workday.

▲ Newsgroups

Newsgroups are collections of electronic bulletin boards, arranged according to topic, where people can read and post messages. Some newsgroups are devoted to current events, but the *news* in *newsgroups* refers to topical discussion groups, not news in the tra-ditional sense. The information or "articles" that make up the news are written by people interested in the topic. Others can read the articles and comment on them. The news-groups exist on a special network called Usenet, one component of the Internet. There are more than 40,000 different newsgroups, with topics ranging from the highly intellectual to the downright weird.

▲ World Wide Web

As mentioned earlier, the **World Wide Web (WWW)** is a network of information sources incorporating hypertext that allows the user to link one piece of information to another. Note that the Web is *part* of the Internet; the two terms are not synonymous. The Web is non-linear. This means that the user does not have to follow a hierarchical path from one piece of information to another. The user can jump from the middle of one document into the middle of another. In addition, the Web incorporates text, graphics, sound, and motion.

Some terminology might be useful at this point. The structure of the Web is based on the Web server, a computer connected to the Internet that facilitates the transfer of hyper-text pages. One server can hold thousands of hypertext pages. A **Web site** is a complete set of hypertext pages linked to each other that contains information about a common topic.

In late 2008, a Florida teenager televised his own suicide over the Internet. The teenager had announced his intention to commit suicide earlier that day in an online forum and linked his Web cam to Justin.tv, a live video-streaming Web site. Estimates vary, but at least a couple hundred people watched the teen take an overdose of drugs and lie back on his bed. After several hours of viewing his motionless body, one of those watching the video feed finally called the police, who arrived on the scene too late to save his life.

This tragic episode is troubling enough, but the behavior of those who read the teen's blog and who watched the video is even more upsetting. Many egged him on and urged him to commit suicide. Some doubted he could do it and called him a coward if he didn't go through with it. Some were convinced that the whole thing was a fake and did nothing. After watching the teen's immobile body for several hours, bloggers speculated that they were seeing a still photo or maybe a recorded tape. Some failed to acknowledge that the scene was authentic even after police broke down the door and unsuccessfully tried to revive the teen. One blogged that the cops looked fake because they didn't have any handcuffs hanging from their belts.

Why does the Internet bring out the malice, cruelty, and cynicism in people? People on the Internet can hide behind a cloak of anonymity. It's easy to spew nastiness when you don't have to own up to your remarks. Anonymity breeds irresponsibility. Then, there is the herd instinct. When they act as part of a group, some people will do and say things that they never would do or say as an individual. Being part of a crowd makes it easy to avoid responsibility. Also, there is the well-documented bystander effect. People in a crowd are less likely to offer help in an emergency if other people are also present. The same phenomenon probably occurs online as well. Finally, there is a lack of connection on the Internet. The person in front of the Web cam can be seen as an object; there is no personal connection between viewer and subject. To many who watched this tragedy, it may have aroused as much emotional connection as a typical YouTube video.

In fairness, this was a complicated case. The teen was obviously suffering from mental problems and had threatened suicide before but never went through with it. Not everybody online egged him on; some took the teen seriously and tried to talk him out of it. Nonetheless, it does bring up the question of what are the ethical obligations of people who are part of forums or online social networks. As we shall see in Chapter 17, there is an ethical principle called the *categorical imperative* that seems to apply here. Simply put, the categorical imperative resembles what we generally call the *Golden Rule:* "Do unto others as you would have them do unto you."

If you were having psychological problems, how would you want others to respond? With jeers, taunts, and callousness? Or would you want them to be understanding and helpful? The same reasoning should apply online. All of us should feel a responsibility to others. If someone is talking about suicide, the matter should be treated seriously and with sympathy. Our obligations to other human beings do not change simply because we are online.

A **Web page** is a hypertext page that is contained within a Web site. The home page of a Web site is the entry or doorway to the site that might contain links to other pages or to various sections of the site.

The protocols for navigating the Web assign each Web page a uniform resource locator (URL) and an Internet address. URLs are structured as follows:

protocol://server.subdomain.top-level domain/directory/filename

For example, the URL for this book is:

http://www.mhhe.com/dominick11e

This means that the page is in the hypertext transfer protocol, the server is linked to the WWW, the subdomain name is *mhhe,* the top-level domain is *com,* and the directory name is dominick 11e.

Their tremendous variety makes it nearly impossible to categorize the types of sites on the Web, but we'll try anyway. Below is a list of some of the more popular types of Web sites:

- *Commercial sites* are maintained by various businesses in order to promote or sell their products. They may contain product descriptions, consumer information, advertising, special offers, and other material. Tide.com, for example, is the home of Tide detergent and ups.com is the home of United Parcel Service. Commercial sites typically end in .com.

- *Organizational sites* are created by many nonprofit groups whose main goal is to provide information to their members and to the general public. Some examples include the sites of the American Medical Association, the National Education Association, the American Association of Retired People, and UNESCO. Organizational sites typically end in .org.

- *Education sites* typically belong to colleges and universities. Harvard.edu and Stanford.edu are examples. Educational sites end in .edu.

- *Government sites,* as the name suggests, are restricted to government entities from the federal to the local level. Thus, USA.gov is the U.S. government's official Web site and Atlanta.gov is the official Web site of the city of Atlanta. Most but not all government sites end in .gov.

- *E-commerce sites* are designed to sell products or services directly from a Web site. Examples are Amazon.com, Overstock.com, and Fandango.com.

- *Personal sites* include information about a person, family, or small group. Genealogy pages, personal pages, blogs, and many other kinds of sites would fall into this category.

- *News and information sites* might be specific in focus—such as globalwood.org with news about the lumber industry and perezhilton.com with entertainment news—or more general, such as CNN.com or abcnews.go.com.

- *Entertainment sites* provide pleasure and amusement. There are a huge number of these sites including hulu.com, youtube.com, jokes.com, and collegehumor.com.

- *Social networking sites* are places such as MySpace, Facebook, LinkedIn, and Twitter where people link up with friends and share information.

- *Search engine sites* display lists of sites related to a user's search term. Google, Yahoo!, MSN, and several others are popular search engines.

- All the other sites that don't fit neatly into one of the above categories.

Many Web sites function as **portals.** A portal, as the name suggests, is an entryway, the first page a person looks at before zooming off into the Web. The strategy behind a successful portal is to offer visitors useful information, such as news headlines, weather, stock information, and bargains, so that they do not go looking for these items at some other site. The longer a person stays at the portal, the greater the chance that she or he might see some of the advertising on the site. Some of the best-known portals are those provided by Yahoo!, Excite, MSNBC, and AOL.

How big is the World Wide Web? The answer is hard to come by because the Web grows every day. As of 2009, the search engine Google estimated that there were more than a trillion unique pages on the Web. However, although it is called the *World Wide Web,* it is primarily a Web for industrialized nations. About 85 percent of the pages on the Web are in English, Japanese, French, or German.

The Evolving Internet

The Internet changes so fast that it is hard to predict its future. Nonetheless, here are several trends that most experts agree will significantly affect the Net in the next few years.

▲ Broadband

Broadband refers to any of the several ways to connect to the Internet that carry information many times faster than conventional dial-up modems. The tremendous gain in speed makes it possible to send huge files in much less time. Downloading a typical music file might take more than half an hour with a dial-up modem but only a minute or so with a broadband connection. In addition, broadband makes it practical to send video over the Internet.

Consumers can access broadband through a satellite modem, a cable modem, or a digital subscriber line (DSL) through their telephone. All three methods are more costly than a dial-up connection, averaging anywhere from $50 to $75 per month.

Technology experts have touted broadband for many years as the wave of the Internet future. In addition to facilitating high-speed Internet access, broadband makes possible many other desirable things, including video-on-demand, interactive television, live streaming video, and downloadable movies.

Thanks to increased marketing efforts and special pricing plans, the number of broadband subscribers has increased over the past few years. At the beginning of 2010, about 90 percent of U.S. households had a broadband connection. Nonetheless, the United States lags behind several other countries in broadband penetration. South Korea, for example, has 93 percent of its subscribers connected to broadband.

▲ Going Mobile: The Wireless Web

Wireless technology will become more and more common during the next decade. There were more than 20 million laptop computers with wireless Net access in 2008, and thanks to the iPhone and other smartphones, more than 42 million people used their cell phone to connect to the Internet. Easier-to-use interfaces and faster networks will probably increase this number in the near future. Fairly soon, the Internet will be available everywhere.

What makes all of this possible is the development of **wireless fidelity,** or **WiFi,** technology. WiFi uses low-power radio signals to connect devices to one another and to the Internet. A base station serves as a transmitter, and computers and cell phone customers can use special hardware and software to hook into the system.

Many WiFi public access locations or "hot spots" have sprung up all over the country—in airport waiting rooms, cafes, and even parks. People who frequent these hot spots can link up with the Internet at no cost. Experts estimate that there are about 100,000 hot spots across the globe.

As mentioned in Chapter 1, mobility is one of the emerging characteristics of modern mass communication. WiFi was the first step in that direction for the Internet. The next step will be **WiMax,** a technology that will bring wireless Internet access to entire metropolitan areas. WiMax works a lot like WiFi, but instead of a short range of 200 feet or so, WiMax permits access across a range of approximately 10 miles. This means an individual could log onto the Net while riding on a commuter train or in the back seat of a car. Wireless companies hope that eventually the WiMax network will be as pervasive as today's cell phone net.

▲ Web 2.0

The growing pervasiveness of broadband made Web 2.0 possible. **Web 2.0** is a label given to the developing Internet and the new, interactive ways that people are putting it to use. It's an inchoate term, capable of many interpretations, but generally referring to a second generation of Web services, characterized by collaboration and sharing, such as social networking sites (like Facebook), user-generated sites (such as YouTube), and group effort sites (such as Wikipedia).

As mentioned in Chapter 1, whereas the first-generation Web was a place where users generally consumed content, Web 2.0 is a place where users generate and share content. Whereas Web 1.0 was static, Web 2.0 is dynamic. With Web 1.0 the audience went to Web pages and looked at content provided by the Web site owner. For example, way back in the late 1990s, eons ago in Internet time, people constructed personal pages on the Web. Visitors could read something about the person who built the site and maybe even look at a few photos, but that was it. Today, people are more likely to have a page on Facebook or MySpace where they can still post basic information, but now they can join groups, send messages back and forth, check on each others' whereabouts and moods, submit and share videos, sell stuff, and link to other sites.

Web 2.0 has also acquired a more pecuniary aspect. Among investors and entrepreneurs, the term refers to a site that requires little risk and could bring huge rewards. Take Flickr.com, for example. With only 10 people on the payroll and the users providing the content, the site attracted millions of visitors. Not surprisingly, it was acquired by Yahoo! for around $40 million. Social networking site dodgeball.com, started by a couple of NYU students, was snapped up by Google. The growth of Web 2.0 has stimulated investment in Internet properties to such an extent that many fear it is creating another Internet "bubble," similar to the one that burst at the end of the 1990s during Web 1.0 and wiped out billions of dollars.

▲ Monetizing the Web

As we have already noted, there is no necessary connection between popularity and financial success. As new Web 2.0 sites attract big numbers of visitors, investors and Web site operators are interested in converting all of these visitors into some form of monetary reward. Hence the emergence of the rather clumsy term *monetizing*, the process of converting something to money. Some solutions are novel. My Second Life sells virtual real estate to real companies so that they can market their products in a virtual world. Shutterfly offers subscribers a chance to upload, edit, and share their photos and charges a small fee for prints. Others are more conventional. Facebook sells display advertising on its pages. Google sells sponsored links next to its search results (see the boxed insert "Counterfeit Clicks"). Hulu runs ads before its programs. YouTube does the same for some of its videos.

No matter what the technique, one thing is certain: Commercialization will continue to increase on the Internet. First, as big companies snap up promising Web 2.0 sites, they will be looking for ways to find a return on their investment. The folks at Yahoo! didn't pay $40 million for Flickr simply because they like to look at pictures. Second, as the traditional media continue to lose audience, advertisers and marketers are looking to the Net to increase the reach of their ads. Heinz, for example, sponsored a contest on YouTube with a $57,000 prize to the person who made the best TV commercial for its catsup. Even the mainstream media recognize the marketing potential of Web 2.0. The producers of the CBS series *How I Met Your Mother* posted a fake video on MySpace to promote an upcoming episode. The tactic worked as viewership among young adults increased by about a million.

S O U N D B Y T E

Even Better Than Cliff's Notes?

Don't have time to read all those novels for your English class? Never fear, the Web is here. Check out rinkworks.com and its Book-a-Minute link for a really bare-bones summary of a plot. For example, with apologies to Charlotte Brontë, here is *Jane Eyre*:

People are mean to Jane Eyre.

Edward:	I have a dark secret. Will you stay with me no matter what?
Jane Eyre:	Yes.
Edward:	I have a lunatic wife.
Jane Eyre:	Bye.

Jane Eyre leaves. Somebody dies. Jane Eyre returns.

Or how about Hemingway's *The Sun Also Rises*:

Stock Hemingway narrating character:	It was Europe after the war. We were depressed. We drank a lot. We were still depressed.

Not a book fan? Not to worry. The site also contains movie summaries, such as this one for *Citizen Kane*:

Orson Welles:	Rosebud. (dies)
Reporter:	What does it mean?
Everybody else:	We don't know.

Internet advertising is big business, generating more than $23 billion in 2008. One of the most common forms of Internet advertising is "pay per click." Whenever you do a search on Google, for example, on the right side of the results page, you will see a number of sponsored links to products or services related to what you are looking for. Search for "satellite radio," and you get nine sponsored links to places that sell satellite radio receivers and hardware. Google gets paid every time someone clicks on one of those links—hence pay per click.

On top of that, Google charges advertisers to feed their sponsored links to various Web sites. (The "Ads by Google" heading usually appears near such links.) These links might appear in blogs, on recipe sites, on the home pages of businesses, and so on. The advertisers also pay Google for each click on these sites. Google, in turn, shares that money with the publisher of the Web page (the blogger, recipe compiler, business owner, and so on).

This system has obvious benefits for advertisers, Web page publishers, consumers, and search engine companies, but it also creates tempting possibilities for abuse—such as "click fraud." Click fraud can work in two ways. The simplest is for a person to generate a lot of false clicks on a competitor's link. Suppose Bob and Barb sell toothbrushes. Barb pays Google $1 every time someone clicks on her sponsored links on a Google search results page. Bob buys a cheap online robot program that repeatedly clicks on Barb's link, costing her $1 each time. Pretty soon, Barb is paying a big chunk of her budget for fraudulent clicks.

The second way is more complicated but no less dishonest. Suppose Barb hires Google to place a sponsored link to her toothbrush site on relevant sites throughout the Web (oral hygiene sites, dental health sites, and so on). She pays Google $1 for every click on her links on these sites. Google passes 50 cents of this fee on to the Web page publisher (the oral hygiene site, dental health site, and so on). Now suppose Bob starts a bogus Web site called "Bob's Bright Smile Blog," and Google places Barb's sponsored link on Bob's blog. Bob next uses his online 'bot program to generate thousands of clicks on Barb's link on his Web site, thus defrauding Barb out of a lot of money.

How prevalent is this kind of fraud? It's hard to say. One 2006 report estimated that around 15 percent of all clicks are false. Google, Yahoo!, and other popular search engines are aware of these scams and have installed click fraud filters that look for patterns and delete phony clicks. Nonetheless, many advertisers claim that the big search engine companies aren't doing enough. Lane's Gifts and Collectibles, for instance, was part of a class action lawsuit that eventually resulted in Google agreeing to a $90-million settlement over charges of click fraud.

Marketing and advertising are even creeping into the blog world (see below). Authors of influential blogs in a certain area might get special treatment from marketers in return for a couple of favorable mentions about their product in the blog. Record companies give advance copies of new releases to music bloggers hoping for some positive comments. The producers of the CBS sitcom *The New Adventures of Old Christine*, a program that features motherhood as a theme, invited the authors of leading "mommy" blogs to the set of the program, where they visited with the stars and received free DVDs. It probably won't come as a surprise that the show got some positive mentions in the blogs.

▲ Blogs

Blog is short for "web log." Blogs are journals in which people write about whatever they want: news, politics, sports, music, movies, quilting, and so on. Blogs are another manifestation of Web 2.0. Readers can post comments and engage in virtual conversations with the blog author. Blogs often contain links to other blogs, news reports, music clips, and video-sharing sites. The book you are reading has its own blog site. Check out http://dynamicsmasscomm.blogspot.com for updates, examples, and discussions of topics covered in this text.

Blogs got their start in the late 1990s but didn't become popular until free software programs made it easy for anybody to put a blog online. And a lot of people did. Technorati, a Web site that tracks these things, reports there were about 130 million blogs in 2009, and the "blogosphere" has been doubling every six months or so. Soon there will be more people writing blogs than reading them. (There is a well-known saying among bloggers: The readership of most blogs is exactly one.)

Mashable.com is one of the most popular blogs on the Web.

Thanks to several surveys, we know a bit about who blogs. North America accounts for about half of all bloggers and Europe for about one-fourth. Three out of four U.S. bloggers are college graduates and two-thirds are male. About half are younger than 30. Most bloggers report they don't blog to make money but to express themselves. That's probably a good thing since most blogs that accept ads from GoogleAdSense make only a couple of dollars a day.

Blogs are a vivid example of how the Internet can make anybody a mass communicator (see Chapter 1). Bloggers can become instant reporters, sharing text and pictures from anywhere in the world. Some of the most dramatic accounts of the Virginia Tech shooting were posted by bloggers.

Blogs have made their influence felt on the traditional media (bloggers generally refer to traditional media as MSM, or mainstream media). When CBS broadcast a report that raised questions about President George W. Bush's military service during the Vietnam era, bloggers questioned the authenticity of the documents that were at the heart of the story. CBS eventually conceded that it could not authenticate the documents and apologized for the report. Ironically, many of the MSM have started their own blogs.

The Internet and the blog have given a voice to those who would not otherwise be heard. As Dan Gillmor puts it in his book *We, the Media:*

> What . . . matters is the fact that people are having their say. This is one of the healthiest media developments in a long time. We are hearing new voices—not necessarily the voices of people who want to make a living by speaking out, but who want to say what they think. (p. 139)

The Economics of the Internet and the Web

We will now look at the general impact of the Internet on the national economy, examine the impact of e-commerce, and then focus on the finances of individual Web sites.

▲ The Internet and the National Economy

After a boom period from 1998 to mid-2000, Internet-related businesses hit hard times in the new century. At the beginning of 2001, it was estimated that stocks of Internet companies had lost more than $1.7 trillion in value. Many dot-com companies folded, and thousands of jobs were lost.

The bust, however, may have a silver lining. The dot-com companies that survived the fallout are those that have sound business plans and good cash flow. At the end of 2004, about 40 percent of publicly traded Internet companies were profitable, including such familiar companies as eBay, Expedia, and Yahoo!. As noted above, Web 2.0 has sparked a new wave of investments and speculation. More than $1.6 billion was invested in Web 2.0 Internet firms in 2006, and as an article in *Fortune* magazine proclaimed, "The Boom Is Back." Will the boom last? The growth of Internet companies such as Google and Yahoo! slowed during the recession at decade's end and e-commerce showed a slight decline, but overall the Internet sector was doing better than most media companies riding out the tough economic times.

More traditional brick-and-mortar stores, such as Wal-Mart and Home Depot, use the Internet as an additional revenue stream. Other corporations are turning to the Net as a business tool, using it to buy parts, handle customer relations, and facilitate worker teamwork. In short, the final economic impact of the Net is yet to be determined, but the long-term outlook seems positive.

▲ E-Commerce

E-commerce is the term used to describe the selling of goods, products, and services online. There are two kinds of e-commerce: (1) the better-known type in which companies sell directly to consumers and (2) a less-visible kind called *B2B* or *e-business* in which companies sell to each other. We will look at consumer e-commerce first.

Statistics reveal the scope of e-commerce. From being nonexistent in the early 1990s, global e-commerce came to account for approximately $250 billion in online spending in 2008. About 10 million consumers purchase something online every week. The products and services that account for most of e-commerce are travel, computer hardware and software, apparel, books, and music.

Impressive as these numbers might be, they pale in comparison to B2B e-commerce. In 2008, according to market research firm IDC, the B2B online market accounted for more than $2 trillion worldwide in sales. The Internet enables businesses to deal directly with one another, sometimes eliminating the middleperson (another example of disintermediation), making the process more efficient. Experts predict that B2B will save American businesses billions of dollars in the years to come.

Now let us take a more specific look at the financial side of individual Web sites.

One way to make money with a Web site is to sell merchandise online as does ecost.com.

▲ Web Site Economics

The tremendous variation in the kinds of people and organizations found on the Internet makes it hard to summarize its economic arrangements. Suffice it to say that the profit motive matters more to some than to others. A company that sells merchandise over the Internet is probably much more concerned with generating revenue than is a government agency or university that maintains a site as a service to its clients. Likewise, Uncle Max is probably not worried whether his blog ever generates a profit.

Cyrano de Bergerac, meet the Internet. You may remember the story of how Cyrano's friend Christian had Cyrano compose poetry for him so that Christian could court the fair Roxanne. Now it seems that lots of people on the Internet are using this same technique, but unlike Christian, they are doing it without the original author's permission or even knowledge.

In order to impress potential Roxannes, online Christians are cutting and pasting the profiles of online Cyranos. This plagiarism occurs most often on online dating sites and social networking sites such as MySpace. In one well-publicized case involving Match.com, more than 50 profiles had copied parts of a witty college-entrance essay that had been published in *Harper's* magazine. (A sample: "I participate in full-contact origami. Years ago I discovered the meaning of life but forgot to write it down.") A recent survey of online daters disclosed that 10 percent admitted to copying some or all of another person's profile.

Why do people copy? For some, it's probably laziness. It's much easier to cut and paste somebody else's clever remarks than think up your own. For others, it's the pressure to make themselves stand out. The pressure is so widespread that a new profession has sprung up: online dating coaches who will help write an attention-getting profile. One service even provides a model profile as a guide. Here's a sample line: "You know the woman who is the first person on the dance floor at every party. That's me." (This line was cut and pasted into more than 90 profiles.)

The Internet may also be to blame. It makes "borrowing" information ridiculously easy. Many college students have become adept at cutting information from online sources and pasting it into their papers. Moreover, some Internet dating guides seem to argue that there's nothing unethical about copying, and several Web sites offer humorous profiles that online daters can purchase. (Sample line: "I'd write more clever things but my train of thought has derailed.")

By the way, one of the online dating-coach sites is E-Cyrano.com. That seems highly appropriate.

The rest of this section examines those online operations for which making money is an important consideration. There are three basic ways to make a profit over the Internet.

The first is to create a site with content so compelling that people will pay to see it. One type of company that follows this model offers specialized information that has value for a large number of customers. The *Wall Street Journal*, one such example, charges a subscription fee to access its online edition. *Consumer Reports* offers access to its product evaluations for $26 a year. Web portals, such as Yahoo!, have also instituted charges for such services as game playing and Web hosting.

The other type of business that uses this pay-for-content model is pornography. At last count there were thousands of these sites, and some were among the most profitable on the Web. Sex sells, even on the Internet.

The second way to make money on the Net is to sell merchandise or services online. Amazon.com, the site that sells everything from laptops to lawn mowers, is the best example of this business model. Although many online retailers went bust in the early years of the new century, many of those that remain are profitable. For example, Amazon had a profit of about $475 million in 2008.

The third moneymaking method is for the site to sell advertising. Advertisers spent more than $23 billion in 2008 for online exposure. Online advertising can be broken down into three main categories: (1) paid search ads, (2) display ads, and (3) classified ads. Of these three, paid search ads (such as those sponsored links that show up on the right side of a Google search) account for the most revenue, followed by display ads (banner ads, pop-ups) and classifieds.

Usually the bigger the audience for a site the more advertising revenue generated, but there are limits. As Facebook, MySpace, and YouTube increase their penetration across the globe, they are discovering that bigger audiences mean more expenses without corresponding ad dollars. As more and more people in developing countries such as Turkey and India log on to video-sharing and social networking sites, Web companies have to provide more servers and more bandwidth in order to meet the demand. Advertisers, however, are less interested in reaching this audience, so ad revenue does not cover the increased costs. One video-sharing site, Veoh, recently blocked its service to Asia, Africa, and Latin America. MySpace and YouTube are both exploring ways to provide an alternative service to these areas that would use less bandwidth.

Suppose you sell shoelaces. Suppose further that you want to sell a lot of your shoelaces online. Suppose even further that you design an attractive, informative, and easy-to-use Web site that shows off your product in the best way possible. It's only a matter of time before people from all over the world are visiting your Web site and buying your shoelaces, right? Not exactly. Even the best-designed Web site is useless if people can't find it.

And how do people find it? Most use search engines like Google and Yahoo!. And the cold fact of the matter is, your site needs to show up near the top of a shoelace shopper's search results page if you expect to make any money.

Just to illustrate: A search for "shoelaces" on Google returned 1.85 million hits. If your Web site was number 678,095 in Google's results, it's unlikely that many people would find it. On the other hand, if you were number one (as was lacesforless.com in this example), you would probably do much better. (Statistics show that the first screen of a search results page accounts for 70 percent of all user clicks.) But what does it take to get a Web site into the top ranks? The answer to that question takes us into the rather arcane world of "search engine optimization," and a consideration of "white hat" versus "black hat" techniques raises ethical questions about online marketing and advertising.

Search engines such as Google and Yahoo! use an algorithm (a set of specific instructions) that determines how their results are ranked. "Spider bots" follow these complex and secret algorithms as they race around the Web at dizzying speed compiling their results for individual searches. If a person knew something about how these algorithms worked, it would be possible to design a Web page that would score high in the ultimate results. Enter a new professional: the search engine optimizer (SEO).

SEOs know that the factors that Google and other search engines use in their algorithms include the number of times search terms turn up in the content of the site, whether the search terms match the key words that describe the site, the number of links to the site, and the "credibility" of those linking sites. Armed with this knowledge, the SEOs redesign the site using "white hat" or legitimate methods, such as making everything on a page visible to the search engine. Product listings, for instance, are moved from an unsearched database to the site itself. Another white-hat technique is participating in a Web ring with other high-quality sites, thus increasing the number of links to the site. A third is making sure that each page has plenty of text that includes relevant terms (search engines don't pay much attention to pictures or graphics).

On the other hand, black-hat techniques are generally considered unethical. These might include "cloaking," creating two versions of a site, one that people see and a bogus site that is visible only to search engines that includes popular search terms, such as "sex." Another is using text containing popular search terms, such as "sex," that users can't see (the background and the foreground colors are the same) but that are visible to spider bots. Yet another is "link farming," using software that automatically generates a huge number of pages with links back to the original site. There are even illegal software programs that can forcibly inject links into sites that search engines score as more credible (such as universities).

Naturally, Google, Yahoo!, and the other search engines are well aware of these scams and do their best to minimize the rigged rankings that result from black-hat techniques. Companies that get caught can have their sites delisted from search results. In 2006, for example, Google accused automaker BMW of using the cloaking technique to enhance its search rankings and dropped the company from its results until the offending procedure was removed. Nonetheless, as revenues from Internet search marketing continue to increase, the struggle between the black hats and the white hats will no doubt continue.

Display ads are becoming more sophisticated and harder to avoid. Most now employ some form of "rich media," using color, motion, and clever layouts to attract attention. Video display ads are becoming more common, and many are displayed as soon as a user visits a Web site.

Well-known Web companies with Web sites that attract lots of visitors dominate online advertising revenue. Google, for example, accounted for about 69 percent of gross online revenue in 2008 while Yahoo! accounted for about 12 percent.

Of course, some Web sites use some combination of one or more of these techniques. For instance, eBay charges for its services, sells advertising, and markets its own customized merchandise.

Feedback for the Internet

As with the other industries mentioned in Part II, independent companies provide information about the Internet audience. Reliable data about audience size are important for advertisers who want to place banner ads on Web sites. The two companies that

Back in the good old days, when your author was in college, if a professor assigned a term paper it meant that students would spend a lot of time in the library, searching for sources, finding relevant information, evaluating its credibility, summarizing it on index cards, and finally organizing the information into a coherent paper. These days, alas, when a research paper is assigned, few students venture into the library. Why go, they ask, when everything you need is available on the Internet?

Most professors will probably agree that when it comes to higher education, the Internet has been a mixed blessing. On the plus side, the Net has made huge amounts of information readily accessible to students. Further, today's students are highly skilled in using the Net quickly to track down facts and figures. Web search engines also help students find many disparate sources of information and encourage them to make connections that were not easily seen before the advent of the Internet.

But there is a downside. My colleagues and I have had the following experience many times. After a research paper is assigned, one or two students will come to us and complain that they cannot find any information on the topic. When asked where they searched, they reply, "Online." When asked if they considered searching in the library, they almost always say no. For many students, if information is not online, it does not exist. Some students are amazed to discover that information specialists report that only about 15 percent of all information can be found online.

Then there is the problem of students cutting and pasting material from the Web into their own research papers. This situation was more severe a few years ago when many students simply downloaded huge chunks of information and pasted it verbatim into papers. Most now realize that professors have antiplagiarism software that can detect this wholesale borrowing. More common today is the practice of lifting a few sentences, changing a word here, cutting a word there, adding a couple of words at the end, and passing off the result as an original thought.

Perhaps most disturbing is the hopscotch nature of information gathering on the Web. So many possible sources show up that students simply jump from one to another, seldom spending much time digesting the contents of one article before going to the next. As a result, students have trouble constructing a valid argument from premise to conclusion and presenting a logical, coherent framework of supporting evidence. The facts are there, but there is not much of an indication that students have thought much about them.

Well, enough ranting. In closing, I would urge all who read this to go to the library and actually touch books. You might be surprised by how much you enjoy and get from the experience.

dominate the audience measurement field are comScore and Nielsen/NetRatings. Both organizations use a panel of consumers to generate their data. comScore samples about 2 million people in the United States, using software that works with a computer's operating system to monitor Internet activity at home and at work. Nielsen uses a similar setup with a sample of about 70,000 people. Both services issue periodic reports that list the most popular Web sites. For example, in March 2009, ComScore reported that Google, Yahoo!, Microsoft, Fox Interactive, and AOL were the parent companies of the top five Web sites.

▲ Audiences

More than a billion people worldwide now use the Internet. The Pew Foundation has sponsored a number of surveys that have focused on the Internet and the people who use it. As one of its reports put it, "At the infant stage, the Internet's user population was dominated by young, white men who had high incomes and plenty of education. As it passed into its childhood years in 1999 and 2000, the population went mainstream; women reached parity with men online, lots more minority families joined the party and more people with modest levels of income and education came online." In short, by 2009 the Internet population resembled the general population.

The Pew report calls the Internet the "new normal" in the American way of life. About two out of three adults use the Internet. On a typical day more than 85 million adults go online to use e-mail, get their news and weather, search for specific information, and simply browse for fun. Teenagers use the Internet even more, with about 8 out of 10 reporting that they go online on a regular basis. Moreover, the first "Internet generation" has come of age, and many of them can't recall what things were like before the Web became a reality.

comScore Inc. measures what Internet sites are most popular.

When people go online, here are the top five things that they do: (1) use e-mail, (2) obtain the latest news, (3) buy things, (4) pay bills, and (5) send instant messages. People also multitask. About 40 percent watch TV while online, another 23 percent listen to the radio.

Web 2.0 has opened up new possibilities. Blogging, sharing videos, social networking, rating products and services, playing online games, and similar activities will doubtless become more popular in the future.

The Social Implications of the Internet

Now that you know some details about the Internet, let's examine some of the social implications. Keep in mind, however, that the Internet is still evolving, and much has yet to be discovered about its impact on society. Nonetheless, a few consequences are already apparent.

▲ A New Model for News

To begin, the Internet supplements the traditional surveillance function of the mass media. As we have seen, when a news event happens, involved or interested parties can post blogs for others to read. Bloggers posted firsthand accounts of the postelection violence in Iran. In the aftermath of Operation Iraqi Freedom, bloggers provided details about life in Baghdad. This represents a shift in traditional journalism in which decisions are made by editors and flow from the top down. Now the news can start at the source and go "sideways," to all who are interested. As some experts have put it, traditional news used to be a lecture; now it's a conversation.

Blogs have questioned the accuracy of news stories in the traditional media and have exposed several instances of sloppy or inaccurate reporting. In response, the news media have attempted to make their techniques more transparent. In short, the Internet provides additional checks and balances to the traditional news media and makes them more accountable to the public.

The Internet has also expanded the interpretation function. Blogs, in particular, have made it possible for everyone to chime in with his or her opinion on news topics and controversial issues. Moreover, many politicians and prominent policymakers read blogs, magnifying their influence even more.

▲ Lack of Gatekeepers

As mentioned in Chapter 1, traditional mass media have a number of gatekeepers. On the Internet, however, there are none. This situation has several implications.

First, the risk of overloading the system with unwanted, trivial, worthless, or inconsequential messages is increased. Do we really need 130 million blogs? Suppose I posted this chapter on every active message board on the Internet and e-mailed it to everybody on every mailing list I could get. Suppose everybody did that with everything they thought was important. The system would get bogged down by all the excess traffic.

Second, gatekeepers also function as evaluators of information. Newspaper editors and television news directors consider the authenticity and credibility of potential news sources. Gatekeepers, however, are not infallible. As detailed in Chapter 13, many mistakes can slip through the gates of even the most established TV networks, newspapers, and magazines. Nevertheless, if the system works properly, bogus news tips, unsubstantiated rumors, and false information are filtered out before they are published or broadcast. Information obtained on the Internet, however, comes without a guarantee. Some of it might be accurate; some of it you must use at your own risk. For example, the UFO-related newsgroups contain several accounts of UFO sightings and abductions by aliens. How credible these reports are is anybody's guess.

Third, having no gatekeepers means having no censorship. The Internet is like a huge city. There are some streets where the whole family feels comfortable and other streets where you probably would not want to take your children.

Of course, there are some potential positive benefits from a lack of gatekeepers. Take blogs, for example. Topics that might be considered too controversial or unfavorable to the economic interests of traditional media can be publicized by bloggers. Further, blogs are not bound by the traditions of mainstream journalism. They can be partisan, in questionable taste, and totally individualistic. This makes for lively and exciting content.

▲ Information Overload

The Internet represents an information retrieval tool that is unparalleled—provided a person knows how to use and understand it. In the days before the Net, students doing research would have to look things up in a text, reference book, or encyclopedia—sources that had some recognized authority. Today, students can post a request for information with a relevant newsgroup or use a search engine to look for the topic. The credibility of responses on a newsgroup, however, is open to debate. A Web search indiscriminately displays a list of "sources," which may number in the millions. Every source on the screen seems to have the same credibility, even though some may be scientific documents and others comic books.

For example, while doing research, I used Google to look for references to "virtual reality." My search turned up 26,900,000 matches, including some that were about virtual reality games, quite a few that were XXX-rated, a large number from multimedia companies that produce virtual reality software, some that described technical background, and one about the use of virtual reality techniques for law enforcement and explosive ordnance training. (Of course, I might have narrowed my search using some advanced techniques, but the fact remains: There is so much on the Web that it is sometimes more overwhelming than useful.) Further, other than making a reasoned

---

guess from the titles, I had no clue as to which sources were more authoritative than the others. (Students doing a conventional search would also have to assess the credibility of their sources, but the profuseness of information and the sheer size of the Net make this extremely difficult to do.)

▲ Privacy Concerns

The Internet also raises a number of privacy concerns. Maintaining a person's privacy in the electronic age is not a new problem, but before the advent of the Internet, compiling a detailed dossier on someone required days or even weeks of searching through records scattered in dozens of places. Today, computerized databases enable a person to accomplish the same things with only a couple of clicks of a mouse. What follows are some illustrations of this growing problem:

- In 2007 department store owner TJX, parent company of T. J. Maxx and Marshall's, reported that hackers stole financial and personal information from at least 45.7 million credit and debit cards, data that could be used to steal the identities of customers.

- In 2009, a list of the names of 250 Los Angeles Police officers under investigation for alleged misconduct was mistakenly posted on the Internet.

- Some states have put the names and addresses of sex offenders on Web sites. Although the motives behind this practice may be understandable, the potential for harm due to incorrect or outdated information is substantial. In North Carolina a family was harassed because their address was listed online as the home of a known sex offender. The sex offender had actually moved away many months earlier, but the entry was never removed from the database. Many companies now charge as much as $150 to do online searches that will disclose someone's current address, Social Security number, bank account number, criminal record, and work history.

- Another growing concern is identity theft. A person can obtain someone's name, Social Security number, and date of birth from the Internet and can then apply for credit cards, get loans, and even commit crimes under another name. Even more unsettling is the fact that the victim may not even know what has been done in his or her name. In California a young man could not figure out why he was always turned down when he applied for retail jobs. He finally learned that someone had stolen his identity using the Internet and had been convicted of shoplifting. Whenever a potential employer ran a background check on the young man, the shoplifting conviction wrongly appeared on his record.

For the past few years, the government has wrestled with this privacy problem, and several bills have been introduced in state legislatures as well as the U.S. Congress that would restrict the availability of personal information. The issue is complicated because many are concerned that government regulation would be so rigid that legitimate searches for information would be difficult. Many prefer voluntary guidelines to laws.

▲ Escapism and Isolation

Finally, does the Internet detach people from other people? Many individuals already spend lots of time engaging in sending e-mail, instant messaging, online chatting, game playing, online shopping, updating their Facebook and Twitter pages, and maybe even cybersex. As more and more attractions go online, will we spend even more of our lives staring at computer screens? Some psychologists have identified a condition known as *Internet addiction,* similar to drug or alcohol addiction. Early studies of Internet users revealed that those who spent many hours online also showed signs of isolation and depression. Subsequent studies, however, have not found such a link, but these studies were done before social networking sites became popular.

The Future: The Evernet

Computers and computer chips keep shrinking. Before long, tiny computers will be part of our household appliances and maybe even our clothes. These devices will be so small that we probably will not even realize they are there. Moreover, experts predict that in the next 10 years advances in technology will enable these microcomputers to carry Web addresses and be connected continuously to the Internet. Imagine a furnace that automatically orders new filters over the Internet whenever it senses that the old ones are dirty. Imagine wearing a tiny computer that automatically unlocks your car, opens your garage door, pays your toll and parking fees, and reminds you that your tires need to be rotated. If you can imagine all of this, you have some idea what the **Evernet,** the successor to the Internet, will be like.

The Evernet (also called the Supranet or Internet II) will mark the convergence of wireless, broadband, and other devices, resulting in a person being connected continuously to the Internet anywhere using any information device. You will no longer have to "log on" to the Net; you and all of the other devices that have computer chips will be automatically "online" all the time and all connected to one another. The Evernet will merge the virtual world with the physical world.

The implications of the Evernet are staggering. A person could send or access information instantly from anywhere in the world. What does that mean for consumers? You could order anything from anywhere at any time. Impulse buying would take on a whole new meaning. Further, shoppers could access price comparison search engines and find out if there was a better deal across the street. What about the implications for business? A manufacturer's assembly lines could be connected to cash registers all over the country. When sales go up, the assembly line works overtime.

What about daily living? "Smart houses" that run themselves would be possible. A smart house would inform you about your daily appointments and chores, monitor security systems, schedule maintenance and repairs, order food when supplies were low, regulate temperature and lighting, start the coffee brewing, and even run a hot bath.

What about health? People wearing pacemakers could have their heart rate and other medical data transmitted continuously to their physicians. If something were amiss, a person would get a call from his or her doctor's computer: "Your blood pressure is too high. Are you taking your pills?"

Granted, all of this sounds a bit like science fiction, and there is always the possibility that new technology will not impress consumers. Nonetheless, just 40 years ago, the Internet also sounded a lot like science fiction.

 **CAREER OUTLOOK >>** ## The Internet and World Wide Web

The Internet and Web are still evolving, so it is difficult to define specific career paths. Some career opportunities that involve the Internet and traditional media have been discussed earlier, such as online journalism and online video; others such as online advertising and online public relations will be covered in later chapters.

The career outlook in the various media industries changes quickly. For a more current description of conditions in the Internet industry and a more detailed look at career options, please consult the book's Web site: www.mhhe.com/dominick11e.

MAIN POINTS

- The computer's ancestors were machines that performed mathematical calculations.

- By the 1970s personal computers using packaged software were on the market.

- The Internet is a network of computer networks. It was started by the U.S. Department of Defense and in its early years was used primarily by scientists. The current Internet started in the 1980s thanks to the efforts of the National Science Foundation.

- The main features of the Internet are e-mail, newsgroups, and the World Wide Web.

- The introduction of broadband Internet connections will encourage the growth of streaming video and microcasting.

- The Internet has had a beneficial impact on the national economy, and e-commerce continues to grow.

- Web 2.0 refers to the contemporary Internet and the new, interactive ways that people are using it.

- The Internet has created social concerns about lack of gatekeepers, information overload, lack of privacy, and isolation.

- The Evernet may be the successor to the Internet.

QUESTIONS FOR REVIEW

1. How did the Internet come into being?
2. Distinguish between a Web site, a Web page, and a portal.
3. What is Web 2.0? How will it affect your life?
4. What's the difference between e-commerce and B2B e-commerce?
5. What are some of the social implications of the Internet?

QUESTIONS FOR CRITICAL THINKING

1. Check out some of the blogs available on the Net. How many did you find useful?
2. Do a Web search for your name. See how much personal information you can find out about yourself on the Web. How easy was it for you to find the information? Could others have found it as well?
3. Do you read blogs? How influential are they among your friends?
4. Some critics (Roger Ebert among them) have suggested that the era of free information on the Internet is almost over and that ultimately we will pay for most of the content we get over the Net. Do you agree? Would you pay to access a search engine? Or a Web site such as CNN.com?
5. Speculate on some of the implications of the Evernet.

KEY TERMS

modem (p. 281)
hypertext (p. 283)
browsers (p. 283)
search engine (p. 283)
protocol (p. 283)
e-mail (p. 284)

spam (p. 284)
newsgroups (p. 284)
World Wide Web (WWW) (p. 284)
Web site (p. 284)
Web page (p. 285)
portals (p. 286)

broadband (p. 286)
wireless fidelity (WiFi) (p. 287)
WiMax (p. 287)
Web 2.0 (p. 287)
Evernet (p. 298)

INTERNET RESOURCES

Online Learning Center

On the Online Learning Center home page, www.mhhe.com/dominick11e, *select* Student Center *and then* Chapter 12.

1. Use the Learning Objectives, Chapter Outline, and Main Points sections to review this chapter.

2. Test your knowledge of the chapter using the multiple choice and flashcard features of the site.

3. Expand your knowledge of concepts and topics discussed in the chapter with additional Questions for Critical Thinking and Internet Exercises.

Surfing the Internet

www.isoc.org/internethistory/
An interactive history of the Internet provided by the Internet Society.

http://www.yahoo.com
The address of one of the many popular Web portals.

www.digitaltrends.com
A site that lists the basics of Web 2.0.

www.powerlineblog.com
One of the more influential politically oriented blogs on the Web.

www.secondlife.com
Get yourself an avatar and see what all the fuss is about.

www.technorati.com
Want to read a blog? Want to read 130 million? This is the site that tries to track them all.

www.twitter.com
What are you doing right now? Tell everybody in just 140 characters.

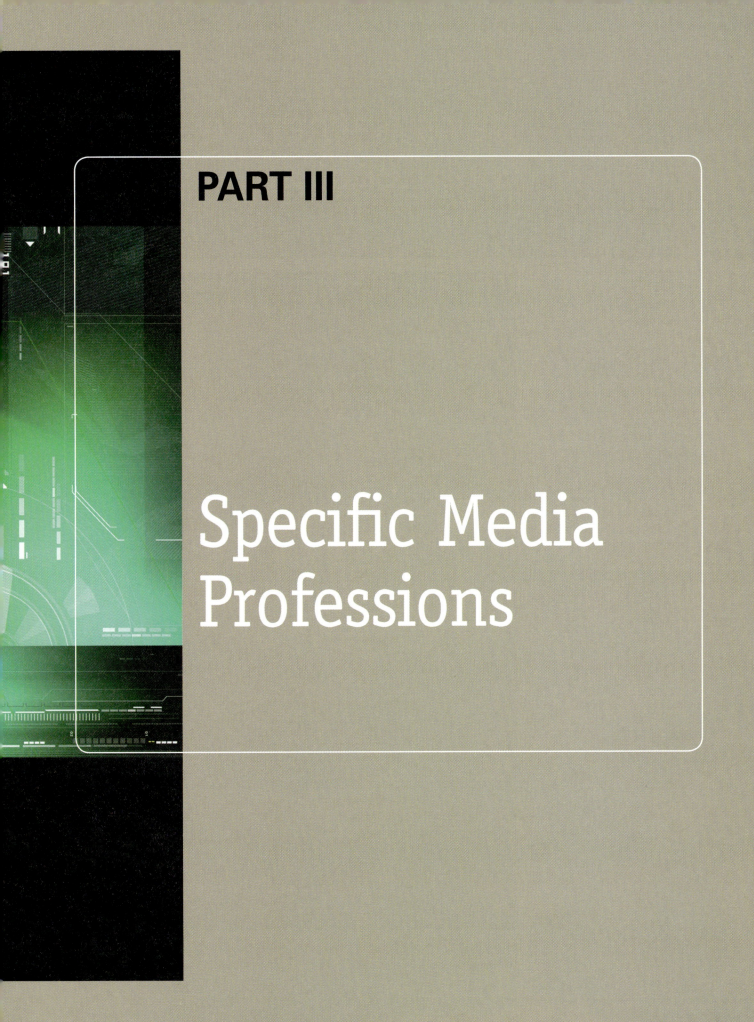

PART III

Specific Media Professions

CHAPTER 13

News Gathering and Reporting

This chapter will prepare you to:

- describe the qualities that characterize news

- identify the three main types of news stories

- understand how the digital revolution has affected news gathering, reporting, and the news business

- recognize the wire services that provide national and international news

- discuss the similarities of broadcast, print, and online journalism

- describe the changes in the news audience over the past several years

Despite strong ratings for Fox News, the total audience for television network news programs continues to decline.

As in the previous edition of this book, we will begin this chapter by examining the most recent report from the Project for Excellence in Journalism. The Project for Excellence in Journalism is sponsored by the prestigious Pew Research Center, which describes itself as "non partisan, non ideological and non political." It is a highly respected, authoritative source whose conclusions are not taken lightly. Here are some excerpts from its latest annual report on American journalism, "The State of the News Media 2009."

This is the sixth edition of our annual report on the State of the News Media in the United States.

It is also the bleakest. . . .

[I]t is now all but settled that advertising revenue—the model that financed journalism for the last century—will be inadequate to do so in this one. . . .

The problem facing American journalism is not fundamentally an audience problem or a credibility problem. It is a revenue problem—the decoupling . . . of advertising from news. . . .

Things are not looking up for the news media. This is not to say, however, that journalism and reporting are on the way out. Although the model and method of delivery may change, Americans still have an appetite for the news, and they now have more control than ever over what information they consume and how and where they consume it. This chapter will take a look at how the digital revolution has transformed the basic principles of journalism, the technology of news gathering, and how stories are reported.

President Barack Obama meets the press.

Deciding What Is News

Deciding what is newsworthy is not an exact science. News values are formed by tradition, organizational policy, and economics, and, more recently, by the digital revolution. Nonetheless, most journalists still agree that there are five core elements that characterize news-worthy events.

1. **Timeliness:** Put glibly, news is new. Yesterday's news is old news. A consumer who picks up the evening paper or turns on the after-noon news or visits a news Web site expects to be told what happened earlier that same day. News is perishable, and stale news is not interesting. The digital revolution has put an additional premium on timeliness. With Web sites that operate 24/7 and bloggers and Twitterers who provide firsthand information about an event minutes after it happens, news no longer has to wait for the morning edition or the evening newscast. As a result, the "shelf life" of news has become shorter.

2. **Proximity:** News happens close by. Readers and viewers want to learn about their neighborhood, town, or country. A train derailment in France, for example, is less likely to be reported than a similar derailment in the local train yard. News media are placing additional emphasis on this factor as they examine the potential of hyperlocal news (see below). Proximity, however, means more than a simple measure of distance. Psychological proximity is also important. Subway rid-ers in San Francisco might show interest in a story about rising vigilantism on the New York subways, even though the story is happening 3,000 miles away. Social media sites have given a new dimension to psychological proximity. A member of MySpace or Facebook can receive news feeds from a specific net-work of friends. In other words, a person can define those individuals with whom he or she feels a psychological proximity. Traditional news media can-not offer this degree of precision.

3. **Prominence:** The more important a person, the more valuable he or she is as a news source. Thus, activities of the president, other heads of state, and sports and entertainment figures attract tremendous media atten-tion. Americans apparently love celebrities and seldom tire of news about them. Even the infamous have news value. The past lives and recent exploits of many criminals are frequently given media coverage.

4. **Consequence:** Events that affect a great many people have built-in news value. The reason an increase in the price of gas is a big story is that it affects nearly everybody in the country. The Internet has given audience members more influence in determining the consequence of certain news items. News media monitor the "clickstream" to see what stories audi-ence members are choosing to read on their Web sites. Stories that rank high are apparently of importance to a great many people and assume added consequence. The negative aspect of this is that some stories that generate lots of clicks tend to be about the bizarre, the sensational, and the unusual rather than the serious and wind up with more coverage than they might otherwise have received. (How much news coverage did Jon and Kate get?)

MEDIA TALK

The Dumbing of America

Clip 3: 4 minutes 39 seconds
You can watch Clip 3 *on the Online Learning Center home page,* www.mhhe.com/dominick11e. *Select* Student Center *and then* Chapter 13. In this clip, authors Noah Oppenheim and Susan Jacoby discuss whether Americans are indeed dumber than in previous years and whether the current pop culture says it is okay to be clueless about current events. Do you feel that the media have made Americans dumber? If so, in what ways? Has increased technology use distracted you from picking up a book and reading? Do you think that most Americans feel it is cool to be clueless about current events? Does pop culture promote igno-rance of current events?

5. **Human interest:** These are stories that arouse some emotion in the audience—stories that are ironic, bizarre, uplifting, or dramatic. Typically, these items concern ordinary people who find themselves in circumstances with which the audience can identify. Thus, when a poor young mother finds a $10 bill and uses the money to buy a $1-million-winning lottery ticket, the story becomes newsworthy.

In addition to these five traditional elements of news value, economics plays a large role. First, some stories cost more to cover than others. It is cheaper to send a reporter or a camera crew to the city council meeting than to assign a team of reporters to investigate city council corruption. Some news operations might not be willing to pay the price for such a story. Conversely, after spending a large sum of money pursuing a story, the news organization might run it, even if it has little traditional news value, simply to justify its cost to management.

By the same token, the cost of new technology is reflected in the types of stories that are covered. When TV stations went to electronic news gathering (ENG), stories that could be covered live became more important. In fact, many organizations, conscious of the scheduling of TV news programs, planned their meetings and/or demonstrations during newscasts to enhance their chances of receiving TV coverage. Further, after helicopters became an expensive investment at many large TV stations, traffic jams, fires, beautiful sunsets, and other stories that lent themselves to airborne journalism suddenly became newsworthy.

The News Business

The business model that has historically supported the news media is a simple one: Advertising pays for most of the cost of gathering and distributing news. There is, however, no necessary connection between advertisers and news. Why should Target, AT&T, and other advertisers pay for a reporter to cover the Supreme Court? Note that this business model works as long as the news media draw the audiences that advertisers want to reach. For almost two centuries the model worked fine, but then the Internet came along. Advertisers discovered that they had other, more efficient ways to reach an audience, and the revenue started to flow away from the news media to the Web. This is what the "State of the News Media" report refers to as the "decoupling" of advertising from news. The revenue declines were considerable: Newspaper income down 23 percent in two years; newsmagazines folding or cutting back; even local TV news, a usually reliable income generator, saw revenue drop by 7 percent. Only the cable news networks were able to stay in the black, thanks to the 2008 elections. The traditional news media cut costs, reduced staff, and were able to shore up some of their losses from their online operations, but it was clear that revenue from their Internet properties would never cover the shortfall.

If that wasn't bad enough, the news media took another hit when the economy went into a recession. As the "State of the News Media" report put it: "Imagine someone about to begin physical therapy following a stroke, suddenly contracting a debilitating secondary illness." In the wake of all of this, the news media were looking for other sources of income and other business models. As we have seen in Chapter 4, newspapers were exploring a nonprofit ownership model and investigating micropayments for access to some of their content. Both television and print media were exploring charging for content downloaded to portable devices such as cell phones and Amazon's Kindle e-book reader.

What does the future hold for the news business? The conclusion drawn by the "State of the News Media" report is not optimistic:

> There are growing doubts within the business, indeed, about whether the generation in charge has the vision and the boldness to reinvent the industry. . . .
>
> Reinvention does not usually come from managers prudently charting course. It tends to come from risk takers trying the unreasonable, seeing what others cannot, imagining what is not there and creating it. We did not see much of it when times were better. Times are harder now.

As we saw in Chapter 2, surveillance is one of the functions performed by the mass media. The media alert us to threats, both short-term and long-term. It seems, however, that the media do a better job alerting the public to more immediate threats, such as an approaching hurricane, than to ones that take longer to unfold.

The financial crisis of 2007–2009 is a case in point. The sudden collapse of the housing market, the failure of huge financial institutions, and the worldwide plunge in stock prices seemed to catch Americans by surprise. Did the media, particularly the business media, fail in their watchdog role?

There are three main viewpoints when it comes to explaining the performance of the media during the recent crisis:

1. The media not only failed to report on the impending crisis, they also made it worse.

2. The media failed to report on the impending crisis, but the causes of the problem were so complex that no journalist should be expected to understand them, let alone report intelligently about them.

3. The media sounded the alert, but nobody listened to them.

Let's take a look at each of these assertions.

The media failed to alert us and made things worse. Critics charge that business coverage has too often taken on a pro-business spin. Newspapers and TV stations make money from advertising, and advertisers don't like bad publicity. Consequently, the pressure was on to report only the good and to ignore the bad. To take a specific example, real estate advertising contributes to a newspaper's bottom line (although not as much as it used to), and most Sunday editions have special real estate sections or pages. Not surprisingly, there were more stories written about the handsome profits made by people who were "flipping" houses and how real estate values kept skyrocketing than there were about what might happen if the bubble were to burst.

Second, the focus of business reporting has changed from consumers to investors. Stories about the positive earnings reports for the financial sector and glowing personality portraits of leading financial figures replaced investigative stories. A flattering profile of Merrill Lynch's CEO concluded that Merrill Lynch couldn't be luckier to have him. In 2007, the CEO was ousted and Merrill Lynch was saved from bankruptcy when it was acquired by Bank of America.

The media failed to alert us, but the problems were too complicated to understand. There is no doubt that the problems underlying the financial crisis were complicated. Intricate financial dealings and arcane investment instruments were certainly part of the predicament. Should we have expected journalists to unravel them for us? Proponents of this view note that federal regulatory bodies failed to predict the collapse. If economic experts couldn't figure out what's going on, why expect journalists, who, as a rule, have little formal training in economics, to figure it out? Further, the economic crisis came at a time when newspapers were cutting back on staff and resources. Covering the financial sector is a huge job and requires a commitment of time and money. Cutbacks in the newsroom may have reduced the number of veteran business journalists, making it harder for those who remained to make sense of the broader picture.

The media sounded the alert, but nobody listened. Several journalists would argue that media did an adequate job of surveillance. An article in the December 2008/January 2009 issue of the *American Journalism Review* summarizes this view: "Well before this year's economic collapse, business journalists shined a spotlight on serious problems in the U.S. economy. But regulators and members of the public didn't pay much attention." The article cites examples of stories in *Fortune* magazine, the *Wall Street Journal,* and the *New York Times* that warned of problems with derivatives, the precarious situation of mortgage lenders, and the housing bubble. But, says the article, no one wanted to hear negative news, particularly when the stock market was climbing and housing values were steadily increasing.

Don't blame the journalists for missing the problem. Blame the financial experts, the regulators, and the public for not listening. The article concludes that business journalists must better educate the public so that when journalists sound the danger signal for the next economic crisis they won't be ignored.

Did the media fail us? The issue is a complex one, and parts of all three perspectives expressed above are valid. There is little doubt that the media did not function as effectively as they might have. A poll of financial journalists found that two-thirds faulted the media for failing to recognize the magnitude of the problem. Too many stories focused on how people were making a quick buck.

Granted that the causes of the crisis were numerous and not easy to understand and explain. Granted also that journalists are not economics experts, but journalists are trained to find experts and to ask the right questions. Reporters should know enough about a topic to be able to dig beneath the surface and make sense of what they find. It's the fundamental responsibility of journalists to understand what they are covering.

Journalism education is also partly to blame. I know from experience that economics and finance courses are not popular among journalism students. Perhaps such specialized training should be required of more of our graduates.

Finally, it is true that many stories were written and aired that did warn of the crisis. But these alarms were probably lost in the far greater number of optimistic articles and glowing CEO portraits that also appeared. Moreover, it is not enough for the media to report two or three stories on an impending problem and then move on. To get the attention of policy makers and the general public, journalists must be persistent.

All in all, one would hope that the media learned lessons from the economic crisis that will help them better report the next one.

News Reporting in the Digital Age

To say that the digital revolution has prompted significant changes in news reporting is an understatement. We will discuss six: (1) increasing number of news sources, (2) blogs, (3) citizen journalism, (4) hyperlocal news, (5) converged journalists, and (6) new reporting tools.

▲ More Sources of News

The Internet has increased the number of available news sources. Audience members can examine (1) general news sites, such as CNN.com or usatoday.com, that offer video, text, and pictures in broad topic areas like world news, national news, technology, entertainment, and politics; (2) news aggregators, such as Google or Yahoo!, that offer a digest of news from other sources; (3) specialized news sites that offer content with a tight focus, such as ESPN for sports news and the *Wall Street Journal*'s Web site for financial news; and (4) blogs.

▲ Blogs

As mentioned above, first and foremost, blogs represent another source of news, one that is free from economic, corporate, political, or advertising considerations. Morsels of news of interest to a small number of people that would otherwise go unreported go into blogs. There are blogs devoted to political news, technology news, entertainment news, and countless other topics. In countries where the government exercises tight control over the media, blogs offer an alternative version of events.

Second, blogs have an agenda-setting effect. They can concentrate the attention of the traditional media on selected events and keep those events in the news cycle. CNN has a special reporter who monitors blogs to see what current issues are being discussed.

Third, blogs provide a check on the traditional media. For example, during the 2004 election campaign, bloggers called into question documents that CBS had publicized in a story about President George W. Bush's National Guard service. CBS ultimately admitted that it could not authenticate the documents. The established media are not used to this level of scrutiny (particularly from people the media regard as amateurs), and this generates a certain amount of friction between bloggers and traditional journalists.

Fourth, blogs represent an additional outlet for reporters to explain why they reported a story the way they did. Why did the reporter frame a story in a certain way? Why were some sources quoted and not others? Why did the reporter use an anonymous source? As Bill Kovach and Tim Rosenstiel, the authors of *The Elements of Journalism*, put it, the audience should be "given a chance to judge the principles by which journalists do their work." Some reporters have started blogs as a first step in this direction. CNN's

Anderson Cooper, for example, authors the 360 blog, where he provides background about stories he is working on.

Finally, blogs have made it possible for everybody to be a newsperson and have opened the way for what's being labeled *citizen journalism.*

▲ Citizen Journalism

As noted earlier, one of the first images of the U.S. Airways plane crash-landing in the Hudson River appeared on a witness's Twitter account. Some of the most spectacular images of wildfires threatening Myrtle Beach, South Carolina, were taken by local residents and posted on CNN's iReport Web site. The demonstrators in Iran made heavy use of YouTube, Twitter, and Facebook. These efforts are all part of a growing trend toward citizen journalism, whereby ordinary citizens become amateur reporters.

The trend was made possible by the development of easy-to-use digital and cell phone video cameras and high-speed Internet access. Its potential was first demonstrated in 2005 when cell phone images of the London Underground bombings and the Asian tsunami were prominently featured on television and in newspapers. More recently, the video of the Virginia Tech shootings was captured by cell phone cameras and shown numerous times.

Citizen journalism is a trend that is actively encouraged by the traditional news media. CNN has iReport, Fox News has uReport, CBS has EyeMobile, and MSNBC has Citizen Journalists. The *New York Times* recently launched several local-community citizen efforts. According to the Knight Citizen News Network, there are nearly 800 citizen media sites in the United States.

Of course, one of the reasons citizen journalism is popular among the mainstream news media is that it is free. In an industry faced with declining audiences and shrinking revenues, citizen input can be a way to cut costs and perhaps eliminate some personnel. Professional journalists, not surprisingly, look upon this trend with some concern. Some argue that these citizen reporters are not journalists at all, but merely witnesses who happen to be in the right place when news breaks out. Legitimate journalism requires balance, fairness, and a sense of ethics, traits that are not necessarily present in amateur reporters.

On the other hand, citizen journalism does empower the audience. News organizations no longer have a monopoly on what gets reported or how it's reported. For example, the official version of the execution of Saddam Hussein was contradicted by a cell phone video shot by someone on the scene.

Citizen journalists often report on news items of interest to a relatively small number of people, a trend labeled *hyperlocal news.*

▲ Hyperlocal News

There's an old maxim in journalism that says "all news is local," but these days it might better be rephrased as "a lot of news is hyperlocal." **Hyperlocal** is another one of those emerging terms that has a wide range of use. Generally, hyperlocal coverage concentrates on the stories, no matter how small, of a particular community or zip code or interest group in a defined geographic area. Most, but not all, hyperlocal coverage can be found on Web sites.

In Naples, Florida, for example, the Web site of the local paper carries detailed news about local real estate prices, restaurant critiques, and extensive information on high school athletics. Other sites might contain coverage of the neighborhood's Little League or soccer teams, rezoning proposals, business start-ups, local crime statistics, and yard sales. The publishers of hyperlocal news hope that the focus on topics that the traditional news media ignore will help them attract the audience that generally does not consume news. MySpace and Facebook are probably the ultimate examples of hyperlocal news. Visitors to these sites can find out news that is of interest to them and their friends.

Making money from hyperlocal coverage presents a challenge. Most Web sites obtain revenue by selling inexpensive ads to local merchants and entrepreneurs who can't afford to buy newspaper space or TV and radio time. A brief tour of some hyperlocal sites revealed ads for neighborhood kids who will work as pet sitters, after-school gymnastics programs, and magicians who perform at local birthday parties. Obviously, these ads may not represent a huge revenue stream, but the cost of hyperlocal news coverage tends to be small. Web sites are simple, without a lot of costly graphics, and much of the content on the site is generated by users.

Hyperlocal news sites may be the beneficiaries of the current crisis in the newspaper industry. As many newspapers stop publication or cut back on local coverage, consumers may turn to hyperlocal sites to fulfill their information needs. Patch.com, for example, offers hyperlocal coverage of communities in northern New Jersey, where the local paper, the *Record,* has made several cutbacks in staff.

The journalists who report hyperlocal news have to be skilled in several areas: writing, video, audio, and photography. In short, they provide yet another example of convergence.

▲ The Converged Journalist

As mentioned in Chapter 4, the converged reporter is one who can write stories for a print medium or a Web site, shoot and post photos online, and do video reports as well. In short, the print journalist and the video journalist have converged to produce the 21st-century version of the news correspondent. In fact, a couple of new terms have been coined to describe this new type of reporter. The **backpack journalist** is a "do-it-all" reporter who carries around a small digital camera, a laptop, and a satellite phone (presumably in a backpack) that enables her or him to produce stories for print, television, and online media. Next-generation reporters who eschew backpacks in favor of the automobile are called **mobile journalists,** or **mojos.** These are staff reporters or freelancers who work out of their cars, covering local news that is usually posted to a Web site or appears in a newspaper print edition.

Whether a traditional reporter or a mojo, journalists in the digital age have a powerful new tool in the Internet.

▲ New Tools

As pointed out by Randy Reddick and Elliot King in *The Online Journ@list,* in the past elite media organizations would send reporters to power centers and other locations where news usually happened to cover events. Today's reporter can sit at his or her desk and instantly access documents, databases, government records, and expert sources. In short, journalists can now bring to their desks information they previously went out to look for.

In order to make the most efficient use of this new tool, however, reporters must learn new skills. The 21st-century journalist must be able to perform Web searches, download data files and analyze them with spreadsheets, set up listservs, and use geographic mapping software. These skills are generally lumped under the term **computer-assisted reporting.**

Although the changes brought about by the move to digital media are extensive, there are still some constants, and we will examine them next.

Categories of News and Reporting

Generally, news can be broken down into three broad categories: (1) hard news, (2) features, or soft news, and (3) investigative reports.

▲ Hard News

Hard news stories make up the bulk of news reporting. They typically embody the first four of the five traditional news values discussed. Hard news consists of basic facts: who, what, when, where, how. It is news of important public events, such as government actions, international happenings, social conditions, the economy, crime, the environment, and science. Hard news has significance for large numbers of people. The front sections of a newspaper or newsmagazine and the lead stories of a radio or TV newscast are usually filled with hard news.

Print Media There is a standard technique used to report hard news. In the print media it is the traditional inverted pyramid form. The main facts of the story are delivered in the first sentence (called the *lead*) in an unvarnished, no-nonsense style. Less important facts come next, with the least important and most expendable facts at the end. This structure aids the reporter (who uses it to compose facts quickly), the editor (who can lop off the last few paragraphs of a story to make it fit the page without doing wholesale damage to the sense of the story), and the reader (who can tell at a glance if he or she is interested in all, some, or none of the story). This format has been criticized for being predictable and old-fashioned. More literary writing styles have been suggested as alternatives, but the inverted pyramid has survived.

Broadcast/Cable Media   In the broadcast/cable media, with the added considerations of limited time, sound, and video, broadcast reporting follows a square format. The information level stays about the same throughout the story. There is usually no time for the less important facts that would come in the last paragraphs of a newspaper story. TV and radio news stories use either a "hard" or a "soft" lead. A hard lead contains the most important information, the basic facts of the story—for example, "The city council has rejected a plan to build the Fifth Street overpass." A soft lead is used to get the viewers' attention; it may not convey much information: "That proposed Fifth Street overpass is in the news again." The lead is then supported by the body of the story, which introduces new information and amplifies the lead. The summation, the final few sentences in the report, can be used to personalize the main point ("This means that the price you pay for gasoline is likely to go up"), introduce another fact, or discuss future developments.

The writing style of broadcast news is completely different from that of print news: It is more informal, conversational, and simple. In addition, it is designed to complement sound bites (recorded comments of the newsmaker) or videotape segments.

Online Media   The writing style for online media is highly variable. Some newspaper sites may simply post the print version of the story with minor editing. Other sites might post the headline and a couple of sentences highlighting the main points of the story with a link that will take readers to the rest of the story. The newspaper inverted-pyramid style is generally used, and photos and video are integrated into the text. Links to other sites that contain supplemental information are often included. Television network and local-station Web sites generally have shorter stories written in the broadcast news style, with video clips that are related to the story.

▲ Soft News

Soft news, or features, covers a wide territory. The one thing that all soft news has in common is that it interests the audience. Features typically rely on human interest for their news value. They appeal to people's curiosity, sympathy, skepticism, or amazement. They can be about places, people, animals, topics, events, or products. Some stories that would be classified as soft news are the birth of a kangaroo at the local zoo, a personality sketch of a local resident who has a small part in an upcoming movie, a cook who moonlights as a stand-up comedian, and a teenager who mistakenly gets a tax refund check for $400,000 instead of $40.

Features are entertaining, and the audience likes them. Many television and print vehicles are based primarily on soft content (*Entertainment Tonight; E!,* the cable entertainment network; *People; Lifestyles of the Rich and Famous; Us* magazine; the "Life" section of *USA Today*). Even prime-time newsmagazines such as *60 Minutes* and *20/20* have substantial amounts of soft news. Likewise, the fiercely competitive early-morning network TV shows are turning more to soft news.

The techniques for reporting features are as varied as the features themselves. In the print media, features seldom follow the inverted-pyramid pattern. The main point of the feature is often withheld until the end, much like the punch line to a joke. Some features are written in chronological order. Others start with a shocking statement, such as "Your secrets just might kill you," and then proceed with an explanation: "If you have a medical problem, you should wear a Medic-Alert bracelet." Still other features are structured in the question-and-answer format.

TV features are more common than radio features. In some large TV markets, one or more reporters cover nothing but features. Almost all stations have a feature file where story ideas are catalogued. If a local station does not have the resources to produce local features, it can look to syndication companies that provide general-interest features for

Anderson Cooper, host of *AC360* on CNN, frequently presents investigative reports.

a fee. Broadcast features also use a variety of formats. Using humorous leads and delaying the main point until the end sometimes work well, a technique often used by Andy Rooney in his features for *60 Minutes.* Other times a simple narrative structure, used in everyday storytelling, is quite effective. The interview format is also popular, particularly when the feature is about a well-known personality.

There are dozens of Web sites, such as *Entertainment Weekly* and *E!* online, that specialize in soft news, particularly celebrity news. Other Web sites may concentrate on a specific topic, such as food (www .food411.com), fashion (www.zoozoom.com), or pets (www.dogster.com).

▲ Investigative Reports

Investigative reports unearth significant information about matters of public importance through the use of nonroutine information-gathering methods. Since the Watergate affair was uncovered by a pair of Washington, D.C., newspaper reporters, investigative reporting has been perceived as primarily concerned with exposing corruption in high places. This connotation is somewhat unfortunate for at least two reasons. In the first place, it encouraged a few short-sighted reporters to look upon themselves as self-appointed guardians of the public good and to indiscriminately pursue all public officials, sometimes using questionable techniques in the hope of uncovering some indiscretion. Much of this investigative journalism turned out to be insignificant. In the second place, this emphasis on exposing political corruption distracted attention from the fact that investigative reporting can concentrate on other topics and perform a valuable public service.

Investigative reports require a good deal of time and money. Because of this heavy investment, they are generally longer than the typical print or broadcast news item. Broadcast investigative reports are usually packaged in documentaries, or in 10- to 15-minute segments of a newsmagazine program (such as *Dateline NBC* or *60 Minutes*). Print investigative pieces are usually run as a series of articles.

Bloggers have also entered the realm of investigative journalism. Bloggers examined a photograph of an Israeli attack on Lebanon published by the Reuters news agency and found evidence that it had been doctored. Conservative blogger Michelle Malkin published an investigative report about the financing of Air America radio.

Some noteworthy examples of recent investigative reports include a 2008 Peabody Award–winning series by KMGH-TV about problems in the Denver Department of Human Services and a Pulitzer Prize–winning report by the *New York Times* concerning how retired generals working as radio and television analysts had ties to companies that benefited from the policies they defended.

The News Flow

As mentioned in Chapter 1, one of the characteristics of traditional mass communication is the presence of a large number of gatekeepers. This fact is seen in the gathering and reporting of news for conventional print and broadcast media. Reporting is a team effort, and quite a few members of the team serve as gatekeepers. Online reporting, in contrast, may have only one or a few gatekeepers. This section will first examine the news flow in the traditional print and broadcast media and then look at online media.

▲ Print Media

There are two main sources of news for a newspaper: staff reports and the wire services. Other, less important sources include feature syndicates and handouts and releases from various sources.

Let us first examine how news is gathered by newspaper personnel. The city editor is the captain of the news-reporting team. He or she assigns stories to reporters and supervises their work. There are two types of reporters: (1) Beat reporters cover some topics on a regular basis, such as the police beat or the city hall beat; and (2) general-assignment reporters cover whatever assignments come up. A typical day for the general-assignment reporter might consist of covering an auto accident, a speech by a visiting politician, and a rock concert. Stories from the reporters are passed along to the city editor, where they are approved and sent to the copy desk for further editing. The managing editor and assistant managing editor are also part of the news team. They are responsible for the overall daily preparation of the paper.

▲ Broadcast/Cable Media

The sources of news for the broadcast media are similar to those for the newspaper. Special wire services cater to TV and radio stations, and local reporters are assigned to cover nearby events. In addition, many broadcast newsrooms subscribe to syndicated news services or, if affiliated with a network, have access to the network's news feeds.

The broadcast newsroom is organized along different lines from its print counterpart. At the local station the news director is in charge of the overall news operation. In large stations most news directors spend their time on administrative work—personnel, budgets, equipment, and so on. In smaller stations most news directors perform other functions (such as being the anchorperson) as well. Next in command is the executive producer. This person supervises all the producers in the newsroom. Typically, producers are assigned to the early-morning, noon, evening, or late-night newscasts. In addition to looking after the other producers, the executive producer might produce the evening news, typically the station's most important program. Here are some of the things that an executive producer does:

1. Decide which stories are covered, who covers them, and how they are covered.
2. Decide the order in which stories appear in the newscast.
3. Determine the amount of time each story is given.
4. Write copy for some stories.
5. Integrate live reports into the newscasts.

The assignment editor, who assigns and monitors the activities of reporters, camera crews, and other people in the field, works closely with the news producer. Since speed is important in broadcast news, there is great pressure on the assignment editor to get the crews to the story in the shortest amount of time.

Then, of course, there are the "glamour" jobs—on-air reporters and anchors. Most reporters in broadcast news function as general-assignment reporters, although the large-market stations might have one or two regularly assigned to a beat, such as the entertainment scene. In many stations anchors occasionally do field reports, but most of the time they perform their work in the studio, preparing for the upcoming newscast. In addition to the people seen on camera, there are quite a few workers whom no one ever sees or hears. Photographers accompany reporters to shoot the video. Tape editors trim the footage into segments that fit within the time allotted to the story. Big stations also have newswriters and production assistants who pull slides and arrange other visuals needed during the newscast.

▲ Online Media

The news flow in an online news department is similar to that in the traditional media. Top executives decide how the site will be structured and how many specialty areas (such as sports, finance, weather, and entertainment) it will contain. Editors decide what content will be used on the Web site, which stories will have additional audio and video files, where the stories will be placed, and how often they will be updated. Reporters revise and update their stories when appropriate. Online news departments that are affiliated with a broadcast or cable network, such as CNN or MSNBC, will use the audio and video that appeared on the parent network but may edit it differently. Other stories may be rewritten from wire copy or from copy that has appeared in print or on the air. Not all online news, however, is recycled. Some online news staffs also employ reporters who do original reporting for the Web site.

The Wire Services

The next time you read your local newspaper, notice how many stories have the initials AP or UPI in the datelines. *AP* stands for Associated Press, and *UPI* for United Press International. These two organizations are called *wire services,* and together they provide you with much of the news about what is going on outside your local community.

In simplified form, here is how the wire services work: A correspondent covers a local news event, such as a fire. He or she reports the event to the bureau chief of the local wire service. If the bureau chief thinks the story is newsworthy enough, the chief will send it on to the state bureau to go out on the state or regional wire. The state bureau chief then decides whether to send it on for inclusion on the national wire. All in all, the wire services are the eyes and ears for local papers and broadcasting stations that cannot afford to have people stationed all over the country.

The AP has about 240 bureaus around the world. Members of the association pay for this service according to their size and circulation. A large paper, such as the *New York Times,* will pay more than a small-town paper. UPI also has dozens of domestic bureaus and a large number of foreign offices. As with the AP, member payment is based on the subscriber's size and audience.

In 2009 the AP had about 16,000 customers worldwide, including about 1,700 member newspapers. It serves about 5,000 radio and TV stations, plus more than 500 international broadcasters. The AP offers a wide range of services to its clients, encompassing a weather wire, a sports wire, and a financial wire along with a broadcast wire used by TV and radio stations.

The Associated Press has shifted its focus in recent years to supplying more content to cable TV and to the Web, including those sites that are in direct competition with newspapers, such as Yahoo! and Google. In fact, broadcasters and digital media have replaced newspapers as the source of most of AP's income. This shift has made many newspaper subscribers unhappy with the AP and has sparked efforts to create alternate sources of reporting. Eight large newspapers in Ohio formed the Ohio News Organization to share information without relying on the AP. Newspapers in Montana have done the same.

In the past few years, UPI has been plagued by financial difficulties. The company was bailed out of bankruptcy in 1992 when it was bought by the Middle Eastern Broadcasting Company, which, in turn, sold it to News World Communications (the publisher of the *Washington Times*) in 2000. As a result of its economic troubles, UPI restructured itself in 2003 to concentrate on two main products: (1) news commentary and analysis and (2) brief news stories tailored for wireless devices, such as PDAs and cell phones, or for Web sites.

AP and UPI are not without competition. Major newspapers, such as the *New York Times,* the *Los Angeles Times,* and the *Washington Post,* offer supplemental news stories generally not covered by other services. Some newspaper groups, such as Gannett, have their own wire services. There is competition overseas as well. The British-based Reuters agency has about 30 bureaus in North America. Agence-France-Presse is another formidable worldwide service.

Media Differences and Similarities in News Coverage

For many years, people argued about what type of journalism is better, print or broadcast. Proponents of print journalism contended that broadcast news was shallow and rarely scratched the service while print could handle in-depth and lengthy reports. Advocates of broadcast journalism pointed out that print media lacked the visual dimension and that print journalism was old-fashioned, slow, and dull.

This debate has subsided now that both newspapers and television emphasize their online versions. A quick glance at a newspaper Web site and a television Web site will reveal that they look pretty much alike. They both have headlines, story summaries, links to full stories, photos, and video. Consequently, it is probably more useful to concentrate on the similarities that cross media lines.

To begin, all professional journalists share the same basic values and journalistic principles.

Honesty in news reporting is crucial for television, online, and newspaper reporters. Stories must be as truthful as possible. The print or online journalist should not invent fictional characters or make up quotations and attribute them to news makers. Broadcast journalists should not stage news events or rearrange the questions and answers in a taped interview.

SOUNDBYTE

We Needed a Study to Tell Us That?

According to an experiment done by the European Society of Psychoanalysis and Psychodynamics, male viewers have trouble paying attention to the news when a pretty female anchor is on the screen. About 75 percent of the men couldn't remember a thing that was said during the first minute of the newscast because they were paying more attention to the anchor's good looks.

Newsatseven.com, a project of the Intelligent Information Laboratory at Northwestern University, is a virtual newscast hosted by avatars. The Web site scans the Web, collects news stories, and edits and formats them for its simulated anchors. The resulting newscast is a blend of images, video, and computer-generated speech.

A sample showed two rather young and hip 2-D anchor-avatars delivering reviews of the movie *Taken*. The text of the reviews was apparently lifted from other sites on the Web and represented a positive and a negative appraisal. As clips from the movie ran in the background, the two avatars disagreed and shared some back-and-forth banter.

The computer-generated speech was understandable but still lacked the natural intonations and shadings of natural talk. (You can probably find the segment on YouTube.) As of 2009, the site was temporarily disabled as its creators were putting together a new version that was scheduled to launch late in the year.

A grant from the National Science Foundation funded the development of the project, but how the site will generate income in the future is not clear.

Will News at Seven replace Katie Couric and the other network anchors? Probably not, but then again you don't have to pay the avatars million-dollar salaries.

Another shared value is accuracy. Checking facts takes time, but it is something that a professional reporter must do for every story.

A third common value is balance. Every story has two or more sides. All journalists must make sure that they do not publicize or promote just one of them. Information should be offered on all sides of a story.

Print, online, and broadcast reporters also share the value of objectivity. Objectivity means that the reporter tries to transmit the news untainted by conscious bias and without personal comment or coloration. Of course, complete and total objectivity is not possible because the process of reporting itself requires countless judgments, each influenced in some way by the reporter's value system. Nonetheless, journalists have traditionally respected the truth, refused to distort facts deliberately, and consciously detached themselves as much as possible from what they were reporting.

Finally, online, print, and broadcast reporters must maintain credibility with their audiences. The news media periodically undergo crises of confidence, during which people begin to doubt the integrity of journalists. Sometimes these crises occur because of excesses in reporting, as happened during the coverage of the death of Anna Nicole Smith in 2007. They may arise following disclosure of violations of journalistic values. Whenever public opinion polls reveal that the news media have slipped another notch or two in credibility, journalists try to regain the lost confidence. After much soul-searching, the crisis usually passes. Credibility, however, is not something that should be examined only during journalistic crises. If a reader or a viewer loses trust or stops believing what is being reported, the fundamental

Forest fires devastated California in 2009. Some images are replayed so often that it's difficult to forget them.

TABLE 13-1

News Audiences, 1980–2008

Year	Network Evening News (total ratings of ABC, NBC, CBS)	Newspapers' Total Weekday Circulation (millions)	Total Readership of Three Major Newsmagazines (millions)
1980	42	62	10.1
1990	30	62	9.8
2000	24	56	9.3
2008	16	48	7.9

contract between audience and reporter is undermined, and the news organization cannot survive. It matters little if the news organization is a newspaper, magazine, radio, online site, or TV station; its credibility is paramount to its viability.

Keep in mind that the above discussion refers to professional journalists. One of the problems with online citizen journalists is that a person is never sure if they subscribe to the same values as do professional reporters. Do citizen journalists check their facts and cross-validate sources? Do they provide the objective stance of a professional, or do they slant their reports because they are trying to promote a personal agenda? Are they aware of the ethics of the profession that prohibit doctored photographs and rearranged quotes? Citizen journalists are a valuable source of news but one that should be treated with caution.

Readership and Viewership

Table 13-1 does not paint a positive picture for the news media. The audience for network news, newspapers, and newsmagazines has been shrinking for the past 30 years. The same trend holds true for local TV news. The audience for cable news fluctuates significantly depending on the occurrence of major news events, but, on average, it too has declined. Further, the audience is getting older. The average age of the typical TV newscast viewer is around 60.

Where is the audience going? Some have dropped out entirely; many people report no interest in following the news. Others go online: On a typical day about 30 percent report visiting a traditional online news site such as MSNBC. Quite a few are looking for news on nontraditional sites, such as YouTube. Still others may get their news via cell phone.

The smaller the audience, of course, the smaller the revenue received from advertising and the smaller the bottom line. This occurrence has already had great impact on those who report the news. Newspapers and TV networks have cut personnel, closed bureaus, and cut back news-gathering costs.

Table 13-2 contains data from two recent Gallup polls about how Americans get their news. An examination of this table reinforces and extends the conclusions of Table 13-1: Only the Internet has shown on increase.

TABLE 13-2

Sources of News, 2002 and 2008

Source: Excerpted from Gallup polls, December 2008 and December 2002. Question was, "How often did you get your news from the following sources?" Numbers in the table are the percentages who answered, "Every day."

Site	2002	2008
Local TV news	57%	51%
Local newspapers	47	40
Cable news networks	41	40
Nightly network news	43	34
Morning network news	29	29
Public TV news	35	28
Radio talk shows	22	18
Internet	15	31
National Public Radio	22	18
National newspapers	11	9

A news council is an independent body composed of journalists and private citizens that unofficially hears and adjudicates disputes over press conduct. People and organizations who feel that they have been wronged by news coverage but lack the time, energy, and money to pursue a libel case turn to news councils to help set the record straight. Those who bring complaints before a news council waive the right to file a lawsuit. Staff members look into complaints, and the council holds hearings on those cases that raise significant issues. The council then votes on whether it thinks the complaint should be upheld. Councils have no legal power to enforce their decisions or to impose penalties. Their power stems from the publicity they bring to the case.

News councils are not a new idea. Wisconsin and Colorado had them; Minnesota and Hawaii still do. There was even a National News Council that operated from 1973 to 1984, but it was discontinued because of lack of money and lack of cooperation from influential media organizations. The idea of news councils resurfaced in 1997 when *60 Minutes* correspondent Mike Wallace suggested that the creation of a news council would help counter public skepticism and the negative feelings that members of the public have about the press. After the program was broadcast, residents from a number of states called the Minnesota News Council to ask how they could start their own councils. In mid-2000 a news council started operation in the state of Washington.

Most members of the news media do not share Wallace's enthusiasm for news councils. They make several arguments to support their view. The argument heard most often is that news councils are the first step toward government regulation. One of the reasons the *New York Times* refused to cooperate with the National News Council was its belief that the council would encourage an atmosphere of regulation in which government intervention might gain public support. Many journalists think that lawmakers would use the public complaints to justify more regulation of the press. A second argument is that news councils would discourage hard-hitting stories. Journalists might be fearful of being unfairly targeted and forced to defend their decisions in controversial stories.

If a council decision goes against a reporter, he or she might be afraid of doing any more such stories. Another argument contends that news councils substitute the judgments of people who do not know much about journalism for the judgments of professionals. How, ask the critics, can laypeople question the merits of a story when they do not know what went into producing it? In short, journalism should be left to the journalists. As one longtime journalist put it, "They have no damn business meddling in our business."

Supporters of the council idea first note that councils can prevent long and costly lawsuits. For example, they could give the principals in a defamation suit another forum in which to present their cases. Proponents also note that councils promote media fairness by making news outlets publicly accountable. Moreover, the councils give news media the chance to explain the reasons behind the choices they made and why they believe their decisions were proper. Such a discussion helps educate the public about some of the problems involved in the everyday practice of journalism and may give the public a greater appreciation for the profession.

Supporters also contend that the press sees no problems in holding up other professions to public scrutiny but is unwilling to subject itself to the same treatment. They note as well that there is wide public support for such an idea. Public opinion polls show that 85 percent of the general public likes the idea.

All things considered, the notion of a news council will be a hard sell to members of the news-gathering profession. Many media outlets are adamantly opposed to the notion. Journalists have never been leading supporters of self-criticism. As Edward R. Murrow once said, when it comes to criticism, "The press is not thin-skinned. It is no-skinned."

There are signs, however, that things may be changing. Although the *New York Times* is still not backing the idea of a news council, the *Times* did agree to appoint a "public editor," who will monitor performance at the paper and look into reader complaints. Moreover, blogs represent an open-to-all form of a news council that scrutinizes media stories and is quick to point out mistakes.

The audience is also becoming less likely to trust the news media. Surveys done by the Pew Research Center for the People and the Press revealed that credibility ratings for local TV news, broadcast news, and cable news had all declined from 2000 to 2008. The same trend showed up for local newspapers, national newspapers, and newsmagazines. All in all, the above data are not encouraging to those in the news-reporting profession.

News Gathering and Reporting

Job prospects for aspiring journalists are fairly bleak. Many news organizations are cutting back staff and reducing hiring. There are a couple of bright spots. Specialized news sources such as Bloomberg News have increased their number of employees in the last few years. Likewise, online journalism may be somewhat of a growth area.

The career outlook in the various media industries changes quickly. For a more current description of conditions in news gathering and reporting and a more detailed look at career options, please consult the book's Web site: www.mhhe.com/dominick11e.

MAIN POINTS

- The qualities that characterize news are timeliness, proximity, prominence, consequence, and human interest. Economics is also important.

- News media are searching for new business models.

- There are three main types of news stories: hard, soft, and investigative.

- The digital revolution has increased the number of available news sources, encouraged the growth of blogs, contributed to the rise of citizen journalism and hyperlocal news, and supplied new tools to reporters.

- The Associated Press and United Press International are two wire services that provide stories to print and broadcast journalists.

- Print, broadcast, and online journalism have their unique strengths and weaknesses.

- All forms of news media strive for credibility.

- Online news enables audience members to select from more news sources and customize their news.

- The audience for news has been declining across all media.

QUESTIONS FOR REVIEW

1. What are the characteristics that determine newsworthiness? Should others be added to the list?

2. What is the difference between hard and soft news? Is it possible to do a hard-news report on a soft-news topic, such as entertainment?

3. How does blogging differ from traditional print and broadcast reporting?

4. How is blogging similar to traditional print and broadcast reporting?

5. What is hyperlocal news?

QUESTIONS FOR CRITICAL THINKING

1. Should news be what the audience wants to know or what the audience needs to know? Who should decide?

2. Where do you get most of your news about what is going on in the world? Why?

3. What news medium is most believable? Print? TV? Online? Why?

4. Why is the audience for news getting smaller?

KEY TERMS

timeliness (p. 304)
proximity (p. 304)
prominence (p. 304)
consequence (p. 304)
human interest (p. 305)

hyperlocal (p. 308)
backpack journalist (p. 309)
mobile journalist (mojo) (p. 309)
computer-assisted reporting
  (CAR) (p. 310)

hard news (p. 310)
soft news (p. 311)
investigative reports (p. 312)

INTERNET RESOURCES

Online Learning Center

On the Online Learning Center home page, www.mhhe.com/dominick11e, *select* Student Center *and then* Chapter 13.

1. Use the Learning Objectives, Chapter Outline, and Main Points sections to review this chapter.

2. Test your knowledge of the chapter using the multiple choice and flashcard features of the site.

3. Expand your knowledge of concepts and topics discussed in the chapter with additional Questions for Critical Thinking and Internet Exercises.

Surfing the Internet

There are hundreds of sites that have a connection to journalism. Only a few are listed here.

www.aim.org
Site of the media watchdog group Accuracy in Media, which critiques the operation of the news media.

www.backfence.com
An example of a hyperlocal news site. Check out what's going on in 50 different communities.

www.cnn.com
CNN Interactive's site. A good example of an online news service. Contains international and national spot news plus links for political, scientific, health, travel, financial, and entertainment news.

www.freedomforum.org
The Freedom Forum is an organization dedicated to exploring and improving journalism.

www.newslink.org
Has links to other media sources as well as research tools.

www.ojr.org
Home of the *Online Journalism Review,* at the Annenberg School of Communications at the University of Southern California. The single best resource for information concerning online journalism.

www.powerlineblog.com
One of the better-known political blogs.

www.stateofthemedia.org/2009/
Read the entire report: "State of the News Media 2009."

CHAPTER 14

Public Relations

This chapter will prepare you to:

- distinguish among *public relations, publicity, press agentry,* and *advertising*

- understand the background of modern public relations

- recognize the impact of the Internet on public relations

- discuss the major areas in which public relations is practiced

- explain the steps involved in developing a public relations campaign

AIG CEO Edward Liddy testifies before Congress. AIG was severely criticized for paying huge bonuses after receiving federal bailout money.

First, some background.

American International Group (AIG) is one of the world's largest insurance firms providing property, life, and auto insurance. In 2006 its total net income was more than $14 billion and it had $1 trillion in assets. Then AIG got involved in a complex form of insurance called a credit default swap in which it offered insurance against losses if loan holders failed to pay back their debts. To make a long, complicated story short, when the housing market imploded and home owners began to default on their mortgages, AIG found itself in severe financial trouble. The U.S. government, however, decided that an AIG failure would seriously damage the economy and bailed out the company with $85 billion of taxpayer money.

What happened next is a classic example of a public relations disaster that illustrates several lessons about public relations in the digital age. Just a few days after the bailout, AIG executives and top salespeople were unwinding at a lavish resort complete with spa treatments, golf outings, and sumptuous catered banquets. Total cost: more than $400,000. When news of the outing broke, AIG was blasted by the news media, commentators, and bloggers all over the world. Even *Saturday Night Live* got into the act during its Weekend Update segment when one of the anchors chided AIG by saying, "Even the mafia knows not to spend the money that soon after a heist." Note that (1) the AIG outing did not include anybody from the AIG division that caused its problems; (2) the outing was planned long in advance of the bailout; (3) such events are a common means of rewarding outstanding employees; and (4) in the long run such retreats are profitable for the company because they generate motivation and increase productivity. Note also that all of those things didn't matter to the general public and members of Congress who lambasted AIG for wasting the taxpayers' money. Lesson One: In troubled times, facts aren't as important as appearances and perceptions.

AIG apparently didn't get the message. As the company was asking for more bailout money, AIG executives were gathering at a luxury resort in Phoenix. This time the company apparently tried to hide its involvement. No AIG logos or signs were evident, and resort employees were told not to mention AIG. Nonetheless, a local TV station heard about the event and secretly taped executives lounging around the pool and enjoying expensive meals. When a reporter for the local station confronted executives at the airport after the meeting, the executives refused to comment and escaped the reporter by entering the first-class check-in area. The story prompted yet another wave of strong criticism. Lesson Two: In an age of bloggers, news tiplines, and cell phone cameras, everybody is a reporter. Companies will have a difficult time attempting to fly under the radar or to cover things up. The new watchword in public relations is transparency.

AIG then hired PR firm Burson-Marsteller to help with its problem. Amid reports that the insurance company might be paying the PR firm as much as $100,000 a month, AIG was criticized for wasting more money on a public relations campaign. Lesson Three: In the age of the Internet, trying to play catch-up when a crisis occurs is difficult. Companies need to have a public relations plan already prepared to handle crises.

Apparently AIG still hadn't learned its lesson. In 2009 it was discovered that the company planned to pay executives $165 million in bonuses. The news was met with public outrage and increased pressure from the government to reduce the payouts. Congress was so incensed that it introduced a bill to ban all bonuses at companies that received bailout funds.

Luckily, AIG's problems may not be typical of those faced by public relations firms and corporate public relations departments, but they do indicate the tremendous importance that public relations can play in the corporate arena, especially in a time of economic crisis when business as usual no longer applies. The rest of this chapter examines the history, structure, and economics of public relations as it is transformed by the digital age.

Defining Public Relations

Before we investigate what public relations is, it may be helpful to compare it with other facets of mass communication. There are, for example, similarities between advertising and public relations. Both are attempts at persuasion, and both involve using the mass media. Public relations, however, is a management function; advertising is a marketing function. Another difference is that advertising uses the mass media and machine-assisted communication settings; unlike PR it does not involve interpersonal communications. A third difference is seen in the fact that advertising is normally sponsored. Public relations messages appear as features, news stories, or editorials, and the space or time involved is not paid for. In many instances, advertising, particularly corporate advertising, is used to help further a public relations program. As we shall see in the next chapter, however, the line between advertising and public relations is becoming blurred as advertisers turn to nontraditional ways of getting their messages to consumers and more businesses adapt the integrated marketing communications perspective. (See the boxed insert "IMC" on page 328.)

A concept that is sometimes confused with public relations is promotion. Promotion involves staging events or planning enterprises that attract media or public attention to a person, product, organization, or cause. Although promotion is useful in some PR campaigns, public relations encompasses a much broader area and involves more than just attracting attention.

Another concept that is sometimes confused with public relations is **publicity,** the placing of stories in the mass media. Publicity is a tool in the public relations process, but it is not equivalent to PR. For example, it is perfectly possible for a firm to have extensive publicity and bad public relations. Further, publicity is primarily one-way communication; public relations is two-way.

Having examined what public relations is *not*, we may now turn to what it *is*. The term *public relations* has many interpretations and meanings. One PR veteran has compiled 500 different ones, ranging from the concise "PR is doing good and getting credit for it" to the 100-word definition in the *Encyclopaedia Britannica*. Most of the leading textbooks on PR usually lead off with a chapter that attempts to define exactly what public relations is or is not. Rather than catalogue these many definitions, we may find it more useful to define PR by examining what PR people do:

1. *Public relations involves working with public opinion.* On the one hand, PR professionals attempt to influence public opinion in a way that is positive to the client. For example, in the AIG episode, the ill-timed public relations campaign was designed to improve Americans' attitudes toward the company.

2. *Public relations is concerned with communication.* Most people are interested in what a given organization is doing to meet their concerns and interests. It is the function of the public relations professional to explain the organization's actions to various **publics** involved with the organization. As noted previously, public relations communication is two-way communication. The PR professional also pays close attention to the thoughts and feelings of the organization's publics. Some experts refer to public relations as a two-way conduit between an organization and its publics.

Note that the word *publics* in the preceding section is plural. This is because an organization typically deals with many different publics in its day-to-day operations. Several PR scholars divide these groups into internal and external publics. *Internal* publics include employees, managers, labor unions, and stockholders. *External* publics consist of consumers, the government, dealers, suppliers, community members, and the mass media. Public relations serves as the link for all these publics.

3. *Public relations is a management function.* It is designed to help a company set its goals and adapt to a changing environment. Public relations practitioners regularly counsel top management. Inherent in the specification of public relations is a planned activity. It is organized and directed toward specific goals and objectives.

Of course, public relations involves much more than just the three functions mentioned. Perhaps it would be easier, for our purposes, to use the following definition approved by the World Assembly of Public Relations:

Public relations is the art and social science of analyzing trends, predicting their consequences, counseling organization leaders, and implementing planned programs of action that serve both the organization's and the public's interest.

A Brief History

If the term *public relations* is interpreted broadly enough, its practice can be traced back to ancient times. The military reports and commentaries prepared by Julius Caesar can be viewed as a triumph in personal and political public relations. During medieval times both the church and the guilds practiced rudimentary forms of public relations.

It was not until the American Revolution that more recognizable public relations activities became evident. The early patriots were aware that public opinion would play an important role in the struggle with England, and they planned their activities accordingly. For example, they staged events, such as the Boston Tea Party, to gain public attention. They also used symbols, such as the Liberty Tree and the Minutemen, that were easily recognized and helped portray their cause in a positive light. Skillful writers such as Samuel Adams, Thomas Paine, Abigail Adams, and Benjamin Franklin used political propaganda to swing public opinion to their side. As a case in point, note

The Boston Tea Party was a PR move calculated to gain support for the colonists' cause. Such an event today would be done in daylight so that TV news crews would have an easier time covering it.

that the altercation between an angry mob and British soldiers became known as the "Boston Massacre," an interpretation well suited to the rebel cause.

Later, the Industrial Revolution and the resulting growth of mass production and mass consumption led to the emergence of big business. Giant monopolies were formed in the railroad, steel, and oil businesses. Many big corporations tended to disregard the interests of the consumer in their quest for more profits. In fact, many executives felt that the less the public knew about their practices and operations, the better. Around the turn of the 20th century, however, public hostility was aroused against unscrupulous business practices. Muckrakers (see Chapter 5) filled the nation's magazines with exposés of industrial corruption and ruthless business tactics. In response, corporations hired communications experts, many of them former newspaper writers, to counteract the effect of these stories. These specialists tried to combat negative publicity by making sure the industry's side of the issue was also presented. These practitioners were the prototypes of what we might call *press agents* or *publicists*.

The debut of modern public relations techniques dates back to the first decade of the 1900s. Most historians agree that the first real public relations pioneer was a man named Ivy Lee. In 1903 Lee and George Parker opened a publicity office. A few years later, Lee became the press representative for the anthracite coal operators and the Pennsylvania Railroad. When these industries were confronted with a strike in the coal industry, Lee issued a "Declaration of Principles." This statement endorsed the concepts of openness and honesty in dealing with the public; it also marked the shift from 19th-century press agentry to 20th-century public relations. Lee went on to have a successful career counseling people such as John D. Rockefeller Jr. Among other achievements Lee is credited with humanizing business and demonstrating that public relations is most effective when it affects employees, customers, and community members. Moreover, Lee would not carry out a public relations program unless it was endorsed and supported by top management.

The government got involved in public relations during World War I when President Woodrow Wilson set up the Creel Committee (named for its chair, journalist George Creel). Creel enlisted the top figures in the public relations field to mount a campaign that per-

Public relations pioneer Ivy Lee.

suaded newspapers and magazines to donate space for ads that urged Americans to save food and to buy war bonds. Creel advised Wilson on communication strategies and was instrumental in publicizing Wilson's war goal "to make the world safe for democracy." The work of the Creel Committee was significant because it demonstrated the power of a well-planned and well-executed public relations campaign. In addition, it helped legitimize the field of public relations.

Following World War I, two more public relations pioneers, Carl Byoir and Edward L. Bernays, appeared on the scene. Bernays is credited with writing the first book on public relations, *Crystallizing Public Opinion*, published in 1923. In 1930 Byoir organized a public relations firm that became one of the world's largest.

The Depression caused many Americans to look upon business with suspicion and distrust. In an attempt to regain public favor, many large corporations established their own public relations departments. The federal government, in its attempt to cope with the bad economic climate, also used good public relations practices to its advantage. President Franklin Roosevelt introduced his New Deal reform program complete with promotional campaigns to win public acceptance. Roosevelt also recognized the tremendous potential of radio in shaping public opinion, and his radio-broadcasted fireside chats were memorable examples of personal public relations. The government intensified its public relations efforts during World War II with the creation of the Office of War Information.

During the second half of the 20th century, changes in American society created an atmosphere in which public relations grew tremendously in importance. What are some of the reasons behind the recent surge in this area?

- Many corporations recognized that they had a social responsibility to serve the public. Finding the means of fulfilling this responsibility was the task of the public relations department.
- A growing tide of consumerism caused many corporations and government agencies to be more responsive to and communicative with their customers or clients, a function served by the public relations department.

Where does PR fit in the organization? Traditional thinking, as mentioned in the chapter, treats PR as a management function. Another philosophy (which emerged during the mid-1990s), called *integrated marketing communications,* or *IMC,* argues that PR should really be part of the marketing function. This distinction involves more than just an organizational war for turf; it holds significant implications for the future of the field. If PR is subsumed within marketing, it loses much of its management component.

Those who advocate IMC point out that, in addition to product and price, public and social issues influence marketing. An integrated approach ensures that a company responds to all these concerns with a single voice. Additionally, proponents of IMC note that clients want their advertising, PR, and marketing activities coordinated and unified. Further, IMC saves a company money since a single IMC department can operate more efficiently than separate departments of advertising, marketing, and PR. Finally, proponents argue that everything that a PR department does—employee communication, crisis management, promotion—boils down to marketing functions.

Opponents of IMC argue that the credibility of PR efforts will be hurt if they are seen as simply another marketing tool. It is already difficult for PR practitioners to maintain perceptions of honesty and believability on the part of the audience, and lumping the PR department with marketing will make the problem even worse. Another argument suggests that IMC hurts the diversity of opinion available to management. A separate PR department makes it more likely that different suggestions and alternative courses of action will be advanced. Finally, opponents argue that PR involves two-way communication that takes into account the needs of various publics, whereas IMC treats everybody as a customer and places top priority on sales.

One of the struggles for the industry in the years to come will be the development of a structure that recognizes the unique contributions of each of the departments that make up the modern organization.

- The growing complexity of modern corporations and government agencies made it difficult for them to get their messages to the public without a department that was specifically assigned that task.
- Increasing population growth along with more specialization and job mobility made it necessary for companies to employ communication specialists whose task it was to interpret the needs of the audience for the organization.

MEDIA TALK

Planting Stories in Iraq

Clip 11: 2 minutes 22 seconds
You can watch Clip 11 *on the Online Learning Center home page,* www.mhhe.com/dominick11e. *Select* Student Center *and then* Chapter 14. This clip discusses the claim that American troops in Iraq are writing articles that are being translated into Arabic and published in Iraqi newspapers while the readers believe that the stories are being written by Iraqi journalists. Is this an effective public relations tactic? What ethical problems are involved? If the stories are factual, has any harm been done? Is this practice any different than U.S. TV stations running video news releases produced by PR firms during their news broadcasts?

WWW

All these trends have combined to make the past 50 or so years the "era of public relations." The profession grew from about 19,000 members in 1950 to more than 200,000 in the United States and 300,000 worldwide in 2006. Along with this growth has come increased professionalization among public relations practitioners. The Public Relations Society of America, founded in 1947, adopted a code of standards in 1954. Public relations education has also made great strides. Recent estimates suggest that about 400 colleges across the country offer courses in public relations. In 1967 the Public Relations Student Society of America was founded. It now has 270 chapters and 8,500 members.

The past decade has seen public relations become even more important. Spin doctors, specialists in political public relations, have assumed prominence in political campaigns and government activities. The Bush administration used public relations extensively to gather public support for Operation Iraqi Freedom in 2003. One facet of this program was the "embedding" of more than 500 journalists with military units to provide firsthand accounts of the action. In the business sector the accounting scandals at major corporations such as Enron, Global Crossing, and Arthur Andersen increased the need for better public relations in order to restore confidence in a company's financial reports and to make top executives more responsible to their employees and shareholders.

The recession caused some firms to cut the amount spent on public relations activities, but overall the PR industry as of 2008 was in fairly good financial shape. The outlook for the future, however, was uncertain. Nonetheless, job opportunities in public relations continued to increase. Finally, as the chapter opener illustrates, public relations takes on added importance during an economic downturn. PR blunders can be magnified by the Internet and hurt the image of a company or even that of a whole industry.

Public Relations in the Digital Age

The Internet has added several new dimensions to public relations. It has opened up new channels of communication between organizations and the public and between public relations practitioners and the media. It has also become a major channel of feedback for organizations interested in their public image.

▲ Communicating with the Audience

Corporate Web sites have become more than just flashy sites that try to sell a product or service. They have become the first line of communication for organizations, consumers, and shareholders. Web sites can be used to help an organization react quickly to a crisis or controversy.

Many public relations firms are counseling their clients to integrate the interactive features of Web 2.0 into their site. The Budweiser site, for example, had a feature called Bud2Bud that allowed visitors (over the age of 21, of course) to invite a friend for a Bud. For those under 21, Pepsi gave consumers a chance to design a new Pepsi can. Most large companies also have pages in Wikipedia. Some agencies place videos for their clients on YouTube.

Several corporations have adopted the podcast as an additional way to get their message out. McDonald's posted a series of podcasts on its Web site with topics ranging from food safety to diversity. Peterson's, the company that publishes information about colleges, offers podcasts on how to prepare for the new SAT.

Social media have opened up new ways for companies to communicate with their publics. Here are just a few examples:

- Starbucks created MyStarbucksIdea whereby customers suggested ideas to the company that were voted on by other customers. The suggestions getting the most votes were then implemented by the company.
- Blender maker Blendtec posts "Will it blend?" videos on YouTube. (The one where the iPhone gets blended has been seen thousands of times.)
- H&R Block has a Facebook fan site where it answers tax questions and promotes local meetings of its fans.
- Zappos uses Twitter to help employees connect with customers.
- McDonald's has a blog that details its social responsibility efforts.

Speaking of blogs, corporations have embraced them as a major public relations tool. A corporate blog can be internal, used for communication with employees and shareholders, or external, used as an outlet to respond to online comments and opinions. Companies are using blogs to resolve consumer complaints before they escalate into real problems. As of 2009, most major companies were engaged in some form of blogging.

Of course, all of these new channels present new challenges. Web sites require people to design and maintain them. Blogs have to be written, and podcasts have to be produced and posted. Social media need to be monitored and updated. Wikis have to be checked periodically to make sure they haven't been maliciously altered. Despite the added cost and labor burden, the Web will likely continue to be a major public relations tool for the foreseeable future.

▲ Communicating with the Media

It didn't take long for public relations practitioners to start using the Internet to streamline their media efforts. E-mail press releases have replaced the traditional paper-mail releases, and e-mail rather than the telephone has become the preferred means of communication between journalists and public relations professionals. Further, the Web has become an important channel in distributing information to the media. PR Newswire's Web site, for example, collects information from agencies and public relations departments and makes this information available to newsrooms across the country. Practitioners can also distribute photos and video clips via the Internet.

The Internet has made it easier for professionals to target their story proposals and press releases to the appropriate sources. A search engine makes it simple to research a given journalist's recent articles to see what kinds of topics he or she might be interested in. Some online Web sites track journalists' job movements. A reporter just starting a new assignment might be particularly interested in story ideas. Finally, database software and e-mail merge programs make it possible for practitioners to efficiently target possible outlets for stories.

New social media tools have added new ways for practitioners to communicate with the media and with themselves. For example, helpareporter.com lets reporters submit questions to PR professionals. Beatblogging.org contains a listing of beat blogs (blogs that generally stick to one topic authored by professionals or amateurs) that PR practitioners can use to make story pitches. Speaking of pitches, yourpitchsucks.com offers a community of professionals who will read a story pitch and make suggestions for improvements.

▲ New Channels of Feedback

It's not surprising that public relations agencies use the Web for feedback on companies, products, and issues. PR Newswire offers eWatch, a service that monitors online news media and related sites for mentions of specific organizations. Technorati can be used to search the blogosphere. Agencies commonly examine customer review sites such as Epinions or Bizrate for their clients to spot positive and negative comments. And, of course, the Web can be used for traditional research, such as surveys and online focus groups, to shape public relations decisions.

Organization of the Public Relations Industry

Public relations activities are generally handled in two ways. Many organizations have their own public relations departments that work with the managers of all other departments. About 85 percent of the 1,500 largest U.S. companies have such departments. In many companies these departments are part of top management, and the PR director is responsible to the president of the company. For example, General Motors and General

This billboard is an example of a public-service PR campaign with a tie-in to a grocery chain.

Electric both employ about a hundred people in their U.S. PR departments. Other organizations hire an external public relations counsel to give advice on press, government, and consumer relations. In business and industry, about one-third of the PR activity is handled by outside counseling firms. Many major corporations retain an outside agency in addition to their own internal public relations department.

Each of these arrangements has its particular advantages and disadvantages. An in-house department can be at work on short notice and has in-depth knowledge about the company; in addition, its operations tend to be less costly. On the other hand, it is hard for a corporate PR team to take an objective view of the company. Further, internal PR departments tend to have trouble coming up with fresh ideas unless new personnel are frequently added. An outside agency offers more services to its clients than does an internal department. Additionally, external counselors have the advantage of being objective observers, and many firms like the prestige associated with being a client of a respected PR firm. On the other side of the coin, outside agencies are expensive, it takes time for them to learn the inner workings of their client's operations, and their involvement may cause resentment and morale problems among the staff of the client's organization.

Internal or external, public relations professionals perform a wide range of services. These include counseling management, preparing annual reports, handling news releases and other forms of media coverage, supervising employee and other internal communications, managing promotions and special events, fund-raising, lobbying, handling community relations, publishing blogs, creating Web sites, and writing speeches.

Public relations is practiced in a variety of settings. Although the general principles are the same, the actual duties of the PR practitioner will vary according to the setting. Following are brief descriptions of a dozen areas in which public relations is practiced:

1. *Business:* Public relations helps the marketing process by instilling in consumers a positive attitude toward the company. Public relations also helps promote healthy employee-management relations and serves as a major liaison between the firm and government regulators. Further, all businesses have to be located somewhere, and the PR department makes sure the company is a good citizen in its community.

2. *Government and politics:* Many government agencies hire PR specialists to help them explain their activities to citizens and to assist the news media in their coverage of the different agencies. These same specialists also communicate the opinions of the public back to the agency. Government PR is big business; its total expenditures on public information rival the budgets of the four major TV networks. The Department of Defense, for instance, produces thousands of films and TV programs every year. The Department of Agriculture sends out thousands of news releases annually. Political public relations is another growing field. A growing number of candidates for public office hire PR experts to help them get their message across to voters.

3. *Education:* PR personnel work in both elementary and higher education. The most visible area of practice in elementary and high school concerns facilitating communication between educators and parents. Other tasks, however, are no less important. In many school systems the PR person also handles relations with the school board, local and state legislative bodies, and the news media. Public relations at the college and university level, although less concerned with parental relations, has its own set of tasks. Fund-raising, legislative relations, community relations, and internal relations with faculty and students would be concerns of most college PR departments.

4. *Hospitals:* The rising cost of health care and greater public expectations of the medical profession have given increased visibility to the PR departments in our nation's hospitals. Some of the publics that hospital PR staffs have to deal with are patients, patients' families, consumers, state insurance commissions, physicians, nurses, and other staff members. Despite the increasing importance of hospital public relations, many hospitals do not have a full-time PR staff. Consequently, this is one area that should see significant growth in the future.

5. *Nonprofit organizations:* The United Way, the Girl Scouts, the American Red Cross, and the Salvation Army are just a few of the organizations that need PR professionals. Probably the biggest PR goal in organizations such as these is fund-raising. Other objectives include encouraging volunteer participation, informing contributors how their money is spent, and working with the individuals served by an organization.

6. *Professional associations:* Organizations such as the American Medical Association, the American Dairy Association, and the American Bar Association employ PR practitioners. In addition to providing news and information to the association's members, other duties of the PR staff are recruiting new members, planning national conferences, influencing government decisions, and working with the news media.

7. *Entertainment and sports:* A significant number of PR experts work for established and would-be celebrities in the entertainment and sports worlds. A practitioner handling this type of client has two major responsibilities: Get the client favorable media coverage, and protect the client from bad publicity. Additionally, many sports and entertainment events (such as the Super Bowl, or a motion picture premiere) have PR campaigns associated with them.

8. *International PR:* Corporations with branches throughout the world, global news media such as CNN, an interrelated world economy, the shifting political scene in Europe—all these factors have combined to make this area one of the fastest growing in public relations. International PR specialists help businesses operating in other countries with local customs, language problems, cultural difficulties, and legal dilemmas.

9. *Investor relations:* This area (called *IR* for convenience) entails building a favorable image for a company and keeping shareholders happy. A public company needs to communicate information, both positive and negative, that might have an impact on its stock price to the financial community in general and shareholders in particular. To do this effectively, IR professionals must know the workings of the financial press and the various channels used to communicate with shareholders, such as annual reports, quarterly reports, and annual meetings. As more and more Americans invest in the stock and bond markets and as financial markets become more global, the importance of IR will surely increase.

10. *Politics:* The importance of PR in political campaigns increases with every election. Building the right personal image, putting the proper spin on the interpretation of events, and responding to the charges of other candidates are all part of the job of a political PR specialist. Many PR firms specialize in political campaigns.

11. *Environment:* Global warming, water conservation, recycling, energy conservation, and other environmental issues have made this area extremely visible in recent years. Practitioners represent both advocacy groups and industries.

12. *Crisis management:* Probably the ultimate test for the PR practitioner is dealing with a crisis. Such crises arise infrequently, but poor handling of a crisis can have long-term negative effects that might cripple a company and/or ruin the reputation of a PR firm. In a crisis the public seeks more information, and the organization involved in the crisis is subjected to increased scrutiny by both the media and the public. Experts in crisis management PR generally counsel their clients to accomplish three goals: terminate the crisis, limit damage, and restore credibility.

As this list suggests, the profession requires PR specialists as well as generalists. In the next section, we will see how the PR function is typically organized and what jobs PR professionals perform.

PR Departments and Staff

At the outset, remember that no two companies have the same exact departmental structure. In one common arrangement for an internal corporate PR department, the director of public relations reports directly to the president of the company. Since PR affects every department, its supervision by the person who runs the entire organization makes sense. Nonetheless, some organizations endorse integrated marketing communications, which puts the PR department in the marketing division. A recent survey noted that about 40 percent of PR departments report to the CEO while 32 percent report to the head of the marketing department. The PR department is further subdivided into three main divisions that are designed to communicate with both internal and external publics: (1) corporate communications, (2) community relations, and (3) press relations. The corporate communications division handles communication with internal publics (workers, shareholders, unions), and the community relations division deals with external publics (community residents, customers, the government). As its name suggests, the press relations division deals with the news media.

The organization of an external PR agency is more complex. One possible arrangement consists of five departments:

1. *Creative services:* Is responsible for ideas and the production of press releases and audio/video media.
2. *Research:* Supervises survey research, focus groups, and data collection.
3. *Publicity and marketing:* Takes charge of merchandising and sales promotions.
4. *Accounts:* Oversees and coordinates relations with clients.
5. *Administration:* Is responsible for the day-to-day personnel, clerical, legal, and financial tasks that keep a business running.

The personnel at a public relations firm include a president and several vice presidents. To succeed in public relations it is necessary for a firm to continually seek out new business or increase the amount of business it does with current clients. The top executives at a PR firm usually spend a good deal of time meeting with prospective clients, preparing proposals, and making presentations.

Account supervisors manage one large account or a number of smaller ones. They are responsible for budgeting, quality control, and managing the workload of project teams. An account executive is responsible for the day-to-day operations involved in dealing with a client. Assistant account executives handle routine work such as writing press releases and conducting basic research.

Firms usually put together account teams to handle large-scale public relations campaigns. Teams may include creative personnel, graphic artists, market researchers, social media designers, and experts in setting up media tours and special events.

The Public Relations Program

Imagine that you are the public relations director for a leading automaker. The company is entering into an agreement with a foreign car manufacturer to produce a foreign model in the United States. Unfortunately, to increase efficiency and centralize its operations, the company will have to close one of its plants located in a midwestern city. About a thousand employees will have to be transferred or find new jobs, and the community will face a significant economic blow. It will be the job of the public relations department to communicate this decision to the community.

The thorny problem just outlined is a typical one for the public relations professional. Handling it requires a planned, organized, and efficient public relations program. This section will trace the four main steps involved in developing a typical PR campaign: (1) information gathering, (2) planning, (3) communication, and (4) evaluation.

▲ Information Gathering

The information-gathering stage is an important one because what is learned from it will influence the remaining stages. **Information gathering** can be achieved through several means. Organizational records, trade journals, public records, and reference books serve as valuable sources of data. Personal contacts, mail to the company, advisory committees, and personnel reports represent other sources of information. If more formal research methods are required, they might be carried out by the PR department or by an outside agency that specializes in public opinion polling or survey research. Return to our example. The PR director at the auto company will need to gather a great deal of information. How much will the company save by its reorganization? Exactly how many workers will be transferred? Will the company help find new jobs for the workers who will be unemployed? What will be the precise economic impact on the community? What will become of the empty buildings that will be left behind? Will the employees believe what the company tells them? What do people expect from the company? Will the company's image be hurt in other areas of the United States?

▲ Planning

Phase 2 is the planning stage. There are two general types of planning: **strategic** and **tactical.** Strategic plans involve long-range, general goals that the organization wishes to achieve. Top management usually formulates an organization's strategic plans. Tactical plans are more specific. They detail the tasks that must be accomplished by every department in the organization to achieve the strategic goals. Some plans that are drawn up might be used only once; others might serve as standing plans that set general organizational policy.

Planning is a vital part of the PR program. Some of the items involved in a PR campaign are framing the objectives, considering the alternatives, assessing the risks and benefits involved in each alternative, deciding on a course of action, figuring out the budget, and securing the necessary approvals from within the organization. In recent years many PR practitioners have endorsed a technique known as **management by objectives (MBO).**

Public relations practitioners almost unanimously sing the praises of social media, but one important question still remains unresolved: How does a public relations firm measure the effectiveness of a social media campaign? A quick glance at Wikipedia lists 16 different variables that might be measured as part of a social media campaign. This long list of possibilities suggests that there is no clear agreement on what exactly should be examined as part of the evaluation process.

The traditional measures of unique visitors, time spent on a site, and page views aren't useful because much of the conversation in social media takes place away from a company's Web site. Some other alternatives need to be developed. One alternative that has been suggested is measuring velocity—how fast something, say a Web video, spreads across Web properties. This metric gauges how popular something is, but it says nothing about impact. For example, your video might have been embedded on 1,000 Facebook pages in a week, but did the video have any influence on behavior or attitude?

Another possibility is counting the mentions of a product or service on blogs, message boards, and comments sections and indicating whether the tone of the comment was positive or negative. (Many companies offer this service.) This technique is most useful when the company has some baseline measure before the campaign and another measure after the campaign has concluded in order to gauge any changes in volume or tone. Moreover, it's probably not enough to look at only the numbers of mentions. PR professionals and their clients should also examine who is making the comments. A disproportionate number may be coming from one or two individuals. Finally, it's hard for a client to know how to interpret these numbers. What makes a successful campaign? One where mentions increase by a factor of two? Of five? The ultimate choice is arbitrary.

A third procedure is to take a qualitative approach. Sometimes just counting the mentions of a product or service obscures important information. A qualitative analysis looks at the context and nature of a comment. Anecdotes, stories, jokes, and whole conversations may be important in determining success. The drawback with qualitative research is that it requires humans to exercise judgment, which makes the analysis take longer and cost more. Nonetheless, it is an approach worth considering.

As clients demand more accountability from their PR counselors, the process of measuring the effectiveness of social media will undoubtedly improve. The Internet is home to many public relations professionals who blog about the topic and discuss new ways to gauge impact and measure success.

Simply put, MBO means that the organization sets observable and measurable goals for itself and allocates its resources to meet those objectives. For example, a corporation might set as a goal increasing sales by 25 percent over the next 2 years. When the time had elapsed, it would be easy to see if the goal had been achieved. This approach is becoming more popular in PR because top management typically thinks in these terms, and if PR practitioners speak the same language as chief executives, they can communicate more effectively with them. It also keeps the department on target in solving PR problems, and it provides concrete feedback about the efficiency of the PR process. In our hypothetical example, some objectives might be informing more than 50 percent of the community about the reasons for the move and making sure community and national attitudes about the company are not adversely affected.

▲ Communication

Phase 3 is the communication phase. After gathering facts and making plans, the organization assumes the role of the source of communication. Several key decisions are made at this stage concerning the nature of the messages and the types of media to be used. Because mass communication media are usually important channels in a PR program, it is necessary for public relations practitioners to have a thorough knowledge of the various media and their strengths and weaknesses. Moreover, PR professionals should know the various production techniques for the print and broadcast media. Some common ways of publicizing a message through the mass media are press releases, video news releases, press kits, photographs, paid advertising, films, videotapes, press conferences, and interviews.

Public relations also makes use of other channels to get messages to its publics. These include both the interpersonal and the machine-assisted settings. House publications, brochures, faxes, letters, bulletins, posters, Web sites, blogs, social media, e-mail, billboards, and bulletin boards are communication channels used by a company to reach its own employees. On a more personal level, public meetings, speeches, demonstrations, staged events, open houses, and tours are other possibilities.

In our hypothetical example, the PR director would probably use a variety of messages and media. News conferences, ads, press releases, and public meetings would be appropriate vehicles for explaining the company's position to its external public. Meanwhile, house publications, bulletin boards, speeches, and letters could be used to reach its internal public.

▲ Evaluation

The last phase concerns **evaluation** of the PR program. How well did it work? The importance of evaluation in public relations is increasing through the use of MBO techniques. If a measurable goal was proposed for the PR program, then an evaluation technique should be able to measure success in reaching that goal. Several different aspects might be measured. One easy method is simply to gauge the volume of coverage that the campaign generated. The number of press releases sent out, letters mailed, speeches made, and so on are simple to compute. In like manner, press clippings and mentions in TV and radio news can be tabulated. It is important to remember, however, that volume does not equal results. A million press clippings mean nothing if they are not read by the audience. Measuring the impact of a campaign on the audience requires more sophisticated techniques of analysis. Some common techniques are questionnaires distributed to random samples of the audience, telephone and Web surveys, panels, reader-interest studies, and experimental campaigns. It is likely that our hypothetical PR director would use many of these techniques.

Before closing, we should note that we have been talking about these four steps as though they were distinct stages. In actuality the PR program is a continuous process, and one phase blends into the next. The results learned in the evaluation stage, for example, are also part of the information-gathering phase of the next cycle of the PR program. In our car company example, the PR department would use the results of surveys and focus

The online home of PR Newswire. More than 100,000 journalists can access press releases through this Web site.

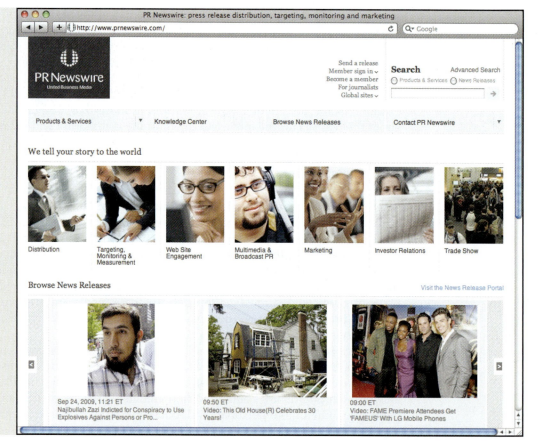

Public relations professionals all agree that the best PR comes from having good word of mouth, or, in the jargon of the trade, a positive buzz—having people say nice things about a product or company. But how do you get the buzz started? How about paying people?

That's the business model behind a Boston company called BzzAgent. The company has recruited a force of about 75,000 worker bees that it describes as "product evangelists" who will go into the streets and tout the virtues of a product to other people, usually without the other people knowing that they've been buzzed. A buzz campaign for the book *The Frog King* illustrates how the process works. Dozens of buzz agents were given free copies of the book and advised to read it on subways, trains, and buses with the cover plainly displayed. Some passages from the book were highlighted to be used as talking points when recommending the book to family and friends. It was also suggested that the agents call local bookstores and ask if the clerk had heard about the book and how many copies were in stock. In three months the book sold more than what the publisher thought it would sell in a year.

The buzz is not cheap. For about $90,000, BzzAgent will provide a client with a thousand specially chosen product evangelists who will spread the word in a 12-week campaign. The agents provide written reports of their activities that are transmitted back to the client. The worker bees get free samples of the product, and they earn points that can be redeemed for books, CDs, and other items.

BzzAgent isn't the only company that commercializes ordinary conversation. Sony Ericsson hired 600 actors to ask passersby to take pictures with its new camera phone. The actors then praised the phone to those who cooperated. Procter & Gamble has more than 200,000 teenagers in its "Tremor" word-of-mouth unit who advocate various products to their peers.

What are some of the ethical questions raised by buzz marketing? Most obviously, there's the issue of deception. BzzAgent suggests that its workers tell others that they are being compensated for their recommendations. There is no way, of course, to know how many, if any, do this. When that key fact is not disclosed, the honesty and integrity of human communication is compromised. Is it possible to have a truthful conversation with someone who has a hidden agenda? The next time someone you know tells you that Sony's new Play Station is great and you should buy one, do you believe it? Those who favor the technique point out that those who participate are not asked to spread the buzz about products that they dislike. People naturally talk about products they use and enjoy. Buzz marketing simply encourages a natural tendency.

A second issue involves privacy. Marketing has invaded almost every facet of American life; consumers are bombarded by hundreds of advertisements every day. Shouldn't there be some circumstances that are marketing-proof? Should a talk with a friend become a paid promotional event? How about the family breakfast table? Should teenagers become paid shills to hawk a breakfast cereal to parents? Is it ethical to take up the time of clerks and salespersons as part of a marketing campaign?

Lastly, as detailed in Chapter 17, there is an ethical philosophy called the *principle of self-determination*. In brief, it maintains that you should not use people as objects or as means to an end. It seems that buzz marketing violates this principle. It values people not for their unique humanness but for the fact that they can be turned into stealth salespeople. The fact that the people involved are willing participants does not change the situation.

Despite these concerns, it's probable that buzz marketing will grow in popularity. It's effective and relatively cheap. There's even a professional organization for those involved: the Word of Mouth Marketing Association (WOMMA).

The WOMMA recently drafted a code of ethics for its members. As noted on WOMMA's Web site, the code can be distilled into three propositions:

- *Honesty of relationship:* You say who you're speaking for.
- *Honesty of opinion:* You say what you believe.
- *Honesty of identity:* You never obscure your identity.

Adherence to the code is voluntary.

groups to determine whether the company's image had suffered, how much credibility the company had with consumers, and if there were any change in customer loyalty. These findings would help in planning the goals of the next PR campaign.

The Economics of Public Relations

The total amount of money spent on corporate public relations activity is hard to measure, but some information is available about the revenues of PR agencies. In 2008 the top 50 independent PR firms in the United States collected about $1.4 billion, up 25 percent from 2006.

The industry is dominated by giant PR firms owned by ad agencies. As of 2009, the biggest PR firms with ad agency parent companies were Porter-Novelli and Fleischman-Hillard (part of the Omnicom Group) and Hill & Knowlton and Burson-Marsteller (part of the WPP Group). The two largest independent PR firms were Edelman and Ruder Finn. The PR business can be volatile, especially for smaller agencies, whose fee income might vary by 40–80 percent from year to year.

PR agencies earn their fees in a variety of ways. Some perform specific projects for specific fees. An annual report, for example, might cost $10,000. Some charge their clients a retainer every month, which might range from a few hundred dollars to considerably more. Other firms keep track of time spent on various projects and charge clients an hourly rate. Still others bill for time plus for extra services and materials.

Public Relations

Despite the economic downturn, job prospects in public relations are better than in other media-related areas. Industry data show that jobs at public relations firms increased by 10 percent from 2006 to 2008. The Bureau of Labor Statistics predicts that the upward trend will continue well into 2015.

The career outlook in the various media industries changes quickly. For a more current description of conditions in the public relations industry and a more detailed look at career options, please consult the book's Web site: www.mhhe.com/dominick11e.

MAIN POINTS

- *Public relations* is difficult to define, but most practitioners agree that PR involves counseling management about communication strategies that can improve public opinion about an organization.

- Modern public relations began around the turn of the 20th century and has steadily increased in importance.

- The Internet is an important part of PR. It is used to provide information to the public and to obtain background information for PR professionals.

- PR is practiced in numerous settings, including business, government, and the nonprofit sector.

- A PR campaign consists of the following stages: information gathering, planning, communication, and evaluation.

QUESTIONS FOR REVIEW

1. Define *public relations.*
2. What are some of the major areas that make use of public relations?
3. What are the stages in a public relations campaign?
4. How have social media changed the practice of public relations?

QUESTIONS FOR CRITICAL THINKING

1. Can you think of any examples of your using PR in your personal life (like putting the best spin on a bad grade in a course)?
2. Why is the term *public relations* so hard to define? Is it important to have a definition that everybody agrees on?
3. How much faith does the public have in the credibility of PR professionals?
4. Many journalists look with disfavor on the field of public relations. What might account for this attitude?

KEY TERMS

publicity (p. 324)	strategic (planning) (p. 334)	evaluation (p. 336)
publics (p. 324)	tactical (planning) (p. 334)	
information gathering (p. 334)	management by objectives (MBO) (p. 334)	

INTERNET RESOURCES

Online Learning Center

On the Online Learning Center home page, www.mhhe.com/dominick11e, *select* Student Center *and then* Chapter 14.

1. Use the Learning Objectives, Chapter Outline, and Main Points sections to review this chapter.

2. Test your knowledge of the chapter using the multiple choice and flashcard features of the site.

3. Expand your knowledge of concepts and topics discussed in the chapter with additional Questions for Critical Thinking and Internet Exercises.

Surfing the Internet

Some of these sites are mentioned in the text. Others appear first on this list. Remember that the Web is always changing. Some sites move, some change their focus, and others simply evaporate.

http://ewatch.prnewswire.com
A site that tracks what the media, investors, consumers, and the competition are saying about an organization.

www.ketchum.com
The home page of Ketchum Public Relations Worldwide. Includes a description of the company, and a list of the worldwide offices and podcasts.

http://aboutpublicrelations.net
A how-to-do-it site for those interested in public relations.

www.prmuseum.com
A museum of public relations. Contains extensive information on the pioneers of PR.

www.prsa.org
The home page of the Public Relations Society of America. Includes general information about the society, a list of relevant publications, and a link to the PR student society. A recently added feature enables members to post their résumés in cyberspace.

CHAPTER 15

Advertising

This chapter will prepare you to:

- define *advertising* and explain how it is classified

- explain how advertising developed

- recognize the impact the Internet has had on advertising

- distinguish among the three main components of the advertising industry

- discuss the components of an advertising campaign

Many organizations and individuals, including the Scottsdale, Arizona, police department, advertise on Facebook.

A male professor colleague recently opened his Facebook page and was greeted by an ad seeking recruits for the Scottsdale, Arizona, police department. Without getting into personal details, suffice it to say that my colleague is a really bad candidate for a law enforcement career in southern Arizona. So why is the Scottsdale, Arizona, PD spending its money on advertising to him? We may never know the exact reason, but the possibilities illustrate some of the intricacies of advertising on the Internet in general and on social media sites in particular.

One possible answer is that the Scottsdale police department doesn't know that it could target its Facebook message to likelier candidates than middle-aged professors. Scottsdale PD, for example, could have chosen to display its ad only to people between 18 and 34 years of age who live in the Southwest. A second possible answer is that the Scottsdale PD was spending so little money on the ad that it didn't matter one way or the other, particularly if it was paying Facebook on a pay-per-click (PPC) basis.

The PPC system works like this: The Scottsdale PD ad is displayed on a number of Facebook sites, but the PD pays Facebook only when somebody clicks on the ad. The click-through rate (the percentage of those seeing the ad who actually click on it) is notoriously low for most Web ads, usually way less than 1 percent. If the click-through rate is .05 percent (.0005) and if your ad is displayed 100,000 times, you'll get 50 people clicking on the ad.

Facebook prices its ads on an auction basis. Potential advertisers bid on what price they are willing to pay per click and set a cap on how much they are willing to pay for an entire campaign. It may be that the Scottsdale PD set aside $10 for Facebook ads and hoped for the best.

It is unknown what kind of bang for the buck the Scottsdale PD achieved, but there is information about other small advertisers and their Facebook efforts. One person wanted to advertise his new baseball-oriented Web site. His bid of 10 cents for a click was accepted, and his ad was displayed 27,105 times over the next two days. He got 6 clicks, a click-through rate of 0.022 percent. Total cost of campaign: 60 cents. Another ad campaign offered 54 cents per click, and the ad was displayed 81,000 times and received 6 clicks, a rate of .01 percent. Total cost: $3.24.

What have we learned so far about advertising on social media sites such as Facebook? (1) Facebook can target ads if a buyer chooses. (2) It doesn't cost a whole lot to run an ad. (3) Don't expect a lot of people to click on your ad, and finally, (4) it's tough for Facebook to make a whole lot of money from small-sized advertisers on the site. To elaborate on that final point, it probably costs Facebook about $100 million a year (maybe more) to stay in business. There are around 7 million college students on its site, and Facebook recommends a bid of 56 cents per click if an advertiser is trying to reach this audience. Just to break even, Facebook would have to sell 178 million clicks (56 cents times 178 million equals just a little less than $100 million). Or to put it another way, every college student in America with a Facebook page would have to click on 25 ads a year. Is this likely? How many ads have you clicked on?

This arithmetic is one reason why popularity of a site doesn't necessarily mean that the site is profitable. Facebook could raise its minimum bid per click, but that might send advertisers over to less expensive sites. Facebook could try to improve its click rate, but that may be difficult given the nature of the site. Facebook generally gets low click-through rates because its members go on the site to socialize rather than to shop. In sum, making a profit based on small- and medium-sized advertisers will be difficult. It should come as no surprise that Facebook is exploring other ways to produce revenue.

Defining Advertising

Simply defined, *advertising* is any form of nonpersonal presentation and promotion of ideas, goods, and services usually paid for by an identified sponsor. Note three key terms in this definition. First, advertising is "nonpersonal"; it is directed toward a large group of anonymous people. Even direct-mail advertising, which may be addressed to a specific person, is prepared by a computer and signed by a machine. Second, advertising typically is "paid for." This fact differentiates advertising from publicity, which is not usually purchased. Sponsors such as Coke and Delta pay for the time and the space they use to get their message across. (Nonprofit organizations, such as the Red Cross or the United Way, advertise but do not pay for time or space. Broadcast stations, newspapers, and magazines run these ads free as a public service.) Third, for obvious reasons, the sponsor of the ad is "identified." In fact, in most instances, identifying the sponsor is the prime purpose behind the ad—otherwise, why advertise? Perhaps the only type of advertising in which the identity of the advertiser may not be self-evident is political advertising. Because of this, broadcasters and publishers will not accept a political ad without a statement identifying those responsible for it.

Before we leave this topic, it should be noted that in the 21st century this definition of advertising has gotten a little blurry around the edges. Many practitioners consider advertising part of the overall marketing mix, along with promotion, branding, word of mouth, and public relations. (Note how this approach is consistent with the integrated marketing communication (IMC) philosophy mentioned in the previous chapter.) Taking that view, differentiating advertising from other forms of marketing is not particularly useful.

▲ Functions of Advertising

Advertising fulfills five basic functions in society. First, it serves a marketing function by helping companies that provide products or services sell their products. Personal selling, sales promotions, and advertising work together to help market the product. Second, advertising is educational. People learn about new products and services, or improvements in existing ones, through advertising. Third, advertising plays an economic role. The ability to advertise enables new competitors to enter the business arena. Competition, in turn, encourages product improvements and can lead to lower prices. Fourth, advertising reaches a mass audience, thus greatly reducing the cost of personal selling and distribution. Finally, advertising performs a definite social function. By vividly displaying the material and cultural opportunities available in a free-enterprise society, advertising helps increase productivity and raises the standard of living.

▲ Types of Advertising

Advertising can be classified in several ways. One useful approach is to distinguish the **target audience**—the specific segment of the population for whom the product or service has a definite appeal. Many target audiences can be defined; the most general are consumers and businesses. **Consumer advertising,** as the name suggests, is targeted at the people who buy goods and services for personal use. For example, Campbell's (known for its soups) uses consumer advertising to direct its ads to the adults and children most likely to buy soup at the grocery store. Most of the advertising that people are exposed to falls into this category. **Business-to-business advertising** is aimed at people who buy products for business use. Industrial, trade, and professional—as well as agricultural—advertising are all part of this category. Consumer advertising is the focus of most of this chapter, but we will also take a brief look at business-to-business advertising.

Geographic focus is another way to classify advertising. International advertising is employed for products and services that are used all over the globe. Coca-Cola and McDonald's, for example, advertise in dozens of countries and in many different languages. National advertising is advertising in many different regions of the same country. Delta, Wal-Mart, and Sprint, for example, run ads on TV networks and in national magazines to reach customers in many different markets across the United States. International

An example of a primary demand ad. The "got milk?" campaign was designed to promote milk drinking, not the purchase of a particular brand of milk.

advertisers, of course, also use national ads. Retail or local advertising is done within one specific market. The neighborhood restaurant or car dealership typically relies on local ads.

Yet a third way to categorize advertising is by purpose. Some ads are for distinct products or services, such as frozen pizzas or muffler repairs, while others try to improve a company's image or influence public opinion on an issue, such as the ads run by oil companies describing their efforts to keep down fuel costs. Another distinction involves primary demand and selective demand ads. A **primary demand ad** has as its purpose the promotion of a particular product category rather than a specific brand. The campaign to encourage milk drinking that shows various celebrities with milk moustaches is an example of this type. A **selective demand ad** is used by an individual company to sell its particular brand, such as a certain brand of milk. Finally, ads can be classified as direct action and indirect action. A **direct action ad** usually contains a toll-free number, coupon, e-mail or Web address, or some similar device to enable the advertiser to see results quickly. In contrast, an **indirect action ad** works over the long run to build a company's image and increase consumer awareness.

A Brief History

Advertising's beginnings are impossible to pinpoint, but several examples date back thousands of years. Clay tablets traced to ancient Babylon have been found with messages that touted an ointment dealer and a shoemaker. The town crier was an important advertising medium throughout England and other countries in Europe during the medieval period.

An ad from the 1900s for Coca-Cola. Included at the bottom is a coupon for a free Coke.

In more recent times, the history of advertising is inextricably entwined with changing social conditions and advances in media technology. For instance, Gutenberg's invention of printing using movable type made possible several new advertising media: posters, handbills, and newspaper ads. The first printed advertisement in English, produced about 1480, was a handbill that announced a prayer book for sale. Its author, evidently wise in the ways of outdoor advertising, tacked his ad to church doors all over England. By the late 1600s, ads were common sights in London newspapers.

Advertising made its way to the American colonies along with the early settlers from England. Ben Franklin, a pioneer of early advertising, made his ads more attractive by using large headlines and considerable white space. From Franklin's time to the early 19th century, newspaper ads resembled what today are called *classified ads*.

The most outspoken critics of advertising charge that it stimulates greed, envy, and avarice—three of the seven deadly sins—a claim that can be made by no other industry. Specifically, foes of advertising claim that it causes people to buy things that they otherwise would not. Flashy ads for new-model cars prompt people to trade in perfectly good older models simply for the prestige and status of owning new ones. Even though the old DVD player works fine, run out and buy the latest version with new bells and whistles. Still wearing last year's clothes? Shame on you. Go out and buy the latest fashions as seen in print and TV ads. In short, advertising *creates* needs and makes people buy things they do not *really* need or want.

In reply to this criticism, advertising practitioners point out that humans have a variety of needs; some are biological (the need for food) and basic (the need for a safe place to live). Others are more complicated (the need for self-esteem and self-actualization). Advertising, say its supporters, caters to a wide variety of needs, not just basic ones. There is nothing wrong with buying a new car every year if it helps a person's self-esteem. Buying the latest fashions can help a person on a quest for self-actualization. Advertising is directed at many forms of need fulfillment, some of them subtle and personal. It is presumptuous of critics to tell consumers what they need or do not need. In this argument advertising is pictured as catering to a variety of needs that are already present in consumers; it does little to create new ones. As further support for this argument, advertisers point out that many heavily advertised products fail, and there is no evidence to suggest that advertising compels people to purchase things they do not want.

A second line of criticism holds that advertising promotes materialistic values and lifestyles. Advertising persuades us to evaluate others not by who they are, but by what they possess. Material objects are portrayed as desirable goals. The people whom advertising presents as models to be emulated are not those who possess admirable personal qualities. Instead, consumers are compelled to emulate people who drive fancy or powerful cars, wear expensive jewelry, write with the best pen, wear the trendiest clothes, or watch TV on the biggest set. Advertising encourages people to spend and acquire and makes consumption the most important activity in life. Critics go on to point out that this aspect of advertising is particularly disruptive for those with low incomes who do not have the means to attain the material goals portrayed in ads.

In response to this argument, supporters of advertising point out that advertising did not create the emphasis on materialism in American life. Writings about rampant materialism in American culture were present as early as 1830. Major holidays in the United States celebrate consumption and materialism. Christmas, for example, encourages gift giving; Thanksgiving, eating. Our basic economic system of capitalism stresses the production and consumption of goods. Advertising simply reflects the larger values of U.S. society and should not be blamed for portraying them.

Finally, advertising is criticized for its intrusiveness. The typical American is the most advertised-to person in the world. U.S. companies spend more than $500 per person on advertising, more than companies in any other country. According to *Business Week,* we are exposed to about 3,000 commercial messages a day. In addition to the ubiquitous commercials on radio, on TV, on the Internet, and in print, advertising is now piped into supermarkets, airports, and doctors' offices; plastered on bathroom walls; splashed on the sides of race cars; snuck into the plots of feature films; displayed on blimps; and printed on the sides of hot dogs. Plans are even in the works to put ads in outer space. The avalanche of ads has made it difficult for advertisers to get consumers to notice their ads, let alone remember them. This leads to additional pressure to find new channels and new attention-getting techniques and results in even more intrusiveness.

Even advertising's supporters agree that advertising is hard to avoid. But they go on to point out that this is a small price to pay for the social and economic benefits that it provides for society. Without advertising, television and radio would not be free, and magazines and newspapers would cost at least twice as much. Advertising that appears on the sides of buses helps keep fares down. The uniforms worn by Little League teams are often given for free in return for plastering the advertiser's name on the back. Would you mind seeing ads for Coke in this textbook if it meant the price was $10 cheaper?

Obviously, these are complicated issues, made even more difficult because there is no simple way to sort out the effects of advertising from the effects of all the other factors in modern life. Nonetheless, because of its high visibility and its role in the well-being of consumers, advertising will continue to be subjected to intense social scrutiny.

The Industrial Revolution caused major changes in American society and in American advertising. Manufacturers, with the aid of newly invented machines, were able to mass-produce their products. Mass production, however, also required mass consumption and a mass market. Advertising was a tremendous aid in reaching this new mass audience.

The impact of increasing industrialization was most apparent in the period from the end of the Civil War to the beginning of the 20th century. In little more than three decades, the following occurred:

- The railroad linked all parts of the country, making it possible for Eastern manufacturers to distribute their goods to the growing Western markets.

- The population of the United States doubled. More people meant larger markets for manufacturers.

- The invention of new communication media—telephone, typewriter, high-speed printing press, phonograph, motion pictures, photography, rural mail delivery— made it easier for people to communicate with one another.

- Economic production increased dramatically, and people had more disposable income to spend on new products.

This improved economic and communication climate helped advertising thrive. Magazines were distributed from coast to coast and made possible truly national advertising. The development of the halftone method for reproducing photographs meant that magazine advertisers could portray their products more vividly. By 1900 it was not unusual for the leading magazines of the period (*Harper's, Cosmopolitan, McClure's*) to run 75–100 pages of ads in a typical issue.

It is not surprising that the increased importance of advertising in the marketing process led to the birth of the **advertising agency,** an organization that specializes in providing advertising services to its clients. The roots of the modern-day agency can be traced to Volney B. Palmer of Philadelphia. In 1842 Palmer bought large amounts of space in various newspapers at a discount and then resold the space at higher rates to advertisers. The actual ad—the copy, layout, and artwork—was still prepared by the company wishing to advertise; in effect, Palmer was a space broker. That situation changed in the late 19th century when the advertising agency of N. W. Ayer & Son was founded. Ayer & Son offered to plan, create, and execute complete advertising campaigns for its customers. By 1900 the advertising agency had become the focal point of creative planning, and advertising was firmly established as a profession.

The 1920s saw the beginning of radio as an advertising medium (see Chapter 7). Network broadcasting made radio an attractive vehicle for national advertisers; by 1930 about $27 million was being spent annually on network advertising, and many of the most popular shows of the day were produced by advertising agencies. However, the stock market crash of 1929 had a disastrous effect on the U.S. economy, and total dollars spent on advertising dropped from $2.8 billion in 1929 to $1.7 billion in 1935. It would take a decade for the industry to recover. During World War II many civilian firms cut back on their advertising budgets. Others simply changed the content of their ads and, instead of selling their products, instructed consumers on how to make their products last until after the war.

World War II was followed by the Cold War, when Americans were concerned about the rise of communism. Despite growth in mass consumption and economic prosperity, the prevailing mood of the country was one of apprehension as many people were afraid that communists were secretly taking over the government and subverting the American way of life. This mood also had an impact on public opinion about advertising. After the Korean War many stories surfaced about brainwashing and mind control of American prisoners. It was not long before advertising was indicted as a form of mind control that seduced people by subtle appeals to subconscious urges. A best-seller called *The Hidden Persuaders* explained how advertisers used psychological research and motivational analysis to sell consumers things they really did not need or want. It was during this time that the concept of subliminal advertising was introduced, which further deepened the suspicions about the advertising industry.

This paranoia gradually subsided during the 1960s, which were characterized by the growth of the creative side of advertising as art directors, copywriters, and TV directors had more input into the way advertising was presented. This trend weakened during the 1970s when a bad economic climate prompted a return to a more direct selling technique and a focus on efficient media planning.

SOUNDBYTE

It's Everywhere! It's Everywhere!

In case you haven't already noticed, it's hard to escape advertising. Eventually, we may get to the point where there is no blank space anywhere. Some of the novel techniques that advertisers are using include the following:

- TV monitors are embedded in the tables at mall food courts and run continuous ads.

- Custom postage stamps bear the logo of a company.

- Ads are stamped on the nozzles of gas pumps.

- In some airports, electrical outlets where commuters plug in laptops contain commercial messages (a plug on a plug?).

- In the Netherlands, sheep grazing by the roadside wear blankets that display ads. (It's called "Lease-a-Sheep.")

- Many companies print advertising on bathroom tissue. (Insert your own joke here.)

Critical / Cultural Issues

Cultural Meaning and Trade Characters

Tony the Tiger, Mr. Clean, the Maytag repairman, Ronald McDonald, the Jolly Green Giant, Betty Crocker, the Keebler Elves—these are examples of trade characters, fictional beings, played by actors or animated, created to help sell a product, service, or idea. Like slogans, trade characters are popular because they are an effective way of linking the product and its advertising so that consumers can easily remember the message. But trade characters do more than slogans; they give a product personality, style, and depth by creating an image with a clear cultural meaning with which the audience can identify.

Created by the Leo Burnett Agency, the Jolly Green Giant has been ho-ho-ho-ing for more than 40 years.

An article by Barbara Phillips in a 1996 issue of the *Journal of Popular Culture* examines the role of trade characters in American culture. Phillips notes that mass-produced products have little cultural meaning. A Duracell battery is hard to distinguish from an Eveready battery, and neither is likely to arouse any emotional response. Trade characters, however, give meaning and significance to otherwise indistinguishable products by linking a product to an image that has a cultural meaning. One way that trade characters create this meaning is by employing commonly accepted mythical symbols—images that convey cultural meaning. Take the Jolly Green Giant, for example. The giant is a common mythical figure whose size connotes strength, power, and authority. His green color is associated with freshness, while his hearty "ho-ho-ho" imparts warmth and humor. The giant's image on a can of peas makes the product less remote and more friendly.

The use of mythical symbols gives trade characters another quality: They communicate messages without having explicitly to state them. Mr. Clean, for example, immaculate in his all-white costume, symbolizes cleanliness and purity. His image suggests that using his product will produce these results, but he never actually says so. In contrast, an ad that proclaims, "Our cleaner will leave your countertop spotless and pure," might be met with some degree of doubt. Since trade characters do not directly state that a product has specific attributes, their "claims" are less likely to be rejected.

There are, of course, some drawbacks to the use of trade characters. Cultural meanings shift over time, and advertisers must be careful to monitor changing attitudes in society. Perhaps the best example of this potential is Aunt Jemima. The Quaker Oats Company started using this trade character in 1889. Over the years, however, the image became an unacceptable stereotype. In 1968, during the civil rights movement, her image changed: She lost 100 pounds and became younger; her red bandana was replaced by a headband. In 1990 she was made over again into an image that was the black equivalent of Betty Crocker, an image the company hoped was more positive. Some trade characters may be entirely inappropriate. Joe Camel, for example, was the subject of much criticism because the cartoon character seemed designed to encourage children to smoke. Camel eventually phased him out.

Trade characters have become an established part of American culture. Their ranks will undoubtedly increase in the future.

The 1980s and 1990s saw the social and media environment for advertising change dramatically. Cable television opened up dozens of new and specialized channels that siphoned advertising dollars away from the major TV networks. New video forms of marketing emerged, such as the infomercial and home shopping. Moreover, improved transportation and communication gave birth to the mega–ad agency with branches throughout the world. Political changes in Europe created new opportunities for global marketing. Changes in society also had an impact. Advertisers were facing a more culturally diverse marketplace that required more selective ads. Consumer attitudes toward products were changing, and new regulations promised to forever alter tobacco advertising. Liquor ads also drew criticism.

Contemporary advertising finds itself coping with technological and social change. As mentioned in Chapter 1, consumers are taking more and more control over their

Those sponsored links at the right side of the results page of a typical Google search brought the search engine company nearly $6 billion in ad revenue in 2009.

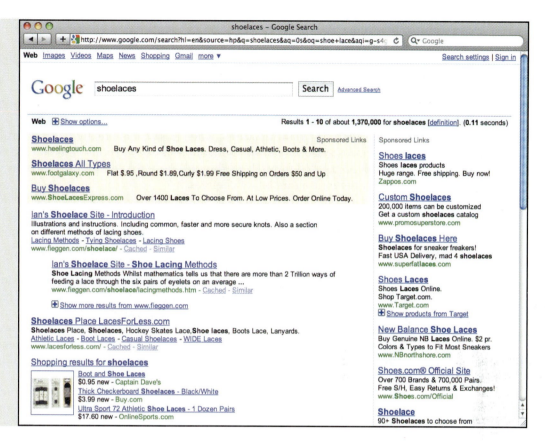

media choices. The Internet, TiVo, the iPod, cell phones, and other technologies have given consumers the power to choose when, where, and how they look for news and entertainment. The traditional advertising model, whereby advertisers interrupt a program or place ads around print articles in the hope that someone sees them, is becoming harder to justify. Couple that trend with the fact that many young people are no longer getting their news and entertainment from traditional media, and it's easy to understand why a lot of advertising money is shifting from the established media to more nontraditional forms, such as text message ads on cell phones, ads on NASCAR race cars, or Internet advertising.

Speaking of Internet advertising, the industry is exploring ways to use this new medium effectively. When it first appeared in the early 1990s, Internet advertising was hailed as the next great advance in advertising reach. As it turned out, however, these hopes were exaggerated. Banner advertising on Internet sites generated little traffic, pop-up blockers screened out pop-up ads, and spam filters quarantined much of e-mail advertising. As a result, advertising professionals had to rethink their Internet strategies. Contemporary Internet advertising is more targeted. Google, for example, lets advertisers buy space on a Web page that displays the results of an individual's Web search. Second, Web ads are becoming more interactive and more engaging. Procter & Gamble's Club Olay Web site encourages women to sign up for special offers and free samples and to receive monthly e-mail from the company.

The recession at the end of the decade had an impact on advertising spending. According to data from Nielsen, total ad revenue declined about 2.5 percent from 2007 to 2008. Advertising in newspapers and magazines dropped the most. Only cable TV and the Internet showed gains.

SOUNDBYTE

Do You Watch the Commercials?

Here are some of the results of a recent survey about what people do during TV commercials:

- 53 percent get annoyed at the number of commercials.
- 52 percent talk to others and don't pay attention.
- 50 percent get up and do something else.
- 43 percent switch to another channel.
- 27 percent mute the sound.
- 13 percent sit and watch the commercial.

Speaking of the Internet, the amount spent on online advertising rose from about $6 billion in 2002 to about $11 billion in 2008, but there were signs that its growth rate was leveling off. The biggest advertisers in 2008 were Procter & Gamble, AT&T, and Verizon.

Advertising in the Digital Age

Online advertising began in 1994 when HotWired, the digital counterpart to the hip *Wired* magazine, started a Web site with about a dozen sponsors who paid to have advertising banners embedded throughout the site. Since that time, advertising as well as the Internet have undergone a number of changes.

▲ Audience Control

As mentioned in Chapter 1, consumers are taking more and more control over their media choices. TiVo, the iPod, video-on-demand, the Internet, and other technologies have given individuals the power to choose when, where, and how they look for news and entertainment. As far as advertising is concerned, consumers are increasingly making media choices that involve avoiding advertising. In a recent survey about half the respondents said that ads spoil their reading or viewing experience. About 18 million people have opted for commercial-free music on satellite radio. Digital video recorders, such as TiVo, are in more than 40 percent of U.S. homes, and the number is increasing daily. As you might expect, about two-thirds of DVR owners fast-forward through the ads. Thousands of commercial-free episodes of TV shows have been downloaded from iTunes. Most people have ad- and spam-blocking software installed on their computers.

These developments have forced advertisers to look for other means to reach the audience. Product placement has become common in movies, TV shows, and even video games. **Viral advertising,** a technique by which companies try to create messages that are so compelling, interesting, funny, or suggestive that consumers willingly and spontaneously share them with others, usually via e-mail, social networking sites, or cell phones, is a hot area. If the technique is successful, word spreads rapidly to a large number of people, much like a virus. For instance, Dove Evolution, a short film posted on YouTube, got more than 1.7 million views thanks to good consumer reaction.

Targeted search advertising, paying for links to a product or service on search results pages, accounted for about $10 billion in revenue in 2008. Finally, some advertisers have turned to "buzz marketing," a technique that pays consumers to talk about products and services.

▲ New Channels

The digital revolution has opened up additional avenues for advertising. Bloggers represent a segment of the population that wields significant influence. Advertisers can use networks such as Blogads to target specific blogs whose readers would be likely customers for their product or service.

Podcasts are another emerging channel. Podtrac, for example, offers advertisers access to 1,500 podcasts, ranging from "This Week in Tech" to "Mugglecast" for Harry Potter fans. Advertisers select the demographics and interests of their target market, and Podtrac selects the most appropriate podcasts. Companies typically sponsor an entire podcast and pay on the basis of how many times the podcast was downloaded.

Not surprisingly, advertising is becoming more common on cell phones. Most high school and college students have one, and young people are the audience segment that many advertisers want to reach. Cell phone companies and advertisers are currently exploring various arrangements. One alternative would let subscribers opt in for ads, agreeing to receive ads on their phones in return for a reduced monthly fee. Another takes advantage of the fact that some phones have global positioning systems. Theoretically at least, a consumer might get a cell phone text message ad when he or she is in the vicinity of a certain store. Consumers who use their phone to access the Internet are already exposed to some advertising. ESPN, for example, includes short video ads along with its video highlights. Advertisers are proceeding cautiously, however, since they fear that cell phone ads might have a boomerang effect and make consumers hostile to the advertised products.

▲ User-Generated Content

As it has in other media areas, user-generated content has become popular with advertisers. Companies such as MasterCard, GM, and Converse have encouraged users to submit homemade commercials. Career Builder ran a user-generated ad contest with the winning entry to be shown during the Super Bowl.

The advantages to advertisers are obvious. Amateur ads cost almost nothing, get consumers to "engage" with the product, and can create word-of-mouth buzz. Companies usually give participants some sort of general theme, simple rules, and a suggested length. Of course, there's a downside. When GM asked users to come up with an ad for their Chevy Tahoe, it got several entries from people who criticized the vehicle for harming the environment.

▲ Decoupling

Finally, mass marketers are no longer as dependent on the mass media as they were 30 years ago, a trend that has serious implications for the media. Back then, if Sony wanted to introduce a new-model TV set, it would advertise in newspapers and magazines and on various television programs or networks. The company realized that much of its advertising would reach people who had absolutely no interest in buying a TV, but Sony would tolerate that inefficiency in order to reach those few who were interested. As department store mogul John Wanamaker once said, "I know half my advertising is wasted but I don't know which half." With the Internet, however, advertisers may be able to figure out how to drastically cut waste.

The Internet lets advertisers target ads at the people most likely to buy the product or service. Search engine ads are the most obvious example. Rather than spending huge amounts of money on TV ads, Sony could pay Google to have an ad displayed next to the search results whenever anybody searched for "television set" or a similar term. To use another example, sites such as Amazon, eBay, and Netflix keep track of what a person buys or rents so that when a person returns to their site, he or she gets a list of recommended items based on his or her search and/or purchasing behavior as well as on the behavior of other people who bought or rented similar items.

Moreover, the Internet makes it easier for advertisers to collect huge amounts of data from large groups of people. Data processing software lets them mine the data for associations that would otherwise seem counterintuitive. One data-mining exercise found that the number-one online activity of people who bought big-screen TVs was visiting military Web sites. Shopping online for TVs ranked 18th. TV set manufacturers would probably devote part of their budget to advertising on military Web sites, something they would probably have never done before the age of data mining.

Further, advertisers are putting more of their budgets into nonmedia sources, such as viral marketing, sponsorship of special events, and public relations efforts. For example, check out the number of advertisers on a typical NASCAR vehicle. Point-of-purchase or in-store advertising is gaining in popularity and attracts more than $10 billion annually.

All of this leads to what we have already called the **"decoupling"** of advertising from mass media (see Chapter 4). There is no compelling reason why advertisers should pay the salaries of TV stars and radio DJs. As companies and organizations find more efficient ways to market their goods and services, there will be a further migration of revenue from the media to other forms of advertising and marketing. This will obviously not happen overnight, but the pattern is clear. The old advertising model is losing more and more of its foundation, and one of these days it may collapse altogether. Traditional ad-supported media are looking for ways to survive the transition.

Organization of the Consumer Advertising Industry

There are three main components of the advertising industry: (1) advertisers, (2) advertising agencies, and (3) the media. We will discuss each of these in turn.

▲ Advertisers

Advertising is an important part of the overall marketing plan of almost every organization that provides a product or a service to the public. Advertisers can range from the small bicycle shop on the corner that spends $4 on an ad in the local weekly paper to huge international corporations such as AT&T, which spends more than $3 billion annually for ads.

At a basic level we can distinguish two different types of advertisers: national and retail. **National advertisers** sell their product or service to customers all across the country. The emphasis in national advertising is on the product or service and not so much on the place where the product or service is sold. For example, the Coca-Cola Company is interested in selling soft drinks. It does not matter to the company if you buy its product at the local supermarket, at a small convenience store, or from a vending machine. **Retail advertisers** (also called *local advertisers*) are companies such as local restaurants, car dealerships, TV repair shops, and other merchants and service organizations that have customers in only one city or trading area. The retail advertiser wants to attract customers to a specific store or place of business. Some companies are both national and local advertisers. Sears and Target, for example, advertise all over the country, but their individual stores use local advertising to highlight their specific sales and promotions. Franchises, such as McDonald's and Burger King, keep up their national image by advertising on network TV, while their local outlets put ads in the paper to attract customers from the local community.

Naturally, the way organizations handle their advertising depends on their size. Some companies have their own advertising departments; a small retail store might have one person who is responsible for advertising and marketing and who may also have other job functions. Whether large or small, all advertisers must attend to several basic functions. These include planning the ads and deciding where they will appear, setting aside a certain amount of money for the advertising budget, coordinating the advertising with other departments in the organization, and, if necessary, supervising the work of an outside agency or company that produces the ad. In addition, some large advertisers have departments that can create and prepare all the advertising materials, purchase the space and airtime for the ads, and check to see if the ads were effective in achieving their goals.

▲ Agencies

According to the American Association of Advertising Agencies, an **agency** is an independent business organization composed of creative people and businesspeople who develop, prepare, and place advertising for sellers seeking to find customers for their goods and services. In the past, advertising agencies were located in a few big cities, such as New York, Chicago, and Los Angeles. That trend has changed, however, and many of the more memorable

The boss as spokesperson. Papa John's founder, John Schnatter, frequently appears in his company's commercials.

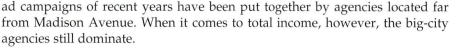

ad campaigns of recent years have been put together by agencies located far from Madison Avenue. When it comes to total income, however, the big-city agencies still dominate.

The past few years in the agency business have seen the spawning of super-agencies, or mega-agencies, resulting from the merger and consolidation of several large ad agencies. In addition, the business has been globalized, since these new mega-agencies have branches all over the world. The five mega-agencies listed in Table 15-1 dominated the industry at the close of 2008.

The global reach of advertising is apparent in the agency business as in many other media. Three of the megagroups in Table 15-1 are foreign-owned.

Agencies can be classified by the range of services they offer. In general terms there are three main types: (1) full-service agencies, (2) media buying services, and (3) creative boutiques.

As the name implies, a **full-service agency** handles all phases of the advertising process for its clients; it plans, creates, produces, and places ads. In addition, it might provide other marketing services, such as sales promotions, trade show exhibits, newsletters, and annual reports. In theory, at least, there is no need for the client to deal with any other company for help promoting its product.

A **media buying service** specializes in buying radio and TV time and reselling it to advertisers and advertising agencies. The service sells time to the advertiser, orders the spots on the various stations, and monitors the stations to see if the ads actually run.

A **creative boutique** (the name was coined during the 1960s and has hung on to the present) is an organization that specializes in the actual creation of ads. In general, boutiques create imaginative and distinctive advertising themes and produce innovative and original ads. A company that uses a creative boutique would have to employ another agency to perform the planning, buying, and administrative functions connected with advertising.

What does a full-service ad agency do for a client? To begin with, the agency studies the product or service and determines what its marketable characteristics are and how it relates to the competition. At the same time, the agency studies the potential market, possible distribution plans, and likely advertising media. The agency then makes a formal presentation to the client detailing its findings and its recommended advertising strategy. If the client agrees, the agency launches the execution phase. This phase entails writing and producing the ads, buying space and time in various media, delivering the ads to the appropriate media, and verifying that all ads actually appear. Finally, the agency works closely with the client's salespeople to make sure they get the greatest possible benefit from the ads.

As advertising continues to move online, several new advertising agencies specializing in creating and delivering ads to Web sites have emerged. These digital ad agencies work with ad networks, organizations that buy Web space from different sites and resell it to advertisers. Once the Web sites have been lined up by the ad network, the ads themselves are distributed by ad-serving firms, such as DoubleClick.

TABLE 15-1	Company	Headquarters	2008 Revenue (in billion U.S. dollars)
Top Five Advertising Agencies, 2008	WPP Group	London	$13.6
	Omnicom	New York	13.4
	Interpublic	New York	6.5
	Publicis	Paris	6.3
	Dentsu	Tokyo	2.9

▲ Media

The final part of the advertising industry consists of the mass media. The media serve as the connection between a company and its customers. The media that are available for advertising include some obvious ones—radio, TV, newspapers, magazines, the Internet—and others that are not so obvious, such as direct mail, billboards, transit cards (bus and car cards), stadium scoreboard ads, point-of-purchase ads, e-mail, chat rooms, and even iPods. Chapters 4, 5, 7, and 10–12 presented an overview of the mainstream mass media and discussed their dependence on various kinds of advertising. This section examines these media from the perspective of an advertiser.

Even the slickest and most imaginative advertising message will fail if it is delivered to the wrong people. To make sure that this does not happen, advertisers employ highly skilled media planners to help them place and schedule their ads.

Advertising specialists evaluate media along four dimensions:

1. *Reach:* How many people can get the message?
2. *Frequency:* How often will the message be received?
3. *Selectivity:* Does the medium actually reach potential customers?
4. *Efficiency:* How much does it cost to reach a certain number of people? (This is usually expressed as cost per thousand people.)

Table 15-2 summarizes how the various media rate on these dimensions.

TABLE 15-2 CHARACTERISTICS	MEDIUM						
Characteristics of Various Media	Newspapers	Magazines	Radio	TV	Outdoor	Direct Mail	Internet
Reach	High	Low	High	High	High	High	Medium
Frequency	High	Low	High	High	High	Medium	Medium
Selectivity	Low	High	High	Medium	Low	High	High
Efficiency	Medium	Medium	Low	High	High	High	Medium

In addition to considering these factors, advertisers have to take into account many others before deciding on which medium to use. An important part of any decision involves considering the creative limitations imposed by the physical properties of each medium. Television, for example, enables the advertiser to show the product in action. On the other hand, TV ads are short and cannot be used to present a great deal of technical information. YouTube advertising videos can be any length, but they may get lost in the plethora of other videos on the site. A magazine ad can be in full color and can present a large amount of data, but it might not have the same impact as a TV ad. Ads on Facebook are relatively cheap, but they reach an audience that is less engaged with advertising in general. All in all, choosing which media to use in the final advertising mix is a difficult decision.

Producing Advertising

▲ Departments and Staff

There are typically four major departments in a big advertising agency: (1) creative services, (2) account services, (3) marketing services, and (4) administration.

The creative department, as the name implies, actually produces the ad. The people in this department write the advertising **copy** (the headline and message of the ad), choose the illustrations, prepare artwork, and/or supervise the scripting and production of radio, TV, and Web ads.

The account services department is responsible for the relationship between the agency and the client. Because the advertising agency is an organization outside the firm doing the advertising, it is necessary to appoint someone, usually called an *account executive* (AE), to promote communication and understanding between client and agency. The AE must represent the viewpoint of the agency to the client but at the same time keep abreast of the needs of the advertiser. Since the AE tends to be the person in the middle, his or her job is obviously an important one in the agency.

The marketing services department is responsible for advising the client as to what media to use for his or her messages. Typically, this department makes extensive use of the data collected by the Audit Bureau of Circulations, Arbitron, Nielsen, MediaMetrix, and the other audience research services mentioned in earlier chapters. This department is also in charge of any sales promotions that are done in connection with the advertising. These may include such things as coupons, premiums, and other aids to dealers.

Netflix is just one of many companies that use pop-up ads. Pop-ups are economical and advertisers think they are effective.

Finally, like any other business, the advertising agency needs a department to take care of the day-to-day administration of the agency. This department is in charge of office management, clerical functions, accounting, personnel, and the training of new employees.

▲ The Advertising Campaign

The best way to illustrate how ads get produced is to present a general discussion of an advertising campaign for a national product. A **campaign** consists of a large number of advertisements, all stressing the same major theme or appeal, that appear in a number of media over a specified time. Following is a discussion, greatly simplified, of the six phases of a typical campaign:

1. Choosing the marketing strategy
2. Selecting the main appeal or theme
3. Translating the theme into the various media
4. Producing the ads
5. Buying space and time
6. Executing and evaluating the campaign

In the first phase, a great deal of research is done to determine the target audience, the marketing objective, the appropriate price for the product or service, and the advertising budget. It is during this phase that the word **positioning** is often heard. Positioning has many interpretations, but in general it means fitting a product or service to one or more segments of the broad market in such a way as to set it apart from the competition without making any change in the product.

Gatorade, for example, for many years used ads that featured sports stars such as Tiger Woods and Mia Hamm in action. In 2009, in an attempt to update the product and to reach consumers who aren't hard-core sports fans, Gatorade was renamed G. Its first round of ads featured athletes, but this time they were casually dressed and not performing. Subsequent advertising portrayed ordinary consumers consuming the product.

Office Max's research revealed that women purchase more than $44 billion in office supplies every year and repositioned itself as a female-friendly store. Ads featured a female walking into a drab office that suddenly bursts into color when she places the Office Max–trademarked ball of colored rubber bands on her desk. The tagline: "Life is beautiful. Work can be too."

Sometimes positioning does not work. Minute Maid orange juice failed in its attempt to reposition its product from simply a breakfast drink to an all-purpose beverage. Despite an $18-million campaign that featured the slogan "Not just for breakfast anymore," sales of orange juice remained flat as customers failed to respond.

After the product or service has been positioned, an overall theme for the campaign is developed and the theme is translated into print, broadcast, and online ads. McDonald's, for example, built a theme around the accent mark in the name of its new coffee brand, McCafé. As one TV spot put it, when you "McCafé your day, a commute becomes a commuté. When a pal drops by your cubicle with an iced mocha, it's a cubiclé." Radio spots talked about how to speak McCafé. The $100-million campaign also featured print ads, a Twitter account, and a McCafé Web site with videos that consumers could share on their social media pages.

Many advertisers like to use well-known celebrities in their ad campaigns. Christina Aguilera, for example, appears in TV commercials for Pepsi and other products.

When it first started back in the 1950s, it was called Kentucky Fried Chicken and its symbol was its founder, Honorary Colonel Harlan Sanders, whose white hair, goatee, and white suit graced many a bucket of fried chicken. In 1991, apparently thinking that "fried" was not the most appropriate descriptor in an increasingly health-conscious society, the name was shortened to KFC, but the restaurant chain still made most of its money by selling fried chicken seasoned with a secret recipe of eleven herbs and spices.

In 2009, however, KFC decided to refocus its advertising emphasis from fried chicken to grilled chicken. Rather than change its name to KGC, the company invested in an expensive ad campaign based on the theme "Unthink KFC." As part of the campaign, KFC enlisted the aid of Oprah Winfrey. Anybody who went to Oprah.com during a one-day window could download and print a coupon that could be redeemed at participating restaurants for two free pieces of grilled chicken, two sides, and a biscuit. Given what happened next, we could ask "What were they unthinking?"

Apparently KFC underestimated Oprah's drawing power and the speed with which news of something free travels over the Internet. It also apparently failed to alert local restaurants to prepare for a stampede of people looking for a free meal. When many customers tried to redeem their coupons, they found that restaurants had no chicken left. Some restaurants simply refused to honor the coupons while others told customers to come back some other time. None of these situations made consumers happy. Twitter was ablaze with people bad-mouthing KFC. News crews interviewed disgruntled customers. People in New York City reportedly staged a protest when they weren't served. KFC finally realized that there was no way it could meet demand, and it pulled the plug on the giveaway.

By the time it ended, there were still more than 6 million coupons that had yet to be redeemed. A person with an unredeemed coupon could go back to a KFC restaurant, fill out a form for a rain check, and wait for another coupon to arrive in the mail (those who did not get a chance to use their coupon during the original promotion would also get a free Pepsi with their meal).

KFC suffered a storm of bad publicity. Mentions on Twitter and blog posts turned negative. Instead of touting the merits of grilled chicken, a KFC spokeswoman was forced to rebut reports that customers had rioted at KFC outlets. Trade magazine *Advertising Age* branded the chicken fiasco a marketing disaster on a par with New Coke. Despite all of the negatives, KFC chose to accentuate the positive, emphasizing that the promotion brought many new customers to the chain's local outlets.

Let's close this probe by contemplating a quote from a KFC spokesperson who was interviewed by a reporter during the promotion. After acknowledging that some KFC restaurants had run out of coleslaw and mashed potatoes and gravy, the spokesperson added "but they are substituting as best they can." Which raises the question: What were they using as substitutes?

The actual production of the ad is done in much the same way that other media content is produced. In the print media the copy, the headline, subheads, any accompanying illustrations, and the layout are first prepared in rough form. The initial step is usually just a thumbnail sketch that can be used to experiment with different arrangements within the ad. The headline might be moved down, the copy moved from right to left, and so on. Next, a **rough layout**—a drawing that is the actual size of the ad—is constructed. Usually, several layouts are prepared, and the best are used to produce the **comprehensive layout,** the one that will be used to produce the ad. Many agencies use outside art studios and printers to help them put together print ads and billboards.

Radio commercials are written and created in much the same way that early radio drama shows were produced. A script is prepared in which dialogue, sound effects, and music are combined to produce whatever effect is desired. The commercial is then either produced in the sound studio or recorded live on location. In either case postproduction editing adds any desired special effects, and eventually, a master disc is prepared for duplication and distribution.

The beginning step in the preparation of a television commercial is a **storyboard,** a series of drawings depicting the key scenes of the planned ad. Storyboards are usually shown to the client before production begins. If the client has any objections or suggestions, changes can be made to the script before production. Once the storyboards are approved, the commercial is ready to go into production. Most TV commercials are shot on film (although some are now switching to videotape). Television commercials are the

There are many blogs across the Web that specialize in writing about travel. People consult them to find out information about airlines, hotels, and tourist attractions. They assume that the blog writer is giving his or her honest and unbiased assessment of a product or service. If the blogger raves about the accommodations at a particular hotel, the reader assumes the blogger is telling the truth.

Well, maybe yes and maybe no. In many instances, advertisers are funneling money to bloggers in return for favorable mentions. Most of the time, the reader is unaware that a payment has been made. The practice is gaining in popularity thanks to the poor economy, as more bloggers look for ways to increase their income. For their part, some bloggers are posting messages on their sites indicating that they accept compensation but that it has no effect on their opinions. Even those bloggers who do not disclose that they are compensated argue that payments have no influence on their opinions.

Of course, many traditional media outlets also take gifts from potential advertisers, but there are ethical guidelines about what they can accept. Advertising professionals also have ethics codes that offer guidance about full disclosure in ads. The code of the Word of Mouth Marketing Association states in part: "We stand against marketing practices whereby the consumer is paid cash by the manufacturer, supplier, or one of their representatives to make recommendations, reviews, or endorsements."

The ethical issues raised here are similar to those mentioned in Chapter 14 with regard to "buzz marketing." The situation is a little different with bloggers because they operate in a different forum. Consumers are probably more skeptical of claims made by a relatively unknown blogger than they would be of claims made by an acquaintance. Nonetheless, if a blogger refuses to acknowledge that he or she accepted a payment from the manufacturer of a product that they are reviewing, deception is involved. It matters little if the blogger claims that payments do not affect their opinions. Deception is still involved, and ethical experts agree that deception is seldom the proper way to act.

What about the ethics of acknowledging a payment but claiming that it didn't affect a review? Ethically speaking, that position is more defensible but the blogger owes his or her readers some proof of that claim. Showing examples of payments for products that eventually received poor reviews might be one way to substantiate the claim of objectivity.

As sometimes happens in a situation where the law and ethics are ambiguous, the government fills in the blanks. In late 2009, the Federal Trade Commission proposed rules to regulate what bloggers and people on social media sites can claim about products. One section of the proposed rules states that if someone is compensated to review a product and then makes false claims about the product, that person could be sued for false representation. If, for example, a medical firm paid a blogger to review a new foot care product and the blogger incorrectly claimed that the product cured athlete's foot, then the FTC could sue the blogger as well as the medical firm.

In any case, like everything else on the Internet, readers should be skeptical of blogs that review products until they can assess the blogger's credibility.

---

most expensive ads to produce. A 30-second spot can easily cost $350,000. Special effects, particularly animation, can drive the costs even higher. In an effort to keep costs down, much of the time spent producing TV commercials consists of planning and rehearsing. As with the print media, many agencies hire outside production specialists to produce their commercials.

While all this is going on, other members of the creative team are preparing Web ads. Banner ads, pop-ups, and pop-unders are still the most common types of online ads, but other configurations are becoming popular. Splash pages are Web pages that appear before a Web page loads and then disappear a short time later. Skyscraper ads are elongated vertical banners that border one or both sides of a Web page. Floating ads move up, down, or across a page as the user scrolls through a Web site. A wallpaper ad changes the background of the page being viewed. Shorter versions of a TV ad might also be prepared to run on the advertiser's Web site or posted on YouTube.

While the creative department is putting together print, Web, and broadcast ads, the marketing department is buying time in those media judged to be appropriate for the campaign. If the product is seasonal (suntan lotion, snowmobiles), the ads are scheduled to reflect the calendar, appearing slightly before and during the time people might begin buying such items. Other products and services might call for a program of steady advertising throughout the year.

This may happen to you in the near future. You're standing in line at a movie theater when all of a sudden your cell phone rings with a message that suggests a Coke and some popcorn would help you enjoy your moviegoing experience. Or you could be at the mall when you get a text message alerting you to Old Navy's big sale.

With advertisers finding it increasingly difficult to reach young people through the traditional mass media, it was only a matter of time before they explored the potential of the nearly ubiquitous cell phone as an advertising medium. The industry calls it "mobile marketing," and it takes various forms: text messages and voice, video, and Web ads on Internet-enabled phones.

The efforts in this area are just beginning. Snapple recently sent 25,000 text messages to selected consumers alerting them to a contest that would reward them with prizes if they found lucky bottle caps from Snapple products. Trans World Entertainment (TWE) is testing a system in which consumers with Bluetooth-capable phones are sent text messages about movie trailers and music downloads as soon as they walk into an f.y.e. or Coconuts store. A 2006 survey revealed that almost 90 percent of major advertisers were considering using the cell phone as an advertising tool.

But what do consumers think about this trend? Most people are irritated when telemarketers interrupt their privacy at home. How will they respond to this possible new intrusion? Not positively, if early indications are typical. One survey disclosed that about 70 percent didn't want ads on their phones. Most were afraid that their cell phones would become as cluttered with ads as their e-mail was with spam.

Faced with this potential resistance, advertisers are looking for ways to make the advertising more attractive. One ad agency is touting the "opt-in" approach—ads will be sent only to those individuals who want them. Another plan offers incentives: Accept ads for a credit on a user's cell phone bill. Consumer groups are also concerned about issues of privacy and intrusiveness raised by cell phone advertising. The Wireless Advertising Industry Association was recently formed to recommend industry guidelines.

As in other areas, advertisers must tread carefully and balance the need to reach consumers with the problems associated with intruding into someone's personal space.

The last phase of the campaign consists of the running of the ads. Testing is done during and after this phase to see if consumers saw and remembered the ads. In addition, sales data are carefully monitored to determine if the campaign had the desired effect on sales.

▲ Advertising Research

Advertising research, which takes place during all phases of the campaign, helps agencies and their clients make informed decisions about their strategy and tactics. **Formative research** is done before the campaign begins to help guide the creative effort. It can take several forms. One is audience definition—identifying the target market, such as "females 18–34" or "all adults." After this is accomplished, audience profiling is done to discover as much as possible about how the target market lives—what they think, what their attitudes are, and how they decide to buy.

The next phase, **message research,** involves pretesting the messages that have been developed for the campaign. At its most basic level, pretesting determines if the audience can actually understand the ads. This type of testing guards against possible double meanings or overlooked sexual connotations that might have eluded the creative staff. In a second type of pretest, researchers show mock-ups of magazines that contain the prototype of the print ad and rough cuts of TV ads to test audiences. Consumers are tested to see whether they recall the main points of the ad and whether their attitude toward the product has shown any change. Some advertising campaigns go through pilot tests in actual markets. A split-cable transmission can show one version of an ad to one group of people and a second version to another group. The ads are compared to see which did a better job. A split-run of a magazine uses the same strategy.

Tracking studies examine how the ads perform during or after the actual campaign. Samples of consumers are studied to see if they recall the ads, if their attitudes about the product have changed, and if they have bought the product or used the service advertised.

The Economics of Advertising

In this section we will examine the economics of advertising on two levels. First, we will look at the total industry and trace expenditures in various media. Second, we will narrow our focus and examine how an advertising agency makes money.

▲ Advertising Volume in Various Media

About $260 billion was spent on advertising in the United States in 2008. Figure 15-1 shows how this money was divided among the various media. Since 1980, newspapers have seen a decrease in their relative share of advertising volumes, as have magazines. Television has shown a significant increase, while outdoor advertising and direct mail have shown modest growth. The Internet will probably account for more of the pie in the future.

▲ Agency Compensation

Historically, the major mass media have allowed advertising agencies a 15 percent commission on the time and space they purchase. Recently, however, the commission system has been declining in popularity. Many advertisers have struck pay-for-performance deals with ad agencies. Payments to ad agencies are based on sales or some other measure of performance. If sales go up, the ad agency gets more money. Other companies pay agencies a fixed fee, and still others use a combination of a flat fee plus performance-based incentives.

FIGURE 15-1

Advertising Expenditures in Various Media, 2008

(Dollar figures are in billions.)

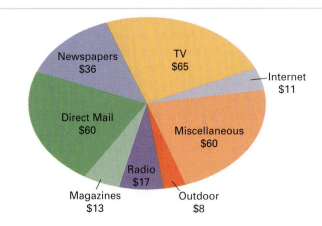

Newspapers $36 · TV $65 · Internet $11 · Miscellaneous $60 · Outdoor $8 · Radio $17 · Magazines $13 · Direct Mail $60

Business-to-Business Advertising

As its name suggests, business-to-business advertising is designed to sell products and services not to general consumers but to other businesses, typically via specialized trade publications, direct mail, e-mail, Web sites, professional journals, and display advertising at trade shows. There are four main categories of business-to-business advertising:

1. *Trade:* Advertising goods and services to wholesalers and retailers who, in turn, resell these items to a more general audience.
2. *Industrial:* Advertising those items that are used in the further production of goods and services, such as copy machines, forklifts, and drill presses.
3. *Professional:* Advertising aimed at doctors, lawyers, architects, nurses, and others who might influence the buying process or use the product in their profession.
4. *Agricultural:* Advertising aimed at farmers and possibly including products such as feed, fertilizer, seed, and chemicals.

Although its visibility might not be high, business-to-business advertising is a multibillion-dollar industry. Some people overlook the potential for a career in business-to-business advertising because they feel it is not as glamorous as consumer advertising. There may be some truth to this: Ads for a chemical solvent, bench-top fermenter, or blast furnace usually are not as flashy as campaigns for sleek new sports cars. In its own way, though, business advertising poses greater creative challenges. Coming up with a theme to sell the sports car is probably much easier than coming up with a winning idea for the chemical solvent.

▲ Consumer Versus Business-to-Business Advertising

There are some obvious differences between advertising directed at consumers and business advertising. In this section we will consider four.

First, the target audience in business advertising is much smaller. In some industries the audience may number in the hundreds. Companies that manufacture storage tanks for petroleum products, for example, have determined that there are only 400 people in the United States authorized to purchase their product. In other areas, the audience may be in the thousands. This means, of course, that the media used to reach the target market must be selected carefully. In the nuclear reactor business, for instance, everyone in the market may read one or two publications.

Second, most of the products that are advertised tend to be technical, complicated, and high-priced. For the advertiser this means that the ads will probably contain a great deal of technical information and will stress accuracy.

The medium of outdoor advertising has grown rapidly over the past decade. Modern billboards use striking new designs and graphics.

Ethical Issues   Advertising and Kids

There is no doubt that advertisers have zeroed in on the child audience. The last few years have seen the growth of kid-specific media: Nickelodeon, Web sites, kid-oriented magazines, movie tie-ins, and even hamburger wrappers. In 2008, about $2 billion was spent on advertising aimed at children.

Part of the reason behind this increase is the fact that kids have become important factors in family buying decisions. First, they have more money to spend. The under-14 set gets allowances, earns money, and receives gifts to the tune of about $20 billion per year. In addition, kids probably influence another $200 billion worth of shopping decisions. Second, the increase in single-parent families and dual-career families means that kids are now making some of the purchasing decisions that were once left to Mom and Dad.

It is not surprising, then, to find that companies are intensifying their efforts to reach this market segment. And it is not just traditional toymakers, cereal companies, and fast-food restaurants that are in the mix. General Motors, for example, placed ads for its new minivan in *Sports Illustrated for Kids* and sent prototype vans to shopping malls where they showed previews of Disney's *Hercules* on a VCR inside the van. GM does not expect many 6-year-olds to go out and buy a van, but the company knows through its research that kids can play an influential role in the decision about which van to buy. In that connection United Airlines kept its younger travelers happy by serving McDonald's Happy Meals.

Market research that examines children's psychology has been used to help sell goods. Researchers know that 7- and 8-year-olds like to collect things. This urge used to be satisfied by bottle caps, seashells, and baseball cards. More recently, the maker of Beanie Babies cashed in on this urge by creating a large number of different animals to collect, limiting production and discontinuing models to create artificial scarcity.

The marketing even extends into schools. Companies donate money, equipment, and educational materials to schools in return for the opportunity to advertise their products. It all started with Channel One, a news program for students. In return for a donation of electronic equipment, schools agreed to show a newscast that contained commercials. Other companies did not take long to follow Channel One. Nike, for example, mailed out shoe assembly kits to schools. Teachers were supposed to help kids make the sneakers while teaching a lesson on environmentally safe manufacturing (presumably by companies like Nike). McDonald's sponsored a seven-week curriculum on how to build a McDonald's restaurant and how to interview for a job there. Some school districts, hard up for cash, have sold advertising space on the sides of school buses and in school hallways.

There are many who feel that all this selling to children is not right. They argue that children are an unsophisticated audience and are vulnerable to the flashy, persuasive techniques of the advertising industry. Not many parents would allow a salesperson to come into their home and talk to their kids; why, then, should they allow TV to target their children? Additionally, critics contend that advertising teaches values that are undesirable. Advertising focuses on the superficial and the material, and it glorifies consumption. Finally, critics contend that advertising creates conflicts between parents and children by encouraging kids to pester their parents for all the products they see advertised. Parents must continually say no and run the risk of possible strife. There is some evidence to support these positions. Even without this support, however, many people feel that advertising to kids is just plain wrong.

The advertisers reply that these critics do not give kids enough credit. They feel that kids are more sophisticated consumers than people realize and learn very quickly to see through the hype and manipulation that may be found in some ads. Additionally, the marketing community points out that kids are going to live in a world saturated by advertising. Coming into contact with it at an early age may help them learn how to deal with it when they become adults. Finally, they argue that kids get valuable information about new products and services from advertising, information that improves their lives.

The issue, of course, has legal as well as ethical overtones. To date, the government has weighed in on the side of kids. The Children's Television Act limits the amount of commercial minutes in TV shows that can be directed at children. The government and the tobacco industry worked out an agreement that prohibited the Camel cigarette company from using the cartoon character Joe Camel in its ads because the character appealed to children. There have been proposals to ban or limit beer, wine, and liquor advertising. Despite these efforts, it is clear that parents will be the ones to confront this issue head-on.

Third, the buyers are professionals—purchasing agents whose only job is to acquire products and services for their company. Generally, the decisions of the purchasing agent are based on reason and research. An error of a penny or two on a large purchase might cost a company thousands of dollars. Consequently, business advertising typically uses the rational approach. Additionally, it is important for advertisers to know exactly who makes buying decisions, since most purchases in large business are generally made in consultation with others in a company.

Fourth, personal selling plays a greater role in the business arena, and advertising is frequently used to support the sales staff in the field. As a result, ad budgets in the business sector may not be as high as those of their consumer counterparts.

▲ Media

The media mix for business advertising is also different from that of consumer advertising. Since the target audience tends to be small, personalized media are best. Business publications tend to be the mainstay of campaigns. One study suggested that about 60 percent of industrial advertising dollars went to business and trade publications. Trade publications can be horizontal, dealing with a job function without regard to industry (such as *Purchasing*), or vertical, covering all job types in an entire industry (such as *LP/Gas*).

Direct mail and e-mail are valuable business advertising tools. Highly differentiated mailing lists can be prepared and ads sent to the most likely prospects. Research has shown that mail is perhaps more effective among businesspeople than among consumers. Whereas a large percentage of direct-mail material is thrown out unopened by the general public, most businesspeople read or at least scan their e-mail and direct-mail ads.

Advertising in trade catalogues is particularly important to companies that sell through distributors rather than via their own sales staff. Since a catalogue is a direct reflection of a company, extra care is taken to make sure it is up-to-date, accurate, and visually appealing.

An example of business-to-business advertising. This ad for Caterpillar industrial equipment contains far more technical information than would be found in a consumer ad.

Exceeding Your Expectations

Cat® 315/315 L:
The New Size in Power and Efficiency

To get the highest return on your machine investment you need an excavator that will do the job efficiently and move on to the next job site quickly. The new Cat 315 is designed to do just that. With all the performance features of the Cat 300 Family and a design which allows it to be hauled on a tag-along trailer, the new 315 can increase your productivity. Here are some of the benefits:

• 300 Family advanced hydraulics with three Power Mode Settings, three Work Mode Settings, Automatic Engine Control and self-diagnostic capabilities for improved productivity, increased fuel efficiency and lower maintenance costs.

© 1994 Caterpillar

• 99 FWHP, turbocharged Cat 3046 Engine designed for more efficient, responsive power and fuel efficiency, plus reduced sound levels.

• Two undercarriage options, standard and long (L), both with a maximum shipping width of less than 9'0" for hassle-free movement from job to job.

• Three stick options to match your job needs: 10'2"   8'6"   7'5"

• Standard auxiliary hydraulic valve for attachment flexibility to do a wider range of jobs more efficiently.

• New control features, including light-touch joysticks...automatic low-to-high-speed travel selection...and winged foot pedals for easier operation.

• Comfortable, efficient cab with large windows for excellent visibility... fully adjustable seat...and sliding joystick consoles.

All these 300 Family advantages...along with your Cat Dealer's unsurpassed service, support and industry-leading parts network...work together to Exceed Your Expectations in every way. Stop in and see the new Cat 315 today!

	315/315 L
Power:	99 FWHP
Operating Weight Up To:	36,000 lb
Ground Level Reach:	30'0"
Maximum Digging Depth:	21'6"
Bucket Capacity Range:	0.68 - 0.97 yd³
Shipping Width, 24" Shoes:	8'6"

CATERPILLAR®

Business-to-business advertising in the mass media used to be rare, but some large companies, such as FedEx, UPS, and Xerox, have used it to great effect. FedEx, for example, found that its business increased more than 40 percent after it started to advertise in consumer media. Purchasing time and space in the mass media must be done skillfully because of the expense and the chance of wasted coverage if the right decision makers are not in the audience. Specialized cable channels have made it possible for many business-to-business advertisers to use more general media with reduced chances of wasted coverage. CNN's *MoneyLine* and several shows on CNBC, for example, attract an audience that contains many business decision makers. General newsmagazines, such as *Time* and *Newsweek*, along with *Forbes*, *BusinessWeek*, and *Fortune*, are rather obvious choices for this type of advertising.

Business advertisers have also increased their use of the Internet. Business-to-business sites can include large amounts of technical data, product descriptions, search engines that allow customers to find the exact product they are interested in, and other information useful to potential purchasers.

▲ Appeals

Close attention is paid to the copy in business-to-business advertising. Many consumer ads depend on impression and style to carry their messages. The copy tends to be brief and can cater to the emotions. Business copy tends to be longer, more detailed, and more factual. A premium is placed on accuracy and completeness. If the ad contains technical inaccuracies or exaggerations, the credibility of the product is compromised. Some of the most-used formats in business advertising are testimonials, case histories, new-product news, and demonstrations.

This is not to say, however, that all industrial ads must be stodgy and dull. In recent years several ad agencies specializing in business ads have introduced warmth, humor, and creativity into their messages. The philosophy behind this movement is that businesspeople are also consumers and that they respond as consumers to business and trade ads.

Advertising

As companies cut back their advertising budgets during the recession at the end of the decade, career prospects in advertising dimmed. The number of jobs at ad agencies dropped by nearly 3 percent from 2008 to 2009, and more cutbacks seemed likely. Those with knowledge of the techniques of online advertising were in most demand from employers.

The career outlook in the various media industries changes quickly. For a more current description of conditions in the advertising industry and a more detailed look at career options, please consult the book's Web site: www.mhhe.com/dominick11e.

MAIN POINTS

- Advertising is any form of nonpersonal presentation and promotion of ideas, goods, and services paid for by an identified sponsor.

- Advertising can be classified by target audience, geographic focus, and purpose.

- Modern advertising began in the late 19th century and grew during the early 20th century as magazines and radio became mass advertising media.

- After World War II, advertising grew at a fast rate, particularly when TV came on the scene.

- The past two decades have seen the start of new channels for advertising, including cable TV and the Internet. Online advertising has grown in the past few years.

- The three main components of the advertising industry are advertisers, agencies, and the media.

- Advertising agencies put together large-scale campaigns for clients, consisting of a market strategy, theme, ads, media time/space, and evaluation.

- Although not as visible as consumer advertising, business-to-business advertising makes up a significant portion of the industry.

QUESTIONS FOR REVIEW

1. What are the three defining characteristics of advertising?

2. Briefly describe the three main components of the advertising industry.

3. What is meant by "decoupling"?

4. What is positioning? Why is it important to advertisers?

5. How does consumer advertising differ from business-to-business advertising?

QUESTIONS FOR CRITICAL THINKING

1. What would society be like without advertising?

2. Is it right to advertise to children? If you think it is appropriate to advertise to children, what special considerations, if any, should be applied to such ads?

3. Check the national media for ongoing advertising campaigns. What are some themes that are currently running?

4. How can you tell if an advertising campaign has been effective?

5. Will "viral marketing" be around five years from now? Why or why not?

6. Review the boxed insert "Cultural Meaning and Trade Characters," and then consider the following. Why do marketers want us to have emotional connections to

mass-produced products? Does the AFLAC duck make you feel more positive toward insurance? In addition to the Aunt Jemima example, how are expectations for and stereotypes of race and gender reflected in trade characters?

KEY TERMS

target audience (p. 342)
consumer advertising (p. 342)
business-to-business advertising (p. 342)
primary demand ad (p. 343)
selective demand ad (p. 343)
direct action ad (p. 343)
indirect action ad (p. 343)
advertising agency (p. 345)

viral advertising (p. 348)
decoupling (p. 349)
national advertisers (p. 350)
retail advertisers (p. 350)
agency (p. 350)
full-service agency (p. 351)
media buying service (p. 351)
creative boutique (p. 351)
copy (p. 353)

campaign (p. 354)
positioning (p. 354)
rough layout (p. 355)
comprehensive layout (p. 355)
storyboard (p. 355)
formative research (p. 357)
message research (p. 357)
tracking studies (p. 357)

INTERNET RESOURCES

Online Learning Center

On the Online Learning Center home page, www.mhhe.com/dominick11e, *select* Student Center *and then* Chapter 15.

1. Use the Learning Objectives, Chapter Outline, and Main Points sections to review this chapter.

2. Test your knowledge of the chapter using the multiple choice and flashcard features of the site.

3. Expand your knowledge of concepts and topics discussed in the chapter with additional Questions for Critical Thinking and Internet Exercises.

Surfing the Internet

The following sites represent just a small sample of the hundreds and hundreds of sites that are relevant to this chapter. All were current as of late 2008. Keep in mind, however, that ad sites change rapidly.

www.aaaa.org
Home of the American Association of Advertising Agencies. Contains agency news, career information, and awards programs.

www.adage.com
Advertising Age is the leading trade publication for the industry. Its Web page has current news, useful statistics, and critiques of Web site advertising.

www.ddb.com
DDB is an ad agency that handles McDonald's and Volkswagen. A sampling of the agency's current and past award-winning work is available.

www.clioawards.com
The Clios are advertising's counterparts to the Oscars. This site has a listing of winners and a searchable archive.

www.womma.com
Learn more about viral advertising at the site of the Word-of-Mouth Marketing Association.

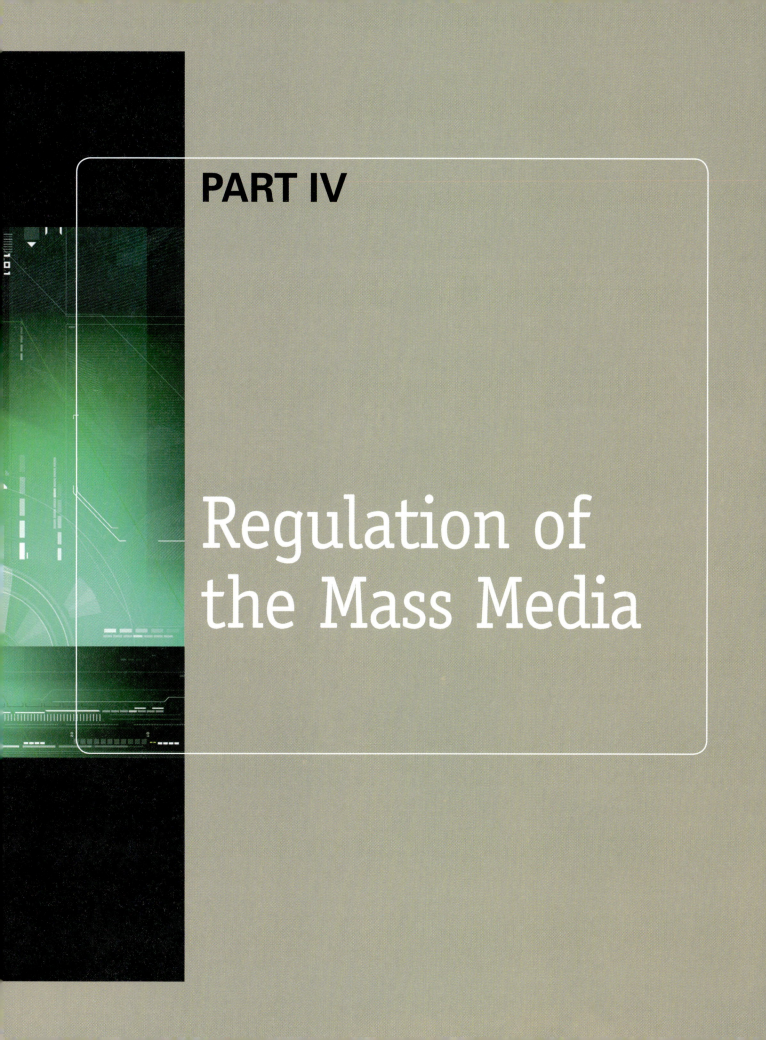

PART IV

Regulation of the Mass Media

CHAPTER 16

Formal Controls: Laws, Rules, Regulations

This chapter will prepare you to:

- define *prior restraint*

- understand the special protective privileges of reporters

- distinguish among *libel, slander, libel per se,* and *libel per quod*

- explain how invasion of privacy can occur

- describe copyright law

- recognize the impact of media regulation of the Internet

EQUAL JUSTICE UNDER LAW

Over the years, court decisions have had a major impact on the operations of mass media.

Let's suppose you wrote a book about how to commit the perfect murder. Your book detailed how to stalk your victim, when to strike, what weapons to use, and how to dispose of the body. Now let's suppose that somebody got a copy of your book and followed your instructions to actually commit a murder. Let's also suppose that relatives of the victim claim that you and your book bear some responsibility for the crime and sue you and your publisher for millions in damages. You have nothing to worry about, right? The First Amendment protects your right to free speech. Even though what you wrote might be objectionable, unpopular, and even repugnant to some, you're still protected.

It might not be that simple. The publisher of *Hit Man: A Technical Manual for Independent Contractors* found itself in the situation described above in 1998 when someone followed the directions in the book to murder three people. Relatives brought a wrongful death suit against the publisher. A federal court ruled that the book was protected by the First Amendment, but an appeals court reversed the decision and ruled that the book merited no First Amendment protection. The Supreme Court declined to hear an appeal and allowed the case to go to trial. Experts predicted that whatever the trial outcome, the case would probably find its way back to the Supreme Court and raise significant First Amendment issues. The case never got back to the Court; the publisher and the relatives reached a settlement before the trial. The vexing issue of what speech falls outside the protection of the law continues to concern those in the mass media. As is clear by now, this chapter is concerned with media law and other regulations dealing with the media.

For purposes of this chapter, formal controls over the media include laws, court decisions that refine those laws, and rules and regulations administered by government agencies. We will examine six areas in which these controls are important: (1) the controversy over a free system of mass communication, (2) copyright, (3) restrictions on obscenity and pornography, (4) regulation of broadcast media, (5) regulation of the Internet, and (6) commercial speech.

Many students have the idea that the field of mass communication law is dull and boring. Nothing could be further from the truth. In what other academic field could you read about raunchy magazines, the CIA, celebrities uttering four-letter words on TV, mass murderers, women in men's locker rooms, juicy divorces, and a man who owned a submarine?

The Press, the Law, and the Courts

▲ A Free Press

As noted in Chapter 4, the idea of a free press did not catch on at first in America. The early colonial papers had problems if they were not "published by authority"—that is, if they were not open to censorship by the Crown. Through the Stamp Act the British government attempted to suppress dissent by taxing printed matter. Recognizing these dangers to a free press, the framers of the Constitution added an amendment (the **First Amendment**) that stated in part that "Congress shall make no law . . . abridging the freedom of speech, or of the press." The precise meaning and interpretation of these words, however, have been open to some debate. Let us examine some key instances in which press and government have come into conflict.

▲ Prior Restraint

When the government censors the press by restraining it from publishing or broadcasting material, that act is called **prior restraint.** Attempts at prior restraint have been relatively rare. Nonetheless, this area does illustrate that the provisions in the First Amendment are not absolute. The Supreme Court has ruled that under certain circumstances prior restraint or censorship of the press is permitted, but the government faces a difficult task in proving that the restraint is justified. There are some obvious examples of legal censorship. During wartime a newspaper could be prevented from publishing the sailing schedules of troop transports, and a radio station could be prohibited from broadcasting the location and numbers of soldiers on the front lines. Other attempts at prior restraint have not been particularly successful; the Supreme Court has generally upheld the right of freedom of the press. There are two seminal cases in this area that are beneficial for us to examine. One is not widely known; the other made the front pages.

The Near Case   During the 1920s the Minnesota legislature passed a law under which newspapers that were considered public nuisances could be curtailed by means of an **injunction** (an order from a court that requires somebody to do something or refrain from doing something). The motives behind this law may have been praiseworthy because it appears to have been designed to prevent abusive attacks on minority groups. Using this public nuisance law, a county attorney sought an injunction against the *Saturday Press* and the paper's manager, J. M. Near, on the grounds that the paper had printed malicious statements about city officials in connection with gangland activities allegedly controlled by minority groups. In 1931 the Supreme Court ruled that the Minnesota law was unconstitutional. Said the Court,

> The fact that for approximately 150 years there has been almost an entire absence of attempts to impose previous restraints upon publications relating to the malfeasance of public officers is significant of the deep-seated conviction that such restraints would violate constitutional rights.

This issue would not be raised again for 40 years.

The Pentagon Papers   U.S. Attorney General John Mitchell was eager to see the Sunday, June 13, 1971, edition of the *New York Times*. Mitchell had attended the wedding of President Richard Nixon's daughter Tricia the day before, and he wanted to see how the *Times* had covered it. On the left side of page 1, Mitchell saw a flattering picture of the president with his daughter on his arm. Next to the wedding picture, another story caught Mitchell's eyes: "Vietnam Archive: Pentagon Study Traces 3 Decades of Growing U.S. Involvement." As Mitchell read further, he realized that the *Times* article was sure to cause problems.

The basis for the story in the *Times* began three years earlier when Secretary of Defense Robert McNamara became disillusioned with the Vietnam War and ordered a massive study of its origins. This study, known eventually as the Pentagon Papers, was put together by 36 different people and ran to more than 7,000 pages. The final report was classified

The first installment of the Pentagon Papers appeared in the *New York Times*. Attempts by the government to halt further publication ended when the Supreme Court ruled in favor of the *Times*.

Source: © 1971 by the New York Times Company.

"Top Secret—Sensitive." During April 1971, one of those Pentagon staff members who compiled the report leaked a copy to a reporter for the *New York Times*. After much study and secrecy, the paper was ready to publish the story in nine installments. The U.S. Justice Department, under John Mitchell's direction, asked a U.S. district court judge to halt publication of the stories on the grounds that they would "cause irreparable injury to the defense interests of the United States." The order was granted, and for the first time in history, a U.S. paper was ordered by the courts to suppress a specific story. By then, however, other newspapers had obtained copies of some or all of the Pentagon documents and started publishing them. The Justice Department sought more restraining orders, but as soon as one paper was ordered to stop publishing, another newspaper in another part of the country would pick up the series. It was obvious that the Supreme Court would eventually have to intervene.

The Court did intervene and with uncharacteristic haste. On June 30, 1971, only 17 days after the story first appeared and only 4 days after hearing oral arguments on the case, the Court decided in favor of the newspapers' right to publish the information. Naturally, the staff at the *New York Times* was delighted. The paper called the decision a "ringing victory for freedom under law." Upon closer examination, however, the victory was not quite as ringing as it was made out to be. The Court did not state that prior restraint could never be invoked against the press. Instead, it pointed out that the government "carries a heavy burden of showing justification" for imposing restraint. The government, in the opinion of the Court, had not shown sufficient grounds for doing this. The government was free, if it wished, to bring other prior restraint cases to the courts to establish exactly how much justification it needed to stifle publication. In addition, each of the nine judges wrote a separate opinion that highlighted the ambiguities and complexities surrounding this topic.

More Recent Cases   After the release of the Pentagon Papers, the prior restraint issue cropped up several times in cases involving ex–CIA agents. In one case the CIA was successful in having portions of a book deleted because they revealed classified information.

In 1983 a principal in Hazelwood, Missouri, deleted from a high school paper an article that dealt with teenage pregnancy and another article about divorce, on the grounds that they were inappropriate. Three student journalists, with the help of the American Civil Liberties Union, filed suit claiming that their First Amendment rights had been violated. The Supreme Court eventually decided the case in favor of the school system. The Court held that since the paper was part of the high school's journalism curriculum and used school supplies and its staff was restricted to journalism students, it was not a public forum and not entitled to First Amendment protection.

Until recently, it appeared that the college press merited more protection. In the fall of 2002, the dean of student affairs and services at Governors State University in Illinois informed the printer of the college's newspaper that prior approval by a university official was required before the paper was printed. The student editors of the paper filed a lawsuit and won a victory when a three-judge panel ruled that the decision in the Hazelwood case did not apply to college newspapers. In 2005, however, the U.S. Court of Appeals reversed that decision declaring that since the newspaper was subsidized by funds from the university, it did not qualify as a public forum. The Supreme Court refused to grant an appeal in the case. Although some states have passed laws providing some degree of protection to student journalists, it appears that high school and college press is entitled to less than the full protection of the First Amendment.

In 1999 a ruling by a district court judge held that the prohibition against prior restraint also included Web sites. The creator of a Web site devoted to news about the Ford Motor Company had posted documents obtained from Ford employees. The company had obtained a ruling that prevented the documents from being posted, but the ruling by the district court judge overturned that prohibition.

Prior restraint received some judicial support in the wake of the rape trial of basketball star Kobe Bryant in 2004. A court reporter mistakenly sent transcripts of confidential proceedings to several media outlets. Upon learning of the error, a judge ordered all copies destroyed and threatened to hold anyone who published the contents in contempt of court. Reporters asked the Colorado Supreme Court to invalidate the order, but the court upheld the restraint, saying that the state's interest in keeping the material secret justified the prior restraint. Further legal action was halted when the judge made public most of the information contained in the transcripts.

Also in 2004, an Alabama district court turned down a government request for prior restraint against a Web site that published the names of investigators for the Drug Enforcement Agency. The court ruled that although the site might make some people uncomfortable it did not present a threat so serious as to justify prior restraint. In 2008, a U.S. Circuit Court of Appeals held that journalists have a right of access to jurors' identities and that a federal judge was wrong to try to empanel an anonymous jury. The court acknowledged that although the press might publish stories about the background of the jurors that could make some less willing to serve, that possibility did not outweigh the judicial system's interest in openness.

In sum, there is a strong constitutional case against prior restraint, but gray areas exist in which censorship might be legal. These areas will probably remain ambiguous until further court cases help define the limits of government authority. It is likely, however, that the barriers against prior restraint will remain formidable.

Protecting News Sources

Before we begin an examination of this topic, it is important to consider that the issues are fairly complicated. Conflicting interests are involved. Reporters argue that if they are forced to disclose confidential sources those sources will dry up and the public's right to know will be adversely affected. Government arguments cite the need for the administration of justice and the rights of an individual to a fair trial.

Perhaps a hypothetical example will help bring these issues into focus. Suppose you are a reporter for a campus newspaper. One of your sources calls you late one night and informs you that several students are running a drug ring that has monopolized the sale of illegal drugs on campus. To check the accuracy of this report, you call another one of your sources, one who in the past has given you reliable information on campus drug dealing. This second source confirms what your caller told you and adds more details. For obvious reasons both of your sources ask not to be identified, and you agree. On the basis of these reports and some additional research, you publish a lengthy article in the campus newspaper about the drug ring. A few days later you are summoned before a grand jury that is investigating criminal drug dealings. You are asked to reveal your sources. If you refuse, you will be charged with contempt and possibly fined or sent to jail. What do you do?

▲ The Reporter's Privilege

Other reporters have found themselves in the same fix. One was Paul Branzburg. In 1969 Branzburg wrote a story for the *Louisville Courier-Journal* in which he described how two local residents were synthesizing hashish from marijuana. His article stated that he had promised not to reveal their identities. Shortly thereafter, Branzburg was subpoenaed (ordered to appear) by the county grand jury. He refused to answer questions about his sources, claiming, in part, that to do so would violate the First Amendment provision for freedom of the press. The case ultimately reached the Supreme Court, which ruled that the First Amendment did not protect reporters from the obligation to testify before grand juries to answer questions concerning a criminal investigation.

Initially, this ruling was viewed as a setback for reporters' rights. However, the Court did suggest some situations in which the reporter's claim to privilege would be valid. These included harassment of news reporters, instances in which grand juries do not operate in good faith, and situations in which there is only a remote connection between the investigation and the information sought. Additionally, the Court suggested that Congress and the states could further define the rights of a reporter to protect sources by enacting legislation (called **shield laws**) to that effect.

After the Branzburg decision, state courts were somewhat inconsistent in their rulings. On the one hand, several cases upheld the reporter's right to keep her or his sources secret. In Florida, Lucy Ware Morgan, a reporter for the *St. Petersburg Times*, refused to disclose her source for a story about a grand jury report on corruption in city government. She was promptly convicted of contempt of court and received a 90-day jail sentence. In 1976, however, the Florida Supreme Court overturned the conviction. Using the Branzburg decision as a guideline, the court concluded that the name of her source was not relevant to the investigation of a crime and that the contempt charge was designed to harass her.

Other decisions have narrowly defined the test of relevancy between the case at hand and the reporter's sources. In Virginia a newspaper reporter refused to identify a source during testimony at a 1978 murder trial. The lawyer for the accused argued that the source was needed to question the credibility of a prosecution witness. The Virginia Supreme Court ruled in favor of the reporter and stated that a reporter's privilege must yield only when the defendant's need for the information is essential. To be essential, said the court, the information had to (1) relate directly to the defendant's guilt or innocence, (2) bear on the reduction of an offense, or (3) concern the mitigation of a sentence.

Just because these cases are taken from the 1970s, do not get the idea that reporters no longer go to jail or get fined. From 1999 to 2000, three reporters in California, a state with what many experts consider the strongest shield law in the country, got into legal trouble when they failed to reveal confidential sources of information. One journalist went to jail for five days, and another was fined $1,000 a day for every day he refused to testify. Fortunately for the reporters, either the sanctions were overturned on appeal or the original requests were dropped. Finally, there is the complicated case of Judith Miller of the *New York Times* and Matthew Cooper of *Time*. The two were subpoenaed and ordered to reveal their confidential sources during an investigation by the Justice Department probing who leaked the name of a covert CIA operative to a newspaper columnist. The reporters declined to cooperate and turned to the legal system for protection. Two federal courts ruled against them, and in mid-2005 the Supreme Court declined to review the case, raising the possibility that the two could serve up to 18 months in prison. In the wake of the Court's action, Cooper's source released him from his promise of confidentiality.

Miller, however, began serving a jail term. Miller was eventually released from jail when she was satisfied that her source had granted permission to reveal his name.

Reporters for the *San Francisco Chronicle* published information leaked from grand jury testimony during investigations concerning the use of performance-enhancing drugs by athletes. In 2006 a new grand jury ordered the reporters to reveal their sources. The reporters appealed the order, but a district court judge ruled that they had to comply with the grand jury's instructions or face a lengthy jail term. The source of the story eventually came forward, and the matter came to a close.

In 2008, a reporter for *USA Today* was ordered to reveal her sources in connection with stories she wrote in a libel case concerning the government's investigation into the 2001 anthrax attacks. The reporter refused, was charged with contempt, and was fined $5,000 a day. The fines were put on hold while the reporter appealed the ruling. The contempt charge was eventually dropped when the original libel case was settled. In another case that same year, an appeals court ruled that the author of a book about Donald Trump was protected by New York's shield law and did not have to reveal his sources. This ruling is interesting in that it appears to extend the protection of the shield law to authors of entertainment books.

The above examples suggest that the nation's courts are taking a more skeptical view of the media's claim to privilege when it comes to revealing sources. In that connection media organizations are counseling reporters to be careful when making promises of confidentiality.

As of 2009, 37 states and the District of Columbia had shield laws. Journalists generally recognize these laws as helpful, but most realize that they are not the powerful protectors of the press that many had hoped for. In addition, the laws themselves represent a bewildering collection of provisions, qualifications, and exceptions. Some states protect only confidential material; some protect the reporter from revealing the name of a source but do not protect the information obtained from sources. Other state laws confer less protection if the reporter is involved in a libel case. In some states shield laws do not apply to reporters subpoenaed by a grand jury. Further, many courts are interpreting the shield laws on a case-by-case basis and ignoring or limiting the interpretation of judgments contained in the law. A federal shield law was introduced in Congress in 2009, but prospects for its passage were uncertain.

▲   Search and Seizure

Finally, there is the troublesome question of protecting notes and other records that might disclose sources or other information relevant to an investigation. In this regard the courts have offered little protection. Three particular cases have disturbed the news media.

In the first case, in 1971, four police officers entered the offices of the *Stanford Daily*, the campus newspaper of Stanford University, and produced a warrant authorizing them to search for photographs of a clash between demonstrators and police that the *Daily* had covered the day before. The newspaper brought suit against the authorities, charging that its First Amendment rights had been violated. In 1978 the Supreme Court ruled that the search was legal. (In 1980, however, Congress extended some protection to newsrooms by passing a bill that would require the government to secure a subpoena to obtain records held by reporters. The scope of a subpoena is somewhat more limited than that of a search warrant. In addition, a subpoena can be challenged.)

In the second case, the U.S. Court of Appeals in the District of Columbia decided another case that further eroded reporters' rights to protect sources. In 1974 the Reporters Committee for Freedom of the Press filed suit against AT&T because the company would not pledge to keep records of reporters' toll calls safe from government scrutiny. (An analysis of these calls might help locate a reporter's source of information.) The court of appeals ruled that it was legal for the government to examine such records without a reporter's knowledge or consent. Another court of appeals ruling in 2006 reinforced this viewpoint when it ruled that the phone records of two *New York Times* reporters who refused to cooperate with a grand jury investigation were not protected by privilege. The court declared that the government's need for the records took precedence over First Amendment concerns.

The third case involved *New York Times* reporter Myron Farber. During 1976 Farber had been reporting on the investigation into mysterious deaths at a New Jersey hospital. The stories led to the indictment of a prominent physician on charges of poisoning five patients. Defense lawyers ultimately subpoenaed notes and documents pertaining to the case that were held by Farber and the *Times.* Both Farber and the paper refused to provide the documents, and both were convicted of contempt of court. Farber was sentenced to 6 months in jail and a $1,000 fine; the *Times* was slapped with a $100,000 fine and was ordered to pay $5,000 every day until it complied with the court's order. The *Times* ultimately turned over its files, but a judge ruled that the paper had "sanitized" them by removing some relevant material, so it reinstated the fine. Farber, meanwhile, had spent 27 days in jail. Eventually, Farber wound up spending 40 days in jail, and the *Times* paid $285,000 in fines. All penalties finally ended with the jury's verdict that the physician was innocent.

In 2005 a freelance journalist/blogger was ordered by a grand jury to turn over to authorities outtakes from videos that he had shot of a violent demonstration in which a police officer was injured. The blogger refused and eventually served 7½ months in federal prison before his lawyer worked out a compromise with prosecutors.

The privacy of computer-stored messages and e-mail received protection from the Electronic Communication Privacy Act, which requires the government to obtain a search warrant before examining online or stored messages intended to be private.

Perhaps the safest conclusion that we can draw is that a reporter's privilege in protecting sources and notes is not absolute. Even those decisions that have favored journalists have been qualified. It also appears that further developments in this area will be put together on a piece-by-piece basis by lower courts unless the Supreme Court issues a precise decision or Congress passes a comprehensive law. As for reporters, they must carefully consider these issues when they promise confidentiality to a news source.

Covering the Courts

On the one hand, the Sixth Amendment guarantees a defendant the right to a trial before an impartial jury; on the other, the First Amendment guarantees freedom of the press. Trial judges are responsible for the administration of justice; reporters are responsible for informing the public about the workings of the legal system. Sometimes these responsibilities clash.

▲ Publicity Before and During a Trial

If a potential jury member has read, seen, or heard stories in the news media about a defendant that appear to indicate that person's guilt, it is possible that the defendant will not receive a fair trial. Although research has not produced definitive evidence linking pretrial publicity to prejudice, this concern has been at the heart of several court decisions that have castigated the news media for trying cases in the newspaper or on television instead of in the courtroom.

The 1960s saw a flurry of cases suggesting that the Supreme Court was taking a close look at pretrial publicity. In 1961 the Court for the first time reversed a criminal conviction entirely because pretrial publicity had made it impossible to select an impartial jury. The case concerned Leslie Irvin, a rather unsavory character who was arrested and charged with six murders. Newspapers carried police-issued press releases that said "Mad Dog"

Donald Trump tried to force the author of *Trump Nation: The Art of Being the Donald* to reveal his sources, but an appeals court ruled the author was protected by New York's shield law.

Irvin had confessed to all six killings. The local media seized upon this story with a vengeance, and many stories referred to Irvin as the "confessed slayer of six." Of the 430 potential jurors examined by attorneys, 90 percent had formed opinions about Irvin's guilt—opinions that ranged from suspicion to absolute certainty that he was guilty. Irvin was convicted—hardly a surprise—and sentenced to death. After six years of complicated legal maneuvers, made even more complicated by Irvin's escape from prison, the case went before the Supreme Court. The Court ruled that the pretrial publicity had ruined the defendant's chances for a fair trial and sent the case back to be retried. (Irvin, who had been recaptured, was again found guilty, but this time was sentenced to life imprisonment.)

Perhaps the most famous case of pretrial publicity concerned an Ohio physician. On July 4, 1954, the wife of Cleveland-area osteopath Dr. Sam Sheppard was found slain in the couple's home. Sheppard became a prime suspect, and the news media, especially the Cleveland newspapers, were impatient for his arrest. "Why Isn't Sam Sheppard in Jail?" and "Why Don't Police Quiz Top Suspect?" were headlines that appeared over page-one editorials. News reports carried the results of alleged scientific tests that cast doubt on Sheppard's version of the crime (these tests were never brought up at the trial). Articles stressed Sheppard's extramarital affairs as a possible motive for the crime. After his arrest the news stories and editorials continued. There were enough of them with headlines such as "Dr. Sam Faces Quiz at Jail on Marilyn's Fear of Him" and "Blood Is Found in Garage" to fill five scrapbooks. Every juror but one admitted to reading about the story in the newspapers. The sensationalized coverage continued during the trial itself, which produced a guilty verdict. Twelve years later the Supreme Court reversed Sheppard's conviction because of the extremely prejudicial publicity. This case assumed added importance because the Court listed six safeguards that judges might invoke to prevent undue influence from publicity. These safeguards included sequestering the jury (that is, moving them into seclusion), moving the case to another county, and placing restrictions on statements made by lawyers, witnesses, or others who might have damaging information.

▲ Gag Rules

Some judges have issued restrictive orders, or **gag rules,** that restrain the participants in a trial (attorneys, witnesses, defendants) from giving information to the media or that limit media coverage of events that occur in court. For example, a superior court judge in a Washington murder trial ordered reporters to report only on events that occurred in front of a jury. Two reporters violated this rule by writing about events that took place in the courtroom while the jury was not present; they were subsequently charged with contempt. The Washington State Supreme Court refused to review this ruling.

The whole question of gag rules reached the Supreme Court in 1976. A Nebraska judge had prohibited reporters from revealing certain information about a mass murder case. The Nebraska Press Association appealed the order to the Supreme Court. The Court ruled on the side of the association and held that reporting of judicial proceedings in open court cannot be prohibited. Once again, upon first examination, this rule appeared to be a significant victory for the press. As time passed, however, it became apparent that the Nebraska decision had left the way open for court-ordered restrictions on what the trial participants could say to the press. It seemed to indicate that some legal proceedings, primarily those that take place before the actual trial begins, might be legitimately closed to the public. By the early 1980s this was exactly what was happening. Although the press was left free to report what it chose, its news sources were muzzled by judicial order. During the late 1970s judges began holding pretrial hearings in private to limit pretrial publicity. A 1979 Supreme Court decision held this practice to be constitutional. In 1980 the Court went on record as stating that the press did, in fact, have a constitutional right to attend criminal trials. *Pretrial* events, however, might still be closed. Because many criminal cases are settled out of court, these pretrial hearings are often the only public hearings held.

In the 1980s the press gained wider access to court proceedings. In 1984 the Supreme Court ruled that the jury selection process should be open to the press except in extreme circumstances, and it established standards that judges must meet before they can close a pretrial hearing. A 1986 Supreme Court decision, however, gave the press a major victory in its efforts to secure access to pretrial proceedings. The Court held that preliminary trial proceedings must be open to the press unless the judge could demonstrate a "substantial probability that the defendant's right to a fair trial would be violated." Additionally, lower courts have held that the First Amendment right of access to trials extends to documents used as evidence. Also in 1986, the Supreme Court ruled that the jury selection process, as well as the trial itself, must ordinarily be open to the public. The Court provided a set of strict guidelines that would justify a private selection of a jury.

In summary, Supreme Court decisions do not give the press an absolute right of access to all court proceedings. Some parts of trials and pretrial hearings may still be closed if the judge can fulfill the Court's guidelines regarding closure. Further, the recent Court decisions have not changed the legal status surrounding the privacy of grand jury hearings—they continue to have the right to secrecy. All in all, it might be safe to conclude that the press has been given a green light to report on matters that occur in open court with little fear of reprisal. But gag orders on news sources and the closing of various legal proceedings threaten to be areas of tension between the press and the judiciary for some time to come.

▲ Cameras and Microphones in the Courtroom

For many years the legal profession looked with disfavor on the idea of cameras and microphones in the courtroom. There was a time when this attitude may have been entirely justified. The whole problem seems to have begun in 1935 when Bruno Hauptmann was put on trial for the kidnapping and murder of the son of national hero Charles Lindbergh. Remember that news photography and radio journalism were still young in 1935, and this fact may have contributed to some of the abuses that occurred during this trial. After the trial the American Bar Association added Canon 35 to its Canons of Professional Ethics. This provision stated that the taking of photographs in the courtroom and the broadcasting (later amended to include telecasting) of court proceedings should not be permitted. Although Canon 35 was not law, its language or some variation of it was adopted as law by every state except Colorado and Texas.

In 1965 the Supreme Court entered the picture when it ruled on the Billie Sol Estes case. Estes was on trial in Texas for allegedly swindling several farmers. The trial judge, over Estes's objections, had allowed the televising of the trial. Estes was found guilty, but he soon appealed that decision to the Supreme Court on the grounds that the presence of television had deprived him of a fair trial. The high court agreed with Estes and argued for the prohibition of television cameras in the courtroom. The Court said that broadcasting a trial would have a prejudicial impact on jurors, would distract witnesses, and would burden the trial judge with new responsibilities. However, the Court went on, there might come a day when broadcast technology would become portable and unobtrusive and television coverage so commonplace that trials might be broadcast. Thus, the decision in the Estes case was not a blanket provision against the televising of trials.

Since 1965 the trend has been toward a general relaxation of the tension between the legal profession and the electronic press. In 1972 the American Bar Association adopted a new code of professional responsibility. Canon 3A(7) of this document superseded the old Canon 35. Canon 3A(7) maintained the ban on taking photographs and broadcasting in the courtroom, but it did allow the judge the discretion to permit televising a trial to a pressroom or to another courtroom to accommodate an overflow crowd. In 1981 the Supreme Court ruled that broadcast coverage of a criminal trial is not inherently prejudicial, thereby clearing the way for the presence of radio and TV in the courtroom. The Court left it up to the states to devise their own systems for implementing such coverage.

As of 2009, all 50 states allowed some form of coverage. The rules for coverage vary state by state. In Georgia, for example, the judge may permit one television camera in the courtroom. In Ohio trial courts, coverage of nonconsenting victims and witnesses is prohibited. Although the situation may change, as of late-2009 cameras are not allowed in federal district courts or at Supreme Court proceedings.

Reporters' Access to Information

▲ Government Information

Reporting the doings of the government can be a frustrating task if the government insists that information about its activities be kept secret. After World War II many members of the press complained that government secrecy was becoming a major problem. Reporters were being restricted from meetings, and access to many government documents was difficult to obtain. Under continuing pressure from journalists and consumer groups, Congress passed the **Freedom of Information Act (FOIA)** in 1966. This law gave the public the right to discover what the federal government was up to—with certain exceptions. The law states that every federal executive-branch agency must publish instructions on what methods a member of the public should follow to get information. If information is improperly withheld, a court can force the agency to disclose what is sought. There are nine areas of exemptions covering material that does not have to be made public, including trade secrets, files of law enforcement investigations, and maps of oil wells. In 2007 a bill was introduced in Congress to streamline the FOIA and make it easier for the public to access government records.

In 2009 President Barack Obama ordered the government to disclose more information under the FOIA. A memo from the Justice Department informed federal agencies that they should disclose information unless there was a legal ban or foreseeable harm in doing so. The agencies were instructed to cooperate with the Office of Government Information Service, an organization established in 2007 to mediate disputes between agencies and those requesting information. In sum, it appears that the media will have an easier time accessing government materials.

In 1996 the Electronic Freedom of Information Act (EFOIA) was passed to make more information available on the Internet. Currently, many government agency Web sites contain a variety of information, ranging from statistics to press releases, that can be accessed online rather than through an FOIA request. Nonetheless, many agencies have been slow to fully implement the requirements of the EFOIA.

A "Sunshine Act" ensures that regular meetings of approximately 50 federal government agencies will be open to the public. There are, however, 10 different situations that might permit an agency to meet behind closed doors, so the right of access to meetings is far from absolute. In addition, many states have their own versions of laws pertaining to information access and open meetings. The degree of compliance with these laws varies widely from state to state.

In the aftermath of the September 11 terrorist attacks, concerns about safety and security came into conflict with guarantees of press freedom. The **USA Patriot Act,** passed in October 2001, gave the government more power to access e-mail and telephone records. This increased monitoring power can be used not only to track terrorists but also to eavesdrop on journalists. In addition, the new law makes it easier for the government to restrict access to official records, and another provision prevents the press from finding out about FBI searches of books bought in bookstores or borrowed from libraries by those suspected of terrorist activities.

▲ Access to News Scenes

We have already examined the issue of access in our discussion of the right of the press to attend certain judicial proceedings. But what about the reporters' right of access to news settings outside the courtroom? The law here appears to be in the developmental stage. In the few decisions that have been handed down, the courts have given little support to the notion that the First Amendment guarantees a right of access. In separate rulings the courts have declared that journalists may be sued for invasion of privacy, for trespassing on private property, and for disobeying a police officer's legitimate command to clear the way at the scene of a serious automobile accident. Most recently, in 2009 a reporter for a Michigan newspaper was convicted of a felony for obstructing police officers at an accident scene. Officers testified that the reporter violated police orders when she crossed a police line in order to take photographs of victims of the accident. Three of the most relevant Supreme Court opinions have focused on the question of access to prisons and prisoners. In these cases the courts have ruled that reporters do not have the right to visit specific parts of a prison, to speak to specific prisoners, or to bring cameras inside. In general, the Court seems to be saying that the access rights of the press are not different from the access rights of the general public. When the public is not admitted, neither is the press.

Some rulings, however, have recognized a limited right of access. A Florida court said that journalists who are customarily invited by police onto private property to view a news scene cannot be prosecuted for trespassing. The courts have also allowed access to news settings in order to halt discrimination among journalists. For example, in one case it was ruled that a female journalist could not be barred from entering a baseball team's locker room if male reporters had been admitted. In sum, the final words on this topic have yet to be written by the courts. A case as influential as the Branzburg or Estes decision has yet to be adjudicated in the area of press access. It is a good bet, however, that such a test will not be long in surfacing.

Defamation

As the preceding discussion makes clear, in its news-gathering activities the press often collides with the government. In addition, the right of free speech and the rights of a free press sometimes come into conflict with the right of an individual to protect his or her reputation. Protection for a person's reputation is found under the laws that deal with **defamation.**

To understand this somewhat complicated area, let us start with some general definitions:

- **Libel:** Libel is written defamation that tends to injure a person's reputation or good name or that diminishes the esteem, respect, or goodwill due a person.

- **Slander:** This is spoken defamation. (In many states, if a defamatory statement is broadcast, it is considered libel even though technically the words are not written. Libel is considered more harmful and usually carries more serious penalties than does slander.)

- **Libel per se:** Some words are always libelous. Falsely written accusations, such as labeling a person a "thief" or a "swindler," automatically constitute libel.

- **Libel per quod:** Words that seem perfectly innocent in themselves can become libelous under certain circumstances. For instance, erroneously reporting that Joe Smith was seen eating a steak dinner last night may seem harmless unless Smith happens to be the president of the Worldwide Vegetarian Society.

For someone to win a libel suit brought against the media, that person must prove five things: (1) that he or she has actually been defamed and harmed by the statements, (2) that he or she has been identified (although not necessarily by name), (3) that the defamatory statements have been published, (4) that the media were at fault, and (5) in most instances that what was published or broadcast was false.

Not every mistake that finds its way into publication is libelous. To report that James Arthur will lead the Fourth of July parade when in fact Arthur James will lead it is probably not libelous because it is improbable that leading a parade will cause harm to a person's reputation. (Courts have even ruled that it is not necessarily libelous to report incorrectly that a person died. Death, said the courts, is no disgrace.) Actual harm might be substantiated by showing that defamatory remarks led to physical discomfort (such as sleepless nights) or loss of income or increased difficulty in performing a job.

Identification need not be by name. If a paper erroneously reports that the professor who teaches Psych 101 at 10 A.M. in Quadrangle Hall is taking bribes from his students, that would be sufficient.

Publication, for our purposes, pertains to a statement's appearance in a mass medium and is self-explanatory.

Fault is a little more complicated. To win a libel suit, some degree of fault or carelessness on the part of the media organization must be shown. As we shall see, the degree of fault that must be established depends on several things: (1) the person who is suing, (2) the subject matter of the suit, and (3) the particular state's laws that are being applied.

A 1986 Supreme Court decision held that private persons (as opposed to public figures) suing for libel must prove that the statements at issue are false, at least when the statements involve matters of public concern. For all practical purposes, however, proving that the media were at fault also involves proving the falsity of what was broadcast or published, so that virtually everyone who brings a libel suit must show the wrongfulness of what was published.

It should be emphasized that a mass medium is responsible for what it carries. It usually cannot hide behind the fact that it only repeated what someone else said. For example, in most situations a magazine could not defend itself against a libel suit by claiming that it simply quoted a hospital worker who said a colleague was stealing drugs. If, in fact, the hospital worker's colleague was not stealing drugs, the magazine would have to look to some other defense against libel. A 2004 decision by the Pennsylvania Supreme Court further clarified this situation when it ruled that the First Amendment does not create a "neutral report privilege" for media when they report newsworthy statements made by one public official about another that might be defamatory. The case stemmed from a story in a local newspaper that quoted one city official calling two other city officials "child molesters." The Pennsylvania court ruled that even though the newspaper reported the story accurately, it could still be sued for defamation if the plaintiff could establish that the paper acted with actual malice.

▲ Defenses Against Libel Suits

What are some of the defenses that can be used? There are three.

The first is truth. If what was reported is proved to be true, there is no libel. This defense, however, is rarely used since it is extremely difficult to prove the truth of a statement. In addition, since the Supreme Court's decision placed the burden of proving the falsity of a statement on the person bringing the libel suit, the truth defense has become even less attractive.

A second defense is privilege. There are certain situations in which the courts have held that the public's right to know comes before a person's right to preserve a reputation. Judicial proceedings, arrest warrants, grand jury indictments, legislative proceedings, and city council sessions are examples of situations that are generally acknowledged to be privileged. If a reporter gives a fair and accurate report of these events, no lawsuits can result, even if what is reported contains a libelous statement.

The third defense is fair comment and criticism. Any person who thrusts him- or herself into the public eye or is at the center of public attention is open to fair criticism. This means that public officials, professional sports figures, cartoonists, artists, columnists, playwrights, and all those who invite public attention are fair game for comment. This defense applies only to opinion and criticism, not to misrepresentations of fact. You can report that a certain director's new movie stank to high heaven without fear of a lawsuit, but you could not report falsely that the director embezzled funds from the company and

Many people are confused by the meaning of the phrase *actual malice* as it applies to defamation. Some individuals mistakenly think that a person who is defamed has to prove evil motives, spite, or ill will on the part of the person or medium that allegedly committed the defamation. Not so. In the famous *New York Times* v. *Sullivan* case, the Supreme Court defined *actual malice* as (1) publishing something that is known to be false ("I know what I'm publishing is not true but I'm going to publish it anyway") or (2) publishing something with reckless disregard for whether it is true or not ("I have good reason to doubt that what I'm publishing is true, but I'm going to publish it anyway").

A libel case involving CBS, Inc., and Walter Jacobson, a news anchor and commentator at WBBM-TV (the CBS affiliate) in Chicago, illustrates this definition. The Brown & Williamson Tobacco Corporation (maker of Viceroy cigarettes) claimed that Jacobson libeled its company when he charged during a TV commentary that Viceroy was using an ad campaign to persuade children to smoke. Viceroy, said Jacobson, was equating cigarette smoking with "wine, beer, shaving, or wearing a bra . . . a declaration of independence and striving for self-identity . . . a basic symbol of the growing-up process." The commentary cited as evidence a Federal Trade Commission report that claimed the company had been advised by its advertising agency to launch such a campaign.

Brown & Williamson, forced to prove actual malice on the part of Jacobson because of the company's position as a public figure, denied ever having launched such a campaign. In fact, company lawyers argued that Brown & Williamson was so outraged by its ad agency's advice that it fired the advertising firm. Further, Brown & Williamson argued that Jacobson knew this fact before he broadcast his commentary. In court one of the officials for the tobacco company testified that a researcher for Jacobson had been told that the ad agency had been fired and that the campaign was not used. During the trial Jacobson said that he had rejected a suggestion from this researcher that a disclaimer should be included in the commentary stating that Brown & Williamson had not used the campaign. Evidently, this fact was enough to convince the jury that Jacobson knew that what he was saying was false—thus establishing actual malice. The jury found in favor of the tobacco company and awarded Brown & Williamson more than $5 million in damages.

For their part Jacobson and CBS maintain that the commentary was an accurate summary of the FTC report and that Brown & Williamson had a strategy directed toward children, even if the company did not fully implement it. In late 1985, CBS announced plans to appeal the decision. The appeal was decided in 1988 in favor of the tobacco company. CBS was ordered to pay $3.05 million in damages.

---

expect protection under fair criticism. However, criticism can be quite severe and caustic and still be protected from lawsuit. In 1990 the Supreme Court ruled that expressions of opinion are not automatically exempt from charges of libel. Opinions that contain an assertion of fact that can be proved false might trigger a defamation suit.

In 1964 the Supreme Court, in the *New York Times* v. *Sullivan* case, significantly expanded the opportunity for comments on the actions of public officials and also changed the nature of the law governing defamation. The case involved the *Times* and an official of the Montgomery, Alabama, police department, L. B. Sullivan, and took place during the civil rights struggle of the early 1960s. A civil rights group published an ad in the *Times* concerning a protest in Montgomery that Sullivan claimed libeled him. Testimony in the case revealed that, indeed, several statements in the ad were false. An Alabama court awarded Sullivan $500,000, but the *Times* appealed the case to the Supreme Court.

The Court reversed the Alabama decision and enumerated three major principles that would affect future decisions concerning defamation:

1. Editorial advertising is protected by the First Amendment.
2. Even statements that are false might qualify for First Amendment protection if they concern the public conduct of public officials.
3. To win a libel suit, public officials must prove that false and defamatory statements were made with actual malice.

The Court also clarified what is meant by *actual malice*—publishing a statement with the knowledge that it is false or publishing a statement in "reckless disregard" of whether it is true or not. A few years later, the Court expanded this protection to include statements made about public figures as well as public officials. In 1971 it appeared that the Supreme Court would even require private individuals who become involved in events of public concern to prove actual malice before collecting for a libel suit. Three years later, the Court seemed to retreat a little from this position when it held that a lawyer involved in a civil lawsuit was not a public figure, that he was not involved in an event of public interest, and that he did not have to prove actual malice.

Even more protection was extended to the private citizen in 1976 in a case concerning the divorce of Mary Alice Firestone and tire heir Russell Firestone Jr. The trial lasted 17 months and received large amounts of media coverage. Ms. Firestone even called several press conferences while the trial was taking place. When *Time* magazine erroneously reported that the divorce had been granted on the grounds of extreme cruelty and adultery, Ms. Firestone sued for libel. (Her husband had charged her with adultery, but adultery was not cited as grounds for the divorce.) *Time* argued that she was a public figure and contended that she had to show not only that the magazine was inaccurate but also that it acted with malice. The Supreme Court ruled that she was not a public figure, despite all the attendant press coverage, and drew a distinction between legitimate public controversies and those controversies that merely interest the public. The latter, said the Court, are not protected, and actual malice need not be proved.

The Court affirmed this distinction in 1979 by noting that the fact that someone is involved in a "newsworthy" event does not make the person a public figure. When a U.S. senator presented a scientist with a satirical award used to denote wasteful spending of government funds, the scientist sued for defamation. The Court ruled that even though the scientist became the subject of media attention, his public prominence before receiving the satirical award did not merit labeling him a public figure. Therefore, he did not have to meet the actual malice standard. Private citizens, however, do have to show some degree of fault or negligence by the media. In many states this means showing that the media did not exercise ordinary care in publishing a story. Establishing this allows a private citizen to collect compensation for any actual damages that stem from the libel. The big bucks, however, come from punitive damages assessed against the media. These awards are designed to punish the media for their past transgressions and serve as a reminder not to misbehave again. To collect punitive damages, even private citizens must show actual malice.

The amount of money that juries award to the winners of libel cases can be substantial. Awards of $1 million or more have become common. Singer Wayne Newton, for example, received a $20-million judgment against NBC. On the other hand, most libel cases are appealed, and about 75 percent either are reversed or have the monetary awards substantially reduced. For example, the Wayne Newton verdict was eventually reversed.

The difficulty that public figures face in successfully bringing a libel suit against the media has prompted some news subjects to look for other remedies. In the past decade several subjects of news stories sued the news media for the way they gathered the news rather than based on the content of the story. Lawsuits concerning trespass and invasion of privacy by the media have become more common.

▲ Defamation and the Internet

The Internet has created new problems with regard to defamation. One problem involves who can be sued for defamation. Suppose you post a defamatory message on an AOL message board. Can someone sue both you and AOL? Congress addressed this issue in the Communications Decency Act of 1996. The law states that Internet service providers such as AOL are not liable for the content that they carry unless they (the providers) are the actual authors of the content. A 2006 decision by a Pennsylvania court seemed to broaden this protection. The court ruled that a person who republished on a Web site a potentially defamatory story written by someone else was also entitled to protection under the act.

Recent court decisions have extended protection to anonymous online speech. In 2009 a Maryland appeals court invalidated a subpoena that sought to identify the authors of online comments. The court went on to enumerate a multipart test that should be applied in future cases. The test included a stipulation to balance the anonymous poster's First Amendment rights against the rights of the person bringing a defamation suit. In a related case, a Tennessee court refused to force the disclosure of the identity of an anonymous

For a private citizen to prevail in a defamation case, he or she must prove some degree of negligence on the part of the media. The standards for determining what constitutes negligence vary from state to state, and as with the actual malice standard, negligence is determined on a case-by-case basis. Nonetheless, some general statements can be made.

A common legal definition of *negligence* states that it is conduct that creates an unreasonable risk of harm. The standard of conduct that the possible negligence is measured against is whether a reasonable person under the same circumstances would behave in the same way. As far as the media are concerned, employees are to be judged against the appropriate practices and customs for their profession. Thus, in many cases the issue of negligence boils down to whether the reporter or editor exercised reasonable care and followed the accepted practices of the profession in determining whether a story was true or false.

Some specific factors might also be taken into account. First, was the story prepared under deadline? If sufficient time and opportunity were available, then reasonable care might require more checking of facts. Second, what was the interest being promoted by the story? Stories covering heated political debates have greater merit than gossip, but gossip can be extremely harmful. Hence, greater care should be exercised in the latter situation.

A concrete example might help illustrate negligence and show how it differs from actual malice. In a 1975 case in Massachusetts, a rookie reporter had been covering a drug trial. The reporter was unaware that a table in the front of the courtroom was reserved for the press. Consequently, he sat in the back, where he had trouble hearing the testimony. One of the defendants was the 20-year-old son of a man named John Stone, who ran the lunchrooms in a public school. When the prosecutor asked a marshal the question of who had the drugs, the reporter thought he heard the marshal say, "Mr. Stone" and assumed he meant John Stone, the only "Mr. Stone" the reporter was aware of. He wrote in his story that John Stone had possession of the drugs. When questioned by his editor, who knew John Stone personally and had a hard time believing that he could have possessed illegal drugs, the reporter said he had heard the name in court. In fact, the marshal was talking about Jeffrey Stone, the son of John Stone. John Stone, naturally enough, sued for libel.

The court found that the reporter was guilty of negligence because he did not sit where he could properly hear and did not check with another source to confirm who the "Mr. Stone" was—two practices that were in keeping with the accepted procedures of journalism. However, the reporter's conduct did not constitute actual malice since he was new in town and did not have reason to doubt that the Stone mentioned in court was the only Stone he knew.

But what about the editor, who knew Mr. Stone personally and had trouble believing the story? The editor had reason to doubt the story but did not even make a phone call to check its accuracy. The court ruled that he had acted with reckless disregard for the truth of the report, which was enough to constitute actual malice.

---

blogger, noting that the request for disclosure would have to pass the test articulated in the Maryland case.

A second vexing question involves jurisdiction. Since the online versions of newspapers, magazines, and newsletters are available all over the world at the click of the mouse, where should a lawsuit be filed? This is an important question because laws governing defamation vary by state. In one recent case, online newspapers in Connecticut published a story about prison conditions in Virginia. A court ruled that the warden of a Virginia prison could sue the newspapers for libel in Virginia because the publications were accessible in that state. This decision, however, was reversed by the court of appeals on the grounds that the newspaper's Web site was not aimed at a Virginia audience. The international situation is muddier. A court in Australia ruled that the Dow Jones Company, based in New Jersey, could be sued for defamation in Australia because the online version of one of its magazines was available for downloading in Australia. Dow Jones eventually lost the case and had to pay out about a half-million dollars in damages. On the other hand, a British appeals court ruled that a Dow Jones publication that was available online could not be sued in England when it was shown that only five people had clicked on the Web site. The court said that there had to be evidence of substantial publication in England before a publication could be sued there.

In that connection, the state of New York passed the Libel Terrorism Protection Act in 2008. The law prevents the enforcement of libel judgments in the state unless a New York court finds that the foreign jurisdiction issuing the ruling has the same free speech protections as guaranteed under U.S. law. In addition, the law allows a citizen of New York to petition a state court to render the foreign verdict unenforceable in New York. A similar measure on the federal level was introduced in Congress but as of this writing was still under consideration.

Invasion of Privacy

▲ The Right to Privacy

Closely related to libel is the issue of privacy. In fact, a single publication will often prompt both types of suits. The big difference between the two is that libel protects a person's reputation, but the right to privacy protects a person's peace of mind and feelings. A second difference is that libel involves the publication of false information; invasion of privacy might be triggered by disclosing the truth.

There are four different ways that the mass media can invade someone's right to privacy.

Intrusion upon Solitude   The first is intruding upon a person's solitude or seclusion. This generally occurs when reporters wrongfully use microphones, surveillance cameras, and other forms of eavesdropping to record someone's private activities. A TV news crew hiding in a van outside your room and secretly taping your activities while you are inside would probably constitute intrusion.

The use of tiny, hidden cameras and microphones by reporters in their quest for news has raised special problems in this area. In a 1999 decision the California Supreme Court ruled that an ABC reporter committed an invasion of privacy when she went to work for a psychic hot line and secretly videotaped a conversation with a coworker. Even though the conversation took place in an open office and was overheard by others, the court ruled that the coworker had a reasonable expectation that a reporter would not secretly videotape his conversations. This decision suggests that reporters should give extra thought to the use of hidden recordings in their news-gathering activities.

Unauthorized Release of Private Information   The second occasion is the unauthorized release of private information. A newspaper's publishing private medical records that reveal that a person has a dread disease is an example in this area. The courts allowed a suit claiming invasion of privacy to be filed when a newspaper published information about a person's sex-change operation without the person's consent.

The Internet has raised new concerns about privacy. In 2008, a federal judge ordered Google to provide information about videos watched on YouTube. The order came in the midst of a copyright suit brought by Viacom against the Internet search company. Viacom wanted access to the data to determine how many times its copyrighted videos were watched on the video-sharing site. Google had resisted providing the information because it might allow Viacom to determine the viewing and video-uploading activity of YouTube users.

Creation of a False Impression   A third method is publicizing people in a false light or creating a false impression of them. This invasion is most closely related to libel because falsity is also involved. Some TV stations get into trouble in this area through the practice of putting new narration over some stock tape footage, which sometimes creates a false impression. For example, a Chicago TV station was sued when it ran stock footage taken three years earlier of a doctor performing a gynecological exam with a story describing how another doctor allegedly used an AIDS-infected swab during a similar exam. The face of the doctor in the stock footage was readily identifiable, and she sued the station, claiming the story made it appear that she had performed the allegedly negligent procedure. (The station settled the suit out of court and paid the doctor an undisclosed amount of money.)

The decision in a 2008 false-light suit in Florida may have implications for invasion-of-privacy laws in other states. The Florida Supreme Court ruled that under Florida law false light was not a legitimate reason to bring a lawsuit. The ruling added, however, that Florida law does recognize defamation by implication, whereby a true statement is reported in such a way as to create a false impression. In short, those bringing cases in Florida for the creation of a false impression will have to show some harm to their reputation; claiming that their feelings have been hurt or that their peace of mind has been harmed will not be enough.

American Apparel is a large clothing manufacturer that has a reputation for edgy advertising campaigns. The company's ads, for example, have featured adult-film actresses in provocative poses and have taken sides in controversies such as immigration. Woody Allen is an Oscar-winning filmmaker whose past life has been the subject of many a sensational tabloid story.

In 2007 American Apparel put up billboards in New York and Los Angeles featuring Allen dressed as an orthodox Jew in a scene from *Annie Hall* and a line of text in Yiddish: "The High Rabbi." American Apparel admitted that the image was taken from the film and was used without Allen's permission. When Allen objected to the ad, American Apparel took down the billboards and apologized. That apparently was not enough for Allen, who sued the company for $10 million claiming that American Apparel appropriated his likeness without permission.

The company argued fair use, claiming that the ads were meant to be social satire and designed to foster discussion about significant public issues. Consequently, it should merit First Amendment protection. Allen's lawyers, of course, disagreed, and some legal experts expected that Allen would prevail in court.

The case, however, never got that far. American Apparel settled out of court, agreeing to pay Allen $5 million. Although this might seem like a high price to pay, the company probably got a few million dollars worth of publicity from the case.

Appropriation of Identity   The last means of invading privacy is through appropriation of a person's name or likeness for commercial purposes. This commonly involves stars and celebrities who find their names or images used without their permission in some business or promotional activity. Model Christie Brinkley, for example, successfully filed suit to stop poster stores from selling her picture without her permission. (See the boxed insert "Woody Allen vs. American Apparel.") The not-so-famous are also protected against appropriation. One man sued because he found that a camera company had used his picture without permission in its instruction manual.

▲ Trespass

Trespass, defined as unauthorized entry into someone else's territory, is a concept that is closely related to invasion of privacy. The close of the 20th century saw a significant increase in the number of trespass cases brought against the news media. These cases highlighted a fundamental question for news reporting: Do journalists have a special First Amendment privilege to break the law in pursuit of a legitimate news story that will advance the public interest? Several recent court decisions suggest that the answer to this question is no.

In one case a Wisconsin court found that a TV photojournalist who had entered private property with permission of a police officer responding to a call was guilty of trespassing. Similarly, a 1999 circuit court ruling found that journalists who enter a private home with law enforcement officers but without consent of the homeowner could be sued for trespass. In another case reporters who followed antinuclear demonstrators through a fence onto the property of a utility company were found guilty of trespassing. A related 1999 Supreme Court case found that law enforcement officers who permitted the news media to accompany them across the threshold of a home when serving a search warrant were violating the Fourth Amendment's provisions against unreasonable searches.

Finally, consider the 1996 case of *Food Lion* v. *ABC.* Reporters for the newsmagazine *Prime Time Live* faked résumés to get jobs at a Food Lion supermarket and used hidden cameras to shoot video to document their story. After the program aired, Food Lion brought suit against the network not for defamation, but for fraud and trespass. Outside the courtroom, lawyers for Food Lion explained that they thought the story was libelous, but they thought they had a better chance of winning on the basis of the trespass and fraud charges. A jury found in favor of Food Lion and awarded the supermarket chain a whopping $5.5 million in damages. A district court judge reduced this amount to $350,000. Eventually, the circuit court of appeals dismissed most of the case, but it did uphold the trespass decision. The original jury awarded Food Lion only $1 in damages for the trespass, but now that the precedent has been set, it is possible that future lawsuits will seek far greater sums for trespass violations.

Copyright law and video-sharing sites have spawned a new entry-level job: video copyright analyst. Basic requirements: keen eyesight, knowledge of media company logos, and ability to sit still for long periods of time.

BayTSP is a company that makes money by checking videos on YouTube to see if there is any material that constitutes copyright infringement. Some of the checking is done by computers that are programmed to search for key words (such as TV show titles) and proper names (such as Chappelle), but automated scanning can't do the whole job. Enter the video copyright analyst whose job it is to watch YouTube videos 8 hours a day looking for copyright violations.

BayTSP employs about 20 of these analysts, called "hashers," who are paid around $11 per hour. When a hasher finds a video that is in violation of the copyright laws, he or she notifies a colleague whose job is to send an e-mail to YouTube demanding that the site remove the offending video. BayTSP's biggest client is Viacom, currently involved in a $1-billion lawsuit against YouTube's owner, Google. Viacom reportedly pays BayTSP about $500,000 a month to trace copyright violations.

The hashers' job is getting harder all the time as uploaders figure out new ways to beat the system. Some deliberately misspell the names of shows or people. Others post music videos and add the word "remix," since music companies are less inclined to remove videos that have been altered by users. The job can be frustrating since many videos are simply re-posted after they have been removed.

Google is working on an automated system designed to keep copyrighted material off YouTube before it is ever posted, but the company has yet to put the system into operation. Such an occurrence would obviously cut into BayTSP's revenue, but the company would probably stay in business since somebody has to check to see if the automated system is working properly.

All of the hashers have one thing in common: None of them watches YouTube videos outside of work.

Copyright

Copyright protects an author against unfair appropriation of his or her work. Although its roots go back to English common law, the basic copyright law of the United States was first enacted in 1909. In 1976, faced with copyright problems raised by the new communications technologies, Congress passed legislation covering literary, dramatic, and musical works, as well as motion pictures, television programs, and sound recordings. The law also states what is not covered. For example, an idea cannot be copyrighted, nor can a news event, a discovery, or a procedure.

For works created on or after January 1, 1978, copyright protection lasts for the life of the author plus 70 years. Works published before that date are eligible for copyright protection for a total of 95 years. To obtain full copyright protection, it is necessary to send a special form, copies of the work, and a small fee to the Register of Copyrights. The owner of a copyrighted work can then reproduce, sell, display, or perform the property.

It is important to note that copyright protection extends only to copying the work in question. If a person independently creates a similar work, there is no copyright violation. As a result, one of the things that a person who brings a copyright suit must prove is that the other person had access to the work under consideration. Thus, if you contend that a hit Hollywood movie was actually based on a pirated script that you had submitted to the company, you must show that the people responsible for the movie had access to your work. (To guard against copyright suits, most production companies will not open the envelopes of what look like unsolicited scripts.) Note, however, that you do not have to prove that someone intentionally or even consciously copied your work.

In addition, the law provides that people can make fair use of copyrighted materials without violating the provisions of the Copyright Act. *Fair use* means that copies of a protected work can be made for such legitimate activities as teaching, research, news reporting, and criticism without penalty. Four factors are taken into consideration in determining fair use:

1.   The purpose of the use (whether for profit or for nonprofit education)
2.   The nature of the copyrighted work
3.   The amount reproduced in proportion to the copyrighted work as a whole
4.   The effect of the use on the potential market value of the copyrighted work

The headline in *Billboard* magazine summed it up: "Grokster Bad; Music Industry Good." The trade press hailed the Supreme Court's 2005 decision in the *MGM* v. *Grokster* case as a monumental victory for the entertainment industry. The Recording Industry Association of America said the Court addressed a significant threat to the U.S. economy and protected "the livelihoods of more than 11 million Americans employed by the copyright industries." Another record executive proclaimed that the Supreme Court drove a stake through "the heart of services that rely on theft as a key competitive advantage." Upon closer examination, however, the decision may not have been the last word about the issue.

At the core of the Court's decision was the manner in which the peer-to-peer systems promoted their services. If a system actively encouraged copyright infringement, as shown by clear expression or other actions and inactions, then the service is liable for the resulting acts of infringement by its users. As far as Grokster was concerned, there was ample evidence that the service touted itself to former Napster users who were looking for another source from which to download copyrighted material. Plus Grokster made no effort to develop a filtering system to diminish infringing material.

But what exactly constitutes encouragement to violate copyright? What if a new file-sharing service emerges exactly like Grokster but tells its users not to copy and share copyrighted works? Is it still responsible for the actions of people who disobey its instruction? What if the service develops filtering software and sends messages to copyright infringers to stop what they are doing? Is the service still responsible for those who ignore its warnings? Those who illegally download, of course, would still be liable for copyright infringement, but they would be in the same situation they were in before the Supreme Court decision. These questions are currently being asked concerning video-sharing sites.

Thus, a teacher who reproduces a passage from a long novel to illustrate writing style to an English class will probably not have to worry about copyright. On the other hand, if a commercial magazine reproduces verbatim a series of articles published in a not-for-profit magazine, it is likely that the copyright statute will be determined to have been violated.

The "fair use" provision on copyright law was in the spotlight in 2008 when J. K. Rowling, the author of the Harry Potter novels, brought suit against a company that planned to publish a *Harry Potter Lexicon.* The judge ruled in Rowling's favor, noting that the proposed book reproduced too much of Rowling's original work and added little that was new or transformative.

Recent cases involving copyright law have dealt with the new communication media. In what is popularly known as the "Betamax case," the Supreme Court ruled in 1984 that viewers who owned videocassette recorders could copy programs off the air for later personal viewing without violating the Copyright Act. Such taping, ruled the Court, was a fair use of the material. In 1991 a federal court ruled that commercial copying companies, such as Kinko's, had to get permission from the publishers before copying and selling copyrighted articles and book excerpts used for college courses.

The 1998 Digital Millennium Copyright Act (DMCA) makes it unlawful to create services that are used to circumvent measures that control access to copyrighted works. In general, service providers, search engines, and Web hosts are immune from copyright infringement liability for simply transmitting information over the Internet. This provision was included to protect companies from having to monitor the activities of everybody who uses the Internet, a practical impossibility. Service providers, search engines, and Web sites do have a responsibility to remove material that appears to constitute copyright infringement when such an infringement is brought to their attention. When that occurs, companies must "expeditiously" remove or block access to the material. However, the DMCA does not provide guidelines on what constitutes an "expeditious" reaction.

The Napster case vividly highlighted some of the copyright problems caused by the Internet. In 1999 the recording industry filed suit against the file-sharing service. Napster argued that its activities were protected by the "fair use" provision of copyright law: Making copies of a song for noncommercial, personal use was the same as videotaping a TV program for personal use. The recording industry argued that Napster was knowingly facilitating the illegal distribution of copyrighted material.

The courts sided with the recording industry and ordered that Napster remove all copyrighted material from its system. The decision spelled the end for Napster, and the

The Pirate Bay is a Swedish Web site that lets visitors find links to TV, music, and film files held on the computers of its 22 million users in order to share those files. In 2008, Swedish prosecutors filed a lawsuit against the owners of the site claiming that the Pirate Bay site helped others violate copyright law. After a lengthy trial, the Swedish court announced a guilty verdict, levied a $3.5-million fine against the owners, and sentenced them to a year in jail. The owners immediately announced they would file an appeal, a process that might take years to resolve.

Swedish law, of course, does not set a precedent in the United States, and the court did not immediately order Pirate Bay to be shut down. Traffic on the Web site did not show any decline after the verdict. Even if Pirate Bay were to cease operation, recent history suggests that some other site would spring up to take its place.

So why did *Billboard* magazine, the main trade publication of the music industry, run this headline: "Could Pirate Bay Verdict Save the Music?" As it turns out, the Pirate Bay case might eventually help the recording industry in its never-ending battle with pirates. The verdict in the earlier Napster case

disallowed hosting of unauthorized material. The ruling in the Grokster case made it illegal to distribute software that encouraged copyright infringements. The Pirate Bay verdict suggested that Web sites could be held liable for merely pointing users to links where they can illegally download copyrighted material, thus giving the recording industry another weapon in its legal battle.

Second, the decision included significant jail time for the defendants. The recording industry hopes that this will have some psychological impact on those planning Pirate Bay clone sites since jail time significantly raises the risk in operating a file-sharing site. In fact, some smaller linking sites did shut down in the wake of the verdict.

Finally, the decision may push illegal file-sharing services to the fringes of the Internet. After each key antipirating decision, those services that remain are forced to try some other method to escape legal action. The industry hopes that eventually file-sharing sites will migrate to virtual private networks where admission is by invitation only. Although this will not entirely solve the problem, it would significantly reduce it since most people would be unaware of how to access the material.

service filed for bankruptcy in 2002. Napster's demise, however, did not put an end to file sharing. New, harder-to-shut-down services, such as Kazaa and Grokster, took its place. By 2004 more people were downloading and sharing music than during Napster's heyday.

The recording industry responded in two ways. First, it filed copyright infringement suits against several hundred individuals for sharing music files on the Internet. Those targeted first were those who had more than a thousand songs stored on their hard drives. Some of those who were sued wound up settling their cases by paying thousands of dollars to the recording companies. As noted in Chapter 8, the recording industry dropped this tactic in 2009. Second, the recording industry joined the movie industry in attempting to sue not just the individuals who illegally downloaded copyrighted material but also the peer-to-peer services, such as Grokster and Streamcast, that made file sharing possible. In mid-2005 the Supreme Court noted that there was substantial evidence that the file-sharing services had promoted their systems as a way in which users could illegally share protected material and thus induced and encouraged their subscribers to violate the law. The Court then ruled that file-sharing services can be sued for the copyright infringement of their customers. The entertainment industry hailed the decision as a great victory, but the ruling failed to address some key questions (see the boxed insert "*MGM* v. *Grokster*"). As we noted in Chapter 8, these decisions have not had a significant effect on file sharing.

Video-sharing sites are the next battleground for copyright issues. In 2007 Viacom and NBC sued YouTube for $1 billion, claiming that the site hosted videos that infringed upon Viacom's and NBC's copyrights. Google, YouTube's parent company, argued that YouTube had complied with the provisions of the DMCA. NBC and Viacom countered that the site should be more proactive about removing copyrighted material and not shift the burden of enforcement to the victims of infringement. They also argued that YouTube had not done enough to stop copyright infringements and that YouTube's lack of zeal in this area actually promoted copyright violations. If NBC and Viacom are successful in showing that YouTube actually promotes the infringement of copyrights by its users, then, under the Supreme Court's *Grokster* ruling, YouTube could face some drastic consequences.

Obscenity and Pornography

Obscenity is not protected by the First Amendment; that much is clear. Unfortunately, nobody has yet come up with a definition of *obscenity* that satisfies everybody. Let us take a brief look at how the definition of this term has changed over the years. (If, when we are done, you are a little confused about this whole issue, do not feel bad. You are not alone.)

For many years the test of whether something was obscene was the **Hicklin Rule,** a standard that judged a book (or any other item) by whether isolated passages had a tendency to deprave or corrupt the mind of the most susceptible person. Thus, if one paragraph of a 500-page book tended to deprave or corrupt the mind of the most suscep-tible person (a 12-year-old child, a dirty old man), then the entire book was obscene. The standard was written in the 1860s and widely used for the next 80 years.

In a 1957 case, *Roth* v. *United States,* the Supreme Court tried its hand at writing a new definition. The new test for detecting obscenity would be the following: whether to the aver-age person, applying contemporary standards, the dominant theme of the material taken as a whole appealed to prurient interests. (*Prurient* means "lewd" or "tending to incite lust.") The Roth test differed from the earlier rule in two significant ways. Not only did the entire work, rather than a single passage, have to be taken into consideration, but the material had to offend the average person, not simply anyone who saw it. Obviously, this standard was less restrictive than the Hicklin Rule, but gray areas remained. Should the community standards be local or national? How exactly would prurient interest be measured?

The next few years produced more obscenity cases to plague the high court. According to other decisions the material had to be "patently offensive" and "utterly without redeeming social value" to be obscene. During the 1960s the Supreme Court began considering the con-duct of the seller or distributor in addition to the character of the material in question. For example, even if material was not considered hard-core pornography, it could be banned if sold to minors, thrust upon an unwilling audience, or advertised as erotic to titillate custom-ers. A 1969 ruling introduced the concept of "variable obscenity" when it stated that certain magazines were obscene when sold to minors but not obscene when sold to adults.

By 1973 so many legal problems were cropping up under the *Roth* guidelines that something had to be done. Consequently, the Supreme Court attempted to close up loop-holes in the case of *Miller* v. *California.* This decision did away with the "utterly without redeeming social value" test and stated that the "community standards" used in defining obscenity could be local standards, which, presumably, would be determined by local juries. The new test of obscenity included three principles:

1. Whether the average person, applying contemporary community standards, would find that the work as a whole appealed to prurient interests
2. Whether the work depicted or described in a patently offensive way certain sexual conduct that was specifically spelled out by a state law
3. Whether the whole work lacked serious literary, artistic, political, or scientific value

Despite this new attempt, problems were not long in coming. The language of the decision appeared to permit a certain amount of local discretion in determining what was obscene. The question of how far a local community can go in setting standards continues to be troublesome. The Supreme Court has since ruled that the motion picture *Carnal Knowledge* is not obscene, even though a state court said that it was. The Court has also said that *Screw* magazine and the *Illustrated Presidential Report of the Commission on Obscenity and Pornography* are obscene no matter what community's standards are invoked. The Court further clarified the third of the *Miller* guidelines in a 1987 case when it ruled that judges and juries must assess the literary, artistic, political, or scientific value of allegedly obscene material from the viewpoint of a "reasonable person" rather than applying community standards. These issues could be decided with the help of experts who would testify about the value of a work. The first two guidelines, however, would still be decided with refer-ence to contemporary community standards.

Over the years the Court has taken a somewhat more lenient view as to what constitutes obscenity. The Miller case suggested that the Court was encouraging the states to deal with the problem at the local level. Given the long history of controversy that surrounded this topic, however, it was unlikely that this predicament would end soon. In fact, the whole issue surfaced again in 1986 when the Justice Department released a report on pornography. The report, which had strong political overtones, called for more stringent laws concerning pornography. One such law, the Child Protection and Obscenity Enforcement Act, took effect in 1988.

More recent problems have concerned the Internet. Child pornography is illegal on the Internet just as it is in other media. The 1988 act specifically mentions computers as one of the channels through which this illegal material might be circulated. Sexual "stalking" over the Net is also prohibited. In an effort to keep pornographic material from children, Congress passed the Communications Decency Act in 1996. Part of the act made it illegal to use a computer to create, solicit, or transmit any obscene, lewd, lascivious, filthy, or indecent communication. The Supreme Court eventually found the act to be unconstitutional and ruled that the Internet should be given the highest level of First Amendment protection, similar to that given to books and newspapers, rather than the more limited rights of broadcasting and cable, where regulation is more common. The Court noted that even though the government has a legitimate interest in trying to protect children from harmful content, this interest does not justify broad suppression of materials directed at adults.

A second attempt at protecting children from pornography also ran into legal difficulty. The Child Online Protection Act required commercial Web sites to demand proof of age before delivering material that might be harmful to minors. In 2000 an appeals court upheld an injunction that blocked implementation of the act, ruling that the act raised serious First Amendment problems. As a result, the act has never been enforced. The law was effectively killed in 2009 when the Supreme Court refused to hear an appeal of the lower court's ruling.

A similar measure, the Children's Internet Protection Act, required libraries that receive federal funds to use filters to block access to pornographic images on their computers. The American Library Association challenged the act, but in 2003 the Supreme Court ruled that the act was constitutional.

As is probably apparent by now, the Internet brings new challenges along with its benefits.

Regulating Broadcasting

The formal controls surrounding broadcasting represent a special case. Not only are broadcasters affected by the laws and rulings previously discussed, but they are also subject to additional controls because of broadcasting's unique position and character. When broadcasting was first developed in the early 20th century, it became clear that more people wanted to operate a broadcasting station than there were suitable frequencies available. As a result, the early broadcasters asked the U.S. Congress to step into the picture. Congress passed the Radio Act of 1927, which held that the airwaves belonged to the public and that broadcasters who wished to use this resource had to be licensed to serve in the public interest. A regulatory body, called the Federal Radio Commission (later known as the Federal Communications Commission), was set up to determine who should get a license and whether those who had a license should keep it. Because of this licensing provision, radio and television are subject to more regulations than are newspapers, magazines, films, and sound recording.

▲ The Federal Communications Commission

The Federal Communications Commission (FCC) does not make law; it interprets the law. One of its big jobs is to interpret the meaning of the phrase "public interest." For example, the FCC may write rules and regulations to implement the Communications Act of 1934

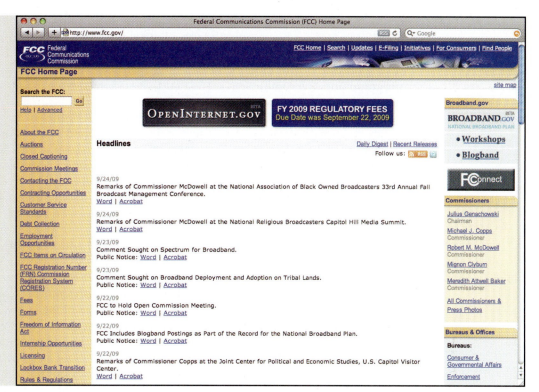

The home page of the FCC. In addition to television and radio, the FCC regulates telephone, telegraph, and personal communication devices.

if these rules serve the public interest. Moreover, the FCC awards and renews licenses if the award or renewal is in the public interest. Over the years several significant FCC rulings have shed some light on this rather ambiguous concept. One of the first things the commission established was that it would examine programming and determine whether the public interest was being served. It was not enough for a station to adhere to the technical operating requirements of its license. It would also have to provide a "well-rounded" program structure. In its 1929 Great Lakes decision, the commission also put broadcasters on notice that the broadcasting of programs that tended to injure the public—fraudulent advertising, attacks on ethnic groups, attacks on religions—would not be in the public interest.

What can the FCC do to stations that do not operate in the public interest? It can take several official actions. At the mildest level, it can fine a station up to $325,000. The next level of severity is to renew a station's license only for a probationary period (usually a year). This action typically puts the station on notice that it has to improve its performance or face even more serious consequences. The most severe form of official action is the revoking or nonrenewal of a license. Revocation/nonrenewal is more of a threat, however, than a reality. From 1934 to 1978, the FCC took away the licenses of only 142 stations. This figure should be weighed against the thousands of renewals that the commission granted each of those years. In fact, it has been calculated that 99.8 percent of all licenses are renewed. Nonetheless, the threat of revocation is a potent one that is universally feared among broadcasters.

During the 1980s, as was the case in many industries, the prevailing philosophy that governed broadcasting was one of deregulation. The FCC and Congress eliminated literally dozens of rules and regulations, including the controversial Fairness Doctrine (see the section devoted specifically to this doctrine). The rush to deregulation slowed during the 1990s as the FCC and Congress established new rules and regulations for broadcasting and cable.

For instance, Congress passed the Children's Television Act, which required that TV stations present programs designed to meet the educational and informational needs of young persons through the age of 16. The bill also created a $2-million endowment to fund children's educational programs. Additionally, the act limited the amount of commercial time during children's programming to 10½ minutes per hour on weekends and 12 minutes per hour on weekdays, a limit that applies to both broadcasters and cable operators. Stations and systems that violate these standards could be subject to a fine. In response to a provision in the law that instructed the FCC to encourage children's programming, the commission mandated that stations devote 3 hours per week to informational and educational programs for children.

The FCC is also involved in policy making through its Office of Strategic Planning and Policy Analysis. This office acts as economic, business, and market consultant to the FCC in order to identify trends and recommend future courses of action. Recent studies have examined the impact of wireless devices that do not require a license and market conditions that would best stimulate the effective use of the Internet.

The FCC has no regulatory control over the Internet or over Internet service providers. The commission does have some indirect influence, however, because it has some regulatory power over telephone and cable companies and can thus affect how you connect to the Internet. In 2005 the FCC issued a policy statement endorsing **Internet neutrality**—a provision that would block Internet service providers from favoring one Web company over another. How much jurisdiction the FCC has over this topic, however, is still open to debate. In 2008, for example, the FCC voted to punish Comcast Corporation for limiting Internet traffic to its consumers in apparent violation of the FCC's network neutrality principles. Comcast admitted to preventing some subscribers from swapping video files over services such as BitTorrent. The FCC didn't fine the company but did require it to stop blocking traffic and disclose more information about its practices to consumers. Comcast argued that the FCC could enforce specific rules but not general principles and appealed the decision. It's likely that this is one issue that will eventually make its way to the Supreme Court.

▲ Indecent Content

When it comes to regulating indecent content, the FCC finds itself caught between the wishes of Congress and the rulings of the federal court system. A 1978 Supreme Court ruling gave the FCC the right to regulate indecency because the pervasive presence of broadcasting made it easily accessible to children. In the late 1980s, after many radio stations began to air raunchy content, Congress passed legislation that instructed the FCC to ban indecent programming 24 hours a day. A federal court declared that this ban was unconstitutional and ordered the FCC to establish a "safe harbor," a time when indecent material could be aired without much chance of reaching children. The FCC responded by banning indecent content between the hours of 6 A.M. and 8 P.M. This did not satisfy Congress (there is some political benefit to be derived from being against indecency), which passed a law banning indecency before midnight. This law was ruled unconstitutional, and finally, a law that banned indecent content between 6 A.M. and 10 P.M. was approved. As should be clear by now, trying to protect children from indecency while protecting the First Amendment rights of adults is an exasperating task.

Indecent content became a hot topic in 2004 thanks in part to Janet Jackson's wardrobe malfunction during the Super Bowl halftime show that revealed more of Janet than many people felt was appropriate. The incident sparked renewed regulatory fervor at the FCC and Congress. The FCC issued more than $3.6 million in fines for indecency in 2004, the most ever recorded. The biggest fine, of more than a million dollars, was issued to Fox Broadcasting for airing *Married by America,* in which bachelors licked whipped cream off of strippers. Fox also got hit with a $550,000 fine for the Super Bowl overexposure. The fine was later tossed out by an appeals court, but a Supreme Court decision ordered the lower court to reexamine its ruling. Moreover, Congress passed stiffer regulations covering indecency.

Everybody would probably agree that fairness is a good idea. We should strive to be equitable and evenhanded in our dealings with others. It's the doctrine part that raises issues.

The Fairness Doctrine was first articulated in 1949 when most communities had one or two TV stations and maybe a few AM radio stations. The rationale behind the doctrine rested on the fact that because of the limited number of broadcast frequencies available, a radio or TV station should not become an advocate of one particular point of view. The public interest was better served if the stations allowed for reasonable opportunity for discussion of contrasting points of view on controversial issues of public importance.

Broadcasters (the rule does not apply to print media) never liked the Fairness Doctrine, arguing that it interfered with their First Amendment rights. A test of the constitutionality of the doctrine came in 1969, and the Supreme Court ruled in favor of the doctrine. The Court held that the First Amendment right of the viewers and listeners to be exposed to different points of view was paramount and overrode the right of the broadcasters. The Court added, however, that if it could be shown at some later date that the doctrine actually restrained free speech, then its constitutionality might be reconsidered.

In the years that followed, broadcasters argued that the doctrine did exactly what the Court feared in restraining free speech. Rather than go to the trouble and expense of seeking out other points of view on controversial issues, broadcasters simply ignored them. Moreover, as more and more radio and TV stations went on the air and cable TV networks were available to more Americans, the scarcity principle underlying the doctrine no longer seemed valid. Conflicting points of view were widely available to the public.

Sentiment at the FCC also turned against the doctrine. The commission found itself spending time and effort evaluating hundreds of complaints that required it to determine what exactly a controversial issue was and what was meant by a reasonable opportunity for discussion. Finally, in the spirit of deregulation during the 1980s, the FCC decided to scrap the doctrine.

Nonetheless, efforts to reinstate the doctrine in one form or another have repeatedly cropped up. Attempts during the administrations of Presidents Reagan and George H. W. Bush both failed. Another attempt in 2005 failed to come to a vote. In 2009, with the Democratic Party in control of the White House and Congress, the Fairness Doctrine was again under consideration. Several members of Congress, including Senator John Kerry and Speaker of the House Nancy Pelosi, have come out in favor of resurrecting the doctrine in some form, but as of late-2009 no legislation had been formally introduced in Congress.

The subtext in this recent debate concerns conservative talk radio. Talk radio blossomed after the demise of the Fairness Doctrine when stations could present partisan programs without fear of being reported to the FCC. Commentators such as Rush Limbaugh and Sean Hannity argued that bringing back the Fairness Doctrine was an effort to curb their influence and limit exposure to a conservative point of view.

Opposition to any reinstatement of the Fairness Doctrine has also come from libertarians, who warn against government regulation of free speech. Other critics point out that the Internet provides ample sources for people who are looking for opposing points of view. In addition, opponents point out that a revived Fairness Doctrine cuts both ways. Conservative talk radio would not be the only medium that would be affected. Stations carrying the liberal talk network Air America would also be subject to the doctrine. Public broadcasting, sometimes charged with being liberal, would also be governed by the doctrine and find its programming open to challenge from conservatives. Even some politically oriented skits on *Saturday Night Live* might trigger a Fairness Doctrine challenge. If, as some propose, the doctrine should be expanded to cover cable TV, then both Fox News and MSNBC would be affected.

Keep in mind that the doctrine deals with controversial issues, those that have already sparked extreme emotions. What seems like balanced coverage to station management might seem biased and unfair to a zealous supporter of a particular issue who would be more than happy to file a Fairness Doctrine complaint. It's not surprising that both broadcasters and the FCC were not fond of the doctrine while it existed.

The maximum amount that a station could be fined for airing indecency was raised to $325,000, 10 times the previous maximum amount.

The FCC continued its crackdown on indecency in 2006. The commission fined CBS and its affiliates more than $3 million for an episode of *Without a Trace* that the FCC ruled obscene. The FCC also changed its policy regarding what it calls "fleeting expletives," such as four-letter words that slip out during a live broadcast. For many years the commission had declined to fine stations for such slips. But in response to a couple of celebrities who used what the FCC termed "the f-word" during awards programs, the commission reversed course and declared that any use of forbidden words, fleeting or not, would invite a fine. The new policy, however, was short-lived. A federal appeals court ruled that the new regulations were arbitrary and declared them null and void. The FCC appealed to the Supreme Court. In a 2009 decision, the Court ruled that the FCC's change in policy was not arbitrary but did not decide if the policy was a violation of broadcasters' First Amendment rights. The Court sent the case back to a lower court for an examination of the free speech issue. It is likely that this case may come before the Court again in the future.

▲ The Equal Opportunities Rule

The **Equal Opportunities Rule** is contained in Section 315 of the Communications Act and is thus federal law. Section 315 deals with the ability of bona fide candidates for public office to gain access to a broadcast medium during political campaigns. In simple terms, this section states that if a station permits one candidate for a specific office to appear on the air, it must offer the same opportunity to all other candidates for that office. If a station gives a free minute to one candidate, all other legally qualified candidates for that office are also entitled to a free minute. If a station sells a candidate a minute for $100, it must make the same offer to all other candidates. Congress has made some exceptions to this law, the most notable of which are legitimate newscasts and on-the-scene coverage of authentic news events.

▲ The Fairness Doctrine

The **Fairness Doctrine** no longer exists. The FCC repealed it in 1987. That does not mean, however, that it is dead and buried. There were several proposals in Congress to revive it, with the most recent attempt in 2009. (See the boxed insert "How Fair Is the Fairness Doctrine?")

When it was still in force, the Fairness Doctrine provided that broadcasters had to seek out and present contrasting viewpoints on controversial matters of public importance. On any issue broadcasters had to make a good-faith effort to cover all the opposing viewpoints. This did not have to take place in one program, but the broadcaster was expected to achieve balance over time. Note that the Fairness Doctrine never said that opposing views were entitled to equal time. It simply mandated that some reasonable amount of time be granted.

Regulating Cable TV

The regulatory philosophy of the FCC and Congress toward cable has shown wide variation over the years. In the 1950s the FCC ruled that it had no jurisdiction over cable. This notion changed in the 1960s when the commission exerted control over the new medium and wrote a series of regulations governing its growth. By 1972 a comprehensive set of rules governing cable was on the FCC's books. The growth of cable during the 1970s led to successful lobbying efforts by the industry to ease many of these restrictions. In the 1980s, in line with the deregulatory philosophy of the Reagan administration, almost all the FCC rules concerning cable were dropped. Moreover, Congress passed the Cable Communications Policy Act in 1984, which gave cable operators great freedom in setting rates and deciding what channels they could carry on their systems. The law also allowed state and local governments the right to grant cable **franchises** (a franchise is an exclusive right to operate in a given territory).

Unlike broadcast stations, cable systems were not licensed by the FCC. Instead, under the 1984 law, the local franchise authority, should it wish to do so, had the power to terminate the franchise at the end of the franchise period. In addition, cable companies were free to set their own rates.

In the years following the passage of this act, many consumers complained that their cable system raised rates and was insensitive to the needs of its customers. Consequently, in 1992 Congress passed the Cable TV Act, which gave the FCC the authority to regulate the rates of most cable systems, required that cable systems carry the signals of any broadcast station with significant viewing in their market, and allowed commercial broadcast stations to waive their right to be carried in exchange for appropriate compensation from the cable system.

Two provisions in this law had important consequences. First, most consumers saw their monthly cable bills go down as the FCC instituted rate reductions of about 17 percent. Second, the provision requiring cable systems to carry the signals of broadcast stations was challenged in federal court as a violation of the First Amendment rights of cable operators. In 1994 the Supreme Court ruled that cable operators deserved more First Amendment protection from government regulation than did broadcasters but not as much as newspapers and magazines. Consequently, the Court declared that it was constitutional for Congress to pass laws to guarantee that the free flow of information not be restricted by a private company that controlled the means of transmission.

The issue of the constitutionality of the specific rules about which stations must be carried by cable systems was decided in 1997 when the Supreme Court ruled in favor of the "must carry" provision. The must-carry provision resurfaced again in 2007 when the FCC issued its dual-carriage rules. The rules specified that cable system operators had to deliver both the analog and digital signals of must-carry stations after the 2009 transition to digital TV. In a compromise worked out with cable operators, the rules would be phased out after three years. In addition, the rules reaffirmed that cable systems also had to carry the stations' high-definition signal.

In 2006–2007, Kevin Martin, the FCC chair, proposed that consumers be given an "a la carte" option when it came to subscribing to cable. Instead of the traditional bundle or tiers of channels that cable systems typically offer, subscribers would be able to choose only those channels that they wanted to receive. Martin argued that the a-la-carte option would enable customers to avoid cable channels that might carry indecent material. With Martin's departure from the FCC in 2009, prospects for the a-la-carte option were not bright.

The Telecommunications Act of 1996

The **Telecommunications Act of 1996** was the first major overhaul of communication laws in more than 60 years. The act contained provisions that affected traditional broadcasters, cable companies, and telephone companies. The following are among the key provisions of the law:

- It removed limits on the number of radio stations that can be owned by one person or organization. Up to eight stations may be owned in a single market. (See Chapter 7.)
- It removed limits on the number of television stations that can be owned as long as stations do not reach more than 35 percent (later changed to 39 percent) of the nation's TV homes.
- It extended the term of broadcast licenses to eight years.
- It allowed telephone companies to enter the cable TV business.
- It allowed cable TV companies to enter the telephone business.
- It deregulated the rates of many cable systems.
- It mandated that newly manufactured TV sets come with the ability to block unwanted programming based on an electronically encoded rating (popularly called the **V-Chip;** see Chapter 17).
- It mandated that the TV industry come up with a voluntary ratings system for violence, sex, and other indecent materials.

Now that the 1996 Telecommunications Act has been in force for several years, we can see evidence of its impact. As mentioned earlier, the removal of the cap on radio station ownership unleashed a wave of consolidation in the industry. The deregulation of cable rates has led to a general increase in cable subscribers' bills. It took a while but competition between phone companies and cable companies has become more vigorous. Phone company AT&T has started U-Verse, a video service with more than 300 channels. Cable giant Cablevision offers telephone service, and many companies are bundling phone, TV, and Internet service into one package.

The rapid changes in the business and technology environment have prompted Congress to reexamine the 1996 act. Some of the issues being examined include network neutrality, a philosophy that prevents Internet service providers from favoring one

Web company over another (for example, charging an extra fee so that one video down-loading service runs faster than competitors), and ways to encourage the spread of broadband.

Regulating Advertising

▲ Deceptive Advertising

The problem of deceptive and potentially harmful advertising has been around a long time. The philosophy of *caveat emptor* (let the buyer beware) was dominant until the early 1900s. Exaggerated claims and outright deception characterized many early adver-tisements, especially those for patent medicines. Spurred on by the muckrakers (see Chapter 5), the government took steps to deal with the problem when it created the Federal Trade Commission (FTC) in 1914. In the early years of its existence, the commis-sion was concerned with encouraging competition through the regulation of questionable business practices, such as bribery, false advertising, and mislabeling of products; protect-ing the consumer was not the main focus. The consumer started to receive some protection in 1938 with the Wheeler-Lea Act, which gave the FTC the power to prevent deceptive advertising that harmed the public, whether or not the advertising had any bad effects on the competition.

Like the FCC, the FTC has several enforcement techniques available to it. First of all, it can issue trade regulations that suggest guidelines for the industry to follow. In 1965, for example, it ruled that auto ads must contain both the city and highway estimates of gas mileage. The FTC also uses the **consent order.** In a consent order the advertiser agrees to halt a certain advertising practice, but at the same time the advertiser does not admit to any violation of the law; there is only an agreement not to continue. Somewhat stronger is a **cease-and-desist order.** This order follows a hearing by the commission that determines that a certain advertising practice does indeed violate the law. Violation of a consent order and failure to comply with a cease-and-desist order can result in fines being levied against the advertiser.

In the late 1960s and the 1970s, the FTC took a more active role in the regulation of advertising. The rising tide of interest in the rights of the consumer and the emergence of consumer activist groups (such as Ralph Nader's Raiders) were probably behind this new direction. A flurry of activity took place. First, the FTC wanted documentation for claims. If Brand Y claimed to be more effective in relieving pain than Brand X, the advertiser was now required to have proof for that claim. The FTC also ordered "corrective advertising," in which some advertisers were required to clarify some of their past claims.

More recently, the FTC has been concerned about advertising inappropriately directed toward children. In 1997 the FTC issued an unfair advertising complaint against the R. J. Reynolds Tobacco Company. The FTC argued that ads featuring Joe Camel, the com-pany's cartoon character, encouraged children to start smoking. In response, Reynolds announced it would no longer use the controversial camel in its ads.

In 2000 the FTC targeted the film industry for marketing R-rated movies to persons under 17. An FTC report found that marketing plans for 28 R-rated films included strategies for reaching children as young as 10. The report criticized Hollywood for routinely aiming its advertising at children for movies that its own rating system labels inappropriate. In response, eight movie studios announced plans to reform their promo-tional efforts. More recently, the FTC has cracked down on products that make deceptive health claims. In 2005, for example, the commission instructed Tropicana orange juice to stop claiming that the product reduced the risk of heart disease and strokes. The FTC also filed lawsuits against six companies whose advertising claimed that people who used their products would lose weight without dieting or exercise. In 2007 the FTC stated that companies that engage in word-of-mouth or "buzz" marketing must disclose these rela-tionships to consumers.

In 2009 the FTC was looking closely at testimonial ads. Under scrutiny were ads for diets and weight-loss programs whereby a person claims to have lost a huge amount of weight using such-and-such a program with this testimonial followed by a disclaimer "Results not typical" or "Your experience may vary." Proposed new FTC guidelines would require that advertisers give some indication of a typical result.

▲ Commercial Speech Under the First Amendment

The 1970s marked a change in judicial thinking about the amount of protection that advertising, or *commercial speech,* as it is called, should receive under the First Amendment. Before the 1970s, advertising had little claim to free-speech protection. In the 1940s F. J. Chrestensen found this out the hard way. Chrestensen owned a former U.S. submarine. There is not much that a private individual can do with a submarine, aside from charging admission to view it. This was Chrestensen's idea, and he wanted to distribute handbills advertising the sub. No way, said the New York City police commissioner. The city's sanitation code did not allow the distribution of advertising matter in the streets. However, handbills of information or of public protest were allowed. Inspired, Chrestensen put his submarine advertising message on one side of the handbill, while the other side was printed with a protest against the City Dock Department. Sorry, said the city, the protest message could be handed out, but the advertising on the other side would have to go. Chrestensen appealed, and two years later the Supreme Court ruled against him and agreed with the city of New York that advertising merited no First Amendment protection.

Since that time, however, the Supreme Court has retreated from this view. In 1964, in the *New York Times* v. *Sullivan* case, it extended First Amendment protection to ads that dealt with important social matters. Seven years later, the Court further extended this protection when a Virginia newspaper ran an ad for an abortion clinic located in New York and thus violated a Virginia law against such advertising. The Supreme Court ruled that the ad contained material in the public interest and merited constitutional protection. More recent cases suggest that in many instances commercial speech falls under the protection of the First Amendment.

In a 1980 ruling concerning advertising by an electric utility company, commonly called the Central Hudson case, the Supreme Court enunciated a four-part test for determining the constitutional protection of commercial speech. First, commercial speech that involves an unlawful activity or advertising that is false or misleading is not protected. Second, the government must have a substantial interest in regulating the commercial speech. Third, the state's regulation must actually advance the government interest

In the 1940s and 1950s, much cigarette advertising promoted the health benefits of smoking. This ad for Camels suggests that doctors endorse not only this brand of cigarette but smoking in general.

involved. Fourth, the state's regulations may be only as broad as necessary to promote the state's interest.

A 1984 ruling illustrated the use of these principles: The Court upheld a prohibition against posting signs on city property. The Court first noted that, although the advertising was for a lawful activity and not misleading, the government has a substantial interest in reducing "visual blight" and that the ordinance directly advanced that interest and was not overly broad. Further, the Court affirmed that corporations also have the right of free speech and granted lawyers, doctors, and professionals the right to advertise their prices. Although all the questions surrounding this issue have not been answered, it seems safe to conclude that at least some commercial speech is entitled to First Amendment protection. Its status, however, is less than that given to political and other forms of noncommercial expression.

Conclusion

The term *half-life* is a useful concept in physics. It refers to the length of time in which one-half of the radioactive atoms present in a substance will decay. We might borrow this term and reshape its meaning so that it is relevant to this book. The half-life of a chapter in this text is the time it takes for half the information contained in the chapter to become obsolete. With that in mind, it is likely that the half-life of this chapter may be among the shortest of any in this book. Laws are constantly changing; new court decisions are frequently handed down, and new rules and regulations are written all the time. All this activity means that what is written in this chapter will need frequent updating. In addition, it means that mass media professionals must continually refresh their understanding of the law. Of course, this also means that there will be a continuing stream of colorful characters, intriguing stories, and high drama as the courts and regulatory agencies further wrestle with the issues and problems involved in mass communication regulation.

MAIN POINTS

- There is a strong constitutional case against prior restraint of the press.

- Reporters have special privileges that protect them in some instances from having to reveal the names of their news sources. These privileges, however, are not absolute.

- Reporters can cover matters that occur in open court with little fear of reprisal. Some pretrial proceedings can still be closed to the press.

- All but two states now allow cameras in the courtroom on a permanent or experimental basis. Cameras and microphones are still barred from federal trial courts and from the Supreme Court.

- Defamation can be either libel or slander. To prevail in a defamation suit, a public figure must show that the published material was false and harmful and that the media acted with actual malice when they published the information. A private citizen must also show that the material was false and harmful and that the media involved acted with negligence.

- Invasion of privacy can occur when the media intrude upon a person's solitude, release private information, create a false impression, or wrongfully appropriate a person's name or likeness.

- Copyright law protects authors from unfair use of their work. There are instances, however, when portions of copyrighted material can be reproduced for legitimate purposes.

- Online file-sharing systems have raised serious questions about copyrights in a digital medium.

- Obscenity is not protected by the First Amendment. To be legally obscene, a work must appeal to prurient interests, depict or describe certain sexual conduct spelled out by state law, and lack serious literary, artistic, political, or scientific value.

- Special regulations and laws apply to broadcasting. The FCC is charged with administering the rules and regulations that deal with cable, TV, and radio. The Telecommunications Act of 1996 had a major impact on the electronic media.

- The FTC oversees advertising. Commercial speech has recently been given more First Amendment protection.

QUESTIONS FOR REVIEW

1. Whom do shield laws protect?
2. Whom do gag orders gag?
3. What is the Freedom of Information Act? How have reporters used it?
4. What is the difference between libel and slander?
5. What factors determine fair use?
6. Briefly explain the significance of the following court cases:
   a. The Betamax case
   b. The Pentagon Papers case
   c. *New York Times* v. *Sullivan*
   d. *Miller* v. *California*

QUESTIONS FOR CRITICAL THINKING

1. Why should reporters have special privileges when other professionals, such as architects, nurses, and accountants, have none?
2. Libel suits can be long and expensive for both sides. What are some other methods of conflict resolution that might cut down the time and the cost but still provide satisfaction for both sides?
3. Why are broadcasting and cable not entitled to the same amount of First Amendment protection as newspapers and magazines? Do you agree with this type of differentiation?
4. Should TV stations be punished if they unexpectedly air a "fleeting expletive"?
5. How can children be protected from exposure to adult-oriented content on the Internet?

KEY TERMS

First Amendment (p. 368)
prior restraint (p. 368)
injunction (p. 368)
shield laws (p. 371)
gag rules (p. 374)
Freedom of Information Act (FOIA) (p. 376)
USA Patriot Act (p. 376)
defamation (p. 377)
libel (p. 377)
slander (p. 377)
libel per se (p. 377)
libel per quod (p. 377)
trespass (p. 383)
Hicklin Rule (p. 387)
Internet neutrality (p. 390)
Equal Opportunities Rule (p. 392)
Fairness Doctrine (p. 392)
franchises (p. 392)
Telecommunications Act of 1996 (p. 393)
V-Chip (p. 393)
consent order (p. 394)
cease-and-desist order (p. 392)

INTERNET RESOURCES

Online Learning Center

On the Online Learning Center home page, www.mhhe.com/dominick11e, *select* Student Center *and then* Chapter 16.

1. Use the Learning Objectives, Chapter Outline, and Main Points sections to review this chapter.
2. Test your knowledge of the chapter using the multiple choice and flashcard features of the site.
3. Expand your knowledge of concepts and topics discussed in the chapter with additional Questions for Critical Thinking and Internet Exercises.

Surfing the Internet

Many Web sites deal with legal matters. The ones listed here seem most helpful for students.

www.fcc.gov
The FCC's home page. Contains an archive of recent speeches, a search engine, and consumer information along with more technical data.

www.freedomforum.org
Contains a summary of recent First Amendment court decisions, relevant law articles, a First Amendment time line, and a full text of relevant Supreme Court rulings.

www.rcfp.org
The Reporters Committee for Freedom of the Press maintains this site, which contains recent court decisions, legal news, and a link to its publication, *The News Media and the Law.*

www.rtnda.org
Home page of the Radio and Television News Directors Association. Contains information about covering the courts, libel, copyright, and other legal issues.

CHAPTER 17

Ethics and Other Informal Controls

This chapter will prepare you to:

- distinguish among the types of informal controls on the media

- explain the most important ethical principles

- explain what the standards departments and performance codes are

- discuss the relationship between the media and their advertisers vis-à-vis ethical practices

- understand the pros and cons of pressure groups

Like a winding road, the path to an ethical decision needs to be carefully navigated.

Laws and regulations are not the only controls on the mass media. Informal controls, stemming from within the media themselves or shaped by the workings of external forces such as pressure groups, consumers, and advertisers, are also important. The following hypothetical examples illustrate some situations in which these controls might spring up:

■ You are the program director for the campus radio station. You get a call one morning from the promotion department of a major record company offering you a free trip to California, a tour of the record company's studios, a ticket to a concert featuring all the company's biggest stars, and an invitation to an exclusive party where you will get to meet all the performers. The company representative explains that this is simply a courtesy to you so that you will better appreciate the quality of her company's products. Do you accept?

■ You are a reporter for the local campus newspaper. The star of the football team, who also happens to be the president of the Campus Crusade for Morality, has been involved in a minor traffic accident, and you have been assigned to cover the story. When you get to the accident scene, you examine the football player's car and find a half-dozen pornographic magazines strewn across the backseat. You have a deadline in 30 minutes; what details do you include in your story?

■ You are the editor of the campus newspaper. One of your reporters has just written a series of articles describing apparent health-code violations in a popular off-campus restaurant. This particular restaurant regularly buys full-page ads in your paper. After you run the first story in the series, the restaurant owner calls and threatens to cancel all her ads unless you stop printing the series. What do you do?

■ You are doing your first story for the campus paper. A local businessperson has promised to donate $5 million to your university so that it can buy new equipment for its mass communication and journalism programs. While putting together a background story on this benefactor, you discover that he was convicted of armed robbery at age 18 and avoided prison only by volunteering for military duty during the closing months of the Korean War. In the more than 50 years that have passed since then, his record has been spotless. He refuses to talk about the incident, claims his wife and his closest friends do not know about it, and threatens to withdraw his donation if you print the story. Naturally, university officials are concerned and urge you not to mention this fact. Do you go ahead and include the incident as simply one element in your overall profile? Do you take the position that the arrest information is not pertinent and not use it? Do you wait until the university has the money and then print the story?

We could go on listing examples, but by now the point is probably clear. There are many situations in the everyday operation of the mass media in which thorny questions about what to do or not to do have to be faced. Most of these situations do not involve laws or regulations but instead deal with the tougher questions of what is right or what is proper. Informal controls over the media usually assert themselves in these circumstances. In this chapter we will discuss the following examples of informal controls: personal ethics; performance codes; internal controls, such as organizational policies, self-criticism, and professional self-regulation; and outside pressures.

Personal Ethics

Ethics are rules of conduct or principles of morality that point us toward the right or best way to act in a situation. Over the years philosophers have developed a number of general ethical principles that serve as guidelines for evaluating our behavior. We will briefly examine five principles that have particular relevance to those working in the mass media professions. Before we begin, however, please note that these principles do not contain magic answers to every ethical dilemma. In fact, different ethical principles often suggest different and conflicting courses of action. There is no perfect answer to every problem. Also, these ethical principles are based on Western thought. Other cultures may have developed totally different systems. Nonetheless, these principles can provide a framework for analyzing what is proper in examining choices and justifying our actions.

▲ Ethical Principles

The Principle of the Golden Mean   Moral virtue lies between two extremes. This philosophical position is typically associated with Aristotle, who, as a biologist, noted that too much food as well as too little food spoils health. Moderation is the key. Likewise, in ethical dilemmas the proper way of behaving lies between doing too much and doing too little. For instance, in the restaurant example mentioned earlier, one extreme would be to cancel the story as requested by the restaurant owner. The other extreme would be to run the series as is. Perhaps a compromise between the two would be to run the series but also give the restaurant owner a chance to reply. Or perhaps the story might contain information about how the restaurant has improved conditions or other tempering remarks.

Examples of the **golden mean** are often found in media practices. For example, when news organizations cover civil disorders, they try to exercise moderation. They balance the necessity of informing the public with the need to preserve public safety by not inflaming the audience.

The Categorical Imperative   What is right for one is right for all. German philosopher Immanuel Kant is identified with this ethical guideline. To measure the correctness of our behavior, Kant suggested that we act according to rules that we would want to see universally applied. In Kant's formulation *categorical* means "unconditional"—no extenuating circumstances, no exceptions. Right is right and should be done, no matter what the consequences. The individual's conscience plays a large part in Kant's thinking. A **categorical imperative** is discovered by an examination of conscience; the conscience informs us what is right. If, after performing an act, we feel uneasy or guilty, we have probably violated our conscience. Applied to mass communication, a categorical imperative might be that all forms of deception in news gathering are wrong and must be avoided. No one wants deception to become a universal practice. Therefore, for example, a reporter should not represent him- or herself as anything other than a reporter when gathering information for a story.

The Principle of Utility   **Utility** is defined as the greatest benefit for the greatest number. Modern utilitarian thinking originated with the 19th-century philosophers Jeremy Bentham and John Stuart Mill. The basic tenet in their formulations is that we are to determine what is right or wrong by considering what will yield the best ratio of good to bad for the general society. Utilitarians ask how much good is promoted and how much evil is restrained by different courses of behavior. Utilitarianism provides a clear method for evaluating ethical choices: (1) Calculate all the consequences, both good and bad, that would result from each of our options; then (2) choose the alternative that maximizes value or minimizes loss.

Looking at the mass communication area, we can easily see several examples of utilitarian philosophy. In 1971 the *New York Times* and other papers printed stolen government documents known as the Pentagon Papers (see Chapter 16). Obviously, the newspapers involved thought that the good that would be achieved by printing these papers far outweighed the harm that would be done. (Note that the Kantian perspective would suggest a different course of action. Theft is bad. Newspapers do not want the government stealing their property, so they should not condone or promote the theft of government property.) Or take the case of a small midwestern paper that chose to report the death of a local teenager who had left town, turned to prostitution and drugs, and been murdered. The paper decided that the potential benefits of this story as a warning to other parents outweighed the grief it would cause the murder victim's family.

The Veil of Ignorance Justice is blind. Philosopher John Rawls argued that justice emerges when everyone is treated without social differentiations. Everybody doing the same job equally well should receive equal pay. Everybody who got an 80 on the test should get the same grade. Rawls advocated that all parties in a problem situation be placed behind a barrier, the **veil of ignorance,** that conceals roles and social differentiations and that each participant be treated as an equal member of society as a whole. Rawls's veil of ignorance suggests that we structure our actions to protect the most vulnerable members of society. It is easy to see the relevance of this principle to the workings of the mass media. If we applied the veil of ignorance to the problem of hammering out the proper relationship between politicians and journalists, the blatant adversarial relationship so often found between the groups would disappear. Behind the veil all newsmakers would be the same. Inherent cynicism and abrasiveness on the part of the press would disappear, as would mistrust and suspicion on the part of the politicians. On a more specific level, consider the case of a financial reporter who frequently gets tips and inside information on deals and mergers that affect the prices of stocks and passes these tips on to friends who use this information for their own profit. The veil of ignorance suggests that the reporter must treat all audience members the same. Personal friends should not benefit from inside information.

The Principle of Self-Determination This principle, closely associated with the Judeo-Christian ethic and also discussed by Kant, might be summarized as "Love your neighbor as yourself." Human beings have unconditional value apart from any and all circumstances. Their basic right to **self-determination** should not be violated by using them as simply a means to accomplish a goal. A corollary to this principle is that no one should allow him- or herself to be treated as a means to someone else's ends. Suppose that sources inside a government investigation on political corruption leak to the press the names of some people suspected of taking bribes, and the press, in turn, publishes the allegations and the names of the suspects. The principle of self-determination suggests that the press is being used by those who leaked the story as a means to accomplish their goal. Perhaps those involved in the investigation want to turn public opinion against those named or simply to earn some favorable publicity for their efforts. In any case, the press should resist being used in these circumstances. The rights, values, and decisions of others must always be respected.

▲ A Model for Individual Ethical Decisions

In numerous situations, personal ethical decisions have to be made about what should or should not be included in media content or what should or should not be done. Every day, reporters, editors, station managers, and other media professionals have to make these decisions. Too often, however, these decisions are made haphazardly, without proper analysis of the ethical dimensions involved. This section presents a model that media professionals can use to evaluate and examine their decisions. This model is adapted from the work of Ralph Potter.[1]

Definitions → *Values* → *Principles* → *Loyalties* → *Action*

---

[1]Ralph Potter, "The Logic of Moral Argument," in *Toward a Discipline of Social Ethics,* P. Deats, ed. (Boston: Boston University Press, 1972).

The *Chicago Tribune* decided to hold off publishing a story about possible wrongdoing by Governor Rod Blagojevich. Cooperating with law enforcement agencies creates special ethical problems for news organizations.

In short, the model asks the individual to consider four aspects of the situation before taking action. First, define the situation. What are the pertinent facts involved? What are the possible actions? Second, determine what values are involved. Which values are more relevant to deciding a course of action? Third, establish what ethical principles apply. We have discussed five that might be involved; there may be others. Fourth, decide where our loyalties lie. To whom do we owe a moral duty? It is possible that we might owe a duty to ourselves, clients, business organizations, the profession, or society in general. To whom is our obligation most important?

Let us examine how this model would work in a real situation. In 2008, reporters for the *Chicago Tribune* were investigating misconduct allegations against Illinois Governor Rod Blagojevich. In the course of their research, they discovered that the governor was also under investigation by U.S. Attorney Patrick Fitzgerald. Following standard operating procedure, the reporters contacted Fitzgerald's office and asked for confirmation and comments about the probe.

When the U.S. attorney's office learned that the *Tribune* was planning to publish the story in the near future, Fitzgerald asked the paper to delay publication of some parts of the story until a key ingredient of their investigation was carried out. The *Tribune* faced a classic ethical dilemma. The paper was on the verge of declaring bankruptcy, and the Blagojevich story was a sensational scoop that would certainly help sell newspapers. On the other hand, publishing the story might compromise or perhaps ruin an investigation into wrongdoing by the state's highest elected official. What course of action should the *Tribune* follow? Let's apply the Potter model and see what we can conclude.

1. *Establish the facts.* Both the paper and the U.S. attorney's office had strong evidence to suggest that the governor was involved in some sort of misconduct. The governor was apparently unaware of many aspects of the investigation. The potential misconduct was evidently serious enough that it might lead to the governor's arrest and removal from office. The investigation was ongoing, and the paper did not know when it might end. Law enforcement officials usually don't ask reporters to hold a story unless something major is involved.

2. *Clarify the values.* Journalists value credibility. Cooperating with law enforcement agencies is generally discouraged because it may harm a journalist's credibility when reporting about law enforcement. Moreover, the *Chicago Tribune* has a long history of exposing political corruption. The newspaper values its role as watchdog, and a story as big as this one would enhance the paper's reputation and maybe help the bottom line. At the same time, however, journalists value the welfare of their audience. Hampering an official investigation of executive misconduct might result in a potentially corrupt public official staying in office and further hurting the public welfare.

3. *State principles.* There are at least three ethical principles that could be involved in this situation. The first is utilitarianism. Did the benefits of publishing the story outweigh the harm that might result? Running the story would raise public awareness about the alleged misconduct and might result in greater public scrutiny of the conduct of all elected officials. On the other hand, running the story might

have prevented law enforcement officials from collecting crucial evidence. The second principle is the golden mean. Reporters could have reported all, some, or none of what they had discovered. The most sensitive stories might be postponed until after the investigation was over. The third principle is the categorical imperative. If a journalist believes that withholding information from the public is never the right course to follow, then the story should be published no matter what the harmful results.

4. *Determine loyalties.* The journalist's primary loyalty is to the audience to report fully the facts of a story, but that is not the journalist's only loyalty. In addition, reporters have a loyalty to society that requires them to act as good citizens in a democracy. Reporters also have a loyalty to all those elected officials who are not corrupt that obliges them to expose those who are dishonest. Finally, journalists owe loyalty to their peers to uphold the standards of the profession.

What actions resulted in this case? The *Chicago Tribune* apparently followed a combination of the ethical principles mentioned above. In keeping with the golden mean, the paper published some stories about the investigation but withheld others in honoring the request of the U.S. attorney's office. The paper did not, however, hold the story indefinitely. As suggested by utilitarianism, the *Tribune* eventually published the story that law enforcement officials wanted withheld, even though publishing the story might have weakened the corruption case against the governor. It appears that the paper thought the good that came from publishing the story would outweigh any harmful impact on the case.

After the governor was arrested, Fitzgerald praised the paper for holding off on the story, stating that had it been published it would have compromised the investigation. The *Tribune*'s editor noted the competing loyalties in the case when he wrote: "The *Chicago Tribune*'s interest in reporting the news flows from its larger obligation of citizenship in a democracy. . . . We strive to make the right decisions as reporters and as citizens. That's what we did in this case."

Performance Codes

Many ethical decisions have to be made within hours or even minutes, without the luxury of lengthy philosophical reflection. In this regard media professionals are not very different from other professionals, such as doctors and lawyers. In these professions, codes of conduct or of ethics have been standardized to help individuals make decisions. If a doctor or a lawyer violates one of the tenets of these codes, he or she may be barred from practice by a decision of a panel of colleagues who oversee the profession. Here the similarity with the mass media ends. Media professionals, thoroughly committed to the notion of free speech, have no professional review boards that grant and revoke licenses. Media codes of performance and methods of self-regulation are less precise and less stringent than those of other organizations. But many of the ethical principles discussed are incorporated into these codes.

▲ The Print Media

During the colorful and turbulent age of jazz journalism (see Chapter 4), several journalists, apparently reacting against the excesses of some tabloids, founded the American Society of Newspaper Editors. This group voluntarily adopted the Canons of Journalism in 1923 without any public or governmental pressure. There were seven canons: responsibility, freedom of the press, independence, accuracy, impartiality, fair play, and decency. By and large, the canons are prescriptive (telling what ought to be done) rather than proscriptive (telling what ought to be avoided). Some of the canons are general and vague, with a great deal of room for individual interpretation. Under *responsibility*, for example, it is stated that "the use a newspaper makes of the share of public attention it gains serves to determine its sense of responsibility, which it shares with every member of its staff." This is a noble thought, but it is of little help when it comes to deciding if a newspaper should include the detail about the pornographic magazines in the star football player's car. Other statements seem simplistic. Under *accuracy,* for example, one learns that "headlines should be fully warranted by the contents of the article they surmount." Nevertheless, these canons should not be dismissed as mere platitudes and empty rhetoric. They do represent the first concrete attempt by journalists to strive for professionalism in their field.

When the canons were first released, *Time* magazine held out grandiose hopes for the future of the profession: "The American Society of Newspaper Editors (ASNE) aims to be to journalism what the American Bar Association is to the legal fraternity." *Time* was overly optimistic. The legal fraternity, through its powerful bar associations, has the power to revoke a member's license to practice. Journalists have fiercely resisted any idea that resembles licensing as a restriction on their First Amendment rights. The ASNE has never proposed licensing or certifying journalists for this reason. In fact, the ASNE has never expelled a member in its history, even though it has had ample reason to do so.

The Society of Professional Journalists (SPJ; formerly Sigma Delta Chi) adopted its code at about the same time as the ASNE. The code was designed to guide journalists working in all media. The SPJ code was unchanged for more than 45 years, but as journalistic ethics became more problematic, the code was revised in 1973, 1984, 1987, and again in 1996. The newly adopted SPJ code is organized around four main principles:

1. *Seek the truth and report it.* Journalists should be honest, fair, and courageous in reporting the news.
2. *Minimize harm.* Journalists should treat sources, subjects, and colleagues as human beings deserving of respect.
3. *Act independently.* Journalists should be free of obligation to any interest other than the public's right to know.
4. *Be accountable.* Journalists should be accountable to their audience and to each other.

In 1975 the Associated Press Managing Editors (APME) association adopted a code that also discussed responsibility, accuracy, integrity, and independence. Revised in 1995, the APME code covers such issues as plagiarism and diversity. As with the ASNE's canons, adherence to the code is voluntary. Neither the SPJ nor the ASNE association has developed procedures to enforce its codes.

In late 1999 the Gannett Company became the first newspaper chain to spell out ethical principles for its papers. Other newspaper chains have companywide guidelines covering general issues, but individual papers can set policy in their own newsrooms. The Gannett guidelines are the first to be newsroom-specific. The decision to establish guidelines stemmed from a growing public distrust of the media and a desire to reassure readers about the fairness and accuracy of newspaper content. The new guidelines forbid, among other things, lying to get a story, fabricating news, and publishing misleading alterations of photographs.

▲ Broadcasting

For many years radio and television broadcasters followed the National Association of Broadcasters (NAB) Code of Good Practice. This code first appeared in 1929 and was revised periodically over the years. It was divided into two parts, one covering advertising and the other covering general program practices. In 1982, however, a court ruled that the code placed undue limitations on advertising, and the NAB suspended the advertising part of its code. The next year, to forestall more legal pressure, the NAB officially dissolved the code in its entirety.

Although the code is gone, its impact lingers. In 1990 the NAB issued voluntary programming principles that addressed four key areas: children's TV, indecency, violence, and drug and substance abuse. The new guidelines were stated in a broad and general way: "Glamorization of drug use and substance abuse should be avoided. . . . Violence . . . should only be portrayed in a responsible manner and should not be used exploitatively." To stay out of trouble with the Justice Department, the NAB declared that there would be no interpretation or enforcement of these provisions and that the standards were not designed to inhibit creativity.

Trying to resurrect a code for broadcasters is a favorite activity among politicians. In 1997 four U.S. senators introduced a bill that would exempt the broadcasting and cable industries from antitrust laws so that they could develop a new code. Other bills that urged broadcasters to develop a voluntary code of conduct were introduced in Congress in 1998 and 1999.

In the broadcast journalism area, the Radio and Television News Directors Association has an 11-part code that covers everything from cameras in the courtroom to invasion of privacy.

The V-Chip and its companion ratings system are an interesting interaction between formal and informal controls. For purposes of this discussion, it is important to point out that the V-Chip represents an example of the government's pressuring the video industry to adopt "voluntary" guidelines that categorize programming. If the industry failed to develop its own program ratings to work with the V-Chip, Congress left the door open for the FCC to do it for them. The threat of government action has been used before to prod broadcasters into reforms that they were reluctant to make on their own. In fact, scholars who have studied the FCC have even given this phenomenon a name: the "raised eyebrow" technique. The V-Chip legislation is a bit stronger than the raised eyebrow, but its end result is the same.

Producers rate program content according to an age-based scale ranging from "TV-G," suitable for a general audience, to "TV-M," for mature audience only. Further, special advisories for specific content are also displayed: "S" for sexual content and "V" for excessive violence. Parents can set the V-Chip to block whatever programming they feel is unacceptable for their children. For example, the V-Chip can be set to block all "TV-M"-rated shows. Interestingly, in its 2007 report on television violence, the FCC declared that the V-Chip, while helpful, was not an effective tool in protecting young people from violent TV content. Despite a public service campaign to educate viewers about the device, a recent survey noted that about 90 percent of respondents didn't use it.

▲ Motion Pictures

Codes of conduct in the motion picture industry emerged during the 1920s. Scandals were racking Hollywood at that time (see Chapter 9), and many states had passed or were considering censorship laws that would control the content of movies. In an attempt to save itself from being tarred and feathered as it were, the industry invited Will Hays, a former postmaster general and elder of the Presbyterian Church, to head a new organization that would clean up films. Hays became the president, chairman of the board, and chairman of the executive committee of a new organization, the Motion Picture Producers and Distributors of America (MPPDA). In 1930 the Motion Picture Production Code was adopted by the new group. The code was mainly proscriptive; it described what should be avoided in order for filmmakers to get their movies past existing censorship boards and listed what topics should be handled carefully so as not to rile existing pressure groups. The 1930 code is remarkable for its specificity; it rambles on for nearly 20 printed pages. The following are some excerpts:

The presentation of scenes, episodes, plots, etc. which are deliberately meant to excite [sex and passion] on the part of the audience is always wrong, is subversive to the interest of society, and is a peril to the human race.

The more intimate parts of the human body are the male and female organs and the breasts of a woman.

a. They should never be uncovered.

b. They should not be covered with transparent or translucent material.

c. They should not be clearly and unmistakably outlined by garments. . . .

There must be no display at any time of machine guns, sub-machine guns or other weapons generally classified as illegal weapons. . . .

Obscene dances are those: which represent sexual actions, whether performed solo or with two or more, which are designed to excite an audience, arouse passion, or cause physical excitement.

A few years after the Production Code was drafted, a Roman Catholic organization, the Legion of Decency (see the boxed insert "The Legion of Decency"), pressured the industry to put teeth into its code enforcement. The MPPDA ruled that no company belonging to its organization would distribute or release any film unless it bore the Production Code Administration's seal of approval. In addition, a $25,000 fine could be levied against a firm that violated this rule. Because of the hammerlock that the major studios had over the movie industry at this time, it was virtually impossible for an independent producer to make or exhibit a film without the aid of a member company. As a result, the Production Code turned out to be more restrictive than many of the local censorship laws it was designed to avoid.

The Production Code was a meaningful force in the film industry for about 20 years. During the late 1940s, however, changes that would ultimately alter the basic structure of the motion picture industry also led to the code being scuttled. In 1948 the Paramount case ended producer-distributor control of theaters, thus allowing independent producers to market a film without the Production Code seal. In addition, economic competition from television prompted films to tackle more mature subjects. The industry responded during the 1950s by liberalizing the code; despite this easing of restrictions, more and more producers began to ignore them. Nonetheless, the code, outdated and unenforceable, persisted into the 1960s. A 1966 revision that tried to keep pace with changing social attitudes proved to be too little too late.

In 1968 the motion picture industry entered into a new phase of self-regulation when the Production Code seal of approval was dropped and a new motion picture rating system was established. Operated under the auspices of the Motion Picture Association of America (successor to the MPPDA), the National Association of Theater Owners, and the Independent Film Importers and Distributors of America, this new system, commonly referred to as the **MPAA rating system,** places films into one of five categories:

G: Suitable for general audiences.

PG: Parental guidance suggested.

PG-13: Some content may be objectionable for children under 13 (a new category added in 1984).

R: Restricted to persons over age 17 unless accompanied by parent or adult guardian.

NC-17: No children under 17 admitted. (This category replaced the X rating in 1990. The MPAA made the change in response to several producers who argued that adult-themed, daring, but nonpornographic films should not be lumped into the same category as porno films.)

Unlike the old Production Code, which regulated film content, the new system leaves producers more or less free to include whatever scenes they like as long as they realize that, by so doing, they may restrict the size of their potential audience. One possible repercussion of this system may be the steady decline in the number of G-rated films released each year. Producers evidently feel that movies in this category will be perceived as children's films and will not be attractive to a more mature audience. During the first 11 years of the rating system's existence, the percentage of films in the G category

After World War I, during the roaringest part of the Roaring Twenties, the films that grossed the most money had titles like *Red Hot Romance, She Could Not Help It, Her Purchase Price,* and *Plaything of Broadway.* One movie ad of the period boasted breathlessly of "brilliant men, beautiful jazz babies, champagne baths, midnight revels, petting parties in the purple dawn." Before long, public opposition to such sensational movies began to form. The appointment of Will Hays, the creation of the Motion Picture Producers and Distributors of America, and the adoption of the Motion Picture Production Code were designed, in part, to forestall this public criticism.

Much of the code was suggested by a Roman Catholic layman, Martin Quigley, and a Roman Catholic priest, Father Daniel Lord. Despite the existence of the code, however, sensational films still appeared in significant numbers. This trend was disturbing to many segments in society, particularly the Catholic Church. Keep in mind that at this time the United States was in the midst of a severe economic depression. Many individuals, including prominent Catholics, connected the country's economic poverty with the nation's moral bankruptcy as evidenced by the films of the period. Additionally, an Apostolic Delegate from Rome took the film industry to task in a blistering speech before the Catholic Charities Convention in New York.

In April 1934 a committee composed of American bishops responded to the speech and to the general tenor of the period by announcing the organization of a nationwide Legion of Decency, whose members were to fight for better films. The legion threatened to boycott those theaters that exhibited objectionable films, and it sometimes made good on its threats. The Chicago chapter of the legion enrolled a half-million members in a matter of days and was matched by equal enrollment in Brooklyn. Detroit Catholics affixed "We Demand Clean Movies" bumper stickers to their cars. Other religious groups joined the legion—Jewish clergy in New York, Lutherans in Missouri. Pope Pius XI praised the legion as an "excellent experiment" and called upon bishops all over the world to imitate it.

There were 20 million Catholics in the United States in 1934, and naturally, the film industry took this group seriously. The Production Code Administration was set up with the power to slap a $25,000 fine on films released without the administration's seal of approval. The Legion of Decency's boycotts hurt enough at the box office to force many theaters to book only films that the legion approved. In Albuquerque, New Mexico, 17 of 21 theaters agreed not to book a film condemned by the legion. In Albany, New York, Catholics pledged to avoid for six months each theater that had screened the condemned film *Baby Doll.* Producers, frightened by this display of economic power, began meeting with legion members to make sure there were no potentially inflammatory elements in their films.

By the 1960s, however, the Legion of Decency was losing most of its clout. The restructuring of the film industry allowed independent producers to market their films without code approval. Many producers did just that and demonstrated that some films could make money even without legion and Production Code approval. The increasingly permissive mood of the country encouraged an avalanche of more mature and controversial films. Moreover, the legion, renamed the National Catholic Office for Motion Pictures, painted itself into a corner when it condemned such artistically worthwhile films as Bergman's *The Silence* and Antonioni's *Blowup,* and endorsed such films as *Godzilla vs. the Thing* and *Goliath and the Sins of Babylon.* By the 1970s this group had effectively lost all its power; it was essentially disbanded in 1980. Nonetheless, during its prime the Legion of Decency was the single most effective private influence on the film industry.

The Motion Picture Association of America's rating is a prominent part of most theater marquees.

dropped, while the percentage of films in the R category increased. X-rated or NC-17-rated films have never accounted for more than 10 percent of the total number of films submitted for review (of course, many low-budget, hard-core pornographic films are never submitted for classification).

In order for the MPAA rating system to work, producers, distributors, theater owners, and parents must all cooperate. There is no governmental involvement in the classification system; there are no fines involved. Moviemakers are not required to submit a film for rating. People evidently think that the system is a good idea. An industry survey done in 2002 disclosed that 74 percent of the adults surveyed considered the ratings "very useful" guides for children's attendance.

▲ The Advertising Industry

In the advertising industry several professional organizations have drafted codes of performance. The American Association of Advertising Agencies first adopted its Standards of Practice in 1924. This code, which covers contracts, credit extension, unfair tactics, and the creative side of advertising, contains provisions prohibiting misleading price claims, offensive statements, and the circulation of harmful rumors about a competitor. The Advertising Code of American Business, developed and distributed by the American Advertising Federation and the Association of Better Business Bureaus International, covers much the same ground. Memberships in these organizations and adherence to the codes are voluntary. In public relations the Public Relations Society of America adopted its first code in 1954 and revised it during the 1980s. As with the other codes, enforcement is essentially voluntary, and the society has no control over a practitioner who is not a member.

Internal Controls

Codes established by professional organizations and individual ethics are not the only informal controls on media behavior. Most media organizations have other internal controls that frequently come into play. Written statements of policy can be found in most newspaper, television, radio, and motion picture organizations. In advertising, a professional organization for self-regulation has existed since 1971.

▲ Organizational Policy: Television Networks' Standards and Practices

For many years each major network maintained a large department that was usually labeled "Standards and Practices" or something similar. Staff members in these departments would make literally thousands of decisions each season on the acceptability of dialogue, plotlines, and visual portrayals. During the late 1980s, however, network budget cuts took their toll, and most of these departments were scaled back dramatically. As criticism of television content increased during the 1990s, these departments were enlarged somewhat, but they still have far fewer people working in them than they did in the early 1980s. The departments at Fox, NBC, and ABC review everything their networks air, including commercials. At CBS the standards department reviews children's programs, docudramas, ads, new shows, and about a dozen existing series. The efforts devoted to monitoring standards vary greatly among cable networks. MTV, for example, closely monitors all its programs; the Discovery Channel rarely has problems regarding taste. Pay channels, such as HBO, have more liberal standards.

The broadcast and cable networks are also relying more and more on the judgment of series producers to determine standards of acceptability. Producers, for their part, have a general notion about how far they can go without raising network displeasure. The networks will generally closely monitor the first few episodes of a series that may cause problems. After that they will put more trust in the producers' standards.

It is probably obvious to any casual observer of broadcast television that network standards have become more liberal over the years. For instance, top-rated *CSI* has broadcast episodes dealing with sadomasochism and sexual fetishes. *Brothers and Sisters* and *Grey's Anatomy* have a gay character as a star.

There are several reasons behind these changes. First, society has become more open-minded. Subjects that were once taboo, such as male impotence, are now discussed routinely in commercials. Second, the broadcast networks have to compete with the more permissive cable networks on which shows such as *Sex and the City* have pushed the envelope of acceptability even further. Finally, the sex scandal involving President Bill Clinton and Monica Lewinsky put sexual topics on the evening newscasts and immediately eliminated many taboos.

Despite this liberalization the networks' standards and practices departments still exercise some caution. Offensive stereotypes are not allowed. Networks traditionally have not aired ads for abortion clinics, contraceptives (some local stations have aired contraceptive ads), or massage parlors.

The Internet can provide an outlet for material that the standards and practices department deems inappropriate for broadcast TV. The unedited versions of comedy skits from network shows such as *Saturday Night Live* sometimes make their way onto YouTube or other video-sharing sites.

In addition to the networks, local stations also exercise self-regulation. Occasionally, a local station will decide that a network show is inappropriate for its audience and decline

The reality series *The Cougar* raised questions about what was acceptable in prime time.

to show it or broadcast it at a later time. For example, more than 20 local stations refused to air *Maxim's Hot 100,* a one-hour special that featured scantily clad females.

Local stations also construct a **policy book.** This book typically spells out the station's philosophy and standards of operation and identifies which practices are encouraged or discouraged. For example, most television and radio stations have a policy against newsroom personnel

NBC's *To Catch a Predator* is part of the newsmagazine show *Dateline NBC*. Its objective is to expose men who use the Internet to meet people below the age of consent for sexual purposes. The program works with an online watchdog group called Perverted Justice. This group has people pretend to be underage children who try to lure pedophiles and sex offenders into online chat rooms in order to set up a face-to-face meeting. When the men show up for the supposed rendezvous, they are surprised by the show's host, who interviews them and quotes explicit sexual passages from their chat room sessions. The men's reactions are recorded by hidden cameras. Sometimes the men are arrested as they leave the house. NBC shares all of its video with law enforcement officers.

Many journalists have condemned the program for its ethical lapses. In the first place, as we have noted earlier in the chapter, journalists rarely work with law enforcement officers and if they do, it is generally for a compelling and narrow purpose as opposed to helping the ratings of a reality TV show.

Second, there is the issue of entrapment, legally defined as when a person is induced or persuaded by law enforcement officers or their agents to commit a crime that they had no previous intent to commit. In some instances, the decoys used by Perverted Justice were the ones who brought up sex, and in some cases they were the ones who suggested a face-to-face meeting. NBC argues that it does not set up the sting operation; that part of the process is handled by Perverted Justice. It turns out, however, that NBC paid Perverted Justice about $75,000 per sting. Further, NBC facilitates the meeting by finding a suitable house and establishing a date and time. Would these men have behaved the same way if Perverted Justice hadn't enticed them and NBC assisted in setting up a meeting? That's difficult to answer, and although at least one judge has ruled that the program's methods may

not necessarily meet the legal definition of entrapment, there are serious ethical questions about NBC's involvement.

Next, there is the issue of punishment. *Dateline*'s official position is that it leaves the punishment to police and prosecutors. Identifying a person as a would-be child molester on national television, however, seems a fairly severe punishment. The program functions as judge and jury, and the men exposed by the undercover operation have little legal recourse. Of course, a person could argue that would-be child molesters should be revealed to the public, but should the media be the one making that judgment? The lives of the men who are caught in the sting are probably ruined by the public exposure. Again, it may be argued that they deserve it, but should the media decide what they deserve? It might be better to conduct such operations without the glare of media exposure and let the courts determine guilt and punishment.

Finally, the program violates the principle of self-determination. The program seems to be exploiting these men for success in the ratings and financial gain. Self-determination maintains that people should not be used as a means to an end. It is certainly true that in the case of potential child molesters it may be argued that the end justifies the means, but that line of reasoning could be used to justify nearly any kind of ethical abuse.

The methods used by *To Catch a Predator* have embroiled it in legal controversy. A producer who claimed she was fired because she objected to the ethical lapses in the program sued for breach of contract. A judge later dismissed the suit. The program also faced a lawsuit over its role in the suicide of a Texas man who was the target of an undercover report. The man failed to show up for his meeting with the decoy, and NBC and the police went to his house, where he took his own life. Amid these developments, NBC canceled the series in December 2008. Reruns, however, still crop up on MSNBC.

---

functioning as commercial spokespersons. Radio stations typically have a policy against airing "homemade" tapes and records. Other stations may have rules against playing songs that are drug-oriented or sexually suggestive. Commercials that make extravagant claims or ads for questionable products and services might also be prohibited under local-station policy.

▲ Organizational Policy: Newspapers and Magazines

Newspapers and magazines create policy statements that take two distinct forms. **Operating policies** cover the everyday problems and situations that crop up during the normal functioning of the paper or magazine. **Editorial policies** are guidelines that the newspaper or magazine follows to persuade the public on certain issues or to achieve specific goals.

Operating policies vary from one paper or magazine to another. In general, however, these policies cover such matters as accepting freebies, using deception to gather information, paying newsmakers for a story or exclusive interview (checkbook journalism), taking junkets, conducting electronic surveillance, using stolen documents, accepting advertising for X-rated films, and publishing the names of rape victims. Also covered are outside employment of reporters and editors and conflicts of interest. Here, for example, are excerpts from *Rules and Guidelines* used by the *Milwaukee Journal:*

> *Free tickets or passes to sports events, movies, theatrical productions, circuses, ice shows, or other entertainment may not be accepted or solicited by staff members.*
>
> *A gift that exceeds token value should be returned promptly with an explanation that it is against our policy. If it is impractical to return it, the company will donate it to a charity.*
>
> *Participating in politics at any level is not allowed, either for pay or as a volunteer. Public relations and publicity work in fields outside the* Journal *should be avoided.*

Some newspapers and magazines are liberal; some are conservative. Some support Democratic candidates; others support Republicans. Some are in favor of nuclear energy; others against. These and other attitudes are generally expressed in the editorial pages of the newspaper. Editorial policy is generally clear at most publications. The *Chicago Tribune* has traditionally expressed a conservative point of view. The *New York Times* has a more liberal policy. The editorial policy of a paper will exert a certain amount of control over the material that is printed on its editorial pages. Of course, the paper has a perfect right to do this. There may be times, however, when the editorial policy of the paper spills over onto its news pages, and this might cause a problem for the paper's reputation for objectivity, responsibility, and integrity.

One problem that crops up periodically is called *boosterism,* a procommunity philosophy that sometimes causes not-so-good news to go unreported. In Flint, Michigan, when the local Fisher Body plant closed, TV networks and newspapers across the country announced the bad news that Flint was about to lose 3,600 jobs. The local Flint paper did not mention the job loss until the 11th paragraph on an inside page. "Good news," however, got prominent play: A story about new shrubs being planted at the local Buick facility earned front-page coverage.

Owners and publishers can exert editorial control over news policy in several ways. They can hire only those people who agree with their editorial views. For example, the *New Orleans Times-Picayune* ran an ad in a trade magazine for a business reporter. One of the qualifications was a "probusiness philosophy." They can also fire people who produce stories that the owner does not like, or they can issue orders to downplay some topics while paying large amounts of attention to others.

What is the significance of these examples for the news-consuming public? For one thing, the sample cases are probably exceptions to the norm rather than the norm itself. Nonetheless, they do illustrate the potential hazards of relying on only one source for news. The intelligent consumer of news and information should rely on several different media to get a more complete picture.

▲ Media Self-Criticism

Some informal control over media content and practices comes from within. Although the amount of internal media criticism has grown in the past few years, it is still small when compared with the amount of investigative reporting and critical analyses that newspapers, magazines, television, and radio conduct about other facets of society. Many newspapers and magazines have media critics and media reporters. The amount of meaningful critical writing done by these journalists, however, is highly variable. Some of the better-known critics in the print media are Ken Auletta of *The New Yorker*, Howard Kurtz of the *Washington Post*, and Tom Shales of *Television Week.*

A few journalism reviews regularly criticize media performance. The *Columbia Journalism Review* is the best known, but its circulation is only about 18,000. Others that are important are the *American Journalism Review* and the *St. Louis Journalism Review.*

The Internet has opened up a new channel for media self-criticism. The Media Channel (www.mediachannel.org), for example, contains news, analysis of issues, and criticism about media across the globe. Journalist Jim Romenesko maintains a similar site at www.poynter.org. The impact of these and similar sites is yet to be determined.

Public editors (the term newspapers use to refer to ombudsmen, or ombuds if you prefer gender-free distinctions) are an endangered species. As newspapers trim their staffs to reduce costs, one of the first positions to go is that of public editor. In 2008, about a dozen papers announced that they were laying off public editors or assigning them to different jobs. (A dozen may not sound like a lot, but remember that there were only about 40 papers that employed public editors.)

Will the disappearance of these positions make newspapers less responsive to their readers? Some editors defend the cuts by noting that newspapers must give priority to news gathering, selling advertising, and customer service in order to stay in business. If the newspaper folds, its responsiveness to readers is a moot point. Other editors contend that the public editor is not the only method that ensures that newspapers keep in touch with their readers. A recent article in the trade publication *Editor & Publisher* quotes the editor of the *Orlando Sentinel:* "Papers can distance themselves too much from readers if everything goes to one person." At the *Sentinel,* every editor is directly accountable to readers. Another argument suggests that technology has made public editors irrelevant. Modern newspapers allow comments on stories, editor blogs, and forums that allow discussion about stories.

There is, of course, another side to the argument. The public editor was the one person that people could contact if they had a problem. Public editors gave readers a voice that wasn't lost in the chatter of story comments or forums. Moreover, the public editor could be an advocate for readers inside the newspapers, and a full-time, in-house advocate is more likely to get a response from management than a comment posted at the end of a story. In addition, suggesting that all editors are responsible to readers spreads the responsibility so thin that it may result in nobody being responsible. Further, public editors developed ties within the community that are lost when the position is eliminated. Losing these ties eliminates another channel of reader-newspaper interaction. Finally, the public editor was a symbol who embodied the idea that newspapers were accountable for their mistakes and their operations were open for public inspection. Eliminating the public editor might hurt the credibility of a publication.

Perhaps the unkindest cut of all occurred when, after having a public editor for more than 40 years, the *Louisville Courier-Journal* decided to eliminate the position. The person who last held the job was also the president of the Organization of News Ombudsmen.

SOUNDBYTE

They Obviously Weren't Listening

Thirty-one engineering students enrolled in a course at a Canadian university were recently punished for cheating. The students had downloaded term papers from the Internet and submitted them as original work. What course were they taking? "Introduction to Ethics."

Cable and broadcast television networks usually offer few programs with serious criticism of the media. Newspapers do a bit more in this area; the *Wall Street Journal* has occasionally run an in-depth study of the problems facing the newspaper industry. In film the industry newspaper *Variety* has sometimes published an article critical of the film industry. *Billboard,* the trade publication of the sound-recording industry, has run analytical, if not critical, pieces on the recording industry.

Some newspapers and other media organizations have tried to incorporate an idea from Scandinavia into their operations to provide some internal criticism. An **ombudsperson** is employed by the company to handle complaints from audience members who feel they have gotten a raw deal. The ombudsperson also criticizes in general the performance of the organization's personnel. Although the number of ombudspersons (sometimes called public editors) in the United States remains small, interest in the position has grown in recent years, primarily because news organizations are worried that they are losing credibility with their audiences. There are about 40 ombudspersons in the United States, just about all at newspapers. The position is almost nonexistent in TV newsrooms. Budget cuts, however, have meant that many ombudspersons are no longer on the job (see the boxed insert "Disappearing Public Editors.")

▲ Professional Self-Regulation in Advertising

In 1971 the leading advertising professional organizations—the Council of Better Business Bureaus, the American Advertising Federation, the American Association of Advertising Industries, and the Association of National Advertisers—formed the National Advertising Review Council. Its objective is to sustain high standards of truth and accuracy in advertising. The council itself is composed of two divisions: the National Advertising Division (NAD) and the National Advertising Review Board (NARB). When a complaint about an ad is made by a consumer or competitor, the complaint goes first to the NAD, which evaluates it. The NAD can dismiss the complaint as unfounded or trivial, or it can contact the advertiser for an explanation or further substantiation. If the NAD is satisfied that the ad in question is accurate, it will dismiss the complaint. If the NAD is not satisfied with the explanation, it can ask the advertiser to change the ad or discontinue the message.

If the advertiser disagrees, the case goes to the NARB, which functions as a court of appeals. Ultimately, if the case does not result in an acceptable solution, the NARB may call it to the attention of the Federal Trade Commission or other appropriate agencies. Sending a case to the FTC happens rarely. In 1993 the board turned over to the FTC the first fraudulent advertising case in the NARB's 22-year history. Most advertisers generally comply with the NAD's wishes. In 2009, for example, the NAD recommended that the Kohler Company discontinue its claim that its toilets were the "global leader in performance toilets," pending evidence to support the claim.

Industry groups also exert control over advertising for their products. For example, the Miller Brewing Company and the Anheuser-Busch Company voluntarily agreed to remove their ads from MTV because they did not want to appear to be encouraging underage drinking.

Outside Influences

The larger context that surrounds a media organization often contains factors that have an influence on media performance. In this section we will discuss four: (1) economics, (2) pressure groups, (3) press councils, and (4) education.

▲ Economic Pressures

Money is a potent influence on media gatekeepers. In commercial media the loss of revenue can be an important consideration in controlling what gets filmed, published, or broadcast. Economic controls come in many shapes and forms. Pressure can be brought to bear by advertisers, by the medium's own business policy, by the general economic structure of the industry, and by consumer groups.

Pressure from Advertisers   The recording industry gets its revenue from the purchase of individual tracks and discs. Consequently, it earns virtually no money from advertisers and is generally immune to their pressures. The film industry makes most of its money from the sale of individual tickets. Advertisers have some limited influence through what is called *product placement*—an arrangement whereby an advertiser pays a movie studio to include its product in a film. *Terminator Salvation,* for example, had several scenes that featured 7-Eleven convenience stores. Nonetheless, in relative terms, advertisers have only modest influence over motion picture content. In the print media, on the other hand, newspapers depend on advertising for about 75 percent of their income, while magazines derive more than 50 percent of their revenues from ads. Radio and television, of course, depend on ads for almost all their income.

The actual amount of control that an advertiser has over media content and behavior is difficult to determine. It is probably fair to say, however, that most news stories and most television and radio programs are put together without much thought as to what advertisers will say about them.

Occasionally, however, you may find examples of pressure:

■   In 2008, a reporter for a Virginia paper wrote unfavorable stories about a local hospital. The hospital complained and pulled all of its advertising from the paper. The reporter was then assigned to another beat. (The paper claimed that the hospital's actions had nothing to do with the reassignment.)

It looked like a good story. The video, posted on YouTube, showed what looked like a stock car race victory celebration at Altamont Motorsports Park. Then, out of nowhere, a man crawled through the open window of the winning car and, while everybody else was celebrating, drove off. Security personnel quickly blocked the track with tow trucks, pulled the thief from the vehicle, and threw him to the ground. It was such a good story that more than a hundred TV stations used the YouTube video on their newscasts.

The problem: The event was staged by TaxBrain.com, an online income tax preparation service, to advertise its services. The car and the race car driver were both sponsored by TaxBrain. The apparent thief was an actor, and the event was filmed by three cameras and professionally edited before it was posted on YouTube. Putting the video clip on YouTube was an attempt by TaxBrain to take advantage of online "viral marketing," creating a buzz about a product on the Internet and then capitalizing on the free publicity. In this case, once the prank was revealed, TaxBrain got the publicity it wanted, but much of it was negative, accusing the company of crossing an ethical line by disguising advertising as news.

Then there's the case of lonelygirl15, an apparent teenager who posted videos on YouTube describing her conflict with her parents and her attempts at romance. Lonelygirl15's video log was hugely popular, generating more than 15 million page views. As it turned out, lonelygirl15 was an aspiring actress, and the videos were a marketing ploy for a planned movie.

Is deceit a legitimate advertising tactic? The Center for Digital Democracy thinks not. The center's position is that all videos that were produced and placed on YouTube and other video-sharing sites for marketing purposes should be labeled as advertising. Some creative executives disagree. They point out that consumers should always be skeptical about the motives and credibility of the people who post videos on the Web.

Finally, there may be a downside to this kind of stealthy promotion. Many of the people who saw the stolen-race-car video recalled absolutely nothing about TaxBrain, the company that put the hoax together in the first place.

- Executives at the *Boston Herald* suspended a reporter who wrote columns critical of a merger between two big Boston banks. One of the banks was a big advertiser in the newspaper and held the mortgage on the newspaper's building. (Management eventually relented and reinstated the journalist.)

Business Policies   Economic pressure on media content is sometimes encouraged by the business practices of the media themselves. When the Massachusetts Supreme Court ruled that a creditor could be sued for harassing those who owed money, the Boston newspapers declined to identify the retail store involved in the suit. The store in question was a big newspaper advertiser. In San Francisco a newspaper killed a column that criticized the Nike Company. It so happened that Nike was the sponsor of the paper's popular "Bay to Breakers" race.

Trading news coverage for advertising time or space is a common problem. A TV station in south Florida sent a flyer to its advertisers offering to do a news story on them in return for $5,000. While trying to negotiate a contract to carry live drawings for the New York State Lottery, a TV station promised lottery officials positive news coverage of lottery events. In both instances the stations withdrew the offers when their breach of ethics was revealed.

Then there is the problem of revenue-related reading matter. This issue crops up when a new shopping center or discount store opens in a community and gets heavy news coverage, maybe more than is justified by ordinary journalistic standards, in return for advertising revenue. Recently, in Waco, Texas, the local newspaper devoted half its front page and two inside pages (with seven color photographs) to the opening of a new supermarket. Not surprisingly, supermarkets spend a lot on newspaper ads.

These examples are not meant to criticize or impugn the reputation of any medium or profession. There are probably countless, less-publicized examples of newspapers, magazines, television, and radio stations resisting advertising and economic pressure. What you should learn from this section is the nature of the close relationship that can sometimes exist between advertisers and media and the pressures that can result. Most of the time, this relationship causes few problems. When professional judgment is compromised by dollar signs, however, then perhaps the economic pressures are performing a dysfunction for the media.

▲ Pressure Groups

Various segments of the audience can band together and try to exert control over the operation of mass media organizations. These groups sometimes use the threat of economic pressure (boycotts) or simply rely on the negative effects of bad publicity to achieve their goals. In radio and television, pressure groups (or *citizens' groups,* as they are often called) can resort to applying legal pressure during the license renewal process. Because of broadcasting's unique legal position, it has been the focus of a great deal of pressure group attention. In 1964, for example, a group of black citizens working with the Office of Communication of the United Church of Christ formed a pressure group and attempted to deny the license renewal of a TV station in Jackson, Mississippi, because of alleged discrimination on the part of station management. After a long and complicated legal battle, the citizens' group succeeded in its efforts. This success probably encouraged the formation of other groups. John Banzhaf III headed an organization called ASH (Action for Smoking and Health), for example, which was instrumental in convincing Congress to ban cigarette advertising from radio and television.

At about the same time, perhaps the most influential of all the pressure groups interested in broadcasting was formed: Action for Children's Television (ACT). From a modest start, this group was successful in achieving the following:

- Persuading the networks to appoint a supervisor for children's programming
- Eliminating drug and vitamin ads from kids' shows
- Instituting a ban on the host's selling in children's programs
- Reducing the amount of advertising during Saturday morning programs
- Helping a bill concerning children's TV pass Congress in 1990

ACT disbanded in 1992. In its final press release, the organization said that its major goal had been achieved with the passage of the 1990 Children's Television Act and that people who want better television for kids now "have Congress on their side."

In the mid-1970s other self-interest groups whose primary interest was not broadcasting began to get involved in television programming. The American Medical Association and the National Parent-Teacher Association both criticized TV violence. The National Organization for Women campaigned for more representative portrayals of women in the mass media. The American-Arab Anti-Discrimination Committee protested that Disney's *Aladdin* featured a song whose lyrics contained a slur against Arabs. Protests by gays and lesbians against the 2000 launch of Dr. Laura Schlessinger's TV show prompted many advertisers to back out from sponsoring the show and several stations to drop it altogether. Dr. Laura eventually apologized for some of her antigay remarks.

As the audiences of traditional media have gotten smaller, pressure group activity has declined. There are, however, some recent examples. The Parents Television Council has urged its members to file complaints with the FCC about certain episodes of *Family Guy,* and the Media Research Center has campaigned against what it perceives as liberal bias in TV news. In addition, issues surrounding the Internet have given rise to a new generation of pressure groups. The Center for Digital Democracy has campaigned on behalf of network neutrality, and the Media and Democracy Coalition has spoken out concerning the recent broadband stimulus program.

We can sum up by saying that there are both positive and negative aspects to the activities of these citizens' groups. On the one hand, they probably have made some media organizations more responsive to community needs and more sensitive to the problems of minorities and other disadvantaged groups. Citizen group involvement with media organizations probably has also increased the feedback between audience and the media industry. On the other hand, these groups are self-appointed guardians of special interests. They are not elected by anyone, and their wishes may not be at all representative of those of the larger population. In addition, many of these groups have exerted unreasonable power, and some extremist groups may actually abuse their influence and do more harm than good.

▲ Education

Education also exerts informal control over the media. Ethics and professionalism are topics that are gaining more and more attention at colleges and universities. In fact, there has been a recent upsurge of interest in teaching ethics at many schools of journalism and mass communication. About 40 percent of the schools in the United States offer a special ethics course to their students. More than half of the approximately 40 books specifically devoted to mass media ethics have been published since 1980. Most of the experts in this area agreed that instead of teaching specific codes of ethics to students, a systematic way of thinking about ethics should be stressed, so that individuals can consider issues and arrive at decisions rationally.

Even this book can be thought of as a means of informal control. The hope is that, after reading it, you will bring a more advanced level of critical thinking and a more sensitive and informed outlook to your media profession or to your role as media consumer.

MAIN POINTS

- There are several types of informal controls on the mass media, including ethics, performance codes, organizational policies, self-criticism, and outside pressures.

- The most important ethical principles that provide guidance in this area are the golden mean, the categorical imperative, the principle of utility, the veil of ignorance, and the principle of self-determination.

- All the media have performance codes that guide professional behavior.

- Many media organizations have standards departments that monitor the content that is published or broadcast.

- The National Advertising Review Council is the main organization that supervises self-regulation in advertising.

- Outside pressures from advertisers can sometimes influence media conduct.

- Special-interest groups, such as Action for Children's Television, have been successful in modifying the content and practices of the TV industry.

QUESTIONS FOR REVIEW

1. What are the main ethical principles discussed in the chapter?

2. Why was the NAB Code of Good Practice discontinued?

3. What is the difference between editorial policies and operating policies?

4. What is an ombudsperson? What does he or she do?

5. What are some ways advertisers can influence news content?

QUESTIONS FOR CRITICAL THINKING

1. How would you handle each of the examples mentioned in the introduction to the chapter?

2. What are some of the advantages and disadvantages of written codes of conduct?

3. Do special-interest groups exert too much power over the media?

4. Do advertisers have too much power over the media?

5. Consider the case of the *Chicago Tribune* discussed at the beginning of the chapter. Did the paper act ethically?

KEY TERMS

golden mean (p. 400)
categorical imperative (p. 400)
utility (p. 400)
veil of ignorance (p. 401)

self-determination (p. 401)
MPAA rating system (p. 406)
policy book (p. 409)
operating policies (p. 410)

editorial policies (p. 410)
ombudsperson (p. 412)

INTERNET RESOURCES

Online Learning Center

On the Online Learning Center home page, www.mhhe.com/dominick11e, *select* Student Center *and then* Chapter 17.

1. Use the Learning Objectives, Chapter Outline, and Main Points sections to review this chapter.

2. Test your knowledge of the chapter using the multiple choice and flashcard features of the site.

3. Expand your knowledge of concepts and topics discussed in the chapter with additional Questions for Critical Thinking and Internet Exercises.

Surfing the Internet

There are few Web sites that deal with the topics discussed in this chapter, but the ones listed here are relevant.

www.mediaethicsmagazine.com
Site that examines practical and theoretical ethical issues in mass media communication.

www.asne.org/ideas/codes/codes.htm
The American Society of Newspaper Editors has collected codes of ethics from about three dozen media organizations.

www.mpaa.org/caramap
Information about the MPAA movie rating system. The MPAA offers Red Carpet Ratings Service—an e-mail update of the ratings of movies about to be released.

www.poynter.org
The Poynter Institute's ethics page. Good for finding out the most current ethical issues.

www.spj.org/ethics.asp
The ethics page of the Society of Professional Journalists. Contains the latest ethics news and an "Ethics Hotline" that you can call for advice.

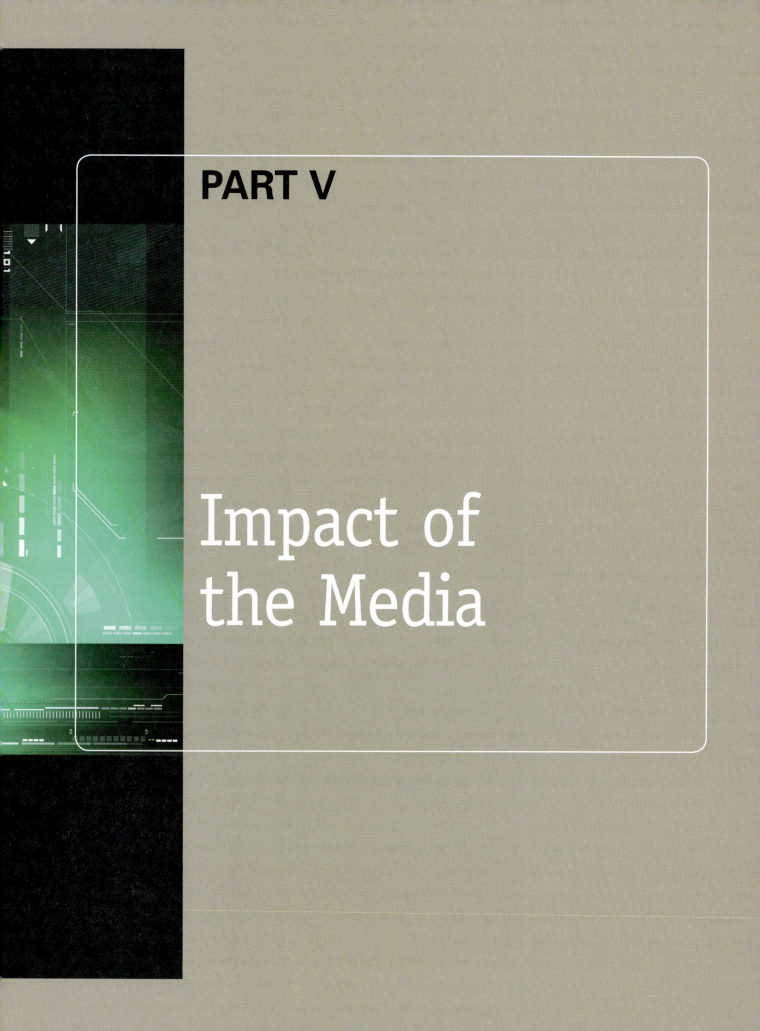

PART V

Impact of the Media

CHAPTER 18

International and Comparative Media Systems

This chapter will prepare you to:

- recognize the global leaders in newspapers, radio, and television

- distinguish among the four main theories of government-press relationships

- categorize media systems by ownership patterns and degree of government control

- understand how politics, culture, geography, history, and economics affect a country's media system

- explain the media systems in Japan, Mexico, and China

The inauguration of President Barack Obama illustrated the variations in media coverage in different nations.

Barack Obama was sworn in as the 44th president of the United States on January 20, 2009. The event was televised live around the world. Examining how different countries covered the occasion is a helpful way to introduce the topics covered in this chapter.

- In the United States the ceremony was televised live by 17 cable and broadcast networks. Nearly 38 million people watched the telecast on TV. Additional millions watched streaming video on more than a dozen different sites, including YouTube and Hulu. Owners of Apple's iPhone could watch the proceedings live on their phones. Internet traffic was so heavy that visitors to many sites had to wait to get connected. The Voice of America broadcast the new president's speech in 45 languages.

- In Japan, the inauguration took place at 2 A.M. local time on January 21. Nonetheless, it was carried live by NHK, the government-run TV network and several commercial networks. Despite the late hour, about 7 percent of households in Japan watched the ceremony. The next day, the three major Japanese newspapers ran extra editions filled with inauguration news.

- In Mexico City, thousands of workers gathered in the streets, offices, and restaurants to watch the event. The Obama inauguration was in stark contrast to the inauguration of Mexico's President Felipe Calderón in 2006. Amid political controversy, Calderón's swearing in took place in a secret nighttime ceremony witnessed only by cabinet members and military personnel. The event was taped and later broadcast over Mexican TV.

- In Russia, the big story of the day was the resolution of the gas war with Ukraine. Russian TV ran the inauguration story in the second half of its broadcast news program. The state-run Rossiya TV offered an analysis of the event, suggesting that people shouldn't hold high expectations.

- In China, the government channel, China Central TV, carried Obama's inauguration speech live with a simultaneous translation, but when Obama talked about earlier generations facing down communism, the coverage broke away from the speech and went back to the Chinese anchor. Broadcast officials claimed that the break from the speech was just part of the normal coverage procedure and that Chinese TV routinely takes breaks even when its own officials are making a speech. The Web site of the *China Daily* newspaper contained a Chinese translation of the speech, but the mention of facing down communism and another sentence about silencing dissent were omitted. An unedited version of the speech, however, appeared on the Web site of Phoenix TV, based in Hong Kong.

This chapter examines the ever-changing world of international media. We will first look at media that are designed to be distributed to other countries. Next, we will examine the media systems that exist in other countries.

International Media Systems

The study of international mass media systems focuses on those media that cross national boundaries. Some media may be deliberately designed for other countries (as is the case with the Voice of Russia, the Voice of America, and the international edition of *Time*); other media simply spill over from one country to its neighbors (as happens between the United States and Canada). Let us look first at those media designed for international consumption.

▲ Global Print Media

Many newspapers provide foreign-language or international editions. The popular ones fall into two categories: general newspapers and financial newspapers. As far as U.S.- and British-based publications are concerned, the following were the leaders at the close of 2009:

- The *International Herald Tribune*, published by the *New York Times* and headquartered in France, has a worldwide circulation of more than 240,000, most of it in Europe. The paper is printed in 36 sites around the world, including New York, Singapore, and Tokyo.

- *WorldPaper*, published by the World Times Company in Boston, is distributed as a newspaper supplement primarily in Latin America, Asia, and the Middle East. It is printed in 25 different countries and boasts a circulation of nearly 1 million.

- The *Financial Times of London*, as its name suggests, specializes in economic news and has a circulation of about 420,000.

- The *Economist*, also based in London, carries financial news and analysis. Readily available in the United States, the weekly is printed in Virginia, London, and Singapore. It reaches about a million readers.

- The *Wall Street Journal*'s international editions reach about 1 million people, mainly in Europe, Asia, and South America.

Other papers that enjoy international status are the *New York Times*, *Le Monde* (France), *El País* (Spain), the *Times* (Great Britain), the *Statesman* (India), and *Al Ahram* (Egypt).

The international flow of news is dominated by global news agencies. Reuters, Associated Press, Agence France-Presse, and ITAR-TASS are the biggest, but in recent years more specialized news organizations, such as the New York Times Syndicate and the Los Angeles Times Syndicate, have also become important.

As far as magazines are concerned, *Reader's Digest* publishes 49 international editions read by about 20 million people in nearly 200 countries. Time Warner, in addition to publishing the international edition of *Time*, which is distributed in about 190 countries, also publishes *Asiaweek* and a newsweekly in Chinese. Hearst Magazines International oversees the distribution of eight major titles—including *Cosmopolitan*, *Good Housekeeping*, and *Redbook*—in more than a hundred countries. *Cosmopolitan* alone is sold in about 50 countries, including Japan, Poland, and Russia.

On the set of CNN International. During its news broadcasts, CNN International links together anchorpersons from CNN bureaus all over the world.

Smaller special-interest magazines are also growing internationally. A Spanish-language version of *Popular Mechanics* is sold throughout Latin America. *Men's Health* publishes a British edition as well as one for Russia. Many business magazines, including *BusinessWeek* and *Fortune*, also have significant foreign readership.

▲ Global Broadcasting

About 150 countries engage in some form of international broadcasting. Many of these services are government run or at least government supervised. Others, like WRMI, Miami, are private operations supported by the sale of commercial time.

In the past, international radio broadcasting was done exclusively in the shortwave part of the radio spectrum (see Chapter 7). Although it goes a long distance, shortwave radio is hard to pick up and prone to interference problems. In an attempt to improve technical quality, major international broadcasters have been striking partnerships with locally operated FM stations. The Voice of America, for instance, has a network of 400 local stations in Latin America that rebroadcast its signal. Further, many international radio services are available in digital form on the Web or carried by satellite.

Listed here are the leading global broadcasters as of 2010:

- The World Service of the British Broadcasting Corporation (BBC) has a worldwide reputation for accurate and impartial newscasts because, in theory at least, it is independent of government ownership. Along with its news, the BBC carries an impressive lineup of music, drama, comedy, sports, and light features. The BBC pioneered the international radio call-in show in which prominent people answer calls from listeners around the globe. The BBC broadcasts 1,120 hours per week in 31 languages and has about 160 million worldwide listeners. The BBC Web site gets about 30 million visitors a month.

- Voice of America (VOA), now in its sixth decade of operation, broadcasts 1,500 weekly hours of news, editorials, and features in more than 40 languages to an audience of about 130 million people, about half of them in Russia and Eastern Europe. The VOA is part of the International Broadcasting Bureau, which also includes Radio Martí, a special AM service aimed at Cuba; its TV counterpart, TV Martí; Arabic-language radio and TV services; Radio Farda, a Persian service; and VOA-TV.

- China Radio International transmits about 1,500 hours of programming weekly in 43 foreign languages. China Radio International carried strident anti-American propaganda until the early 1970s, when improved relations led to a mellowing of its tone. Most of China Radio International's programming consists of news, analysis, commentary, and cultural information about China. China Radio International can also be heard on several AM stations in the United States.

- Deutsche Welle (DW), "German Wave," broadcasts about a thousand hours per week in 30 languages. DW's transmitters are located in Germany, Africa, and Asia. It has a large audience, particularly in Africa.

- Radio France International (RFI) broadcasts more than 300 hours a week to 45 million listeners, many on the African continent, in 20 languages. RFI programming consists of a blend of music, news, commentary, and locally produced features.

The biggest change in international broadcasting in recent years has been the proliferation of global news, sports, and music channels. The pioneer in this area was CNN, which now reaches millions of hotel rooms and numerous cable systems in Europe, Africa, and Asia. CNN International (CNNI), started in 1990, reaches more than 170 million homes in about 200 countries. CNN International is organized into five networks that serve (1) Europe, the Middle East, and Africa, (2) North Asia and the Pacific, (3) South Asia, (4) Latin America, and (5) North America. CNN International has also started broadcasting newscasts in several local languages as well as in English. CNBC offers 24-hour business news to 147 million households in 70 countries worldwide. In addition, BBC World, a full-time news channel, is available in Europe, Asia, Africa, and some U.S. locations. Russia is also joining the global news business. Russia Today, a 24-hour satellite news channel, began broadcasting in 2005. The news service has bureaus in Washington, London, Jerusalem, and Brussels. The TV services of Deutsche Welle and China Radio International also show up on many cable and satellite systems.

In the aftermath of the 9/11 attacks, many Americans asked why so many people in the world have anti-American attitudes. Several theories were proposed. Some accused the U.S. of cultural insensitivity; others cited U.S. foreign policy in the Middle East. Still others blamed international mass communication. They argued that most people in the world come into contact with U.S. culture through American TV shows and movies that are shown in their home countries. Anybody who watched a steady diet of shows such as *Friends, CSI,* and *Desperate Housewives* and movies such as *The Departed* and *Grindhouse* and listened to hip-hop music might come away with the notion that Americans are violent and sexually immoral people.

This theory was the subject of a study reported in the April-June 2007 issue of *Mass Communication and Society.*[1] The researchers conducted a survey among college students in Singapore. They measured students' attitudes toward Americans and also tabulated the students' exposure to American media content. They found that these young people were heavily exposed to U.S.-produced material, particularly music, films, and TV shows.

Was there a relationship between consuming U.S. content and attitudes toward Americans? There was, but it was not in the direction that the theory mentioned above would have predicted. Instead, there was a slight positive correlation between exposure to U.S. content and attitudes toward Americans. In short, those who consumed a lot of American media had slightly more positive attitudes toward Americans.

A correlation, of course, does not establish causation (see the next chapter). It may be that students who already have favorable attitudes toward Americans were the ones who saw and heard a lot of U.S. media content while those with negative attitudes avoided the same material. In addition, the sample came from only one country, and the correlation, although statistically significant, was small and did not explain much of the variability in student attitudes. Nonetheless, the study indicates that researchers need to dig more deeply into the effects of exposure to international media.

[1]See J. Fullerton, M. Hamilton, and A. Kendrick, "U.S.-Produced Entertainment Media and Attitude Toward Americans," *Mass Communication and Society* (2007), Vol. 10, No. 2, pp. 171–188.

Sports and music channels also have audiences all over the world. MTV is available almost everywhere, reaching more than 400 million households. ESPN International (ESPNi) is the biggest global provider of sports programming. Launched in 1988, the service is seen in more than 140 countries and territories and reaches about 90 million households. ESPNi serves Canada, Asia, Latin America, the Pacific Rim, Africa, and the Middle East. The News Corporation also operates satellite services that beam news and sports programming to more than 180 million viewers in Europe and Asia. The Cartoon Network, TNT, and Nickelodeon also have large global audiences.

▲ Film and TV

Although American films still do well overseas, they are becoming less dominant as locally produced films grow in popularity. Nevertheless, they still contribute mightily to Hollywood's bottom line. In 2008, foreign box office revenue was more than double the domestic total. Some films do even better overseas than in the United States. *Mamma Mia!,* for example, earned about $144 million in the United States and Canada and about $460 million overseas. There are signs, however, that things are changing. A decade ago, 9 out of the top 10 box office leaders in other countries were American-produced. In mid-2009, 6 of the top 10 in Japan were local productions. In France, 5 of the 10 were local; in Italy 4 out of 10.

The major Hollywood studios have recognized this trend and have started international branches that produce movies in other countries. In 2008, for example, Warner Brothers helped produce 44 films in 12 countries. Sony has projects under development in Russia, and Fox is involved with local companies in Japan and Brazil.

The same trend is evident in the television arena. The United States still leads the international television market but is no longer as influential as it once was. Local programs provide strong competition and rule prime time in many countries. Further, the economic downturn has prompted many countries to produce cheaper local programs rather than buy expensive imports. The U.S. situation has also been hampered by the lack of new hit TV series that would attract foreign networks. But as long as programs such as *House, CSI,* and *Grey's Anatomy* are around, the United States will continue to do well overseas.

As more countries produce their own TV content, many U.S. production companies, especially those that produce game and reality shows, have concentrated on licensing formats to overseas producers who turn them into local versions. There are dozens of foreign variations of *Wheel of Fortune, Jeopardy, Pimp My Ride,* and *World Poker Tour.* There are two Spanish and one Portuguese versions of *Desperate Housewives.* Viewers in Russia can watch local versions of *Home Improvement* and *The Golden Girls.*

Another aspect of international media is the problem of cross-border spillover. TV signals, of course, know no national boundaries, and the programs of one nation can be received easily in another country. The problem has caused some friction between the United States and Canada. Shows on ABC, NBC, and CBS are just as popular in Canada as they are in the United States, and they take away audiences from Canadian channels. Fearful of a cultural invasion of U.S. values and aware of the potential loss of advertising revenue to U.S. stations, the Canadian government has instituted content regulations that specify the minimum amount of Canadian content that must be carried by Canadian stations. Not surprisingly, spillover is also a problem on the crowded European continent. More than a third of TV viewing time in Finland, Ireland, and Belgium involves programs from another country's TV service. In Switzerland 60 percent of viewing is "out of country."

World Media Online

The World Wide Web provides access to worldwide media on a scale never before possible. Radio stations in other countries, for example, are available on the Net. A scan of Web sites in early 2009 found stations in Japan, the Philippines, Hong Kong, Russia, Brazil, Great Britain, and many other countries broadcasting on the Net. Streaming video from other countries is becoming more available on the Web. Jump TV has a selection of more than 250 channels from 70 countries. Many of the major international and domestic TV systems in many countries have Web sites with streaming video. And, of course, video-sharing sites such as YouTube contain video clips submitted from across the globe.

Individuals who want to read newspapers or magazines from other countries now have a wide selection at their disposal. In addition to the U.S. papers that have an international readership, such as the *New York Times* and *Wall Street Journal,* papers from France (*Le Monde*), Germany (*Die Welt*), Great Britain (*London Times*), Japan (*Asahi Shimbun*), Australia (*Sydney Morning Herald*), and many other countries make available online versions as well. International magazines that have established Web sites include *Asia Week, Asia Online, Beat* (Australia), *Der Spiegel* (Germany), *Tokyo Journal* (Japan), and *Hennes* (Sweden).

We need to keep in mind, however, that although it is called the *World Wide Web,* this new medium is far from globally accessible. In 2009 it was estimated that around 1.5 billion people were online. This sounds like a large number, but it represents only about 24 percent of the world's population. The Internet is most accessible to those in the developed countries. More than 250 million are online in North America compared to 54 million in Africa.

Probably the last place you might expect to find the ultrahip, mildly risqué network is in the conservative Middle East, but as of 2007 MTV Arabia has been bringing the network's edgy programming to the Arab world. Viewers in Egypt, Lebanon, the United Arab Emirates, and other Middle Eastern countries can now enjoy such shows as *Cribs, Pimp My Ride,* and *The Hills.*

MTV Arabia has a potential audience of nearly 200 million people. About 65 percent of its audience is under 25, a demographic coveted by advertisers such as auto dealers, food and beverage manufacturers, and electronics companies. Further, mobile phone penetration is high in the area (in the United Arab Emirates there are more mobile phone contracts than people), opening an additional channel for advertisers.

When it comes to content, MTV Arabia has to do a complicated balancing act. On the one hand, MTV has to satisfy the young audience that is looking for cutting-edge content and contemporary popular music. On the other, MTV has to be aware of the region's culture that has many viewers looking for more conservative and spiritual programming. The channel uses a panel of local viewers to help determine programming, and some of the international music videos are edited to show less skin. Nonmusic programming takes up more than half of the schedule and is a mix of MTV-produced series and local fare. On a recent Thursday night, MTV Arabia featured *50 Cent, Road Rules,* and *Waslati,* a local show featuring user-generated video clips. One of the more popular series was *Hip Hop Na,* a talent show hosted by Fredwreck Nassar that tried to find the Middle East's next hip-hop star.

MTV Arabia does not run religious programming, but the channel refrains from airing music videos during the holy month of Ramadan. In addition, on Friday, the Muslim holy day, MTV runs a small pop-up graphic to remind viewers that it is time for the traditional Muslim noon prayer.

News from Russia is easily available on the Web. Interfax Russia has subscribers in more than a hundred countries.

Comparative Media Systems

Let us now turn our attention to media systems as they exist in individual nations. Before we start, we should note that the media system that exists in a country is directly related to the political system in that country. The political system determines the exact relationship between the media and the government. Over the years several theories have developed concerning this relationship. In the sections that follow are examples of these theories in operation.

▲ Theories of the Press

Since the 16th century, scholars and philosophers have attempted to describe the relationship between the government and the media and its implications with regard to freedom and control. Over the years, as political, economic, and social conditions have changed, various theories of the press have developed to articulate and explain this relationship. All theories, however, fall somewhere between two "isms" that reflect polar opposites in the amount of control the government exerts over the media—authoritarianism and libertarianism (see Figure 18-1). Current theories of the press represent modifications of these two fundamental principles. Let us look at each of them.

The **authoritarian theory** arose in 16th-century England, at about the same time as the introduction of the printing press in that country. Under the authoritarian system the prevailing belief was that the ruling elite should guide the masses, whose intellectual ability was held in low esteem. Public dissent and criticism were considered harmful to both the government and the people and were not tolerated. Authoritarians used various devices to force compliance of the press, including licensing, censorship of material before publication, the granting of exclusive printing rights to favored elements of the press, and the swift, harsh punishment of government critics.

The **libertarian theory** is directly opposed to authoritarianism. Libertarians assume that human beings are rational and capable of making their own decisions and that governments exist to serve the individual. Libertarians believe that the common citizen has a right to hear all sides of an issue to distinguish truth from falsehood. Since any government restriction on the expression of ideas infringes on the rights of the citizen, the government can best serve the people by not interfering with the media. In short, the press must be free from control.

The libertarian theory fit well with the freewheeling political climate and rugged individualism of early America. By the mid-20th century, however, two world wars and a depression had changed world politics, media industries had become big business, and broadcasting had made it possible to reach millions of people instantaneously. As a result, new theories of the press emerged. In 1956 a book titled *Four Theories of the Press* reexamined the libertarian and authoritarian philosophies and described two more modern approaches. The **social responsibility theory** (also referred to as the *Western concept*) incorporates part of the original libertarian approach but introduces some new elements as well. This approach holds that the press has a right to criticize government and other institutions, but it also has a responsibility to preserve democracy by properly informing the public and by responding to society's needs and interests. The press does not have the freedom to do as it pleases; it is obligated to respond to society's requirements. The government may involve itself in media operations by issuing regulations if the public

FIGURE 18-1

Theories of Media-
Government
Relationships

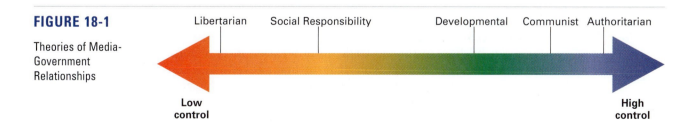

Libertarian   Social Responsibility   Developmental   Communist   Authoritarian

**Low
control**

**High
control**

"The Repeal, or the Funeral Procession of Miss Americ-Stamp." Colonial newspapers operated under an authoritarian philosophy as practiced by the British government. This English cartoon, published in 1766, satirized the repeal of the Stamp Act, an attempt to suppress hostile opinion by placing a tax on the pages of colonial newspapers.

interest is not being adequately served. The regulation of broadcasting by the Federal Communications Commission is a good example of this latter provision. The United States, Japan, Britain, and many other European countries are examples of countries that subscribe to this theory.

The other theory spelled out in *Four Theories of the Press* is the **communist theory.** This theory is a variant on the authoritarian scheme. The media are "owned" by the people as represented by the state. Their purpose is to support the Marxist system and to achieve the goals of the state as expressed through the Communist Party. Recent history has shown that the communist approach to the press works best in a closed society in which information is tightly controlled by the government. Once information is available from competing sources, people give little credibility to the official media.

This fact was illustrated by events in Russia and Eastern Europe at the end of the 1980s. The British Broadcasting Corporation (BBC), Voice of America, CNN, Radio Liberty, and Radio Free Europe unraveled the Communist Party's media monopoly. TV viewers in Eastern Europe saw Western TV shows beamed from West Germany or sent via satellite. Hollywood movies on videocassette were widely available. The people of Eastern Europe and Russia saw the shortcomings of their political and economic systems and clamored for change. As a result, the communist theory of the press has few proponents today. China, Cuba, and North Korea are about the only places where it can be found, and even in those countries the official version of the theory often bears little resemblance to the actual practices of the media. In short, the communist theory has been rendered obsolete by history.

A more recent formulation is the **developmental theory,** which would fall more toward the authoritarian side of the spectrum. In this ideology the government mobilizes the media to serve national goals in economic and social development. Information is considered a scarce natural resource that must be carefully managed by the government to achieve national goals. Some of the goals the media are expected to help achieve include political integration, literacy, economic self-sufficiency, and the eradication of disease. Until recently, many emerging countries espoused the developmental approach, but changing economic and political conditions have made it less prevalent. Many emerging countries, such as Brazil and Chile, have replaced dictatorships with democracies, and democracies typically look with disfavor upon government control over the media. In addition, even in those countries where democracy has yet to appear, the government has either privatized the formerly state-run media or allowed competition from independent channels. Consequently, the government has less control over the flow of information

Although the Russian government is less repressive than it was in the days of the old U.S.S.R., it is still highly sensitive toward criticism, particularly when that criticism is carried on television. All of the major Russian TV networks are owned by the government or people friendly to the government, making them easy to control.

A puppet show that poked fun at Russian leader Vladimir Putin was canceled during Putin's first term as president and never reappeared. During Russia's equivalent of the Oscars, a couple of actors made jokes about the government. Their remarks were cut from the broadcast. The Russian rock group Televizor (Russian for TV set) had a booking on a TV show canceled after they appeared at a demonstration for an opposing political party.

During a TV talk show that was taped in advance of broadcast, one of the panel members, Mikhail Delyagin, made critical remarks about the government's economic policy. When the show aired, Delyagin's remarks were cut and he

was digitally erased from the program. The Russian technicians, however, did a sloppy job. In one scene you can see Delyagin's disembodied legs and one hand in a chair next to the moderator.

Delyagin was one of several government critics whose names were on a "stop list," a roster of people who are not permitted on Russian newscasts and talk shows. Government officials denied the existence of such a list and explained that people who disagreed with the administration were simply not newsworthy or had nothing new to say.

Although television is the major focus of the government's attention, many radio stations and newspapers also apparently abide by the stop list and rarely give attention to dissenters. Interestingly, Russia does not censor the Internet, perhaps because relatively few in the population have access to it (about 25 percent in 2008). In contrast, television newscasts reach large audiences and are usually among the top 10 highest-rated programs.

and is less able to promote the developmental approach. All in all, the growth of democracy and the growing popularity of free-marketplace economics have resulted in more countries endorsing the social responsibility approach.

▲ Control and Ownership of the Media

One helpful way of distinguishing among the various media systems throughout the world is to classify them along the dimensions of (1) ownership and (2) control. Finnish Professor Osmo Wiio has developed a useful analysis scheme, presented in Figure 18-2. As can be seen, ownership can range from private to public (*public ownership* usually means some form of government ownership), and control can range from centralized to decentralized. Note that this typology is an oversimplification. Many countries have mixed media systems in which part of the broadcasting system is owned by the government and part by private interests. In some countries the print media could be placed in one cell of the matrix and the broadcasting system in another. Nonetheless, this model is helpful for displaying some of the major differences among systems.

FIGURE 18-2

Typology of Media Ownership and Control

Source: From "The Mass Media Role in the Western World" by Osmo A. Wiio, in *Comparative Mass Media Systems* by L. John Martin and Anju Grover Chaudhary. Copyright © 1983 by Longman Inc. Reprinted by permission of Allyn and Bacon.

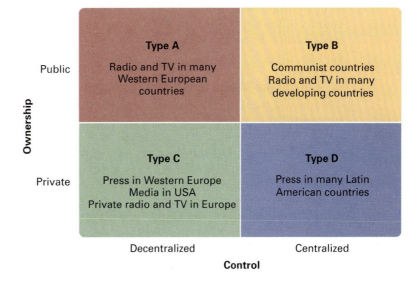

	Decentralized	Centralized
Public	**Type A** Radio and TV in many Western European countries	**Type B** Communist countries Radio and TV in many developing countries
Private	**Type C** Press in Western Europe Media in USA Private radio and TV in Europe	**Type D** Press in many Latin American countries

Ownership / Control

In the upper-left cell are type A systems. These represent decentralized control and public ownership, a type best illustrated by the broadcasting systems in European countries such as France, Denmark, and Italy. Some of the broadcasting media are publicly owned, but no single political or special-interest group can control their messages. In Great Britain, for example, the BBC is a government-chartered, publicly owned corporation that is relatively immune to government censorship and interference. Private broadcasting systems also operate in these countries.

In the upper-right cell are type B systems. This arrangement is typical of communist or socialist countries in which the media are publicly owned and controlled by the dominant political party. China is an example.

In the lower-left cell is the decentralized-control, private-ownership model. This is the system that currently operates in the United States and in many European countries. The media are owned by private companies, and there is little, if any, centralized control.

The lower-right cell is the centralized-control, privately owned system. In many countries, particularly the developing countries of Africa and Latin America, the media are owned by private organizations but are firmly controlled by the government. Venezuela would seem to fit in this category.

Far fewer countries today would fall into cell B of the matrix than would have a few years ago. Only a handful of nations still exemplify the communist or socialist media model. (Cuba, China, and North Korea are examples.) In these countries the ruling party exercises control, and freedom of the press belongs to the state, not to the media. Communist countries feel that it is necessary to speak with one voice, and antigovernment or antiparty criticism is forbidden.

Press control is exercised in several ways. First, the government controls the source. Printing and broadcasting equipment are given only to approved organizations. In Cuba, for example, there is a newsprint shortage, and only the government newspaper is supplied with it. Next, journalists are state-trained and state-approved. Finally, news agencies are state-owned, and news sources state-controlled. In China the regime keeps a close eye on the Internet. The government blocks certain Web sites and filters the output from search engines, such as Google, so that a search for certain forbidden terms will yield no results. Blogs, postings on bulletin boards, and Internet chat rooms are also closely monitored.

Those countries that have abandoned the communist philosophy have generally moved into cells A and C of the matrix. The state-run media organizations have seen much of their control taken away, and private media outlets are permitted. Individual media outlets are given much more freedom to criticize the government.

The most significant trend in those countries that fall into cell A of the matrix has been a move toward pluralism in their broadcasting systems. State-owned monopolies in many countries, including France, Italy, Greece, Spain, and some of the Scandinavian countries, have given way to privately owned and commercially sponsored broadcasting systems. In addition, cable promises to bring even more video diversity to these countries.

▲ Role of the Media in Various Countries

The role of a mass media system in a given country will differ according to its place in the typology. For example, as mentioned, in many developing countries where there is strong centralized control over the media, the principal role of mass communication is to help develop and build the nation. Not surprisingly, many less-developed countries are concerned primarily with economic and political development. This concern is translated into a rather focused definition of the role of mass media. In general, the media are expected to help achieve modernization or other national goals. In fact, a new term, *developmental journalism*, has been coined to describe this philosophy. In short, **developmental journalism** means that the role of the media is to support national interests with regard to economic and social development and to support objectives such as national unity, stability, and cultural integrity.

On the one hand, developmental journalism entails finding ways to make abstract stories about commodity pricing, agricultural policies, and educational goals understandable to readers and to highlight the developmental goals achieved by the nation. On the other hand, developmental journalism can also mean that the press refrains from any criticism of the government and prints only what the government deems helpful to its cause. The philosophy of many Asian, Latin American, and African developing nations falls somewhere between these two conceptions of developmental journalism.

The role of the media under the communist theory is straightforward: They are tools of propaganda, persuasion, and education. They function only secondarily as sources of information and entertainment. This philosophy dates back to Lenin, who decreed that the communist press was to help further the revolution.

As we saw in Chapter 2, Western media inform and entertain, but their content is somewhat different from that of communist and less-developed nations' media. Most of the information carried by the media in the Western democracies is geared to the specific political and economic needs of the audience. An examination of the press in the United States and Canada, for example, would reveal a large amount of news about the local and national government, some of it unfavorable and critical. The role of government watchdog, based on the ideas presented in the social responsibility theory, is a function that would be unsettling to many of the countries in cells B and D of the matrix in Figure 18-2. Moreover, a great deal of content in the Western media is consumer oriented, consisting of advertising, news, and entertainment. Further, there is, relatively speaking, little regulation of the content of the entertainment media. Aside from some regulations governing pornography and prohibitions against certain content on the broadcast media, the government takes little interest in entertainment content.

It is the interpretation or editorial function in which the biggest differences are found. The United States and other Western countries have a tradition of press freedom that recognizes the right of the media to present ideas to try to persuade the audience to some point of view. The philosophy of the **free marketplace of ideas** is endorsed by most countries in cells A and C of Figure 18-2. All relevant ideas concerning an issue are examined in the media, and a "self-righting" process occurs. Given the autonomous nature of the Western media, it would be difficult for the government to mobilize the media to support some national goal, as is typically done in developing and communist countries. There is a built-in tension and adversarial relationship between press and government that makes such efforts rare.

▲ Economic Differences in Media Systems

In the United States advertising plays a key role in media support (see Chapter 15). Newspapers, magazines, radio, and television all derive a significant amount of their total income from the sale of advertising time or space. Direct government subsidy or support of the media is minimal, limited to the funds given to public broadcasting. (Of course, the government also indirectly helps support the media by buying a lot of advertising.) In Western Europe several countries provide indirect subsidies to the media, such as cheaper mailing privileges and tax concessions. Some Scandinavian countries have a system whereby newspapers controlled by various political parties are given direct financial assistance. Several different systems are used to support broadcasting. In the United Kingdom, for example, the BBC is state-chartered and gets its operating funds from an annual license fee paid by the owners of TV sets. At the same time, the independent TV networks make their money from the sale of advertising time, in much the same way their U.S. counterparts do. Many other Western countries follow this same model.

It is difficult to generalize about the means of economic support for media in less-developed countries. Where the print media are privately owned, money comes from circulation fees and advertising. Publishers are generally free to keep all profits, but in many countries space must be provided free of charge for government announcements. Advertising and license fees are the two major sources of income for broadcasting.

In those few communist countries that still exist, most economic support for the media comes directly from the government. Since the media are state-owned, money for their operation is simply set aside from the government's budget. Because of this subsidy, the single-copy costs of newspapers and magazines tend to be cheap. Advertising used to be a minuscule source of income in communist countries, but recently, these governments have welcomed it as an important revenue stream.

Examples of Other Media Systems

Let us now take a more detailed look at the mass media in three different countries: (1) Japan, an industrialized nation, (2) Mexico, a developing nation, and (3) China, a communist country.

▲ Japan

More than 127 million people live on this nation of islands. Japan's geography, culture, history, and economy have shaped its current media system. Education is highly valued in Japan, where the literacy rate is nearly 100 percent. This has helped the country develop a strong print media industry.

There are more than 120 newspapers in Japan with a combined circulation of about 67 million, a total that exceeds that of U.S. papers. Japan has more than 10 newspapers with circulation above the million mark; the United States has only 3. Some of the major

Critical / Cultural Issues

Cultural Imperialism?

Cultural domination refers to the process in which national cultures are overwhelmed by the importing of news and entertainment from other countries—mainly from the United States. Residents of many countries are concerned that their national and local heritage will be replaced by one global culture dominated by U.S. values. They point out that American music, books, TV shows, and films are popular around the world. Many are fearful that audiences will become persuaded to adopt the values portrayed in this content—capitalism, materialism, consumption, and so forth. As a result, many countries, including Canada, Spain, and France, have placed quotas on the amount of foreign material that can be carried on their broadcasting systems.

The notion of cultural domination also spills over into the news area. For many years the representatives of many developing nations have been arguing for a New World Information Order. They point out that the existing flow of news is one way: from the industrialized West to the developing nations, sometimes referred to as the *third world*. Under such a system, say the developing countries, news from the third world is scant, and what news there is reflects unfavorably upon the developing nations. For example, what do you know about South America? Most people will mention two things—revolutions and drugs—the two topics that dominate the news coverage. Most know little else about the whole continent. To remedy this imbalance, developing countries have advocated controls over the news and other media content that come across their borders. A resolution reflecting this philosophy was passed by the United Nations Educational, Scientific, and Cultural Organization (UNESCO) in the 1980s. The United States looked with disfavor on this proposal, and it was one of the factors that prompted the United States to withdraw from UNESCO back in the mid-1980s.

Is this charge of cultural imperialism a valid one? One claim of those who urge a New World Information Order has substance. News coverage of third world nations is unbalanced. In response, the Western media have attempted to report more non-Western news and have started programs to train journalists of former third world countries. In addition, several other alternative news agencies have developed—including the Inter Press Third World News Agency, the South North News Service, and the Pan African News Agency—that supplement and enlarge the coverage of the major Western news organizations.

Any consideration of this debate must also acknowledge that the whole controversy has economic implications. Those who champion the free flow of information across borders also champion their right to profit from the sale of their products across borders. Those who advocate controls in the name of avoiding cultural domination are also assuring themselves of less competition in the marketplace. If a country limits foreign television programs to 30 percent of its schedule, the other 70 percent must be produced locally. How much of the cultural imperialism debate is based on principle and how much on cash is hard to determine.

The cultural imperialism argument seems to assume that people in other countries are weak and simply absorb and accept cultural messages. One of the key things that the critical/cultural analysts point out is that the audience is anything but passive. It is likely that audiences in other cultures pin their own meanings and interpretations on media content. Those in other countries will reinterpret what they receive in light of their own culture and personal experiences.

The changing world political scene and the increasing trend toward market-driven economies and less oppressive governments have increased support for the Western model. The proponents of the New World Information Order received considerable backing from the former communist countries of the Soviet Union and Eastern Europe. Now that these countries have changed governments, there is less support for the notion of increased media control. Consumers the world over seem to welcome the changes.

Those who campaign against cultural imperialism contend that American values are becoming dominant. This raises the question of exactly what American values are. The United States is currently experiencing a wave of multiculturalism, and the heritages of many ethnic and racial groups have influenced the cultural tastes and values of the entire country. In the music area, for example, reggae—which came from Jamaica—found a following among white Americans and went on to influence the development of African American rap music. Is the global popularity of rap a manifestation of Jamaican, African American, or white American values?

national newspapers are *Yomiuri Shimbun, Asahi Shimbun,* and *Mainichi Shimbum.* (As you may have deduced by now, *shimbun* is the Japanese word for "newspaper.") The *Yomiuri Shimbun* has a daily circulation of about 14 million, making it the world leader. By comparison, *USA Today* has a circulation of about 2 million. Along with the national papers, Japan supports many other regional and local dailies. Tokyo alone has a dozen newspapers, several of them in English.

As in other countries, however, newspaper readership is declining, especially among younger readers. Competition from the Internet, video games, cell phones, and television has made it difficult for newspapers to attract a younger audience. Again, much like their counterparts in the United States, the major Japanese newspapers have Web sites that add another revenue stream.

Japan also has several newsmagazines and an influential business magazine. Leisure and lifestyle publications are popular. Asian editions of familiar publications such as *Time, Forbes,* and *Reader's Digest* are widely available. Comic books in Japan sell millions of copies every year. These publications, although they bear a surface resemblance to American comics, are deeply rooted in Japanese culture and are read by young and old. Many Japanese comic books are available in America.

Broadcasting in Japan started in the 1920s when the Japanese government adopted the British model of a noncommercial system headed by a public corporation. Commercial broadcasting started after World War II, a result in part of the influence of the American forces that occupied the country. Japan's economy has helped it become one of the world's leaders in the development of electronic media, and Japan has one of the most technologically advanced broadcasting systems in the world.

The state-run, noncommercial Japan Broadcasting Corporation (*Nippon Hoso Kyokai,* or NHK) is patterned after the BBC. It has an annual budget of more than $5 billion, all of which comes from a license fee imposed on all TV sets in Japan—about $150 a year. Competing with the five NHK channels are five commercial TV networks and two satellite channels. (The most-viewed networks are commercial ones: Fuji Television, Nippon TV, and the Tokyo Broadcasting System, but NHK is not far behind.) TV and radio reach virtually 100 percent of the population as 11,000 transmitters blanket the country. Almost all the programs on Japanese TV are locally produced; American series do not do well in Japan. About 40 percent of all Japanese homes are equipped for cable. At present, however, cable is used to retransmit regular TV into areas that suffer poor TV reception. About 90 percent of all homes have VCRs or DVD players, and the video software business is booming.

Because of its mountainous terrain, Japan pioneered the development of a direct broadcast satellite (DBS) system. NHK has spent about $2 billion in DBS research and now operates three satellite channels that beam entertainment, sports, movies, music, and specials directly from satellite to living room. NHK's system has about 4 million subscribers, but other privately operated satellite systems are struggling to stay in the black. Japan was one of the pioneers of HDTV. However, NHK backed an analog system of HDTV, which has since been surpassed by the digital version (see Chapter 10). In early 1997, NHK finally announced that it too was backing a new digital system. With an eye toward the future, NHK is conducting research on a system of ultrahigh-definition TV, whose picture resolution is 16 times better than the current HDTV system, and is also investigating superthin, flexible display panels.

American films tend to dominate the Japanese box office, but recently, some locally produced movies have provided some unexpected competition. Sony, the huge Japan-based conglomerate, is heavily involved in making Hollywood movies through its Sony Pictures Entertainment unit. *Quantum of Solace* and *Spider-Man 3* are two of the studio's recent releases.

Japan has been a leader in developing new technologies. As we have already discussed, cell phone use, especially text messaging, is extremely popular in Japan, and many people rely on their cell phones to connect to the Internet. Speaking of the Internet, 73 companies provide Internet service to about 94 million Japanese, about 74 percent of the population.

Clearly, the digital revolution has come to Japan. Newspapers and magazines are searching for new ways to make money from their online versions; TV networks are struggling with the transition from analog to digital; and the influence of the Internet and mobile media is growing. Japan recently launched a service that provides streaming video to cell phones using the electromagnetic spectrum rather than the Internet. In sum, Japan is a media-rich country whose media industries face many of the same problems and challenges found in Great Britain and the United States.

▲ Mexico

The media situation in Mexico is typical of that of many developing countries. It demonstrates some of the myriad challenges faced by nations as they strive to form indigenous systems. The media system in Mexico has been influenced by economics, politics, and geography. A country with 111 million inhabitants and a literacy rate of 92 percent, Mexico has been saddled with massive foreign debt and high inflation. Sharp divisions exist between the rich and the poor. Many urban areas are characterized by relative prosperity, and some rural areas are mired in poverty. Literacy is higher in the cities than in the countryside. Moreover, various governments have taken different attitudes toward the media, vacillating between strict control and relative leniency. Finally, Mexico's media system always operates in the shadow of its neighbor to the north, the United States.

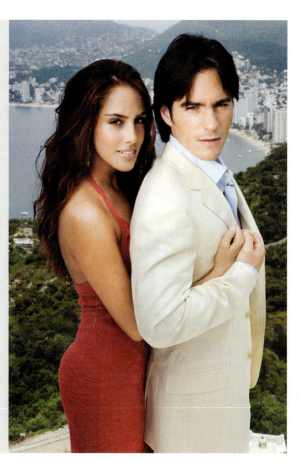

An ad for one of the steamy tele-novelas popular in Mexico and among Spanish-speaking residents of the United States.

Mexico has approximately 300 daily newspapers. Total daily circulation is about 9 million. For many years the *Excelsior*, published in Mexico City, was the country's leading newspaper. Ownership and labor problems, however, have plagued the newspaper in recent years. Some provincial newspapers, such as *El Norte* in Monterrey, are also influential. Most large newspapers have their own Web sites.

Mexico publishes more than 200 periodicals. Media conglomerate Televisa is the world's largest publisher of Spanish-language magazines, including many that are aimed at Hispanics living in the United States. Televisa's best-known publication is the women's magazine *Vanidades*.

Freedom of the press has a checkered history in Mexico. For many years the government kept the press in check by controlling the national supply of news-print. Publications that were critical of the government often found their supply of paper cut off. The government also controlled broadcasting permits and could force radio and TV stations off the air if their reports offended the regime. Finally, the government and ruling political party exerted power by bribing journalists.

At the turn of the century, a new political party came into power and promised press freedoms. A survey by WorldAudit.org, a group that monitors press freedom, gave Mexico a rating of "partly free." Mexico scored 48 out of 100 on WorldAudit's scale of freedom (the lower the score, the more press freedom). Since that time, however, press freedoms have deteriorated. In its most recent evaluation, WorldAudit gave Mexico a rating of 71, down significantly from its earlier score. Part of the reason for the decline was the continuing bloodshed associated with drug trafficking. Drug gangs have used threats and violence to discourage journalists from investigating their activities, and the government has been unable or unwilling to protect them. As a result, Mexico is the most dangerous country in Latin America for journalists. Since 2000, more than 25 reporters have been killed or reported missing.

Radio broadcasting developed in Mexico about the same time as it did in the United States. An official broadcast service signed on in 1923, and the model followed was heavily influenced by the U.S. system. In addition to state-run educational and cultural services, a system of private ownership of stations and commercial support was instituted. During the 1950s the state sold most of its stations to private interests. Today, there are more than 800 commercial radio stations and only 50 noncommercial stations, along with more than a dozen commercial networks. Most stations also stream their programs on the Web.

Television broadcasting was modeled directly on the U.S. system. It began as a commercially supported private enterprise, but a 1960 law dictated that TV had to perform certain social functions, such as promoting moral principles and preserving human dignity. Government became more involved in TV during the 1970s when an agreement with station owners set aside 12.5 percent of the broadcast day for government-produced programs. The government also acquired a Mexico City station as an outlet for its programs.

The private television and radio sector is dominated by Televisa, which controls about 70 of the 120 TV stations in the country. Televisa is the parent company of Univision, a U.S. Spanish TV network, and Televisa produces and exports telenovelas, the Spanish versions of U.S. soap operas, which are tremendously popular throughout Latin America. For most of its existence, Televisa held a virtual monopoly on TV broadcasting, sometimes reaching 95 percent of all Mexican TV homes. In the past few years, however, it has faced competition from TV Azteca, which was government-owned until it was sold to a private firm in the mid-1990s. Broadcasting a program lineup that featured racy telenovelas, TV Azteca attracted about 40 percent of the audience in 2008, and some big advertisers were abandoning Televisa in favor of the younger network.

Some U.S. TV programming is popular in Mexico, but, as in many other countries, the top-rated shows are generally Mexican productions of situation comedies or telenovelas. Some American shows that were carried by Mexican TV in 2009 were *Criminal Minds*, *Monk*, and *House*.

DVD penetration tops 65 percent, one of the highest figures in Latin America. About 20,000 different video releases are available in video rental stores. Like many developing countries, Mexico has a problem with pirated videotapes and DVDs. One authority calculated that about 25 percent of all videos for rent in Mexico City are pirated copies.

U.S. films do well in Mexico. *The Dark Knight*, *Kung-Fu Panda*, and *Iron Man* were box office leaders in 2009. Some recent films made in Mexico, such as *El Crimen del Padre Amaro*

Newspapers in China are sometimes posted in public places for passersby to read.

and *Y Tu Mamá Tambien,* got favorable critical reviews and were also box office successes in the United States. In addition to competing in the television arena, Televisa and TV Azteca are competing on the big screen. Both companies now distribute films in Mexico. Televisa also produces films, finances films, and owns a chain of movie theaters.

The growth of new media has been slow in Mexico. About 25 percent of the population has access to the Internet. Cell phones have been adopted more rapidly, but as of 2009, they were in the hands of only 55 percent of the population. Nonetheless, cell phone use is expected to grow rapidly.

In sum, the media scene in Mexico is changing. More competition is present, and longtime giant Televisa is losing a little of its dominance. In addition, Mexico's proximity to the United States has had many effects. Although a good deal of news and entertainment content flows from the United States to Mexico, there is now a significant flow in the other direction as well. The large Mexican American population in the United States constitutes an enthusiastic audience for Mexico's media. In fact, although hard figures are difficult to find, it is likely that Mexico exports more media content to the United States than does any other nation. This trend is likely to continue.

▲ China

The 2008 Beijing Olympic Games focused world attention on China and its mass media. The media in China have been expanding rapidly, particularly in the past 20–25 years. The past decade or so, with some exceptions, has seen a trend toward less government control and a more diverse media landscape. This trend is due in part to China's move toward a free-market economy and a greater dependence on advertising to support the media. Owners of many print and broadcast outlets are responsive to profit-and-loss considerations and act accordingly. As a result, the marketplace rather than the Communist Party is now the major influence on the content of Chinese media.

The country has about 2,200 newspapers, many started since 1980, with a combined circulation of nearly 120 million. China recently replaced Japan as the country with the largest newspaper circulation and now has 24 newspapers that rank among the top 100 in circulation. China is one of the few countries where newspaper circulation and advertising revenue are both increasing. Newspaper advertising revenue was $4.9 billion in 2008, up significantly from 2005.

China has several national newspapers. The party-controlled *People's Daily* once dominated newspaper circulation, but since 1980 its circulation has dropped from 7 million to 2.8 million. Three other papers—*Yangtse Evening Post, Yangcheng Evening News,* and the *Sichuan Ribao*—boast circulations of more than a million. One English-language paper, *China Daily,* is aimed at foreigners living in China and interested foreigners living in America and Europe. Business and sports publications have proliferated, and China now publishes more than a hundred financial newspapers. Xinhua, the Chinese state-run news service, has a hundred overseas bureaus and transmits more than 50,000 words every day to Chinese media.

For decades state-owned newspapers enjoyed a captive audience. People who worked for the Chinese government, a large number of the workforce, were forced to subscribe to government publications. Recent reforms have done away with this practice, and it is expected that the *People's Daily,* the official newspaper of the Communist Party, will see its circulation tumble even more.

The relaxation of government media control has prompted many independent newspapers to start operation. The government's more liberal attitude toward the press was demonstrated during the SARS virus outbreak in 2003. After some initial hesitation, Beijing encouraged newspapers to pursue the story aggressively, and many did just that. This renewed spirit has helped these publications succeed in attracting both readers and advertising revenue. During the 2008 Olympics, the Chinese government relaxed its restrictions on foreign media. Authorities promised that the foreign press would have the same freedom in Beijing as it had during previous Olympics in other countries. Despite this promise, many reporters complained that the government blocked their access to some Internet sites and limited their ability to report on news occurring in other parts of China.

The total number of magazines published in China is probably somewhere near 10,000. *Reader* and *Trends,* the two most popular magazines, attract significant advertising revenue. In addition, Chinese editions of popular titles, such as *Elle China* and *Business Week China,* are best-sellers.

Most Chinese live in rural areas where literacy rates are lower than in cities. Consequently, many people rely on radio for news and entertainment. The country's 700 radio stations reach more than 95 percent of the population. China National Radio administers 10 national radio networks that broadcast on the AM, FM, and shortwave bands. Many local communities also have their own FM stations. Many Chinese stations stream their programming on the Internet.

Television in China showed remarkable growth during the 1980s and the 1990s. As of 2009, TV penetration was about 98 percent, or about 380 million households, making China the largest television market in the world. China Central Television provides 18 channels with 200 hours of programming every day. CCTV-1, the primary service, broadcasts news, entertainment, and special events. The other channels are more specialized, featuring science, children's programming, and music. In addition to CCTV, there are several thousand local and regional TV stations. As of 2007, the hottest show in China was *Super Girl,* sort of a Chinese version of *American Idol.*

The trend toward a free-market economy has encouraged the growth of TV advertising. Commercials are now a common sight on Chinese TV. China's entry into the World Trade Organization and the Beijing Olympics brought additional advertising revenue to the country. In 2008, about $35 billion was spent on advertising in China, making it the world's second-biggest advertising market, behind only the United States. China Central Television's advertising revenue grew by 15 percent from 2007 to 2008.

Despite its more liberal attitudes, the Chinese government occasionally takes steps to limit what can be shown in the country. Regulations limit local stations to no more than 25 percent imported programming. The government limits the amount of commercials in prime time to no more than 9 minutes per hour. Many foreign news programs are not allowed to be shown in China.

China has a fairly active motion picture industry, much of it centered in Hong Kong. In 2007 about 400 movies made in China were released. Competition from foreign films is limited by a quota that allows no more than 20 films to be imported per year. Imported films are also subject to government censorship. *Brokeback Mountain* was not screened in China, and *Pirates of the Caribbean: At World's End* had several scenes deleted before it premiered in Chinese theaters. Despite these restrictions, most of the top Hollywood films are shown in China. An occasional Chinese film, such as *Crouching Tiger, Hidden Dragon,* coproduced with Sony, is successful in the United States.

Internet penetration was about 22 percent in 2008, but this number is deceiving since many Chinese access the Internet not at home but at Internet cafes. Blogging has

Freedom House is an organization that supports press freedom across the globe. It issues an annual report summarizing the state of press freedom in 195 countries and territories. For the last seven years, the report has indicated that press freedom has declined.

To construct its report, Freedom House looks at indicators of journalistic independence in three broad categories: legal environment, political environment, and economic environment. Each country is rated across these categories (with higher numbers meaning less freedom) and the ratings are summed. A score of 0–30 puts a country in the "free press" category, a score of 31–60 in the "partly free" group, while a score of 61 or above puts the country in the "not free" group.

The 2009 report found that the lowest level of press freedom was in the Middle East and North Africa. Restrictions on reporters covering the Gaza violence in 2008 resulted in Israel dropping from the free to the partly free category. Press freedom also declined in the Palestinian Authority territory. Western Europe had the highest level of freedom, although Italy's rating declined because of media concentration and intimidation of journalists by organized crime.

The biggest year-to-year decline came in central and eastern Europe due to attacks on journalists in Bulgaria, Bosnia, and Croatia. Russia's score declined because of government intimidation of the press.

The report also noted some of the reasons for this declining movement in press freedom. Emerging democracies such as Mexico, Argentina, and the Philippines have yet to fully realize the meaning of a free press. Some states, such as Russia, Ethiopia, and Gambia, have seen the emergence of more authoritarian governments that have cracked down on reporters. In many countries, violence toward reporters has increased, and many governments have been unable to stop the bloodshed. As the world economy struggles, it is expected that even more curbs to press freedom might result.

As a matter of interest, the country that was rated the most free was Iceland. Scandinavian countries made up the rest of the top five. The United States tied for 24th along with the Czech Republic and Lithuania. The three countries at the bottom of the list were Togo, Djibouti, and Burundi.

---

become popular, with about 40 million Chinese posting blogs with a total readership of more than 100 million. Internet advertising revenue is growing, as well. The Chinese government is increasingly concerned about the potential power of the Internet. Most Internet users are blocked from accessing Web sites that the government deems inappropriate or harmful. Internet service providers are required to record information that can help track users' Web trails and immediately halt the transmission of subversive material.

The government has instituted tight rules on video-sharing Web sites. Access to YouTube has been limited, and in 2008 China issued new rules that would restrict the broadcasting of Internet video to Web sites run by the state. It is unclear how this new rule would affect privately owned Chinese video-sharing sites, since they already monitor their videos for pornographic or politically sensitive content. It is also uncertain how the rules would affect foreign video sites. No matter what happens, the stricter rules indicate that the government realizes that the Internet poses a threat to the Communist Party's control of information.

Mobile media are also becoming popular. About 45 percent of the population has a cell phone. Cell phones have played an important role in communication. The earliest news of the SARS outbreak in China was not carried by the mainstream media but was spread by individuals sending text messages on their cell phones.

In the years to come, it is likely that the trend toward a free-marketplace economy will continue to have an impact on China's mass media. In turn, the mass media may also influence the country's political climate.

In sum, the media systems in these three countries illustrate the varying influences that economics, culture, geography, and politics have on the development of mass communication systems. Because of these and other factors, each nation will create a media system that is best suited to its own needs.

MAIN POINTS

- Communications across international boundaries have increased in the past two decades.

- Newspapers designed for international consumption include the *International Herald Tribune, USA Today International,* and financial papers. Many magazines also have international editions.

- Global radio broadcasters include the Voice of America, the BBC, China Radio International, Deutsche Welle, and RFI.

- The leaders in global television are CNN, MTV, ESPN, BBC World, and CNBC.

- Comparative analysis of media systems allows us to view alternative ways of structuring the mass media.

- The four main theories of government-media relationships are authoritarian, libertarian, social responsibility, and developmental.

- Media systems can be categorized by examining ownership patterns and degree of government control.

- The development of media systems in various countries is influenced by politics, culture, geography, history, and economics.

- The media systems in Japan, Mexico, and China illustrate how the theories of government-media relationships have operated in other countries and how numerous factors have affected those systems.

QUESTIONS FOR REVIEW

1. Name the major international newspapers and broadcasting services.

2. Compare and contrast the four major theories of the press.

3. Distinguish between public and private ownership of mass media.

4. What is developmental journalism?

5. How has geography shaped the mass communication systems in Japan, Mexico, and China?

QUESTIONS FOR CRITICAL THINKING

1. Given the ubiquity of the Internet, is it possible for any nation today to use the authoritarian approach?

2. American media products are easily available in other countries. What media products from other countries are easily available here? Why is there such a difference?

3. As China moves more and more toward a free-market economy, what will happen to the country's media system?

4. Review the "Cultural Imperialism" box on page 433, and consider the following: To what extent do you agree that American media products can influence the traditional values held in other societies? If you were a political leader in another country, would you favor quotas on the amount of foreign material that could be broadcast? Why or why not?

KEY TERMS

authoritarian theory (p. 427)
libertarian theory (p. 427)
social responsibility theory (p. 427)

communist theory (p. 428)
developmental theory (p. 428)

developmental journalism (p. 430)
free marketplace of ideas (p. 431)

INTERNET RESOURCES

Online Learning Center

On the Online Learning Center home page, www.mhhe.com/dominick11e, *select* Student Center *and then* Chapter 18.

1. Use the Learning Objectives, Chapter Outline, and Main Points sections to review this chapter.

2. Test your knowledge of the chapter using the multiple choice and flashcard features of the site.

3. Expand your knowledge of concepts and topics discussed in the chapter with additional Questions for Critical Thinking and Internet Exercises.

Surfing the Internet

Many sites deal with international mass communication in general, and many others are the home pages of international media. Those listed here are a sampling of both.

www.aib.org.uk
Home page of the Association for International Broadcasting. Contains links to many international broadcasting stations.

www.cctv.com/english
Home page of China Central Television. Includes a program schedule.

http://global.nytimes.com
Home of the *International Herald Tribune,* also known as the global edition of the *New York Times.*

www.ipl.org/div/news
The Internet Public Library has links to online papers in every region of the globe.

www.mtv.com/mtvinternational
Check out the various configurations of all the foreign MTV networks. Find out what is the number-one music video in India, and generally keep up-to-date with this Web site.

www.tvradioworld.com
A directory of Internet radio and TV stations that includes the major international outlets.

CHAPTER 19

Social Effects of Mass Communication

This chapter will prepare you to:

- explain how scientists use surveys and experiments to study the effects of mass communication

- describe how the media can serve as agents of socialization

- discuss the impact of televised violence

- define the *agenda-setting effect* and *agenda building*

- explain how the media can help crystallize a viewer's political choices

- describe how the Internet may affect social involvement

The video game *Grand Theft Auto IV* has been linked to several violent incidents.

Released in North America in April 2008, *Grand Theft Auto IV* features the adventures of Nico Bellic, an Eastern European veteran who comes to Liberty City (a fictionalized version of New York City) to pursue his dreams but is pulled into a life of crime. The game includes instances of muggings, robberies, and carjacking. *Grand Theft Auto IV* has been hugely popular, selling more than 13 million copies. It has also been the cause of much controversy.

In June 2008, a gang of teens who were fans of *Grand Theft Auto IV* went on a 2-hour crime spree in Garden City, Long Island. The teens were sitting in a local park looking for something to do when one of them came up with the idea to live out the game. According to police reports, the gang first mugged a man at a bus stop near the park and beat him up. They next broke into garages and stole bats and crowbars, which they used as weapons in a robbery of a motorist. The gang had surrounded another car in an attempted carjacking when police arrived and put an end to their escapade.

This was not the only incident involving *Grand Theft Auto*. To cite just two, in August 2008 a teenager in Thailand who spent much of his spare time playing the game killed a cab driver during a robbery attempt. The teenager told police that he wanted to find out if it was as easy to rob a cab driver in real life as it was in the game. A few years earlier, a teen in Alabama killed three people in an apparent attempt to act out a scene from an earlier version of the game.

Obviously, not everybody who plays *Grand Theft Auto* is inspired to commit murder and mayhem. These few examples do, however, highlight the possible connection between media exposure and behavior. Accordingly, this final chapter examines the social effects of mass communication. The first part looks at the impact of media on people's attitudes, perceptions, and knowledge. The second part looks at how the media affect the way people behave. Before we discuss these effects, however, we need to examine how they have been investigated.

Investigating Mass Communication Effects

There are many ways to investigate what is or is not an effect of mass communication. Some people claim that personal observation is the best way to establish proof. As we noted in Chapter 2, the critical/cultural analysts focus on the various meanings that audience members construct from specific texts. Others rely on expert opinions and evaluations; still others point to common sense when they wish to support their views. All these methods are valuable, but this chapter will focus on the results of scientific studies of the media's impact on individuals. Keep in mind, however, that the scientific approach is only one of many ways to examine this topic.

When it comes to gathering information about media effects, scientists have typically used two main methods:

- A **survey** is carried out in the real world. It usually consists of a large group of individuals answering questions put to them via a questionnaire. Although the survey is usually not sufficient proof of cause and effect, it does help establish associations. A special kind of survey, a **panel study,** enables researchers to be more confident about attributing patterns of cause and effect in survey data. The panel study collects data from the same people at two or more points in time. As a result, it is possible, for example, using sophisticated techniques that control the effects of other variables, to determine if viewing televised violence at an early age is related to aggressive behavior at a later date. Panel studies are expensive and take a long time to complete.

- An **experiment** is performed in a laboratory and usually consists of the controlled manipulation of a single factor to determine its impact on another factor. A special kind of experiment, a **field experiment,** is conducted in a real-life setting. Experiments are useful because they help establish causality.

In the remainder of this chapter, we will focus on scientific findings about the effects of media on knowledge, attitudes, perceptions, and behavior.

Effects of Mass Communication on Knowledge and Attitudes

The dividing line between attitudes and behaviors is fuzzy. In many instances we can only infer that an attitude or perception exists by observing relevant behavior. Thus, many of the studies mentioned in this section involve the measurement of *both* behavior and attitudes.

We will examine three topics that have generated the most research interest: (1) the role of the media in socialization, (2) cultivation analysis, and (3) agenda setting.

▲ Media and Socialization

In Chapter 2 we defined *socialization* as the ways in which individuals come to adopt the behavior and values of a group. In this section we will concentrate on the socialization of children. Socialization is a complex process extending over a number of years and involving various people and organizations, called **agencies of socialization,** who contribute in some degree to the socialization process. Figure 19-1 presents a simplified diagram of some of the more common agencies.

In many situations the media's contribution to socialization will be slight. Parents might have greater influence ("Eat your spinach; it's good for you"). So might friends ("Don't be a tattletale"). So might direct experience ("I'd better not take my sister's stuff because the last time I did, she popped me one").

On the other hand, the media, especially television, may play an important role in socialization when it comes to certain topics. Let us now look at evidence pinpointing some of these areas.

FIGURE 19-1

Agencies of
Socialization

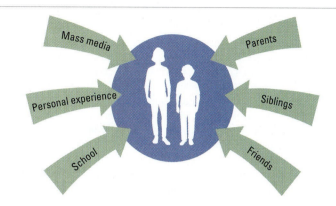

Could a media celebrity, such as Miley Cyrus, serve as an agency of socialization for young women? Could she influence their attitudes about what behaviors are appropriate for teens?

▲ The Media as a Primary Source of Information

Learning is an important part of the socialization process, and the media serve as important sources of information for a wide range of topics, especially politics and public affairs. For example, a survey of sixth and seventh graders found that 80 percent named a mass medium as the source of most information about the president and vice president, 60 percent named a mass medium as the primary source of information about Congress, and half named a mass medium as the chief information source about the Supreme Court.

Other research has shown that the media, primarily TV, serve as primary information sources for many age groups about a wide range of topics. More than 90 percent of Americans cited television as their primary source of information about the September 11 terrorist attacks. Television is the source of most information for local and congressional elections. This phenomenon is not limited to political and public affairs information. There is reason to believe that media presentations, including those in entertainment programs, are important sources of information on topics such as occupations, crime, law enforcement, alcohol and drug usage, the environment, and minorities. One recent study of high school students, for example, found that about 1 in 4 listed rock music as an important source of information about moral values and that 1 in 4 specified it as an important source of information about interpersonal relationships. Another survey found that many young people listed Comedy Central's *The Daily Show* as their main source of news.

▲ Shaping Attitudes, Perceptions, and Beliefs

The mass media also play an important role in the transmission of attitudes, perceptions, and beliefs. Several writers have suggested that under certain conditions the media (especially TV) may become important socialization agencies in determining the attitudes of young people. Specifically, TV will be an influential force when the following factors are operative:

- The same ideas, people, or behaviors recur consistently from program to program; that is, they are presented in a stereotyped manner.

New perspectives on the effects of television are coming from a surprising source: economists. The biggest problem in determining the social effects of television is isolating the TV effect from that of parents, peers, social class, ethnicity, and a host of other variables. In the past 30 or 40 years, however, economic researchers have developed new, high-power statistical methods that have made it a little easier to determine what causes what in complex relationships. These new techniques have sparked research into issues not commonly investigated by traditional economists, such as why most drug dealers live with their mothers and how a person's income is influenced by the condition of his or her teeth.

Some economists have used these new statistical methods to take advantage of "natural experiments" to investigate the effects of television viewing. One such test was made possible when the FCC froze the construction of new TV stations from 1948 to 1952, resulting in some cities having TV while others did not. The researchers looked at 1965 test scores from elementary and high school students, and after controlling for numerous sociological variables, they discovered that children who had more exposure to television had better scores than those with less exposure. This effect was even more pronounced in households where English was not the primary language.

Another economist looked at the impact of Brazilian telenovelas (soap operas) on the fertility rate. There are few children in these programs because it would be difficult for viewers to keep track of shows with large numbers of characters. Because one company has a virtual monopoly on the airing of Brazilian telenovelas, the researchers were able to look at when the broadcasts were shown in various parts of the country. They then looked at changes in the fertility rate, again controlling for numerous other influences. After the broadcasts appeared, the number of average births per woman consistently declined. Interestingly, exposure to a competing TV network that aired Mexican and American shows did not have the same effect.

Scholars interested in the effects of TV can no longer confine their research to the traditional mass communication journals; these days they must scan the economics journals as well.

- A child is heavily exposed to TV content.
- A child has limited interaction with parents and other socializing agents and lacks an alternative set of beliefs to serve as a standard against which to assess media portrayals.

All this means that under certain conditions TV will be an influential force in shaping what children think about certain topics. Complicated though the task is, some researchers have identified some of the conditions, the topics, and the children to which this theory applies. Moreover, they have specified some of the effects that may result when television does the socializing.

Stereotypes   In the study of media socialization, it is helpful to identify consistent themes or stereotypes present in media content. For instance, consider how television programs typically portray law enforcement and crime. Programs about crime and law enforcement are a staple of prime-time television; 20–35 percent of all program time consists of shows dealing with cops and criminals. However, the large percentage of law enforcement characters portrayed on TV does not accurately reflect the actual percentage employed in this capacity in real life. Further—on television, at least—crime doesn't pay. One study found that some 90 percent of TV crimes were solved; real-life law enforcement agencies are not nearly as effective.

Further, consider how social roles as seen on television are influenced by gender. In one study published in 2008, researchers examined all comedy, drama, and reality programs that aired during prime time on the six broadcast networks. They found that female characters were significantly more likely than male characters to appear in interpersonal roles that centered on romance, family, and friends. In contrast, male characters were significantly more likely to appear in work-related roles. This gender distinction in social roles has been found by similar research done in the 1970s, 1980s, and 1990s.

In sum, evidence suggests that the TV world often presents images that are at odds with reality. Stereotyping has also characterized, in addition to police dramas and gender-role portrayals, the depiction of occupations, methods of problem solving, portrayals of scientists, the depiction of mental illness, and many other topics.

The Effects of Heavy Viewing   It seems probable that youngsters who are heavy TV viewers would display a pattern of beliefs and perceptions consistent with media portrayals. The earliest research in this area, completed in the 1930s, found that frequent viewing of crime and gangster movies could change attitudes on topics such as capital punishment and prison reform. More recently, other researchers have noted a connection between heavy viewing of violent TV programs and favorable attitudes toward the use of violence in real life. Further, children who are heavy viewers of cops-and-robbers TV programs are likely to believe that police are more successful in apprehending criminals than are children who are not fans of these shows.

In other areas several studies have linked high levels of television viewing with attitudes favoring traditional gender roles. In other words, children who are heavily exposed to television are more likely to feel, among other things, that men make better doctors and that women make better nurses or that raising children is a job for women rather than men.

To be fair, we must again stress that this type of research *assumes* but does not necessarily *prove* that the mass media play a significant part in creating the attitudes held by these youngsters. Surveys can only highlight associations, not prove causality. Although some experimental evidence points to the media as the cause of certain attitudes, we cannot entirely rule out other interpretations. Nevertheless, it is likely that the link between media exposure and certain attitudes demonstrates reciprocal causation. What this means is best shown by an example. Watching violent TV

Do TV programs such as *Ugly Betty* represent the most important source of information about Hispanic families for white viewers? Mass media researchers are interested in how television influences attitudes toward minorities.

shows might cause a youngster to hold favorable attitudes toward aggression. These favorable attitudes might then prompt him or her to watch more violent TV, which, in turn, might encourage more aggressive attitudes, and so on. The two factors might be said to be mutually causing each other.

The Absence of Alternative Information   Although research evidence is less consistent in this area than in others, it appears that under some circumstances television can affect young people's attitudes about matters for which the environment fails to provide firsthand experience or alternative sources of information. One survey that examined the potential impact of TV on dating behavior found that teenagers are more likely to turn to TV for guidance when they have limited real-life experience with dating.

Where media influence is indirect, it is difficult to pinpoint. This is particularly true when the media operate simultaneously with other agencies of socialization and when interpersonal channels outweigh media channels in forming attitudes and opinions. In the area of politics, for instance, the media probably supply youngsters with information and viewpoints that are subsequently commented on by parents and friends. Political beliefs and attitudes evolve out of this double context. In such cases the socializing impact of parents and other interpersonal sources is more important than that of the media. One study dealing with attitudes toward police found that, although children spend a great deal of time watching TV cop shows, friends and family are the important socializing agents. The point is this: The media play a significant role in socialization. Sometimes this role is easy to detect; sometimes it is indirect and harder to see; at still other times it is apparently slight. Clearly, numerous factors are influential in determining how a child comes to perceive the world. The media (and television, in particular), however, have become important factors in the socialization process.

▲ Cultivation Analysis

Directly related to socialization is an area of research called **cultivation analysis.** Developed by George Gerbner and his colleagues at the University of Pennsylvania, cultivation analysis suggests that heavy TV viewing "cultivates" perceptions of reality consistent with the view of the world presented in television programs. Cultivation analysis concentrates on the long-term effects of exposure—on both adults and children—rather than on the short-term impact on attitudes and opinions.

Methodology   The first stage in cultivation analysis is a careful study of television content to identify predominant themes and messages. Not surprisingly, television portrays a rather idiosyncratic world that is unlike reality along many dimensions. For example, television's world is usually populated by a preponderance of males: Two-thirds to three-quarters of all leading characters are men. Moreover, television overemphasizes the professions of—and, as previously mentioned, overrepresents the proportion of workers engaged in—law enforcement and the detection of crime. Last, the TV world is a violent one—around 50 percent of all programs contain at least one instance of violence.

The second stage involves examining what, if anything, viewers absorb from heavy exposure to the world of television. Respondents are presented with questions concerning social reality and are asked to check one of two possible answers. One of these answers (the "TV answer") is in line with the way things are portrayed on television; the other (the "real-world answer") resembles actual life. Here is an example:

What percentage of all males who have jobs work in law enforcement and crime detection? Is it _____ 1 percent or _____ 10 percent?

On television about 12 percent of all male characters hold such jobs; thus, 10 percent would be the TV answer. In reality about 1 percent are employed in law enforcement; thus, 1 percent is the real-world answer. The responses of a large sample of heavy TV viewers are then compared with those of light TV viewers. If heavy viewers show a definite tendency to choose TV answers, we would have evidence that a cultivation effect is occurring.

People with DVRs who fast-forward through ads can't escape at least some of the commercial message. A 2007 study done by NBC had one group of people watch TV ads live at normal speed while other groups fast-forwarded through them at up to six times normal speed. The next day 69 percent of the live viewers remembered what ads they saw, but so did 25 percent of the viewers who watched at the fastest possible speed.

The research also disclosed that the ads that were best remembered in the fast-forward mode had several things in common: They used simple story lines, kept the brand logo in the middle of the screen, and used familiar characters. Ads that the viewer had seen before were also better remembered. The researchers speculated that people remember ads in the fast-forward mode because they are actually paying more attention to them while they look for cues that the program is back on.

By the way, the two ads that were best remembered by those who zipped through the commercials featured Matt Damon (in an ad for the latest "Bourne" movie) and Mr. Mucus (in an ad for Mucinex cough syrup).

Research Findings   Is there evidence to suggest such an effect? Most findings suggest that among some people TV cultivates distorted perceptions of the real world. In one survey of approximately 450 New Jersey schoolchildren, 73 percent of heavy viewers compared with 62 percent of light viewers gave the TV answer to a question about the number of people involved in violence in a typical week. Youngsters who were heavy viewers were also more fearful about walking alone at night in a city. They overestimated how many people commit serious crimes, how often police find it necessary to use force, and how frequently police shoot at fleeing suspects.

Other cultivation research has focused specifically on college students. In one study students' exposure to pornography was examined to see if stereotyped perceptions were being cultivated. Among males, those who were heavy users of pornography were more apt to report that they had less confidence in females doing certain jobs (such as mechanic or mayor). They also tended to agree more with stereotypes of sexuality ("Men have stronger sexual urges than women; women say 'no' to sex when they don't really mean it") than did light users. These relationships held even after rigorous statistical controls removed possible influences of other factors. Women showed no such effects from exposure. A 2007 study looked at the cultivation impact of TV's portrayal of mental health. Content analysis revealed that in prime-time programs the mentally ill were 10 times more likely to be violent criminals than those without mental problems. In line with cultivation, a survey disclosed that heavy television viewers were more fearful of having a mental health facility located in their neighborhood and were less likely to support living next to someone who was mentally ill. A 2009 study examined viewers of *Grey's Anatomy* and their perceptions of doctors. Heavy viewers thought the program presented a credible portrayal of doctors. Heavy viewers were also more likely to believe that real-world doctors were courageous and reported more satisfaction with their own real-world doctors than did light viewers.

Although the results of cultivation analysis studies are evocative and fascinating, conclusions are clouded by three problems. First, it is difficult to determine cause and effect. For example, does heavy TV viewing cause people to be fearful of walking alone at night, or does being fearful cause them to stay home and watch more TV?

The second problem concerns the fact that people differ in ways other than their TV viewing habits. Consequently, factors other than TV watching might affect the differences in

How many doctors are like the acerbic but brilliant Dr. House on the Fox show of the same name? Cultivation analysis suggests that for some heavy viewers, TV portrayals might influence their perceptions of real life.

perceptions and attitudes between heavy and light viewers. When certain factors that appear relevant to the cause-and-effect relationship (such as age, sex, and education) are statistically controlled, one factor at a time, the association between TV watching and perceptions is evident but somewhat weakened. When two or more factors are controlled simultaneously (such as examining the relationship between TV viewing and anxiety while simultaneously controlling for effects of both sex and age), some overall relationships disappear. We cannot conclude, however, that a relationship does not exist. In fact, recent research indicates that certain subgroups will show a cultivation effect and others will not.

One group of researchers, for example, detected a phenomenon they labeled **mainstreaming,** whereby differences apparently due to cultural and social factors tend to diminish among heavy TV viewers. They have also found evidence for what they call **resonance,** a situation in which the respondent's real-life experiences are congruent with those of the television world, thereby leading to a greater cultivation effect.

Third, technical decisions about the way TV viewing and attitudes are measured can have a significant impact on findings. For example, the precise wording of the questions has been shown to be important. In addition, some researchers argue that exposure to a particular kind of program (such as violent shows) gives a more accurate picture of cultivation than simply measuring overall TV viewing. Others note that deciding on the number of hours of viewing that differentiates heavy and light viewers has a bearing on the magnitude of cultivation.

To sum up and perhaps oversimplify, we can say that, although not all mass communication scholars are totally convinced by the reasoning underlying cultivation analysis, a growing body of evidence suggests that the cultivation effect is indeed real for many people.

▲ Agenda Setting

One influence of mass media that has turned up in many studies of mass communication is the **agenda-setting effect.** (An agenda is a list of things to be considered or acted upon.) When we say that the media have an impact on agenda setting, we mean that they have the ability to choose and emphasize certain topics, thereby causing the public to perceive these issues as important. To paraphrase Bernard Cohen in his book *The Press and Foreign Policy,* we can say that the media may not always be successful in telling people what to think, but they are usually successful in telling people what to think about.

Agenda-setting studies typically concern themselves with information media: newsmagazines, newspapers, television, and radio. Much of the research on agenda setting has been carried out during political campaigns. There are two reasons for this. First, messages generated by political campaigns are usually designed to set agendas (politicians call this tactic "emphasizing the issues"). Second, political campaigns have a clear-cut beginning and end, thus making the time period for study unambiguous.

TV coverage of news events, such as the postelection violence in Iran, can shape the public's agenda.

One typical agenda-setting study was an investigation of the 1968 presidential election. The researchers asked a sample of voters to rank what they believed to be the key issues of the campaign. While this was going on, the researchers examined newsmagazines, newspapers, and television newscasts and ranked the campaign issues according to the time and space the media devoted to each issue. When the media's ranking was compared with the voters' ranking, there was a strikingly high degree of correspondence. In other words, the voters perceived as important those issues that the media judged important, as evidenced by the amount of coverage they received. Similar studies of more recent elections have found similar results. Although such studies strongly suggest a relationship between personal agendas and media agendas, they do not address the question of causation, an issue that we have encountered before.

Some studies indicate that there are situations in which the direction of cause and effect is unclear—or will even depend on the medium under consideration. At least two studies report that newspapers exert a greater agenda-setting effect than does television. In fact, one survey found that during a political campaign television appeared to alter its coverage to conform to voter interest, and newspapers appeared to shape the voters' agendas.

Recent reviews published in scholarly journals noted two new directions of research interest. The first pertains to the notion of **framing,** the general way a news topic is treated by the media. This line of research posits that not only do the media tell us what to think about, they also tell us how to think about it by the way the story is framed. For example, suppose Congress is considering changes in the food stamp program. One way the media might frame this story is by concentrating on both the increased efficiency that might result from the changes and the savings to taxpayers. Alternatively, the media might choose to emphasize the hardships that might be experienced by people who will no longer qualify for the program. The particular choice of frames will affect the salience of the story and our attitudes toward the revised program.

A second direction concerns **agenda building.** Research on this topic examines how the media build their agenda of newsworthy items. Some factors that seem to have an impact are presidential press conferences, congressional hearings, and public relations efforts. One recent study, for example, found that a public relations effort by the Christian Coalition was influential in shaping the media agenda some three months later. Another recent study suggested that a journalist's own personal agenda (the issues that he or she considers important) might also have an impact on the media agenda. A study published in 2005 suggested that entertainment programs that focus on crime and law enforcement are influential in building the audience's personal agenda, which may eventually have an impact on polling data that help shape the media agenda.

Research into the impact of online media on agenda setting is a growing area. There is obvious evidence that bloggers can set the news media agenda, as seen in the controversy over CBS News's airing of questionable documents relating to President George W. Bush's military service during the Vietnam era. Bloggers first raised questions about the authenticity of the documents, and the story was quickly picked up by the mainstream media. Two studies of the 2004 presidential election found that topics frequently mentioned in blogs were related to the media agenda.

Media Effects on Behavior: A Short History

The political effects of the mass media, especially radio, prompted much of the early research. Many people feared that a skilled political demagogue might use the new medium of radio to gain political power. As a result, large-scale studies were conducted during the 1940s to gauge the extent of media influence. Somewhat surprisingly, these early surveys found that the media had little direct effect on political decision making. Personal influence was more important, and individuals labeled "opinion leaders" were thought to be more important in transmitting political orientations.

President Franklin D. Roosevelt used radio effectively as a political communications tool during his "fireside chats" with the nation. The increasing importance of radio as a tool prompted several large-scale studies during the 1940s.

The explosive growth of TV during the 1950s and 1960s shifted the research focus to young people. Early large-scale surveys noted that television could influence children's values and perceptions of the world. In addition, the new medium might adversely affect social relationships and skills necessary for success in school. The impact of media portrayals of violence was of special concern as evidenced by Senate subcommittee hearings on the topic in 1961 and 1964. In 1967 a national commission concluded that a steady diet of media violence had "an adverse effect on human character and attitudes."

The topic was revisited again in 1970 when the United States Surgeon General issued a report that linked exposure to TV violence with antisocial behavior. A 1982 follow-up study reinforced the conclusions of the original report. Media violence remained the center of attention during the 1990s. As mentioned in previous chapters, the Telecommunications Act of 1996 contained provisions for program ratings and a V-Chip that enabled parents to block violent and other unwanted programming from their TVs. Televised violence came under the spotlight again in 1999 after the Columbine shootings and yet again after the Virginia Tech massacre.

We will next examine more closely some of the topics mentioned in the 1970 report summary, beginning with the topic that has generated the most research attention: the effects of TV violence.

The Impact of Televised Violence

Does television viewing prompt violent or other antisocial behaviors on the part of the viewer? As we have just seen, this question has been debated for four decades. It is a complicated issue, and the definitive answer has not yet been found. Nonetheless, enough evidence has been gathered that we can begin to point to some preliminary conclusions. To arrive at these conclusions, we must examine research data from surveys and from experiments.

▲ Survey Results

Table 19-1 contains abbreviated and modified questionnaire items taken from surveys designed to analyze the viewing of TV violence and aggressive behavior.

TABLE 19-1

Questionnaire Items

	Almost always	Often	Sometimes	Never
1. About how often do you watch the following TV programs?				
NCIS	____	____	____	____
Scrubs	____	____	____	____
Cold Case	____	____	____	____
The Office	____	____	____	____
CSI	____	____	____	____
Law & Order	____	____	____	____

2. Next, what would you do if these things happened to you?
   a. Pretend somebody you know took something from you and would not give it back. What would you do?
   ____ Hit the other person and take my property back.
   ____ Call the police.
   ____ Ask the person to return it.
   ____ Nothing.
   b. Pretend somebody was telling lies about you. What would you do?
   ____ Hit the person and make the person stop.
   ____ Ask the person to stop telling lies.
   ____ Nothing.

What makes some children imitate the violent acts they see on TV? Scientists have been studying this question since the early 1950s.

As you can see, with measures such as the ones in the table (assuming, of course, a questionnaire that was much longer), it would be possible to index a person's viewing of programs that generally contain violence. It would also be possible to measure that same person's tendency to report his or her willingness to use violence in everyday situations. If viewing violent TV does affect behavior, we would expect to find some relationship between reported heavy viewing of violence and an individual's own self-report of aggressive tendencies. If we do not find such a link, we might assume that exposure to media violence has no impact on subsequent aggressive tendencies. If, however, we do find a connection, we might suspect that media violence actually causes aggression. We could not be sure, however, because survey data alone are not sufficient to establish a cause-and-effect relationship. We must also keep in mind that there are different ways of measuring exposure to TV violence and aggressive tendencies.

Viewed as a whole, surveys compiled over the years are difficult to summarize. Perhaps the most concise generalization is one that appeared in a recent summary of television research findings. After carefully analyzing all survey results, the authors of this summary "conclude that the evidence to date indicates that there is a significant correlation between the viewing of violent television programs and aggressive behavior in day-to-day life."

Nevertheless, as already mentioned, a relationship is not necessarily evidence of cause and effect. Remember, however, that the special survey technique known as a *panel study* gives us a little more confidence in making cause-and-effect statements based on survey data. However, since panel studies cost a lot and sometimes take years to complete, not many exist. Further, the results from those that are available are not as clear as we might like them to be. One panel study whose methods might have been stronger was included in the 1970 Surgeon General's report on television and social behavior. It found evidence that viewing violent TV shows at an early age was a cause of aggression in later life.

Additional survey evidence appeared in 1982 with the publication of *Television and Aggression: A Panel Study*. This book reported the results of a three-year research project sponsored by NBC. Data on aggression, TV viewing, and a large number of sociological variables were collected on six different occasions from children in two midwestern cities. Eventually, about 1,200 boys in grades two through six participated in the main survey.

Lengthy and detailed analysis of the data suggested that there was no relationship between the viewing of TV violence and subsequent aggressive behavior. Later, other researchers were given the opportunity to reanalyze the NBC data. One reexamination did find some partial evidence of a causal relationship between TV violence and aggression, but its impact was tiny. In sum, if a causal relationship was present in the NBC data, it was extremely weak and hard to find.

In 1986 an international team of scientists reported the results of panel studies done in five countries: the United States, Finland, Australia, Israel, and Poland. The U.S. study and the Polish study found that early TV viewing was significantly related to later aggression. The Finnish study reached a similar conclusion for boys but not for girls. In Israel viewing TV violence seemed to be a cause of subsequent aggression among boys and girls who lived in urban areas but not among those who lived in rural areas. The panel study done in Australia was not able to find a causal relationship. Despite these differences the five panels were consistent in at least two findings. First, the relationship between the viewing of violence and aggression tended to be somewhat weak. Second, there was a pattern of circularity in causation. Viewing violent TV caused some children to become more aggressive. Being aggressive, in turn, caused some children to watch more violent TV.

The results of an extensive panel survey reported in 2002 found that teens who watched more than one hour of TV a day were more likely to commit violent acts in later years than were teens who watched less. The survey tracked 707 children for more than 17 years. The researchers interviewed the participants several times and also checked arrest records to document violent behavior. The relationship between TV viewing and aggressive acts was still evident after other factors such as low family income and a prior history of violence were controlled statistically. The results of the study were weakened, however, by the fact that the researchers measured the total amount of TV exposure rather than exposure to violent content. It is difficult to explain why general TV exposure, much of it to nonviolent programs, would be related to aggression.

A study published in 2004 found results consistent with past research. More than 400 third, fourth, and fifth graders were surveyed at the beginning and at the end of the school year. The researchers found that children who were exposed early in the school year to media violence in TV, movies, and video games were more likely to see the world as a hostile place and to behave more aggressively at the end of the year. A 2007 panel study done by researchers at the Child Health Institute at the University of Washington found that viewing violent TV at ages 3–5 was associated with increased risk of antisocial behavior for boys but not for girls at ages 7–10.

What are we to make of all these panel studies? On the whole, they seem to suggest that there is a mutual causal connection between watching TV violence and performing aggressive acts. This connection, however, is small and influenced by individual and cultural factors. At this point, we will turn to the results of laboratory studies to aid us further in forming a conclusion about what causes what.

▲ Experimental Results

Imagine that it is a cold winter night. As part of the requirements of Psychology 100, a course in which you are enrolled, you are required to serve as a subject in 3 hours of research. Tonight is your night to fulfill part of your obligation. Thus, you find yourself trudging across campus to the Psychology Building. Upon arriving, you join several dozen other students in a large auditorium. Before long, an individual enters the room, introduces himself as Professor So-and-So, and tells you that you are about to begin your first experiment of the evening.

Professor So-and-So has a new IQ test that he is trying to develop, and he needs your cooperation. The test booklet is passed out, and you are told to begin. As soon as you start the test, you realize that it is unlike any IQ test you have ever seen before. There are questions about advanced calculus, early Greek architecture, and organic chemistry, which you have no idea how to answer. In a few minutes the professor starts making sarcastic comments: "You'll never finish college if this simple test takes you so long"; "It looks as if this group will certainly flunk out"; "High school students have finished this test by now." Finally, with an air of exasperation, the professor says, "There's no hope for you. Hand in the papers. Since most of you won't be in school after this semester's grades, let me say good-bye to you now." With that the professor storms out of the room.

A few minutes go by, and then another individual enters the room and calls out two lists of names. Each group is assigned to another room down the hall. When you report to your assigned room, you find another professor already there. She tells you that this is the second experiment you will participate in tonight. It is a study to see how much people remember from films. You are going to be shown a brief excerpt from a film, and then you will be asked questions about it. The lights go out, and all of a sudden you are watching an 8-minute fight scene from a Kirk Douglas film called *The Champion.* In the movie Douglas, playing a boxer, gets the stuffing beaten out of him as he competes for the title. (Unknown to you, that other group of students is also seeing a film. At the same time you are watching Douglas get battered, they are viewing a scene from the film *Canal Boats in Venice.*) When the film ends, you are asked several questions about its content.

You are then directed to yet another room. Once in this cubicle, you are told that the third and last experiment is to begin. You are seated in front of a rather strange-looking machine with a dial that can be moved from a setting of 1 to 11. You also notice a button and a light connected to something behind the machine. The researcher explains that you are to be part of an experiment designed to investigate memory. In another room, but wired up to this same machine, is a student who is learning a word-association test. Every time this other student makes a mistake, you are to punish him by giving him a shock. The dial on your panel determines the intensity of the shock; when you press the button, it will be administered. You can choose any level you like; you can hold the button down as long as you like. The experimenter then gives you a level-2 shock to show you what it feels like. You jump and wonder why you did not take poly sci instead of psych. Your thoughts are interrupted, however, when the little light on the panel flashes on. The other student has made a mistake. It is your job to administer punishment. Your hand reaches for the dial. . . .

▲ The Catharsis Versus Stimulation Debate

This is an abstracted, simplified, and condensed version of the prototype experimental design used in several key studies to investigate the impact of media violence. The idea behind this experiment is to test two rival theories about the effects of watching violence. The first theory is thousands of years old; it is called the **catharsis theory** and can be traced back to Aristotle. This theory holds that viewing scenes of aggression can actually purge the viewer's own aggressive feelings. Thus, a person who sees a violent television program or movie might end up less likely to commit violence. The other theory, called the **stimulation theory,** argues just the opposite: Seeing scenes of violence will actually stimulate an individual to behave more violently afterward.

As you may have understood, in the hypothetical experiment, everybody was first insulted and presumably angered (this part of the experiment gave you some hostility to be purged); one group saw a violent film, and the other saw a nonviolent film. Both groups were then given a turn at the punishment machine. If catharsis was at work, then the group that saw *The Champion* would have given less intense shocks; if stimulation was at work, then *The Champion* group would have given more intense shocks.

The catharsis versus stimulation debate was one of the earliest to surface in the study of mass media's effects. One early study seemed to point to catharsis, but a series of studies carried out by psychologist Leonard Berkowitz and his colleagues at the University of Wisconsin found strong support for the stimulation hypothesis. Since that time, the bulk of the evidence seems consistent: Watching media violence tends to stimulate aggressive behavior on the part of the viewer. There is little evidence for catharsis.

▲ Field Experiments

In field experiments people are studied in their typical environment, where they probably react more naturally than they do in the lab. Field experiments are therefore subject to the contaminating influences of outside events.

At least two field experiments done in the early 1970s revealed no link between TV and aggression. On the other hand, five field experiments have yielded data consistent with the survey and lab data. Their main conclusion is that people who watch a steady diet of violent programs tend to exhibit more antisocial or aggressive behavior.

One of the more elaborate field experiments involved a Canadian town that did not receive a TV signal until 1974. Two similar towns were selected for comparison—one could get only Canadian TV, and the other could get Canadian and U.S. channels. The research team gathered data from all three towns in 1974 and again two years later. Children in the town that had recently received access to U.S. TV showed an increase in their rate of aggressive acts that was more than three times higher than that of children living in the other two towns. Taken as a whole, the results from the field experiments tend to support the notion that viewing TV violence fosters aggressive behavior.

▲ What Can We Conclude?

Let us now try to summarize the results of these surveys and experiments. Although no single survey or experiment can provide a conclusive answer, and although every study has certain shortcomings, there appears to be a thread of consistency running throughout these studies. Surveys and panel studies have shown a relationship between the viewing of violent programs and aggressive behavior. Lab and field experiments also have shown that watching violence increases the possibility of behaving aggressively. Taken as a whole, these results encourage a tentative acceptance of the proposition that watching violence on television increases aggressiveness on the part of at least some viewers.

However, viewing TV violence is only one of many factors that might prompt a person to behave aggressively, and in relative terms its influence is not particularly strong. But is a weak relationship an inconsequential relationship? Much of the recent debate about TV violence has centered on this question. In statistical terms researchers gauge the strength of any relationship by the amount of variability in one measure that is accounted for by the other. For example, height and weight are two factors that are related. If I know how tall you are, I can make a better guess about your weight than if I do not know your height. I may not get your weight exactly right, but at least I will be closer to the correct figure. Consequently, height "explains" some of the variability associated with weight. If two factors are perfectly related, one explains 100 percent of the variability of the other. If two factors are not related (for example, weight and IQ), one explains 0 percent of the variability of the other. Exposure to TV violence typically explains from about 2–9 percent of the variability of aggression. In other words, about 91–98 percent of the variability in aggression is due to something else. Given these figures, can we conclude that the impact of TV violence is really that important?

The answer to that question is more political and philosophical than scientific, but research does provide some benchmarks for comparison. In psychology the relationship between undergoing psychotherapy and being "cured" of your mental ailment is only slightly stronger than that between TV violence and aggression. Further, the effect size for TV violence's impact on antisocial behavior is only slightly less than that of the effect size between viewing *Sesame Street* and readiness for school. *Sesame Street*, of course, was regarded as a great success. Lastly, the Food and Drug Administration has released for general use several drugs whose therapeutic effect is about the same as or even less than the effect of TV violence on aggression. Thus, although the effect might be small, it is not necessarily trivial.

▲ Video Game Violence

As noted at the beginning of the chapter, violent video games have raised many of the same concerns about violence as have TV programs. The techniques used to study televised violence—surveys, experiments, panel studies—have also been employed to investigate the impact of violent video games. Although there have been some exceptions, the results of these studies generally parallel the results found for TV violence.

Experimental evidence is mixed. Several experiments have noted that playing violent video games results in a short-term increase in aggressive behavior, aggressive thoughts, and aggressive emotions. Others have found no effects. Complicating variables such as the age of the player, the type of game, and the time spent playing all have an impact on experimental results. Surveys have shown a small but nonrandom connection between playing violent games and antisocial behavior in the real world. Only one panel study has looked at long-term effects of violent game playing. This study examined young people in Japan and the United States and found that in both countries children who played violent games became more aggressive over time. In sum, as is the case for TV violence, there is a weak connection between playing violent video games and performing antisocial behavior.

Encouraging Prosocial Behavior

Most early research into the effects of mass communication dealt with the negative or antisocial effects of the media. Toward the end of the 1960s, however, sparked perhaps by the success of public television's *Sesame Street*, researchers recognized that positive

A recent experiment suggests that there are several factors that influence the performance of prosocial behavior. Subjects were first given a test that measured their "need for approval," a personality trait. At a later date, half of the subjects were directed to go to a room where they thought they were to participate in another experiment. When they got to the room, an experimenter noted the presence of a security camera and casually mentioned that the building was under constant video surveillance. At this point, the experimenter "accidentally" dropped an armful of questionnaires. An observer noted if the subjects helped to collect and sort the questionnaires—this was a measurement of public prosocial behavior. The subjects then filled out a survey that contained an item about how willing the subjects were to donate to a charitable organization—this was a measure of private prosocial behavior. The other half of the subjects went through the same procedure except that they were taken to a room with no security camera.

What were the results? The subjects in the room with the camera offered more help to the experimenter than subjects in the room with no camera. People with a high need for approval were also more likely to help than those with a low need for approval. The presence of the camera, however, had no effect on the private prosocial behavior. There was no difference between the groups in their willingness to donate to charity, nor did need for approval make a difference. In short, prosocial behavior is a function of a person's desire for approval and the expectation that the prosocial act will be witnessed by others who will reward the person with their approval.

behaviors could be promoted by television programs. (These behaviors are generally referred to by the umbrella term **prosocial behavior** and can include actions such as sharing, cooperating, developing self-control, and helping.)

▲ Experiments

Lab experiments have shown that films and TV programs can affect the performance of prosocial behavior, including such things as exercising self-control, cooperating, sharing, and helping. These experiments typically show a brief segment from a television program demonstrating one of these behaviors to one group of children and show a different program or no program at all to another group. After watching the segment, the children are given a chance to exercise self-control (such as by following directions from the experimenter) or to share (such as by winning money in a game and giving some to charity).

▲ Surveys

Surveys measure what TV programs children watch and how often they perform prosocial acts in real life. A wide range of prosocial behaviors have been examined, including altruism, sharing, friendliness, and peaceful conflict resolution. Some surveys ask children how often they have performed the above behaviors while others rely on parents' or teachers' reports of these actions.

▲ Research Results

Do prosocial messages actually influence day-to-day behavior? Generalizing about the results of research in this area is difficult because the term *prosocial behavior* covers so many different areas. The best summary available comes from a 2006 review published in *Media Psychology* that examined the results of 34 studies, both experiments and surveys, conducted between 1970 and 1990. The authors noted that experimental results showed a moderate short-term impact of exposure to prosocial material. Children who were exposed to prosocial programs were slightly more likely to perform prosocial acts in a laboratory setting. Interestingly, surveys that measured voluntary exposure to prosocial programs revealed a moderate positive impact, about as strong as the negative effect that resulted from viewing violent content. The one prosocial behavior that was affected the most by exposure to prosocial media content was altruism, a behavior that was simple and easy to imitate. In sum, as the authors concluded, "Television has the potential to foster positive social interactions . . . and encourage viewers to be more tolerant and helpful."

Shows such as *Between the Lions* carry an obvious prosocial message.

Political Behavior Effects

Trying to summarize the many studies that have been conducted about the influences of the media on politics would require far more space than we have available. Consequently, we will restrict our discussion to the more central findings. At the core of our current discussion will be an examination of the individual's most important political behavior, the ultimate payoff in any political campaign—namely, voting behavior.

▲ Negative Advertising

Recent political campaigns have centered attention on negative political advertising. Although there is no standard definition of this term, most political experts interpret it as a personal attack on the opposing candidate or an attack on what the opposing candidate stands for. There was much speculation that negative advertising would turn off voters, make them distrustful of politics, and make them less inclined to participate in the political process. Both survey and laboratory research suggested that most of these fears were unfounded. When compared with those who did not view negative ads, voters who were exposed to negative ads were just as likely to vote, were just as involved, and showed little difference in the amount of trust they placed in the political system. There was a tendency, however, for negative advertising to be related to more polarized attitudes, but this polarization did not seem to have much impact on political behavior.

More recent surveys indicate that those candidates who use a lot of negative advertising tend to receive a lower proportion of the vote. This does not necessarily mean that negative ads are ineffective; it may be that candidates who are behind in preelection polls turn to negative advertising since they have little to lose. (For a summary of

---

Critical / Cultural Issues

The Question of Technological Determinism and the Kennedy-Nixon Debate Myth

Contributed by Paul Myron Hillier, assistant professor, University of Tampa   The first-ever televised presidential debate took place on September 26, 1960, between the youthful, "telegenic" Senator John Kennedy of Massachusetts and the makeup-free Vice President Richard Nixon. Erika Tyner Allen of the Museum of Broadcast Communications writes, "Those who heard the first debate on the radio pronounced Nixon the winner. But the 70 million who watched television saw a candidate still sickly and obviously discomforted by Kennedy's smooth delivery and charisma. Those television viewers focused on what they saw, not what they heard. Studies of the audience indicated that, among television viewers, Kennedy was perceived the winner of the first debate by a very large margin."[1]

Kennedy defeated Nixon in their first debate primarily due to the appearance of the presidential candidates and the power of televised images, the story goes. Television exposed Nixon as uncomfortable, and perhaps sinister, while Kennedy came across as articulate and sincere.

And to support this argument that television made the difference—some go so far as to say changed the nature of politics itself—many scholars and commentators have suggested that the majority of the audience who listened to the debate on the radio thought Nixon "won" while those who watched the debate on TV declared Kennedy the "winner." Indeed, this claim is made so often and by so many different people that one might get the impression there's something more than anecdotal evidence to support the argument.

"One of the most perplexing legacies of the first Kennedy-Nixon debate is the claim that radio listeners and television viewers came to opposite conclusions about the debate winner," David L. Vancil and Sue D. Pendell wrote in their 1987 article, "The Myth of Viewer-Listener Disagreement in the First Kennedy-Nixon Debate."[2] Vancil and Pendell convincingly and exhaustively demonstrated that none of the empirical research done during the period supports or even reports this viewer-listener disagreement.

In fact, as the authors unpack all of the major polling organizations' surveys, they confirm that the polls "could not have shown Nixon as having 'a clear advantage' among radio listeners" because none of the organizations distinguished between the radio and television audience to begin with.

While questions of audiences' interpretations and political discourse in the age of TV are interesting and important, this myth of a viewer-listener disagreement highlights some key presumptions about the role and function of communication technologies in society. The argument that different communication technologies, like radio and television, have different "effects," and that the Kennedy-Nixon debate is a watershed moment that illustrates the social and cultural consequence of television, for good or ill, is commonplace, even logical to assume. However, it is important to recognize and emphasize that no technology operates—indeed, has no meaning—outside of cultural and social conditions. Television itself does not determine its uses or readings.

Vision is a fundamental element in the Kennedy-Nixon debate myth, but the assumption that Nixon's appearance caused people to look unfavorably upon him, that he "lost" the debate because of the way he looked, is problematic on a number of levels. Addressing this point, Vancil and Pendell sensibly note, "Appearance problems, such as Nixon's perspiring brow, *could* have had a negative impact on viewer perceptions, but it is also possible for viewers to be sympathetic to such problems, or to interpret them as evidence of attractive or desirable qualities."[3] Appearance alone does not lead one to any natural or essential conclusions. One person's "used-car salesman" can be another's "best bud." Reading a person's perspiration as evidence of a dishonest character isn't a natural reaction to a televised image but rather a socially constructed one. An important detail missing from this attention to how a person appears is context.

It is tempting to address those arguments that emphasize visual "effects" at the same level of sense. A whole set of complicating and contrary positions can be imagined. On what basis can one really claim that what we see trumps what we hear? Would this be true in every instance and in all contexts? Someone eloquently advocating criminal behavior on the radio has more of an effect on those who listen as opposed to those who see the person speaking is an obese man in a burlap sack? However, to critique television or any technology in terms of the senses is to miss the larger picture. The championing of a kind of polished image, a blue suit, a youthful complexion, certain types of gestures, and a particular body image did not happen because of *television,* but because of social and cultural goals, desires, and ends, all advanced and chosen by people. Television altered nothing *by itself.*

Forms of technological determinism show up everywhere, from academia to popular culture. They are found in rationalizations and histories of the steam engine, the cotton gin, the automobile, and the computer. Internet video, DVRs, blogs, interactive TV, and video game systems are all said to have changed or will change the world. As Raymond Williams perceived of the ways most people talk about technology, "It is either a self-acting force which creates new ways of life, or it is a self-acting force which provides materials for new ways of life. These positions are so deeply established, in modern social thought, that it is very difficult to think beyond them."[4] But think beyond them we must. Seeing communication technologies as social practices, not in terms of independent objects, effects, problems, or answers alone, is to underscore the material fact that technologies are not independent of people and context.

---

[1]Erika Tyner Allen, "The Kennedy-Nixon Presidential Debates, 1960," The Museum of Broadcast Communications, http://www.museum.tv/archives/etv/K/htmlk/kennedy-nixon/kennedy-nixon.htm (17 April 2007).

[2]David L. Vancil and Sue D. Pendell, "The Myth of Viewer-Listener Disagreement in the First Kennedy-Nixon Debate," in *Central State Speech Journal,* Spring 1987, 38(1), 16–27.

[3]Vancil and Pendell, 17.

[4]Raymond Williams, *Television: Technology and Cultural Form* (London and New York: Routledge Classics, 2003), 2.

---

the rather voluminous research literature on negative advertising, see "The Effects of Negative Political Campaigns: A Meta-Analytic Reassessment," *Journal of Politics,* 2007, pp. 1176–1209.)

▲ Mass Media and Voter Choice

A person's decision to vote for a particular candidate is affected by not only the mass media but also many other factors, both social and psychological. Still, some tentative generalizations can be made.

It would appear that conversion (changing your vote from Republican to Democrat, for example) is unlikely to result from media exposure, because it is difficult for the media to persuade someone whose mind is already made up to change and because most people (roughly two-thirds) have already made up their minds before the campaign begins. Far more common are two effects that have a direct bearing on voter choice: reinforcement and crystallization. **Reinforcement** means the strengthening or support of existing attitudes and opinions. **Crystallization** means the sharpening and elaboration of vaguely held attitudes or predispositions. If a person approaches a campaign undecided or neutral, then crystallization is likely to occur. If the person has already made up his or her mind, then reinforcement will probably take place.

In recent national elections there has been an increase in ticket splitting (supporting one party's candidate for president and another's for governor, for example). This phenomenon may be due to crystallization, which in turn results from exposure to mass media. The flow of information during the campaign evidently crystallizes a voter's vague intention, and in many instances these new choices do not square with party loyalty. On the other hand, when partisan voters are exposed to the media, reinforcement is likely.

These findings do not necessarily mean that the media are not influential. A key factor in winning any election is to keep the party faithful loyal (reinforcement) and to persuade enough of the undecideds to vote for one side or the other (crystallization). Thus, even though widespread conversion is not usually seen, the media are still influential. Even more importantly, the media may have significant indirect influence on the electorate. By serving as important sources of political news, by structuring "political reality," and by creating an image of candidates and issues, the media may have a potent effect on a person's attitudes toward the political system. Furthermore, our discussion has been mainly concerned with the effects of the media in national elections. Local elections present a somewhat different picture. Most research evidence indicates that the media, especially local newspapers, might be highly influential in affecting voter choice in a city, county, or district election.

▲ Televised Debates

The first series of presidential debates between John Kennedy and Richard Nixon during the 1960 election prompted more than 30 different studies. Most concluded that the main effect of the debates was reinforcement, since most people had made up their minds before the debates. There was also evidence of a crystallization effect as independent voters shifted to the Kennedy camp. Although the crystallization effect was small, the 1960 election was decided by a tenth of a percentage point, suggesting that even small effects can have significant results.

The reinforcement effect was found again during the 1984 and 1988 debates. In 1996 the debates between Bill Clinton and Bob Dole seemed to have little impact on voter choice. Any effect of the debates between Al Gore and George W. Bush in the 2000 election was difficult to detect. The audience for these debates was the smallest ever due to competition from sporting events and entertainment programs. Most surveys done about the 2004 debates between Bush and John Kerry indicated that Kerry was perceived the winner in all of them. Nonetheless, Bush still won reelection, suggesting that winning a debate does not necessarily translate into winning an election. In 2008, surveys consistently found that Barack Obama was perceived as the winner in his debates with John McCain. Obama maintained a clear lead in the polls throughout the campaign and went on to win the election.

▲ Television and the Political Behavior of Politicians

On a general level, it is clear that the emergence of television has affected the political behavior of politicians and political campaigns. A comparison of pre-TV practices with those occurring after TV's adoption reveals the following:

- Nominating conventions are now planned with television in mind. They are designed not so much to select a candidate as to make a favorable impression on the public.
- Television has increased the cost of campaigning.
- Television has become the medium around which most campaigns are organized.

- Campaign staffs now typically include one or more television consultants whose job it is to advise the candidate on his or her television image.

- The Internet has become an important channel of political communication and a new means of fund-raising. Many influential blogs are concerned with politics.

Research About the Social Effects of the Internet

For obvious reasons, research concerning the effects of spending time on the Internet is still in a formative stage. Nonetheless, we can already identify two major trends in Net studies: (1) the impact of Internet use on other media and (2) the relationship between Internet use and social involvement.

The Internet seems to have had the most impact on television usage. This is not surprising since much Internet use takes place during the evening—the same time that most TV viewing generally takes place. Magazine and newspaper reading, radio listening, and moviegoing seem not to have been significantly affected.

As mentioned in Chapter 13, the Internet is becoming more important as a source of news. At the same time, there has been a decline in the number of people who rely on broadcast TV and newspapers as their main sources of news. A 2008 survey found that TV was still the main source for national and international news but that the percentage who named it as their main source had dropped from 82 percent in 2002 to 70 percent in 2008. Meanwhile, the Internet had overtaken the newspaper as the main source of news, with 40 percent naming the Internet and 35 percent citing the newspaper. The percentage relying on the Internet will doubtlessly increase in the next several years.

Early studies that looked at the Internet and social involvement suggested that people who were heavy users of the Internet were also those who reported greater feelings of loneliness and social isolation. More recent surveys, however, have discovered just the opposite. One survey found that Internet use was related to more social involvement in the local community; another found that those who spent a great deal of time on the Internet were more politically involved and had more contacts than those who did not spend time online. Yet another found that Internet users were the ones with the most social contacts. Apparently, both the audiences and the Internet have changed over the past few years, and innovations such as instant messaging encourage greater social contact. Not all demographic groups, however, are benefiting from the expanding Internet. One 2004 study revealed that Internet use had no impact on social involvement or psychological well-being among low-income Americans.

All in all, surveys that have studied people's Internet use support the "rich get richer" model. Extroverted people are the ones who gain the most social contacts through the Internet. To them, it is just another channel to use to link up with friends. Conversely, introverted people who go online tend to shy away from social contacts.

Communication in the Future: The Social Impact

Let us close this chapter (and this book) with an examination of some of the relevant questions about the impact of the new communications technology on society. Advances in media technology usually have an upside and a downside. The telephone, for example, made communication at a distance much more convenient. It also meant that we could be interrupted, awakened, or bothered at any hour of the day or night. Radio and television brought immediate access to information and entertainment but also encouraged the proliferation of couch potatoes. What might the future bring?

▲ Threats to Privacy

Computers have opened up threats to privacy. Some systems enable supervisors to monitor every keystroke of their employees to observe productivity. E-mail, no matter how personal, can be read by anyone with access to the system. Consumers who subscribe to computerized data services run the risk of having their personal files examined by unauthorized persons or, even worse, having their identities stolen.

Some scary examples: In 2008, the Bank of New York Mellon lost a box of computer backup tapes containing names, social security numbers, and bank account numbers of more than 12 million customers. The next year the National Archives lost a hard disk drive that contained sensitive data from the Clinton administration including social security numbers and Secret Service operating procedures. At the University of California, Berkeley, a database containing personal information on 160,000 present and former students was accessed by hackers. Credit card details of 19,000 British shoppers including names, addresses, and account numbers accidentally appeared on the Web and could be found using Google. Unfortunately, there are plenty of other examples (see www.privacyrights .org/ar/ChronDataBreaches.htm#CP for a detailed list of recent security breaches).

In the past, spying on our personal habits was made difficult simply because information was scattered about in different places. Now computers store huge amounts of information about us in one centralized place, the computer's memory, that is easily accessed from anywhere over phone lines. We willingly provide much of this information when we apply for a credit card, buy a car or a house, take out insurance, file a lawsuit, claim unemployment benefits, and so on. What many consumers do not know is that much of this information is sold to other organizations for other purposes. This is one of the reasons many of us are hit with barrages of spam from organizations we have never heard of.

Computer scanning systems used at the checkout counters of supermarkets and drug and discount stores now record your every purchase. Such information is invaluable to marketers. For instance, the makers of Mylanta can offer discounts to people who regularly buy Tums to get them to switch to their product. Bumble Bee tuna can send free samples to Chicken of the Sea buyers. Although this is great for marketing purposes, it is troubling for consumers. If you are like the rest of us, there are some purchases you make that you might like to keep private. Do you want everybody to know what kind of birth control method you use?

▲ Fragmentation and Isolation

The mass media are increasingly serving the needs of more specialized audiences. Magazines, radio stations, satellite radio, cable TV networks, and broadband TV channels, with their highly targeted niche audiences, are the best examples of this trend, but the other media are moving in this direction. Technology is increasingly directing individuals toward more selective content exposure as demonstrated by the iPod, TiVo, and Facebook. If this trend continues, it might result in a generation of consumers fragmented into smaller and smaller interest groups with little in common with the rest of society. If people are overspecialized in their interests, they may run the risk of being ignorant about the rest of the world.

This phenomenon has been labeled the *cocoon effect* by sociologists. From their perspective it refers to the process whereby people surround themselves with only the political and social information that they find comforting, appealing, or acceptable. It is as though people retreat into their informational cocoon to escape some of the uncertainty of modern life and to help reduce the multitude of choices that have to be made in today's society. It seems possible that this cocooning could generalize into cultural and recreational use of knowledge as well, further increasing an individual's isolation from society.

Moreover, as telecommuting becomes more popular, more and more people will stay at home. The computer will enable people to work, bank, shop, and be entertained at home. Books, groceries, flowers, movies, meals, medicines, diapers, and deodorants can be delivered directly to a consumer's door. With worries over personal safety mounting daily, will people decide to just stay at home?

> ### SOUNDBYTE
>
> **Technology Improves Relationships**
>
> A survey of DVR owners found that 80 percent of married couples claimed that the DVR has actually improved their relationship. Among the survey respondents with children, 81 percent said the DVR has improved their family life. They reported fewer fights about what to watch and more family time gathered to watch TV. Just another example of better living through technology.

▲ Communication Overload

Innovations in communication technology have made us better connected, but that connectivity has come with a price. We now put up with people talking loudly into their cell phones, cell phones going off during movies and plays, people constantly updating their Twitter accounts, people texting while talking, and people ignoring us while they tap and touch their iPhones.

Furthermore, it's becoming increasingly difficult to keep up with the flood of messages that we send or receive daily. E-mailing, texting, IMing, blogging, updating Twitter and Facebook pages, talking on cell phones, and uploading photos and videos now consume a significant portion of our time—perhaps too much. Psychiatrists have identified a new ailment called FAD, or Facebook Addiction Disorder, among people who spend inordinate amounts of time on Facebook. Texting while driving has been the cause of numerous automobile accidents. About 80 percent of all e-mail is spam, and the time that employees spend deleting these unwanted messages costs corporations more than $20 billion a year.

The increased availability of these new communication channels has created a tremendous drain on our time. For example, a typical teenager in 2008 spent about 31 hours a week online—that's only 9 hours short of a full workweek. About 9 hours were spent on social media, another 2 hours watching YouTube, about 3 hours doing school-related searches, and the rest spent on general information and entertainment sites. In addition, the average teen sends and receives about 80 text messages every day and spends more than an hour a day talking on the phone. In all, not counting sleep or school, in an average week the typical teen spends about half of his or her time in some form of communication. It's entirely possible that many young people have trouble managing their time in the face of this commitment to communication.

▲ Escape

The issue of escape has been around almost since the time that the mass media were invented. Many parents and educators were worried that young people would much prefer to spend time in the media world instead of the real world. Social critics have painted bleak pictures of mesmerized children attending to various forms of media: radio, movies, TV, video games, and Net surfing. In the future this concern might have more validity since the media realities that are available are becoming more and more like life outside the media. Home theaters that duplicate the theater experience are already on the market. Big-screen HDTV sets with stereo sound and interactive features are also available. Manufacturers of video games are experimenting with ways to make their displays three-dimensional. And who knows what advances will be made in the virtual reality area? What happens when it is far more fun to be in some media-generated reality than in real life? In fact, virtual reality simulations raise the question "What exactly is 'real' life anyway?" Will large numbers of us abandon socially relevant pursuits for a romp in the media world?

And what happens farther down the road? In William Gibson's 1984 novel *Neuromancer*, people plug computer chips, called *stims*, directly into their brains. Stims provide experiences for all the senses and are usually preprogrammed, but there is also the possibility of becoming a *rider*, traveling through the world computer matrix (which bears an eerie resemblance to the Internet) or even shifting yourself into another person's reality and experiencing the world as the other person experiences it. Could this be the ultimate media experience? Alternate realities hardwired into the cerebral cortex? You decide.

Will isolation increase as more people interact online and not in person?

MAIN POINTS

- Surveys and experiments are the two main quantitative techniques used to study the effects of mass communication.

- Media can serve as socialization forces when they are the primary sources of information about a topic and that information is presented in a consistent manner.

- Media can cultivate false perceptions of reality among some heavy users.

- The media can set the priority of certain issues for the public.

- TV violence shows a small but persistent correlation with antisocial behavior among heavy viewers.

- Experiments have shown that TV can produce prosocial behavior, and some evidence of this effect has been found in surveys.

- The media are more effective in reinforcing or crystallizing a person's voting choice. TV has had a significant impact on the conduct of politicians and political campaigns.

- The main topics of research concerning the Internet are its effects on the usage of other media and the relationship between social isolation and online media use.

- Other concerns about the effects of mass communications focus on the areas of privacy, isolation, communication overload, and escape.

QUESTIONS FOR REVIEW

1. What are the two main methods that social scientists use to investigate media effects?

2. What gets cultivated in a cultivation analysis?

3. Summarize the catharsis versus stimulation debate. What viewpoint does research evidence favor?

4. What is the difference between the public's agenda and the media's agenda?

5. How do the media influence the voting choices of the audience?

QUESTIONS FOR CRITICAL THINKING

1. Why is it difficult to establish the effects of mass communication?

2. Young children are not the only ones who go through a socialization period. College students have to be socialized as well. What were the main socialization agencies that prepared you to fit into college life? How important were the media?

3. How are college students portrayed on prime-time TV? Do these portrayals perpetuate any stereotypes?

4. Why has the debate over media violence gone on so long? Will scientists ever amass enough evidence to satisfy everybody? Why or why not?

5. What sorts of research projects should be developed to study the social impact of the Internet?

6. Review the boxed insert on page 458, "The Question of Technological Determinism and the Kennedy-Nixon Debate Myth," and consider the following: Can you think of other forms of technological determinism that surround the Internet? The cell phone? Blogs? What does this analysis suggest about uncritical acceptance of empirical research findings?

KEY TERMS

survey (p. 444)
panel study (p. 444)
experiment (p. 444)
field experiment (p. 444)
agencies of socialization (p. 444)
cultivation analysis (p. 448)

mainstreaming (p. 450)
resonance (p. 450)
agenda-setting effect (p. 450)
framing (p. 451)
agenda building (p. 451)
catharsis theory (p. 455)

stimulation theory (p. 455)
prosocial behavior (p. 457)
reinforcement (p. 460)
crystallization (p. 460)

INTERNET RESOURCES

Online Learning Center

On the Online Learning Center home page, www.mhhe.com/dominick11e, *select* Student Center *and then* Chapter 19.

1. Use the Learning Objectives, Chapter Outline, and Main Points sections to review this chapter.

2. Test your knowledge of the chapter using the multiple choice and flashcard features of the site.

3. Expand your knowledge of concepts and topics discussed in the chapter with additional Questions for Critical Thinking and Internet Exercises.

Surfing the Internet

In addition to Web sites, several newsgroups and listservs are useful to those interested in mass media effects. The listings that follow represent only a small sample.

www.aber.ac.uk/media/Documents/short.cultiv.html
Contains a thorough description of the history, techniques, and issues connected to cultivation analysis.

www.surgeongeneral.gov/library/youthviolence/chapter4/sec1.html
Thorough discussion of risk factors for youth violence, including a summary of the research on TV violence.

www.wimmerdominick.com
Contains a discussion of media effects and related readings.

http://allpsych.com/researchmethodsintroduction.html
Good introduction to basic research methods used in the social sciences.

>> Glossary

advertising agency A company that handles both the creative and the business side of an advertising campaign for its clients.

agencies of socialization The various people or organizations that contribute to the socialization of an individual.

agency An organization that handles basic needs of advertisers.

agenda building The ways the media decide what is newsworthy.

agenda-setting effect The influence of the mass media created by emphasizing certain topics, thus causing people to perceive those same issues as important.

AM Amplitude modulation of radio waves.

Arbitron The professional research organization that measures radio audiences.

Audit Bureau of Circulations (ABC) An organization formed by advertisers and publishers in 1914 to establish ground rules for counting circulation data.

authoritarian theory The prevailing belief that a ruling elite should guide the intellectually inferior masses.

backpack journalist A reporter who can prepare news stories for print, electronic, and online media.

best-seller lists The ranking of best-selling books based on retail sales.

beware surveillance A media function that occurs when the media inform the public of short-term, long-term, or chronic threats.

Billboard The sound recording industry trade publication that tabulates record popularity.

block booking A policy of major film studios that required theater owners to show several of a studio's low-quality films before they could receive the same studio's top-quality films.

blog A personal journal kept on the Web.

broadband Increased bandwidth for Internet connections, which speeds up downloads.

browsers A type of software that enables individuals to search for content on the Web.

buffering Storing video signals for video transmitted via the Internet.

business-to-business advertising Advertising directed not at the general public but at other businesses.

C3 rating The ratings for average commercial minutes in live programming plus three days of DVR playback.

campaign In advertising, a large number of ads that stress the same theme and appear over a specified length of time.

carriage fee A fee paid by cable systems to carry a cable network.

categorical imperative The ethical principle that people should behave as they wish all others would behave.

catharsis A release of pent-up emotion or energy.

catharsis theory The theory that viewing aggression will purge the viewer's aggressive feelings.

cease-and-desist order A Federal Trade Commission order notifying an advertiser that a certain practice violates the law; failure to comply with a cease-and-desist order can result in fines being levied against the advertiser.

channels Pathways by which a message travels from sender to receiver.

circulation The total number of copies of a publication delivered to newsstands, vending machines, and subscribers.

clock hour A radio format that specifies every element of the program.

commercial television Television programs broadcast by local stations whose income is derived from selling time on their facilities to advertisers.

Communications Act of 1934 An act of Congress creating the Federal Communications Commission.

communist theory The theory of the press that the media should promote the goals of the ruling political party.

comprehensive layout The finished model of a print ad.

computer-assisted reporting (CAR) Skills involved in using the Internet to aid reporting.

concept testing A type of feedback in which a one- or two-paragraph description for a new series is presented to a sample of viewers for their reactions.

consent order A Federal Trade Commission order in which the advertiser agrees to halt a certain advertising practice without admitting any violation of the law.

consequence The importance or weightiness of a news story.

consumer advertising Advertising directed at the general public.

controlled circulation A type of circulation in which publications are sent free or distributed to a select readership, such as airline passengers or motel guests.

convergence   The blending of communication technologies, operations, or businesses.

conversational currency   Topic material presented by the media that provides a common ground for social conversations.

copy   The headlines and message in an ad.

corporate convergence   The merging of companies with holdings in one medium with companies that have assets in other media.

creative boutique   An advertising organization that specializes in the creative side of advertising.

credibility   The trust that the audience holds for media that perform surveillance functions.

critical/cultural approach   An analytical technique that examines power relationships in society and focuses on meanings people find in texts.

crystallization   The sharpening and elaboration of a vaguely held attitude or predisposition.

cultivation analysis   An area of research that examines whether television and other media encourage perceptions of reality that are more consistent with media portrayals than with actuality.

culture   Common values, behaviors, attitudes, and beliefs that bind a society together.

custom magazines   Free magazines published by corporations for current and prospective customers.

cycle   In all-news radio, the amount of time that elapses before the program order is repeated.

decoding   The activity in the communication process by which physical messages are translated into a form that has eventual meaning for the receiver.

decoupling   A separation of the connection between two entities. In mass communication, it refers to the breaking of the traditional link between advertising support and content.

defamation   The act of harming the reputation of another by publishing false information.

demo   A demonstration disk used to sell a musical performer or group.

developmental journalism   A type of journalism, practiced by many less-developed countries, that stresses national goals and economic development.

developmental theory   The assumption that government uses media to further national, economic, and social goals.

device convergence   The tendency for functions once served by separate machines to be merged into a single device.

Digital Millennium Copyright Act   Protects Internet service providers from copyright suits for simply transmitting over the Internet information provided by others.

digital technology   A system that encodes information—sound, text, data, video—into a series of on and off pulses that are usually denoted as zeros and ones.

digital television (DTV)   Television signals consisting of binary signals that enable improved picture quality.

digital video recorder (DVR)   A device, like TiVo, that records television content on a hard disc.

digital videodisc (DVD)   A disc that stores audio, movies, video, and graphics in a digital format that is compatible with DVD players and home computers.

direct action ad   An ad that contains a direct response item (such as a toll-free number) that enables advertisers to see results quickly.

direct broadcast satellite (DBS)   A system in which a home TV set receives a signal directly from an orbiting satellite.

disintermediation   The process of delivering a product or service directly to the consumer.

distribution system   The cables that deliver the signals to subscribers.

double features   The practice started by theaters in the 1930s of showing two feature films on the same bill.

dummy   A rough version of a magazine that is used for planning how the final version will look.

dysfunctions   Consequences that are undesirable from the point of view of the welfare of society.

e-book   A digital version of a book, which can be read by using a computer or a special reader.

editorial policies   Guidelines the print media follow to persuade the public on certain issues or to achieve specific goals.

e-mail   Electronic messages sent from computer to computer.

encoding   The activity in the communication process by which thoughts and ideas from the source are translated into a form that may be perceived by the senses.

encryption   Scrambling video signals so that only those with the proper decoding hardware can receive them.

Equal Opportunities rule   Part of the Communications Act of 1934; Section 315 allows bona fide candidates for public office to gain access to a broadcast medium during political campaigns.

evaluation   Research done to measure the effectiveness of an advertising or a public relations campaign.

Evernet   The successor to the Internet; an arrangement by which an individual is constantly connected to the Internet using various information devices.

experiment   A research technique that stresses controlled conditions and manipulates variables.

Fairness Doctrine   A now defunct FCC doctrine that required broadcast stations to provide various points of view on a controversial issue.

Federal Communications Commission (FCC)   A regulatory agency, composed of five individuals appointed by the president, whose responsibilities include broadcast and wire regulation.

feedback   The responses of the receiver that shape and alter subsequent messages from the source.

field experiment   An experiment that is conducted in a natural setting as opposed to a laboratory.

First Amendment   The first amendment of the Bill of Rights, stating that Congress shall make no law abridging the freedom of speech or of the press.

FM   Frequency modulation of radio waves.

focus group   A group of 10–15 people led by a moderator that discusses predetermined topics.

format   Consistent programming designed to appeal to a certain segment of the audience.

format wheel   A visual aid that helps radio programmers plan what events happen during a given time period.

formative research   Advertising research done before developing a campaign.

framing   The general way a news medium treats a topic.

franchises   Exclusive rights to operate a business in a given territory.

Freedom of Information Act (FOIA)   A law stating that every federal executive-branch agency must publish instructions on the methods a member of the public should follow to get information.

free marketplace of ideas   A press philosophy that endorses the free flow of information.

full-service agency   An ad agency that handles all phases of advertising for its clients.

functional approach   A methodology that holds that something is best understood by examining how it is used.

gag rules   Judicial orders that restrict trial participants from giving information to the media or that restrain media coverage of events that occur in court.

gatekeepers   Individuals who decide whether a given message will be distributed by a mass medium.

geosynchronous satellite   A satellite whose orbit keeps it over the same spot on Earth.

golden mean   The ethical principle that moderation is the key to virtue.

gramophone   A "talking machine" patented in 1887 by Emile Berliner that utilized a disk instead of a cylinder.

graphophone   A recording device similar to the phonograph but utilizing a wax cylinder rather than tinfoil.

hard news   Timely stories with significance for many people.

head end   The antenna and related equipment of the cable system that receives and processes distant television signals so that they can be sent to subscribers' homes.

heavy metal   A counterculture musical trend of the 1960s–1970s, characterized by a vaguely threatening style and heavy use of amplification and electronic equipment.

hegemony   The dominance of one entity over another.

Hicklin Rule   A long-standing obscenity standard based on whether a book or other item contains isolated passages that might deprave or corrupt the mind of the most susceptible person.

HD Radio   Digital radio service with greatly improved quality.

HDTV   A supersharp television system that delivers about twice the resolution of traditional TV.

house drop   The section of the cable that connects the feeder cable to the subscriber's TV set.

human interest   A news value that emphasizes the emotional, bizarre, offbeat, or uplifting nature of a news story.

hyperlocal   News that concentrates on stories from a small geographic area.

hypertext   A digital navigational tool that links one electronic document to another.

ideology   A particular set of beliefs or ideas.

independents   Radio or TV stations unaffiliated with any network.

indirect action ad   An advertisement that works over the long run to build a company's image.

information gathering   A phase of a public relations campaign in which pertinent data are collected.

injunction A court order that requires an individual to do something or to stop doing something.

instrumental surveillance A media function that occurs when the media transmit information that is useful and helpful in everyday life.

Internet neutrality The idea that Internet service providers cannot favor one company over another.

Internet-only radio stations Radio stations that exist only online.

Internet TV Sending video signals over the Internet.

interpersonal communication A method of communication in which one person (or group) interacts with another person (or group) without the aid of a mechanical device.

investigative reports News reporting that requires extraordinary efforts to gather information about matters of public importance.

jazz A form of popular music that emerged during the Roaring Twenties and was noted for its spontaneity and disdain of convention.

jazz journalism Journalism of the Roaring Twenties that was characterized by a lively style and a richly illustrated tabloid format.

joint venture A method of movie financing in which several companies pool resources to finance films.

Kinetoscope The first practical motion picture camera and viewing device, developed by William Dickson in 1889.

libel Written defamation that tends to injure a person's reputation or good name or that diminishes the esteem, respect, or goodwill due a person.

libel per quod Written material that becomes libelous under certain circumstances.

libel per se Falsely written accusations (such as labeling a person a "thief" or a "swindler") that automatically constitute libel.

libertarian theory The assumption that all human beings are rational decision makers and that governments exist to serve the individual.

limited partnership A method of movie financing in which a number of investors put up a specified amount of money for a film.

linkage The ability of the mass media to join different elements of society that are not directly connected by interpersonal channels.

machine-assisted interpersonal communication A method of communication involving one or more persons and a mechanical device (or devices) with one or more receivers.

macroanalysis A sociological perspective that considers the functions performed by a system (such as mass media) for the entire society.

magazines Printed publications that contain an assortment of materials that appear on a regular basis.

mainstreaming In cultivation analysis the tendency of differences to disappear among heavy-TV-viewing people, apparently because of cultural and social factors.

management by objectives (MBO) A management technique that sets observable, measurable goals for an organization to achieve.

marketing Developing, pricing, distributing, and promoting an idea, a good, or a service.

mass communication The process by which a complex organization, with the aid of one or more machines, produces and transmits public messages that are directed at large, heterogeneous, and scattered audiences.

mass media The channels and the institutions of mass communication.

meaning The interpretation an audience makes of text.

media buying service An organization that specializes in buying media time to resell to advertisers.

Mediamark Research Inc. (MRI) A company that measures magazine readership.

media vehicle A single component of a mass medium, such as a newspaper or TV network.

message The actual physical product in the communication process that the source encodes.

message research Pretesting messages in an ad campaign.

microanalysis A sociological perspective that considers the functions performed by a system (such as mass media) for the individual.

microcasting Sending an audio or video message to a small group of interested people.

mobile journalists (mojos) Reporters who work out of cars covering local community news.

mobile parenting An arrangement by which parents keep track of children by using cell phones and pagers.

modem A device that enables computers to communicate via phone lines.

Motion Picture Patents Company (MPPC) An organization formed by the nine leading film and film equipment manufacturers in 1908 for the purpose of controlling the motion picture industry.

MPAA rating system   The G, PG, PG-13, R, NC-17 rating system for movies administered by the Motion Picture Association of America.

muckrakers   A term coined by Theodore Roosevelt to describe the reform movement undertaken by leading magazines in the 1890s to expose corrupt practices of business and government to the general public.

national advertisers   Advertisers who sell a product all across the country.

National Public Radio (NPR)   A noncommercial U.S. radio network.

network   An organization composed of interconnecting broadcasting stations that cuts costs by airing the same programs.

newsgroups   A section of the Internet devoted to message boards that are organized according to topic.

newshole   The amount of space available each day in a newspaper for news.

nickelodeons   The popular name for the many penny arcades and amusement centers that emerged around the beginning of the 20th century and specialized in recordings and film.

noise   In communication, anything that interferes with the delivery of a message.

noncommercial television   Television programs broadcast by those stations whose income is derived from sources other than the sale of advertising time.

nonduplication rule   An FCC rule passed in 1965, stating that an AM-FM combination may not duplicate its AM content on its FM channel for more than 50 percent of the time.

ombudsperson   An individual in a media organization assigned to handle complaints from audience members.

one-stops   Individuals who sell records to retail stores and jukebox operators who are not in a position to buy directly from the record company.

operating policies   Guidelines that cover the everyday problems and situations that crop up during the operation of a media organization.

operational convergence   A system used in media organizations whereby one staff produces content for two media.

paid circulation   A type of circulation in which the reader must purchase a magazine through a subscription or at a newsstand.

panel study   A research method in which data are collected from the same individuals at different points in time.

paradigm   A model used for analysis.

parasocial relationship   A situation whereby audience members develop a sense of kinship or friendship with media personalities.

pass-along audience   That portion of a magazine's total audience composed of individuals who pick up copies of a magazine while at the doctor's office, at work, while traveling, and so on.

payola   Bribes of gifts and money paid to DJs by record companies in order to gain favorable airplay for their releases.

pay-per-view (PPV)   A system that enables cable TV subscribers to pay a one-time fee to view one specific program or movie.

penny press   The mass-appeal press of the early 19th century.

persistence of vision   The quality of the human eye that enables it to retain an image for a split second after the image has disappeared.

personal digital assistants (PDAs)   Digital devices that keep track of addresses, schedules, and other useful information.

phi phenomenon   The tendency of the human perceptual system to perceive continuous motion between two stationary points of light that blink on and off; the basis for the illusion of motion in motion pictures.

phonograph   A "talking machine" developed by Thomas Edison in the late 1870s; the hand-cranked device preserved sound on a tinfoil-wrapped cylinder.

photojournalism   Journalism in which written text is secondary to photographs in news stories.

pickup   A technique of financing a motion picture.

pilot   The first episode of a projected television series.

pilot testing   A process that involves showing a sample audience an entire episode of a show and recording their reactions.

podcasting   Prerecording programs prepared for the iPod that can be downloaded and played at the listener's convenience.

policy book   At radio and TV stations, a book that spells out philosophy and standards of operation and identifies practices that are encouraged or discouraged.

political press   Newspapers and magazines of the 1790–1820 era that specialized in publishing partisan political articles.

polysemic   Having many meanings.

Portable People Meter (PPM)   A small device carried by an individual that automatically records radio and television exposure.

portals   The first pages a person sees when opening an Internet browser.

positioning   In advertising, stressing the unique selling point of a product or service to differentiate it from the competition.

primary audience   That portion of a magazine's total audience made up of subscribers or those who buy it at the newsstand.

primary demand ad   An advertisement that promotes a specific product category, such as milk.

printing on demand   One-at-a-time printing of books that exist in a digital database.

prior restraint   An attempt by the government to censor the press by restraining it from publishing or broadcasting material.

prominence   News value that stresses the importance of the person involved in the event.

protocol   A common language accepted by computer programmers.

proximity   News value based on the location of a news event.

Public Broadcasting Act of 1967   A congressional act that established the Public Broadcasting Service.

publicity   The placing of stories in the mass media.

publics   The various audiences served by public relations.

publishers   A segment of the print media industry responsible for the creation of content.

rack jobbers   Individuals who service record racks located in variety and large department stores by choosing the CDs to be sold in each location.

Radio Act of 1927   A congressional act establishing the Federal Radio Commission, a regulatory body that would issue broadcasting licenses and organize operating times and frequencies.

rate base   The number of buyers guaranteed by a magazine and used to compute advertising rates.

rating   The ratio of listeners to a particular radio station to all people in the market; the ratio of viewers of a particular TV program to the number of households in the market equipped with TV.

receiver   The target of the message in the communication process.

reinforcement   Support of existing attitudes and opinions by certain messages.

resonance   In cultivation analysis the situation in which a respondent's life experiences are reinforced by what is seen on TV, thus reinforcing the effect of TV content.

retail advertisers   Businesses that have customers in only one trading area.

rough layout   An early version of a print ad.

search engine   Software that enables users to search the Internet for specific information.

selective demand ad   An ad that stresses a particular brand.

self-determination   The ethical principle that human beings deserve respect for their decisions.

share of the audience   The ratio of listeners to a particular radio station to the total number of listeners in the market; the ratio of the number of households watching a particular TV program to the number of households watching TV at that time.

shield laws   Legislation that defines the rights of a reporter to protect sources.

slander   Spoken defamation; in many states, if a defamatory statement is broadcast, it is considered libel, even though technically the words are not written; libel is considered more harmful and usually carries more serious penalties than does slander.

sliding scale   An arrangement between a motion picture exhibitor and a distributor that details how much box office revenue will be kept by the movie theater.

social media   A set of Internet tools that encourage content sharing and community relationships.

social responsibility theory   The belief that the press has a responsibility to preserve democracy by properly informing the public and by responding to society's needs.

social utility   The media function that addresses an individual's need to affiliate with family, friends, and others in society.

socialization   The ways an individual comes to adopt the behavior and values of a group.

soft news   Features that rely on human interest for their news value.

source   A person who initiates communication.

spam   The electronic equivalent of junk mail.

stimulation theory   A theory that suggests viewing violence will actually stimulate an individual to behave more violently.

storyboard   A series of drawings depicting the key scenes in a TV ad.

strategic planning   A management technique that sets long-range, general goals.

subsidiary rights   Rights given by a publisher to others, allowing them to reproduce certain content.

surveillance   The news and information function of the mass media.

survey   A technique of gathering data that typically uses a questionnaire.

tabloids   Heavily illustrated publications usually half the size of a normal newspaper page.

tactical planning   A management technique that sets short-range, specific goals.

target audience   In advertising, the segment of the population for whom the product or service has an appeal.

technological determinism   The theory that contends technology drives historical change.

Telecommunications Act of 1996   A major revision of U.S. communication laws that affected broadcasting, cable, and telephone industries.

text   The object of analysis in the critical/cultural approach.

timeliness   News value that stresses when an event occurred.

time shifting   Recording programs and playing them back at times other than when they are aired.

time softening   Tendency of cell phone users to treat appointed times with more flexibility.

tracking studies   Studies that examine how ads perform during or after a campaign.

trespass   Illegal entry onto another's property.

UHF   The ultra-high-frequency band of the electromagnetic spectrum; channels 14–69 on the TV set.

underground press   A type of specialized reporting that emerged in the mid-to-late 1960s, with emphasis on politically liberal news and opinion and cultural topics such as music, art, and film.

USA Patriot Act   A law that gave the government increased powers of surveillance.

uses-and-gratifications model   A model proposing that audience members have certain needs or drives that are satisfied by using both nonmedia and media sources.

utility   The ethical principle that stresses the greatest good for the greatest number.

Variety   The entertainment industry trade publication.

V-Chip   A device installed in a TV set that restricts the reception of violent or objectionable material.

veil of ignorance   The ethical principle that everyone should be treated equally.

VHF   The very-high-frequency band of the electromagnetic spectrum; channels 2–13 on the TV set.

video-on-demand   A system by which a cable TV system can provide movies to customers at times of the customers' choosing.

viral advertising   Technique of creating messages so interesting that consumers spontaneously share them.

voice-over-Internet protocol (VoIP)   Method for sending a phone call over the Internet.

voice tracking   A technique in radio in which a disc jockey prerecords the voice portion of a shift that is later broadcast on several stations.

Web 2.0   The label given to the current version of the Web that emphasizes interactivity and sharing.

Web page   A hypertext page contained within a Web site.

Web site   A set of hypertext pages linked to each other that contain information about a common topic.

WiMax   Technology that allows wireless Internet access over a wide area.

wireless fidelity (WiFi)   A system by which personal computers and other information devices connect to the Internet without wires.

World Wide Web (WWW)   A network of information sources that uses hypertext to link one piece of information to another.

yellow journalism   Sensationalized journalism, appearing during the 1890s, noted for its emphasis on sex, murder, popularized medicine, pseudoscience, self-promotion, and human-interest stories.

zoned editions   Newspapers that have special sections for specific geographic areas.

>> Photo Credits

Chapter 1 p. 2, © Mikael Karlsson; p. 6, © AP/Wide World Photos; p. 8, © Raymond Reuter/Corbis Sygma; p. 11, © Paramount/Courtesy Everett Collection; p. 15, Photo: ABC/Danny Feld, © ABC/Courtesy Everett Collection; p. 24, © Karen Bleier/Time Life Pictures **Chapter 2** p. 28, Warner Brothers/DC Comics/The Kobal Collection; p. 31, © Tony Freeman/PhotoEdit; pp. 34, 39, © AP/Wide World Photos; p. 42, © Sergio Dionisio/Getty Images; p. 44, TM & Copyright © Fox 2000 Pictures. All rights reserved./Courtesy Everett Collection; p. 45, Courtesy Everett Collection **Chapter 3** p. 50, © Robert Brenner/PhotoEdit; p. 53, © Brown Brothers; pp. 57, 58, 59, 61, © The Granger Collection, New York; p. 64, © TLC/Courtesy Everett Collection; p. 70, © Creatas/PunchStock; p. 72, © Dan Kitwood/Getty Images **Chapter 4** p. 80, © AP/Wide World Photos; p. 82, © Brown Brothers; p. 83, © General Research and Reference Division. Schomberg Center for Research in Black Culture. The New York Public Library. Astor, Lenox and Tilden Foundations; p. 84, © Collection of The New York Historical Society, #54956; p. 86, © Brown Brothers; p. 95, © Cynthia Johnson/Getty Images; p. 96, © The McGraw-Hill Companies, Inc./Erica S. Leeds, photographer; p. 102, Courtesy FMC Corporation **Chapter 5** p. 108, © The McGraw-Hill Companies, Inc./Mark Dierker, photographer; p. 111, © The Granger Collection, New York; p. 112T, © Timepix; p. 112B, © Margaret Bourke-White/Timepix/Getty Images; p. 118, © Michael Dwyer/Stock Boston; p. 123T, © Mark Zemnick; p. 123B, Courtesy Johnson Publishing Company, Inc. **Chapter 6** p. 130, Courtesy Everett Collection; p. 132, © PhotoEdit; p. 133, © Eric Sander/Getty Images; p. 138, © AP/Wide World Photos; p. 145, © Brad Barket/Getty Images **Chapter 7** p. 148, Russell Illig/Getty Images; p. 150, National Archives; p. 152, Stock Montage; p. 153, © Culver Pictures/Art Archive; p. 157, © 2003 ABC News/ABC Photography Archives; p. 161, Courtesy Carole Dominick; p. 163, © AP/Wide World Photos; p. 165, © Scott Olson/Getty Images **Chapter 8** p. 176, © Alexandra Wyman/WireImage/Getty Images; p. 178, © Brown Brothers; p. 180T, © Nina Leer/Timepix/Getty Images; p. 180B, © Getty Images; p. 182T, © Russ Einhorn/Getty Images; pp. 182B, 183L, Courtesy Everett Collection; p. 183R, © Getty Images; p. 184, © Shirlaine Forrest/WireImage/Getty Images; p. 190, © Scott Legato/FilmMagic/Getty Images; p. 193, Mitch Leigh Studio, Walters/Storyk Design Group. Photo by Robert Wolsh Designs **Chapter 9** p. 200, Columbia Pictures/Kobal Collection; p. 202, © Bettmann/Corbis; pp. 205, 206, 207, Photofest; p. 208, © J.R. Eyerman/Timepix/Getty Images; p. 212, © Paramount/Courtesy Everett Collection; p. 215, Photofest; p. 217, © Michele Burgess/Stock Boston; p. 218, Columbia/Danjaq/Eon/The Kobal Collection; p. 225, © Chelsea Lauren/WireImage/Getty Images **Chapter 10** p. 228, © Kevin Winter/Getty Images; p. 231T, © Bettmann/Corbis; p. 231B, Courtesy Everett Collection; p. 233, © Ed Carlin/Index Stock Imagery/Photolibrary; p. 240, © David Frazier/The Image Works; p. 241, © Frances Roberts/Alamy; p. 245, Photo: Scott Garfield/© ABC /Courtesy Everett Collection; p. 249, © Frederick M. Brown/Getty Images; p. 250, © AP/Wide World Photos **Chapter 11** p. 268, © AP/Wide World Photos **Chapter 12** p. 278, Courtesy of the author; p. 280, Courtesy University of Pennsylvania's School of Engineering and Applied Science **Chapter 13** p. 302, © Chester Higgins, Jr./The New York Times/Redux; p. 304, © Mark Wilson/Getty Images; p. 312, © Karen Ballard/Redux; p. 316, © AP/Wide World Photos **Chapter 14** p. 322, © Paul J. Richards/AFP/Getty Images; p. 326, © Bettmann/Corbis; p. 331, © Bob Daemmrich/The Image Works **Chapter 15** p. 343T, Serena and Venus Williams © 1999 National Fluid Milk Processor Promotion Board; p. 343B, © Culver Pictures/Art Archive; p. 346, © Tony Freeman/PhotoEdit; p. 350, Courtesy Papa John's International; p. 354, © Clive Brunskill/Getty Images; p. 359, Institute of Outdoor Advertising; p. 361, Courtesy Caterpillar **Chapter 16** p. 366, © Royalty-Free/Corbis; p. 369, © 2010 by The New York Times Co. Reprinted by permission; p. 373, © Mike Coppola/FilmMagic/Getty Images; p. 395, PAR Archive **Chapter 17** p. 398, © Royalty-Free/Corbis; p. 402, © AP/Wide World Photos; p. 407, © The McGraw-Hill Companies, Inc./Mark Dierker, photographer; p. 409, © TV Land/Courtesy Everett Collection **Chapter 18** p. 420, © Jonathan Torgovnik/Getty Images; p. 422, © The CNN Inc.; p. 428, © The Granger Collection, New York; p. 435, © Telemundo/Photofest; p. 437, © Dave Saunders/Stone/Getty Images **Chapter 19** p. 442, © AP/Wide World Photos; p. 445, © Jason Merritt/Getty Images; p. 447, Photo: Dean Hendler/© ABC/Courtesy: Everett Collection; p. 449, © 20th Century Fox Film Corp. All rights reserved./Courtesy Everett Collection; p. 450, © Oliver Laban-Mattei/AFP/Getty Images; p. 451, © Bettmann/Corbis; p. 453, © Edouard Berne/Stone/Getty Images; p. 458, Courtesy Everett Collection; p. 463, BananaStock/Jupiterimages

>> Text & Illustration Credits

>> Index